STUDENT'S SOLUTIONS MANUAL

JOHN C. JACOBS

INTERMEDIATE ALGEBRA THROUGH APPLICATIONS

Geoffrey Akst   Sadie Bragg

Borough of Manhattan Community College,
City University of New York

PEARSON

Addison
Wesley

Boston San Francisco New York
London Toronto Sydney Tokyo Singapore Madrid
Mexico City Munich Paris Cape Town Hong Kong Montreal

Reproduced by Pearson Addison-Wesley from electronic files supplied by the author.

Copyright © 2006 Pearson Education, Inc.
Publishing as Pearson Addison-Wesley, 75 Arlington Street, Boston, MA 02116.

ISBN   0-201-66230-2

7 8 OPM 08 07

PEARSON

Addison
Wesley

CONTENTS

Chapter 1 Algebra Basics

Pretest

1. -0.5 is 0.5 units to the left of zero.

2. -8 is 8 units from zero, therefore $|-8| = 8$.

3. -2.7 is to the left of -2.5 on the number line $-2.7 < -2.5$.

4. Commutative Property of Addition.

5. Rewrite as addition $-7 - 6 = (-7) + (-6)$

    Add their absolute values and keep the sign.

    $(-7) + (-6) = -13$

6. Rewrite as addition.

    $12 - 18 + (-3) - (-4) =$

    $(+12) + (-18) + (-3) + (+4)$

    Use the commutative property of addition.

    $(+12) + (+4) + (-18) + (-3)$

    Add numbers with the same sign. $(+16) + (-21)$

    Find the difference of absolute values; take sign of number with largest absolute value.

    $(+16) + (-21) = -5$

7. Evaluate the inside of the absolute value first. The product of numbers with opposite signs is negative.

    $|5(-2)(4)| = |(-10)(4)| = |-40| = 40$

8. $(-6)^2 = (-6)(-6)$

    The product of numbers with the same sign is positive.

    $(-6)(-6) = 36$

9. $2^0 = 1$

10. $3(10-8) - (7-13)^2 \div 12$

    Evaluate inside parentheses first.

    Change to addition.

    $3(10+(-8)) - (7+(-13))^2 \div 12$

    $3(2) - (-6)^2 \div 12 =$

    Evaluate exponents.

    $3(2) - (36) \div 12 =$

    Change to addition.

    $3(2) + (-36) \div 12 =$

    Multiply and divide before adding.

    $6 + -3 = 3$

11. $6[2(\underline{5-3}) - (\underline{4+1})]^2 = 6[2(5+(-3)) - (5)]^2 =$

    Change subtraction to addition of the opposite,

Evaluate inside of parentheses first.

$6[2(2) + (-5)]^2 =$

Multiplication before addition.

$6[4 + (-5)]^2$

Change subtraction to addition of the opposite.

$= 6[-1]^2 =$

Evaluate exponents before multiplication.

$6[1] = 6$

12. $\dfrac{(-2)^2 - (-8)}{15 - 11} =$ Evaluate exponents first.

    $\dfrac{4 - (-8)}{15 - 11} =$

    Change subtraction to addition of opposite.

    $\dfrac{4 + (+8)}{15 + (-11)} =$

    Perform addition and divide.

    $\dfrac{12}{4} = 3$

13. Add exponents when multiplying.

    $\dfrac{y^6 \bullet y}{y^5} = \dfrac{y^6 \bullet y^1}{y^5} = \dfrac{y^{6+1}}{y^5} = \dfrac{y^7}{y^5}$

    Subtract exponents when dividing.

    $= \dfrac{y^7}{y^5} = y^{7-5} = y^2$

14. Multiply exponents

    $-(3a^4 b^2)^3 = -(3^{1\bullet 3} a^{4\bullet 3} b^{2\bullet 3}) = -(3^3 a^{12} b^6) =$

    Evaluate 3^3.

    $-27a^{12} b^6$

15. Negative exponents mean reciprocal.

    $-9x^{-7} = -\dfrac{9}{x^7}$

16. "More than" means add, "product" means multiply.

    $10 + 2ab$ or $2ab + 10$

17. Substitute $3(4) - 6(-2) + (-1)$

    Evaluate $12 + 12 - 1 = 23$

18. Distribute the negative 3.

    $-15u - 3(7) - (-3)(8u) + 11 =$

    $-15u - 21 + 24u + 11 =$

    Use the commutative property.

    $-15u + 24u - 21 + 11 =$

    Use the distributive property.

    $(-15 + 24)u - 21 + 11 =$

    $9u - 10$

19. $-259.34 < -210$
      Nitrogen melts at a higher temperature.
20. $t = 1003 - 1995 = 8$
      $$-0.32(8)^3 + 4.5(8)^2 - 0.5(8) + 636 =$$
      $$-0.32 \cdot 512 + 4.5 \cdot 64 - 4.0 + 636 =$$
      756 or 756,000

Exercise 1.1 Introduction to Real Numbers

		Whole Numbers	Integers	Rational Numbers
1.	-5		X	X
3.	−3.9			X
5.	7	X	X	X
7.	$\sqrt{3}$			

		Irrational Numbers	Real Numbers
1.	−5		X
3.	−3.9		X
5.	7		X
7.	$\sqrt{3}$	X	X

9.   4
11. −3.5
13. $\dfrac{5}{4}$

15. The opposite of –5 is +5.
17. The opposite of $\dfrac{1}{4}$ is $-\dfrac{1}{4}$.

	Number	Additive Inverse
19.	−12	12
21.	2.7	−2.7

23. $\left|\dfrac{1}{4}\right| = \dfrac{1}{4}$
25. $|-9| = 9$
27. $-|-2| = -(2) = -2$
29. $-|5.3| = -(5.3) = -5.3$
31. $|+6| = 6$ AND $|-6| = 6;$ 6 and −6
33. Absolute value is always zero or greater. No number has an absolute value that is negative.
35. False, −5 is to the left of –1 on the number line.
37. False, $\dfrac{5}{4} = \dfrac{15}{12} \leq \dfrac{20}{12} = \dfrac{5}{3}$
39. True, all negative numbers are less than zero.

41. True $-|3| = -3 \geq -3$
43. False $1.2 \not\leq 0.5$
45. $0 > -7$
47. $-4 > -6$
49. $-7.4 < -7$
51. $|8| = |-8|$ because $8 = 8$
53. $-|4.1| < |-4.1|$ because $-4.1 < 4.1$
55.
      $-4, -\dfrac{2}{5}, \dfrac{3}{4}$, and 5
57.
      $-3.5, -1.8, 1$, and 4.3
59.
      $[-4, \infty)$
61.
      $(-\infty, 3)$
63.
      $[-4, 3]$
65. It is warmer in January at the South Pole.
      $-16^o F > -74^o F$
67. $-27m > -400m$
69. a. States that gained seats: Arizona, California, Florida, and Texas. States that lost seats: Illinois, New York, Ohio, Pennsylvania and Wisconsin.
      b. In 1990, New York's population was greater than that of Texas. In 2000, Texas had the greater population. Apportionment of seats to the U. S. House of Representatives is based on population.
      c. Arizona and Wisconsin have the same number of representatives in 2000 as do Illinois and Pennsylvania. States with the same number of representatives have about the same population.
71. This month's price < Last month's price.
      Therefore, $x < y$ or $y > x$.
73. SUV price > Minivan price.
      Therefore, $x > y$ or $y < x$.
75. a,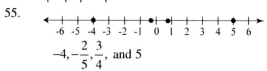
      b. Zero would represent a score of par.
      c. Clink.

Exercise 1.2 Operations with Real Numbers

1. $-7 + 9 = 2$
3. $2 - (-2) = 2 + (+2) = 4$

5. $-1+(-10)=-11$

7. $3-4=3+(-4)=-1$

9. $-1-7=-1+(-7)=-8$

11. The sum of a number and its opposite is 0.

13. $5.6+(-9.2)=-3.6$

15. $-3.7-(-4)=-3.7+(+4)=0.3$

17. $\left(-\dfrac{1}{4}\right)+\left(-\dfrac{3}{4}\right)=-\dfrac{4}{4}=-1$

19. $\dfrac{7}{10}+\left(-\dfrac{9}{10}\right)=-\dfrac{2}{10}=-\dfrac{1}{5}$

21. $-\dfrac{2}{5}-\dfrac{3}{5}=-\dfrac{2}{5}+\left(-\dfrac{3}{5}\right)=-\dfrac{5}{5}=-1$

23. $-4.9-(-9.3)=-4.9+(+9.3)=4.4$

25. $7.23-(-7.23)=7.23+(+7.23)=14.46$

27. 40   Product of two factors with like signs is positive.

29. -40 Product of two factors with different signs is negative.

31. 7   Quotient of two factors with like signs is positive.

33. -5 Quotient of two factors with different signs is negative.

35. -5 Quotient of two factors with different signs is negative.

37. -11.5 Product of two factors with different signs is negative.

39. 8.75   Product of two factors with like signs is positive.

41. -2.2 Quotient of two factors with different signs is negative.

43. 30   Quotient of two factors with like signs is positive.

45. $\left(-\dfrac{3}{\cancel{4}_{1}}\right)\left(-\dfrac{\cancel{8}^{2}}{1}\right)=6$ Product of two factors with like signs is positive.

47. $6\div\left(-\dfrac{1}{4}\right)=\dfrac{6}{1}\bullet\left(-\dfrac{4}{1}\right)=-24$ Product of two factors with different signs is negative.

49. $\left(-\dfrac{1}{\cancel{2}_{1}}\right)\left(\dfrac{\cancel{2}^{1}}{3}\right)=-\dfrac{1}{3}$ Product of two factors with different signs is negative.

51. $\left(-\dfrac{2}{5}\right)\div\left(-\dfrac{3}{5}\right)=\left(-\dfrac{2}{\cancel{5}}\right)\left(\bullet-\dfrac{\cancel{5}}{3}\right)=\dfrac{2}{3}$ Product of two factors with like signs is positive.

53. $4^{3}=4\bullet4\bullet4=64$

55. $(-3)^{2}=(-3)(-3)=9$ The negative sign is inside the parentheses; this is the product of two negative numbers.

57. $-2^{2}=-(2)(2)=-4$ The negative sign does NOT go with the exponent unless there are parentheses. -2^{2} is the same as $(-1)(2)^{2}$.

59. $-3(5-11)-6=-3(5+(-11))-6=$
$-3(-6)-6=18-6=12$

61. $-3\left[-5-(1+7)\right]=$
$-3[-5-8]=-3[-13]=39$

63. $-2(10)-4(-7)=-2(10)+(-4)(-7)=$
$-20+28=8$

65. Multiply and divide from left to right.
$-36\div(-4)(-3)=9(-3)=-27$

67. Multiply and divide from left to right.
$6(-8)\div(-16)(5)=-48\div(-16)(5)=3(5)=15$

69. Evaluate the inside of parentheses first. $2\left[3(5-8)+2(6-7)\right]=$
$2\left[3(-3)+2(-1)\right]=2\left[\underline{-9-2}\right]=2[-11]=-22$

71. Evaluate numerators and denominators before dividing. $\dfrac{(-4)(7)+8(-1)}{5-11}=\dfrac{-28-8}{-6}=\dfrac{-36}{-6}=6$

73. $(2)(10)-\underline{3^{2}}=(2)(10)-(3)(3)=20-9=11$

75. Evaluate the insides of parentheses first, then exponents followed by multiplication and division done left to right.
$-3+4^{2}\div8(\underline{5-6})^{2}=-3+\underline{4^{2}}\div8(\underline{-1})^{2}=$
$-3+\underline{16\div8}(1)=-3+\underline{2(1)}=-3+2=-1$

77. $-5\left[3^{2}-4(\underline{32\div16})^{3}\div8\right]+25$
$-5\left[\underline{3^{2}}-4(\underline{2})^{3}\div8\right]+25=$
$-5[9-\underline{4\bullet8}\div8]+25=$
$-5[9-\underline{32\div8}]+25=-5[\underline{9-4}]+25=$
$-5[5]+25=-25+25=0$

79. $\dfrac{12-15}{-3}+\dfrac{-5-11}{-4}=\dfrac{-3}{-3}+\dfrac{-16}{-4}=1+4=5$

81. Evaluate the inside of the absolute value first.
$|\underline{2-9}|=|-7|=7$

83. $-|6|+|-15|=-6+15=9$

85. $-|6-\underline{4^{2}}|-|(2)(-7)|=-|\underline{6-16}|-|(2)(-7)|=$
$-|-10|-|-14|=-10-14=-24$

87. Evaluate the inside of the radical first adding left to right. $\sqrt{\underline{8+1}-4}=\sqrt{\underline{9-4}}=\sqrt{5}$

89. $\sqrt{2(12-8-1)} = \sqrt{2(4-1)} = \sqrt{2(3)} = \sqrt{6}$

91. Change = last − first $31,000 - 26,000 = 5,000$ ft

93. $10^{\circ}F - 12^{\circ}F = 10^{\circ}F + (-12^{\circ}F) = -2^{\circ}F$

The temperature at 6:00 P.M. was −2°F

95. $-16(3^2) + 160 = \underline{-16 \bullet 9} + 160 =$

$-144 + 160 = 16$ft.

97. a.

Player	Score	Score with Respect to Par
Annika Sorenstam	68	−4
Juli Inkster	75	+3
Karrie Webb	70	−2
Se Ri Pak	71	−1
Dottie Pepper	74	+2

b. The golfers scored below par.

99. $\dfrac{22+27+(-1)+(-9)+(-2)+(-13)+(-9)}{7} =$

$\dfrac{49+(-34)}{7} = \dfrac{15}{7} = 2\dfrac{1}{7} \approx 2^{\circ}F$

101. a. $3\left(1\dfrac{1}{2}\right) \bullet 10 = \dfrac{3}{1} \bullet \dfrac{3}{\cancel{2}_1} \bullet \dfrac{\cancel{10}^5}{1} = \dfrac{45}{1} = 45$ mg.

b. $3\left(1\dfrac{1}{2}\right)(10) = \dfrac{3}{1} \bullet \dfrac{3}{\cancel{2}_1} \bullet \dfrac{\cancel{10}^5}{1} = \dfrac{45}{1} = 45$ tablets.

103. a. 2002: $19.9 - 17.3 = 2.6$
     2003: $18.2 - 19.9 = -1.7$
     2004: $16.7 - 18.2 = -1.5$
     2005: $17.8 - 16.7 = 1.1$

Year	2002	2003	2004	2005
Change in revenue from Previous Year (in millions of dollars).	+2.6	−1.7	−1.5	+1.1

b. $\dfrac{+2.6+(-1.7)+(-1.5)+1.1}{4} = \dfrac{0.5}{4} =$

0.125 million = $125,000

c. $\dfrac{17.3+19.9+18.2+16.7+17.8}{5} = \dfrac{89.9}{5} =$

17.98 million = $17,980,000 average.

Exercise 1.3 Properties of Real Numbers

1. $3.7 + 2 = 2 + 3.7$

3. $\left[(-1)+(-6)\right]+7 = (-1)+\left[(-6)+7\right]$

5. $-3 + 0 = -3$

7. $3(1+9) = 3 \bullet 1 + 3 \bullet 9$

9. $(2+7) \bullet 5 = 5(2+7)$

11. $2a + 2b = 2(a+b)$

13. Commutative property of multiplication.

15. Commutative property of addition.

17. Distributive property.

19. Multiplication property of zero.

21. Additive inverse property.

23. Associative property of addition.

25. Associative property of multiplication.

27. $(6.1)(0) = 0$

29. $(-7.2)(0) = 0$

31. $8 + \underline{(-3)+(-5)} = 8 + (-8) = 0$ or

$\underline{8+(-3)}+(-5) = 5 + (-5) = 0$

33. Rearrange the numbers by sign.

$2 + (-3.8) + 9.13 + (-1) =$

$\underline{2+9.13} + \underline{(-3.8)+(-1)} = 11.13 + (-4.8) = 6.33$

35. $\underline{(-7)(-2)}(3) = (14)(3) = 42$

37. $\underline{(-2)(-2)}(-2) = (4)(-2) = -8$

39. $\underline{(-5)(-7)}(-2)(10) = \underline{(35)(-2)}(10) =$

$(-70)(10) = -700$

41. $0 \div 3 = 0$ Division into zero always gives zero.

43. Not possible, dividing by zero is undefined.

45. The additive inverse of 2 is -2.

47. The additive inverse of -7 is 7.

49. The multiplicative inverse of 7 is $\dfrac{1}{7}$.

51. The multiplicative inverse of -1 is $\dfrac{1}{-1} = -1$.

53. $(-4)(2+5) = (-4)(2)+(-4)(5)$

55. $(x+10) \bullet 3 = 3 \bullet x + 3 \bullet 10 = 3x + 30$

57. $-(a+6b) = (-1)(a)+(-1)(6b) =$

$-a + (-6b)$ or $-a - 6b$

59. $n \cdot n - n \cdot 2 = n^2 - 2n$
61. a. The commutative property of multiplication.
    b. The associative property of multiplication.
    c. Multiplication of real numbers.
63. a. The associative property of multiplication.
    b. The multiplicative inverse property.
    c. The multiplicative identity property.
65. Yes, by the commutative property of addition.
    (Distance traveled on bus) + (distance walked) =
    (distance walked) + (distance traveled on bus).
67. Yes, by the distributive property. $r(p+q) = rp + rq$
69. Using the additive identity property: $p + 0 = p$, his
    weight at the end of the week is p.
71. Yes, by the commutative property of multiplication:
    $\frac{1}{2} \cdot 9 \cdot 12 = \frac{1}{2} \cdot 12 \cdot 9$. The calculations give the same
    result.

Exercise 1.4 Laws of Exponents and Scientific Notation

1. $7 \cdot 7 \cdot 7 \cdot 7 = 7^4$
3. $a \cdot a \cdot a \cdot a \cdot a = a^5$
5. $(-5x)(-5x)(-5x)(-5x) = (-5x)^4$
7. $(a+b)(a+b)(a+b) = (a+b)^3$
9. $4^2 = 4 \cdot 4 = 16$
11. There are three negative signs in this product.
    $(-3)^3 = (-3)(-3)(-3) = -27$
13. There is only one negative sign in this product.
    $-3^3 = -3 \cdot 3 \cdot 3 = -27$
15. There are two negative signs in this
    product. $(-10)^2 = (-10)(-10) = 100$
17. $7^0 = 1$
19. The exponent zero goes only with the letter n.
    $-4n^0 = -4(1) = -4$
21. $(-2y)^0 = 1$
23. $(3n)^1 = 3n$
25. $(3a+b)^0 = 1$
27. $3^3 \cdot 3^1 = 3^{3+1} = 3^4 = 81$
29. $n^8 \cdot n^5 = n^{8+5} = n^{13}$
31. The bases are not the same so the expression cannot
    be simplified.
33. $x^0 \cdot x^5 = 1 \cdot x^5 = x^5$ or
    $x^0 \cdot x^5 = x^{0+5} = x^5$
35. $(x+2)^3 \cdot (x+2)^1 = (x+2)^{3+1} = (x+2)^4$
37. $\frac{6^7}{6^3} = 6^{7-3} = 6^4$

39. $\frac{x^{12}}{x^7} = x^{12-7} = x^5$
41. The bases are not the same so the expression cannot
    be simplified.
43. $\frac{t^8}{t^1} = t^{8-1} = t^7$
45. $(2n+1)^4 \div (2n+1)^1 = (2n+1)^{4-1} = (2n+1)^3$
47. $y^4 \cdot y^3 \cdot y^7 = y^{4+3+7} = y^{14}$
49. Use the commutative property of multiplication to
    reorder the factors. $(p^5q^9)(pq) = p^5q^9p^1q^1 =$
    $p^5p^1q^9q^1 = p^{5+1}q^{9+1} = p^6q^{10}$
51. Use the commutative property of multiplication to
    reorder the factors.
    $(y^2x^2)(-xz^2)(7yz^4) =$
    $y^2x^2 \cdot (-1)x^1z^2 \cdot 7y^1z^4 =$
    $(-1)(7)x^2x^1y^2y^1z^2z^4 =$
    $-7x^{2+1}y^{2+1}z^{2+4} = -7x^3y^3z^6$
53. $\frac{n^6 \cdot n^2 \cdot n^4}{n^8} = \frac{n^{6+2+4}}{n^8} = \frac{n^{12}}{n^8} = n^{12-8} = n^4$
55. $\frac{r^9 \cdot r^7}{r^{13} \cdot r^1} = \frac{r^{9+7}}{r^{13+1}} = \frac{r^{16}}{r^{14}} = r^{16-14} = r^2$
57. $5^{-2} = \frac{1}{5^2}$
59. $t^{-8} = \frac{1}{t^8}$
61. $n^{-10} = \frac{1}{n^{10}}$
63. $(-3y)^{-1} = -\frac{1}{3y}$
65. $(a+6)^{-5} = \frac{1}{(a+6)^5}$
67. $\frac{1}{x^{-6}} = x^6$
69. $-n^{-8} = -\frac{1}{n^8}$
71. $x^{-4}y^2 = \frac{y^2}{x^4}$
73. $2^{-1}y^2 = \frac{y^2}{2^1} = \frac{y^2}{2}$
75. $-3t^{-2} = -\frac{3}{t^2}$
77. $\frac{2}{x^{-4}} = 2x^4$
79. $-\frac{p^3}{5q^{-1}} = -\frac{p^3q}{5}$

81. $\dfrac{3a^{-2}}{b} = \dfrac{3}{a^2 b}$

83. $\dfrac{n^{-2}}{n^{-5}} = n^{-2-(-5)} = n^{-2+5} = n^3$ or

$\dfrac{n^{-2}}{n^{-5}} = \dfrac{n^5}{n^2} = n^{5-2} = n^3$

85. $\dfrac{\left(x^{-7}\right)\left(x^3\right)}{\left(x^4\right)\left(x^{-1}\right)} = \dfrac{x^{-7+3}}{x^{4+(-1)}} = \dfrac{x^{-4}}{x^3} = \dfrac{1}{x^4 x^3} = \dfrac{1}{x^{4+3}} = \dfrac{1}{x^7}$

or

$\dfrac{\left(x^{-7}\right)\left(x^3\right)}{\left(x^4\right)\left(x^{-1}\right)} = \dfrac{x^3 \bullet x^1}{x^4 \bullet x^7} = \dfrac{x^{3+1}}{x^{4+7}} = \dfrac{x^4}{x^{11}} = \dfrac{1}{x^{11-4}} = \dfrac{1}{x^7}$

87. $\left(5^2\right)^4 = 5^{2\bullet 4} = 5^8$

89. $-\left(x^3\right)^5 = -\left(x^{3\bullet 5}\right) = -x^{15}$

91. $\left(n^4\right)^{-3} = n^{4\bullet(-3)} = n^{-12} = \dfrac{1}{n^{12}}$ or

$\left(n^4\right)^{-3} = \dfrac{1}{\left(n^4\right)^3} = \dfrac{1}{n^{4\bullet 3}} = \dfrac{1}{n^{12}}$

93. $-\left(a^{-5}\right)^{-1} = -\left(a^{(-5)\bullet(-1)}\right) = -a^5$

95. The exponent does not affect the negative sign.

$-\left(2p\right)^4 = -\left(2^4 p^4\right) = -16p^4$

97. The exponent does affect the negative sign.

$\left(-2p\right)^4 = \left(-2\right)^4 p^4 = 16p^4$

99. The outermost exponent does affect the negative sign.

$\left(-a^5 b^2\right)^2 = \left((-1)a^5 b^2\right)^2 = \left(-1\right)^2 a^{5\bullet 2} b^{2\bullet 2} =$

$a^{10} b^4$

101. The outermost exponent does affect the negative sign.

$\left(-3n^5\right)^3 = \left(-3\right)^3 n^{5\bullet 3} = -27n^{15}$

103. $-2\left(a^2 b^3\right)^4 = -2a^{2\bullet 4} b^{3\bullet 4} = -2a^8 b^{12}$

105. $\left(x^{-9} y^4\right)^3 = x^{-9\bullet 3} y^{4\bullet 3} = x^{-27} y^{12} = \dfrac{y^{12}}{x^{27}}$ or

$\left(x^{-9} y^4\right)^3 = \left(\dfrac{y^4}{x^9}\right)^3 = \dfrac{y^{4\bullet 3}}{x^{9\bullet 3}} = \dfrac{y^{12}}{x^{27}}$

107. $\left(8^{-1} a^8 b^{-8}\right)^{-2} = 8^{-1\bullet(-2)} a^{8\bullet(-2)} b^{-8\bullet(-2)} =$

$8^2 a^{-16} b^{16} = \dfrac{64b^{16}}{a^{16}}$

109. $\left(\dfrac{x}{2}\right)^3 = \left(\dfrac{x^1}{2^1}\right)^3 = \dfrac{x^{1\bullet 3}}{2^{1\bullet 3}} = \dfrac{x^3}{2^3} = \dfrac{x^3}{8}$

111. $\left(\dfrac{-p^5}{q^3}\right)^4 = \left(\dfrac{(-1)p^5}{q^3}\right)^4 = \dfrac{(-1)^4 p^{5\bullet 4}}{q^{3\bullet 4}} = \dfrac{p^{20}}{q^{12}}$

113. $-\left(-\dfrac{2n^3}{5m^2}\right)^2 = -\left(\dfrac{(-2)n^3}{5m^2}\right)^2 = -\dfrac{(-2)^2 n^{3\bullet 2}}{5^2 m^{2\bullet 2}} =$

$-\left(\dfrac{4n^6}{25m^4}\right) = -\dfrac{4n^6}{25m^4}$

115. $\left(\dfrac{-4r^2}{st^4}\right)^3 = \dfrac{(-4)^3 r^{2\bullet 3}}{s^3 t^{4\bullet 3}} = -\dfrac{64r^6}{s^3 t^{12}}$

117. $\left(\dfrac{3b^{-1}}{a^{-3}}\right)^2 = \dfrac{3^2 b^{-1\bullet 2}}{a^{-3\bullet 2}} = \dfrac{9b^{-2}}{a^{-6}} = \dfrac{9a^6}{b^2}$ or

$\left(\dfrac{3b^{-1}}{a^{-3}}\right)^2 = \left(\dfrac{3a^3}{b^1}\right)^2 = \dfrac{3^2 a^{3\bullet 2}}{b^{1\bullet 2}} = \dfrac{9a^6}{b^2}$

119. $\left(\dfrac{3u^4}{4v^3}\right)^{-2} = \dfrac{3^{-2} u^{4\bullet(-2)}}{4^{-2} v^{3\bullet(-2)}} = \dfrac{3^{-2} u^{-8}}{4^{-2} v^{-6}} = \dfrac{4^2 v^6}{3^2 u^8} = \dfrac{16v^6}{9u^8}$

121. $-\left(\dfrac{p^{-2} q^2}{r^2 t}\right)^{-2} = -\left(\dfrac{p^{-2\bullet(-2)} q^{2\bullet(-2)}}{r^{2\bullet(-2)} t^{1\bullet(-2)}}\right) =$

$-\left(\dfrac{p^4 q^{-4}}{r^{-4} t^{-2}}\right) = -\dfrac{p^4 r^4 t^2}{q^4}$

123. Move the decimal point 8 places to the left.
4×10^8

125. Move the decimal point 11 places to the left.
9.26×10^{11}

127. Move the decimal point 6 places to the right.
4.2×10^{-6}

129. Move the decimal point 10 places to the right.
7.4×10^{-10}

131. Move the decimal place 6 places to the right.
$2,430,000$

133. Move the decimal point three places to the left.
0.003027

135. Move the decimal point 6 places to the left.
0.000001

137. $\left(2 \times 10^2\right)\left(5 \times 10^4\right) = 2 \bullet 5 \times 10^{2+4} =$

$10 \times 10^6 = 10^7$ or 1×10^7

139. $\left(2.7 \times 10^{-2}\right)\left(3 \times 10^{-3}\right) = 2.7 \bullet 3 \times 10^{-2+(-3)} =$

8.1×10^{-5}

141. $\left(6.9 \times 10^5\right) \div \left(3 \times 10^2\right) = \dfrac{6.9 \times 10^5}{3 \times 10^2} =$

$2.3 \times 10^{5-2} = 2.3 \times 10^3$

143. $\left(5.4 \times 10^{10}\right) \div \left(9 \times 10^4\right) = \dfrac{5.4 \times 10^{10}}{9 \times 10^4} =$

$0.6 \times 10^{10-4} = 6 \times 10^{-1} \times 10^6 = 6 \times 10^5$

145. $\left(2.613 \times 10^9\right)\left(5.391 \times 10^{-12}\right) =$

$14.086683 \times 10^{9+(-12)} = 1.4086683 \times 10^1 \times 10^{-3} =$

$1.4086683 \times 10^{1+(-3)} = 1.4086683 \times 10^{-2}$

147. $\left(9.821\times10^{20}\right)\div\left(3.732\times10^{12}\right)=\dfrac{9.821\times10^{20}}{3.732\times10^{12}}=$

$2.631564845\times10^{20-12}=2.631564845\times10^{8}$

149. No. The volume of the original locker is x^3 and the volume of the locker with half the dimension on each edge is $\left(\dfrac{1}{2}x\right)^3=\left(\dfrac{x}{2}\right)^3=\dfrac{x^3}{8}$ or only one eighth the volume of the original locker.

151. $\left(2^3\right)^2 n=2^{3\bullet2}n=2^6 n=64n$ bacteria .

153. Move the decimal point 7 places to the left. $6\times10^7\,$m

155. Move the decimal point nine places to the left. 0.000000001

157. a. There are 60 months in 5 years. You will have deposited $60\bullet\$100=\$6000$.

b. $100\left[\left(1.00375^{12}\right)^5-1\right]\div0.00375$

$\dfrac{100\left[1.00375^{60}-1\right]}{0.00375}=\$6714.56$

c. Total interest earned was $\$6714.56-\$6000=\$714.56$.

159. People per square mile $=\dfrac{\text{people}}{\text{area}}$.

$\dfrac{1.272\times10^8\ \text{people}}{3.78\times10^5\ \text{sq Km}}=0.3365\times10^{8-5}=$

$3.37\times10^{-1}\times10^3=3.37\times10^2=337$

In 2010, there will be about 337 people per square kilometer in Japan.

161. Income taxes: $46.2\%\left(1.836218\times10^{12}\right)=$

$0.848332716\times10^{12}=8.48332716\times10^{1}\times10^{10}=$

8.48332716×10^{11}

Corporate taxes: $7.8\%\left(1.836218\times10^{12}\right)=$

$0.143225004\times10^{12}=1.43225004\times10^{11}$

Social Security: $39.6\%\left(1.836218\times10^{12}\right)=$

$0.727142328\times10^{12}=7.27142328\times10^{11}$

Other: $6.4\left(1.836218\times10^{12}\right)=$

$0.117517952\times10^{12}\approx1.18\times10^{11}$

163. $\dfrac{2.16\times10^{28}}{9\times10^{16}}\bullet60=0.24\times10^{28-16}\left(60\right)=$

$14.4\times10^{12}=1.44\times10^{13}$ kg

1.44×10^{13} kg of matter is converted in an hour.

Exercise 1.5 Algebraic Expressions: Translating, Evaluating, and Simplifying

Answers may vary in translations.

1. $\dfrac{1}{2}n$ is one-half times n or one-half of n.

3. $x-8$ is eight less than x or eight subtracted from x or x decreased by eight.

5. $\dfrac{y}{5}$ is y divided by five or the quotient of y and five.

7. $a+(-2)$ is a added to negative two or a increased by negative two.

9. $3x$ is the product of three and x or three times x.

11. $2a-b$ is twice a decreased by b or b less than the double of a.

13. $9+6n$ is nine more than the product of six and n or nine increased by six times n.

15. $-3(x+y)$ is negative three times the sum of x and y or the product of negative three and the sum of x and y.

17. $7(a-b)$ is seven times the difference between a and b or the product of seven and a decreased by b.

19. $\dfrac{r+s}{9}$ is the quotient of the sum of r and s with nine or the sum of r and s all divided by nine.

21. $\dfrac{-3}{x+y}$ is the quotient of negative three and the sum of x and y or negative three divided by the quantity x plus y.

23. $4p-5q$ is the difference between four times p and 5 times q or the product of four and p decreased by the product of five and q.

25. $\dfrac{2xy}{x-y}$ is the quotient of the product of two, x, and y with the difference between x and y or twice x times y, divided by the quantity x minus y.

27. One-fourth of a number is $\dfrac{1}{4}n$ or $\dfrac{n}{4}$.

29. The sum of a number and -3 is $n+(-3)$.

31. The difference between x and -2 is $x-(-2)$.

33. The ratio of b to a is $\dfrac{b}{a}$.

35. The product of -4 and y is -4y.

37. The sum of x and $-y$ is $x+(-y)$.

39. Seven less than the product of h and 3 is $3h-7$.

41. The sum of p and -3 is $p+(-3)$.

43. The quantity p minus q divided by the quantity p plus q is $\dfrac{p-q}{p+q}$.

45. Negative two times the quantity a plus 5 is $-2(a+5)$.

47.

x	$3x+2$
−2	$3(-2)+2=-4$
−1	$3(-1)+2=-1$
0	$3(0)+2=2$
1	$3(1)+2=5$
2	$3(2)+2=8$

49.

y	$2y-1.5$
0	$2(0)-1.5=-1.5$
1	$2(1)-1.5=0.5$
2	$2(2)-1.5=2.5$
3	$2(3)-1.5=4.5$
4	$2(4)-1.5=6.5$

51.

x	$-0.5x$
−4	$-0.5(-4)=2$
−2	$-0.5(-2)=1$
0	$-0.5(0)=0$
2	$-0.5(2)=-1$
4	$-0.5(4)=-2$

53.

n	$-\dfrac{n}{3}$
−6	$-\dfrac{(-6)}{3}=2$
−3	$-\dfrac{(-3)}{3}=1$
0	$-\dfrac{(0)}{3}=0$
3	$-\dfrac{(3)}{3}=-1$
6	$-\dfrac{(6)}{3}=-2$

55.

g	$-2g^2$
−2	$-2(-2)^2=-2(4)=-8$
−1	$-2(-1)^2=-2(1)=-2$
0	$-2(0)^2=-2(0)=0$
1	$-2(1)^2=-2(1)=-2$
2	$-2(2)^2=-2(4)=-8$

57.

a	a^2-3a+2
−2	$(-2)^2-3(-2)+2=$ $(4)+6+2=12$
−1	$(-1)^2-3(-1)+2=$ $(1)+3+2=6$
0	$(0)^2-3(0)+2=$ $(0)+0+2=2$
1	$(1)^2-3(1)+2=$ $1-3+2=0$
2	$(2)^2-3(2)+2=$ $4-6+2=0$

59. a. $x=-2,\ y=4$

$$-2x+3y=-2(-2)+3(4)=4+12=16$$

b. $x=-2$

$$6x^2=6(-2)^2=6(4)=24$$

c. $w=-1,\ z=5$

$$3(5w-z)=3(5(-1)-(5))=$$
$$3(-5-5)=3(-10)=-30$$

d. $y=4,\ w=-1$

$$y^2-3w^3=(4)^2-3(-1)^3=$$
$$16-3(-1)=16+3=19$$

61. a. $a=-1,\ c=-4$

$$\frac{3c}{5+a}=\frac{3(-4)}{5+(-1)}=\frac{-12}{4}=-3$$

b. $a=-1,\ b=2$

$$\frac{a+b}{a-b}=\frac{(-1)+(2)}{(-1)-(2)}=\frac{1}{-3}=-\frac{1}{3}$$

c. $c=-4\quad -c^2=-(-4)^2=-(16)=-16$

d. $a=-1,\ b=2\quad (-a+b)^2=$

$$(-(-1)+(2))^2=(1+2)^2=(3)^2=9$$

63. $3a$ and $5b$ are unlike terms.

65. x and $-7x$ are like terms.

67. $2x^2$ and $-6x$ are unlike terms.

69. $8a^2b$ and $-5a^2b$ are like terms.

71. $x+5x=(1+5)x=6x$

73. $12a^2-2a^2=(12-2)a^2=10a^2$

75. $9t-2t+7=(9-2)t+7=7t+7$

77. $x-9+5x=x+5x-9=(1+5)x-9=6x-9$

79. $9x - 10x^2 + 7x^2 = 9x + (-10 + 7)x^2 =$

$9x - 3x^2$ or $-3x^2 + 9x$

81. $6x^2 + 6x$ cannot be simplified, they are not like terms.

83. $-5a^2b + 2a^2b = (-5 + 2)a^2b = -3a^2b$

85. $\frac{1}{2}(x - 2) - 6 = \left(\frac{1}{2}\right)x - \left(\frac{1}{2}\right) \cdot 2 - 6$

$= \frac{1}{2}x - 1 - 6 = \frac{1}{2}x - 7$

87. $-(3y - 1) =$

$(-1)(3y - 1) = (-1)(3y) - (-1)(1) = -3y + 1$

89. $4x - 6 - (x + 7) = 4x - 6 + (-1)(x + 7) =$

$4x - 6 + (-1)(x) + (-1)(7) = 4x - 6 - x - 7 =$

$4x - x - 6 - 7 = (4 - 1)x - 13 = 3x - 13$

91. $(15a + 2) - 3(5a + 8) =$

$15a + 2 + (-3)(5a + 8) =$

$15a + 2 + (-3)(5a) + (-3)(8) =$

$15a + 2 - 15a - 24 = 15a - 15a + 2 - 24 =$

$(-15 + 15)a - 22 = (0)a - 22 = -22$

93. $9 + 4\left[-3(y - 1) + 5x\right] =$

$9 + 4\left[(-3)(y) - (-3) \cdot 1 + 5x\right] =$

$9 + 4\left[-3y + 3 + 5x\right] =$

$9 + (4)(-3y) + (4) \cdot 3 + (4)(5x) =$

$9 - 12y + 12 + 20x = 20x - 12y + 21$

95. $7 + 3\left[-2(x - 7) + 2x\right] =$

$7 + 3\left[(-2)x - (-2) \cdot 7 + 2x\right] =$

$7 + 3\left[-2x + 14 + 2x\right] = 7 + 3\left[-2x + 2x + 14\right] =$

$7 + 3\left[(-2 + 2)x + 14\right] = 7 + 3\left[(0)x + 14\right] =$

$7 + 3[14] = 7 + 42 = 49$

97. $3n - \left\{5\left[2(9n - 1) - 3(n + 4)\right] + 2(8 - 5n)\right\} =$

$3n - \left\{5[18n - 2 - 3n - 12] + 2(8 - 5n)\right\} =$

$3n - \left\{5[15n - 14] + 2(8 - 5n)\right\} =$

$3n - \left\{75n - 70 + 16 - 10n\right\} =$

$3n - \left\{65n - 54\right\}$

$= 3n - 65n + 54 = -62n + 54$

99. Evaluate $2.47b + 21.6$ when $b = 16.8$

$2.47(16.8) + 21.6 = 41.496 + 21.6 = 63.096$

63.096 rounds to approximately 63 in. tall.

101. Evaluate $2116.8 + 62d$ when $d = 8$

$2116.8 + 62(8) = 2116.8 + 496 =$

2612.8 pounds per square foot.

103. Perimeter is twice the length plus twice the width for a rectangle. The length is $(x) + (x + 4) + (x) = 3x + 4$ and the width is $x + 4$. Two widths + two lengths is $2(3x + 4) + 2(x + 4) = 6x + 8 + 2x + 8 = 8x + 16$.

105. a. Quotient of h to b is $\frac{h}{b}$.

b.

Player	Number of Hits h	Number of Times at bat b	Batting Average $\frac{h}{b}$
Barry Bonds	133	390	$\frac{133}{390} = .341$
Manny Ramirez	185	569	$\frac{185}{569} = .325$
Alex Rodriguez	181	607	$\frac{181}{607} = .298$
Ichiro Suzuki	212	679	$\frac{212}{679} = .312$

107. a.

Year	x	Hourly Earnings $0.5x + 17.5$
2000	0	$0.5(0) + 17.5 = \$17.50$
2001	1	$0.5(1) + 17.5 = \$18.00$
2002	2	$0.5(2) + 17.5 = \$18.50$
2003	3	$0.5(3) + 17.5 = \$19.00$

b. The average hourly earnings are increasing by $0.50 each year.

c. 2005 is 5 years since 2000.

$0.5x + 17.5 = 0.5(5) + 17.5 = \$20.00$

2010 is 10 years since 2000

$0.5x + 17.5 = 0.5(10) + 17.5 = \$22.50$

109. The value of the laptop will be $1350 - $115 for each year or $(1350 - 115t)$ dollars after t years.

111. Perimeter is twice the width plus twice the length. If the width is w, then the length is

$w + 5$ and the perimeter will be

$2 \bullet \text{width} + 2 \bullet \text{length} = 2w + 2(w + 5) =$

$2w + 2w + 10 = 4w + 10$

She needs to buy $(4w + 10)$ ft of fencing.

113. a. $10.5h$

Number of Hours, h	Weekly Pay $10.5h$ (in dollars)
30	$10.5(30) = 315$
32.5	$10.5(32.5) = 341.25$
35	$10.5(35) = 367.50$
38	$10.5(38) = 399$
40	$10.5(40) = 420$

   b. $10.5h + 5.25(h - 40) = 10.5h + 5.25h - 210 =$
   $(15.75h - 210)$ dollars.

   c. $15.75(54) - 210 = 850.50 - 210 = 640.50$
   Her weekly pay is $640.50.

115. If x theaters have 400 seats, then the rest or $15 - x$ must have 200 seats. The total seats will be
   $x(400) + (15 - x)(200) =$
   $400x + 3000 - 200x = 200x + 3000$

117. If there are n 3½ diskettes, the rest, or $350 - n$ will be Zip disks. Their value will be:
   $n(4.75) + (350 - n)(30.00) =$
   $4.75n + 10500 - 30.00n =$
   $(10,500 - 25.25n)$ dollars.

Chapter 1 Review Exercises

1.   False, $\sqrt{2}$ is irrational.
2.   True, -5 is an integer.
3.
4.   The additive inverse of -8 is 8.
5.   The value of $|-6| = 6$
6.   False $-2 > -7$
7.   True $0 \geq -6.1$
8.   a.
     b. $(-\infty, 0]$
9.   Subtract their absolute values, use the sign of the number with the largest absolute value. $3.4 + (-5.9) = -2.5$

10. Do not subtract, add the opposite. $5 - (-2) = 5 + (+2) = 7$
11. The product of two factors with like signs is positive.
     $(-4.5)(-3) = 13.5$
12. $\left(\dfrac{1}{4}\right)^2 = \left(\dfrac{1}{4}\right)\left(\dfrac{1}{4}\right) = \dfrac{1}{16}$
13. The quotient of two factors with like signs is positive.
     $(-8) \div (-4) = \dfrac{-8}{-4} = 2$
14. $-3(4 - 10) = -3(4 + (-10)) =$
     $-3(-6) = 18$
15. $\left[3(\underline{5 + 6}) - 3(\underline{4 - 5})\right] = \left[3(11) - 3(-1)\right] =$
     $[33 + 3] = 36$
16. Evaluate the numerator before dividing.
     $\dfrac{-1 + (-9)}{5} = \dfrac{-10}{5} = -2$
17. $(-5)^2 - 3^2 = 25 - 9 = 16$
18. $|3 - 9| = |-6| = 6$
19. $-|-1| - |6| = -(1) - (6) = -7$
20. $\sqrt{29 - 16} = \sqrt{13}$
21. $3 + 9 = 9 + 3$
22. $(-3)(1 + 9) = (-3)(1) + (-3)(9)$
23. $(3x + y) + z = 3x + (y + z)$
     Associative property of addition.
24. $-(x + 1) + (x + 1) = 0$
     Additive inverse property.
25. $10 + (-2) + (-1) = 8 + (-1) = 7$
26. $(-4)(-5)(-2)(4) = (20)(-2)(4) =$
     $(-40)(4) = -160$
27. The additive inverse of 4 is –4.
28. The multiplicative inverse of $\dfrac{2}{3}$ is $\dfrac{3}{2}$.
29. $3(a - 4b) = 3(a) - 3(4b) = 3a - 12b$
30. $-(x - 5) = (-1)(x - 5) = (-1)(x) - (-1)(5) =$
     $-x + 5$
31. $(-5x)(-5x)(-5x) = (-5x)^3$
32. $(-4)^3 = (-4)(-4)(-4) = -64$
33. $13^0 = 1$
34. $(-3xy)^1 = -3xy$
35. $7^{-2} = \dfrac{1}{7^2}$
36. $(2y)^{-1} = \dfrac{1}{2y}$

37. $n^8 n^4 = n^{8+4} = n^{12}$

38. $\left(ab^2\right)\left(a^2 b\right) = a^{1+2} b^{2+1} = a^3 b^3$

39. $\dfrac{a^5}{b^2}$ cannot be simplified. The bases

    are not the same.

40. $\left(2n+1\right)^4 \div \left(2n+1\right) = \dfrac{\left(2n+1\right)^4}{\left(2n+1\right)^1} =$

    $\left(2n+1\right)^{4-1} = \left(2n+1\right)^3$

41. $\left(-y^3\right)^5 = \left(\left(-1\right)^1 \left(y^3\right)\right)^5 =$

    $\left(-1\right)^{1\bullet 5}\left(y^{3\bullet 5}\right) = -y^{15}$

42. $\left(pq^3\right)^4 = \left(p^1 q^3\right)^4 = p^{1\bullet 4} q^{3\bullet 4} =$

    $p^4 q^{12}$

43. $\left(\dfrac{-u^3}{uv^2}\right)^4 = \left(\dfrac{-u^{3-1}}{v^2}\right)^4 = \left(\dfrac{(-1)\left(u^2\right)}{v^2}\right)^4 =$

    $\dfrac{(-1)^4 \left(u^8\right)}{v^8} = \dfrac{u^8}{v^8}$

44. $-4t^{-2} = -\dfrac{4}{t^2}$

45. $\dfrac{2p^3}{q^{-1}} = 2p^3 q$

46. $x^5 \bullet x^{-4} = x^{5-4} = x^1 = x$

47. $\left(-2p^2 q^{-5}\right)^{-2} = \left(-2\right)^{-2} p^{2\bullet(-2)} q^{-5\bullet(-2)} =$

    $\dfrac{1}{\left(-2^2\right)} p^{-4} q^{10} = \dfrac{q^{10}}{4p^4}$

48. $\left(\dfrac{x^4}{3y}\right)^{-2} = \dfrac{x^{4\bullet(-2)}}{3^{-2} y^{-2}} = \dfrac{x^{-8}}{3^{-2} y^{-2}} =$

    $\dfrac{3^2 y^2}{x^8} = \dfrac{9 y^2}{x^8}$ or

    $\left(\dfrac{x^4}{3y}\right)^{-2} = \left(\dfrac{3y}{x^4}\right)^2 = \dfrac{3^2 y^2}{x^{4\bullet 2}} = \dfrac{9 y^2}{x^8}$

49. Move the decimal point eight units to the left.
    $200,000,000 = 2\times 10^8$

50. Move the decimal point four places to the
    right. $0.00031 = 3.1\times 10^{-4}$

51. Move the decimal point five places to the right.
    $2.86\times 10^5 = 286,000$

52. Move the decimal point three places to the left.
    $5.02\times 10^{-3} = 0.00502$

53. $\left(3\times 10^2\right)\left(5\times 10^4\right) = 3\bullet 5\times 10^{2+4} =$

    $15\times 10^6 = 1.5\times 10^1 \times 10^6 = 1.5\times 10^7$

54. $\left(8\times 10^5\right) \div \left(2\times 10^3\right) = \dfrac{8\times 10^5}{2\times 10^3} =$

    $4\times 10^{5-3} = 4\times 10^2$

55. $x-4$ is four less than x or x decreased by four.

56. $\dfrac{3}{p+q}$ is three divided by the sum of p and

    or the quotient of three and the sum of

    p and q.

57. The difference between x and -5 is $x-\left(-5\right)$.

58. The quantity p plus q divided by the quantity q minus

    p is $\dfrac{p+q}{q-p}$.

59.

x	$2x-5$
-2	$2(-2)-5 = -4-5 = -9$
-1	$2(-1)-5 = -2-5 = -7$
0	$2(0)-5 = 0-5 = -5$
1	$2(1)-5 = 2-5 = -3$
2	$2(2)-5 = 4-5 = -1$

60. $w=-3$ and $z=2$

    $3\left(w-5z\right) = 3\left(\left(-3\right)-5\left(2\right)\right) =$

    $3\left(-3-10\right) = 3\left(-13\right) = -39$

61. The terms are $2a$ and $5b$.
    They are unlike.

62. The terms are $3a^2 b$ and $-a^2 b$.
    They are like terms.

63. $x-5x = x\left(1-5\right) = -4x$

64. $-4ab^2 + 7ab^2 = \left(-4+7\right)ab^2 = 3ab^2$

65. $6t-3t+2 = \left(6-3\right)t+2 = 3t+2$

66. $5x^2 - 7x + 9x^2 + x = 5x^2 + 9x^2 - 7x + x =$

    $\left(5+9\right)x^2 + \left(-7+1\right)x = 14x^2 - 6x$

67. $-\left(5y-1\right) = \left(-1\right)\left(5y-1\right) =$

    $\left(-1\right)\left(5y\right) - \left(-1\right)\left(1\right) = -5y+1$

68. $6+3\left[-2\left(x-6\right)+4x\right] = 6+3\left[\underline{-2x}+12+\underline{4x}\right] =$

    $6+3\left[2x+12\right] = 6+6x+36 = 6x+42$

69. a. Wednesday.
    b. $-16 < -15$
    c. $\dfrac{-13-16-24-10-15-11-4}{7} = \dfrac{-93}{7} \approx -13$

    The average temperature was about -13°F for the
    week.

70. a.

    b. The company showed losses in the second and
    fourth quarters.

c. $\dfrac{1.7+-0.5+3.8+-1.75}{4}=$

$\dfrac{3.25}{4}=\$0.8125$ million $=\$812,500$

The average profit was $812,500.

71. $\$578.37-585.00=-\$6.63$

72. $23\%\times1300=299$

An 8-oz glass of milk contains about 300 mg of calcium.

73.   Mt. McKinley elevation – Death Valley elevation.

$6194-(-86)=6194+86=6280m.$

74.   a.

Year	Revenue – Expenditures (in millions)
1999	$\$1,827,454-\$1,701,891=\$125,563$
2000	$\$2,025,218-\$1,788,773=\$236,445$
2001	$\$1,991,194-\$1,863,895=\$127,299$
2002	$\$1,853,173-\$2,010,975=-\$157,802$
2003	$\$1,863,218-\$2,140,377=-\$277,159$
2004	$\$1,922,025-\$2,229,425=-\$307,400$

b.   The sum of the surpluses is:

$125,563+236,445+127,299=489,307$

The sum of the deficits is:

$-157,802-304,159-307,400=-769,361$

The average change was:

$\dfrac{489304+(-769,361)}{6}=\dfrac{-280,053}{6}=$

$-46,675.5$ rounded to the nearest million

$-\$46,676$ million $=-\$46,676,000,000$

75.   Earth's radius $=\dfrac{\text{Sun's radius}}{109}=$

$\dfrac{6.955\times10^{8}\,\text{m}}{109}=\dfrac{6.955\times10^{8}\,\text{m}}{1.09\times10^{2}}=$

$6.381\times10^{8-2}\,\text{m}=6.381\times10^{6}\,\text{m}.$

The radius of the planet earth is approximately 6.4×10^{6} meters.

76. $4.2\times10^{7}=42,000,000$

$42,000,000$ Total people

$\underline{-3,200,000}$ Children

$38,800,000$ Adults who were living with HIV/AIDS in 2002.

77. $-4.9(2)^{2}-3(2)+100=-4.9(4)-3(2)+100=$

$-19.6-6+100=-25.6+100=74.4m$

The object is 74.4 m above the ground.

78. $6(71-60)+106=6(11)+106=$

$66+106=172$ lbs.

79.   a. $\dfrac{A\bullet n}{60}$ $A=100,\ n=15$

$\dfrac{(100)\bullet(15)}{60}=\dfrac{1500}{60}=25$ drops per min.

b.   Millileters per hour means $\dfrac{\text{milliliters}}{\text{hours}}=$

$\dfrac{1500\ \text{ml.}}{12\ \text{hr.}}=125$ milliters per hour.

c. $\dfrac{A\bullet n}{60}$ $A=125,\ n=15$

$\dfrac{(125)\bullet(15)}{60}=\dfrac{1875}{60}\approx31$ drops per minute.

80.

time, t (in seconds)	Height (in feet) $-16t^{2}+20t+300$
0	$-16(0)^{2}+20(0)+300=$ 300
1	$-16(1)^{2}+20(1)+300=$ $-16\bullet1+20+300=304$
2	$-16(2)^{2}+20(2)+300=$ $-16\bullet4+40+300=$ $-64+40+300=276$
3	$-16(3)^{2}+20(3)+300=$ $-16(9)+60+300=$ $-144+60+300=216$
4	$-16(4)^{2}+20(4)+300=$ $-16\bullet16+80+300=$ $-256+80+300=124$
5	$-16(5)^{2}+20(5)+300=$ $-16(25)+100+300=$ $-400+100+300=0$

81.   Dividing $45,000 into two accounts gives investments of x and $\$45,000-x$.

$5\%x+6\%(\$45,000-x)=$

$0.05x+0.06(45000-x)=$

$0.05x+2700-0.06x=$

$(2,700-0.01x)$ dollars.

82.   If h is hours parked, only hours after the one is charged at $1.50. The first hour costs $5. That makes the charge $\$5+\$1.50(h-1)=$

$5+1.50h-1.50=(1.50h+3.50)$ dollars.

Chapter 1 Posttest

1. -3.5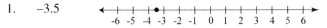

2. $|-9| = 9$

3. False, $-2 \not< -5$

4. $-4 + (x + y) = (-4 + x) + y$

5. $3 - (-6) = 3 + (+6) = 9$

6. $10 + |(-2) + (-1)| = 10 + |-3| = 10 + 3 = 13$

7. $\underline{(-3)(5)}(-1)(-2) = \underline{(-15)(-1)}(-2) =$
   $\underline{(15)(-2)} = -30$

8. $-13^0 = (-1)(13^0) = (-1)(1) = -1$

9. $-\left(-\dfrac{1}{2}\right)^2 = -\left(-\dfrac{1}{2}\right)\left(-\dfrac{1}{2}\right) = -\dfrac{1}{4}$

10. $(12)(-7) \div (-6)(3) + (-2)^2 =$
    Multiply and divide left to right.
    $(12)(-7) \div (-6)(3) + 4 =$
    $\underline{-84 \div (-6)}(3) + 4 = \underline{14(3)} + 4 = 42 + 4 = 46$

11. $-\left[6(\underline{7+4}) - 3^2(\underline{8-1})\right]^3 = -\left[6 \bullet 11 - \underline{3^2}(7)\right]^3 =$
    $-[6 \bullet 11 - \underline{9 \bullet 7}]^3 = -[\underline{66 - 63}]^3 = -[3]^3 = -27$

12. $\dfrac{-4 - \underline{(-2)^4}}{4(\underline{5^2} - 13 \bullet 2)} = \dfrac{-4 - 16}{4(25 - \underline{13 \bullet 2})} = \dfrac{-4 - 16}{4(\underline{25 - 26})} =$
    $\dfrac{-4 + (-16)}{4(-1)} = \dfrac{-20}{-4} = 5$

13. $\dfrac{2p^3}{q^{-2}} = 2p^3 q^2$

14. $\left(ab^4\right)^3\left(a^6 b\right) = a^{1 \bullet 3} b^{4 \bullet 3} a^6 b = a^3 b^{12} a^6 b =$
    $a^{3+6} b^{12+1} = a^9 b^{13}$

15. $\left(\dfrac{x^4 y^2}{z^{-1}}\right)^{-2} = \left(\dfrac{z^{-1}}{x^4 y^2}\right)^2 = \left(\dfrac{1}{x^4 y^2 z}\right)^2 =$
    $\dfrac{1}{x^{4 \bullet 2} y^{2 \bullet 2} z^{1 \bullet 2}} = \dfrac{1}{x^8 y^4 z^2}$ or
    $\left(\dfrac{x^4 y^2}{z^{-1}}\right)^{-2} = \dfrac{x^{4(-2)} y^{2(-2)}}{z^{-1(-2)}} = \dfrac{x^{-8} y^{-4}}{z^2} = \dfrac{1}{x^8 y^4 z^2}$

16. Four times the difference between p and q or the product of four and the quantity q subtracted from p.

17. $2(x - 3y)$ when $x = -1$ and $y = 5$
    $2((-1) - 3(5)) = 2(-1 - 15) = 2(-16) = -32$

18. $4 + 3\left[-8(x-1) + 4x\right] = 4 + 3\left[\underline{-8x} + 8 \underline{+4x}\right] =$
    $4 + 3\left[-4x + 8\right] = 4 + -12x + 24 = -12x + 28$

19. a. \$5000 plus \$80 per guest$=$
    $(5000 + 80x)$ dollars.
    b. $5000 + 80x$ when $x = 200$
    $5000 + 80(200) = 5000 + 16000 = \$21,000$

20. 0.7 astronomical units $=$
    $0.7(9.3 \times 10^7) = 6.51 \times 10^7$ miles.
    The distance from the Sun to the planet Venus is approximately 6.5×10^7 miles.

Chapter 2 Linear Equations and Inequalities

Pretest

1. Substitute -2 for x.

$\frac{1}{2}(-2)-6\overset{?}{=}7$

$-1-6=-7\ne 7$

-2 is not a solution.

2. $2x-10=-5$

$2x-10+10=-5+10$

$2x=5$

$\frac{2x}{2}=\frac{5}{2}$

$x=\frac{5}{2}$

3. $5x+9=3x+13$

$5x+9-3x=3x-3x+13$

$2x+9=13$

$2x+9-9=13-9$

$2x=4$

$\frac{2x}{2}=\frac{4}{2}$

$x=2$

4. $4-6n=2(1-2n)$

$4-6n=2-4n$

$4-6n+4n=2-4n+4n$

$4-2n=2$

$4-4-2n=2-4$

$-2n=-2$

$\frac{-2n}{-2}=\frac{-2}{-2}$

$n=1$

5. $4x-3y=6$

$4x-4x-3y=-4x+6$

$-3y=-4x+6$

$\frac{-3y}{-3}=\frac{-4x+6}{-3}$

$y=\frac{-4x}{-3}+\frac{6}{-3}$

$y=\frac{4}{3}x-2$

6. Substitute 5 into the inequality.

$8-2(5)\overset{?}{\le}7$

$8-10\overset{?}{\le}7$

$-2\le 7$ True

5 is a solution to the inequality.

7. $x-5\le 2x+1$

$x-2x-5\le 2x-2x+1$

$-x-5\le 1$

$-x-5+5\le 1+5$

$-x\le 6$

$\frac{-x}{-1}\ge \frac{6}{-1}$ Reverse direction of inequality.

$x\ge -6$

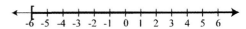

8. $4x+3<7$ $\qquad$ and $5x-1\ge -16$

$4x+3-3<7-3$ $\qquad$ $5x-1+1\ge -16+1$

$4x<4$ $\qquad\qquad$ $5x\ge -15$

$\frac{4x}{4}<\frac{4}{4}$ $\qquad\qquad$ $\frac{5x}{5}\ge \frac{-15}{5}$

$x<1$ $\qquad\qquad\quad$ $x\ge -3$

9. $\frac{2}{3}x+4\le 0$ $\qquad$ or $10-9x\le 19$

$\qquad\qquad\qquad\qquad$ $10-10-9x\le 19-10$

$\frac{2}{3}x+4-4\le 0-4$ $\qquad$ $-9x\le 9$

$\frac{2}{3}x\le -4$ $\qquad\qquad$ $\frac{-9x}{-9}\ge \frac{9}{-9}$

$\left(\frac{3}{2}\right)\frac{2}{3}x\le -4\left(\frac{3}{2}\right)$ $\qquad$ $x\ge -1$

$x\le -6$

10. $-17<6x+13<25$

$-17-13<6x+13-13<25-13$

$-30<6x<12$

$\frac{-30}{6}<\frac{6x}{6}<\frac{12}{6}$

$-5<x<2$

11. $\left|-3.7-2.2\right|=\left|-5.9\right|=5.9$

12. $\left|x+9\right|=5$

$x+9=5$ $\qquad$ or $x+9=-5$

$x+9-9=5-9$ $\qquad$ $x+9-9=-5-9$

$x=-4$ $\qquad\qquad$ $x=-14$

13. $\left|y\right|-2=-1$

$\left|y\right|-2+2=-1+2$

$\left|y\right|=1$ means $y=1$ or $y=-1$

14. $\left|4x+3\right|=\left|x-9\right|$ means

$4x+3 = x-9$ or $4x+3 = -(x-9)$

$4x-x+3 = x-x-9$ $4x+3 = -x+9$

$3x+3 = -9$ $4x+x+3 = -x+x+9$

$3x+3-3 = -9-3$ $5x+3 = 9$

$3x = -12$ $5x+3-3 = 9-3$

$\dfrac{3x}{3} = \dfrac{-12}{3}$ $5x = 6$

$x = -4$ $\dfrac{5x}{5} = \dfrac{6}{5}$

                    $x = \dfrac{6}{5}$

15. $|2x-1| \geq 1$ means

     $2x-1 \geq 1$ or $2x-1 \leq -1$

     $2x-1+1 \geq 1+1$ $2x-1+1 \leq -1+1$

     $2x \geq 2$ $2x \leq 0$

     $\dfrac{2x}{2} \geq \dfrac{2}{2}$ $\dfrac{2x}{2} \leq \dfrac{0}{2}$

     $x \geq 1$ $x \leq 0$

16.   If y is the number of years the copier is in service, then the current value of the copier will be: $\$5000 - \$840y$. This will be $\$800$ when

     $5000 - 840y = 800$

     $5000 - 5000 - 840y = 800 - 5000$

     $-840y = -4200$

     $\dfrac{-840y}{-840} = \dfrac{-4200}{-840}$

     $y = 5$ The copier will have the value of $\$800$ in 5 years.

17.

Action	Substance	Amount	Amount of Salt
Start	65% Saline	6 L	$0.65 \bullet 6 =$ 3.9 L
Add	Water	4 L	0
Finish	?% New	10 L	3.9 L

     Concentration $= \dfrac{\text{Total Salt}}{\text{Total amount}} =$

     $\dfrac{3.9 \text{ L}}{10 L} = 0.39 = 39\%$

18.   In a five-day week, he will be allowed $5 \bullet \$150$ for meals and $0.30m$ for driving m miles.

     $5 \bullet 150 + 0.30m \leq 900$

     $750 + 0.30m \leq 900$

$750 - 750 + 0.30m \leq 900 - 750$

$0.30m \leq 150$

$\dfrac{0.30m}{0.30} \leq \dfrac{150}{0.30}$

$m \leq 500$

He can drive at most 500 mi in a 5-day workweek.

19. $\$7500 < \text{cost} < \$9000$

     $7500 < 4500 + 0.6b < 9000$

     $\underline{-4500 \quad\quad -4500 \quad\quad\quad\quad -4500}$

     $3000 < \quad\quad\quad 0.6b < 4500$

     $\dfrac{3000}{0.6} < \dfrac{0.6b}{0.6} < \dfrac{4500}{0.6}$

     $5000 < b < 7500$

     Between 5000 and 7500 bottles of juice should be produced each month.

20. $|\text{cost} - 12000| \leq 2500$

     $|c - 12000| \leq 2500$

     $-2500 \leq c - 12000 \leq 2500$

     $\underline{+12000 \quad\quad +12000 \;\; +12000}$

     $9500 \leq c \quad\quad\quad\quad \leq 14500$

     $9500 \leq c \leq 14500$

The homeowner could pay a minimum of $\$9,500$ to a maximum of $\$14,500$ for kitchen remodeling.

Exercises 2.1 Solving Linear Equations

1.   Does $2x - 1 = 5$ when $x = 2$?

     $2(2) - 1 \overset{?}{=} 5$

     $4 - 1 \overset{?}{=} 5$

     $3 \neq 5$ 2 is not a solution.

3.   Does $1 - \dfrac{t}{4} = -2$ when $t = -4$?

     $1 - \dfrac{-4}{4} \overset{?}{=} -2$

     $1 - (-1) \overset{?}{=} -2$

     $1 + 1 \overset{?}{=} -2$

     $2 \neq -2$ -4 is not a solution.

5.   Does $5y - 6 = 7y - 5$ when $y = -\dfrac{1}{2}$?

     $5\left(-\dfrac{1}{2}\right) - 6 \overset{?}{=} 7\left(-\dfrac{1}{2}\right) - 5$

     $-\dfrac{5}{2} - \dfrac{12}{2} \overset{?}{=} -\dfrac{7}{2} - \dfrac{10}{2}$

     $-\dfrac{17}{2} = -\dfrac{17}{2}$ $-\dfrac{1}{2}$ is a solution.

7.   Does $2n - 10 = 4(3n - 15)$ when $n = 7$?

$2(7) - 10 \overset{?}{=} 4(3(7) - 15)$

$14 - 10 \overset{?}{=} 4(21 - 15)$

$4 \overset{?}{=} 4(6)$

$4 \neq 24$ 7 is not a solution

9.   Does $\frac{1}{2}\left(9 - \frac{x}{4}\right) + x = \frac{x}{3} - 2$ when $x = -12$

$\frac{1}{2}\left(9 - \frac{-12}{4}\right) + (-12) \overset{?}{=} \frac{-12}{3} - 2$

$\frac{1}{2}(9 + 3) - 12 \overset{?}{=} -4 - 2$

$\frac{1}{2}(12) - 12 \overset{?}{=} -6$

$6 - 12 \overset{?}{=} -6$

$-6 = -6$ -12 is a solution.

11. $x + 4 = 2$

$x + 4 - 4 = 2 - 4$

$x = -2$

Check

$(-2) + 4 \overset{?}{=} 2$

$2 = 2$ True.

13. $x - 3.7 = -2$

$x - 3.7 + 3.7 = -2 + 3.7$

$x = 1.7$

Check

$(1.7) - 3.7 = -2$

$-2 = -2$ True.

15. $\frac{3}{4} + y = -\frac{5}{8}$

$\frac{3}{4} - \frac{3}{4} + y = -\frac{5}{8} - \frac{3}{4}$

$y = -\frac{5}{8} - \frac{6}{8} = -\frac{11}{8}$

Check

$\frac{3}{4} + \left(-\frac{11}{8}\right) \overset{?}{=} -\frac{5}{8}$

$\frac{6}{8} - \frac{11}{8} \overset{?}{=} -\frac{5}{8}$

$-\frac{5}{8} = -\frac{5}{8}$ True.

17. $\frac{n}{5} = -1$

$(5)\left(\frac{n}{5}\right) = -1(5)$

$n = -5$

Check

$\frac{(-5)}{5} \overset{?}{=} -1$

$-1 = -1$ True.

19. $16 - 4y = 0$

$16 - 16 - 4y = 0 - 16$

$-4y = -16$

$\left(-\frac{1}{4}\right)(-4y) = -16\left(-\frac{1}{4}\right)$

$y = 4$

Check

$16 - 4(4) \overset{?}{=} 0$

$16 - 16 = 0$

$0 = 0$ True.

21. $\frac{2}{3}n = \frac{4}{9}$

$\left(\frac{3}{2}\right)\frac{2}{3}n = \left(\frac{\overset{1}{\cancel{3}}}{\cancel{2}}\right)\frac{\overset{2}{\cancel{4}}}{\underset{3}{\cancel{9}}}$

$n = \frac{2}{3}$

Check

$\frac{2}{3}\left(\frac{2}{3}\right) \overset{?}{=} \frac{4}{9}$

$\frac{4}{9} = \frac{4}{9}$ True.

23. $-8.1 = 0.9a$

$\frac{-8.1}{0.9} = \frac{0.9}{0.9}a$

$-9 = a$

Check

$-8.1 = 0.9(-9)$

$-8.1 = -8.1$ True.

25. $5x + 1 = -4$

$5x + 1 - 1 = -4 - 1$

$5x = -5$

$\frac{5}{5}x = \frac{-5}{5}$

$x = -1$

Check

$$5(-1)+1\overset{?}{=}-4$$

$$-5+1\overset{?}{=}-4$$

$$-4=-4 \text{ True.}$$

27. $12-x=-10$

$$12-12-x=-10-12$$

$$-x=-22$$

$$\frac{-x}{-1}=\frac{-22}{-1}$$

$$x=22$$

Check

$$12-(22)\overset{?}{=}-10$$

$$-10=-10 \text{ True.}$$

29. $-4n-6=10$

$$-4n-6+6=10+6$$

$$-4n=16$$

$$\frac{-4}{-4}n=\frac{16}{-4}$$

$$n=-4$$

Check

$$-4(-4)-6\overset{?}{=}10$$

$$16-6\overset{?}{=}10$$

$$10=10 \text{ True.}$$

31. $9+8n=9$

$$9-9+8n=9-9$$

$$8n=0$$

$$\frac{8n}{8}=\frac{0}{8}$$

$$n=0$$

Check

$$9+8(0)\overset{?}{=}9$$

$$9+0\overset{?}{=}9$$

$$9=9 \text{ True.}$$

33. $\dfrac{t}{3}-5=2$

$$\frac{t}{3}-5+5=2+5$$

$$\frac{t}{3}=7$$

$$(3)\frac{t}{3}=(3)7$$

$$t=21$$

Check

$$\frac{21}{3}-5\overset{?}{=}2$$

$$7-5\overset{?}{=}2$$

$$2=2 \text{ True.}$$

35. $4-\dfrac{3}{5}x=13$

$$4-4-\frac{3}{5}x=13-4$$

$$-\frac{3}{5}x=9$$

$$\left(-\frac{5}{3}\right)\left(-\frac{3}{5}x\right)=\left(-\frac{5}{\cancel{3}}\right)\overset{3}{\cancel{9}}$$

$$x=-15$$

Check

$$4-\frac{3}{\cancel{5}}\left(-\overset{3}{\cancel{15}}\right)\overset{?}{=}13$$

$$4-3(-3)\overset{?}{=}13$$

$$4+9\overset{?}{=}13$$

$$13=13 \text{ True.}$$

37. $0.2=-1.2n-7$

$$0.2+7=-1.2n-7+7$$

$$7.2=-1.2n$$

$$\frac{7.2}{-1.2}=\frac{-1.2}{-1.2}n$$

$$-6=n$$

Check

$$0.2\overset{?}{=}-1.2(-6)-7$$

$$0.2\overset{?}{=}7.2-7$$

$$0.2=0.2 \text{ True.}$$

39. $8y=y$

$$8y-y=y-y$$

$$7y=0$$

$$\frac{7}{7}y=\frac{0}{7}$$

$$y=0$$

Check

$$8(0)\overset{?}{=}0$$

$$0=0 \text{ True.}$$

41. $10-5x=x+18$

$$10-5x-x=x-x+18$$
$$10-6x=18$$
$$10-10-6x=18-10$$
$$-6x=8$$
$$\frac{-6}{-6}x=\frac{8}{-6}$$
$$x=-\frac{4}{3}$$

Check
$$10-5\left(-\frac{4}{3}\right)\overset{?}{=}-\frac{4}{3}+18$$
$$\frac{30}{3}+\frac{20}{3}\overset{?}{=}-\frac{4}{3}+\frac{54}{3}$$
$$\frac{50}{3}=\frac{50}{3}\ \text{True.}$$

43. $7y-8=12y-8$
$$7y-12y-8=12y-12y-8$$
$$-5y-8=-8$$
$$-5y-8+8=-8+8$$
$$-5y=0$$
$$\frac{-5}{-5}y=\frac{0}{-5}$$
$$y=0$$

Check
$$7(0)-8\overset{?}{=}12(0)-8$$
$$-8=-8\ \text{True.}$$

45. $8a-3-5a=15$
$$3a-3=15$$
$$3a-3+3=15+3$$
$$3a=18$$
$$\frac{3}{3}a=\frac{18}{3}$$
$$a=6$$

Check
$$8(6)-3-5(6)\overset{?}{=}15$$
$$48-3-30\overset{?}{=}15$$
$$45-30\overset{?}{=}15$$
$$15=15\ \text{True.}$$

47. $16n=7n-15-6n$
$$16n=n-15$$
$$16n-n=n-n-15$$
$$15n=-15$$
$$\frac{15}{15}n=\frac{-15}{15}$$
$$n=-1$$

Check
$$16(-1)\overset{?}{=}7(-1)-15-6(-1)$$
$$-16\overset{?}{=}-7-15+6$$
$$-16\overset{?}{=}-22+6$$
$$-16=-16\ \text{True.}$$

49. $2.4-0.6x+3.3=1.3x$
$$-0.6x+5.7=1.3x$$
$$-0.6x+0.6x+5.7=1.3x+0.6x$$
$$5.7=1.9x$$
$$\frac{5.7}{1.9}-\frac{1.9}{1.9}x$$
$$3=x$$

Check
$$2.4-0.6(3)+3.3=1.3(3)$$
$$2.4-1.8+3.3\overset{?}{=}3.9$$
$$3.9=3.9\ \text{True.}$$

51. $18-12n=16+3n-11$
$$18-12n=5+3n$$
$$18-12n-3n=5+3n-3n$$
$$18-15n=5$$
$$18-18-15n=5-18$$
$$-15n=-13$$
$$\frac{-15}{-15}n=\frac{-13}{-15}$$
$$n=\frac{13}{15}$$

Check
$$18-\overset{4}{\cancel{12}}\left(\frac{13}{\underset{5}{\cancel{15}}}\right)=16+\overset{1}{\cancel{3}}\left(\frac{13}{\underset{5}{\cancel{15}}}\right)-11$$
$$18-\frac{52}{5}\overset{?}{=}16+\frac{13}{5}-11$$
$$\frac{90}{5}-\frac{52}{5}\overset{?}{=}\frac{80}{5}+\frac{13}{5}-\frac{55}{5}$$
$$\frac{38}{5}=\frac{38}{5}\ \text{True.}$$

53. $23t+11-15t=6t-18+7$
$$8t+11=6t-11$$
$$8t-6t+11=6t-6t-11$$
$$2t+11=-11$$
$$2t+11-11=-11-11$$
$$2t=-22$$
$$\frac{2}{2}t=\frac{-22}{2}$$
$$t=-11$$

Check

$23(-11)+11-15(-11)=6(-11)-18+7$

$-253+11+165\overset{?}{=}-66-18+7$

$-77=-77$ True.

55. $11y+24-18y=13y-21-10y$

$24-7y=3y-21$

$24-7y-3y=3y-3y-21$

$24-10y=-21$

$24-24-10y=-21-24$

$-10y=-45$

$\dfrac{-10}{-10}y=\dfrac{-45}{-10}$

$y=\dfrac{9}{2}$

Check

$11\left(\dfrac{9}{2}\right)+24-18\left(\dfrac{9}{2}\right)=13\left(\dfrac{9}{2}\right)-21-10\left(\dfrac{9}{2}\right)$

$\dfrac{99}{2}+\dfrac{48}{2}-\dfrac{162}{2}\overset{?}{=}\dfrac{117}{2}-\dfrac{42}{2}-\dfrac{90}{2}$

$-\dfrac{15}{2}=-\dfrac{15}{2}$ True.

57. $5.7+3.6x-7.2=0.6x+2.5-2x$

$3.6x-1.5=-1.4x+2.5$

$3.6x+1.4x-1.5=-1.4x+1.4x+2.5$

$5.0x-1.5=2.5$

$5.0x-1.5+1.5=2.5+1.5$

$5.0x=4.0$

$\dfrac{5.0}{5.0}x=\dfrac{4.0}{5.0}$

$x=\dfrac{4}{5}$ or $x=0.8$

Check

$5.7+3.6(0.8)-7.2=0.6(0.8)+2.5-2(0.8)$

$5.7+2.88-7.2\overset{?}{=}0.48+2.5-1.6$

$1.38=1.38$ True.

59. $-2(x-6)=4$

$-2x+12=4$

$-2x+12-12=4-12$

$-2x=-8$

$\dfrac{-2}{-2}x=\dfrac{-8}{-2}$

$x=4$

Check

$-2((4)-6)\overset{?}{=}4$

$-2(-2)\overset{?}{=}4$

$4=4$ True.

61. $7-(3n-8)=-6$

$7-3n+8=-6$

$-3n+15=-6$

$-3n+15-15=-6-15$

$-3n=-21$

$\dfrac{-3}{-3}n=\dfrac{-21}{-3}$

$n=7$

Check

$7-(3(7)-8)\overset{?}{=}-6$

$7-(21-8)\overset{?}{=}-6$

$7-(13)=-6$

$-6=-6$ True.

63. $-4(7+3x)=-5(2x+8)$

$-28-12x=-10x-40$

$-28-12x+10x=-10x+10x-40$

$-28-2x=-40$

$-28+28-2x=-40+28$

$-2x=-12$

$\dfrac{-2}{-2}x=\dfrac{-12}{-2}$

$x=6$

Check

$-4(7+3(6))\overset{?}{=}-5(2(6)+8)$

$-4(7+18)\overset{?}{=}-5(12+8)$

$-4(25)\overset{?}{=}-5(20)$

$-100=-100$ True.

65. $\dfrac{1}{2}(16n-12)=9n+11$

$8n-6=9n+11$

$8n-9n-6=9n-9n+11$

$-n-6=11$

$-n-6+6=11+6$

$-n=17$

$\dfrac{-n}{-1}=\dfrac{17}{-1}$

$n=-17$

Check

$$\frac{1}{2}(16(-17)-12) \overset{?}{=} 9(-17)+11$$

$$\frac{1}{2}(-272-12) \overset{?}{=} -153+11$$

$$\frac{1}{2}(-284) \overset{?}{=} -142$$

$$-142 = -142 \text{ True.}$$

67. $5x-2(x+6) = 6(x-1)-8$

$5x-2x-12 = 6x-6-8$

$3x-12 = 6x-14$

$3x-6x-12 = 6x-6x-14$

$-3x-12 = -14$

$-3x-12+12 = -14+12$

$-3x = -2$

$\dfrac{-3}{-3}x = \dfrac{-2}{-3}$

$x = \dfrac{2}{3}$

Check

$$5\left(\frac{2}{3}\right)-2\left(\left(\frac{2}{3}\right)+6\right) \overset{?}{=} 6\left(\left(\frac{2}{3}\right)-1\right)-8$$

$$\frac{10}{3}-2\left(\frac{2}{3}+\frac{18}{3}\right) \overset{?}{=} 6\left(\frac{2}{3}-\frac{3}{3}\right)-8$$

$$\frac{10}{3}-2\left(\frac{20}{3}\right) \overset{?}{=} 6\left(-\frac{1}{3}\right)-8$$

$$\frac{10}{3}-\frac{40}{3} \overset{?}{=} -\frac{6}{3}-\frac{24}{3}$$

$$-\frac{30}{3} = -\frac{30}{3} \text{ True.}$$

69. $13-9(2n+3) = 4(6n+1)-15n$

$13-18n-27 = 24n+4-15n$

$-18n-14 = 9n+4$

$-18n-9n-14 = 9n-9n+4$

$-27n-14 = 4$

$-27n-14+14 = 4+14$

$-27n = 18$

$\dfrac{-27}{-27}n = \dfrac{18}{-27}$

$n = -\dfrac{2}{3}$

Check

$$13-9\left(2\left(-\frac{2}{3}\right)+3\right) \overset{?}{=} 4\left(6\left(-\frac{2}{3}\right)+1\right)-15\left(-\frac{2}{3}\right)$$

$$13-9\left(-\frac{4}{3}+\frac{9}{3}\right) \overset{?}{=} 4(-4+1)+10$$

$$13-9\left(\frac{5}{3}\right) \overset{?}{=} 4(-3)+10$$

$$13-15 \overset{?}{=} -12+10$$

$$-2 = -2 \text{ True.}$$

71. $3[1-(4x-5)] = 5(6-2x)$

$3[1-4x+5] = 30-10x$

$3[6-4x] = 30-10x$

$18-12x = 30-10x$

$18-12x+10x = 30-10x+10x$

$18-2x = 30$

$18-18-2x = 30-18$

$-2x = 12$

$\dfrac{-2}{-2}x = \dfrac{12}{-2}$

$x = -6$

Check

$$3[1-(4(-6)-5)] \overset{?}{=} 5(6-2(-6))$$

$$3[1-(-24-5)] \overset{?}{=} 5(6+12)$$

$$3[1-(-29)] \overset{?}{=} 5(18)$$

$$3[30] \overset{?}{=} 90$$

$$90 = 90 \text{ True.}$$

73. $\dfrac{1}{2}(18-6n)+5n = 10-\dfrac{1}{4}(16n+20)$

$9-3n+5n = 10-4n-5$

$2n+9 = -4n+5$

$2n+4n+9 = -4n+4n+5$

$6n+9 = 5$

$6n+9-9 = 5-9$

$6n = -4$

$\dfrac{6}{6}n = \dfrac{-4}{6}$

$n = -\dfrac{2}{3}$

Check

$$\frac{1}{2}\left(18-6\left(-\frac{2}{3}\right)\right)+5\left(-\frac{2}{3}\right) \overset{?}{=} 10-\frac{1}{4}\left(16\left(-\frac{2}{3}\right)+20\right)$$

$$\frac{1}{2}(18+4)-\frac{10}{3} \overset{?}{=} 10-\frac{1}{4}\left(-\frac{32}{3}+\frac{60}{3}\right)$$

$$\frac{1}{2}(22)-\frac{10}{3} \overset{?}{=} 10-\frac{1}{4}\left(\frac{28}{3}\right)$$

$$11-\frac{10}{3} \overset{?}{=} 10-\frac{7}{3}$$

$$\frac{33}{3}-\frac{10}{3}\overset{?}{=}\frac{30}{3}-\frac{7}{3}$$

$$\frac{23}{3}=\frac{23}{3} \quad \text{True.}$$

75. $12y-\big[9(2-y)-8\big]=5y+3(6-4y)$

$12y-[18-9y-8]=5y+18-12y$

$12y-[-9y+10]=-7y+18$

$12y+9y-10=-7y+18$

$21y-10=-7y+18$

$21y+7y-10=-7y+7y+18$

$28y-10=18$

$28y-10+10=18+10$

$28y=28$

$\frac{28}{28}y=\frac{28}{28}$

$y=1$

Check

$12(1)-\big[9(2-(1))-8\big]\overset{?}{=}5(1)+3(6-4(1))$

$12-\big[9(1)-8\big]\overset{?}{=}5+3(6-4)$

$12-[9-8]\overset{?}{=}5+3(2)$

$12-[1]\overset{?}{=}5+6$

$11=11$ True.

77. $6(3x-8)-4(4x-9)=3(5x+3)-(7x+1)$

$18x-48-16x+36=15x+9-7x-1$

$2x-12=8x+8$

$2x-8x-12=8x-8x+8$

$-6x-12=8$

$-6x-12+12=8+12$

$-6x=20$

$\frac{-6}{6}x=\frac{20}{-6}$

$x=-\frac{10}{3}$

Check

$6(3\left(-\frac{10}{3}\right)-8)-4\left(4\left(-\frac{10}{3}\right)-9\right)\overset{?}{=}$

$\qquad 3\left(5\left(-\frac{10}{3}\right)+3\right)-\left(7\left(-\frac{10}{3}\right)+1\right)$

$6(-10-8)-4\left(\frac{-40}{3}-\frac{27}{3}\right)\overset{?}{=}$

$\qquad 3\left(-\frac{50}{3}+\frac{9}{3}\right)-\left(-\frac{70}{3}+\frac{3}{3}\right)$

$6(-18)-4\left(-\frac{67}{3}\right)\overset{?}{=}3\left(-\frac{41}{3}\right)-\left(-\frac{67}{3}\right)$

$-108+\frac{268}{3}\overset{?}{=}-\frac{123}{3}+\frac{67}{3}$

$-\frac{324}{3}+\frac{268}{3}\overset{?}{=}-\frac{56}{3}$

$-\frac{56}{3}=-\frac{56}{3}$ True.

79. $\frac{1}{2}x-\frac{3}{4}x+5=\frac{1}{6}(10-3x)-\frac{2}{3}$

$\frac{2}{4}x-\frac{3}{4}x+5=\frac{10}{6}-\frac{3}{6}x-\frac{2}{3}$

$-\frac{1}{4}x+5=-\frac{1}{2}x+\frac{5}{3}-\frac{2}{3}$

$-\frac{1}{4}x+5=-\frac{1}{2}x+\frac{3}{3}$

$-\frac{1}{4}x+5=-\frac{1}{2}x+1$

$-\frac{1}{4}x+\frac{1}{2}x+5=-\frac{1}{2}x+\frac{1}{2}x+1$

$-\frac{1}{4}x+\frac{2}{4}x+5=1$

$\frac{1}{4}x+5-5=1-5$

$\frac{1}{4}x=-4$

$(4)\frac{1}{4}x=(4)(-4)$

$x=-16$

Check

$\frac{1}{2}(-16)-\frac{3}{4}(-16)+5\overset{?}{=}\frac{1}{6}(10-3(-16))-\frac{2}{3}$

$-8+12+5\overset{?}{=}\frac{1}{6}(10+48)-\frac{2}{3}$

$9\overset{?}{=}\frac{1}{6}(58)-\frac{2}{3}$

$9\overset{?}{=}\frac{29}{3}-\frac{2}{3}$

$9\overset{?}{=}\frac{27}{3}$

$9=9$ True.

81. a. The price of the book at the on-line retailer is the cost less shipping $\$33.59-\$3.99=\$29.60$.
20% less than list means list – 20% of list.
Let $l=$ list price

$29.60=l-.20l$

$29.60=0.80l$

$$\frac{29.60}{0.80} = l$$

$$37 = l$$

The Original list price was $37.00.

b. $37.00 - 29.60 = 7.40$ saved.

c. $\text{Discount} = \dfrac{\text{Change in price}}{\text{Original price}} =$

$$\frac{37.00 - 33.59}{37.00} = \frac{3.41}{37} \approx .09$$

The actual discount was about 9%.

83. There are nine spaces between the first and last hurdle. The distance to the first hurdle, the nine spaces, and the distance from the last hurdle to the finish is 400 meters.

$$45 + 9d + 40 = 400$$

$$9d + 85 = 400$$

$$9d + 85 - 85 = 400 - 85$$

$$9d = 315$$

$$\frac{9}{9}d = \frac{315}{9}; \quad d = 35$$

The distance between the hurdles is 35 meters.

85. For how many minutes will plan A equal plan B?

$$39.95 = 14.95 + 4 + 0.07m$$

$$39.95 = 18.95 + 0.07m$$

$$39.95 - 18.95 = 18.95 - 18.95 + 0.07m$$

$$21.00 = 0.07m$$

$$\frac{21.00}{0.07} - \frac{0.07}{0.07}m$$

$$300 = m$$

Plans A and B cost the same when plan B uses 300 minutes.

87. If s is the number of small pillows, then $18 - s$ is the number of large pillows. The fabric used in making the small pillows plus the fabric used in making the large pillows is 18 sq yd.

$$\frac{1}{2}s + 2(18 - s) = 18$$

$$\frac{1}{2}s + 36 - 2s = 18$$

$$\frac{1}{2}s - \frac{4}{2}s + 36 = 18$$

$$-\frac{3}{2}s + 36 = 18$$

$$-\frac{3}{2}s + 36 - 36 = 18 - 36$$

$$-\frac{3}{2}s = -18$$

$$\left(-\frac{2}{3}\right)\left(-\frac{3}{2}s\right) = -18\left(-\frac{2}{3}\right)$$

$$s = 12 \quad 18 - s = 6$$

Twelve small pillows and 6 large pillows are made.

89. If n represents the number of nonmembers registered, then the total registration less the number of nonmembers or $2017 - n$ are the number of members registered. The sum of the fees paid by each group must give the total collected.

$$200n + 120(2017 - n) = 268120$$

$$200n + 242040 - 120n = 268120$$

$$80n + 242040 = 268120$$

$$80n + 242040 - 242040 = 268120 - 242040$$

$$80n = 26080$$

$$\frac{80}{80}n = \frac{26080}{80}$$

$$n = 326$$

326 nonmembers registered for the conference.

91. Let n be the number of the first employee. The second employee is $n + 1$ and the third is $n + 2$.

$$n + (n + 1) = 2407$$

$$n + n + 1 = 2407$$

$$2n + 1 = 2407$$

$$2n + 1 - 1 = 2407 - 1$$

$$2n = 2406$$

$$\frac{2n}{2} = \frac{2406}{2}$$

$$n = 1203, \ n + 1 = 1204, \ n + 2 = 1205$$

The number assigned to the third employee was 1205.

93. $$4x + 5 = (3x - 7) + (2x - 16)$$

$$4x + 5 = 5x - 23$$

$$4x - 5x + 5 = 5x - 5x - 23$$

$$-x + 5 = -23$$

$$-x + 5 - 5 = -23 - 5$$

$$-x = -28$$

$$\frac{-x}{-1} = \frac{-28}{-1}$$

$$x = 28$$

$$3(28) - 7 = 84 - 7 = 77$$

$$2(28) - 16 = 56 - 16 = 40$$

The measure of the angles are 40° and 77°.

95. Let t = hours needed to finish the marathon.

Distance = rate $\times$ time

$$10 = 4t$$

$$\frac{10}{4} = \frac{4}{4}t$$

$$\frac{5}{2} = t$$

$$2\frac{1}{2} = t$$

It will take her 2 ½ to finish the walkathon.

97. Let t = the time the mother takes to catch up to her son.

The mother's distance = the son's distance.

Note that the rate is in miles per hour so the time must be expressed in hours.

Rate × time = distance

Mother	32	t	32t
Son	8	$t+\dfrac{15}{60}$	$8\left(t+\dfrac{15}{60}\right)$

$15\text{min} = \dfrac{15}{60}\text{Hr.}$

$32t = 8\left(t+\dfrac{15}{60}\right)$

$32t = 8t + 8\left(\dfrac{1}{4}\right)$

$32t = 8t + 2$

$32t - 8t = 8t - 8t + 2$

$24t = 2$

$\dfrac{24}{24}t = \dfrac{2}{24}$

$t = \dfrac{1}{12}\text{hours.}$

$\dfrac{1}{12}(60) = 5\text{minutes}$

The mother took 5 minutes to catch up with her son.

99. Let t = the time for the second group to catch the first group. The distance traveled by each group must be the same. Times must be expressed as parts of hours because speed is in miles per hour.

Rate × time = distance

1st Group	60	$t+\dfrac{20}{60}-\dfrac{10}{60}$	$60\left(t+\dfrac{20}{60}-\dfrac{10}{60}\right)$
2nd Group	75	t	$75t$

First group distance = second group distance.

rate × (time + 20 min − 10 min) = rate × time

$60\left(t+\dfrac{20}{60}-\dfrac{10}{60}\right) = 75t$

$60\left(t+\dfrac{10}{60}\right) = 75t$

$60t + 10 = 75t$

$60t - 60t + 10 = 75t - 60t$

$10 = 15t$

$\dfrac{10}{15} = \dfrac{15}{15}t$

$\dfrac{2}{3} = t \qquad t = \dfrac{2}{3}$ hours.

$t = \dfrac{2}{3}(60) = 40$ minutes.

The second group catches up to the first group 40 minutes after they leave. 8:20 + :40 = 9:00.

101. Together, the two friends must walk the entire 2.2 miles. The time for each person is the same.

$\left(24\text{ Minutes} = \dfrac{24}{60}\text{ Hours}\right)$

Rate × time = distance

1st Person	r	$\dfrac{24}{60}$	$r\left(\dfrac{24}{60}\right)$
2nd Person	$r+\dfrac{1}{2}$	$\dfrac{24}{60}$	$\left(r+\dfrac{1}{2}\right)\left(\dfrac{24}{60}\right)$

$\text{Distance}_{1^{st}\text{ Person}} + \text{Distance}_{2^{nd}\text{Person}} = 2.2$

$r\left(\dfrac{24}{60}\right)+\left(r+\dfrac{1}{2}\right)\left(\dfrac{24}{60}\right) = 2.2$

$0.4r + 0.4r + 0.2 = 2.2$

$0.8r + 0.2 = 2.2$

$0.8r + 0.2 - 0.2 = 2.2 - 0.2$

$0.8r = 2$

$\dfrac{0.8}{0.8}r = \dfrac{2}{0.8}$

$r = 2.5 \qquad r+\dfrac{1}{2} = 3$

The rates of the two friends are 2.5 mph and 3 mph.

103. The two investments are x and $12,000 - x$.

The gain from the 7% investment less the loss from the 9% investment totals $200.

Principal × Rate = Profit

1st fund	x	7%	$7\%(x)$
2nd fund	$12000 - x$	9%	$9\%(12000 - x)$

$7\%(x) - 9\%(12000 - x) = 200$

$.07(x) - .09(12000 - x) = 200$

$0.07x - 1080 + .09x = 200$

$0.16x - 1080 = 200$

$0.16x - 1080 + 1080 = 200 + 1080.$

$0.16x = 1280$

$\dfrac{0.16}{0.16}x = \dfrac{1280}{0.16}$

$x = 8000$

$8,000 was invested at 7% and $4,000 was invested at 9%.

105. Let h = the amount invested in the high-risk mutual fund. $3h$ becomes the amount invested in the low-risk fund. The return on the low-risk mutual fund and the

loss on the high-risk mutual fund equals a loss of $525.

Principal × Rate = Profit

Hi-risk	h	3%	$3\%(h)$
Low-risk	$3h$	12%	$12\%(3h)$

$3\%(3h) - 12\%(h) = -525$

$0.03(3h) - 0.12(h) = -525$

$0.09h - 0.12h = -525$

$-0.03h = -525$

$\dfrac{-0.03}{-0.03}h = \dfrac{-525}{-0.03}$

$h = 17500 \qquad 3h = 3(17500) = 52500$

$17,500 was invested in the high-risk mutual fund and $52,500 was invested in the low-risk mutual fund for a total investment of $70,000.

107. 9% alcohol solution means 9% of the solution is alcohol. Alcohol is added here.

Solution × Rate = Alcohol

Alcohol	x	100%	$100\%(x)$
Solution	24 ml	9%	$9\%(24)$
Final mix	$x+24$	16%	$16\%(x+24)$

The alcohol added plus the alcohol in the original mixture equals the alcohol in the final solution.

$100\%x + 9\%(24) = 16\%(x+24)$

$1x + .09(24) = 0.16(x+24)$

$x + 2.16 = 0.16x + 3.84$

$x - 0.16x + 2.16 = 0.16x - 0.16x + 3.84$

$0.84x + 2.16 = 3.84$

$0.84x + 2.16 - 2.16 = 3.84 - 2.16$

$0.84x = 1.68$

$\dfrac{0.84}{0.84}x = \dfrac{1.68}{0.84}$

$x = 2$

2 milliliters of pure alcohol are needed to make the 16% solution.

109. Ten gallons gets split into x and $10 - x$. Octane is an anti-knocking rating.

Amount × Rate = Total rating

87-Octane	x	87%	$87\%(x)$
92-Octane	$10-x$	92%	$92\%(10-x)$
90-Octane	10	90%	$90\%(10)$

$87\%(x) + 92\%(10-x) = 90\%(10)$

$0.87x + .92(10-x) = .90(10)$

$0.87x + 9.2 - 0.92x = 9.0$

$-0.05x + 9.2 = 9.0$

$-0.05x + 9.2 - 9.2 = 9.0 - 9.2$

$-0.05x = -0.2$

$\dfrac{-0.05}{-0.05}x = \dfrac{-0.2}{-0.05}$

$x = 4$

She needs 4 gallons of the 87-octane gasoline and 6 gallons of the 92-octane gasoline.

b.   Amount × Rate = Cost

87-Octane	4	1.59	$4(1.59)$
92-Octane	6	2.09	$6(2.09)$
90-Octane			$4(1.59)+6(2.09)$

total $= 4(1.59) + 6(2.09)$

total $= 6.36 + 12.54$

total $= 18.90$

She paid $18.90 to fill her gas tank.

Exercises 2.2 Solving Literal Equations and Formulas

1. $7m + n = 2$

$7m - 7m + n = 2 - 7m$

$n = 2 - 7m$

3. $9a - 3b = 0$

$9a - 3b + 3b = 0 + 3b$

$9a = 3b$

$\dfrac{9a}{9} = \dfrac{3b}{9}$

$a = \dfrac{b}{3}$

5. $\dfrac{2}{3}xy = z$

$(3)\dfrac{2}{3}xy = (3)z$

$2xy = 3z$

$\dfrac{2xy}{2y} = \dfrac{3z}{2y}$

$x = \dfrac{3z}{2y}$

7. $5a + b = c$

$5a + b - b = c - b$

$5a = c - b$

$\dfrac{5a}{5} = \dfrac{c-b}{5}$

$a = \dfrac{c-b}{5}$

9. $ax - by = c$

$ax - ax - by = -ax + c$

$-by = -ax + c$

$$\frac{-by}{-b} = \frac{-ax+c}{-b}$$

$$y = -\frac{-ax+c}{b} \quad \text{or} \quad \frac{-(-ax+c)}{b} = \frac{ax-c}{b}$$

11. $qrs + t = 0$

$qrs + t - t = 0 - t$

$qrs = -t$

$$\frac{qrs}{qs} = \frac{-t}{qs}$$

$$r = -\frac{t}{qs}$$

13. $\dfrac{x}{y} - z = v$

$$\frac{x}{y} - z + z = v + z$$

$$\frac{x}{y} = v + z$$

$$(y)\frac{x}{y} = (y)(v+z)$$

$x = y(v+z) \quad \text{or} \quad x = yv + yz$

15. $\dfrac{a-b}{c} = -d$

$$\frac{c}{1}\left(\frac{a-b}{c}\right) = -d\left(\frac{c}{1}\right)$$

$a - b = -cd$

$a - a - b = -cd - a$

$-b = -cd - a$

$$\frac{-b}{-1} = \frac{-cd-a}{-1}$$

$b = cd + a$

17. $\dfrac{rs}{t} = v + w$

$$\left(\frac{t}{1}\right)\frac{rs}{t} = (v+w)\left(\frac{t}{1}\right)$$

$rs = t(v+w)$

$$\frac{rs}{r} = \frac{t(v+w)}{r}$$

$$s = \frac{t(v+w)}{r}$$

19. $wx - y = u + s$

$wx - y + y = u + s + y$

$wx = u + s + y$

$$\frac{wx}{x} = \frac{u+s+y}{x}$$

$$w = \frac{u+s+y}{x}$$

21. $a(b+c) = d - g$

$ab + ac = d - g$

$ab - ab + ac = d - g - ab$

$ac = d - g - ab$

$$\frac{ac}{a} = \frac{d-g-ab}{a}$$

$$c = \frac{d-g-ab}{a}$$

23. $V = IR$

$$\frac{V}{I} = \frac{IR}{I}$$

$$\frac{V}{I} = R \quad \text{or}$$

$$R = \frac{V}{I}$$

25. $F = \dfrac{mv^2}{r}$

$$(r)F = \frac{mv^2}{r}(r)$$

$Fr = mv^2$

$$\frac{Fr}{v^2} = \frac{mv^2}{v^2}$$

$$\frac{Fr}{v^2} = m \quad \text{or}$$

$$m = \frac{Fr}{v^2}$$

27. $P = 2(l+w)$

$P = 2l + 2w$

$P - 2l = 2l - 2l + 2w$

$P - 2l = 2w$

$$\frac{P-2l}{2} = \frac{2w}{2}$$

$$\frac{P-2l}{2} = w \quad \text{or}$$

$$w = \frac{P-2l}{2}$$

29. $A = \pi s(r_1 + r_2)$

$A = \pi s r_1 + \pi s r_2$

$A - \pi s r_2 = \pi s r_1 + \pi s r_2 - \pi s r_2$

$A - \pi s r_2 = \pi s r_1$

$$\frac{A-\pi s r_2}{\pi s} = \frac{\pi s r_1}{\pi s}$$

$$\frac{A-\pi s r_2}{\pi s} = r_1 \quad \text{or}$$

$$r_1 = \frac{A-\pi s r_2}{\pi s}$$

31. $S = \dfrac{n(a_1 + a_n)}{2}$

$S = \dfrac{na_1 + na_n}{2}$

$\left(\dfrac{2}{1}\right)S = \dfrac{na_1 + na_n}{2}\left(\dfrac{2}{1}\right)$

$2S = na_1 + na_n$

$2S - na_1 = na_1 - na_1 + na_n$

$2S - na_1 = na_n$

$\dfrac{2S - na_1}{n} = \dfrac{na_n}{n}$

$\dfrac{2S - na_1}{n} = a_n$ or $a_n = \dfrac{2S - na_1}{n}$

33. a. Note that V and v are not the same.

$V^2 = v^2 + 2as$

$V^2 - v^2 = v^2 - v^2 + 2as$

$V^2 - v^2 = 2as$

$\dfrac{V^2 - v^2}{2s} = \dfrac{2as}{2s}$

$\dfrac{V^2 - v^2}{2s} = a$ or $a = \dfrac{V^2 - v^2}{2s}$

b. $s = 125$ m $V = 0$ $v = 20$ m/s

$a = \dfrac{V^2 - v^2}{2s} = \dfrac{(0)^2 - (20)^2}{2(125)} =$

$\dfrac{-400}{250} = -1.6$ m per sec^2

35. a. $I = 6(h - 60) + 106$

$I = 6h - 360 + 106$

$I = 6h - 254$

$I + 254 = 6h - 254 + 254$

$I + 254 = 6h$

$\dfrac{I + 254}{6} = \dfrac{6h}{6}$

$\dfrac{I + 254}{6} = h$

$h = \dfrac{I + 254}{6}$

b. $I = 190$

$h = \dfrac{I + 254}{6} = \dfrac{190 + 254}{6}$

$h = \dfrac{444}{6} = 74$

The man is 74 inches or 6 feet 2 inches tall.

37. a. $E = 9.6w + 1.7h - 4.7y + 655$

$E - 9.6w = 9.6w - 9.6w + 1.7h - 4.7y + 655$

$E - 9.6w = 1.7h - 4.7y + 655$

$E - 9.6w - 1.7h = 1.7h - 1.7h - 4.7y + 655$

$E - 9.6w - 1.7h = -4.7y + 655$

$E - 9.6w - 1.7h - 655 = -4.7y + 655 - 655$

$E - 9.6w - 1.7h - 655 = -4.7y$

$\dfrac{E - 9.6w - 1.7h - 655}{-4.7} = \dfrac{-4.7y}{-4.7}$

$-\dfrac{E - 9.6w - 1.7h - 655}{4.7} = y$

$y = -\dfrac{E - 9.6w - 1.7h - 655}{4.7}$ or

$y = \dfrac{-E + 9.6w + 1.7h + 655}{4.7}$

b. $E = 1305$ $w = 55$ $h = 160$

$y = \dfrac{-E + 9.6w + 1.7h + 655}{4.7}$

$y = \dfrac{-1305 + 9.6(55) + 1.7(160) + 655}{4.7}$

$y = \dfrac{-1305 + 528 + 272 + 655}{4.7}$

$y = \dfrac{150}{4.7} = 31.91$

The woman is approximately 32 years old.

39. a. $E = 9\left(\dfrac{R}{I}\right)$

b. $E = 9\left(\dfrac{R}{I}\right) = \dfrac{9R}{I}$

$E\left(\dfrac{I}{9}\right) = \left(\dfrac{I}{9}\right)\dfrac{9R}{I}$

$\dfrac{EI}{9} = R$

$R = \dfrac{EI}{9}$ or $R = \dfrac{1}{9}EI$

c.

Pitcher	E	I	$R = \dfrac{1}{9}EI$
Schilling	2.95	168.0	$\dfrac{1}{9}(2.95)(168.0) =$ 55
Martinez	2.22	186.2	$\dfrac{1}{9}(2.22)(186.2) =$ 46
Nomo	3.09	218.1	$\dfrac{1}{9}(3.09)(218.1) =$ 75
Vasquez	3.24	230.2	$\dfrac{1}{9}(3.24)(230.2) =$ 83

41. a. $A = \dfrac{100}{d}$

b. $d = 12.5$

$A = \dfrac{100}{d} = \dfrac{100}{12.5} = 8$

The person needs an accommodation of 8 diopters.

Exercise 2.3 Solving Linear Inequalities

1. Is 2 a solution for $3x - 7 > -2$?

$3(2) - 7 \overset{?}{>} -2$

$6 - 7 \overset{?}{>} -2$

$-1 > -2$

2 is a solution.

3. Is -8 a solution for $\dfrac{n}{4} + 10 \le 8$?

$\dfrac{-8}{4} + 10 \overset{?}{\le} 8$

$-2 + 10 \overset{?}{\le} 8$

$8 \le 8$

-8 is a solution.

5. Is 10 a solution for $23 - 5x \ge 2x + 9$?

$23 - 5(10) \overset{?}{\ge} 2(10) - 9$

$23 - 50 \overset{?}{\ge} 20 - 9$

$-17 \overset{}{\ngeq} 11$

10 is not a solution.

7. Is -12 a solution for $\dfrac{2}{3}y + 8 < \dfrac{3}{4}y + 6$?

$\dfrac{2}{3}(-12) + 8 \overset{?}{<} \dfrac{3}{4}(-12) + 6$

$-8 + 8 \overset{?}{<} -9 + 6$

$0 \overset{}{\nless} -3$

-12 is not a solution.

9. Is $-\dfrac{3}{8}$ a solution for $4(24n + 1) + 16 > 40n - 2$?

$4\left(24\left(-\dfrac{3}{8}\right) + 1\right) + 16 \overset{?}{>} 40\left(-\dfrac{3}{8}\right) - 2$

$4(-9 + 1) + 16 \overset{?}{>} -15 - 2$

$4(-8) + 16 \overset{?}{>} -17$

$-32 + 16 \overset{?}{>} -17$

$-16 > -17$

$-\dfrac{3}{8}$ is a solution.

11. $(-\infty, -1)$

13. $[2, \infty)$

15. $\left(-3\dfrac{1}{2}, \infty\right)$

17. $(-\infty, 7.5]$

19. $n + 5 \ge 3$

$n + 5 - 5 \ge 3 - 5$

$n \ge -2;\ [-2, \infty)$

21. $y - 3 < -7$

$y - 3 + 3 < -7 + 3$

$y < -4;\ (-\infty, -4)$

23. $x + \dfrac{1}{2} > -1\dfrac{1}{2}$

$x + \dfrac{1}{2} - \dfrac{1}{2} > -1\dfrac{1}{2} - \dfrac{1}{2}$

$x > -2;\ (-2, \infty)$

25. $-6.5 \ge y - 4.5$

$-6.5 + 4.5 \ge y - 4.5 + 4.5$

$-2 \ge y$ or $y \le -2;\ (-\infty, -2]$

27. $2x - 9 < x - 6$

$2x - x - 9 < x - x - 6$

$x - 9 < -6$

$x - 9 + 9 < -6 + 9$

$x < 3;\ (-\infty, 3)$

29. $9x + 5 \ge 8x + 5$

$9x - 8x + 5 \ge 8x - 8x + 5$

$x + 5 \ge 5$

$x + 5 - 5 \ge 5 - 5$

$x \ge 0;\ [0, \infty)$

31. $1.7 - 2.8x \le 3.2 - 3.8x$

$1.7 - 2.8x + 3.8x \le 3.2 - 3.8x + 3.8x$

$1.7 + x \le 3.2$

$1.7 - 1.7 + x \le 3.2 - 1.7$

$x \le 1.5;\ (-\infty, 1.5]$

33. $\dfrac{4}{5}x \ge -8$

$\left(\dfrac{5}{4}\right)\dfrac{4}{5}x \ge -8\left(\dfrac{5}{4}\right)$

$x \ge -10;\ [-10, \infty)$

35. $-3n < 15$

$\dfrac{-3n}{-3} > \dfrac{15}{-3}$ Change inequality direction when

multiplying or dividing by a negative number.

$n > -5;\ (-5, \infty)$

37. $-90 \le -15y$

$\dfrac{-90}{-15} \ge \dfrac{-15y}{-15}$ Change inequality direction

when multiplying or dividing by a negative

number.

$6 \ge y$ or $y \le 6;\ (-\infty, 6]$

39. $-\dfrac{3}{8}x > \dfrac{9}{16}$

$\left(-\dfrac{8}{3}\right)\left(-\dfrac{3}{8}x\right) < \dfrac{9}{16}\left(-\dfrac{8}{3}\right)$ Change inequality

direction when multiplying or dividing by a

negative number.

$x < -\dfrac{3}{2};\ \left(-\infty, -\dfrac{3}{2}\right)$

41. $2 - x \le 1$

$2 - 2 - x \le 1 - 2$

$-x \le -1$

$(-1)(-x) \ge (-1)(-1)$

$x \ge 1$ Choice c.

43. $-11 < 2x - 9$

$-11 + 9 < 2x - 9 + 9$

$-2 < 2x$

$\dfrac{-2}{2} < \dfrac{2x}{2}$

$-1 < x$ or $x > -1$ Choice d.

45. $2x + 5 \le 13$

$2x + 5 - 5 \le 13 - 5$

$2x \le 8$

$\dfrac{2x}{2} \le \dfrac{8}{2}$

$x \le 4;\ (-\infty, 4]$

47. $9 - \dfrac{x}{3} < -5$

$9 - 9 - \dfrac{x}{3} < -5 - 9$

$-\dfrac{x}{3} < -14$

$(-3)\left(-\dfrac{x}{3}\right) > (-3)(-14)$ Change inequality

direction when multiplying or dividing by a

negative.

$x > 42;\ (42, \infty)$

49. $11y + 9 \ge 8y$

$11y - 8y + 9 \ge 8y - 8y$

$3y + 9 \ge 0$

$3y + 9 - 9 \ge 0 - 9$

$3y \ge -9$

$\dfrac{3y}{3} \ge \dfrac{-9}{3}$

$y \ge -3;\ [-3, \infty)$

51. $6y < -18y$

$6y + 18y < -18y + 18y$

$24y < 0$

$\dfrac{24y}{24} < \dfrac{0}{24}$

$y < 0;\ (-\infty, 0)$

53. $3y - 13 > 15 - y$

$3y + y - 13 > 15 - y + y$

$4y - 13 > 15$

$4y - 13 + 13 > 15 + 13$

$4y > 28$

$\dfrac{4y}{4} > \dfrac{28}{4}$

$y > 7;\ (7, \infty)$

55. $\dfrac{2}{3}x + 6 \ge \dfrac{4}{5}x + 9$

$\dfrac{2}{3}x - \dfrac{4}{5}x + 6 \ge \dfrac{4}{5}x - \dfrac{4}{5}x + 9$

$\dfrac{10}{15}x - \dfrac{12}{15}x + 6 \ge 9$

$$-\frac{2}{15}x+6\geq 9$$

$$-\frac{2}{15}x+6-6\geq 9-6$$

$$-\frac{2}{15}x\geq 3$$

$$\left(-\frac{15}{2}\right)\left(-\frac{2}{15}x\right)\leq \left(-\frac{15}{2}\right)(3)$$

$$x\leq -\frac{45}{2};\ \ \left(-\infty,-\frac{45}{2}\right]$$

57. $2.8z-1.3>-1.6z-0.2$

$$2.8z+1.6z-1.3>-1.6z+1.6z-0.2$$

$$4.4z-1.3>-0.2$$

$$4.4z-1.3+1.3>-0.2+1.3$$

$$4.4z>1.1$$

$$\frac{4.4z}{4.4}>\frac{1.1}{4.4}$$

$$z>0.25;\ \ (0.25,\infty)$$

59. $3n-2-n>5n+19$

$$2n-2>5n+19$$

$$2n-5n-2>5n-5n+19$$

$$-3n-2>19$$

$$-3n-2+2>19+2$$

$$-3n>21$$

$$\frac{-3n}{-3}<\frac{21}{-3}$$

$$n<-7;\ \ (-\infty,-7)$$

61. $17n-8n+14\leq 13n-10+6$

$$9n+14\leq 13n-4$$

$$9n-13n+14\leq 13n-13n-4$$

$$-4n+14\leq -4$$

$$-4n+14-14\leq -4-14$$

$$-4n\leq -18$$

$$\frac{-4n}{-4}\geq \frac{-18}{-4}$$

$$n\geq \frac{9}{2};\ \ \left[\frac{9}{2},\infty\right)$$

63. $3(2x-1)-4\geq 7x-12$

$$6x-3-4\geq 7x-12$$

$$6x-7\geq 7x-12$$

$$6x-7x-7\geq 7x-7x-12$$

$$-x-7\geq -12$$

$$-x-7+7\geq -12+7$$

$$-x\geq -5$$

$$\frac{-x}{-1}\leq \frac{-5}{-1}$$

$$x\leq 5;\ \ (-\infty,5]$$

65. $15n-4(5-6n)<32-(17-18n)$

$$15n-20+24n<32-17+18n$$

$$39n-20<15+18n$$

$$39n-18n-20<15+18n-18n$$

$$21n-20<15$$

$$21n-20+20<15+20$$

$$21n<35$$

$$\frac{21n}{21}<\frac{35}{21}$$

$$n<\frac{5}{3};\ \ \left(-\infty,\frac{5}{3}\right)$$

67. $\frac{3}{4}(12x-16)+20>25\left(\frac{2}{5}x-1\right)+9x$

$$9x-12+20>10x-25+9x$$

$$9x+8>19x-25$$

$$9x-19x+8>19x-19x-25$$

$$-10x+8>-25$$

$$-10x+8-8>-25-8$$

$$-10x>-33$$

$$\frac{-10x}{-10}<\frac{-33}{-10}$$

$$x<\frac{33}{10};\ \ \left(-\infty,\frac{33}{10}\right)$$

69. $\frac{1}{4}\left[2-9\left(6+\frac{2}{3}x\right)\right]+19\leq 17-\frac{1}{2}(8+7x)$

$$\frac{1}{4}[2-54-6x]+19\leq 17-4-\frac{7}{2}x$$

$$\frac{2}{4}-\frac{54}{4}-\frac{6}{4}x+19\leq 13-\frac{7}{2}x$$

$$\frac{1}{2}-\frac{27}{2}-\frac{3}{2}x+19\leq 13-\frac{7}{2}x$$

$$-\frac{26}{2}-\frac{3}{2}x+19\leq 13-\frac{7}{2}x$$

$$-13-\frac{3}{2}x+19\leq 13-\frac{7}{2}x$$

$$-\frac{3}{2}x+6\leq 13-\frac{7}{2}x$$

$$-\frac{3}{2}x+\frac{7}{2}x+6\leq 13-\frac{7}{2}x+\frac{7}{2}x$$

$$\frac{4}{2}x+6\leq 13$$

$$2x+6\leq 13$$

$$2x+6-6\leq 13-6$$

$$2x \leq 7$$

$$\frac{2x}{2} \leq \frac{7}{2}$$

$$x \leq \frac{7}{2}; \quad \left(-\infty, \frac{7}{2}\right]$$

71. Let d be the number of days for dialing parking.

$$5d < 60$$

$$\frac{5d}{5} < \frac{60}{5}$$

$$d < 12$$

The daily rate is better if one parks for fewer than 12 days.

73. Let m be the number of minutes for calls outside the network.

$$29.95 + 0.79m < 50$$

$$29.95 - 29.95 + 0.79m < 50 - 29.95$$

$$0.79m < 20.05$$

$$\frac{0.79m}{0.79} < \frac{20.05}{0.79}$$

$$m < 25.4$$

You can make at most 25 minutes of calls outside the network.

75. The total expenses must be less or equal to $2500.

$$486 + 170 + 654 + \text{ remaining expenses} \leq 2500$$

$$1310 + \text{ remaining expenses} \leq 2500$$

$$1310 - 1310 + \text{ remaining expenses} \leq 2500 - 1310$$

$$\text{remaining expenses} \leq 1190$$

$$\text{Daily expenses} = \frac{1190}{7} = 170$$

The nurse can spend $170 per day on remaining expenses.

77. The sum of the four quarterly profits divided by four must be equal to or greater than $100,000. Let f be the fourth quarter profit.

$$\frac{120,356 + 96,147 + 85,502 + f}{4} \geq 100,000$$

$$\frac{302005 + f}{4} \geq 100000$$

$$\frac{4}{1}\left(\frac{302005 + f}{4}\right) \geq \left(\frac{4}{1}\right)100,000$$

$$302005 + f \geq 400000$$

$$302005 - 302005 + f \geq 400000 - 302005$$

$$f \geq 97995$$

The fourth quarter profit must be at least $97,995.

79. The distance the woman travels in the 20 minutes must be greater to or equal to the distance the man travels. The man traveled 15 minutes longer than the woman. Time must be expressed as parts of an hour because the rate is in miles per hour. Let r be the rate of the woman.

For the man:

Distance = rate × time

$$\text{Distance} = 6\left(\frac{20}{60} + \frac{15}{60}\right)$$

For the woman:

Distance = rate × time

$$\text{Distance} = r\left(\frac{20}{60}\right)$$

$$r\left(\frac{20}{60}\right) \geq 6\left(\frac{20}{60} + \frac{15}{60}\right)$$

$$r\left(\frac{1}{3}\right) \geq 6\left(\frac{35}{60}\right)$$

$$r\left(\frac{1}{3}\right) \geq \overset{1}{6}\left(\frac{7}{\underset{2}{12}}\right)$$

$$r\left(\frac{1}{3}\right) \geq \frac{7}{2}$$

$$r\left(\frac{1}{3}\right)\left(\frac{3}{1}\right) \geq \left(\frac{7}{2}\right)\left(\frac{3}{1}\right)$$

$$r \geq \frac{21}{2}$$

$$r \geq 10.5$$

The woman must travel at least 10.5 miles per hour.

81. Let c be the amount invested in the certificates of deposit . Then, $30000 - c$ will be the amount invested in the risky stocks.

$$6\%c + 12\%(30000 - c) > 2460$$

$$0.06c + 0.12(30000 - c) > 2460$$

$$0.06c + 3600 - 0.12c > 2460$$

$$-0.06c + 3600 > 2460$$

$$-0.06c + 3600 - 3600 > 2460 - 3600$$

$$-0.06c > -1140$$

$$\frac{-0.06c}{-0.06} < \frac{-1140}{-0.06} \quad \text{Change the direction of the}$$

inequality when multiplying or dividing by a negative quantity.

$$c < 19000$$

She invested less than $19,000 in CDs.

83. The fixed costs plus the variable costs must be less than the income produced. Let d be the number of deliveries needed for a profit.

$$1500 + 0.85d < 6d$$

$$1500 - 1500 + 0.85d < 6d - 1500$$

$$0.85d < 6d - 1500$$

$$0.85d - 6d < 6d - 6d - 1500$$

$-5.15d < -1500$

$$\frac{-5.15d}{-5.15} > \frac{-1500}{-5.15}$$

$d > 291.2$

The service must make at least 292 deliveries per month for a profit.

85. For how many months will $2500 plus $109 a month be less than $2000 plus $129 a month. Let m equal the number of months.

$2500 + 109m < 2000 + 129m$

$2500 + 109m - 129m < 2000 + 129m - 129m$

$2500 - 20m < 2000$

$2500 - 2500 - 20m < 2000 - 2500$

$-20m < -500$

$$\frac{-20m}{-20} > \frac{-500}{-20}$$

$m > 25$

The first option should be selected on a car to be leased for more than 25 months.

Exercises 2.4 Solving Compound Inequalities

1. $2 < x < 5$ $(2,5)$

3. $-3 \le x < 0$ $[-3,0)$

5. $x < -4$ or $x > 3$ $(-\infty, -4) \cup (3, \infty)$

7. $x < -2$ or $x \ge 0.5$ $(-\infty, -2) \cup [0.5, \infty)$

9. $2x > -10$ and $3x - 1 < 8$

$\dfrac{2x}{2} > \dfrac{-10}{2}$ $3x - 1 + 1 < 8 + 1$

$x > -5$ $3x < 9$

                $\dfrac{3x}{3} < \dfrac{9}{3}$

                $x < 3$

$-5 < x < 3$ $(-5, 3)$

11. $\dfrac{2}{3}t > -4$ and $9 - 4t \ge -11$

$\left(\dfrac{3}{2}\right)\left(\dfrac{2}{3}t\right) > -4\left(\dfrac{3}{2}\right)$ $9 - 9 - 4t \ge -11 - 9$

                $-4t \ge -20$

$t > -6$ $\dfrac{-4t}{-4} \le \dfrac{-20}{-4}$

                $t \le 5$

$-6 < t \le 5$ $(-\infty, 5]$

13. $7 \le 6x + 1$ and $-4x \ge 28$

$7 - 1 \le 6x + 1 - 1$ $\dfrac{-4x}{-4} \le \dfrac{28}{-4}$

$6 \le 6x$ $x \le -7$

$\dfrac{6}{6} \le \dfrac{6x}{6}$

$1 \le x$ or $x \ge 1$

x cannot be both greater or equal to 1 and less than or equal to -7. There is no solution.

15. $-41 < 9a - 5 \le 13$

$-41 + 5 < 9a - 5 + 5 \le 13 + 5$

$-36 < 9a \le 18$

$\dfrac{-36}{9} < \dfrac{9a}{9} \le \dfrac{18}{9}$

$-4 < a \le 2$ $(-4, 2]$

17. $-13 < \dfrac{4x}{5} - 9 < -7$

$-13 + 9 < \dfrac{4x}{5} - 9 + 9 < -7 + 9$

$-4 < \dfrac{4x}{5} < 2$

$-4\left(\dfrac{5}{4}\right) < \left(\dfrac{5}{4}\right)\left(\dfrac{4x}{5}\right) < \left(\dfrac{5}{4}\right)2$

$-5 < x < \dfrac{5}{2}$ $\left(-5, \dfrac{5}{2}\right)$

19. $8 \le 12 - h$ and $-\dfrac{2}{3}h > 1$

$8 - 12 \le 12 - 12 - h$

$-4 \le -h$ $\left(-\dfrac{3}{2}\right)\left(-\dfrac{2}{3}h\right) < 1\left(-\dfrac{3}{2}\right)$

$\dfrac{-4}{-1} \ge \dfrac{-h}{-1}$ $h < -\dfrac{3}{2}$

$4 \ge h$ or $h \le 4$

For $h \le 4$ and $h < -\dfrac{3}{2}$, $h < -\dfrac{3}{2}$ suffices. $\left(-\infty, -\dfrac{3}{2}\right)$

21. $0 \le -8x - 20 \le 24$

$0 + 20 \le -8x - 20 + 20 \le 24 + 20$

$20 \le -8x \le 44$

$\dfrac{20}{-8} \ge \dfrac{-8x}{-8} \ge \dfrac{44}{-8}$

$-\dfrac{5}{2} \ge x \ge -\dfrac{11}{2}$ or $-\dfrac{11}{2} \le x \le -\dfrac{5}{2}$ $\left[-\dfrac{11}{2}, -\dfrac{5}{2}\right]$

23. $2x-3<-5$ or $3x+4>10$

  $2x-3+3<-5+3$ $3x+4-4>10-4$

  $2x<-2$ $3x>6$

  $\dfrac{2x}{2}<\dfrac{-2}{2}$ $\dfrac{3x}{3}>\dfrac{6}{3}$

  $x<-1$ $x>2$

  $x<-1$ or $x>2$ $(-\infty,-1)\cup(2,\infty)$

25. $6-r>14$ or $-11\le 3r-8$

  $6-6-r>14-6$ $-11+8\le 3r-8+8$

  $-r>8$ $-3\le 3r$

  $\dfrac{-r}{-1}<\dfrac{8}{-1}$ $\dfrac{-3}{3}\le\dfrac{3r}{3}$

  $r<-8$ $-1\le r$

  $r<-8$ or $r\ge-1$ $(-\infty,-8)\cup[-1,\infty)$

27. $18-10x\ge 23$ or $26+9x\ge-28$

  $18-18-10x\ge 23-18$ $26-26+9x\ge-28-26$

  $-10x\ge 5$ $9x\ge-54$

  $\dfrac{-20x}{-10}\le\dfrac{5}{-20}$ $\dfrac{9x}{9}\ge\dfrac{-54}{9}$

  $x\le-\dfrac{1}{2}$ $x\ge-6$

The two intervals overlap. The solution is all real numbers. $(-\infty,\infty)$

29. $-17\le 16-11a$ or $-5<-7a-12$

  $-17-16\le 16-16-11a$ $-5+12<-7a-12+12$

  $-33\le-11a$ $7<-7a$

  $\dfrac{-33}{-11}\ge\dfrac{-11a}{-11}$ $\dfrac{7}{-7}>\dfrac{-7a}{-7}$

  $3\ge a$ $-1>a$

            $a<-1$

  $a\le 3$ $(-\infty,3]$

31. $\dfrac{n}{2}+8>11$ or $9-\dfrac{2n}{3}\ge 6$

  $\dfrac{n}{2}+8-8>11-8$ $9-9-\dfrac{2n}{3}\ge 6-9$

  $\dfrac{n}{2}>3$ $-\dfrac{2n}{3}\ge-3$

  $2\left(\dfrac{n}{2}\right)>2\bullet 3$ $\left(-\dfrac{3}{2}\right)\left(-\dfrac{2n}{3}\right)\le\left(-\dfrac{3}{2}\right)(-3)$

  $n>6$ $n\le\dfrac{9}{2}$

  $n\le\dfrac{9}{2}$ or $n>6$ $\left(-\infty,\dfrac{9}{2}\right]\cup(6,\infty)$

33. $4x+19>-19$ or $15-3x\ge 26$

  $4x+19-19>-19-19$ $15-15-3x\ge 26-15$

  $4x>-38$ $-3x\ge 11$

  $\dfrac{4x}{4}>\dfrac{-38}{4}$ $\dfrac{-3x}{-3}\le\dfrac{11}{-3}$

  $x>-\dfrac{19}{2}$ $x\le-\dfrac{11}{3}$

Since $-\dfrac{11}{3}>-\dfrac{19}{2}$ the two intervals overlap and the solution is all real numbers. $(-\infty,\infty)$

35. $7x-9>4x-18$ and $6x+5<x$

  $7x-4x-9>4x-4x-18$ $6x+5<x$

  $3x-9>-18$ $6x-x+5<x-x$

  $3x-9+9>-18+9$ $5x+5<0$

  $3x>-9$ $5x+5-5<0-5$

  $\dfrac{3x}{3}>\dfrac{-9}{3}$ $5x<-5$

  $x>-3$ $\dfrac{5x}{5}<\dfrac{-5}{5}$

            $x<-1$

  $-3<x<-1$

37. $5x+9\le 6x-3$

  $5x-6x+9\le 6x-6x-3$

  $-x+9\le-3$

  $-x-9+9\le-3-9$

  $-x\le-12$

  $\dfrac{-x}{-1}\ge\dfrac{-12}{-1}$

  $x\ge 12$

  or $10x-7<4x+5$

  $10x-7<4x+5$

  $10x-4x-7<4x-4x+5$

  $6x-7<5$

  $6x-7+7<5+7$

  $6x<12$

  $\dfrac{6x}{6}<\dfrac{12}{6}$

  $x<2$

  $x<2$ or $x\ge 12$

39. $3x-9\le-2-\dfrac{x}{2}$

  $3x+\dfrac{x}{2}-9\le-2-\dfrac{x}{2}+\dfrac{x}{2}$

  $\dfrac{6x}{2}+\dfrac{x}{2}-9\le-2$

$$\frac{7x}{2}-9\le-2$$

$$\frac{7x}{2}-9+9\le-2+9$$

$$\frac{7x}{2}\le7$$

$$\left(\frac{2}{7}\right)\left(\frac{7x}{2}\right)\le\left(\frac{2}{7}\right)7$$

$$x\le2$$

$$15x-20x<-40$$

$$-5x<-40$$

$$\frac{-5x}{-5}>\frac{-40}{-5}$$

$$x>8$$

No real value of x can satisfy both conditions $x\le2$ and $x>8$. There is no solution.

41. $\dfrac{1}{2}x-21<\dfrac{1}{4}x-10$

$$\frac{1}{2}x-\frac{1}{4}x-21<\frac{1}{4}x-\frac{1}{4}x-10$$

$$\frac{2}{4}x-\frac{1}{4}x-21<-10$$

$$\frac{1}{4}x-21<-10$$

$$\frac{1}{4}x-21+21<-10+21$$

$$\frac{1}{4}x<11$$

$$4\left(\frac{1}{4}x\right)<4\bullet11$$

$$x<44\bullet$$

or

$$6x+19>4x+5$$

$$6x-4x+19>4x-4x+5$$

$$2x+19>5$$

$$2x+19-19>5-19$$

$$2x>-14$$

$$\frac{2x}{2}>\frac{-14}{2}$$

$$x>-7$$

For $x<44$ or $x>-7$, x can be any real number. The solution is all real numbers.

43. $2(5x+1)>9x+1$

$$10x+2>9x+1$$

$$10x-9x+2>9x-9x+1$$

$$x+2>1$$

$$x+2-2>1-2$$

$$x>-1$$

and

$$11x-7\ge4x$$

$$11x-4x-7\ge4x-4x$$

$$7x-7\ge0$$

$$7x-7+7\ge0+7$$

$$7x\ge7$$

$$\frac{7x}{7}\ge\frac{7}{7}$$

$$x\ge1$$

For $x>-1$ and $x\ge1$, the solution is

$$x\ge1.$$

45. $-15\le5(x-7)<20$

$$-15\le5x-35<20$$

$$-15+35\le5x-35+35<20+35$$

$$20\le5x<55$$

$$\frac{20}{5}\le\frac{5x}{5}<\frac{55}{5}$$

$$4\le x<11$$

47. $1\le-\dfrac{1}{3}(4x-27)<17$

$$1\le-\frac{4x}{3}+9<17$$

$$1-9\le-\frac{4x}{3}+9-9<17-9$$

$$-8\le-\frac{4x}{3}<8$$

$$\left(-\frac{3}{4}\right)(-8)\ge\left(-\frac{3}{4}\right)\left(-\frac{4x}{3}\right)>\left(-\frac{3}{4}\right)8$$

$$6\ge x>-6 \text{ or } -6<x\le6$$

49. $13\le8x-3(4x+1)\le25$

$$13\le8x-12x-3\le25$$

$$13\le-4x-3\le25$$

$$13+3\le-4x-3+3\le25+3$$

$$16\le-4x\le28$$

$$\frac{16}{-4}\ge\frac{-4x}{-4}\ge\frac{28}{-4}$$

$$-4\ge x\ge-7 \text{ or } -7\le x\le-4$$

51. $-8.3<1.7-0.5(7x-1)<3.95$

$$-8.3<1.7-3.5x+0.5<3.95$$

$$-8.3<2.2-3.5x<3.95$$

$$-8.3-2.2<2.2-2.2-3.5x<3.95-2.2$$

$$-10.5<-3.5x<1.75$$

$$\frac{-10.5}{-3.5}>\frac{-3.5x}{-3.5}>\frac{1.75}{-3.5}$$

$$3>x>-0.5 \text{ or } -0.5<x<3$$

53. Let t be the fourth test score. The average of the four grades must be between 83 and 87.

$$83 < \frac{87 + 82 + 80 + t}{4} < 87$$

$$83 < \frac{249 + t}{4} < 87$$

$$4 \bullet 83 < \frac{4}{1}\left(\frac{249 + t}{4}\right) < 4 \bullet 87$$

$$332 < 249 + t < 348$$

$$332 - 249 < 249 - 249 + t < 348 - 249$$

$$83 < t < 99$$

The possible scores on the fourth exam to have a B average must be between 83 and 99.

55. Unhealthy weights result in
BMI < 18.5 or BMI > 24.9.

$$h = 68 \quad \text{BMI} = \frac{703w}{h^2} = \frac{703w}{68^2} = \frac{703w}{4624}$$

$$\frac{703w}{4624} < 18.5$$

$$\frac{703w}{4624}(4624) < 18.5(4624)$$

$$703w < 85544$$

$$\frac{703w}{703} < \frac{85544}{703}$$

$$w < 121.7$$

$$\frac{703w}{4624} > 24.9$$

$$\frac{703w}{4624}(4624) > 24.9(4624)$$

$$703w > 115137.6$$

$$\frac{703w}{703} > \frac{115137.6}{703}$$

$$w > 163.8$$

Unhealthy weights for a person 5 feet 8 inches tall are less than 122 pounds or more than 164 pounds.

57. Let s be the speed of the plane. The Mach number is

$$\frac{s}{740}.$$

$$1 < \frac{s}{740} < 2$$

$$1(740) < \frac{s}{740}(740) < 2(740)$$

$$740 < s < 1480$$

The range of speeds for aircrafts whose mach numbers are between 1.0 and 2.0 are between 740 mph and 1480 mph.

59. Let g be the number of guests.

$$7500 < 2500 + 50g < 10000$$

$$7500 - 2500 < 2500 - 2500 + 50g < 10000 - 2500$$

$$5000 < 50g < 7500$$

$$\frac{5000}{50} < \frac{50g}{50} < \frac{7500}{50}$$

$$100 < g < 150$$

The couple can invite between 100 and 150 guests.

61. Let b be the number of baskets sold. The revenue from each basket is $45b$ and the cost is $200 + 5b$. The profit is $45b - (200 + 5b)$.

$$1000 < 45b - (200 + 5b) < 2000$$

$$1000 < 45b - 200 - 5b < 2000$$

$$1000 < 40b - 200 < 2000$$

$$1000 + 200 < 40b - 200 + 200 < 2000 + 200$$

$$1200 < 40b < 2200$$

$$\frac{1200}{40} < \frac{40b}{40} < \frac{2200}{40}$$

$$30 < b < 55$$

The owner must sell between 30 and 55 gift baskets per month.

Exercises 2.5 Solving Absolute Value Equations and Inequalities

1. $|-3 - 3| = |-6| = 6$

   or $|3 - (-3)| = |6| = 6$

3. $|-11 - (-4)| = |-11 + 4| = |-7| = 7$

   or $|-4 - (-11)| = |-4 + 11| = |7| = 7$

5. $|1.5 - 9| = |-7.5| = 7.5$

   or $|9 - 1.5| = |7.5| = 7.5$

7. $x = 7$ or $x = -7$

9. $n = \frac{2}{3}$ or $n = -\frac{2}{3}$

11. $6x = 24$ or $6x = -24$

$$\frac{6x}{6} = \frac{24}{6} \qquad \frac{6x}{6} = \frac{-24}{6}$$

$$x = 4 \qquad\qquad x = -4$$

13. $2|y| = -1.6$

$$\frac{2}{2}|y| = \frac{-1.6}{2}$$

$|y| = -0.8$ No solution, $|y| \geq 0$

15. $|x| + 1 = 1$

$$|x| + 1 - 1 = 1 - 1$$

$$|x| = 0$$

$$x = 0$$

17. $|x| - 4 = -2$

$$|x| - 4 + 4 = -2 + 4$$

$$|x| = 2$$

$$x = 2 \text{ or } x = -2$$

19. $3|n|+10=7$

$3|n|+10-10=7-10$

$3|n|=-3$

$\dfrac{3}{3}|n|=\dfrac{-3}{3}$

$|n|=-1$ No solution, $|n|\geq 0$

21. $12-4|y|=-16$

$12-12-4|y|=-16-12$

$-4|y|=-28$

$\dfrac{-4}{-4}|y|=\dfrac{-28}{-4}$

$|y|=7$

$y=7$ or $y=-7$

23. $|4x|+9=15$

$|4x|+9-9=15-9$

$|4x|=6$

$4x=6$ or $4x=-6$

$\dfrac{4x}{4}=\dfrac{6}{4}$ $\quad$ $\dfrac{4x}{4}=\dfrac{-6}{4}$

$x=\dfrac{3}{2}$ $\quad\quad$ $x=-\dfrac{3}{2}$

25. $\left|\dfrac{2}{3}n\right|-5=-1$

$\left|\dfrac{2}{3}n\right|-5+5=-1+5$

$\left|\dfrac{2}{3}n\right|=4$

$\dfrac{2}{3}n=4$ $\quad$ or $\quad$ $\dfrac{2}{3}n=-4$

$\left(\dfrac{3}{2}\right)\dfrac{2}{3}n=4\left(\dfrac{3}{2}\right)$ $\quad$ $\left(\dfrac{3}{2}\right)\dfrac{2}{3}n=-4\left(\dfrac{3}{2}\right)$

$n=6$ $\quad\quad\quad$ $n=-6$

27. $|y+7|=4$

$y+7=4$ $\quad$ or $\quad$ $y+7=-4$

$y+7-7=4-7$ $\quad$ $y+7-7=-4-7$

$y=-3$ $\quad\quad\quad$ $y=-11$

29. $|x-3|=-1$ has no solution as $|x-3|\geq 0$.

31. $|2z+13|=21$

$2z+13=21$ $\quad$ or $\quad$ $2z+13=-21$

$2z+13-13=21-13$ $\quad$ $2z+13-13=-21-13$

$2z=8$ $\quad\quad\quad$ $2z=-34$

$\dfrac{2z}{2}=\dfrac{8}{2}$ $\quad\quad$ $\dfrac{2z}{2}=\dfrac{-34}{2}$

$z=4$ $\quad\quad\quad$ $z=-17$

33. $|4x-11|=17$

$4x-11=17$ $\quad$ or $\quad$ $4x-11=-17$

$4x-11+11=17+11$ $\quad$ $4x-11+11=-17+11$

$4x=28$ $\quad\quad\quad$ $4x=-6$

$\dfrac{4x}{4}=\dfrac{28}{4}$ $\quad\quad$ $\dfrac{4x}{4}=\dfrac{-6}{4}$

$x=7$ $\quad\quad\quad$ $x=-\dfrac{3}{2}$

35. $2|3n-1|=16$

$\dfrac{2}{2}|3n-1|=\dfrac{16}{2}$

$|3n-1|=8$

$3n-1=8$ $\quad$ or $\quad$ $3n-1=-8$

$3n-1+1=8+1$ $\quad$ $3n-1+1=-8+1$

$3n=9$ $\quad\quad\quad$ $3n=-7$

$\dfrac{3n}{3}=\dfrac{9}{3}$ $\quad\quad$ $\dfrac{3n}{3}=-\dfrac{7}{3}$

$n=3$ $\quad\quad\quad$ $n=-\dfrac{7}{3}$

37. $-|10-6z|=7$

$\dfrac{-|10-6z|}{-1}=\dfrac{7}{-1}$

$|10-6z|=-7$

No solution. $|10-6z|\geq 0$

39. $-\dfrac{1}{3}|8-7n|=-12$

$\left(-\dfrac{3}{1}\right)\left(-\dfrac{1}{3}\right)|8-7n|=\left(-\dfrac{3}{1}\right)(-12)$

$|8-7n|=36$

$8-7n=36$ $\quad$ or $\quad$ $8-7n=-36$

$8-8-7n=36-8$ $\quad$ $8-8-7n=-36-8$

$-7n=28$ $\quad\quad\quad$ $-7n=-44$

$\dfrac{-7n}{-7}=\dfrac{28}{-7}$ $\quad\quad$ $\dfrac{-7n}{-7}=\dfrac{-44}{-7}$

$n=-4$ $\quad\quad\quad$ $n=\dfrac{44}{7}$

41. $|5x|=|7x-24|$

$5x=7x-24$

$5x-7x=7x-7x-24$ $\quad\quad$ $5x=-(7x-24)$

$-2x=-24$ $\quad\quad\quad\quad$ $5x=-7x+24$

$\dfrac{-2x}{-2}=\dfrac{-24}{-2}$ $\quad$ or $\quad$ $5x+7x=-7x+7x+24$

$x=12$ $\quad\quad\quad\quad$ $12x=24$

$\quad\quad\quad\quad\quad\quad$ $\dfrac{12x}{12}=\dfrac{24}{12}$

$\quad\quad\quad\quad\quad\quad$ $x=2$

43. $\frac{1}{2}x + 3 = \frac{1}{4}x$

$\frac{1}{2}x - \frac{1}{4}x + 3 = \frac{1}{4}x - \frac{1}{4}x$ $\frac{1}{2}x + 3 = -\frac{1}{4}x$

$\frac{2}{4}x - \frac{1}{4}x + 3 = 0$ $\frac{1}{2}x + \frac{1}{4}x + 3 = -\frac{1}{4}x + \frac{1}{4}x$

$\frac{1}{4}x + 3 = 0$ $\frac{2}{4}x + \frac{1}{4}x + 3 = 0$

$\frac{1}{4}x + 3 - 3 = 0 - 3$ or $\frac{3}{4}x + 3 = 0$

$\frac{1}{4}x = -3$ $\frac{3}{4}x + 3 - 3 = 0 - 3$

$4\left(\frac{1}{4}x\right) = 4(-3)$ $\frac{3}{4}x = -3$

$x = -12$ $\left(\frac{4}{3}\right)\left(\frac{3}{4}x\right) = -3\left(\frac{4}{3}\right)$

$x = -4$

45. $2x - 3 = x + 9$

$2x - x - 3 = x - x + 9$ or $2x - 3 = -(x + 9)$

$x - 3 = 9$ $2x - 3 = -x - 9$

$x - 3 + 3 = 9 + 3$ $2x + x - 3 = -x + x - 9$

$x = 12$ $3x - 3 = -9$

$3x - 3 + 3 = -9 + 3$

$3x = -6$

$\frac{3x}{3} = \frac{-6}{3}$

$x = -2$

47. $5y + 1 = 6y - 1$

$5y - 6y + 1 = 6y - 6y - 1$ or $5y + 1 = -(6y - 1)$

$-y + 1 = -1$ $5y + 1 = -6y + 1$

$-y + 1 - 1 = -1 - 1$ $5y + 6y + 1 = -6y + 6y + 1$

$-y = -2$ $11y + 1 = 1$

$\frac{-y}{-1} = \frac{-2}{-1}$ $11y + 1 - 1 = 1 - 1$

$y = 2$ $11y = 0$

$\frac{11y}{11} = \frac{0}{11}$

$y = 0$

49. $11 - 7x = 5 - 9x$

$11 - 7x + 9x = 5 - 9x + 9x$

$11 + 2x = 5$

$11 - 11 + 2x = 5 - 11$

$2x = -6$

$\frac{2x}{2} = \frac{-6}{2}$

$x = -3$

or

$11 - 7x = -(5 - 9x)$

$11 - 7x = -5 + 9x$

$11 - 7x - 9x = -5 + 9x - 9x$

$11 - 16x = -5$

$11 - 11 - 16x = -5 - 11$

$-16x = -16$

$\frac{-16x}{-16} = \frac{-16}{-16}$

$x = 1$

51. $x + 7 = x + 1$

$x - x + 7 = x - x + 1$

$7 \neq 1$

This part does not lead to a solution.

$x + 7 = -(x + 1)$

$x + 7 = -x - 1$

$x + x + 7 = -x + x - 1$

$2x + 7 = -1$

$2x + 7 - 7 = -1 - 7$

$2x = -8$

$\frac{2x}{2} = \frac{-8}{2}$

$x = -4$ is the only solution.

53. $4 - n = -(n - 2)$

$4 - n = -n + 2$

$4 - n + n = -n + n + 2$

$4 \neq 2$ This part does not lead to a solution.

or

$4 - n = n - 2$

$4 - n - n = n - n - 2$

$4 - 2n = -2$

$4 - 4 - 2n = -2 - 4$

$-2n = -6$

$\frac{-2n}{-2} = \frac{-6}{-2}$

$n = 3$ is the only solution.

55. $\frac{-|3t + 4|}{-1} = \frac{-|2t - 1|}{-1}$

$|3t + 4| = |2t - 1|$

$3t + 4 = 2t - 1$

$3t - 2t + 4 = 2t - 2t - 1$

$t + 4 = -1$

$t + 4 - 4 = -1 - 4$

$t = -5$

or

$3t + 4 = -(2t - 1)$

$3t + 4 = -2t + 1$

$3t + 2t + 4 = -2t + 2t + 1$

$5t + 4 = 1$

$5t + 4 - 4 = 1 - 4$

$5t = -3$

$\dfrac{5t}{5} = \dfrac{-3}{5}$

$t = -\dfrac{3}{5}$

57. $|8 - a| \geq 0$ making $-|8 - a| \leq 0$

$|4a + 7| \geq 0$ There is no solution.

59. $x > 3$ of $x < -3$; $(-\infty, -3) \cup (3, \infty)$

61. $-\dfrac{1}{2} \leq x \leq \dfrac{1}{2}$; $\left[-\dfrac{1}{2}, \dfrac{1}{2}\right]$

63. $7x \geq 21$ or $7x \leq -21$

$\dfrac{7x}{7} \geq \dfrac{21}{7}$ $\qquad$ $\dfrac{7x}{7} \leq \dfrac{-21}{7}$

$x \geq 3$ $\qquad$ $x \leq -3$

$(-\infty, -3] \cup [3, \infty)$

65. $-4 < x + 4 < 4$

$-4 - 4 < x + 4 - 4 < 4 - 4$

$-8 < x < 0$; $(-8, 0)$

67. $x - 5 \geq 3$ $\qquad$ or $\qquad$ $x - 5 \leq -3$

$x - 5 + 5 \geq 3 + 5$ $\qquad$ $x - 5 + 5 \leq -3 + 5$

$x \geq 8$ $\qquad$ $x \leq 2$

$(-\infty, 2] \cup [8, \infty)$

69. $|x| + 5 \geq 6$

$|x| + 5 - 5 \geq 6 - 5$

$|x| \geq 1$ $\quad$ $x \geq 1$ or $x \leq -1$

$(-\infty, -1] \cup [1, \infty)$

71. $|x| - 3 < -2$

$|x| - 3 + 3 < -2 + 3$

$|x| < 1$ $\quad$ $-1 < x < 1$; $(-1, 1)$

73. $2x + 3 \geq 11$ $\qquad$ or $\qquad$ $2x + 3 \leq -11$

$2x + 3 - 3 \geq 11 - 3$ $\qquad$ $2x + 3 - 3 \leq -11 - 3$

$2x \geq 8$ $\qquad$ $2x \leq -14$

$\dfrac{2x}{2} \geq \dfrac{8}{2}$ $\qquad$ $\dfrac{2x}{2} \leq \dfrac{-14}{2}$

$x \geq 4$ $\qquad$ $x \leq -7$

$(-\infty, -7] \cup [4, \infty)$

75. $-9 < 6 - 3x < 9$

$-9 - 6 < 6 - 6 - 3x < 9 - 6$

$-15 < -3x < 3$

$\dfrac{-15}{-3} > \dfrac{-3x}{-3} > \dfrac{3}{-3}$

$5 > x > -1$ or $-1 < x < 5$; $(-1, 5)$

77. Absolute value is always greater than or equal to zero. Any value of x will work. The solution is all real numbers: $(-\infty, \infty)$.

Analytically:

$\dfrac{2}{3}x + 4 \geq 0$ $\qquad$ or $\qquad$ $\dfrac{2}{3}x + 4 \leq 0$

$\dfrac{2}{3}x + 4 - 4 \geq 0 - 4$ $\qquad$ $\dfrac{2}{3}x + 4 - 4 \leq 0 - 4$

$\dfrac{2}{3}x \geq -4$ $\qquad$ $\dfrac{2}{3}x \leq -4$

$\left(\dfrac{3}{2}\right)\left(\dfrac{2}{3}x\right) \geq -4\left(\dfrac{3}{2}\right)$ $\qquad$ $\left(\dfrac{3}{2}\right)\left(\dfrac{2}{3}x\right) \leq -4\left(\dfrac{3}{2}\right)$

$x \geq -6$ $\qquad$ $x \leq -6$

$(-\infty, -6] \cup [-6, \infty) = (-\infty, \infty)$

79. $\dfrac{-|2x - 7|}{-1} > \dfrac{-6}{-1}$

$|2x - 7| > 6$

$2x - 7 > 6$ $\qquad$ or $\qquad$ $2x - 7 < -6$

$2x - 7 + 7 > 6 + 7$ $\qquad$ $2x - 7 + 7 < -6 + 7$

$2x > 13$ $\qquad$ $2x < 1$

$x > \dfrac{13}{2}$ $\qquad$ $\dfrac{2x}{2} < \dfrac{1}{2}$

$\qquad\qquad\qquad\qquad$ $x < \dfrac{1}{2}$

$\left(-\infty, \dfrac{1}{2}\right) \cup \left(\dfrac{13}{2}, \infty\right)$

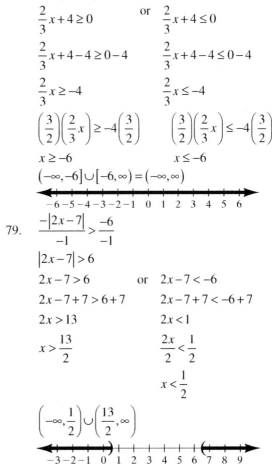

81. $|4x-3|-6 \le 5$

$|4x-3|-6+6 \le 5+6$

$|4x-3| \le 11$

$-11 \le 4x-3 \le 11$

$-11+3 \le 4x-3+3 \le 11+3$

$-8 \le 4x \le 14$

$\dfrac{-8}{4} \le \dfrac{4x}{4} \le \dfrac{14}{4}$

$-2 \le x \le \dfrac{7}{2}; \quad \left[-2, \dfrac{7}{2}\right]$

83. Let t be the possible temperature reading.

$|t-36.8| \le 0.4$

$-0.4 \le t-36.8 \le 0.4$

$-0.4+36.8 \le t-36.8+36.8 \le 0.4+36.8$

$36.4 \le t \le 37.2$

The maximum possible temperature is 37.2°C and the minimum possible temperature is 36.4°C.

85. Let s be the speed of the car.

$|s-37| \le 1$

$-1 \le s-37 \le 1$

$-1+37 \le s-37+37 \le 1+37$

$36 \le s \le 38$

The maximum possible speed was 38 mph and the minimum possible speed was 36 mph.

87. a. $|x-68| \le 4$

b. $-4 \le x-68 \le 4$

$-4+68 \le x-68+68 \le 4+68$

$64 \le x \le 72$

Between 64% and 72% of the residents oppose the construction of the runway.

89. Let I be the income of the resident.

a. $|I-39000| > 5000$

b. $I-39000 > 5000$

$I-39000+39000 > 5000+39000$

$I > 44000$

or

$I-39000 < -5000$

$I-39000+39000 < -5000+39000$

$I < 34000$

The resident makes less than $34,000 or more than $44,000.

91. The average speed between the maximum and minimum speeds is $\dfrac{35+55}{2} = \dfrac{90}{2} = 45$. 45 is ten units from both 35 and 55.

The speed must satisfy $|s-45| \le 10$.

Chapter 2 Review Exercises

1. Substitute 4 for x in $2x+5=6x-11$.

$2(4)+5 \overset{?}{=} 6(4)-11$

$8+5 \overset{?}{=} 24-11$

$13 = 13$

4 is a solution.

2. Substitute -1 for x in $12-7x=4(3x+1)$.

$12-7(-1) \overset{?}{=} 4(3(-1)+1)$

$12+7 \overset{?}{=} 4(-3+1)$

$19 \overset{?}{=} 4(-2)$

$19 \ne -8$ -1 is not a solution.

3. Substitute -2 for x in $\dfrac{2}{3}(9x-12)=-(8-3x)$

$\dfrac{2}{3}(9(-2)-12)=-(8-3(-2))$

$\dfrac{2}{3}(-18-12) \overset{?}{=} -(8+6)$

$\dfrac{2}{3}(-30) \overset{?}{=} -14$

$-20 \ne -14$ -2 is not a solution.

4. Substitute $-\dfrac{1}{3}$ for x in $3x+\dfrac{1}{2}(8x+12)=6-(1-4x)$.

$3\left(-\dfrac{1}{3}\right)+\dfrac{1}{2}\left(8\left(-\dfrac{1}{3}\right)+12\right) \overset{?}{=} 6-\left(1-4\left(-\dfrac{1}{3}\right)\right)$

$-1+\dfrac{1}{2}\left(-\dfrac{8}{3}+\dfrac{36}{3}\right) \overset{?}{=} 6-\left(\dfrac{3}{3}+\dfrac{4}{3}\right)$

$-1+\dfrac{1}{2}\left(\dfrac{28}{3}\right) \overset{?}{=} 6-\dfrac{7}{3}$

$-\dfrac{3}{3}+\dfrac{14}{3} \overset{?}{=} \dfrac{18}{3}-\dfrac{7}{3}$

$\dfrac{11}{3}=\dfrac{11}{3}$ $-\dfrac{1}{3}$ is a solution.

5. $\left(-\dfrac{3}{2}\right)\left(-\dfrac{2}{3}x\right)=4\left(-\dfrac{3}{2}\right)$

$x=-6$

Check

$-\dfrac{2}{3}(-6) \overset{?}{=} 4$

$4=4$ True.

6. $3n+4-4=-8-4$

$3n=-12$

$\dfrac{3n}{3}=\dfrac{-12}{3}$

$n=-4$

Check

$$3(-4)+4\overset{?}{=}-8$$

$$-12+4\overset{?}{=}-8$$

$$-8=-8 \text{ True.}$$

7. $$7x-9x-16=9x-9x$$

$$-2x-16=0$$

$$-2x-16+16=0+16$$

$$-2x=16$$

$$\frac{-2x}{-2}=\frac{16}{-2}$$

$$x=-8$$

Check

$$7(-8)-16\overset{?}{=}9(-8)$$

$$-56-16\overset{?}{=}-72$$

$$-72=-72 \text{ True.}$$

8. $$17-2t+10t=11-10t+10t$$

$$17+8t=11$$

$$17-17+8t=11-17$$

$$8t=-6$$

$$\frac{8t}{8}=\frac{-6}{8}$$

$$t=-\frac{3}{4}$$

Check

$$17-2\left(-\frac{3}{4}\right)\overset{?}{=}11-10\left(-\frac{3}{4}\right)$$

$$17+\frac{3}{2}\overset{?}{=}11+\frac{15}{2}$$

$$\frac{34}{2}+\frac{3}{2}\overset{?}{=}\frac{22}{2}+\frac{15}{2}$$

$$\frac{37}{2}=\frac{37}{2} \text{ True.}$$

9. $$-4n+12=0$$

$$-4n+12-12=0-12$$

$$-4n=-12$$

$$\frac{-4n}{-4}=\frac{-12}{-4}$$

$$n=3$$

Check

$$4(3)-3-8(3)+15\overset{?}{=}0$$

$$12-3-24+15\overset{?}{=}0$$

$$0=0 \text{ True.}$$

10. $$-0.5-1.9a=1.1a-2.6$$

$$-0.5-1.9a-1.1a=1.1a-1.1a-2.6$$

$$-0.5-3a=-2.6$$

$$-0.5+0.5-3a=-2.6+0.5$$

$$-3a=-2.1$$

$$\frac{-3a}{-3}=\frac{-2.1}{-3}$$

$$a=0.7$$

Check

$$3.5-1.9(0.7)-4\overset{?}{=}1.1(0.7)-2.6$$

$$3.5-1.33-4\overset{?}{=}0.77-2.6$$

$$-1.83=-1.83 \text{ True.}$$

11. $$\frac{3}{2}x-8=-15$$

$$\frac{3}{2}x-8+8=-15+8$$

$$\frac{3}{2}x=-7$$

$$\left(\frac{2}{3}\right)\left(\frac{3}{2}x\right)=-7\left(\frac{2}{3}\right)$$

$$x=-\frac{14}{3}$$

Check

$$\frac{1}{2}\left(3\left(-\frac{14}{3}\right)-16\right)\overset{?}{=}-15$$

$$\frac{1}{2}(-14-16)\overset{?}{=}-15$$

$$\frac{1}{2}(-30)\overset{?}{=}-15$$

$$-15=-15 \text{ True.}$$

12. $$12y+24=-28+36y$$

$$12y-36y+24=-28+36y-36y$$

$$-24y+24=-28$$

$$-24y+24-24=-28-24$$

$$-24y=-52$$

$$\frac{-24y}{-24}=\frac{-52}{-24}$$

$$y=\frac{13}{6}$$

Check

$$3\left(4\left(\frac{13}{6}\right)+8\right)\overset{?}{=}-4\left(7-9\left(\frac{13}{6}\right)\right)$$

$$3\left(\frac{26}{3}+\frac{24}{3}\right)\overset{?}{=}-4\left(\frac{14}{2}-\frac{39}{2}\right)$$

$$3\left(\frac{50}{3}\right)\overset{?}{=}-4\left(-\frac{25}{2}\right)$$

$$50=50 \text{ True.}$$

13. $6y - 2 + 2y = 12y + 18$

$8y - 2 = 12y + 18$

$8y - 12y - 2 = 12y - 12y + 18$

$-4y - 2 = 18$

$-4y - 2 + 2 = 18 + 2$

$-4y = 20$

$\dfrac{-4y}{-4} = \dfrac{20}{-4}$

$y = -5$

Check

$6(-5) - 2\big(1 - (-5)\big) \overset{?}{=} 12(-5) + 18$

$-30 - 2(6) \overset{?}{=} -60 + 18$

$-30 - 12 \overset{?}{=} -42 \quad -42 = -42$ True.

14. $4[1 - 5x + 2] + 11x = 7 - 7x + 7$

$4[3 - 5x] + 11x = 14 - 7x$

$12 - 20x + 11x = 14 - 7x$

$-9x + 12 = 14 - 7x$

$-9x + 7x + 12 = 14 - 7x + 7x$

$-2x + 12 = 14$

$-2x + 12 - 12 = 14 - 12$

$-2x = 2$

$\dfrac{-2x}{-2} = \dfrac{2}{-2}$

$x = -1$

Check

$4\big[1 - (5(-1) - 2)\big] + 11(-1) \overset{?}{=} 7 - (7(-1) - 7)$

$4[1 - (-5 - 2)] - 11 \overset{?}{=} 7 - (-7 - 7)$

$4\big[1 - (-7)\big] - 11 \overset{?}{=} 7 - (-14)$

$4[8] - 11 \overset{?}{=} 7 + 14$

$32 - 11 \overset{?}{=} 21$

$21 = 21$ True.

15. $10x - 10x + 2y = -10x - 2$

$2y = -10x - 2$

$\left(\dfrac{1}{2}\right) 2y = \left(\dfrac{1}{2}\right)(-10x - 2)$

$y = -5x - 1$

16. $y - y - 4x = -y + 8$

$-4x = -y + 8$

$\left(-\dfrac{1}{4}\right)(-4x) = \left(-\dfrac{1}{4}\right)(-y + 8)$

$x = \dfrac{y}{4} - 2$

17. $ab - ab + cd = 0 - ab$

$cd = -ab$

$\dfrac{cd}{d} = \dfrac{-ab}{d}$

$c = -\dfrac{ab}{d}$

18. $6xy - v + v = v + z$

$6xy = v + z$

$\dfrac{6xy}{6y} = \dfrac{v + z}{6y}$

$x = \dfrac{v + z}{6y}$

19. $ab - ac = d$

$ab - ac + ac = ac + d$

$ab = ac + d$

$\dfrac{ab}{a} = \dfrac{ac + d}{a}$

$b = \dfrac{ac + d}{a}$

20. $q - rs - rt = p$

$q - rs - q + rs - rt = p - q + rs$

$-rt = p - q + rs$

$\dfrac{-rt}{-r} = \dfrac{p - q + rs}{-r}$

$t = -\dfrac{p - q + rs}{r}$

21. $A - 2\pi r^2 = 2\pi r^2 - 2\pi r^2 + 2\pi rh$

$A - 2\pi r^2 = 2\pi rh$

$\dfrac{A - 2\pi r^2}{2\pi r} = \dfrac{2\pi rh}{2\pi r}$

$\dfrac{A - 2\pi r^2}{2\pi r} = h$ or $h = \dfrac{A - 2\pi r^2}{2\pi r}$

22. $150D = 150\left(\dfrac{Ay}{150}\right)$

$150D = Ay$

$\dfrac{150D}{y} = \dfrac{Ay}{y}$

$\dfrac{150D}{y} = A$ or $A = \dfrac{150D}{y}$

23. $\dfrac{PV}{nR} = \dfrac{nRT}{nR}$

$\dfrac{PV}{nR} = T$ or $T = \dfrac{PV}{nR}$

24. $\dfrac{V}{lh} = \dfrac{lhw}{lh}$

$\dfrac{V}{lh} = w$ or $w = \dfrac{V}{lh}$

25. Substitute –2 for n in $4n-7 > 3n-6$.

$$4(-2)-7 \overset{?}{>} 3(-2)-6$$

$$-8-7 \overset{?}{>} -6-6$$

$-15 \not> -12$ –2 is not a solution.

26. Substitute 15 for y in $\frac{1}{4}(y+5) \le 10-\frac{1}{3}y$.

$$\frac{1}{4}(15+5) \overset{?}{\le} 10-\frac{1}{3}(15)$$

$$\frac{1}{4}(20) \overset{?}{\le} 10-5$$

$5 \le 5$ 15 is a solution.

27. b.
28. a.
29. d.
30. c.

31. $10\left(-\dfrac{3}{5}\right) < 10\left(\dfrac{1}{10}x\right)$

$-6 < x$ or $x > -6$

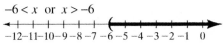

32. $2n-7+7 \le 9+7$

$2n \le 16$

$\dfrac{2n}{2} \le \dfrac{16}{2}$

$n \le 8$

33. $11-5y+4y \le 11-4y+4y$

$11-y \le 11$

$11-11-y \le 11-11$

$-y \le 0$

$\dfrac{-y}{-1} \ge \dfrac{0}{-1}$

$y \ge 0$

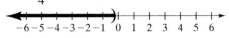

34. $-3x-x > x-x+1$

$-4x > 1$

$\dfrac{-4x}{-4} < \dfrac{1}{-4}$

$x < -\dfrac{1}{4}$

35. $4y+6 \ge 9y-9$

$4y-9y+6 \ge 9y-9y-9$

$-5y+6 \ge -9$

$-5y+6-6 \ge -9-6$

$-5y \ge -15$

$\dfrac{-5y}{-5} \le \dfrac{-15}{-5}$

$y \le 3;\ (-\infty, 3]$

36. $12-3x \le -12$

$12-12-3x \le -12-12$

$-3x \le -24$

$\dfrac{-3x}{-3} \ge \dfrac{-24}{-3}$

$x \ge 8;\ [8, \infty)$

37. $10-4x-14 < -10x-16$

$-4x-4 < -10x-16$

$-4x+10x-4 < -10x+10x-16$

$6x-4 < -16$

$6x-4+4 < -16+4$

$6x < -12$

$\dfrac{6x}{6} < \dfrac{-12}{6}$

$x < -2;\ (-\infty, -2)$

38. $\dfrac{1}{3}[7-24n+11] > 26-13n$

$\dfrac{1}{3}[18-24n] > 26-13n$

$6-8n > 26-13n$

$6-8n+13n > 26-13n+13n$

$6+5n > 26$

$6-6+5n > 26-6$

$5n > 20$

$\dfrac{5n}{5} > \dfrac{20}{5}$

$n > 4;\ (4, \infty)$

39. $(-4, 1]$

40. $[-2, 3)$

41. $(-\infty, 0] \cup [2.5, \infty)$

42. $(-\infty, -3) \cup (4, \infty)$

43. $2x-3+3 > 1+3$ and $x+7-7 < 12-7$

$2x > 4$ $x < 5$

$\dfrac{2x}{2} > \dfrac{4}{2}$

$x > 2$

$2 < x < 5;\ (2,5)$

44. $2\left(\dfrac{1}{2}x\right) \ge 2(-2)$ and $1-1-3x > -8-1$

$x \ge -4$ $-3x > -9$

$\dfrac{-3x}{-3} < \dfrac{-9}{-3}$

$x < 3$

$-4 \le x < 3;\ [-4,3)$

45. $-11-4 < 5x+4-4 \le 14-4$

$-15 < 5x \le 10$

$\dfrac{-15}{5} < \dfrac{5x}{5} \le \dfrac{10}{5}$

$-3 < x \le 2;\ (-3,2]$

46. $0-2 \le 2-2-4x \le 18-2$

$-2 \le -4x \le 16$

$\dfrac{-2}{-4} \ge \dfrac{-4x}{-4} \ge \dfrac{16}{-4}$

$\dfrac{1}{2} \ge x \ge -4$ or

$-4 \le x \le \dfrac{1}{2};\ \left[-4,\dfrac{1}{2}\right]$

47. $3x+1-1 < -2-1$ or $4x-7+7 \ge 7+7$

$3x < -3$ $4x \ge 14$

$\dfrac{3x}{3} < \dfrac{-3}{3}$ $\dfrac{4x}{4} \ge \dfrac{14}{4}$

$x < -1$ $x \ge \dfrac{7}{2}$

$x < -1$ or $x \ge \dfrac{7}{2};\ (-\infty,-1)\cup\left[\dfrac{7}{2},\infty\right)$

48. $\dfrac{1}{4}x+3-3 < 6-3$ or $2-2-5x < 12-2$

$\dfrac{1}{4}x < 3$ $-5x < 10$

$4\left(\dfrac{1}{4}x\right) < 4(3)$ $\dfrac{-5x}{-5} > \dfrac{10}{-5}$

$x < 12$ $x > -2$

$(-\infty,12)\cup(-2,\infty) = (-\infty,\infty)$

All real numbers.

49. $8x-2x+12 \le 2x-2x$ or $x-3x < 3x-3x$

$6x+12 \le 0$ $-2x < 0$

$6x+12-12 \le 0-12$ $\dfrac{-2x}{-2} > \dfrac{0}{-2}$

$6x \le -12$ $x > 0$

$\dfrac{6x}{6} \le \dfrac{-12}{6}$

$x \le -2$

50. $7x-8x-6 \le 8x-8x-4$

$-x-6 \le -4$

$-x-6+6 \le -4+6$

$-x \le 2$

$\dfrac{-x}{-1} \ge \dfrac{2}{-1}$

$x \ge -2$

and

$19-x+4x \le 10-4x+4x$

$19+3x \le 10$

$19-19+3x \le 10-19$

$3x \le -9$

$\dfrac{3x}{3} \le \dfrac{-9}{3}$

$x \le -3$

$x > -2$ and $x \le -3$ are disjoined sets.

There is no solution.

51. $|-2-9| = |-11| = 11$

or

$|9-(-2)| = |11| = 11$

52. $|-6.4-(-5.7)| = |-6.4+5.7| = |-0.7| = 0.7$

or

$|-5.7-(-6.4)| = |-5.7+6.4| = |0.7| = 0.7$

53. $x = 15$ or $x = -15$

54. $4y = 24$ or $4y = -24$

$\dfrac{4y}{4} = \dfrac{24}{4}$ $\dfrac{4y}{4} = \dfrac{-24}{4}$

$y = 6$ $y = -6$

55. $|n|-12+12 = -3+12$

$|n| = 9$

$n = 9$ or $n = -9$

56. $11-11-2|x| = 9-11$

$-2|x| = -2$

$\dfrac{-2}{-2}|x| = \dfrac{-2}{-2}$

$|x| = 1$

$x = 1$ or $x = -1$

57. $|y+2| \geq 0$ for all values of y.

There is no solution.

58. $13-13-|5-6y| = 12-13$

$-|5-6y| = -1$

$\dfrac{-1}{-1}|5-6y| = \dfrac{-1}{-1}$

$|5-6y| = 1$

$\begin{array}{ll} 5-6y = 1 & \text{or} \quad 5-6y = -1 \\ 5-5-6y = 1-5 & \quad 5-5-6y = -1-5 \\ -6y = -4 & \quad -6y = -6 \\ \dfrac{-6y}{-6} = \dfrac{-4}{-6} & \quad \dfrac{-6y}{-6} = \dfrac{-6}{-6} \\ y = \dfrac{2}{3} & \quad y = 1 \end{array}$

59. $3x-9 = 4x+15$

$3x-4x-9 = 4x-4x+15$

$-x-9 = 15$

$-x-9+9 = 15+9$

$-x = 24$

$\dfrac{-x}{-1} = \dfrac{24}{-1}$

$x = -24$

or

$3x-9 = -(4x+15)$

$3x-9 = -4x-15$

$3x+4x-9 = -4x+4x-15$

$7x-9 = -15$

$7x-9+9 = -15+9$

$7x = -6$

$\dfrac{7x}{7} = \dfrac{-6}{7}$

$x = -\dfrac{6}{7}$

60. $x-1 = x+1$

$x-x-1 = x-x+1$

$-1 \neq 1$ No solution from this part.

$x-1 = -(x+1)$

$x-1 = -x-1$

$x+x-1 = -x+x-1$

$2x-1 = -1$

$2x-1+1 = -1+1$

$2x = 0$

$\dfrac{2x}{2} = \dfrac{0}{2}$

$x = 0$

61. $-1.5 < x < 1.5;\ (-1.5, 1.5)$

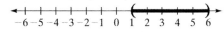

62. $-3 \leq x-4 \leq 3$

$-3+4 \leq x-4+4 \leq 3+4$

$1 \leq x \leq 7;\ [1,7]$

63. $|x|+2-2 \geq 2-2$

$|x| \geq 0$ is true for all possible values of x.

All real numbers; $(-\infty, \infty)$

64. $\begin{array}{ll} 2x-5 > 4 & \text{or} \quad 2x-5 < -4 \\ 2x-5+5 > 4+5 & \quad 2x-5+5 < -4+5 \\ 2x > 9 & \quad 2x < 1 \\ \dfrac{2x}{2} > \dfrac{9}{2} & \quad \dfrac{2x}{2} < \dfrac{1}{2} \\ x > \dfrac{9}{2} & \quad x < \dfrac{1}{2} \end{array}$

$\left(-\infty, \dfrac{1}{2}\right) \cup \left(\dfrac{9}{2}, \infty\right)$

65. $\dfrac{-|4x=9|}{-1} \geq \dfrac{-1}{-1}$

$|4x-9| \geq 1$

$\begin{array}{ll} 4x-9 \geq 1 & \text{or} \quad 4x-9 \leq -1 \\ 4x-9+9 \geq 1+9 & \quad 4x-9+9 \leq -1+9 \\ 4x \geq 10 & \quad 4x \leq 8 \\ \dfrac{4x}{4} \geq \dfrac{10}{4} & \quad \dfrac{4x}{4} \leq \dfrac{8}{4} \\ x \geq \dfrac{5}{2} & \quad x \leq 2 \end{array}$

$\left(-\infty, 2\right] \cup \left[\dfrac{5}{2}, \infty\right)$

66. $|2x-7|-1+1 < 4+1$

$|2x-7| < 5$

$-5 < 2x-7 \leq 5$

$-5+7 \leq 2x-7+7 \leq 5+7$

$2 < 2x < 12$

$\dfrac{2}{2} < \dfrac{2x}{2} < \dfrac{12}{2}$

$1 < x < 6;\ (1,6)$

67. Let w be the width of the floor space.

$48w = 1440$

$$\frac{48w}{48} = \frac{1440}{48}$$

$x = 30$

30 inches are required for the width.

68. Let l be the list price of the textbook.

$l + 25\%l = 96$

$l + 0.25l = 96$

$1.25l = 96$

$$\frac{1.25l}{1.25} = \frac{96}{1.25}$$

$l = 76.8$

The list price of the textbook is $76.80.

69. Let s be the amount the driver was exceeding the speed limit.

$50 + 10(s - 10) = 120$

$50 + 10s - 100 = 120$

$10s - 50 = 120$

$10s - 50 + 50 = 120 + 50$

$10s = 170$

$$\frac{10s}{10} = \frac{170}{10}$$

$s = 17$

The driver was going 17 mph over the 55 mph limit or going 72 mph.

70. Let q be the number of quilts in order for the cost to be equal to the revenue.

$90q = 2450 + 20q$

$90q - 20q = 2450 + 20q - 20q$

$70q = 2450$

$$\frac{70q}{70} = \frac{2450}{70}$$

$q = 35$

The cost will be equal to the revenue if 35 quilts are sold.

71. $(x) + (x+1) + (x+2) + (x+3) = 18$

$x + x + 1 + x + 2 + x + 3 = 18$

$4x + 6 = 18$

$4x + 6 - 6 = 18 - 6$

$4x = 12$

$$\frac{4x}{4} = \frac{12}{4}$$

$x = 3, \ x + 1 = 4, \ x + 2 = 5, \ x + 3 = 6$

The last four digits of the phone number are 3456.

72. The perimeter is $2 \bullet \text{width} + 2 \bullet \text{length}$.

$2(2w) + 2(w) = 24$

$4w + 2w = 24$

$6w = 24$

$$\frac{6w}{6} = \frac{24}{6}$$

$w = 4$ ft, $2w = 8$ ft

The length is 8 ft, the width is 4 ft.

$A = \text{length} \times \text{width}$.

$A = (8)(4)$

$A = 32$ sq ft.

The area of the tapestry is 32 sq ft.

73. Distance = rate × time. The distances traveled by the bus and car are the same. The bus traveled ten minutes $\frac{10}{60} = \frac{1}{6}$ hour more than the car. Let t be the time the car traveled.

Car distance = bus distance.

$$60t = 50\left(t + \frac{1}{6}\right)$$

$$60t = 50t + \frac{50}{6}$$

$$60t - 50t = 50t - 50t + \frac{50}{6}$$

$$10t = \frac{50}{6}$$

$$\frac{1}{10}(10t) = \frac{1}{10}\left(\frac{50}{6}\right)$$

$$t = \frac{50}{60} = \frac{5}{6}$$

The car caught up to the bus in $\frac{5}{6}$ hr. or 50 minutes.

74. Distance = rate × time. The sum of the distances traveled by the two friends is 5.5 miles. Let r be the rate of the faster person.

$$r\left(\frac{5}{60}\right) + (r - 6)\left(\frac{5}{60}\right) = 5.5$$

$$r\left(\frac{1}{12}\right) + (r - 6)\left(\frac{1}{12}\right) = 5.5$$

$$\frac{1}{12}r + \frac{1}{12}r - \frac{1}{2} = 5.5$$

$$\frac{2}{12}r - \frac{1}{2} = 5.5$$

$$\frac{1}{6}r - \frac{1}{2} + \frac{1}{2} = 5.5 + \frac{1}{2}$$

$$\frac{1}{6}r = 6$$

$$6\left(\frac{1}{6}r\right) = 6(6)$$

$r = 36, \ r - 6 = 30$

The two friends drove at a rate of 36 mph and 30 mph.

75. 15% alcohol solution means 15% of the solution is alcohol. Alcohol is added here. If the total solution is 8 liters, then the two parts will be s and $8-s$.

Solution × Rate = Alcohol

15% Alcohol	s	15%	$15\%(s)$
75% Alcohol	$8-s$	75%	$75\%(8-s)$
39% Alcohol	s	39%	$39\%(8)$

$0.15s + 0.75(8-s) = 0.39(8)$

$0.15s + 6 - 0.75s = 3.12$

$-0.60s + 6 = 3.12$

$-0.60s + 6 - 6 = 3.12 - 6$

$-0.60s = -2.88$

$\dfrac{-0.60s}{-0.60} = \dfrac{-2.88}{-0.60}$

$s = 4.8, \ 8 - s = 3.2$

4.8 liters of the 15% solution and 3.2 liters of the 75% solution are needed.

76. Let h be the amount of money invested in a high-risk fund.

Fund	Investment	Rate	Profit
Low Risk	$3h$	4.5%	$4.5\%(3h)$
High Risk	h	8%	$8\%(h)$
Total	$h+3h$		$1075

$0.045(3h) + 0.08(h) = 1075$

$0.135h + 0.08h = 1075$

$0.215h = 1075$

$\dfrac{0.215h}{0.215} = \dfrac{1075}{0.215}; \quad h = 5000, \ 3h = 15000$

$15,000 was invested in the low-risk fund and $5,000 was invested in the high-risk fund.

77. a. $I = \text{Pr}t$

$\dfrac{I}{Pt} = \dfrac{\text{Pr}t}{Pt}$

$\dfrac{I}{Pt} = r$ or $r = \dfrac{I}{Pt}$

b. $P = 1000, \ I = 275, \ t = 5$

$r = \dfrac{I}{Pt} = \dfrac{275}{1000 \bullet 5} = \dfrac{275}{5000} = 0.055$

The interest rate was 5.5%.

78. a. $D = Ay \div (y + 12)$

$D = \dfrac{Ay}{y + 12}$

$A = 120, \ y = 4$

b. $D = \dfrac{Ay}{y + 12} = \dfrac{120 \bullet 4}{4 + 12} = \dfrac{480}{16} = 30$

The correct dose of the medication is 30 mg.

79. length + width + height ≤ 62

$l + w + h \leq 62$

$l = 30, \ w = 20$

$30 + 20 + h \leq 62$

$50 + h \leq 62$

$50 - 50 + h \leq 62 - 50$

$h \leq 12$

The maximum height is 12 inches.

80. Let m be the number of miles. The first mile costs $1.50 and the remaining miles, $(m-1)$, are charged at the $1.60 rate.

$1.50 + 1.60(m - 1) > 30$

$1.50 + 1.60m - 1.60 > 30$

$1.60m - 0.10 > 30$

$1.60m - 0.10 + 0.10 > 30 + 0.10$

$1.60m > 30.10$

$\dfrac{1.60m}{1.60} > \dfrac{30.10}{1.60}$

$m > 18.8$

The taxi fare will exceed $30 for 19 miles or more.

81. Let m be the number of miles the trucks are driven.

$15 + 0.20m < 35 + 0.10m$

$15 + 0.20m - 0.10m > 35 + 0.10m - 0.10m$

$15 + 0.10m > 35$

$15 - 15 + 0.10m > 35 - 15$

$0.10m > 20$

$45(7) + 1.20(w - 25)(7) \leq 420$

$315 + 8.40(w - 25) \leq 420$

$315 + 8.40w - 210 \leq 420$

$105 + 8.40w \leq 420$

$105 - 105 + 8.40w \leq 420 - 105$

$8.40w \leq 315$

$\dfrac{8.40w}{8.40} \leq \dfrac{315}{8.40}$

$w \leq 37.5$

82. Let w be the number of words in the ad. The first 25 words are covered by the $45 charge so $(w - 25)$ words are charged at the rate of $1.20 a word each day for seven days.

Moving company B is better if more than 200 miles are driven.

$\dfrac{0.10m}{0.10} > \dfrac{20}{0.10}$

$m > 200$

The ad can have 37 words at most.

83. Let d be the distance driven in 3 hours.

Distance = rate × time.

$$D = rt$$

$$\frac{D}{t} = \frac{rt}{t}$$

$$\frac{D}{t} = r \ \text{ or } \ r = \frac{D}{t}$$

The rate must be from 45 to 65 mph.

$$45 \le \frac{D}{3} \le 65$$

$$3(45) \le 3\left(\frac{D}{3}\right) \le 3(65)$$

$$135 \le D \le 195$$

The range of distances is 135 miles to 195 miles in three hours.

84. $a = 35$

$$220 - 2R \le 35$$

$$220 - 220 - 2R \le 35 - 220$$

$$-2R \le -185$$

$$\frac{-2R}{-2} \ge \frac{-185}{-2}$$

$$R \ge 92.5$$

or

$$220 - \frac{10}{7}R \ge 35$$

$$220 - 220 - \frac{10}{7}R \ge 35 - 220$$

$$-\frac{10}{7}R \ge -185$$

$$\left(-\frac{7}{10}\right)\left(-\frac{10}{7}\right)R \le (-185)\left(-\frac{7}{10}\right)$$

$$R \le 129.5$$

The target heart rate is between and including 92.5 to 129.5 beats per minute.

85. Let l be the length of the inseam.

$$|l - 30| \le \frac{1}{2}$$

$$l - 30 \le \frac{1}{2} \qquad \text{or} \quad l - 30 \ge -\frac{1}{2}$$

$$l - 30 + 30 \le \frac{1}{2} + 30 \qquad l - 30 + 30 \ge -\frac{1}{2} + 30$$

$$l \le 30\frac{1}{2} \qquad\qquad l \ge 29\frac{1}{2}$$

The maximum length is 30½ in. and the minimum length is 29½ in.

86. Let r be the approval rating.

$$|r - 49| \le 2$$

$$r - 49 \le 2 \qquad \text{or} \quad r - 49 \ge -2$$

$$r - 49 + 49 \le 2 + 49 \qquad r - 49 + 49 \ge -2 + 49$$

$$r \le 51 \qquad\qquad r \ge 47$$

The approval rating are between and including 47% to 51%.

Chapter 2 Posttest

1. Substitute -3 for x.

$$\frac{1}{3}(-3) - 8 \stackrel{?}{=} -9$$

$$-1 - 8 \stackrel{?}{=} -9$$

$$-9 = -9$$

Yes, -3 is a solution.

2. $4x + 7 = 5$

$$4x + 7 - 7 = 5 - 7$$

$$4x = -2$$

$$\frac{4x}{4} = \frac{-2}{4}$$

$$x = -\frac{1}{2}$$

3. $2n - 11 = 6n + 17$

$$2n - 6n - 11 = 6n - 6n + 17$$

$$-4n - 11 = 17$$

$$-4n - 11 + 11 = 17 + 11$$

$$-4n = 28$$

$$\frac{-4n}{-4} = \frac{28}{-4}$$

$$n = -7$$

4. $3(1 + 3t) = -(5t - 17)$

$$3 + 9t = -5t + 17$$

$$3 + 9t + 5t = 5t - 5t + 17$$

$$3 + 14t = 17$$

$$3 - 3 + 14t = 17 - 3$$

$$14t = 14$$

$$\frac{14}{14}t = \frac{14}{14}$$

$$t = 1$$

5. $a(x + y) - b = c$

$$ax + ay - b = c$$

$$ax - ax + ay - b + b = c - ax + b$$

$$ay = c - ax + b$$

$$\frac{ay}{a} = \frac{c - ax + b}{a}$$

$$y = \frac{c - ax + b}{a}$$

6. Substitute -1 for n.

$$2(-1) - 7 \stackrel{?}{>} -9$$

$$-2 - 7 \stackrel{?}{>} -9$$

$$-9 \not> -9$$

No, -1 is not a solution.

7. $5x+9>3(x+9)$

$5x+9>3x+27$

$5x-3x+9>3x-3x+27$

$2x+9>27$

$2x+9-9>27-9$

$2x>18$

$\dfrac{2x}{2}>\dfrac{18}{2}$

$x>9$

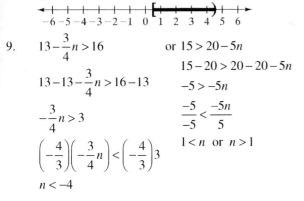

8. $2x-7<2$　　　and　　$x-1>-x$

$2x-7+7<2+7$　　$x+x-1>-x+x$

$2x<9$　　　　　　$2x-1>0$

$\dfrac{2x}{2}<\dfrac{9}{2}$　　　　$2x-1+1>0+1$

$x<\dfrac{9}{2}$　　　　　　$2x>1$

　　　　　　　　$\dfrac{2x}{2}>\dfrac{1}{2}$

　　　　　　　　$x>\dfrac{1}{2}$

$\dfrac{1}{2}<x<\dfrac{9}{2}$

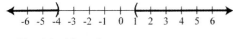

9. $13-\dfrac{3}{4}n>16$　　　or　$15>20-5n$

　　　　　　　　　　$15-20>20-20-5n$

$13-13-\dfrac{3}{4}n>16-13$　　$-5>-5n$

$-\dfrac{3}{4}n>3$　　　　　$\dfrac{-5}{-5}<\dfrac{-5n}{5}$

　　　　　　　　　$1<n$ or $n>1$

$\left(-\dfrac{4}{3}\right)\left(-\dfrac{3}{4}n\right)<\left(-\dfrac{4}{3}\right)3$

$n<-4$

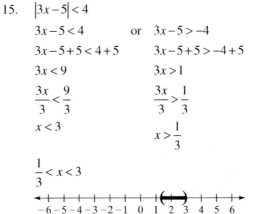

10. $-10\le14-12x<8$

$-10-14\le14-14-12x<8-14$

$-24\le-12x<-6$

$\dfrac{-24}{-12}\ge\dfrac{-12x}{-12}>\dfrac{-6}{-12}$

$2\ge x>\dfrac{1}{2}$ or $\dfrac{1}{2}<x\le2$

11. $\left|-9.4-(-5.6)\right|=\left|-9.4+5.6\right|=\left|-3.8\right|=3.8$

12. $\left|3x-5\right|=4$

$3x-5=4$　　　　or　$3x-5=-4$

$3x-5+5=4+5$　　　$3x-5+5=-4+5$

$3x=9$　　　　　　$3x=1$

$\dfrac{3x}{3}=\dfrac{9}{3}$　　　　　$\dfrac{3x}{3}=\dfrac{1}{3}$

$x=3$　　　　　　$x=\dfrac{1}{3}$

13. $-\left|2y+1\right|+2=-9$

$-\left|2y+1\right|+2-2=-9-2$

$-\left|2y+1\right|=-11$

$\dfrac{-\left|2y+1\right|}{-1}=\dfrac{-11}{-1}$

$\left|2y-1\right|=11$

$2y-1=11$　　　or　$2y-1=-11$

$2y-1+1=11+1$　　$2y-1+1=-11+1$

$2y=12$　　　　　$2y=-10$

$\dfrac{2y}{2}=\dfrac{12}{2}$　　　　$\dfrac{2y}{2}=\dfrac{-10}{2}$

$y=6$　　　　　　$y=-5$

14. $\left|x-6\right|=\left|x-7\right|$

$x-6=x-7$　　　or　$x-6=-(x-7)$

$x-x-6=x-x-7$　　$x-6=-x+7$

$-6\ne-7$　　　　　$x+x-6=-x+x+7$

No solution from　　$2x-6=7$

this part.　　　　　$2x-6+6=7+6$

　　　　　　　　$2x=13$

　　　　　　　　$\dfrac{2x}{2}=\dfrac{13}{2}$

　　　　　　　　$x=\dfrac{13}{2}$

15. $\left|3x-5\right|<4$

$3x-5<4$　　　or　$3x-5>-4$

$3x-5+5<4+5$　　$3x-5+5>-4+5$

$3x<9$　　　　　$3x>1$

$\dfrac{3x}{3}<\dfrac{9}{3}$　　　　$\dfrac{3x}{3}>\dfrac{1}{3}$

$x<3$　　　　　　$x>\dfrac{1}{3}$

$\dfrac{1}{3}<x<3$

16. Let r be the number of relaxation massages. Then 53 $-r$ is the number of deep tissue massages.

$70r + (53 - r)90 = 3930$

$70r + 4770 - 90r = 3930$

$-20r + 4770 = 3930$

$-20r + 4770 - 4770 = 3930 - 4770$

$-20r = -840$

$\dfrac{-20r}{-20} = \dfrac{-840}{-20}$

$r = 42, \quad 53 - r = 11$

42 relaxation and 11 deep tissue massages were provided.

17. Let l be the amount of money invested in the fund that lost money. $\$50,000 - l$ is the money invested in the account that gained money.

Fund	Investment	Rate	Profit
Lost	l	-8%	$-8\%(l)$
Gained	$50000 - l$	6%	$6\%(50000 - l)$
Total	50000		-850

$-0.08l + 0.06(50000 - l) = -850$

$-0.08l + 3000 - 0.06l = -850$

$-0.14l + 3000 = -850$

$-0.14l + 3000 - 3000 = -850 - 3000$

$-0.14l = -3850$

$\dfrac{-0.14l}{-0.14} = \dfrac{-3850}{-0.14}; \quad l = 27500, \ 50000 - l = 22500$

$\$27,500$ was invested in the account that lost 8% and $\$22,500$ was invested in the account that gained 6%.

18. Let h be the number of hours the gym is used under option B.

$50 < 20 + 1.50h$

$50 - 20 < 20 - 20 + 1.50h$

$30 < 1.50h$

$\dfrac{30}{1.50} < \dfrac{1.50h}{1.50}$

$20 < h \ \text{ or } \ h > 20$

Option A is better if the gym is used more than 20 hours per week.

19. The cost of 1000 postcards printed and mailed will be $(1.40 + .15)1000 = (1.55)1000 = 1550$.

That leaves $1700 - 1550 = 150$ to

$1600 - 1550 = 50$ to be spent on flyers.

Let f be the number of flyers.

$50 < f(.10) < 150$

$\dfrac{50}{.10} < \dfrac{f(.10)}{.10} < \dfrac{150}{.10}$

$500 < f < 1500$

Between 500 and 1500 flyers can be printed.

20. Let l be the length and width of the sheets.

$|48 - l| \le 0.001$

$48 - l \le 0.001 \qquad \text{or } 48 - l \ge -0.001$

$48 - 48 - l \le 0.001 - 48 \qquad 48 - 48 - l \ge -0.001 - 48$

$-l \le -47.999 \qquad\qquad -l \ge -48.001$

$\dfrac{-l}{-1} \ge \dfrac{47.999}{-1} \qquad\qquad \dfrac{-l}{-1} \le \dfrac{-48.001}{-1}$

$l \ge 47.999 \qquad\qquad l \le 48.001$

The area will be between the square of the smallest length and width and the largest length and width.

$(47.999)^2 \le A \le (48.001)^2$

$2303.904 \le A \le 2304.096$

The area will be from 2303.904 sq in to 2304.096 sq in.

Cumulative Review Exercises

1. $7 - \left[12 - (1+3)^2\right] \div -4 = 7 - \left[12 - 4^2\right] \div -4 =$

$7 - [12 - 16] \div -4 = 7 - (-4) \div -4 = 7 - 1 = 6$

2. $2 \bullet (3 + 5) = 2 \bullet (5 + 3)$

3. $\left(a^3 b\right)^2 = a^{3 \bullet 2} b^{1 \bullet 2} = a^6 b^2$

4. $6n^{-1} = 6 \bullet \dfrac{1}{n^1} = \dfrac{6}{n}$

5. $\dfrac{1}{3}(2n + 9) \ \text{ or } \ \dfrac{2n + 9}{3}$

6. $x = -2, \ y = 0.5, \ z = -1$

$4(-2)^2 (0.5) - ((-1) + 2(0.5)) =$

$4 \bullet 4 \bullet (0.5) - (-1 + 1) = 16 \bullet (0.5) - (0) = 8 - 0 = 8$

7. $7x + 8 - 9x + 5 + 3(x - 7) =$

$7x + 8 - 9x + 5 + 3x - 21 =$

$7x - 9x + 3x + 8 + 5 - 21 =$

$x(7 - 9 + 3) + 13 - 21 = x - 8$

8. $\dfrac{2.793 \times 10^9}{9.3 \times 10^7} = \dfrac{2.793}{9.3} \times 10^{9-7} = 0.3003 \times 10^2 = 30.03$

Neptune is about 30 astronomical units from the sun.

9. $\dfrac{0.12 + (-0.23) + (-0.14) + 0.13 + (-0.08)}{5} = \dfrac{-0.20}{5} =$

-0.04

10. a. $m = \dfrac{s}{5}$

   b. $m = 2.5$

   $2.5 = \dfrac{s}{5}$

   $(5)(2.5) = \dfrac{s}{5}(5)$

   $12.5 = s$

   $s = 12.5$

   You will hear the thunder in 12.5 sec.

Chapter 3 Graphs, Linear Equations and Inequalities, and Functions

Pretest

1.

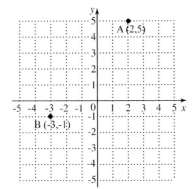

2. $m = \dfrac{y_2 - y_1}{x_2 - x_1} = \dfrac{-11-1}{3-(-6)} = \dfrac{-12}{9} = -\dfrac{4}{3}$

3. Slope of $\dfrac{3}{4}$ means $\dfrac{\text{change in } y \text{ is } 3}{\text{change in } x \text{ is } 4}$

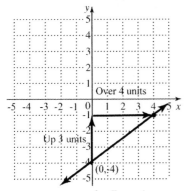

4. $m_{\overline{pq}} = \dfrac{y_2 - y_1}{x_2 - x_1} = \dfrac{3-7}{5-1} = \dfrac{-4}{4} = -1$

   $m_{\overline{rs}} = \dfrac{y_2 - y_1}{x_2 - x_1} = \dfrac{-3-(-10)}{-15-(-8)} = \dfrac{7}{-7} = -1$

   The slopes are the same so the lines are parallel.

5. Substitute 3 for x and -2 for y.

   $3(3) + 2(-2) \overset{?}{=} 5$

   $9 - 4 = 5$ Yes, $(3, -2)$ is a solution.

6. x-intercept is where $y = 0$.

   $4(0) - 6x = 12 \quad -6x = 12 \quad x = -2 \quad (-2, 0)$

   y-intercept is where $x = 0$.

   $4y - 6(0) = 12 \quad 4y = 12 \quad y = 3 \quad (0, 3)$

7. Computation for points.

x	$y = 3x+1$	(x, y)
0	$3(0)+1 = 1$	$(0, 1)$
1	$3(1)+1 = 4$	$(1, 4)$

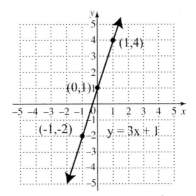

8. $12x - 6 = 0 \quad 12x = 6 \quad x = \dfrac{6}{12}$

   $x = \dfrac{1}{2}$ is a vertical line.

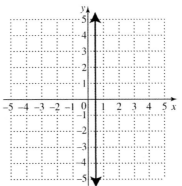

9. $4x - 3y = -9$

x	y
0	$\begin{array}{l} 4(0) - 3y = -9 \\ -3y = -9 \\ y = 3 \end{array}$
$\begin{array}{l} 4x - 3(0) = -9 \\ 4x = -9 \\ x = -\dfrac{9}{4} \end{array}$	0
-3	$\begin{array}{l} 4(-3) - 3y = -9 \\ -12 - 3y = -9 \\ -3y = 3 \\ y = -1 \end{array}$

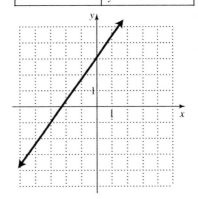

10. $y - y_1 = m(x - x_1)$

$y - 5 = 2(x - (-1))$

$y - 5 = 2(x + 1)$;   Point-slope form.

$y - 5 = 2x + 2$

$y = 2x + 7$;   slope-intercept form

11. $m = \dfrac{y_2 - y_1}{x_2 - x_1} = \dfrac{2 - (-1)}{-2 - 0} = \dfrac{3}{-2} = -\dfrac{3}{2}$

$y - y_1 = m(x - x_1)$

$y - (-1) = -\dfrac{3}{2}(x - 0)$

$y + 1 = -\dfrac{3}{2}(x - 0)$;   Point-slope form

$y + 1 = -\dfrac{3}{2}x$

$y = -\dfrac{3}{2}x - 1$;   Slope-intercept form

12. $4(-3) - 2(4) \overset{?}{>} -2$

$-12 - 8 \overset{?}{>} -2$

$-20 \not> -2$; $(-3, 4)$ is not a solution.

13. First graph the corresponding equation: $y = \dfrac{1}{2}x + 3$

and draw a dashed line.

x	$y = \dfrac{1}{2}x + 3$	$(x, y))$
0	$\dfrac{1}{2}(0) + 3 = 3$	$(0, 3)$
2	$\dfrac{1}{2}(2) + 3 = 4$	$(2, 4)$
4	$\dfrac{1}{2}(4) + 3 = 5$	$(4, 5)$

Using $(0, 0)$ as a test point, we check the relationship

$y < \dfrac{1}{2}x + 3$

$0 \overset{?}{<} \dfrac{1}{2}(0) + 3$

$0 < 3$

and shade the half plane containing $(0, 0)$.

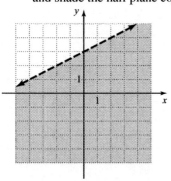

14. First graph the corresponding equation: $-2x - 6y = 6$
and draw a solid line.

$-6y = 2x + 6$

$y = \dfrac{2}{-6}y + \dfrac{6}{-6}$

$y = -\dfrac{1}{3}x - 1$

x	$y = -\dfrac{1}{3}x - 1$	(x, y)
0	$-\dfrac{1}{3}(0) - 1 = -1$	$(0, -1)$
3	$-\dfrac{1}{3}(3) - 1 = -2$	$(3, -2)$
-3	$-\dfrac{1}{3}(-3) - 1 = 0$	$(-3, 0)$

Using the test point $(0, 0)$, we check the relationship

$-2(0) - 6(0) \overset{?}{\leq} 6$; $0 \leq 6$ and shade the half plane

containing $(0, 0)$.

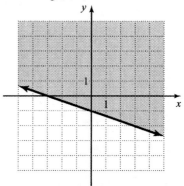

15. $f(x) = |2x - 8|$

$f(-6) = |2(-6) - 8| = |-12 - 8| = |-20| = 20$

16. $f(x) = 1 - 1.5x$ for $x \geq -2$

x	$f(x) = 1 - 1.5x$	$(x, f(x))$
-2	$1 - 1.5(-2) = 4$	$(-2, 4)$
0	$1 - 1.5(0) = 1$	$(0, 1)$
2	$1 - 1.5(2) = -2$	$(2, -2)$

Domain: $[-2, \infty)$, Range: $(-\infty, 4]$

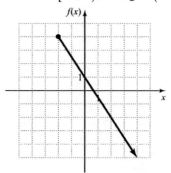

17. a.

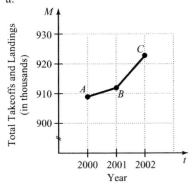

b. $m = \dfrac{y_2 - y_1}{x_2 - x_1}$

$m_{\overline{AB}} = \dfrac{911,917 - 908,989}{2001 - 2000} = 2,928$

$m_{\overline{BC}} = \dfrac{922,817 - 911,917}{2002 - 2001} = 10,900$

c. Since the slopes of the lines are not equal, the number of takeoffs and landings did not increase at the same rate over the 3 years.

18. a. $B = 0.08k + 18$

b.

k	$B = 0.08k + 18$	(k, B)
0	$0.08(0) + 18 = 18$	$(0, 18)$
200	$0.08(200) + 18 = 34$	$(200, 34)$
400	$0.08(400) + 18 = 50$	$(400, 50)$

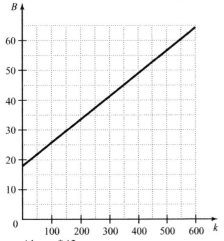

c. About \$42

19. a. $(2, 24)$ and $(4, 8)$

$m = \dfrac{s_2 - s_1}{t_2 - t_1} = \dfrac{8 - 24}{4 - 2} = -8$

$s - s_1 = m(t - t_1)$

$s - 24 = -8(t - 2)$

$s - 24 = -8t + 16$

$s = -8t + 40$

b. Slope = –8. This represents the rate of decrease of the car's velocity, that is, its deceleration.

c. The y-intercept is (0, 40) represents the speed of the car when the brakes were applied: 40 mph.

d. The y-intercept is (5, 0). The car comes to a complete stop in 5 seconds.

20. a. $1.50x + 1.00y < 20$

b. The inequality is < so the boundary line is dashed. Graph the corresponding equation:

$1.5x + y = 20$

$y = -1.5x + 20$

x	$y = -1.5x + 20$	(x, y)
0	$-1.5(0) + 20 = 20$	$(0, 20)$
4	$-1.5(4) + 20 = 14$	$(4, 14)$
8	$-1.5(8) + 20 = 8$	$(8, 8)$

Draw a dashed line

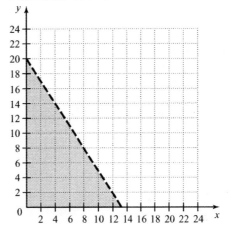

c. The point (10,8) does not lie within the solution set, the customer cannot make 10 point-of-sale transactions.

Exercises 3.1 The Rectangular Coordinate System

1.

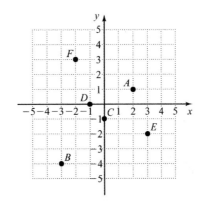

3.

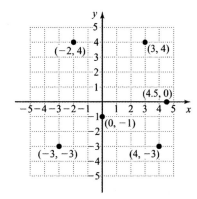

5.   II
7.   IV
9.   I
11. III
13. II
15. I
17. a. A: $(400, 340)$
         B: $(450, 400)$
         C: $(475, 590)$
         D: $(520, 720)$
         E: $(600, 500)$
     b. Students C and D.
     c. The sum of the coordinates represents the student's combined SAT score.

19.

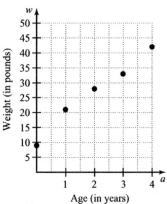

21. a.

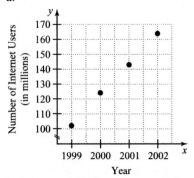

     b. The points indicate an upward trend. Each year the number of Internet users increased.
23. a. $1.64
     b. The average was below $1.50 in August, September, October, November, December, and January.

c. The greatest increase in price occurred between January and February. The increase was about $0.20.

25. Graph II best illustrates the trip to the beach. As the friends drive to the beach, the distance from their apartment increases (line segment slants up to the right). When they get to the beach, the distance from their apartment does not change (horizontal line segment). As they head home the distance from the apartment decreases (line segment slants down to the right). When they stop for dinner, the distance from the apartment does not change (horizontal line segment). finally, as they complete the drive home, their distance from the apartment decreases and eventually returns to 0 (line segment slants down to the right).

Exercises 3.2 Slope

1. $m = \dfrac{y_2 - y_1}{x_2 - x_1} = \dfrac{2 - 0}{2 - 4} = -1$

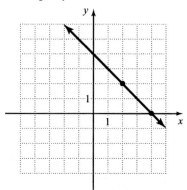

3. $m = \dfrac{y_2 - y_1}{x_2 - x_1} = \dfrac{-2 - (-1)}{-1 - 3} = \dfrac{-1}{-4} = \dfrac{1}{4}$

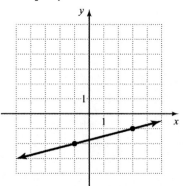

5. $m = \dfrac{y_2 - y_1}{x_2 - x_1} = \dfrac{0 - (-4)}{5 - 0} = \dfrac{4}{5}$

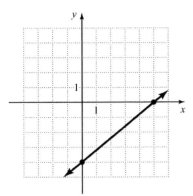

7. $m = \dfrac{y_2 - y_1}{x_2 - x_1} = \dfrac{0-0}{-3-(-1)} = \dfrac{0}{-2} = 0$

The line is horizontal.

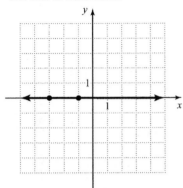

9. $m = \dfrac{y_2 - y_1}{x_2 - x_1} = \dfrac{-2-2}{-4-(-4)} = \dfrac{-4}{0}$

m is undefined. The line is vertical.

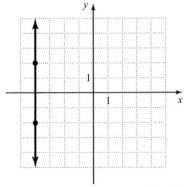

11. $m = \dfrac{y_2 - y_1}{x_2 - x_1} = \dfrac{-1-5}{3-(-1)} = \dfrac{-6}{4} = -\dfrac{3}{2}$

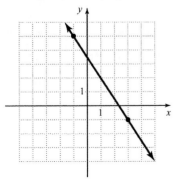

13. $m = \dfrac{y_2 - y_1}{x_2 - x_1} = \dfrac{-3-(-1.5)}{0.5-(-0.5)} = \dfrac{-1.5}{1} = -1.5$

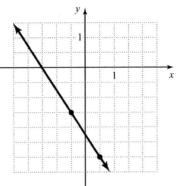

15. Negative slope.
17. Undefined slope.
19. Positive slope.
21. Zero slope.

23. $m_{\overline{AB}} = \dfrac{-1-6}{0-6} = \dfrac{-7}{-6} = \dfrac{7}{6}$

$m_{\overline{CD}} = \dfrac{-2-2}{3-(-3)} = \dfrac{-4}{6} = -\dfrac{2}{3}$

25. Slope $= \dfrac{\text{Rise}}{\text{Run}} = -3 = \dfrac{-3}{1}$

From $(0,0)$ move 3 units down, 1 unit right to $(1,-3)$.

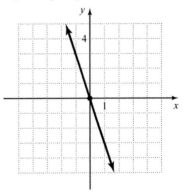

27. Slope $= \dfrac{\text{Rise}}{\text{Run}} = \dfrac{1}{4}$

From $(-2,4)$ move 1 unit up, 4 units right to $(2,5)$.

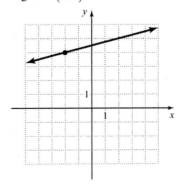

29.   Slope $= \dfrac{\text{Rise}}{\text{Run}} = 0 = \dfrac{0}{1}$

From $(-3,-2)$ move 0 units up-down,

1 unit right to $(-2,-2)$.

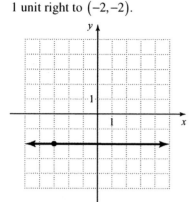

31.   Answers may vary

$(x_1 + a, y_1 + ma)$, $a = 1,\ 2$.

$(0+1, 4+(2)1) = (1,6)$

$(0+2, 4+(2)2) = (2,8)$

33.   Answers may vary

$(x_1 + a, y_1 + ma)$, $a = 1,\ 2$

$(-5+1, 2+(-4)1) = (-4,-2)$

$(-5+2, 2+(-4)2) = (-3,-6)$

35.   Answers may vary

$(x_1 + a, y_1 + ma)$, $a = 2,\ 4$

$\left(-4+2, 1+\left(\dfrac{1}{2}\right)2\right) = (-2,2)$

$\left(-4+4, 1+\left(\dfrac{1}{2}\right)4\right) = (0,3)$

37.   Answers may vary

$(x_1 + a, y_1 + ma)$, $a = 4,\ 8$

$\left(-8+4, -1+\left(-\dfrac{3}{4}\right)4\right) = (-4,-4)$

$\left(-8+8, -1+\left(-\dfrac{3}{4}\right)8\right) = (0,-7)$

39.   Answers may vary

$(x_1 + a, y_1 + ma)$, $a = 1,\ 2$

$\left(\dfrac{1}{2}+1, -7+(1)0\right) = \left(\dfrac{3}{2}, -7\right)$

$\left(\dfrac{1}{2}+2, -7+(2)0\right) = \left(\dfrac{5}{2}, -7\right)$

41.   Answers may vary

m is undefined. The line is vertical and the

x-value does not change.

$(-2.4, 2)$ and $(-2.4, 7)$

43. $m_{\overline{PQ}}\ \dfrac{2-1}{3-5} = -\dfrac{1}{2}$ $m_{\overline{RS}}\ \dfrac{6-4}{9-8} = 2$

Perpendicular

45. $m_{\overline{PQ}}\ \dfrac{-10-(-4)}{-1-0} = 6$ $m_{\overline{RS}}\ \dfrac{0-6}{-13-(-12)} = 6$

Parallel

47. $m_{\overline{PQ}}\ \dfrac{-4.8-3.2}{-2.4-1.6} = 2$ $m_{\overline{RS}}\ \dfrac{10.5-0.5}{0.9-5.9} = -2$

Neither

49. $m = \dfrac{\text{change in height}}{\text{change in distance}} = \dfrac{4}{84} = \dfrac{1}{21}$

$\dfrac{1}{21} < \dfrac{1}{20}$

The ramp does meet the guideline.

51.   a. The slope is positive.

b. A positive slope indicates that as the amount of the purchase increases, so too does the amount of the sales tax.

c. Using the endpoints $(100,5)$ and $(0,0)$.

$m = \dfrac{y_2 - y_1}{x_2 - x_1} = \dfrac{5-0}{100-0} = \dfrac{1}{20} = 0.05 = 5\%$

The slope is $\dfrac{1}{20} = 0.05$; it represents the sales tax rate, which is 5% or \$5 for every \$100 purchased.

53.   a. The slope represents the cost of the coffee per pound.

b. Since the slope of the line for Coffee shop A, 5, is greater than the slope of the line for Coffee shop B, 4.5, Coffee shop A charges more for Kona coffee.

55.   a.

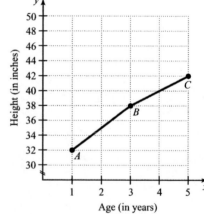

b. $m_{\overline{AB}} = \dfrac{38-32}{3-1} = 3$ $m_{\overline{BC}} = \dfrac{42-38}{5-3} = 2$

c. Since the slopes are not the same, the child's rate of growth was not constant throughout her first five years.

57. $m_A = \dfrac{11-7.5}{50-0} = 0.07$ $m_B = \dfrac{8.5-5}{50-0} = 0.07$

The slope of the line for provider A is $\dfrac{7}{100} = 0.07$,

and the slope of the line for provider B is $\dfrac{7}{100} = 0.07$.

Since the slopes are equal, the providers charge the same per-minute fee, namely 7 cents.

59. To be a rectangle, adjacent sides must be perpendicular.

$m_{\overline{AB}} = \dfrac{-5-(-2)}{1-(-2)} = -1$ $m_{\overline{BC}} = \dfrac{-8-(-5)}{-2-1} = 1$

$m_{\overline{CD}} = \dfrac{-5-(-8)}{-5-(-2)} = -1$ $m_{\overline{DA}} = \dfrac{-5-(-2)}{-5-(-2)} = 1$

The slope of $\overline{AB}$ is –1, the slope of $\overline{BC}$ is 1, the slope of $\overline{CD}$ is -1, and the slope of $\overline{AD}$ is 1. Since the slopes of each adjacent pair of line segments $\overline{AB}$ and $\overline{BC}$, $\overline{BC}$ and $\overline{CD}$, $\overline{CD}$ and $\overline{AD}$, and $\overline{AB}$ and $\overline{AD}$ are negative reciprocals, the sides are perpendicular and the quadrilateral is a rectangle.

61. Plan A charges a monthly flat fee for up to a certain number of call minutes (horizontal line segment) and a per-minute fee for any number of call minutes (positive sloped line). Plan B charges a flat monthly fee plus a smaller per-minute fee for each minute of calling.

Exercises 3.3 Graphing Linear Equations

1. $-1\overset{?}{=}\dfrac{1}{4}(4)$

$-1 \neq 1$

It is not a solution.

3. $5\overset{?}{=}-3(-2)-1$

$5\overset{?}{=}6-1$

$5 = 5$

It is a solution.

5. $2(-3)-3(-7)\overset{?}{=}15$

$-6+21\overset{?}{=}15$

$15 = 15$

It is a solution.

7. $10(-1.4)+6(0.5)\overset{?}{=}11$

$-14+3\overset{?}{=}11$

$-11 \neq 11$

It is not a solution.

9. $8 = 8$

It is a solution.

11. Graph b. has a positive slope of 2 and has a y-intercept of -1.

13. Graph d. has a slope of negative 2 and a y-intercept of -1.

15. x-intercept means $y = 0$.

$0 = x-4$

$x = 4$ $(4,0)$

y-intercept means $x = 0$.

$y = 0-4$

$y = -4$ $(0,-4)$

17. x-intercept means $y = 0$.

$0 = \dfrac{1}{3}x+3$

$-3 = \dfrac{1}{3}x$

$-9 = x$ $(-9,0)$

y-intercept means $x = 0$.

$y = \dfrac{1}{3}(0)+3$

$y = 3$ $(0,3)$

19. x-intercept means $y = 0$.

$4x+2(0) = -8$

$4x = -8$

$x = -2$ $(-2,0)$

y-intercept means $x = 0$.

$4(0)+2y = -8$

$2y = -8$

$y = -4$ $(0,-4)$

21. x-intercept means $y = 0$.

$5x-2(0) = 10$

$5x = 10$

$x = 2$ $(2,0)$

y-intercept means $x = 0$.

$5(0)-2y = 10$

$-2y = 10$

$y = -5$ $(0,-5)$

23. x-intercept means $y = 0$.

$8(0)-6x+2 = 0$

$-6x+2 = 0$

$-6x = -2$

$x = \dfrac{-2}{-6} = \dfrac{1}{3}$ $\left(\dfrac{1}{3},0\right)$

y-intercept means $x = 0$.

$8y - 6(0) + 2 = 0$

$8y + 2 = 0$

$8y = -2$

$y = \dfrac{-2}{8} = -\dfrac{1}{4}$ $\quad \left(0, -\dfrac{1}{4}\right)$

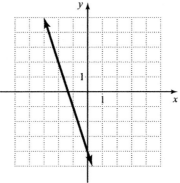

25. x-intercept means $y = 0$.

$10(0) \neq -15$

There is no x-intercept.

y-intercept means $x = 0$.

$10y = -15$

$y = \dfrac{-15}{10} = -\dfrac{3}{2}$ $\quad \left(0, -\dfrac{3}{2}\right)$

27. x-intercept means $y = 0$.

$-3x = -18$

$x = 6$ $\quad (6, 0)$

y-intercept means $x = 0$.

$-3(0) \neq -18$

There is no y-intercept.

29.

x	$y = x + 2$	(x, y)
0	$0 + 2 = 2$	$(0, 2)$
1	$1 + 2 = 3$	$(1, 3)$
2	$2 + 2 = 4$	$(2, 4)$

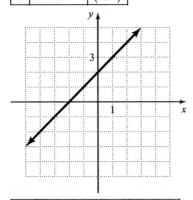

31.

x	$y = -3x - 4$	(x, y)
-2	$-3(-2) - 4 = 2$	$(-2, 2)$
-1	$-3(-1) - 4 = -1$	$(-1, -1)$
0	$-3(0) - 4 = -4$	$(0, -4)$

33. $2x - y = 4$

$2x = y + 4$

$2x - 4 = y$

$y = 2x - 4$

x	$y = 2x - 4$	(x, y)
0	$2(0) - 4 = -4$	$(0, -4)$
1	$2(1) - 4 = -2$	$(1, -2)$
2	$2(2) - 4 = 0$	$(2, 0)$

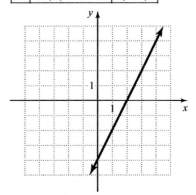

35. $x + 4y = 12$

$4y = -x + 12$

$y = -\dfrac{1}{4}x + 3$

x	$y = -\dfrac{1}{4}x + 3$	(x, y)
-4	$-\dfrac{1}{4}(-4) + 3 = 4$	$(-4, 4)$
0	$-\dfrac{1}{4}(0) + 3 = 3$	$(0, 3)$
4	$-\dfrac{1}{4}(4) + 3 = 2$	$(4, 2)$

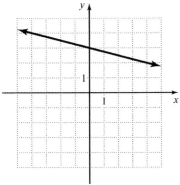

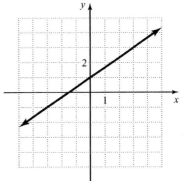

37. $3x + 3y = -6$

$3y = -3x - 6$

$y = \dfrac{-3x - 6}{3}$

$y = -x - 2$

x	$y = -x - 2$	(x, y)
-2	$-(-2) - 2 = 0$	$(-2, 0)$
0	$-(0) - 2 = -2$	$(0, -2)$
2	$-(2) - 2 = -4$	$(2, -4)$

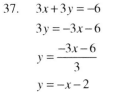

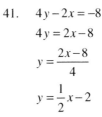

41. $4y - 2x = -8$

$4y = 2x - 8$

$y = \dfrac{2x - 8}{4}$

$y = \dfrac{1}{2}x - 2$

x	$y = \dfrac{1}{2}x - 2$	(x, y)
-2	$\dfrac{1}{2}(-2) - 2 = -3$	$(-2, -3)$
0	$\dfrac{1}{2}(0) - 2 = -2$	$(0, -2)$
2	$\dfrac{1}{2}(2) - 2 = -1$	$(2, -1)$

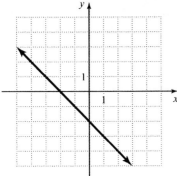

39. $2x - 3y = -3$

$-3y = -2x - 3$

$y = \dfrac{-2x - 3}{-3}$

$y = \dfrac{2}{3}x + 1$

x	$y = \dfrac{2}{3}x + 1$	(x, y)
-3	$\dfrac{2}{3}(-3) + 1 = -1$	$(-3, -1)$
0	$\dfrac{2}{3}(0) + 1 = 1$	$(0, 1)$
3	$\dfrac{2}{3}(3) + 1 = 3$	$(3, 3)$

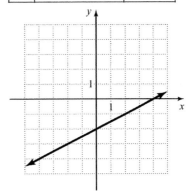

43. $4x + 5y - 10 = 0$

$5y = -4x + 10$

$y = \dfrac{-4x + 10}{5}$

$y = -\dfrac{4}{5}x + 2$

x	$y = -\dfrac{4}{5}x + 2$	(x, y)
-3	$-\dfrac{4}{5}(-3) + 2 =$ $\dfrac{12}{5} + \dfrac{10}{5} = \dfrac{22}{5} =$ $4\dfrac{2}{5}$	$\left(-3, 4\dfrac{2}{5}\right)$
0	$-\dfrac{4}{5}(0) + 2 = 2$	$(0, 2)$
3	$-\dfrac{4}{5}(3) + 2 =$ $-\dfrac{12}{5} + \dfrac{10}{5} = -\dfrac{2}{5}$	$\left(3, -\dfrac{2}{5}\right)$

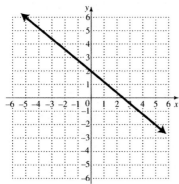

45. $20 - 10y = 0$

$-10y = -20$

$y = 2$

x	$y = 2$	(x, y)
-2	2	$(-2, 2)$
0	2	$(0, 2)$
2	2	$(2, 2)$

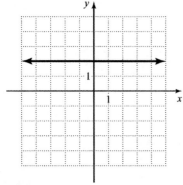

47. $9x = -27$

$x = -3$

$x = -3$	y	(x, y)
-3	-2	$(-3, -2)$
-3	0	$(-3, 0)$
-3	2	$(-3, 2)$

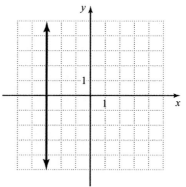

49. $1.4x - 0.35 = 0.7y$

$\dfrac{1.4x - 0.35}{0.7} = y$

$y = 2x - 0.5$

x	$y = 2x - 0.5$	(x, y)
-1	$2(-1) - 0.5 = -2.5$	$(-1, -2.5)$
0	$2(0) - 0.5 = -0.5$	$(0, -0.5)$
1	$2(1) - 0.5 = 1.5$	$(1, 1.5)$

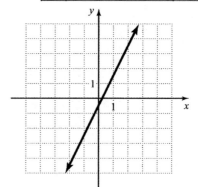

51. $0.5y + 1 = -0.25x$

$0.5y = -0.25x - 1$

$y = \dfrac{-0.25x - 1}{0.5}$

$y = -0.5x - 2$

x	$y = -0.5x - 2$	(x, y)
-2	$-0.5(-2) - 2 = -1$	$(-2, -1)$
0	$-0.5(0) - 2 = -2$	$(0, -2)$
2	$-0.5(2) - 2 = -3$	$(2, -3)$

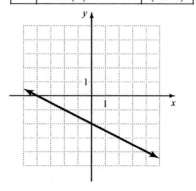

53. a. $A = 40t + 1000$

t	A
0	$40(0) + 1000 = 1000$
2	$40(2) + 1000 = 1080$
4	$40(4) + 1000 = 1160$
6	$40(6) + 1000 = 1240$

b.

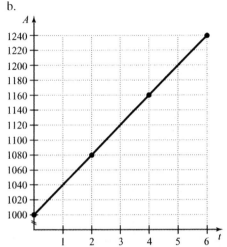

c. The A-intercept represents the initial amount of money deposited into the savings account.

d. From the graph, it appears that it will take 5 years for the account to grow to $1200.

55. a. $A = 200w + 50$

b.

w	$A = 200w + 50$	(w, A)
0	$200(0) + 50 = 50$	$(0, 50)$
2	$200(2) + 50 = 450$	$(2, 450)$
4	$200(4) + 50 = 850$	$(4, 850)$

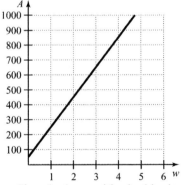

c. Since both quantities in this situation are positive, only points whose coordinates are positive need be considered. The only points in the coordinate plane for which both coordinates are positive lie in Quadrant I.

57. $c = 10m$

m	$c = 10m$	(m, c)
0	$10(0) = 0$	$(0, 0)$
5	$10(5) = 50$	$(5, 50)$
10	$10(10) = 100$	$(10, 100)$

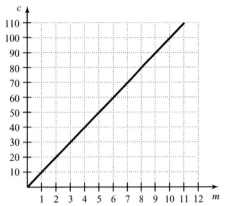

59. a. $c = 45n + 99$

b.

n	$c = 45n + 99$	(n, c)
0	$45(0) + 99 = 99$	$(0, 99)$
6	$45(6) + 99 = 369$	$(6, 369)$
10	$45(10) + 99 = 549$	$(10, 549)$

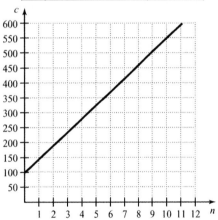

c. The total cost for 6 months service is about $370.

61. a. $A + B = 1800$

b. $A + B = 1800$

$B = -A + 1800$

A	$B = -A + 1800$	(A, B)
0	$-(0) + 1800 = 1800$	$(0, 1800)$
600	$-(600) + 1800 = 1200$	$(600, 1200)$
1800	$-(1800) + 1800 = 0$	$(1800, 0)$

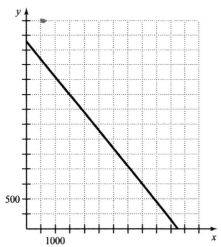

c. The A-intercept is (1800, 0). The B-intercept is (0, 1800). The A-intercept represents the number of associate's degrees awarded if no bachelor's degrees were awarded. The B-intercept represents the number of bachelor's degrees awarded if no associate's degrees were awarded.

d. Only positive integer values make sense in this situation since the college cannot award fractions of degrees.

63. a. $300m + 100c = 1000$

b. $100c = -300m + 1000$

$$c = \frac{-300m + 1000}{100}$$

$$c = -3m + 10$$

m	$c = -3m + 10$	(m, c)
0	$-3(0) + 10 = 10$	$(0, 10)$
1	$-3(1) + 10 = 7$	$(1, 7)$
2	$-3(2) + 10 = 4$	$(2, 4)$

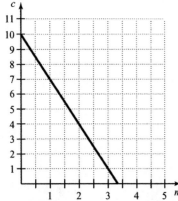

c. The m-intercept represents the number of servings she would need to meet the daily minimum requirement if she only uses milk as her source of calcium. The c-intercept represents the number of servings she would need to meet the daily minimum requirement if she only uses cottage cheese as her source of calcium.

Exercises 3.4 More on Graphing Linear Equations

1. $y - 2x = 0$

$y = 2x$

$y = mx + b \quad m = 2 \quad b = 0$

Slope $= 2$ y-intercept is $(0, 0)$.

3. $12x + 3y = -18$

$3y = -12x - 18$

$$y = \frac{-12x - 18}{3}$$

$y = -4x - 6$

$y = mx + b \quad m = -4 \quad b = -6$

Slope $= -4$ y-intercept is $(0, -6)$.

5. $3x - 6y = 6$

$-6y = -3x + 6$

$$y = \frac{-3x + 6}{-6}$$

$$y = \frac{1}{2}x - 1$$

$y = mx + b \quad m = \dfrac{1}{2} \quad b = -1$

Slope is $\dfrac{1}{2}$ y-intercept is $(0, -1)$.

7. $10y - 8x = 100$

$10y = 8x + 100$

$$y = \frac{8x + 100}{10}$$

$$y = \frac{4}{5}x + 10$$

$y = mx + b \quad m = \dfrac{4}{5} \quad b = 10$

Slope is $\dfrac{4}{5}$ y-intercept is $(0, 10)$.

9. $3x + 2y - 1 = 0$

$2y = -3x + 1$

$$y = \frac{-3x + 1}{2}$$

$$y = -\frac{3}{2}x + \frac{1}{2}$$

$y = mx + b \quad m = -\dfrac{3}{2} \quad b = \dfrac{1}{2}$

Slope is $-\dfrac{3}{2}$ y-intercept is $\left(0, \dfrac{1}{2}\right)$.

11. $y-5=-3(x-8)$

$y-5=-3x+24$

$y=-3x+29$

$y=mx+b \quad m=-3 \quad b=29$

Slope is -3 y-intercept is $(0,29)$.

13. $3x-6y=12$

$-6y=-3x+12$

$y=\dfrac{-3x+12}{-6}$

$y=\dfrac{1}{2}x-2$

$y=mx+b \quad m=\dfrac{1}{2} \quad b=-2$

Slope is $\dfrac{1}{2}$, y-intercept is $(0,-2)$.

Graph b.

15. $6x+2y=-4$

$2y=-6x-4$

$y=\dfrac{-6x-4}{2}$

$y=-3x-2$

$y=mx+b \quad m=-3 \quad b=-2$

Slope is -3, y-intercept is $(0,-2)$.

Graph a.

17. $y=2x+3$

$y=mx+b \quad m=2 \quad b=3$

Slope is 2, y-intercept is $(0,3)$.

Move up 2, right 1 to $(1,5)$.

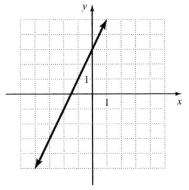

19. $y=-\dfrac{1}{3}x-1$

$y=mx+b \quad m=-\dfrac{1}{3} \quad b=-1$

Slope is $-\dfrac{1}{3}$, y-intercept is $(0,-1)$.

Move right 3, down 1 to $(3,-2)$.

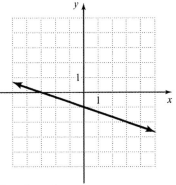

21. $2x-3y=9$

$-3y=-2x+9$

$y=\dfrac{-2x+9}{-3}$

$y=\dfrac{2}{3}x-3$

$y=mx+b \quad m=\dfrac{2}{3} \quad b=-3$

Slope is $\dfrac{2}{3}$, y-intercept is $(0,-3)$.

Move up 2, right 3 to $(3,-1)$.

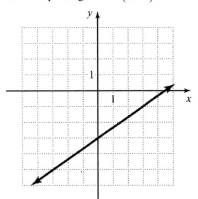

23. $4x+y=0$

$y=-4x$

$y=mx+b \quad m=-4 \quad b=0$

Slope is -4, y-intercept is $(0,0)$.

Move down 4, right 1 to $(1,-4)$.

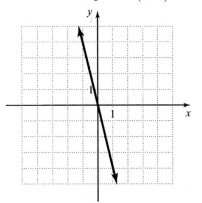

25. $y - 2 = -2(x + 2)$

$y - 2 = -2x - 4$

$y = -2x - 2$

$y = mx + b \quad m = -2 \quad b = -2$

Slope is -2, y-intercept is $(0, -2)$.

Move down 2, right 1 to $(1, -4)$.

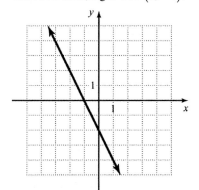

27. $y = 0.5x + 1.5$

$y = mx + b \quad m = 0.5 \quad b = 1.5$

y-intercept is $(0, 1.5)$.

Move up 0.5, right 1 to $(1, 2)$.

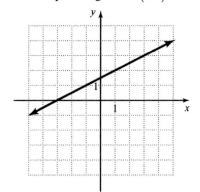

29.

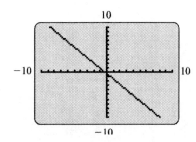

31.

33. $m = -\dfrac{3}{5}$ y-intercept is $(0, 8)$.

$y - y_1 = m(x - x_1)$

$y - 8 = -\dfrac{3}{5}(x - 0)$; point-slope form.

$y = mx + b; \quad m = -\dfrac{3}{5}, \quad b = 8$

$y = -\dfrac{3}{5}x + 8$; slope-interecept form.

35. $3x + 9y = 18$

$9y = -3x + 18$

$y = \dfrac{-3x + 18}{9}$

$y = -\dfrac{1}{3}x + 2$

Parallel lines have the same slope.

$m = -\dfrac{1}{3}$ y-intercept is $(0, -4)$.

$y - y_1 = m(x - x_1)$

$y + 4 = -\dfrac{1}{3}(x - 0)$; point-slope form.

$y = mx + b; \quad m = -\dfrac{1}{3}, \quad b = -4$

$y = -\dfrac{1}{3}x - 4$; slope-interecept form.

37. $2y - 4x - 14 = 0$

$2y = 4x + 14$

$y = \dfrac{4x + 14}{2}$

$y = 2x + 7$

For perpendicular lines, the slopes are negative reciprocals of each other.

$m = -\dfrac{1}{2}$ Passes through $(-5, 0)$.

$y - y_1 = m(x - x_1)$

$y - 0 = -\dfrac{1}{2}(x + 5)$; point-slope form.

$y = -\dfrac{1}{2}x - \dfrac{5}{2}$; slope-interecept form.

39. A vertical line has an undefined slope and is of the form $x = $ a constant. $x = -2.3$.

41. $m = -1$ Passes through $(3, 2)$.

$y - y_1 = m(x - x_1)$

$y - 2 = -1(x - 3)$; point-slope form.

$y - 2 = -x + 3$

$y = -x + 5$; slope-interecept form.

43. $m = \dfrac{3}{2}$ Passes through $(-6, 5)$.

$y - y_1 = m(x - x_1)$

$y - 5 = \dfrac{3}{2}(x + 6)$; point-slope form.

$y - 5 = \dfrac{3}{2}x + 9$

$y = \dfrac{3}{2}x + 14$; slope-interecept form.

45. $2x + 4y = 1$

$4y = -2x + 1$

$y = \dfrac{-2x + 1}{4}$

$y = -\dfrac{1}{2}x + \dfrac{1}{4}$

Parallel lines have the same slope.

$m = -\dfrac{1}{2}$ Passes through $(2, -1)$.

$y - y_1 = m(x - x_1)$

$y + 1 = -\dfrac{1}{2}(x - 2)$; point-slope form.

$y + 1 = -\dfrac{1}{2}x + 1$

$y = -\dfrac{1}{2}x$; slope-interecept form.

47. $5x - 4y = 12$

$-4y = -5x + 12$

$y = \dfrac{-5x + 12}{-4}$

$y = \dfrac{5}{4}x - 3$

For perpendicular lines, the slopes are negative reciprocals of each other.

$m = -\dfrac{4}{5}$ Passes through $(-10, -6)$.

$y - y_1 = m(x - x_1)$

$y + 6 = -\dfrac{4}{5}(x + 10)$; point-slope form.

$y + 6 = -\dfrac{4}{5}x - 8$

$y = -\dfrac{4}{5}x - 14$; slope-interecept form.

49. $m = \dfrac{y_2 - y_1}{x_2 - x_1} = \dfrac{9 - 7}{5 - 3} = 1$

$m = 1$ Passes through $(3, 7)$.

$y - y_1 = m(x - x_1)$

$y - 7 = 1(x - 3)$; point-slope form.

or $m = 1$ Passes through $(5, 9)$.

$y - 9 = 1(x - 5)$; point-slope form.

$y - 9 = x - 5$

$y = x + 4$; slope-interecept form.

51. $m = \dfrac{y_2 - y_1}{x_2 - x_1} = \dfrac{-4 - 1}{3 - 0} = -\dfrac{5}{3}$

Point slope form using $(0, 1)$.

$y - 1 = -\dfrac{5}{3}(x - 0)$

Point slope form using $(3, -4)$.

$y + 4 = -\dfrac{5}{3}(x - 3)$

$y = mx + b$ Using $(0, 1)$, $b = 1$

$y = -\dfrac{5}{3}x + 1$; slope-intercept form.

53. $m = \dfrac{y_2 - y_1}{x_2 - x_1} = \dfrac{-2 - 1}{-4 - 6} = \dfrac{3}{10}$

Point slope form using $(-4, -2)$.

$y + 4 = \dfrac{3}{10}(x + 2)$

Point slope form using $(6, 1)$.

$y - 1 = \dfrac{3}{10}(x - 6)$

$y - 1 = \dfrac{3}{10}x - \dfrac{18}{10}$

$y = \dfrac{3}{10}x - \dfrac{9}{5} + 1$

$y = \dfrac{3}{10}x - \dfrac{9}{5} + \dfrac{5}{5}$

$y = \dfrac{3}{10}x - \dfrac{4}{5}$; slope-intercept form.

55. a. $A = 40x + 100$

b.

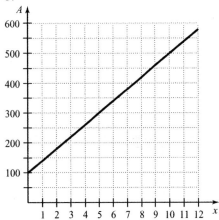

c. The A-intercept represents the initial consultation fee.

57. a. $m = \dfrac{C_2 - C_1}{F_2 - F_1} = \dfrac{-30 - 0}{-22 - 32} = \dfrac{-30}{-54} = \dfrac{5}{9}$

Using $(32, 0)$

$C - 0 = \dfrac{5}{9}(F - 32); \quad C = \dfrac{5}{9}(F - 32)$

b. $-85 = \dfrac{5}{9}(F - 32)$

$-85\left(\dfrac{9}{5}\right) = \left(\dfrac{9}{5}\right)\left(\dfrac{5}{9}\right)(F - 32)$

$-153 = F - 32$

$-153 + 32 = F; \quad F = -121$

Hydrogen boils at -121°F.

59. a. $(2, 20)$ and $(4, -44)$

$m = \dfrac{v_2 - v_1}{t_2 - t_1} = \dfrac{-44 - 20}{4 - 2} = \dfrac{-64}{2} = -32$

Using $(2, 20)$

$v - 20 = -32(t - 2)$

$v - 20 = -32t + 64$

$v = -32t + 84$

b.

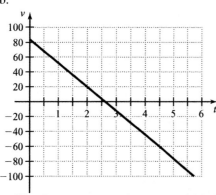

c. The slope represents the rate at which the velocity changes.

d. The t-intercept is the point at which the object changes from an upward direction to a downward direction.

61. a. $(0, 1.25)$ and $(6, 10.25)$

$m = \dfrac{y_2 - y_1}{x_2 - x_1} = \dfrac{10.25 - 1.25}{6 - 0} = \dfrac{9}{6} = 1.50$

Using $(0, 1.25)$ $b = 1.25$

Fare $= 1.50m + 1.25$

b. The slope represents the per-mile meter rate.

c. Fare $= 1.50m + 1.25$

$20.75 = 1.50m + 1.25$

$19.50 = 1.50m$

$\dfrac{19.50}{1.50} = m$

$m = 13$

The passenger was driven 13 miles.

63. Distance = rate × time.
Time must be in hours.

Rate $= \dfrac{\text{change in distance}}{\text{change in time}} = \dfrac{170 - 142}{.5} = 56$

Using the trucker's starting point $(0, 0)$ $b = 0$

$d = 56t$

65. Points are $(0, 26)$ and $(3, 83)$.

$m = \dfrac{83 - 26}{3 - 0} = \dfrac{57}{3} = 19$

Using $(3, 83)$

$n - 83 = 19(t - 3);$ point-slope form.

Using $(0, 26)$

$n - 26 = 19(t - 0)1$ point-slope form.

Using $(0, 26)$ $b = 26$

$n = 19t + 26;$ slope-intercept form.

Exercises 3.5 Graphing Linear Inequalities

1. $3 \overset{?}{>} 5 - 2(2)$

$3 \overset{?}{>} 5 - 4$

$3 > 1$ $(2, 3)$ is a solution.

3. $-2 \overset{?}{\leq} \dfrac{1}{2}(-6) + 1$

$-2 \overset{?}{\leq} -3 + 1$

$-2 \leq -2$ $(-6, -2)$ is a solution.

5. $3\left(\dfrac{2}{3}\right) + 2\left(\dfrac{1}{2}\right) \overset{?}{<} 2$

$2 + 1 \overset{?}{<} 2$

$3 \not< 2$ $\left(\dfrac{2}{3}, \dfrac{1}{2}\right)$ is not a solution.

7. $8(1) - 5(4) \overset{?}{\geq} -11$

$8 - 20 \overset{?}{\geq} -11$

$-12 \not\geq -11$ $(4, 1)$ is not a solution.

9. The inequality is > so the line must be dashed. The line forming the border is:

$x - 3y = 9$

$-3y = -x + 9$

$y = \dfrac{-x + 9}{-3}; \quad y = \dfrac{1}{3}x - 3$

This line has a slope of $\dfrac{1}{3}$ and a y-intercept of $(0, -3)$.

Choice c.

11. The inequality is $\geq$ so the line is solid. The line forming the border is:

$6x + 9y = -9$

$9y = -6x - 9$

$y = \dfrac{-6x - 9}{9}$

$y = -\dfrac{2}{3}x - 1$

This line has a slope of $-\dfrac{2}{3}$ and passes through $(0, -1)$. Choice a.

13. The inequality is > so the boundary line is dashed.

x	$y = 2x$	(x, y)
0	0	$(0,0)$
1	$2(1) = 2$	$(1,2)$
2	$2(2) = 4$	$(2,4)$

Test point is $(4,0)$ because $(0,0)$ is on the line.

$0 \overset{?}{>} 4$

$0 \not> 4$

Shade the half-plane NOT containing $(4, 0)$.

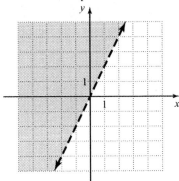

15. The inequality is < so the boundary line is dashed.

x	$y = x - 4$	(x, y)
0	$0 - 4 = -4$	$(0,-4)$
2	$2 - 4 = -2$	$(2,-2)$
4	$4 - 4 = 0$	$(4,0)$

Test point is $(0,0)$.

$0 \overset{?}{<} 0 - 4$

$0 \not< -4$

Shade the half-plane NOT containing $(0,0)$.

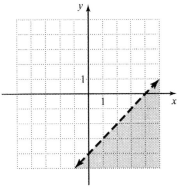

17. The inequality is $\geq$ so the boundary line is solid.

x	$y = \dfrac{1}{2}x + 3$	(x, y)
-2	$\dfrac{1}{2}(-2) + 3 = 2$	$(-2,2)$
0	$\dfrac{1}{2}(0) + 3 = 3$	$(0,3)$
2	$\dfrac{1}{2}(2) + 3 = 4$	$(2,4)$

Test point is $(0,0)$.

$0 \overset{?}{\geq} \dfrac{1}{2}(0) + 3$

$0 \not\geq 3$

Shade the half plane NOT containing $(0,0)$.

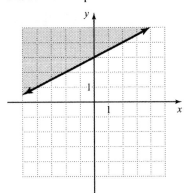

19. The inequality is $\leq$ so the boundary line is solid.

x	$y = 2 - 3x$	(x, y)
0	$2 - 3(0) = 2$	$(0,2)$
1	$2 - 3(1) = -1$	$(1,-1)$
2	$2 - 3(2) = -4$	$(2,-4)$

Test point is $(0,0)$.

$0 \overset{?}{\leq} 2 - 3(0)$

$0 \leq 2$

Shade the half-plane containing $(0,0)$.

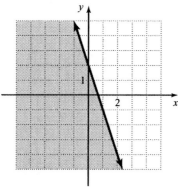

21. The inequality is $<$ so the boundary line is dashed.

$x = -1.5$	y	(x, y)
-1.5	0	$(-1.5, 0)$
-1.5	2	$(-1.5, 2)$
-1.5	4	$(-1.5, 4)$

Test point is $(0, 0)$.

$0 \overset{?}{<} -1.5$

$0 \not< -1.5$

Shade the half-plane NOT containing $(0, 0)$.

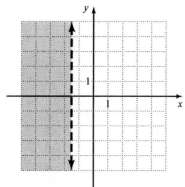

23. The inequality is $\leq$ so the boundary line is solid.

x	$y = 4$	(x, y)
0	4	$(0, 4)$
2	4	$(2, 4)$
4	4	$(4, 4)$

Test point is $(0, 0)$.

$0 \overset{?}{\leq} 4$

$0 \leq 4$

Shade the half-plane containing $(0, 0)$.

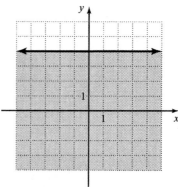

25. The inequality is $>$ so the boundary line is solid.

$4x + 2y = -2$

$2y = -4x - 2$

$y = \dfrac{-4x - 2}{2}$

$y = -2x - 1$

x	$y = -2x - 1$	(x, y)
-2	$-2(-2) - 1 = 3$	$(-2, 3)$
0	$-2(0) - 1 = -1$	$(0, -1)$
1	$-2(1) - 1 = -3$	$(1, -3)$

Test point is $(0, 0)$.

$4(0) + 2(0) \overset{?}{\geq} -2$

$0 \geq -2$

Shade the half-plane containing $(0, 0)$.

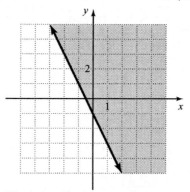

27. The inequality is $\leq$ so the boundary line is solid.

$2x - 3y = -6$

$-3y = -2x - 6$

$y = \dfrac{-2x - 6}{-3}$

$y = \dfrac{2}{3}x + 2$

x	$y = \dfrac{2}{3}x + 2$	(x, y)
-3	$\dfrac{2}{3}(-3) + 2 = 0$	$(-3, 0)$
0	$\dfrac{2}{3}(0) + 2 = 2$	$(0, 2)$
3	$\dfrac{2}{3}(3) + 2 = 4$	$(3, 4)$

Test point is $(0, 0)$.

$2(0) - 3(0) \overset{?}{\leq} -6$

$0 \not\leq -6$

Shade the half-plane NOT containing $(0, 0)$.

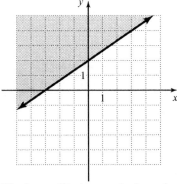

29.   The inequality is > so the boundary line is dashed.

$5y - 3x + 20 = 0$

$5y = 3x - 20$

$y = \dfrac{3x - 20}{5}$

$y = \dfrac{3}{5}x - 4$

x	$y = \dfrac{3}{5}x - 4$	(x, y)
-2	$\dfrac{3}{5}(-2) - 4 = -5\dfrac{1}{5}$	$\left(-2, -5\dfrac{1}{5}\right)$
0	$\dfrac{3}{5}(0) - 4 = -4$	$(0, -4)$
5	$\dfrac{3}{5}(5) - 4 = -1$	$(5, -1)$

Test point is $(0, 0)$.

$5(0) - 3(0) + 20 \overset{?}{>} 0$

$20 > 0$

Shade the half-plane containing $(0, 0)$.

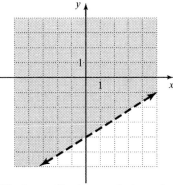

31.   The inequality is < so the boundary line is dashed.

$0.4x - 0.3y = 1.2$

$-0.3y = -0.4x + 1.2$

$y = \dfrac{-0.4x + 1.2}{-0.3}$

$y = \dfrac{4}{3}x - 4$

x	$y = \dfrac{4}{3}x - 4$	(x, y)
0	$\dfrac{4}{3}(0) - 4 = -4$	$(0, -4)$
2	$\dfrac{4}{3}(2) - 4 = -\dfrac{4}{3}$	$\left(2, -\dfrac{4}{3}\right)$
3	$\dfrac{4}{3}(3) - 4 = 0$	$(3, 0)$

Test point is $(0, 0)$.

$0.4(0) - 0.3(0) \overset{?}{<} 1.2$

$0 < 1.2$

Shade the half-plane containing $(0, 0)$.

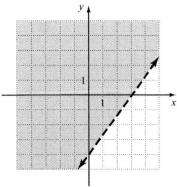

33.   a. $p \geq 0.04b$

b. The inequality is $\geq$ so the boundary line will be solid.

b	$p = 0.04b$	(p, b)
0	$0.04(0) = 0$	$(0, 0)$
500	$0.04(500) = 20$	$(500, 20)$
1000	$0.04(1000) = 40$	$(1000, 40)$

The test point is (0, 30) because (0,0) is on the boundary line.

$$30 \overset{?}{\geq} 0.04(0)$$

$$30 \geq 0$$

Shade the half-plane containing the point (0, 30).

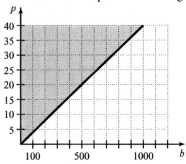

c. $p \geq 0.04(650)$

$p \geq 26$

Answers may vary. Possible answer: $30.

35. Let x be the shares of technology stock and y be the shares of media stock.

a. $30x + 21y \leq 5000$

b. The inequality is $\leq$ so the boundary line is solid.
$$30x + 21y = 5000$$

$$21y = -30x + 5000$$

$$y = \frac{-30x + 5000}{21}$$

$$y = -\frac{10}{7}x + \frac{5000}{21}$$

x	$y = -\dfrac{10}{7}x + \dfrac{5000}{21}$	(x, y)
0	$-\dfrac{10}{7}(0) + \dfrac{5000}{21} \approx 238$	$(0, 238)$
50	$-\dfrac{10}{7}(50) + \dfrac{5000}{21} \approx 167$	$(50, 167)$
100	$-\dfrac{10}{7}(100) + \dfrac{5000}{21} = 95$	$(100, 95)$

Test point is (0,0).

$$30(0) + 21(0) \overset{?}{\leq} 5000$$

$$0 \leq 5000$$

Shade the half plane containing the point (0,0).

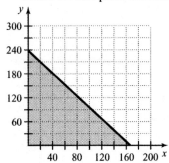

c. Since the point (100,100) does not lie in the shaded region, the investor cannot purchase 100 shares of each stock.

37. Let a be the number of adults and c be the number of children on the elevator.

a. $160a + 60c \leq 2000$

b. The inequality is $\leq$ so the boundary line is solid.
$$160a + 60c = 2000$$

$$60c = -160a + 2000$$

$$c = \frac{-160a + 2000}{60}$$

$$c = -\frac{8}{3}a + \frac{100}{3}$$

a	c	(a, c)
0	$-\dfrac{8}{3}(0) + \dfrac{100}{3} = 33.3$	$(0, 33.3)$
5	$-\dfrac{8}{3}(5) + \dfrac{100}{3} = 20$	$(5, 20)$
10	$-\dfrac{8}{3}(10) + \dfrac{100}{3} = 6.7$	$(10, 6.7)$

Test point is (0,0).

$$160(0) + 60(0) \overset{?}{\leq} 2000$$

$$0 \leq 2000$$

Shade the half-plane containing the point (0,0).

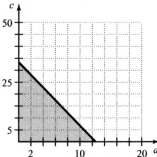

c. Answers may vary. Possible answer: 10 adults and 5 children.

39. a. $12c + 8r \leq 360$

b. The inequality is $\leq$ so the boundary line will be solid.
$$12c + 8r = 360$$

$$8r = -12c + 360$$

$$r = \frac{-12c + 360}{8}$$

$$r = -\frac{3}{2}c + 45$$

r	$c = -\dfrac{3}{2}r + 45$	(r, c)
0	$-\dfrac{3}{2}(0) + 45 = 45$	$(0, 45)$
10	$-\dfrac{3}{2}(10) + 45 = 30$	$(10, 30)$
30	$-\dfrac{3}{2}(30) + 45 = 0$	$(30, 0)$

Test point is $(0, 0)$

$12(0) + 8(0) \overset{?}{\leq} 360$

$0 \leq 360$

Shade the half–plane containing the point $(0, 0)$

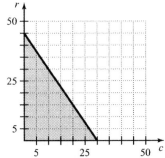

c. Yes since the solution point $(20, 15)$ lies on the boundary line and all points on the boundary line are solutions to the inequality.

41. a. Time must be expressed in terms of minutes.
$0.5T + R \leq 60$

b. The inequality is $\leq$ so the boundary line is solid.
$0.5T + R = 60$

$R = -0.5T + 60$

T	$R = -0.5T + 60$	(T, R)
0	$-0.5(0) + 60 = 60$	$(0, 60)$
60	$-0.5(60) + 60 = 30$	$(60, 30)$
120	$-0.5(120) + 60 = 0$	$(120, 0)$

Test point is $(0, 0)$.

$0.5(0) + 0 \overset{?}{\leq} 60$

$0 \leq 60$

Shade the half-plane containing the point $(0, 0)$

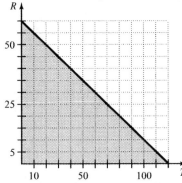

c. No, since the point $(50, 40)$ does not lie within the solution region.

Exercises 3.6 Introduction to Functions

1. A function. No two ordered pairs have the same first element.

3. Not a function. The ordered pairs $(-2, -3)$ and $(-2, 3)$ have the same first element.

5. Not a function. The ordered pairs $(3, 4)$ and $(3 - 4)$ have the same first element.

7. A function. No two ordered pairs have the same first element.

9. Domain: $\{-2, -1, 0, 1, 2\}$

    Range: $\{6, 8, 10, 12, 14\}$

11. Domain: $\{-3, -1, 0, 1, 3\}$

    Range: $\{-27, -1, 0, 1, 27\}$

13. Domain: $\{-4, -3, -2, -1, 1, 2, 3, 4\}$

    Range: $\{-8, -5, 0, 7\}$

15. Domain: $\{-4, -2, 0, 1, 2, 3.5, 5\}$

    Range: $\{1, 2, 3\}$

17. Domain: $\{-7, -3, -1, 2, 4\}$

    Range: $\{-4, -2, 1, 3, 7\}$

19. Domain: $\{2000, 2001, 2002, 2003, 2004\}$

    Range: $\{20, 23, 32, 34, 38\}$

21. a. $f(2) = 8 - 5(2) = 8 - 10 = -2$

    b. $f(-1) = 8 - 5(-1) = 8 + 5 = 13$

    c. $f\left(\dfrac{3}{5}\right) = 8 - 5\left(\dfrac{3}{5}\right) = 8 - 3 = 5$

    d. $f(1.8) = 8 - 5(1.8) = 8 - 9 = -1$

23. a. $g(5) = 2.4(5) - 7 = 12 - 7 = 5$

    b. $g(-2) = 2.4(-2) - 7 = -11.8$

    c. $g(a) = 2.4(a) - 7 = 2.4a - 7$

    d. $g(a^2) = 2.4(a^2) - 7 = 2.4a^2 - 7$

25. a. $\left|\dfrac{1}{2}(0) + 3\right| = |3| = 3$

    b. $\left|\dfrac{1}{2}(-8) + 3\right| = |-4 + 3| = |-1| = 1$

    c. $\left|\dfrac{1}{2}(-4t) + 3\right| = |-2t + 3|$

    d. $\left|\dfrac{1}{2}(t - 6) + 3\right| = \left|\dfrac{1}{2}t - 3 + 3\right| = \left|\dfrac{1}{2}t\right|$

27. a. $h(2) = 3(2)^2 - 6(2) - 9 =$
       $3(4) - 12 - 9 = 12 - 12 - 9 = -9$

    b. $h(-1) = 3(-1)^2 - 6(-1) - 9 =$
       $3(1) + 6 - 9 = 0$

c. $h(-n) = 3(-n)^2 - 6(-n) - 9 =$

$3n^2 + 6n - 9$

d. $h(2n) = 3(2n)^2 - 6(2n) - 9 =$

$3(4n^2) - 12n - 9 = 12n^2 - 12n - 9$

29. a. $g(7) = 10$

b. $g(-150) = 10$

c. $g(t) = 10$

d. $g(5 - 9t) = 10$

31. $f(x) = 5x - 4$

x	$f(x) = 5x - 4$	(x, y)
0	$5(0) - 4 = -4$	$(0, -4)$
$\dfrac{1}{5}$	$5\left(\dfrac{1}{5}\right) - 4 = -3$	$\left(\dfrac{1}{5}, -3\right)$
$\dfrac{4}{5}$	$5\left(\dfrac{4}{5}\right) - 4 = 0$	$\left(\dfrac{4}{5}, 0\right)$

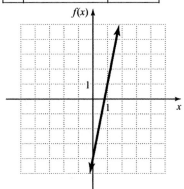

Domain: $(-\infty, \infty)$

Range: $(-\infty, \infty)$

33. $g(x) = |x| + 2$

x	$f(x) = |x| + 2$	(x, y)
-2	$|-2| + 2 = 2 + 2 = 4$	$(-2, 4)$
-1	$|-1| + 2 = 1 + 2 = 3$	$(-1, 3)$
0	$|0| + 2 = 0 + 2 = 2$	$(0, 2)$
1	$|1| + 2 = 1 + 2 = 3$	$(1, 3)$
2	$|2| + 2 = 2 + 2 = 4$	$(2, 4)$

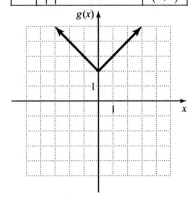

Domain: $(-\infty, \infty)$

Range: $[2, \infty)$

35. $f(x) = -5$

x	$f(x) = -5$	(x, y)
-4	-5	$(-4, -5)$
0	-5	$(0, -5)$
4	-5	$(4, -5)$

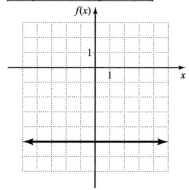

Domain: $(-\infty, \infty)$

Range: $\{-5\}$

37. $f(x) = -\dfrac{1}{4}x - 1$ for $x \le 0$

x	$f(x) = -\dfrac{1}{4}x - 1$	(x, y)
0	$-\dfrac{1}{4}(0) - 1 = -1$	$(0, -1)$
-2	$-\dfrac{1}{4}(-2) - 1 = -\dfrac{1}{2}$	$\left(-2, -\dfrac{1}{2}\right)$
-4	$-\dfrac{1}{4}(-4) - 1 = 0$	$(-4, 0)$

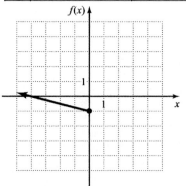

Domain: $(-\infty, 0]$

Range: $[-1, \infty)$

39. $h(x) = |x+1|$ for $x \geq -2$

x	$h(x) = |x+1|$	(x,y)
-2	$|-2+1| = |-1| = 1$	$(-2,1)$
-1	$|-1+1| = |0| = 0$	$(-1,0)$
0	$|0+1| = |1| = 1$	$(0,1)$
1	$|1+1| = |2| = 2$	$(1,2)$
2	$|2+1| = |3| = 3$	$(2,3)$

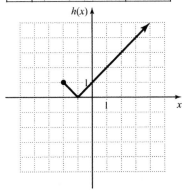

Domain: $[-2, \infty)$ Range: $[0, \infty)$

41. $f(x) = x^2$ for $x \leq 0$

x	$f(x) = x^2$	(x,y)
0	$(0)^2 = 0$	$(0,0)$
-1	$(-1)^2 = 1$	$(-1,1)$
-2	$(2)^2 = 4$	$(-2,4)$

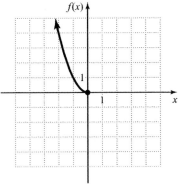

Domain: $(-\infty, 0]$ Range: $[0, \infty)$

43. A function. No vertical line will cross the graph more than once.

45. No, not a function. The vertical part of the graph fails the vertical line test.

47. A function. No vertical line will cross the graph more than once.

49. A function. No vertical line will cross the graph more than once.

51. a. $d(a) = 0.20a$

b. $d(150) = 0.20(150) = 30$

The discount is $30 so $30 was saved.

c.

a	$d(a) = 0.20a$	(a,d)
0	$0.20(0) = 0$	$(0,0)$
200	$0.20(200) = 40$	$(200,40)$
400	$0.20(400) = 80$	$(400,80)$

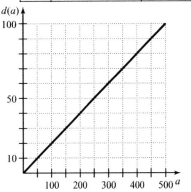

d. Domain: $[0, \infty)$ Range: $[0, \infty)$

53. a. $V(t) = 22500 - 1875t$

b. $V(6)$ represents the value of the car 6 years after it is purchased.

$V(6) = 22500 - 1875(6) =$

$22500 - 11250 = 11250$

The value of the car after 6 years is $11,250.

c.

t	$V(t) = 22500 - 1850t$	$(t, V(t))$
0	$22500 - 1850(0) =$ 22500	$(0, 22500)$
6	$22500 - 1875(6) =$ 11250	$(6, 11250)$
12	$22500 - 1875(12) = 0$	$(12, 0)$

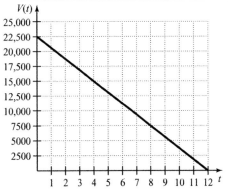

d. Domain: $[0, 12]$ Range: $[0, 22500]$

55. a. $d(x) = 500 - 50x$

b. $d(2) = 500 - 50(2) = 500 - 100 = 400$

After two weeks the patient's dosage is 400 mg.

c.

x	$d(x) = 500 - 50x$	$(x, d(x))$
0	$500 - 50(0) =$ $500 - 0 = 500$	$(0, 500)$
5	$500 - 50(5) =$ $500 - 250 = 250$	$(5, 250)$
10	$500 - 50(10) =$ $500 - 500 = 0$	$(10, 0)$

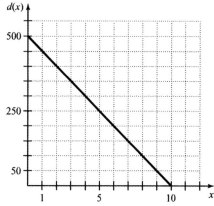

Domain: $[0, 10]$

Range: $[0, 500]$

57.   a. $h(0.5) = 180$

$h(3) = 160$

b.   No. $t > 5$ is not in the domain. The objects reaches
the ground in 5 seconds.

Chapter 3 Review Exercises

1.

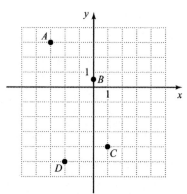

2. $A(5, 4)$, $B(-2, 0)$, $C(-5, -3)$, $D(4, -5)$

3.   Quadrant IV.

4.   Quadrant III.

5.   Quadrant I or quadrant III.

6.   Quadrant II or quadrant IV.

7. $m = \dfrac{y_2 - y_1}{x_2 - x_1} = \dfrac{-2 - 4}{-3 - 0} = 2$

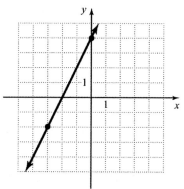

8. $m = \dfrac{y_2 - y_1}{x_2 - x_1} = \dfrac{2 - 3}{-6 - (-3)} = \dfrac{1}{3}$

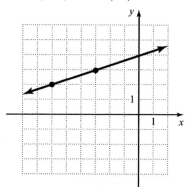

9. $m = \dfrac{y_2 - y_1}{x_2 - x_1} = \dfrac{3 - (-1)}{1.5 - 1.5} = \dfrac{4}{0}$

Slope is undefined.

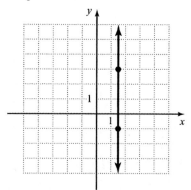

10. $m = \dfrac{y_2 - y_1}{x_2 - x_1} = \dfrac{4 - (-1)}{2 - 5} = -\dfrac{5}{3}$

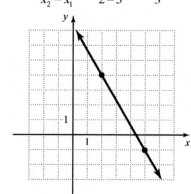

11. Positive slope.
12. Undefined slope.
13. Zero slope.
14. Negative slope.
15. Slope $= \dfrac{\text{Rise}}{\text{Run}} = \dfrac{1}{1}$

From $(2,3)$ move 1 unit up, 1 unit right

to $(3,4)$.

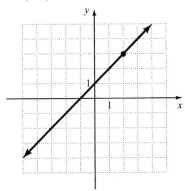

16. Slope $= \dfrac{\text{Rise}}{\text{Run}} = -\dfrac{2}{3} = \dfrac{-2}{3}$

From $(0,1)$ move 2 units down, 3 units

right to $(3,-1)$.

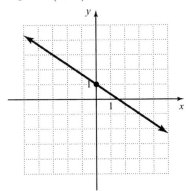

17. Slope $= \dfrac{\text{Rise}}{\text{Run}} = -\dfrac{1}{2} = \dfrac{-1}{2}$

From $(-3,-1)$ move 1 unit down, 2 units

right to $(-1,-2)$.

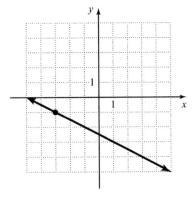

18. Slope $= \dfrac{\text{Rise}}{\text{Run}} = 0 = \dfrac{0}{1}$

From $(-4,4)$ move 0 units up-down,

1 unit right to $(-3,4)$.

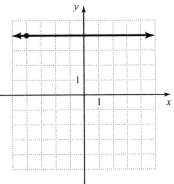

19. Answers may vary.

$(x_1 + a,\, y_1 + ma)$, $a = 1,\ 2$

$(-5+1, 3+(-4)(1)) = (-4,-1)$

$(-5+2, 3+(-4)(2)) = (-3,-5)$

20. Answers may vary.

$(x_1 + a,\, y_1 + ma)$, $a = 1,\ 2$

$(6+1, -9+(3)(1)) = (7,-6)$

$(6+2, -9+(3)(2)) = (8,-3)$

21. Answers may vary.

$(x_1 + a,\, y_1 + ma)$, $a = 1,\ 2$

$(1.6+1, -1+(0)(1)) = (2.6,-1)$

$(1.6+2, -1+(0)(2)) = (3.6,-1)$

22. Answers may vary.

$(x_1 + a,\, y_1 + ma)$, $a = 5,\ -5$

$\left(-4+5, -7+\left(-\dfrac{3}{5}\right)(5)\right) = (1,-10)$

$\left(-4-5, -7+\left(-\dfrac{3}{5}\right)(-5)\right) = (-9,-4)$

23. $m_{\overline{PQ}} = \dfrac{y_2 - y_1}{x_2 - x_1} = \dfrac{6-4}{-2-1} = -\dfrac{2}{3}$

$m_{\overline{RS}} = \dfrac{y_2 - y_1}{x_2 - x_1} = \dfrac{-2-(-5)}{11-9} = \dfrac{3}{2}$

Slopes are negative reciprocals. The lines are
perpendicular.

24. $m_{\overline{PQ}} = \dfrac{y_2 - y_1}{x_2 - x_1} = \dfrac{7-(-3)}{-1.8-3.2} = \dfrac{10}{-5} = -2$

$m_{\overline{RS}} = \dfrac{y_2 - y_1}{x_2 - x_1} = \dfrac{12-4}{1-5} = \dfrac{8}{-4} = -2$

Slopes are the same. The lines are parallel.

25. $0\overset{?}{=}\dfrac{1}{3}(6)-2$

$0\overset{?}{=}2-2$

$0=0$

$(6,0)$ is a solution.

26. $5(-1)-2(-3)\overset{?}{=}-1$

$-5+6\overset{?}{=}-1$

$1\neq -1$

$(-1,-3)$ is not a solution.

27. x-intercept means $y=0$.

$0=3x-9$

$x=3\quad (3,0)$

y-intercept means $x=0$.

$y=0-9$

$y=-9\quad (0,-9)$

28. x-intercept means $y=0$.

$2x+8=0$

$x=-4\quad (-4,0)$

y-intercept means $x=0$.

$2(0)+8\neq 0$

There is no y-interecept.

29. x-intercept means $y=0$.

$24\neq 12(0)$

There is no x-intercept.

y-intercept means $x=0$.

$24=12y$

$y=2\quad (0,2)$

30. x-intercept means $y=0$.

$4(0)-9x=6$

$x=-\dfrac{2}{3}\quad \left(-\dfrac{2}{3},0\right)$

y-intercept means $x=0$.

$4y-9(0)=6$

$y=\dfrac{3}{2}\quad \left(0,\dfrac{3}{2}\right)$

31.

x	$y=2x-1$	(x,y)
0	$2(0)-1=-1$	$(0,-1)$
1	$2(1)-1=1$	$(1,1)$
2	$2(2)-1=3$	$(2,3)$

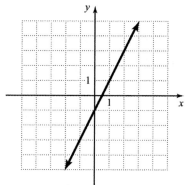

32.

x	$y=-\dfrac{1}{3}x+2$	(x,y)
-3	$-\dfrac{1}{3}(-3)+2=3$	$(-3,3)$
0	$-\dfrac{1}{3}(0)+2=2$	$(0,2)$
3	$-\dfrac{1}{3}(3)+2=1$	$(3,1)$

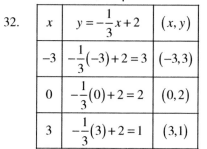

33. $2y=-3x+6$

$y=\dfrac{-3x+6}{2}$

$y=-\dfrac{3}{2}x+3$

x	$y=-\dfrac{3}{2}x+3$	(x,y)
0	$-\dfrac{3}{2}(0)+3=3$	$(0,3)$
2	$-\dfrac{3}{2}(2)+3=0$	$(2,0)$
4	$-\dfrac{3}{2}(4)+3=-3$	$(4,-3)$

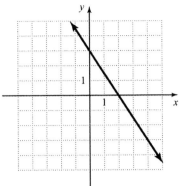

34. $-4y = -12x - 8$

$y = \dfrac{-12x - 8}{-4}$

$y = 3x + 2$

x	$y = 3x + 2$	(x, y)
-2	$3(-2) + 2 = -4$	$(-2, -4)$
-1	$3(-1) + 2 = -1$	$(-1, -1)$
0	$3(0) + 2 = 2$	$(0, 2)$

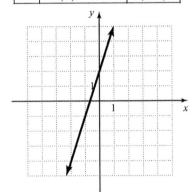

35. $y = \dfrac{-12}{6}$

$y = -2$

x	$y = -2$	(x, y)
-4	-2	$(-4, -2)$
0	-2	$(0, -2)$
4	-2	$(4, -2)$

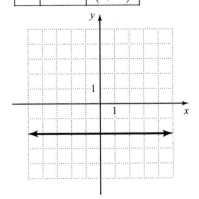

36. $x = \dfrac{-25}{-10}$

$x = \dfrac{5}{2}$

$x = \dfrac{5}{2}$	y	(x, y)
$\dfrac{5}{2}$	-2	$\left(\dfrac{5}{2}, -2\right)$
$\dfrac{5}{2}$	0	$\left(\dfrac{5}{2}, 0\right)$
$\dfrac{5}{2}$	2	$\left(\dfrac{5}{2}, 2\right)$

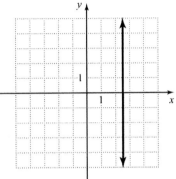

37. $5x - y = 1$

$-y = -5x + 1$

$y = \dfrac{-5x + 1}{-1}$

$y = 5x - 1$

$y = mx + b \quad m = 5 \quad b = -1$

Slope is 5.

y-intercept is $(0, -1)$.

38. $6y - 4x = -18$

$6y = 4x - 18$

$y = \dfrac{4x - 18}{6}$

$y = \dfrac{2}{3}x - 3$

$y = mx + b \quad m = \dfrac{2}{3} \quad b = -3$

Slope is $\dfrac{2}{3}$.

y-intercept is $(0, -3)$.

39. $7y + 2x - 14 = 0$

$7y = -2x + 14$

$y = \dfrac{-2x + 14}{7}$

$y = -\dfrac{2}{7}x + 2$

$y = mx + b \quad m = -\dfrac{2}{7} \quad b = 2$

Slope is $-\dfrac{2}{7}$.

y-intercept is $(0, 2)$.

40. $y - 8 = -\dfrac{3}{2}(x - 2)$

$y - 8 = -\dfrac{3}{2}x + 3$

$y = -\dfrac{3}{2}x + 11$

$y = mx + b \quad m = -\dfrac{3}{2} \quad b = 11$

Slope is $-\dfrac{3}{2}$.

y-intercept is $(0, 11)$.

41. $y = -\dfrac{1}{4}x + 3$

$y = mx + b \quad m = -\dfrac{1}{4} \quad b = 3$

y-intercept is $(0, 3)$.

Move down 1, right 4 to $(4, 2)$.

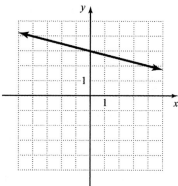

42. $y = 4x - 5$

$y = mx + b \quad m = 4 \quad b = -5$

y-intercept is -5.

Move up 4, right 1 to $(1, -1)$.

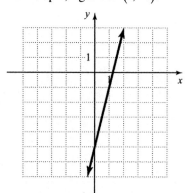

43. $3x - 5y = 20$

$-5y = -3x + 20$

$y = \dfrac{-3x + 20}{-5}$

$y = \dfrac{3}{5}x - 4$

$y = mx + b \quad m = \dfrac{3}{5} \quad b = -4$

y-intercept is $(0, -4)$.

Move up 3, right 5 to $(5, -1)$.

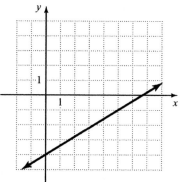

44. $4y + 6x = -24$

$4y = -6x - 24$

$y = \dfrac{-6x - 24}{4}$

$y = -\dfrac{3}{2}x - 6$

$y = mx + b \quad m = -\dfrac{3}{2} \quad b = -6$

y-intercept is $(0, -6)$.

Move up 3, left 2 to $(-2, -3)$.

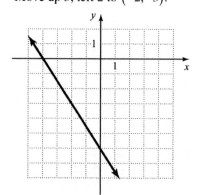

45. $y - 3 = -6(x - (-1))$

$y - 3 = -6(x + 1)$; point-slope form.

$y - 3 = -6x - 6$

$y = -6x - 3$; slope-intercept form.

46. $y - 7 = \dfrac{2}{5}(x - 5)$; point-slope form.

$y - 7 = \dfrac{2}{5}x - 2$

$y = \dfrac{2}{5}x + 5$; slope-intercept form.

47. Horizontal lines have a slope of 0.

$y - (-2.4) = 0(x - 1.2)$

$y + 2.4 = 0$

$y = -2.4$

48. $-8y = -2x + 40$

$y = \dfrac{-2x + 40}{-8}$

$y = \dfrac{1}{4}x - 5$

Slope is $\dfrac{1}{4}$

Parallel lines have the same slope.

$y - 1 = \dfrac{1}{4}(x - (-8))$

$y - 1 = \dfrac{1}{4}(x + 8)$; point-slope form.

$y - 1 = \dfrac{1}{4}x + 2$

$y = \dfrac{1}{4}x + 3$; slope-intercept form.

49. $-3y = 15x - 9$

$y = \dfrac{15x - 9}{-3}$

$y = -5x + 3$

Slope is -5.

Perpendicular lines have slopes that are negative reciprocals.

$y - 7 = \dfrac{1}{5}(x - 0)$; point-slope form.

$y - 7 = \dfrac{1}{5}x$

$y = \dfrac{1}{5}x + 7$; slope-intercept form.

50. $m = \dfrac{y_2 - y_1}{x_2 - x_1} = \dfrac{-8 - (-5)}{-1 - (-2)} = \dfrac{-3}{1} = -3$

Using $(-2, -5)$

$y - (-5) = -3(x - (-2))$

$y + 5 = -3(x + 2)$; point-slope form.

Using $(-1, -8)$

$y - (-8) = -3(x - (-1))$

$y + 8 = -3(x + 1)$; point slope form.

$y + 8 = -3x - 3$

$y = -3x - 11$; slope -intercept form.

51. $5(2) - 6\left(-\dfrac{2}{3}\right) \overset{?}{>} 20$

$10 + 4 \overset{?}{>} 20$

$14 \not> 20$

$\left(2, -\dfrac{2}{3}\right)$ is not a solution.

52. $4(-2) - 2(-3) \overset{?}{\le} -1$

$-8 + 6 \overset{?}{\le} -1$

$-2 \le -1$

$(-3, -2)$ is a solution.

53. The inequality is $\ge$ so the boundary line is solid.

x	$y = -\dfrac{2}{3}x + 3$	(x, y)
-3	$-\dfrac{2}{3}(-3) + 3 = 5$	$(-3, 5)$
0	$-\dfrac{2}{3}(0) + 3 = 3$	$(0, 3)$
3	$-\dfrac{2}{3}(3) + 3 = 1$	$(3, 1)$

Test point is $(0, 0)$.

$0 \overset{?}{\ge} -\dfrac{2}{3}(0) + 3$

$0 \not\ge 3$

Shade the half-plain not containing the point $(0, 0)$.

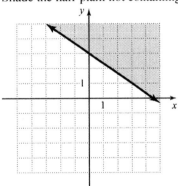

54. The inequality is $<$ so the boundary line is dashed.

x	$y = 1$	(x, y)
0	1	$(0, 1)$
2	1	$(2, 1)$
4	1	$(4, 1)$

Test point is $(0, 0)$.

$0 < 1$

Shade the half-plane containing the point $(0, 0)$.

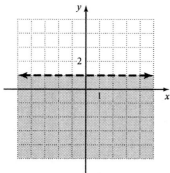

55. The inequality is $\geq$ so the boundary line is solid.

$-4y = -4x + 12$

$y = \dfrac{-4x + 12}{-4}$

$y = x - 3$

x	$y = x - 3$	(x, y)
0	$0 - 3 = -3$	$(0, -3)$
1	$1 - 3 = -2$	$(1, -2)$
3	$3 - 3 = 0$	$(3, 0)$

The test point is $(0, 0)$.

$4(0) - 4(0) \overset{?}{\geq} 12$

$0 \not\geq 12$

Shade the area not containing the point $(0, 0)$.

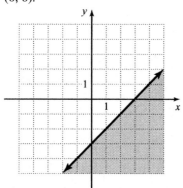

56. The inequality is $>$ so the boundary line is dashed.

$5y = -3x - 10$

$y = \dfrac{-3x - 10}{5}$

$y = -\dfrac{3}{5}x - 2$

x	$y = -\dfrac{3}{5}x - 2$	(x, y)
-5	$-\dfrac{3}{5}(-5) - 2 = 1$	$(-5, 1)$
0	$-\dfrac{3}{5}(0) - 2 = -2$	$(0, -2)$
5	$-\dfrac{3}{5}(5) - 2 = -5$	$(5, -5)$

Test point is $(0, 0)$.

$3(0) + 5(0) \overset{?}{>} -10$

$0 > -10$ true

Shade the area containing the point $(0, 0)$.

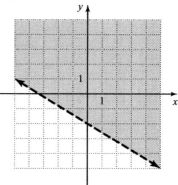

57. A function. No two ordered pairs have the same first element.

58. Not a function $(3, -2)$ and $(3, 4)$ have the same first element and different second elements.

59. Domain: $\{-7, -5, -3, -1\}$.

Range: $\{3\}$.

60. Domain: $\{-6, -4, -3, -2, 0, 2, 3, 4, 6\}$.

Range: $\{-6, -3, 0, 1, 2, 5, 8\}$.

61. Domain: $\{-27, -8, -1, 0, 1, 8, 27\}$.

Range: $\{-3, -2, -1, 0, 1, 2, 3\}$.

62. Domain: $\{20, 24, 26, 30, 32, 38\}$.

Range: $\{190, 228, 247, 285, 304, 361\}$.

63. a. $f(-9) = \dfrac{1}{3}(-9) + 6 = -3 + 6 = 3$

b. $f(3.6) = \dfrac{1}{3}(3.6) + 6 = 1.2 + 6 = 7.2$

c. $f(3a) = \dfrac{1}{3}(3a) + 6 = a + 6$

d. $f(6a - 12) = \dfrac{1}{3}(6a - 12) + 6 =$

$2a - 4 + 6 = 2a + 2$

64. a. $g(3) = |4(3) - 7| = |12 - 7| = |5| = 5$

b. $g\left(-\dfrac{3}{4}\right) = \left|4\left(-\dfrac{3}{4}\right) - 7\right| =$

$|-3 - 7| = |-10| = 10$

c. $g(2n) = |4(2n) - 7| = |8n - 7|$

d. $g\left(\dfrac{1}{4}n + 1\right) = \left|4\left(\dfrac{1}{4}n + 1\right) - 7\right| =$

$|n + 4 - 7| = |n - 3|$

65. $f(x) = 4 - \dfrac{1}{2}x$

x	$f(x) = 4 - \dfrac{1}{2}x$	(x, y)
0	$4 - \dfrac{1}{2}(0) = 4$	$(0,4)$
2	$4 - \dfrac{1}{2}(2) = 3$	$(2,3)$
4	$4 - \dfrac{1}{2}(4) = 2$	$(4,2)$

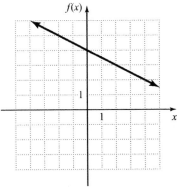

Domain: $(-\infty, \infty)$

Range: $(-\infty, \infty)$

66. $f(x) = -x^2$

x	$f(x) = -x^2$	(x, y)
-2	$-(-2)^2 = -4$	$(-2,-4)$
-1	$-(-1)^2 = -1$	$(-1,-1)$
0	$-(0)^2 = 0$	$(0,0)$
1	$-(1)^2 = -1$	$(1,-1)$
2	$-(2)^2 = -4$	$(2,-4)$

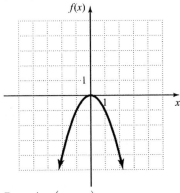

Domain: $(-\infty, \infty)$

Range: $(-\infty, 0]$

67. $g(x) = -|x| + 5$

x	$g(x) = -|x| + 5$	(x, y)
-5	$-|-5| + 5 = 0$	$(-5,0)$
-3	$-|-3| + 5 = 2$	$(-3,2)$
0	$-|0| + 5 = 5$	$(0,5)$
3	$-|3| + 5 = 2$	$(3,2)$
5	$-|5| + 5 = 0$	$(5,0)$

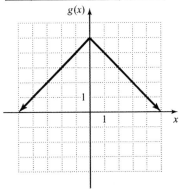

Domain: $(-\infty, \infty)$

Range: $(-\infty, 5]$

68. $g(x) = 4x - 9$ for $x \geq 1$

x	$g(x) = 4x - 9$	(x, y)
1	$4(1) - 9 = -5$	$(1,-5)$
2	$4(2) - 9 = -1$	$(2,-1)$
3	$4(3) - 9 = 3$	$(3,3)$

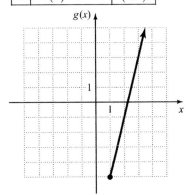

Domain: $[1, \infty)$

Range: $[-5, \infty)$

69. No, not a function. The y-axis crosses the graph twice failing the vertical line test.

70. A function. No vertical line will cross the graph more than once.

71. a. The slope represents the employee's hourly pay rate.

b. For Employee A

using $(0,0)$ and $(12,90)$

$$m = \frac{y_2 - y_1}{x_2 - x_1} = \frac{90 - 0}{12 - 0} = \frac{90}{12} = 7.5$$

For employee B

using $(0,0)$ and $(6,80)$

$$m = \frac{y_2 - y_1}{x_2 - x_1} = \frac{80 - 0}{6 - 0} = 13\frac{1}{3}$$

Employee B has a higher hourly pay, since the slope of the line for Employee A (7.5) is less than the slope for Employee B $\left(13\frac{1}{3}\right)$.

72.   The childcare center chargers a flat fee for a certain number of minutes (horizontal line segment). In addition, a per-minute fee is charged for any number of minutes thereafter (line segment slants up).

73.   a.

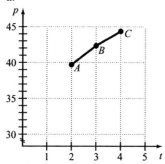

   b. $m_{\overline{AB}} = \frac{y_2 - y_1}{x_2 - x_1} = \frac{42.34 - 39.68}{3 - 2} = 2.66$

$$m_{\overline{BC}} = \frac{y_2 - y_1}{x_2 - x_1} = \frac{44.37 - 42.34}{4 - 3} = 2.03$$

Slope of $\overline{AB}$ is 2.66; slope of $\overline{BC}$ is 2.03.

   c.   Since the slopes of $\overrightarrow{AB}$ and $\overrightarrow{BC}$ are not the same, the increase in the average ticket price was not constant over the 3 years.

74.   a. $y = 4.95x + 10$

x	$y = 4.95x + 10$	(x, y)
0	$4.95(0) + 10 = 10$	$(0, 10)$
6	$4.95(6) + 10 = 39.70$	$(6, 39.70)$
10	$4.95(10) + 10 = 59.50$	$(10, 59.50)$

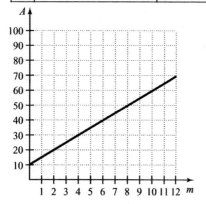

   b.   The slope of the line is 4.95. It represents the monthly fee the company charges.

   c.   The y-intercept is (0, 10). It represents the initial subscription fee.

   d.   A customer pays about $70 for 1 yr of service.

75.   a. $1.50x + 1.25y = 1200$

   b. $1.25y = -1.50x + 1200$

$$y = \frac{-1.50x + 1200}{1.25}$$

$$y = -1.2x + 960$$

x	$y = -1.2x + 960$	(x, y)
0	$-1.2(0) + 960 = 960$	$(0, 960)$
500	$-1.2(500) + 960 = 360$	$(500, 360)$
800	$-1.2(800) + 960 = 0$	$(800, 0)$

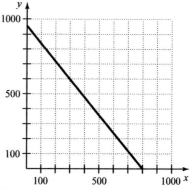

   c.   The x-intercept is $(800, 0)$ and the y-intercept is $(0, 960)$. The x-intercept represents the number of cups of coffee sold at Friday night's game if no hot chocolate was sold. The y-intercept represents the number of cups of hot chocolate sold if no coffee were sold.

   d.   If 300 cups of hot chocolate was sold, then about 550 cups of coffee were sold.

76.   a.   Slope = -170

   Point: $(3, 850)$

$$b - 850 = -170(n - 3)$$

$$b - 850 = -170n + 510$$

$$b = -170n + 1360$$

   b.

n	$b = -170n + 1360$	(n, b)
0	$-170(0) + 1360 = 1360$	$(0, 1360)$
3	$-170(3) + 1360 = 850$	$(3, 850)$
8	$-170(8) + 1360 = 0$	$(8, 0)$

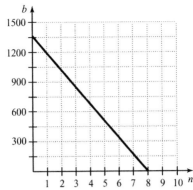

c. The n-intercept represents the number of months a customer will pay in order to pay off the balance. The b-intercept represents the annual premium amount.

77. a. Slope $= \dfrac{b_2 - b_1}{m_2 - m_1} = \dfrac{330 - 165}{6 - 3} = 55$

Using $(3, 165)$

$b - b_1 = \text{slope}(m - m_1)$

$b - 165 = 55(m - 3)$

Using $(6, 330)$

$b - b_1 = \text{slope}(m - m_1)$

$b - 330 = 55(m - 6)$

b. Slope indicates the machine can fill 55 bottles per minute.

c. 1 hour is 60 minutes. $60 \times 55 = 3300$

The machine can fill 3300 bottles in one hour.

78. a. $P(x) = 1.20x + 300$

b. $P(200) = 1.20(200) + 300 = 540$

The company makes a monthly profit of $540 for selling 200 bottles.

c.

x	$P(x) = 1.20x + 300$	(x, y)
0	$1.20(0) + 300 = 300$	$(0, 300)$
200	$1.20(200) + 300 = 540$	$(200, 540)$
500	$1.20(500) + 300 = 900$	$(500, 900)$

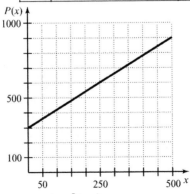

d. Domain: $[0, \infty)$

Range: $[300, \infty)$

79. a. $5v + 10d \geq 500$

b. The inequality is $\geq$ so the boundary line is solid.

$10d = -5v + 500$

$d = \dfrac{-5v + 500}{10}; \quad d = -\dfrac{1}{2}v + 50$

v	$d = -\dfrac{1}{2}v + 50$	(v, d)
0	$-\dfrac{1}{2}(0) + 50 = 50$	$(0, 50)$
50	$-\dfrac{1}{2}(50) + 50 = 25$	$(50, 25)$
100	$-\dfrac{1}{2}(100) + 50 = 0$	$(100, 0)$

Test point is $(0, 0)$.

$5(0) + 10(0) \overset{?}{\geq} 500; \quad 0 \not\geq 500$

Shade the half-plane not containing the point $(0, 0)$.

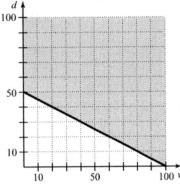

c. No, since the point $(30, 25)$ does not lie in the solution region.

80. a. $0.59x + 1.49y \leq 100$

b. The inequality is $\leq$ so the boundary line is solid.

$1.49y = -0.59x + 100$

$y = \dfrac{-0.59x + 100}{1.49}$

$y = -\dfrac{0.59}{1.49}x + \dfrac{100}{1.49}$

x	$y = -\dfrac{0.59}{1.49}x + \dfrac{100}{1.49}$	(x, y)
0	$-\dfrac{0.59}{1.49}(0) + \dfrac{100}{1.49} = 67.11$	$(0, 67)$
50	$-\dfrac{0.59}{1.49}(50) + \dfrac{100}{1.49} = 47.32$	$(50, 47)$
100	$-\dfrac{0.59}{1.49}(100) + \dfrac{100}{1.49} = 27.52$	$(100, 28)$

Test point is $(0, 0)$.

$0.59(0) + 1.59(0) \overset{?}{\leq} 100$

$0 \leq 100$

Shade the half-plane containing the point $(0, 0)$.

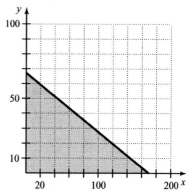

c. Answers may vary. Possible answer: 100 min of calling within the network and 20 min of calls outside the network.

Chapter 3 Posttest

1.

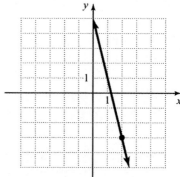

2. $m = \dfrac{y_2 - y_1}{x_2 - x_1} = \dfrac{4 - (-1)}{1.7 - 4.2} = \dfrac{5}{-2.5} = -2$

3. Slope $= \dfrac{\text{Rise}}{\text{Run}} = -4 = \dfrac{-4}{1}$

From $(2, -3)$ move 4 units down and 1 unit right to $(3, -7)$ or move 4 units up and 1 unit left to $(1, 1)$.

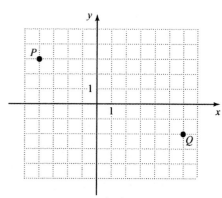

4. $m_{\overline{PQ}} = \dfrac{y_2 - y_1}{x_2 - x_1} = \dfrac{-5 - 9}{-8 - (-6)} = \dfrac{-14}{-2} = 7$

$m_{\overline{RS}} = \dfrac{y_2 - y_1}{x_2 - x_1} = \dfrac{11 - 10}{-3 - 4} = \dfrac{1}{-7} = -\dfrac{1}{7}$

The lines are perpendicular because the slopes of perpendicular lines are negative reciprocals.

5. $3\left(\dfrac{1}{2}\right) - 2\left(-\dfrac{1}{4}\right) \overset{?}{=} 1$

$\dfrac{3}{2} + \dfrac{2}{4} \overset{?}{=} 1$

$\dfrac{6}{4} + \dfrac{2}{4} \overset{?}{=} 1$

$\dfrac{8}{4} = 2 \neq 1$

$\left(\dfrac{1}{2}, -\dfrac{1}{4}\right)$ is not a solution.

6. x-intercept means $y = 0$.

$6x - 9(0) + 3 = 0$

$6x = -3$

$x = \dfrac{-3}{6} = -\dfrac{1}{2}; \quad \left(-\dfrac{1}{2}, 0\right)$

y-intercept means $x = 0$.

$6(0) - 9y + 3 = 0$

$-9y = -3$

$y = \dfrac{-3}{-9} = \dfrac{1}{3}; \quad \left(0, \dfrac{1}{3}\right)$

7.

x	$y = -\dfrac{3}{5}x + 3$	(x, y)
0	$-\dfrac{3}{5}(0) + 3 = 3$	$(0, 3)$
2	$-\dfrac{3}{5}(2) + 3 = \dfrac{9}{5}$	$\left(2, \dfrac{9}{5}\right)$
5	$-\dfrac{3}{5}(5) + 3 = 0$	$(5, 0)$

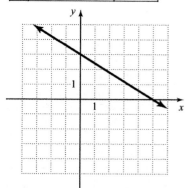

8. $\dfrac{24}{-8} = y$

$y = -3$

x	$y = -3$	(x, y)
-2	-3	$(2, -3)$
0	-3	$(0, -3)$
2	-3	$(2, -3)$

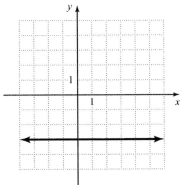

9. $-14y = -7x + 56$

$$y = \frac{-7x + 56}{-14}$$

$$y = \frac{1}{2}x - 4$$

x	$y = \frac{1}{2}x - 4$	(x, y)
-2	$\frac{1}{2}(-2) - 4 = -5$	$(-2, -5)$
0	$\frac{1}{2}(0) - 4 = -4$	$(0, -4)$
2	$\frac{1}{2}(2) - 4 = -3$	$(2, -3)$

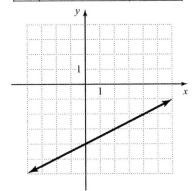

10. $y = 4x + 7$

$y = mx + b; \quad m = 4$

$y - y_1 = m(x - x_1)$

$y - (-1) = 4(x - 0)$

$y + 1 = 4(x - 0);$ point-slope form.

$y + 1 = 4x$

$y = 4x - 1;$ slope-intercept form.

11. $m = \dfrac{y_2 - y_1}{x_2 - x_1} = \dfrac{-2 - 5}{0 - 2} = \dfrac{-7}{-2} = \dfrac{7}{2}$

Using $(2, 5)$

$y - 5 = \dfrac{7}{2}(x - 2);$ point-slope form.

Using $(0, -2)$

$y + 2 = \dfrac{7}{2}(x - 0);$ point-slope form.

$y + 2 = \dfrac{7}{2}x$

$y = \dfrac{7}{2}x - 2;$ slope-intercept form.

12. $g(x) = -2x + 11$

$g(a + 3) = -2(a + 3) + 11$

$g(a + 3) = -2a - 6 + 11$

$g(a + 3) = -2a + 5$

13.

x	$f(x) = -|x| + 1$	(x, y)
-5	$-|-5| + 1 = -4$	$(-5, -4)$
-2	$-|-2| + 1 = -1$	$(-2, -1)$
0	$-|0| + 1 = 1$	$(0, 1)$
2	$-|2| + 1 = -1$	$(2, -1)$
5	$-|5| + 1 = -4$	$(5, -4)$

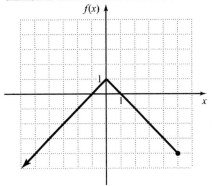

14. $0.4(-10) - 1.2(-20) \overset{?}{\le} -15$

$-4 + 24 \overset{?}{\le} -15$

$20 \not\le -15$

$(-10, -20)$ is not a solution.

15. The inequality is $>$ so the boundary line is dashed.

x	$y = -3x + 3$	(x, y)
0	$-3(0) + 3 = 3$	$(0, 3)$
1	$-3(1) + 3 = 0$	$(1, 0)$
2	$-3(2) + 3 = -3$	$(2, -3)$

Test point is $(0, 0)$

$0 \overset{?}{>} -3(0) + 3$

$0 \not> 3$

Shade the half-plane not containing the point $(0, 0)$.

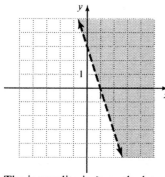

16. The inequality is ≥ so the boundary line is solid.

$$-8y = -2x - 16$$

$$y = \frac{-2x - 16}{-8}$$

$$y = \frac{1}{4}x + 2$$

x	$y = \frac{1}{4}x + 2$	(x, y)
-4	$\frac{1}{4}(-4) + 2 = 1$	$(-4, 1)$
0	$\frac{1}{4}(0) + 2 = 2$	$(0, 2)$
4	$\frac{1}{4}(4) + 2 = 3$	$(4, 3)$

Test point is (0, 0).

$$2(0) - 8(0) \overset{?}{\geq} -16$$

$$0 \geq -16$$

Shade the half-plane containing the point (0, 0).

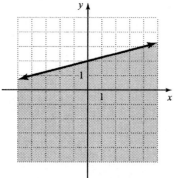

17. a.

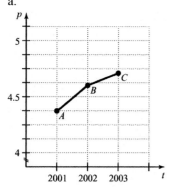

b. $m_{\overleftrightarrow{AB}} = \frac{y_2 - y_1}{x_2 - x_1} = \frac{4.60 - 4.37}{2002 - 2001} = \frac{0.23}{1} = 0.23$

$m_{\overleftrightarrow{BC}} = \frac{y_2 - y_1}{x_2 - x_1} = \frac{4.71 - 4.60}{2003 - 2002} = \frac{0.11}{1} = 0.11$

The slope of $\overleftrightarrow{AB}$ is 0.23 and the slope of $\overleftrightarrow{BC}$ is 0.11.

c.   No. Since the slopes of $\overleftrightarrow{AB}$ and $\overleftrightarrow{BC}$ are not the same, the price of silver did not increase at the same rate over the 3 years.

18. a. $4r + 8l = 1200$

b. $8l = -4r + 1200$

$$l = \frac{-4r + 1200}{8}$$

$$l = -\frac{1}{2}r + 150$$

r	$l = -\frac{1}{2}r + 150$	(r, l)
0	$-\frac{1}{2}(0) + 150 = 150$	$(0, 150)$
150	$-\frac{1}{2}(150) + 150 = 75$	$(150, 75)$
300	$-\frac{1}{2}(300) + 150 = 0$	$(300, 0)$

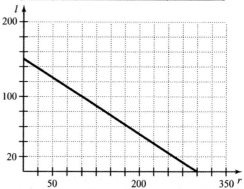

c.   The r-intercept is (300, 0) and the l-intercept is (0, 150) The r-intercept represents the number of roses used in a floral arrangement with no lilies. The l-intercept represents the number of lilies used in the floral arrangements with no roses.

d.   75 lilies are used with 150 roses.

19. a. $\left(5, \frac{5}{8}\right)$ and $\left(20, 2\frac{1}{2}\right)$

$$m = \frac{d_2 - d_1}{t_2 - t_1} = \frac{2\frac{1}{2} - \frac{5}{8}}{20 - 5} = \frac{\frac{20}{8} - \frac{5}{8}}{15} =$$

$$\frac{\frac{15}{8}}{15} = \frac{15}{8} \times \frac{1}{15} = \frac{1}{8}$$

Using $\left(5, \dfrac{5}{8}\right)$

$d - \dfrac{5}{8} = \dfrac{1}{8}(t-5)$

$d - \dfrac{5}{8} = \dfrac{1}{8}t - \dfrac{5}{8}; \quad d = \dfrac{1}{8}t$

b. The slope of $\dfrac{1}{8}$ represents the joggers speed in mi per min.

c. $10 = \dfrac{1}{8}t$

$80 = t$

$t = 80$ minutes $= \dfrac{80}{60}$ hours $= 1\dfrac{1}{3}$ hours.

It will take the jogger $1\dfrac{1}{3}$ hours to run 10 miles.

20. a. $8x + 14y \geq 4000$

b. The inequality is $\geq$ so the boundary line is solid.

$14y = -8x + 4000$

$y = \dfrac{-8x + 4000}{14}$

$y = -\dfrac{4}{7}x + \dfrac{2000}{7}$

x	$y = -\dfrac{4}{7}x + \dfrac{2000}{7}$	(x, y)
0	$-\dfrac{4}{7}(0) + \dfrac{2000}{7} = \dfrac{2000}{7} = 285.7$	$(0, 286)$
200	$-\dfrac{4}{7}(200) + \dfrac{2000}{7} = 171.4$	$(200, 171)$
500	$-\dfrac{4}{7}(500) + \dfrac{2000}{7} = 0$	$(500, 0)$

The test point is $(0, 0)$.

$8(0) + 14(0) \overset{?}{\geq} 4000$

$0 \ngeq 4000$

Shade the half-plane not containing the point $(0, 0)$.

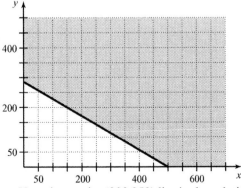

c. Yes, since point $(200, 250)$ lies in the solution region.

Cumulative Review Exercises

1. $4\left[25 - 3(\underline{8-11})^2\right] \div 2 + (-6) =$

$4\left[25 - 3(\underline{-3})^2\right] \div 2 + (-6) =$

$4\left[25 - \underline{3 \bullet 9}\right] \div 2 + (-6) =$

$4\left[\underline{25 - 27}\right] \div 2 + (-6) =$

$\underline{4\left[-2\right]} \div 2 + (-6) =$

$\underline{-8 \div 2} + (-6) = -4 + (-6) = -10$

2. The distributive property.

3. $\left(\dfrac{2x^2}{y^{-1}}\right)^{-3} = \left(2x^2y\right)^{-3} = 2^{-3}x^{-6}y^{-3} = \dfrac{1}{8x^6y^3}$

4. $-5n - 2(1-n) + 7 = -5n - 2(1) - 2(-n) + 7 =$

$-5n - 2 + 2n + 7 = -5n + 2n - 2 + 7 =$

$n(-5+2) - 2 + 7 = -3n + 5$

5. $12 - (4x+9) = 8 - 7x$

$12 - (1)(4x) - (1)(9) = 8 - 7x$

$12 - 4x - 9 = 8 - 7x$

$12 - 9 - 4x = 8 - 7x$

$3 - 4x = 8 - 7x$

$3 - 4x + 7x = 8 - 7x + 7x$

$3 + 3x = 8$

$3 - 3 + 3x = 8 - 3$

$3x = 5$

$\dfrac{3x}{3} = \dfrac{5}{3}$

$x = \dfrac{5}{3}$

6. $-6 < 14 - 2x \leq 0$

$-6 - 14 \leq 14 - 14 - 2x \leq 0 - 14$

$-20 < -2x \leq -14$

$\dfrac{-20}{-2} > \dfrac{-2x}{-2} \geq \dfrac{-14}{-2}$

$10 > x \geq 7$ or

$7 \leq x < 10$

<~+~+~+~+~+~[~+~)~+~+~>
0 1 2 3 4 5 6 7 8 9 10 11 12

7. One solution is to plot $(2, 5)$ and use the slope.

$m = 1 = \dfrac{1}{1}$, move up 1 and right 1 to $(3, 6)$.

Another solution is to solve for y and make a table of values.

$y - 5 = 1(x - 2)$

$y - 5 = x - 2$

$y = x + 3$

x	$y = x + 3$	(x, y)
-3	$-3 + 3 = 0$	$(-3, 0)$
0	$0 + 3 = 3$	$(0, 3)$
2	$2 + 3 = 5$	$(2, 5)$

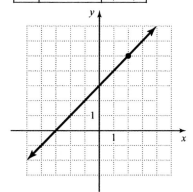

8. $10 - |3x + 8| = 4$

$-|3x + 8| = -6$

$$\dfrac{-|3x + 8|}{-1} = \dfrac{-6}{-1}$$

$|3x + 8| = 6$

$3x + 8 = 6$ or $3x + 8 = -6$

$3x = -2$ $3x = -14$

$$\dfrac{3x}{3} = \dfrac{-2}{3}$$ $$\dfrac{3x}{3} = \dfrac{-14}{3}$$

$x = -\dfrac{2}{3}$ $x = -\dfrac{14}{3}$

9.   Let s be the shipping charge and d be the amount of the order.

$s = 5 + 0.05(d - 100)$

$8.75 = 5 + 0.05(d - 100)$

$8.75 = 5 + 0.05d - 5$

$8.75 = 0.05d$

$$\dfrac{8.75}{0.05} = \dfrac{0.05d}{0.05}$$

$175 = d$

$d = 175$

The total order was $175.

10.   45% saline solution means 45% of the solution is salt. Salt is added in this problem. Splitting 20 liters into two quantities gives x and $20 - x$.

Action	Substance	Amount	Amount of Salt
Start	80% Saline	x	$0.80x$
Add	30% Saline	$(20 - x)$	$0.30(20 - x)$
Finish	45% Saline	20	$0.45(20)$

$0.80x + 0.30(20 - x) = 0.45(20)$

$0.80x + 6 - 0.30x = 9$

$0.50x + 6 = 9$

$0.50x = 3$

$$\dfrac{0.50x}{0.50} = \dfrac{3}{0.50}$$

$x = 6$

$20 - x = 14$

She needs 6 liters of the 80% solution and 14 liters of the 30% solution to make the required solution.

Chapter 4 Systems of Linear Equations and Inequalities

Pretest

1. $2(1)-3(4)\overset{?}{=}-10$ $5(1)+2(4)\overset{?}{=}13$

    $2-12\overset{?}{=}-10$ $5+8\overset{?}{=}13$

    $-10=-10$ True $13=13$ True

    Yes, it is a solution.

2.

x	$y=3x-4$	(x,y)
0	$3(0)-4=-4$	$(0,-4)$
1	$3(1)-4=-1$	$(1,-1)$

x	$y=-(2x-1)$	(x,y)
0	$-(2(0)-1)=1$	$(0,1)$
1	$-(2(1)-1)=-1$	$(1,-1)$

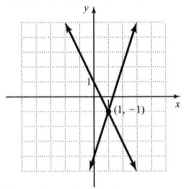

The solution is $(1,-1)$.

3. $9x-4y=-8;$ $-4y=-9x-8$

    $y=\dfrac{9}{4}x+2$

x	$y=\dfrac{9}{4}x+2$	(x,y)
-2	$\dfrac{9}{4}(-2)+2=-\dfrac{5}{2}$	$\left(-2,-\dfrac{5}{2}\right)$
0	$\dfrac{9}{4}(0)+2=2$	$(0,2)$

$-3x+2y=4;$ $2y=3x+4$

$y=\dfrac{3}{2}x+2$

x	$y=\dfrac{3}{2}x+2$	(x,y)
-2	$\dfrac{3}{2}(-2)+2=-1$	$(-2,-1)$
0	$\dfrac{3}{2}(0)+2=2$	$(0,2)$

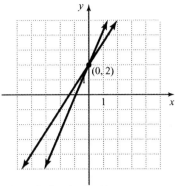

The solution is $(0, 2)$.

4. $5y-20=0$

    $5y=20$ $y=4$

x	$y=4$	(x,y)
0	4	$(0,4)$
2	4	$(2,4)$

$6x+8y=8$

$8y=-6x+8$

$y=-\dfrac{3}{4}x+1$

x	$y=-\dfrac{3}{4}x+1$	(x,y)
0	$-\dfrac{3}{4}(0)+1=1$	$(0,1)$
4	$-\dfrac{3}{4}(4)+1=-2$	$(4,-2)$

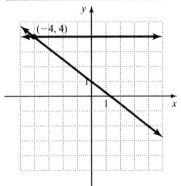

The solution is $(-4, 4)$.

5. $y=8\left(\dfrac{1}{2}y-1\right)+5$

    $y=4y-8+5$

    $y=4y-3$

    $-3y=-3$ $y=\dfrac{-3}{-3}=1$

    $x=\dfrac{1}{2}(1)-1$ $x=-\dfrac{1}{2}$

    $\left(-\dfrac{1}{2},1\right)$

6. $4x - 2(3 + 2x) = 9$

$4x - 6 - 4x = 9$

$-6 = 9$ False

No solution.

7. $u = -7v + 8$

$6(-7v + 8) - v = 5$

$-42v + 48 - v = 5$

$-43v + 48 = 5$

$-43v = -43$

$v = \dfrac{-43}{-43} = 1$

$u + 7(1) = 8$

$u + 7 = 8$

$u = 1$

$u = 1,\ v = 1$

8. $x + y = 10$

$\dfrac{3x - y = 6}{4x\ \ \ \ = 16}$

$x = \dfrac{16}{4} = 4$

$(4) + y = 10$

$y = 6$

$(4, 6)$

9. $5a - 3b = -1 \xrightarrow{\times(-1)} -5a + 3b = 1$

$13a - 3b = 1 \qquad\qquad \dfrac{13a - 3b = 1}{8a\ \ \ \ = 2}$

$a = \dfrac{1}{4}$

$5\left(\dfrac{1}{4}\right) - 3b = -1$

$\dfrac{5}{4} - 3b = -1$

$-3b = -\dfrac{4}{4} - \dfrac{5}{4} = -\dfrac{9}{4}$

$b = -\dfrac{9}{4}\left(-\dfrac{1}{3}\right) = \dfrac{3}{4}$

$a = \dfrac{1}{4},\ b = \dfrac{3}{4}$

10. $0.5x - 1.5y = 1.25 \xrightarrow{\times 12} 6x - 18y = 15$

$-6x + 18y = -15 \qquad \dfrac{-6x + 18y = -15}{0 = 0}$

Infinitely many solutions.

11. $2(2) - (-3) + (1) \overset{?}{=} 8$

$4 + 3 + 1 \overset{?}{=} 8$

$8 = 8$ True

$3(2) + 2(-3) + (1) \overset{?}{=} 1$

$6 - 6 + 1 \overset{?}{=} 1$

$1 = 1$ True

$(2) + 3(-3) - 3(1) \overset{?}{=} 10$

$2 - 9 - 3 \overset{?}{=} 10$

$-10 = 10$ False

No, it is not a solution.

12. $\begin{aligned} x + y + \ z &= 0 \\ \underline{2x - y + 3z} &\underline{= 3} \\ 3x\ \ \ \ + 4z &= 3 \end{aligned}$

$2x - y + 3z = 3 \xrightarrow{\times 2} 4x - 2y + 6z = 6$

$x + 2y - z = -3 \qquad \begin{aligned} x + 2y - \ z &= -3 \\ \underline{} & \\ 5x\ \ \ \ + 5z &= 3 \end{aligned}$

$3x + 4z = 3 \xrightarrow{\times 5} 15x + 20z = 15$

$5x + 5z = 3 \xrightarrow{\times(-3)} \dfrac{-15x - 15z = -9}{5z = 6}$

$z = \dfrac{6}{5}$

$5x + 5\left(\dfrac{6}{5}\right) = 3$

$5x + 6 = 3$

$5x = -3$

$x = -\dfrac{3}{5}$

$-\dfrac{3}{5} + y + \dfrac{6}{5} = 0$

$y + \dfrac{3}{5} = 0$

$y = -\dfrac{3}{5}$

$\left(-\dfrac{3}{5}, -\dfrac{3}{5}, \dfrac{6}{5}\right)$

13. $\dfrac{1}{2}y - \dfrac{1}{4}z = 1 \xrightarrow{\times(-8)} -4y + 2z = -8$

$x - 2z = 2 \qquad \begin{aligned} x - 2z &= 2 \\ \underline{-4y + x\ \ \ \ = -6} & \\ x - 4y &= -6 \end{aligned}$

$x - 4y = -6 \qquad\qquad x - 4y = -6$

$3x - 2y = -13 \xrightarrow{\times(-2)} \dfrac{-6x + 4y = 26}{-5x\ \ \ = 20}$

$x = -4$

$3(-4) - 2y = -13$

$-12 - 2y = -13$

$-2y = -1$

$y = \dfrac{-1}{-2} = \dfrac{1}{2}$

$-4 - 2z = 2$

$-2z = 6$

$z = \dfrac{6}{-2} = -3$

$\left(-4, \dfrac{1}{2}, -3\right)$

14.   Augmented matrix:

$$\begin{bmatrix} 4 & 5 & -1 & | & -4 \\ 1 & -2 & 1 & | & 5 \\ 2 & 1 & 0 & | & 5 \end{bmatrix}$$

Interchange row 1 and row 2

$$\begin{bmatrix} 1 & -2 & 1 & | & 5 \\ 4 & 5 & -1 & | & -4 \\ 2 & 1 & 0 & | & 5 \end{bmatrix}$$

Multiply row 3 by -2 and add to row 2

$$\begin{bmatrix} 1 & -2 & 1 & | & 5 \\ 4+2(-2) & 5+1(-2) & -1+0(-2) & | & -4+5(-2) \\ 2 & 1 & 0 & | & 5 \end{bmatrix}$$

$$\begin{bmatrix} 1 & -2 & 1 & | & 5 \\ 0 & 3 & -1 & | & -14 \\ 2 & 1 & 0 & | & 5 \end{bmatrix}$$

Multiply row 1 by -2 and add to row 3

$$\begin{bmatrix} 1 & -2 & 1 & | & 5 \\ 0 & 3 & -1 & | & -14 \\ 2+1(-2) & 1+(-2)(-2) & 0+1(-2) & | & 5+5(-2) \end{bmatrix}$$

$$\begin{bmatrix} 1 & -2 & 1 & | & 5 \\ 0 & 3 & -1 & | & -14 \\ 0 & 5 & -2 & | & -5 \end{bmatrix}$$

Multiply row 2 by 2 and subtract row 3

$$\begin{bmatrix} 1 & -2 & 1 & | & 5 \\ 0 & 2(3)-5 & 2(-1)-(-2) & | & 2(-14)-(-5) \\ 0 & 5 & -2 & | & -5 \end{bmatrix}$$

$$\begin{bmatrix} 1 & -2 & 1 & | & 5 \\ 0 & 1 & 0 & | & -23 \\ 0 & 5 & -2 & | & -5 \end{bmatrix}$$

Multiply row 2 by -5 and add to row 3.

$$\begin{bmatrix} 1 & -2 & 1 & | & 5 \\ 0 & 1 & 0 & | & -23 \\ 0 & 5+(-5)(1) & -2+(-5)(0) & | & -5+(-5)(-23) \end{bmatrix}$$

$$\begin{bmatrix} 1 & -2 & 1 & | & 5 \\ 0 & 1 & 0 & | & -23 \\ 0 & 0 & -2 & | & 110 \end{bmatrix}$$

Multiply row 3 by $-\dfrac{1}{2}$

$$\begin{bmatrix} 1 & -2 & 1 & | & 5 \\ 0 & 1 & 0 & | & -23 \\ 0 & 0 & -2\left(-\dfrac{1}{2}\right) & | & 110\left(-\dfrac{1}{2}\right) \end{bmatrix}$$

$$\begin{bmatrix} 1 & -2 & 1 & | & 5 \\ 0 & 1 & 0 & | & -23 \\ 0 & 0 & 1 & | & -55 \end{bmatrix}$$

$z = -55 \quad y = -23 \quad x - 2y + z = 5$

$x - 2(-23) - 55 = 5$

$x + 46 - 55 = 5$

$x - 9 = 5$

$x = 14$

$(14, -23, -55)$

15. $y < \dfrac{1}{2}x - 1$

The boundary line is dashed

x	$y = \dfrac{1}{2}x - 1$	(x, y)
0	$\dfrac{1}{2}(0) - 1 = -1$	$(0, -1)$
2	$\dfrac{1}{2}(2) - 1 = 0$	$(2, 0)$

The test point is $(0, 0)$.

$0 \overset{?}{<} \dfrac{1}{2}(0) - 1$

$0 \not< -1$

Shade the half-plane not containing $(0, 0)$.

$y \geq -3x + 1$

The boundary line is solid.

x	$y = -3x + 1$	(x, y)
0	$-3(0) + 1 = 1$	$(0, 1)$
1	$-3(1) + 1 = -2$	$(1, -2)$

Test point is $(0,0)$.

$0 \overset{?}{\geq} -3(0)+1$

$0 \not\geq 1$, shade the half-plane not containing $(0,0)$.

$y \geq -4$

The boundary line is solid.

x	$y = -4$	(x, y)
0	-4	$(0,-4)$
2	-4	$(2,-4)$

The test point is $(0,0)$.

$0 \geq -4$, shade the half-plane containing $(0,0)$.

The solutions to the system are all the points that lie in all three overlapping shaded regions.

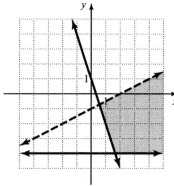

16.   Let C be the total charge and m be the miles of the ride.

$C = 1.25 + 1.30(m-1)$

$C = 1.75 + 1.20(m-1)$

$1.25 + 1.30(m-1) = 1.75 + 1.20(m-1)$

$1.25 + 1.30m - 1.30 = 1.75 + 1.20m - 1.20$

$1.30m - 0.05 = 1.20m + 0.55$

$0.10m = 0.60$

$m = 6$

Both taxi companies will charge the same amount for a 6-mile ride.

17.   Let d be the distance and t be the time.

$d = 54t$

$d = 60t$

When will their distances total 171 miles?

$54t + 60t = 171$

$114t = 171$

$t = \dfrac{171}{114} = 1.5$

The busses will be 171 miles apart after $1\frac{1}{2}$ hr.

18.   Let a be the amount of 25% solution and b be the amount of 50% solution.

Action	Percent of Alcohol	Amount of Solution (L)	Amount of Alcohol (L)
Start	25%	a	$0.25a$
Add	50%	b	$0.50b$
Finish	40%	20	$0.40(20)$

1) $a + b = 20$

2) $.25a + .50b = 0.40(20)$

Multiply equation 1) by -0.25 and add to 2).

$-0.25a - 0.25b = -0.25(20)$

$-0.25a - 0.25b = -5$

$\underline{0.25a + 0.50b = 8}$

$0.25b = 3$

$b = \dfrac{3}{0.25} = 12$

$a + 12 = 20$

$a = 8$

She can combine 8 L of the 25% alcohol solution with 12 L of the 50% alcohol solution to obtain the required amount.

19.   Let s be the number of small bags.
Let m be the number of medium bags.
Let l be the number of large bags.

1) $s + m + l = 807$

2) $l = 10 + 2m$

3) $2.50s + 3.00m + 3.75l = 2282$

Substituting the expression for l from 2) into equations 1) and 3):

$s + m + (10 + 2m) = 807$

$s + m + 10 + 2m = 807$

4) $s + 3m = 797$

$2.5s + 3m + 3.75(10 + 2m) = 2282$

$2.5s + 3m + 37.5 + 7.5m = 2282$

5) $2.5s + 10.5m = 2244.5$

Solving equation 4) for s and substituting into equation 5):

$s = 797 - 3m$

$2.5(797 - 3m) + 10.5m = 2244.5$

$1992.5 - 7.5m + 10.5m = 2244.5$

$3m = 252$

$m = 84$

$s = 797 - 3m = 797 - 3(84) = 545$

$l = 10 + 2m = 10 + 2(84) = 178$

545 small, 84 medium, and 178 large bags of popcorn were sold on Wednesday.

20.   a. $x + y \le 10000$

$0.05x + 0.06y \ge 300$

b. $x + y \le 10000$

$y \le -x + 10000$

The boundary line is solid.

x	$y = -x + 10000$	(x, y)
0	$-(0) + 10000 = 10000$	$(0, 10000)$
10000	$-(10000) + 10000 = 0$	$(10000, 0)$

Test point is $(0, 0)$.

$(0) + (0) \overset{?}{\le} 10000$

$0 \le 10000$, shade the half plane

containing $(0, 0)$.

$0.05x + 0.06y \ge 300$

$0.06y \ge -0.05x + 300$

$y \ge -\dfrac{5x}{6} + 5000$

The boundary line is solid.

x	$y = -\dfrac{5x}{6} + 5000$	(x, y)
0	$-\dfrac{5}{6}(0) + 5000 = 5000$	$(0, 5000)$
6000	$-\dfrac{5}{6}(6000) + 5000 = 0$	$(6000, 0)$

The test point is $(0, 0)$. $0.05(0) + 0.06(0) \overset{?}{\ge} 300$

$0 \overset{}{\ngeq} 300$

The half plane not containing $(0, 0)$ is shaded.

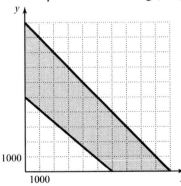

The solutions are all points between and including
the two lines.

c. Answers may vary. Possible answer: $2500 in
the account earning 5% simple interest and %5000
in the account earning 6% simple interest.

Exercises 4.1 Solving Systems of Linear Equations by Graphing

1. $2 + 4 \overset{?}{=} 6 \qquad 3(2) - 4 \overset{?}{=} 2$

$6 = 6$ True

$6 - 4 \overset{?}{=} 2$

$2 = 2$ True

A solution.

3. $3(1) - 5(-1) \overset{?}{=} 8 \qquad 4(1) - 4(-1) \overset{?}{=} 0$

$3 + 5 \overset{?}{=} 8 \qquad\qquad 4 + 4 \overset{?}{=} 0$

$8 = 8$ True $8 = 0$ False

Not a solution.

5. $16\left(\dfrac{1}{4}\right) - 10\left(-\dfrac{1}{2}\right) \overset{?}{=} 9 \qquad 2\left(\dfrac{1}{4}\right) + 3\left(-\dfrac{1}{2}\right) \overset{?}{=} -1$

$4 + 5 \overset{?}{=} 9 \qquad\qquad \dfrac{1}{2} - \dfrac{3}{2} \overset{?}{=} -1$

$9 = 9$ True

$-1 = -1$ True

A solution.

7.   Intersection from graph a. is $(2, -3)$.

$3(2) + 5(-3) \overset{?}{=} 9$

$6 - 15 \overset{?}{=} 9$

$-9 = 9$ False

$(2, -3)$ is not a solution.

Intersection from graph d. is $(-2, 3)$.

$3(-2) + 5(3) \overset{?}{=} 9 \qquad 3(-2) - 2(3) \overset{?}{=} -12$

$-6 + 15 \overset{?}{=} 9 \qquad\qquad -6 - 6 \overset{?}{=} -12$

$9 = 9$ True $-12 = -12$ True

$(-2, 3)$ is a solution.

Choice d.

9. $2x - 3y = 6 \qquad\qquad 4x - 6y = -18$

$-3y = -2x + 6 \qquad -6y = -4x - 18$

$y = \dfrac{2}{3}x - 2 \qquad\qquad y = \dfrac{2}{3}x + 3$

Slope: $\dfrac{2}{3}$ Slope: $\dfrac{2}{3}$

y-interecept is $(0, -2)$ y-intercept is $(0, 3)$

The lines are parallel. Choice c.

11.

x	$y = 2x$	(x, y)
1	$2(1) = 2$	$(1, 2)$
2	$2(2) = 4$	$(2, 4)$

x	$y = \frac{1}{3}x$	(x, y)
-3	$\frac{1}{3}(-3) = -1$	$(-3, -1)$
3	$\frac{1}{3}(3) = 1$	$(3, 1)$

x	$y = \frac{4}{3}x - \frac{1}{3}$	(x, y)
-2	$\frac{4}{3}(-2) - \frac{1}{3} = -3$	$(-2, -3)$
1	$\frac{4}{3}(1) - \frac{1}{3} = 1$	$(1, 1)$

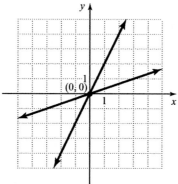

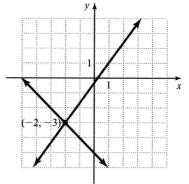

The solution is (0, 0).

The solution is (−2, −3).

13.

x	$y = -\frac{1}{2}x + 1$	(x, y)
0	$-\frac{1}{2}(0) + 1 = 1$	$(0, 1)$
2	$-\frac{1}{2}(2) + 1 = 0$	$(2, 0)$

x	$y = x - 5$	(x, y)
0	$0 - 5 = -5$	$(0, -5)$
2	$2 - 5 = -3$	$(2, -3)$

17. $x - y = -3$

$-y = -x - 3$

$y = x + 3$

x	$y = x + 3$	(x, y)
0	$0 + 3 = 3$	$(0, 3)$
2	$2 + 3 = 5$	$(2, 5)$

$y = 7 - 3x$

x	$y = -3x + 7$	(x, y)
1	$-3(1) + 7 = 4$	$(1, 4)$
2	$-3(2) + 7 = 1$	$(2, 1)$

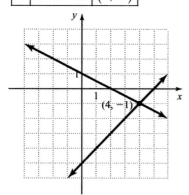

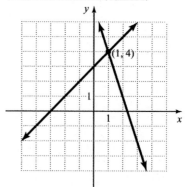

The solution is (4, −1).

The solution is (1, 4)

15. $x + y = -5$

$y = -x - 5$

19. $4x = 12 - 3y$

$4x - 12 = -3y$

x	$y = -x - 5$	(x, y)
-3	$-(-3) - 5 = -2$	$(-3, -2)$
0	$-(0) - 5 = -5$	$(0, -5)$

$-\frac{4}{3}x + 4 = y$

$y = -\frac{4}{3}x + 4$

$4x - 3y = 1$

$-3y = -4x + 1$

$y = \frac{4}{3}x - \frac{1}{3}$

x	$y=-\dfrac{4}{3}x+4$	(x,y)
0	$-\dfrac{4}{3}(0)+4=4$	$(0,4)$
3	$-\dfrac{4}{3}(3)+4=0$	$(3,0)$

$-6y=8x+6$

$y=-\dfrac{4}{3}x-1$

x	$y=-\dfrac{4}{3}x-1$	(x,y)
0	$-\dfrac{4}{3}(0)-1=-1$	$(0,-1)$
3	$-\dfrac{4}{3}(3)-1=-5$	$(3,-5)$

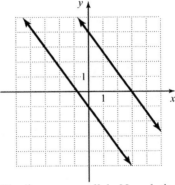

The lines are parallel. No solution.

21. $y-5=-2 \quad y=3$

x	$y=3$	(x,y)
-2	3	$(-2,3)$
2	3	$(2,3)$

$3x=6 \quad x=2$

$x=2$	y	(x,y)
2	-2	$(2,-2)$
2	2	$(2,2)$

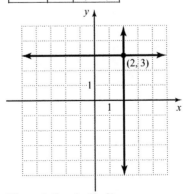

The solution is (2, 3)

23. $3x-6y=12$

$-6y=-3x+12$

$y=\dfrac{1}{2}x-2$

x	$y=\dfrac{1}{2}x-2$	(x,y)
0	$\dfrac{1}{2}(0)-2=-2$	$(0,-2)$
2	$\dfrac{1}{2}(2)-2=-1$	$(2,-1)$

$4y+8=2x$

$4y=2x-8$

$y=\dfrac{1}{2}x-2$

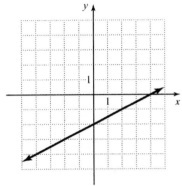

$3x-6y=12$ and $4y+8=2x$ form the same graph.
There are infinitely many solutions.

25. $-2x+8y=12$

$8y=2x+12$

$y=\dfrac{1}{4}x+\dfrac{3}{2}$

x	$y=\dfrac{1}{4}x+\dfrac{3}{2}$	(x,y)
-2	$\dfrac{1}{4}(-2)+\dfrac{3}{2}=1$	$(-2,1)$
2	$\dfrac{1}{4}(2)+\dfrac{3}{2}=2$	$(2,2)$

$3x+2y=-4$

$2y=-3x-4$

$y=-\dfrac{3}{2}x-2$

x	$y=-\dfrac{3}{2}x-2$	(x,y)
-2	$-\dfrac{3}{2}(-2)-2=1$	$(-2,1)$
0	$-\dfrac{3}{2}(0)-2=-2$	$(0,-2)$

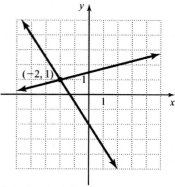

Solution is (–2, 1).

27. $0.5x - 1.5y = 1$

$-1.5y = -0.5x + 1$

$y = \dfrac{1}{3}x - \dfrac{2}{3}$

x	$y = \dfrac{1}{3}x - \dfrac{2}{3}$	(x, y)
-1	$\dfrac{1}{3}(-1) - \dfrac{2}{3} = -1$	$(-1, -1)$
2	$\dfrac{1}{3}(2) - \dfrac{2}{3} = 0$	$(2, 0)$

$2x - 6y - 4 = 0$

$-6y = -2x + 4$

$y = \dfrac{1}{3}x - \dfrac{2}{3}$

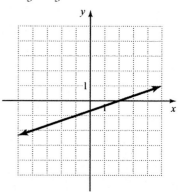

$0.5x - 1.5y = 1$ and $2x - 6y - 4 = 0$ form the same graph. There are infinitely many solutions.

29. $6x - 5y = 9$

$-5y = -6x + 9$

Enter $y_1 = (-6x + 9) \div -5$ into the calculator.

Enter $y_2 = 3x - 2$ into the calculator.

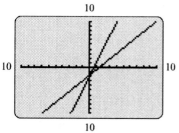

The approximate solution is (0.111, –1.667).

31. $3.7x + 2.1y = -4$

$2.1y = -3.7x - 4$

Enter $y_1 = (-3.7x - 4) \div 2.1$ into the calculator.

$-0.6x - 2y = 6.8$

$-2y = 0.6x + 6.8$

Enter $y_2 = (0.6x + 6.8) \div -2$ into the calculator.

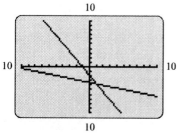

The approximate solution is $(1.023, -3.707)$.

33.   a. $x + y = 12000$

$x = 3y$

b. $y = -x + 12000$

x	$y = -x + 12000$	(x, y)
0	$-(0) + 12000 = 12000$	$(0, 12000)$
12000	$-(12000) + 12000 = 0$	$(12000, 0)$

$y = \dfrac{1}{3}x$

x	$y = \dfrac{1}{3}x$	(x, y)
0	$\dfrac{1}{3}(0) = 0$	$(0, 0)$
12000	$\dfrac{1}{3}(12000) = 4000$	$(12000, 4000)$

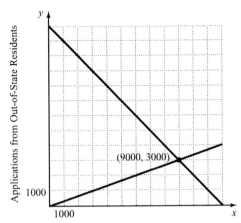

Solution is (9000, 3000)

c. 9000 applications were from in-state residents and 3000 were from out-of-state residents.

35. a. $w = l + 2500$

$w + l = 11500$

b. $l = w - 2500$

w	$l = w - 2500$	(w, l)
2500	$2500 - 2500 = 0$	$(2500, 0)$
10000	$10000 - 2500 = 7500$	$(10000, 7500)$

$l = -w + 11500$

w	$l = -w + 11500$	(w, l)
0	$-(0) + 11500 = 11500$	$(0, 11500)$
10000	$-(10000) + 11500 = 1500$	$(10000, 1500)$

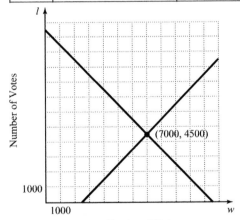

Solution is (7000,4500)

c. The winning candidate received 7000 votes and the losing candidate received 4500 votes.

37. a. $C = 20$

$C = 1.75n + 2.5$

b.
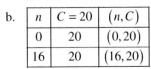

n	$C = 20$	(n, C)
0	20	$(0, 20)$
16	20	$(16, 20)$

n	$C = 1.75n + 2.5$	(n, C)
0	$1.75(0) + 2.5$	$(0, 2.5)$
16	$1.75(16) + 2.5 = 30.5$	$(16, 30.5)$

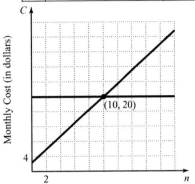

Solution is (10, 20).

c. The monthly costs will be the same if 10 movies are rented.

d. From the graph: at 8 months, Webflix charges $20 and Movie-net charges $16.50. Movie-net is a better deal since it would cost $3.50 less per month if 8 movies are rented.

39. Let $C(x)$ be the cost of manufacturing x plastic sharps containers and $R(x)$ be the revenue from selling x plastic sharps containers.

$C(x) = 1.50x + 875$

$R(x) = 4x$

x	$y = C(x) = 1.5x + 875$	(x, y)
0	$1.5(0) + 875 = 875$	$(0, 875)$
400	$1.5(400) + 875 = 1475$	$(400, 1475)$

x	$y = R(x) = 4x$	(x, y)
0	$4(0) = 0$	$(0, 0)$
400	$4(400) = 1600$	$(400, 1600)$

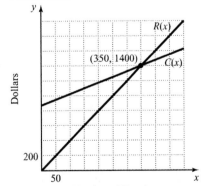

Solution is (350, 1400).

From the graph, the company must sell 350 containers in order to break even.

41.   Let x be the hours worked at the coffee shop and y be the hours worked at the office.

$$x + y = 20$$

$$8x + 12y = 216$$

$$y = -x + 20$$

x	$y = -x + 20$	(x, y)
0	$-(0) + 20 = 20$	$(0, 20)$
15	$-(15) + 20 = 5$	$(15, 5)$

$$12y = -8x + 216$$

$$y = -\frac{2}{3}x + 18$$

x	$y = -\frac{2}{3}x + 18$	(x, y)
0	$-\frac{2}{3}(x) + 18 = 18$	$(0, 18)$
15	$-\frac{2}{3}(15) + 18 = 8$	$(15, 8)$

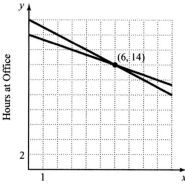

Solution is (6, 14).
From the graph, she works 6 hr at the coffee shop and 14 hr at the office.

Exercises 4.2 Solving Systems of Linear Equations Algebraically by Substitution or Elimination

1. $y = x - 3 \quad y = 2x + 1$

$x - 3 = 2x + 1 \qquad y = (-4) - 3$

$-x = 4 \qquad\qquad y = -7$

$x = -4$

$(-4, -7)$

3. $y = \frac{1}{2}x + 3 \quad x = 4y + 6$

$y = \frac{1}{2}(4y + 6) + 3 \qquad x = 4(-6) + 6$

$y = 2y + 3 + 3 \qquad\qquad x = -18$

$-y = 6 \quad y = -6$

$(-18, -6)$

5. $3x + 2y = -8 \quad y = -4x + 11$

$3x + 2(-4x + 11) = -8 \qquad y = -4(6) + 11$

$3x - 8x + 22 = -8 \qquad\qquad y = -13$

$-5x = -30$

$x = 6$

$(6, -13)$

7. $x + y = 13 \quad x = -(y - 13)$

$-(y - 13) + y = 13$

$-y + 13 + y = 13$

$13 = 13$

This is a true statement for all values of x.
Infinitely many solutions.

9. $7y = 21 - 14x \quad -5y = 20x$

$y = -4x$

$7(-4x) = 21 - 14x \qquad -5y = 20\left(-\frac{3}{2}\right)$

$-28x = 21 - 14x \qquad -5y = -30$

$-14x = 21 \qquad\qquad y = 6$

$x = -\frac{3}{2}$

$\left(-\frac{3}{2}, 6\right)$

11. $10a - b = 5 \quad 10a + 3b = -7$

$b = 10a - 5 \qquad\qquad 10\left(\frac{1}{5}\right) - b = 5$

$10a + 3(10a - 5) = -7 \qquad 2 - b = 5$

$10a + 30a - 15 = -7 \qquad -b = 3$

$40a = 8 \qquad\qquad b = -3$

$a = \frac{1}{5}$

$a = \frac{1}{5}, \ b = -3$

13. $x - 5y = -1 \quad 7x - y = 10$

$x = 5y - 1 \qquad\qquad x - 5\left(\frac{1}{2}\right) = -1$

$7(5y - 1) - y = 10$

$35y - 7 - y = 10 \qquad x - \frac{5}{2} = -\frac{2}{2}$

$34y = 17$

$y = \frac{1}{2} \qquad\qquad x = \frac{3}{2}$

$\left(\frac{3}{2}, \frac{1}{2}\right)$

15. $2x + 12 = -2y \quad x + y = 6$

$x = -y + 6$

$2(-y + 6) + 12 = -2y$

$-2y + 12 + 12 = -2y$

$24 = 0$ False

No solution.

17. $8s - 4t = 36$ $3s + 5t = 20$

$-4t = -8s + 36$

$t = 2s - 9$ $3(5) + 5t = 20$

$3s + 5(2s - 9) = 20$ $15 + 5t = 20$

$3s + 10s - 45 = 20$ $5t = 5$

$13s = 65$ $t = 1$

$s = 5$

$s = 5, \ t = 1$

19. $6x - 9y - 27 = 0$ $10x - 12y - 29 = 0$

$6x = 9y + 27$

$x = \dfrac{3}{2}y + \dfrac{9}{2}$

$10\left(\dfrac{3}{2}y + \dfrac{9}{2}\right) - 12y - 29 = 0$ $\quad 6x - 9\left(-\dfrac{16}{3}\right) - 27 = 0$

$15y + 45 - 12y - 29 = 0$ $\qquad 6x + 48 - 27 = 0$

$3y + 16 = 0$ $\qquad\qquad\quad 6x + 21 = 0$

$3y = -16$ $\qquad\qquad\quad 6x = -21$

$y = -\dfrac{16}{3}$ $\qquad\qquad x = -\dfrac{7}{2}$

$\left(-\dfrac{7}{2}, -\dfrac{16}{3}\right)$

21. $x + y = 3$

$\dfrac{x - y = 5}{2x \quad\ \ = 8}$

$x = 4$

$4 + y = 3$

$y = -1$

$(4, -1)$

23. $-3x + 2y = -2$

$\dfrac{3x - 3y = 1}{\quad -y = -1}$

$y = 1$

$3x - 3(1) = 1$

$3x = 4$

$x = \dfrac{4}{3}$

$\left(\dfrac{4}{3}, 1\right)$

25. $2x - 5y = 7$ $\qquad\qquad 2x - 5y = 7$

$6x - 5y = -3 \xrightarrow{\times(-1)} \dfrac{-6x + 5y = 3}{-4x \quad\ \ = 10}$

$x = -\dfrac{5}{2}$

$2\left(-\dfrac{5}{2}\right) - 5y = 7$

$-5 - 5y = 7$

$-5y = 12$

$y = -\dfrac{12}{5}$

$\left(-\dfrac{5}{2}, -\dfrac{12}{5}\right)$

27. $7c + 3d = 0$ $\qquad\qquad 7c + 3d = 0$

$7c - 9d = 0 \xrightarrow{\times(-1)} \dfrac{-7c + 9d = 0}{12d = 0}$

$d = 0$

$7c + 3(0) = 0$

$7c = 0$

$c = 0$

$c = 0, \ d = 0$

29. $3x - 6y = -10 \xrightarrow{\times(-2)} -6x + 12y = 20$

$6x - 12y = -20 \qquad\qquad \dfrac{6x - 12y = -20}{0 = 0}$

Infinitely many solutions.

31. $\dfrac{1}{8}x - \dfrac{3}{5}y = -7$ $\qquad \dfrac{1}{8}x - \dfrac{3}{5}y = -7$

$\dfrac{1}{2}x + \dfrac{1}{5}y = -2 \xrightarrow{\times 3} \dfrac{\dfrac{3}{2}x + \dfrac{3}{5}y = -6}{\dfrac{1}{8}x + \dfrac{3}{2}x = -13}$

$\dfrac{1}{8}x + \dfrac{12}{8}x = -13$

$\dfrac{13}{8}x = -13$

$x = -13\left(\dfrac{8}{13}\right) = -8$

$\dfrac{1}{8}(-8) - \dfrac{3}{5}y = -7$

$-1 - \dfrac{3}{5}y = -7$

$-\dfrac{3}{5}y = -6$

$y = -6\left(-\dfrac{5}{3}\right) = 10$

$(-8, 10)$

33. $9x - 13 = 7y + 11x$

$-2x - 7y = 13 \xrightarrow{\times 2} -4x - 14y = 26$

$4x + 8y = -17 \qquad\qquad \dfrac{4x + 8y = -17}{-6y = 9}$

$y = -\dfrac{3}{2}$

$$-2x - 7\left(-\frac{3}{2}\right) = 13$$

$$-2x + \frac{21}{2} = \frac{26}{2}$$

$$-2x = \frac{5}{2}$$

$$x = \frac{5}{2}\left(-\frac{1}{2}\right) = -\frac{5}{4}$$

$$\left(-\frac{5}{4}, -\frac{3}{2}\right)$$

35. $2x + 3y = 6y - 4$

$2x - 3y = -4$

$-\dfrac{1}{2}(4x - 6y) = 7$

$-2x + 3y = 7$

$\underline{2x - 3y = -4}$

$\qquad 0 = -3$ False

No solution.

37. $3x + 4y = 1 \xrightarrow{\times 3} 9x + 12y = 3$

$2x - 3y = 12 \xrightarrow{\times 4} \underline{8x - 12y = 48}$

$\qquad\qquad\quad 17x \qquad = 51$

$x = 3$

$3(3) + 4y = 1$

$9 + 4y = 1$

$4y = -8$

$y = -2$

$(3, -2)$

39. $5x + 2y = 11 \xrightarrow{\times 4} 20x + 8y = 44$

$4x + 7y = -2 \xrightarrow{\times(-5)} \underline{-20x - 35y = 10}$

$\qquad\qquad\qquad\qquad -27y = 54$

$y = -2$

$5x + 2(-2) = 11$

$5x - 4 = 11$

$5x = 15$

$x = 3$

$(3, -2)$

41. $16x + 12y = -2 \xrightarrow{\times 3} 48x + 36y = -6$

$12x + 9y = -1.5 \xrightarrow{\times(-4)} \underline{-48x - 36y = 6}$

$\qquad\qquad\qquad\qquad\qquad 0 = 0$

Infinitely many solutions.

43. $2.5a - 1.25b = -4 \xrightarrow{\times 3} 7.5a - 3.75b = -12$

$-3a - 0.2b = -2 \xrightarrow{\times 2.5} \underline{-7.5a - 0.5b = -5}$

$\qquad\qquad\qquad\qquad\qquad -4.25b = -17$

$b = 4$

$-3a - 0.2(4) = -2$

$-3a - 0.8 = -2$

$-3a = -1.2$

$a = 0.4$

$a = 0.4, \ b = 4$

45.   a. Let C be the total cost of the tow and d be the days stored.

$C = 25d + 60$

$C = 20d + 75$

b. $25d + 60 = 20d + 75$

$5d = 15$

$d = 3$

   The companies charge the same for 3 days of storage.

47.   Let l be the length of the garden and w be the width of the garden. The perimeter is twice the width plus twice the length.

$w = l - 4$

$2l + 2w = 52$

$2l + 2(l - 4) = 52$

$2l + 2l - 8 = 52$

$4l = 60$

$l = 15$

$w = 15 - 4 = 11$

The length of the garden is 15 ft and the width is 11 ft.

49.   Let x be the speed of the boat in still water and y be the speed of the current in the Wailua River.

a. $x - y = 18$

$\quad x + y = 22$

b. $x - y = 18$

$\quad \underline{x + y = 22}$

$\quad 2x \quad\ = 40$

$\quad x = 20$

$\quad 20 + y = 22$

$\quad y = 2$

The speed of the boat is 20 mph and the speed of the current is 2 mph.

51.   Let s be the number of 12-oz cups sold and l be the number of 20-oz cups sold.

$s + l = 508$

$3s = l$

$s + 3s = 508$

$4s = 508$

$s = 127; \quad 3(127) = 381$

127 12-oz cups of coffee were sold and 381 20-oz cups were sold.

53. Let s be the number of small storage lockers and l be the number of large storage lockers.

$$s+l=54 \xrightarrow{\times(-200)} -200s-200l=-10800$$

$$200s+800l=22800 \quad \underline{200s+800l=22800}$$

$$600l=12000$$

$$l=20$$

The facility has 20 large storage lockers.

55. Let l represent the money invested in the low-risk fund and h represent the money invested in the high-risk fund.

$$2l=h$$

$$0.06l-0.09h=-210$$

$$0.06l-0.09(2l)=-210$$

$$0.06l-0.18l=-210$$

$$-0.12l=-210$$

$$l=1750$$

$$2(1750)=h$$

$$3500=h$$

$$h=3500$$

$1,750 was invested in the low-risk fund and $3,500 was invested in the high-risk fund.

57. Let h represent the number of liters of the higher concentration 65% alcohol solution and l represent the number of liters of the 25% solution.

Action	Percent of Alcohol	Amount of Solution (L)	Amount of Alcohol (L)
First	25%	l	$0.25l$
Second	65%	h	$0.65h$
Finish	40%	10	$0.40(10)$

$$h+l=10$$

$$0.65h+0.25l=0.40(10)$$

$$0.65h+0.25l=4 \xrightarrow{\times(-4)} -2.6h-l=-16$$

$$h+l=10 \qquad \underline{h+l=10}$$

$$-1.6h=-6$$

$$h=3.75$$

$$l+3.75=10$$

$$l=6.25$$

She must combine 3.75 L of the 65% solution with 6.25 L of the 25% solution.

Exercises 4.3 Solving Systems of Linear Equations in Three Variables

1. $(2)+(-3)-(5)\overset{?}{=}-6$

$-1-5\overset{?}{=}-6$ $\qquad -6=-6$ True

$2(2)-(-3)+(5)\overset{?}{=}12$

$4+3+5\overset{?}{=}12$ $\qquad 12=12$ True

$-3(2)-2(-3)-4(5)\overset{?}{=}-20$

$-6+6-20\overset{?}{=}-20$ $\qquad -20=-20$ True

A solution.

3. $2(-2)-2\left(-\dfrac{1}{2}\right)-4(-1)\overset{?}{=}1$

$-4+1+4\overset{?}{=}1$ $\qquad 1=1$ True

$5(-2)-8\left(\dfrac{-1}{2}\right)+3(-1)\overset{?}{=}9$

$-10+4-3\overset{?}{=}9$ $\qquad -9=9$ False

$-(-2)+6\left(-\dfrac{1}{2}\right)+5(-1)\overset{?}{=}-8$

$2-3-5\overset{?}{=}-8$ $\qquad -6=-8$ False

Not a solution.

5. $\dfrac{3}{5}(20)-\dfrac{1}{4}(8)\overset{?}{=}10$

$12-2\overset{?}{=}10$ $\qquad 10=10$ True

$\dfrac{3}{20}(20)+2(7)\overset{?}{=}17$

$3+14\overset{?}{=}17$ $\qquad 17=17$ True

$-9(8)+10(7)\overset{?}{=}-2$

$-72+70\overset{?}{=}-2$ $\qquad -2=-2$ True

A solution.

7. $2x=8$

$x=4$

$(4)-4z=12$

$-4z=8$

$z=-2$

$3(4)-2y+(-2)=0$

$12-2y-2=0$

$-2y=-10$

$y=5$

$(4,5,-2)$

9. $x+y+z=-1$

$\underline{2x-y-z=-5}$

$3x\qquad=-6$

$x=-2$

$-2+y+z=-1\longrightarrow y+z=1$

$-2+2y-z=6\longrightarrow \underline{2y-z=8}$

$3y\qquad=9$

$y=3$

$-2+3+z=-1$

$1+z=-1$

$z=-2$

$(-2,3,-2)$

11. $3x-y+5z=-20\xrightarrow{\times4}12x-4y+20z=-80$

$2x+4y-2z=15\longrightarrow\underline{2x+4y-2z=15}$

$14x+18z=-65$

$2x+4y-2z=15\longrightarrow2x+4y-2z=15$

$-4x-2y-z=-1\xrightarrow{\times2}\underline{-8x-4y-2z=-2}$

$-6x-4z=13$

$14x+18z=-65\xrightarrow{\times2}28x+36z=-130$

$-6x-4z=13\xrightarrow{\times9}\underline{-54x-36z=117}$

$-26x=-13$

$x=\dfrac{1}{2}$

$-6\left(\dfrac{1}{2}\right)-4z=13$

$-3-4z=13$

$-4z=16$

$z=-4$

$2\left(\dfrac{1}{2}\right)+4y-2(-4)=15$

$1+4y+8=15$

$4y=6$

$y=\dfrac{3}{2}$

$\left(\dfrac{1}{2},\dfrac{3}{2},-4\right)$

13. $-2x+6y-3z=0\longrightarrow-2x+6y-3z=0$

$x-y+z=2\xrightarrow{\times2}\underline{2x-2y+2z=4}$

$4y-z=4$

$-2x+6y-3z=0$

$\underline{2x-5y-z=1}$

$y-4z=1$

$y-4z=1\longrightarrowy-4z=1$

$4y-z=4\xrightarrow{\times(-4)}\underline{-16y+4z=-16}$

$-15y=-15$

$y=1\quad4(1)-z=4\quad x-(1)+0=2$

$z=0x=3$

$(3,1,0)$

15. $8y+3z=3\xrightarrow{\times(-2)}-16y-6z=-6$

$10x+6z=4\longrightarrow\underline{10x+6z=4}$

$10x-16y=-2$

$5x+4y=2\xrightarrow{\times4}20x+16y=8$

$10x-16y=-2\longrightarrow\underline{10x-16y=-2}$

$30x=6$

$x=\dfrac{1}{5}$

$5\left(\dfrac{1}{5}\right)+4y=2\quad8\left(\dfrac{1}{4}\right)+3z=3$

$1+4y=22+3z=3$

$4y=13z=1$

$y=\dfrac{1}{4}z=\dfrac{1}{3}$

$\left(\dfrac{1}{5},\dfrac{1}{4},\dfrac{1}{3}\right)$

17. $\dfrac{2}{3}x-\dfrac{1}{2}y=1\xrightarrow{\times6}4x-3y=6$

$\dfrac{1}{4}y+\dfrac{1}{3}z=2\xrightarrow{\times12}3y+4z=24$

$\dfrac{1}{3}x-\dfrac{1}{2}z=-5\xrightarrow{\times6}2x-3z=-30$

$4x-3y=6\longrightarrow4x-3y=6$

$2x-3z=-30\xrightarrow{\times(-2)}\underline{-4x+6z=60}$

$-3y+6z=66$

$3y+4z=24$

$\underline{-3y+6z=66}$

$10z=90$

$z=9$

$3y+4(9)=244x-3(-4)=6$

$3y+36=244x+12=6$

$3y=-124x=-6$

$y=-4x=-\dfrac{3}{2}$

$\left(-\dfrac{3}{2},-4,9\right)$

19. $x+4y-2z=6$

$\underline{2x+3y+2z=7}$

$3x+7y=13$

$x+4y-2z=6\xrightarrow{\times2}2x+8y-4z=12$

$x-y+4z=1\longrightarrow\underline{x-y+4z=1}$

$3x+7y=13$

$3x+7y=13\longrightarrow3x+7y=13$

$3x+7y=13\xrightarrow{\times(-1)}\underline{-3x-7y=-13}$

$0=0$

Infinitely many solutions.

21.
$$4x+3y-2z=-7 \xrightarrow{\times 2} 8x+6y-4z=-14$$
$$5x-3y+4z=24 \longrightarrow \underline{5x-3y+4z=24}$$
$$13x+3y =10$$

$$4x+3y-2z=-7 \longrightarrow 4x+3y-2z=-7$$
$$8x+2y+z=10 \xrightarrow{\times 2} \underline{16x+4y+2z=20}$$
$$20x+7y =13$$

$$20x+7y=13 \xrightarrow{\times 3} 60x+21y=39$$
$$13x+3y=10 \xrightarrow{\times(-7)} \underline{-91x-21y=-70}$$
$$-31x =-31$$

$$x=1$$
$$20(1)+7y=13 \qquad 4(1)+3(-1)-2z=-7$$
$$7y=-7 \qquad\qquad 1-2z=-7$$
$$y=-1 \qquad\qquad -2z=-8$$
$$\qquad\qquad\qquad z=4$$

$$(1,-1,4)$$

23.
$$4x-y+8z=-2 \longrightarrow 4x-y+8z=-2$$
$$x+2y+4z=3 \xrightarrow{\times(-2)} \underline{-2x-4y-8z=-6}$$
$$2x-5y =-8$$

$$2x-5y=-8 \longrightarrow 2x-5y=-8$$
$$2x-5y=1 \xrightarrow{\times(-1)} \underline{-2x+5y=-1}$$
$$0=-9 \text{ False}$$

No solution.

25.
$$7x-6y+3z=13 \xrightarrow{\times 2} 14x-12y+6z=26$$
$$2x+3y+2z=-2 \xrightarrow{\times-7} \underline{-14x-21y-14z=14}$$
$$-33y-8z=40$$

$$2x+3y+2z=-2 \xrightarrow{\times(-3)} -6x-9y-6z=6$$
$$6x-5y+7z=-11 \longrightarrow \underline{6x-5y+7z=-11}$$
$$-14y+z=-5$$

$$-33y-8z=40 \longrightarrow -33y-8z=40$$
$$-14y+z=-5 \xrightarrow{\times 8} \underline{-112y+8z=-40}$$
$$-145y =0$$

$$y=0$$
$$-14(0)+z=-5 \qquad 7x-6(0)+3(-5)=13$$
$$z=-5 \qquad\qquad 7x-15=13$$
$$\qquad\qquad\qquad 7x=28$$
$$\qquad\qquad\qquad x=4$$

$$(4,0,-5)$$

27. Let b be the number of beef dinners, c be the number of chicken dinners and f be the number of fish dinners.
$$50b+42c+48f=8988$$
$$b=2f$$

$$b+c+f=192$$
$$50(2f)+42c+48f=8988$$
$$148f+42c=8988$$
$$(2f)+c+f=192$$
$$3f+c=192 \xrightarrow{\times(-42)} -126f-42c=-8064$$
$$148f+42c=8988 \longrightarrow \underline{148f+42c=8988}$$
$$22f =924$$

$$f=42$$
$$b=2(42) \qquad 84+c+42=192$$
$$b=84 \qquad\quad c+126=192$$
$$\qquad\qquad\qquad c=66$$

84 beef dinners, 66 chicken dinners and 42 fish dinners were ordered.

29. Let l be the length of the package, w be the width and h be the height of the package.
$$l+w+h=65$$
$$h=w-5$$
$$2l=3w$$
$$l=\frac{3}{2}w$$

$$\frac{3}{2}w+(w-5)+w=65 \qquad l=\frac{3}{2}(20)=30$$
$$\frac{3}{2}w+2w-5=65 \qquad 30+20+h=65$$
$$\frac{7}{2}w=70 \qquad\qquad h=15$$
$$w=70\left(\frac{2}{7}\right)$$
$$w=20$$

$$l+2w+2h=30+2(20)+2(15)=$$
$$30+40+30=100 \quad 100<130$$
The combined length and girth is 100 in which is less than 130 in. The package does meet the parcel post restrictions.

31. Let n be the thickness of a nickel, d be the thickness of a dime and q be the thickness of a quarter.
$$n+d+q=5.05$$
$$4n+2q+2d=14$$
$$n=d+0.6$$
$$(d+0.6)+d+q=5.05$$
$$2d+q=4.45$$
$$4(d+0.6)+2q+2d=14$$
$$4d+2.4+2q+2d=14$$

$$6d + 2q = 11.6 \longrightarrow \quad 6d + 2q = 11.6$$

$$2d + q = 4.45 \xrightarrow{\times(-2)} -4d - 2q = -8.90$$

$$2d \quad\quad = 2.70$$

$$d = 1.35$$

$$n = 1.35 + 0.6 \quad\quad 1.95 + 1.25 + q = 5.05$$

$$n = 1.95 \quad\quad\quad 3.20 + q = 5.05$$

$$q = 1.85$$

The thickness of a nickel is 1.95 mm, of a dime 1.35 mm, and of a quarter is 1.75 mm.

33. Let x be the number of par-3 holes, y be the number of par-4 holes, and z be the number of par-5 holes on the golf course.

$$x + y + z = 18$$

$$3x + 4y + 5z = 72$$

$$y - 6 = z$$

$$x + y + y - 6 = 18$$

$$x + 2y = 24$$

$$3x + 4y + 5(y - 6) = 72$$

$$3x + 4y + 5y - 30 = 72$$

$$3x + 9y = 102 \longrightarrow 3x + 9y = 102$$

$$x + 2y = 24 \xrightarrow{\times(-3)} -3x - 6y = -72$$

$$3y = 30$$

$$y = 10 \quad 10 - 6 = z \quad x + 10 + 4 = 18$$

$$z = 4 \quad\quad x = 4$$

There are 4 par-3 holes, 10 par-4 holes, and 4 par-5 holes on the course.

35. Let x be the amount invested at 8.5%, y be the amount invested at 6%, and z be the amount invested at 5%.

$$x + y + z = 15000$$

$$2z = x$$

$$0.085x + 0.06y + 0.05z = 1040$$

$$2z + y + z = 15000$$

$$y + 3z = 15000$$

$$x + y + z = 15000 \xrightarrow{\times -0.085}$$

$$-0.085x - 0.085y - 0.085z = -1275$$

$$\underline{0.085x + 0.06y + 0.05z = 1040}$$

$$-0.025y - 0.035z = -235$$

$$y + 3z = 15000 \xrightarrow{\times 0.025} 0.025y + 0.075z = 375$$

$$\underline{-0.025y - 0.035z = -235}$$

$$0.04z = 140$$

$$z = 3500$$

$$y + 3z = 15000 \quad\quad 2z = x$$

$$y + 3(3500) = 15000 \quad\quad 2(3500) = x$$

$$y + 10500 = 15000 \quad\quad x = 7000$$

$$y = 4500$$

She invested \$7000 in the account earning 8.5% interest, \$4500 in the account earning 6% interest and \$3500 in the account earning 5% interest.

Exercises 4.4 Solving Systems of Linear Equations by Using Matrices

1. $\begin{bmatrix} 1 & -7 & | & 12 \\ 1 & -4 & | & 6 \end{bmatrix}$ Add $(-1)\times$ row 1 to row 2

$$\begin{bmatrix} 1 & -7 & | & 12 \\ 1 + (-1)(1) & -4 + (-1)(-7) & | & 6 + (-1)(12) \end{bmatrix}$$

$$\begin{bmatrix} 1 & -7 & | & 12 \\ 0 & 3 & | & -6 \end{bmatrix} \text{Multiply row 2 by } \left(\frac{1}{3}\right)$$

$$\begin{bmatrix} 1 & -7 & | & 12 \\ 0 & 3\left(\frac{1}{3}\right) & | & -6\left(\frac{1}{3}\right) \end{bmatrix}$$

$$\begin{bmatrix} 1 & -7 & | & 12 \\ 0 & 1 & | & -2 \end{bmatrix}$$

$$y = -2$$

$$x - 7y = 12$$

$$x - 7(-2) = 12$$

$$x + 14 = 12$$

$$x = -2$$

$$(-2, -2)$$

3. $\begin{bmatrix} 3 & 4 & | & -1 \\ 2 & 3 & | & -1 \end{bmatrix}$ Add $(-1)\times$ row 2 to row 1

$$\begin{bmatrix} 3 + (-1)(2) & 4 + (-1)(3) & | & -1 + (-1)(-1) \\ 2 & 3 & | & -1 \end{bmatrix}$$

$$\begin{bmatrix} 1 & 1 & | & 0 \\ 2 & 3 & | & -1 \end{bmatrix} \text{Add } (-2)\times \text{ row 1 to row 2}$$

$$\begin{bmatrix} 1 & 1 & | & 0 \\ 2 + (-2)(1) & 3 + (-2)(1) & | & -1 + (-2)(0) \end{bmatrix}$$

$$\begin{bmatrix} 1 & 1 & | & 0 \\ 0 & 1 & | & -1 \end{bmatrix}$$

$$y = -1$$

$$x + y = 0$$

$$x + (-1) = 0$$

$$x = 1$$

$$(1, -1)$$

5. $\begin{bmatrix} 9 & -15 & | & 12 \\ -3 & 5 & | & -4 \end{bmatrix}$ Multiply row 1 by $\left(\frac{1}{9}\right)$

$$\begin{bmatrix} 9\left(\dfrac{1}{9}\right) & -15\left(\dfrac{1}{9}\right) & \Big| & 12\left(\dfrac{1}{9}\right) \\ -3 & 5 & \Big| & -4 \end{bmatrix}$$

$$\begin{bmatrix} 1 & -\dfrac{5}{3} & \Big| & \dfrac{4}{3} \\ -3 & 5 & \Big| & -4 \end{bmatrix} \text{ Add } 3\times \text{ row 1 to row 2}$$

$$\begin{bmatrix} 1 & -\dfrac{5}{3} & \Big| & \dfrac{4}{3} \\ -3+3(1) & 5+3\left(-\dfrac{5}{3}\right) & \Big| & -4+3\left(\dfrac{4}{3}\right) \end{bmatrix}$$

$$\begin{bmatrix} 1 & -\dfrac{5}{3} & \Big| & \dfrac{4}{3} \\ 0 & 0 & \Big| & 0 \end{bmatrix}$$

$$x - \dfrac{5}{3}y = \dfrac{4}{3}$$

The solution is a linear equation. There are infinitely many solutions.

7. $$\begin{bmatrix} \dfrac{1}{2} & -\dfrac{1}{3} & \Big| & -7 \\ 3 & 5 & \Big| & 21 \end{bmatrix} \text{ multiply row 1 by 2}$$

$$\begin{bmatrix} \dfrac{1}{2}(2) & -\dfrac{1}{3}(2) & \Big| & -7(2) \\ 3 & 5 & \Big| & 21 \end{bmatrix}$$

7. (cont)

$$\begin{bmatrix} 1 & -\dfrac{2}{3} & \Big| & -14 \\ 3 & 5 & \Big| & 21 \end{bmatrix} \text{ add } (-3)\times \text{ row 1 to row 2}$$

$$\begin{bmatrix} 1 & -\dfrac{2}{3} & \Big| & -14 \\ 3+(-3)(1) & 5+(-3)\left(-\dfrac{2}{3}\right) & \Big| & 21+(-3)(-14) \end{bmatrix}$$

$$\begin{bmatrix} 1 & -\dfrac{2}{3} & \Big| & -14 \\ 0 & 7 & \Big| & 63 \end{bmatrix} \text{ Multiply row 2 by } \left(\dfrac{1}{7}\right)$$

$$\begin{bmatrix} 1 & -\dfrac{2}{3} & \Big| & -14 \\ 0 & 7\left(\dfrac{1}{7}\right) & \Big| & 63\left(\dfrac{1}{7}\right) \end{bmatrix}$$

$$\begin{bmatrix} 1 & -\dfrac{2}{3} & \Big| & -14 \\ 0 & 1 & \Big| & 9 \end{bmatrix}$$

$$y = 9$$

$$x - \dfrac{2}{3}y = -14$$

$$x - \dfrac{2}{3}(9) = -14$$

$$x = -14 + 6$$

$$x = -8$$

$$(-8, 9)$$

9. $$\begin{bmatrix} 1 & 3 & -2 & \Big| & 10 \\ 3 & -2 & -1 & \Big| & 9 \\ 4 & -1 & 5 & \Big| & 1 \end{bmatrix} \text{ add } (-3)\times \text{ row 1 to row 2} \rightarrow \begin{bmatrix} 1 & 3 & -2 & \Big| & 10 \\ 3+(-3)(1) & -2+(-3)(3) & -1+(-3)(-2) & \Big| & 9+(-3)(10) \\ 4 & -1 & 5 & \Big| & 1 \end{bmatrix}$$

$$\begin{bmatrix} 1 & 3 & -2 & \Big| & 10 \\ 0 & -11 & 5 & \Big| & -21 \\ 4 & -1 & 5 & \Big| & 1 \end{bmatrix} \text{ add } (-4)\times \text{ row 1 to row 3} \rightarrow \begin{bmatrix} 1 & 3 & -2 & \Big| & 10 \\ 0 & -11 & 5 & \Big| & -21 \\ 4+(-4)(1) & -1+(-4)(3) & 5+(-4)(-2) & \Big| & 1+(-4)(10) \end{bmatrix}$$

$$\begin{bmatrix} 1 & 3 & -2 & \Big| & 10 \\ 0 & -11 & 5 & \Big| & -21 \\ 0 & -13 & 13 & \Big| & -39 \end{bmatrix} \begin{array}{l} \text{Multiply row 3 by } \left(-\dfrac{1}{13}\right) \\ \text{and interchange it with row 2} \end{array} \rightarrow \begin{bmatrix} 1 & 3 & -2 & \Big| & 10 \\ 0 & -13\left(-\dfrac{1}{13}\right) & 13\left(-\dfrac{1}{13}\right) & \Big| & -39\left(-\dfrac{1}{13}\right) \\ 0 & -11 & 5 & \Big| & -21 \end{bmatrix}$$

$$\begin{bmatrix} 1 & 3 & -2 & | & 10 \\ 0 & 1 & -1 & | & 3 \\ 0 & -11 & 5 & | & -21 \end{bmatrix} \text{ Add 11} \times \text{ row 2 and add to row 3} \rightarrow \begin{bmatrix} 1 & 3 & -2 & | & 10 \\ 0 & 1 & -1 & | & 3 \\ 0 & -11+(11)(1) & 5+(11)(-1) & | & -21+(11)(3) \end{bmatrix}$$

$$\begin{bmatrix} 1 & 3 & -2 & | & 10 \\ 0 & 1 & -1 & | & 3 \\ 0 & 0 & -6 & | & 12 \end{bmatrix} \text{ Multiply row 3 by } \left(-\frac{1}{6}\right) \rightarrow \begin{bmatrix} 1 & 3 & -2 & | & 10 \\ 0 & 1 & -1 & | & 3 \\ 0 & 0 & -6\left(-\frac{1}{6}\right) & | & 12\left(-\frac{1}{6}\right) \end{bmatrix}$$

$$\begin{bmatrix} 1 & 3 & -2 & | & 10 \\ 0 & 1 & -1 & | & 3 \\ 0 & 0 & 1 & | & -2 \end{bmatrix}$$

$z = -2$

$y - z = 3$ $x + 3y - 2z = 10$

$y - (-2) = 3$ $x + 3(1) - 2(-2) = 10$

$y = 1$ $x + 3 + 4 = 10$

                    $x = 3$

$(3, 1, -2)$

11.

$$\begin{bmatrix} 6 & -4 & -3 & | & -4 \\ 2 & 8 & -7 & | & -11 \\ -1 & 2 & 1 & | & 2 \end{bmatrix} \begin{array}{c} \text{Multiply row 3 by} \\ (-1) \text{ and interchange} \\ \text{it with row 1} \end{array} \rightarrow \begin{bmatrix} -1(-1) & 2(-1) & 1(-1) & | & 2(-1) \\ 2 & 8 & -7 & | & -11 \\ 6 & -4 & -3 & | & -4 \end{bmatrix}$$

$$\begin{bmatrix} 1 & -2 & -1 & | & -2 \\ 2 & 8 & -7 & | & -11 \\ 6 & -4 & -3 & | & -4 \end{bmatrix} \begin{array}{c} \text{add row 1} \\ \times (-2) \text{ to row 2} \end{array} \rightarrow \begin{bmatrix} 1 & -2 & -1 & | & -2 \\ 2+(-2)(1) & 8+(-2)(-2) & -7+(-2)(-1) & | & -11+(-2)(-2) \\ 6 & -4 & -3 & | & -4 \end{bmatrix}$$

$$\begin{bmatrix} 1 & -2 & -1 & | & -2 \\ 0 & 12 & -5 & | & -7 \\ 6 & -4 & -3 & | & -4 \end{bmatrix} \text{ add row 1} \times (-6) \text{ to row 3} \rightarrow \begin{bmatrix} 1 & -2 & -1 & | & -2 \\ 0 & 12 & -5 & | & -7 \\ 6+(-6)(1) & -4+(-6)(-2) & -3+(-6)(-1) & | & -4+(-6)(-2) \end{bmatrix}$$

$$\begin{bmatrix} 1 & -2 & -1 & | & -2 \\ 0 & 12 & -5 & | & -7 \\ 0 & 8 & 3 & | & 8 \end{bmatrix} \text{ Multiply row 2 by } \left(\frac{1}{12}\right) \rightarrow \begin{bmatrix} 1 & -2 & -1 & | & -2 \\ 0 & 12\left(\frac{1}{12}\right) & -5\left(\frac{1}{12}\right) & | & -7\left(\frac{1}{12}\right) \\ 0 & 8 & 3 & | & 8 \end{bmatrix}$$

$$\begin{bmatrix} 1 & -2 & -1 & | & -2 \\ 0 & 1 & -\frac{5}{12} & | & -\frac{7}{12} \\ 0 & 8 & 3 & | & 8 \end{bmatrix} \text{ add } -8 \times \text{ row 2 to row 3} \rightarrow \begin{bmatrix} 1 & -2 & -1 & | & -2 \\ 0 & 1 & -\frac{5}{12} & | & -\frac{7}{12} \\ 0 & 8+(-8)(1) & 3+(-8)\left(-\frac{5}{12}\right) & | & 8+(-8)-\frac{7}{12} \end{bmatrix}$$

$$\begin{bmatrix} 1 & -2 & -1 & | & -2 \\ 0 & 1 & -\frac{5}{12} & | & -\frac{7}{12} \\ 0 & 0 & \frac{19}{3} & | & \frac{38}{3} \end{bmatrix} \text{ Multiply row 3 by } \frac{3}{19} \rightarrow \begin{bmatrix} 1 & -2 & -1 & | & -2 \\ 0 & 1 & -\frac{5}{12} & | & -\frac{7}{12} \\ 0 & 0 & \frac{19}{3}\left(\frac{3}{19}\right) & | & \frac{38}{3}\left(\frac{3}{19}\right) \end{bmatrix} \rightarrow \begin{bmatrix} 1 & -2 & -1 & | & -2 \\ 0 & 1 & -\frac{5}{12} & | & -\frac{7}{12} \\ 0 & 0 & 1 & | & 2 \end{bmatrix}$$

$$z = 2$$

$$y - \frac{5}{12}z = -\frac{7}{12} \qquad x - 2y - z = -2$$

$$y - \frac{5}{12}(2) = -\frac{7}{12} \qquad x - 2\left(\frac{1}{4}\right) - 1(2) = -2$$

$$y - \frac{10}{12} = -\frac{7}{12} \qquad x - \frac{1}{2} - 2 = -2$$

$$y = \frac{3}{12} \qquad x - \frac{5}{2} = -2$$

$$y = \frac{1}{4} \qquad x = \frac{1}{2} \qquad \left(\frac{1}{2}, \frac{1}{4}, 2\right)$$

13.
$$\begin{bmatrix} 5 & 7 & 3 & | & -48 \\ -8 & 2 & 4 & | & 24 \\ 12 & -6 & -9 & | & -21 \end{bmatrix} \text{Multiply row 2 by } \frac{1}{2} \rightarrow \begin{bmatrix} 5 & 7 & 3 & | & -48 \\ -8\left(\frac{1}{2}\right) & 2\left(\frac{1}{2}\right) & 4\left(\frac{1}{2}\right) & | & 24\left(\frac{1}{2}\right) \\ 12\left(\frac{1}{3}\right) & -6\left(\frac{1}{3}\right) & -9\left(\frac{1}{3}\right) & | & -21\left(\frac{1}{3}\right) \end{bmatrix} \rightarrow \begin{bmatrix} 5 & 7 & 3 & | & -48 \\ -4 & 1 & 2 & | & 12 \\ 4 & -2 & -3 & | & -7 \end{bmatrix}$$
and row3 by $\left(\frac{1}{3}\right)$

$$\begin{bmatrix} 5 & 7 & 3 & | & -48 \\ -4 & 1 & 2 & | & 12 \\ 4 & -2 & -3 & | & -7 \end{bmatrix} \begin{matrix} \text{add row 2 to} \\ \text{row 1, add} \\ \text{row 2 to row 3} \end{matrix} \rightarrow \begin{bmatrix} 5+(-4) & 7+(1) & 3+(2) & | & -48+(12) \\ -4 & 1 & 2 & | & 12 \\ 4+(-4) & -2+(1) & -3+(2) & | & -7+(12) \end{bmatrix} \rightarrow \begin{bmatrix} 1 & 8 & 5 & | & -36 \\ -4 & 1 & 2 & | & 12 \\ 0 & -1 & -1 & | & 5 \end{bmatrix}$$

$$\begin{bmatrix} 1 & 8 & 5 & | & -36 \\ -4 & 1 & 2 & | & 12 \\ 0 & -1 & -1 & | & 5 \end{bmatrix} \begin{matrix} \text{add 4× row 1} \\ \text{to row 2} \end{matrix} \rightarrow \begin{bmatrix} 1 & 8 & 5 & | & -36 \\ -4+4(1) & 1+4(8) & 2+4(5) & | & 12+4(-36) \\ 0 & -1 & -1 & | & 5 \end{bmatrix} \rightarrow \begin{bmatrix} 1 & 8 & 5 & | & -36 \\ -4 & 1 & 2 & | & 12 \\ 0 & -1 & -1 & | & 5 \end{bmatrix}$$

$$\begin{bmatrix} 1 & 8 & 5 & | & -36 \\ 0 & 33 & 22 & | & -132 \\ 0 & -1 & -1 & | & 5 \end{bmatrix} \begin{matrix} \text{add 33×} \\ \text{row 3 to} \\ \text{row 2} \end{matrix} \rightarrow \begin{bmatrix} 1 & 8 & 5 & | & -36 \\ 0 & 33+33(-1) & 22+33(-1) & | & -132+33(5) \\ 0 & -1 & -1 & | & 5 \end{bmatrix} \rightarrow \begin{bmatrix} 1 & 8 & 5 & | & -36 \\ 0 & 0 & -11 & | & 33 \\ 0 & -1 & -1 & | & 5 \end{bmatrix}$$

$$\begin{bmatrix} 1 & 8 & 5 & | & -36 \\ 0 & 0 & -11 & | & 33 \\ 0 & -1 & -1 & | & 5 \end{bmatrix} \begin{matrix} \text{Multiply row 3 by} \\ (-1) \text{ and interchange} \\ \text{with row 2} \end{matrix} \rightarrow \begin{bmatrix} 1 & 8 & 5 & | & -36 \\ 0 & -1(-1) & -1(-1) & | & 5(-1) \\ 0 & 0 & -11 & | & 33 \end{bmatrix} \rightarrow \begin{bmatrix} 1 & 8 & 5 & | & -36 \\ 0 & 1 & 1 & | & -5 \\ 0 & 0 & -11 & | & 33 \end{bmatrix}$$

$$\begin{bmatrix} 1 & 8 & 5 & | & -36 \\ 0 & 1 & 1 & | & -5 \\ 0 & 0 & -11 & | & 33 \end{bmatrix} \begin{matrix} \text{Multiply row} \\ \text{3 by } \left(-\frac{1}{11}\right) \end{matrix} \rightarrow \begin{bmatrix} 1 & 8 & 5 & | & -36 \\ 0 & 1 & 1 & | & -5 \\ 0 & 0 & -11\left(-\frac{1}{11}\right) & | & 33\left(-\frac{1}{11}\right) \end{bmatrix} \rightarrow \begin{bmatrix} 1 & 8 & 5 & | & -36 \\ 0 & 1 & 1 & | & -5 \\ 0 & 0 & 1 & | & -3 \end{bmatrix}$$

$$\begin{bmatrix} 1 & 8 & 5 & | & -36 \\ 0 & 1 & 1 & | & -5 \\ 0 & 0 & 1 & | & -3 \end{bmatrix} \qquad \begin{matrix} z = -3 \\ \\ \end{matrix} \quad \begin{matrix} y + z = -5 \\ y + (-3) = -5 \\ y = -2 \end{matrix} \quad \begin{matrix} x + 8y + 5z = -36 \\ x + 8(-2) + 5(-3) = -36 \\ x - 16 - 15 = -36 \\ x = -5 \end{matrix} \qquad (-5, -2, -3)$$

15.
$$\begin{bmatrix} 7 & -1 & 8 & | & -9 \\ 3 & 3 & -10 & | & -5 \\ 3.5 & -0.5 & 4 & | & -14 \end{bmatrix} \begin{matrix} \text{Multiply} \\ \text{row 3 by 2} \end{matrix} \rightarrow \begin{bmatrix} 7 & -1 & 8 & | & -9 \\ 3 & 3 & -10 & | & -5 \\ 7 & -1 & 8 & | & -28 \end{bmatrix}$$

$$\begin{bmatrix} 7 & -1 & 8 & | & -9 \\ 3 & 3 & -10 & | & -5 \\ 7 & -1 & 8 & | & -28 \end{bmatrix} \begin{matrix} \text{add } (-1)\text{row} \\ \times 3 \text{ to row 1} \end{matrix} \rightarrow \begin{bmatrix} 7+(-1)(7) & -1+(-1)(-1) & 8+(-1)(8) & | & -9+(-1)(-28) \\ 3 & 3 & -10 & | & -5 \\ 7 & -1 & 8 & | & -28 \end{bmatrix}$$

$$\begin{bmatrix} 0 & 0 & 0 & | & 19 \\ 3 & 3 & -10 & | & -5 \\ 7 & -1 & 8 & | & -28 \end{bmatrix}$$ The first row implies $0z = 19$, which has no solution.

17. $\begin{bmatrix} 0 & 1 & 5 & | & -15 \\ 4 & -4 & 0 & | & -20 \\ 8 & 0 & -2 & | & 8 \end{bmatrix}$ Multiply row 2 by $\left(\dfrac{1}{4}\right)$ and row 3 by $\left(\dfrac{1}{2}\right)$ $\rightarrow \begin{bmatrix} 0 & 1 & 5 & | & -15 \\ 4\left(\dfrac{1}{4}\right) & -4\left(\dfrac{1}{4}\right) & 0\left(\dfrac{1}{4}\right) & | & -20\left(\dfrac{1}{4}\right) \\ 8\left(\dfrac{1}{2}\right) & 0\left(\dfrac{1}{2}\right) & -2\left(\dfrac{1}{2}\right) & | & 8\left(\dfrac{1}{2}\right) \end{bmatrix} \rightarrow \begin{bmatrix} 0 & 1 & 5 & | & -15 \\ 1 & -1 & 0 & | & -5 \\ 4 & 0 & -1 & | & 4 \end{bmatrix}$

$\begin{bmatrix} 0 & 1 & 5 & | & -15 \\ 1 & -1 & 0 & | & -5 \\ 4 & 0 & -1 & | & 4 \end{bmatrix}$ interchange rows 1 and 2 $\rightarrow \begin{bmatrix} 1 & -1 & 0 & | & -5 \\ 0 & 1 & 5 & | & -15 \\ 4 & 0 & -1 & | & 4 \end{bmatrix}$

$\begin{bmatrix} 1 & -1 & 0 & | & -5 \\ 0 & 1 & 5 & | & -15 \\ 4 & 0 & -1 & | & 4 \end{bmatrix}$ add $-4\times$ row 1 to row 3 $\rightarrow \begin{bmatrix} 1 & -1 & 0 & | & -5 \\ 0 & 1 & 5 & | & -15 \\ 4+(-4)(1) & 0+(-4)(-1) & -1+(-4)(0) & | & 4+(-4)(-5) \end{bmatrix}$

$\begin{bmatrix} 1 & -1 & 0 & | & -5 \\ 0 & 1 & 5 & | & -15 \\ 0 & 4 & -1 & | & 24 \end{bmatrix}$ add $-4\times$ row 2 to row 3 $\rightarrow \begin{bmatrix} 1 & -1 & 0 & | & -5 \\ 0 & 1 & 5 & | & -15 \\ 0 & 4+(-4)(1) & -1+(-4)(5) & | & 24+(-4)(-15) \end{bmatrix} \rightarrow \begin{bmatrix} 1 & -1 & 0 & | & -5 \\ 0 & 1 & 5 & | & -15 \\ 0 & 0 & -21 & | & 84 \end{bmatrix}$

$\begin{bmatrix} 1 & -1 & 0 & | & -5 \\ 0 & 1 & 5 & | & -15 \\ 0 & 0 & -21 & | & 84 \end{bmatrix}$ Multiply row 3 by $\left(-\dfrac{1}{21}\right)$ $\rightarrow \begin{bmatrix} 1 & -1 & 0 & | & -5 \\ 0 & 1 & 5 & | & -15 \\ 0 & 0 & -21\left(-\dfrac{1}{21}\right) & | & 84\left(-\dfrac{1}{21}\right) \end{bmatrix} \rightarrow \begin{bmatrix} 1 & -1 & 0 & | & -5 \\ 0 & 1 & 5 & | & -15 \\ 0 & 0 & 1 & | & -4 \end{bmatrix}$

$\begin{array}{llll} z = -4 & y + 5z = -15 & x - y = -5 \\ & y + 5(-4) = -15 & x - 5 = -5 \\ & y - 20 = -15 & x = 0 \\ & y = 5 \end{array}$

$(0, 5, -4)$

19. $\begin{bmatrix} 2 & 3 & 0 & | & 7 \\ 0 & -11 & -4 & | & -5 \\ 1 & 1 & -6 & | & 0 \end{bmatrix}$ interchange rows 1 and 3 $\rightarrow \begin{bmatrix} 1 & 1 & -6 & | & 0 \\ 0 & -11 & -4 & | & -5 \\ 2 & 3 & 0 & | & 7 \end{bmatrix}$

$\begin{bmatrix} 1 & 1 & -6 & | & 0 \\ 0 & -11 & -4 & | & -5 \\ 2 & 3 & 0 & | & 7 \end{bmatrix}$ Add $(-2)\times$ row 1 to row 3 $\rightarrow \begin{bmatrix} 1 & 1 & -6 & | & 0 \\ 0 & -11 & -4 & | & -5 \\ 2+(-2)(1) & 3+(-2)(1) & 0+(-2)(-6) & | & 7+(-2)(0) \end{bmatrix} \rightarrow \begin{bmatrix} 1 & 1 & -6 & | & 0 \\ 0 & -11 & -4 & | & -5 \\ 0 & 1 & 12 & | & 7 \end{bmatrix}$

$\begin{bmatrix} 1 & 1 & -6 & | & 0 \\ 0 & -11 & -4 & | & -5 \\ 0 & 1 & 12 & | & 7 \end{bmatrix}$ Interchange rows 2 and 3 $\rightarrow \begin{bmatrix} 1 & 1 & -6 & | & 0 \\ 0 & 1 & 12 & | & 7 \\ 0 & -11 & -4 & | & -5 \end{bmatrix}$

$\begin{bmatrix} 1 & 1 & -6 & | & 0 \\ 0 & 1 & 12 & | & 7 \\ 0 & -11 & -4 & | & -5 \end{bmatrix}$ add $(11)\times$ row 2 to row 3 $\rightarrow \begin{bmatrix} 1 & 1 & -6 & | & 0 \\ 0 & 1 & 12 & | & 7 \\ 0 & -11+(11)(1) & -4+(11)(12) & | & -5+(11)(7) \end{bmatrix} \rightarrow \begin{bmatrix} 1 & 1 & -6 & | & 0 \\ 0 & 1 & 12 & | & 7 \\ 0 & 0 & 128 & | & 72 \end{bmatrix}$

$$\begin{bmatrix} 1 & 1 & -6 & | & 0 \\ 0 & 1 & 12 & | & 7 \\ 0 & 0 & 128 & | & 72 \end{bmatrix} \begin{matrix} \text{Multiply row 3} \\ \text{by } \left(\dfrac{1}{128}\right) \end{matrix} \rightarrow \begin{bmatrix} 1 & 1 & -6 & | & 0 \\ 0 & 1 & 12 & | & 7 \\ 0 & 0 & 128\left(\dfrac{1}{128}\right) & | & 72\left(\dfrac{1}{128}\right) \end{bmatrix} \rightarrow \begin{bmatrix} 1 & 1 & -6 & | & 0 \\ 0 & 1 & 12 & | & 7 \\ 0 & 0 & 1 & | & \dfrac{9}{16} \end{bmatrix}$$

$z = \dfrac{9}{16}$ $\quad y + 12z = 7 \qquad x + y - 6z = 0$

$\qquad\qquad\quad y + 12\left(\dfrac{9}{16}\right) = 7 \quad x + \dfrac{1}{4} - 6\left(\dfrac{9}{16}\right) = 0$

$\qquad\qquad\quad y + \dfrac{27}{4} = 7 \qquad x + \dfrac{1}{4} - \dfrac{27}{8} = 0$

$\qquad\qquad\quad y = \dfrac{28}{4} - \dfrac{27}{4} \qquad x = \dfrac{27}{8} - \dfrac{2}{8}$

$\qquad\qquad\quad y = \dfrac{1}{4} \qquad\qquad x = \dfrac{25}{8}$

$\left(\dfrac{25}{8}, \dfrac{1}{4}, \dfrac{9}{16}\right)$

21. let x be the amount of 15% solution and y be the amount of 40% solution.

Action	Percent of Alcohol	Amount of Solution (L)	Amount of Alcohol (L)
Start	15%	x	$0.15x$
Add	40%	y	$0.40y$
Finish	25%	5	$0.25(5)$

$\begin{matrix} x + y = 5 \\ 0.15x + 0.40y = 0.25(5) \end{matrix} \rightarrow \begin{bmatrix} 1 & 1 & | & 5 \\ 0.15 & 0.40 & | & 1.25 \end{bmatrix} \begin{matrix} \text{add } (-0.15)\times \\ \text{row 1 to row2} \end{matrix} \rightarrow \begin{bmatrix} 1 & 1 & | & 5 \\ 0.15 + & 0.40 + & | & 1.25 + \\ (-0.15)(1) & (-0.15)(1) & | & (-0.15)(5) \end{bmatrix}$

$\begin{bmatrix} 1 & 1 & | & 5 \\ 0 & 0.25 & | & 0.50 \end{bmatrix} \begin{matrix} \text{Multiply row 2} \\ \text{by } \left(\dfrac{1}{0.25}\right) \end{matrix} \rightarrow \begin{bmatrix} 1 & 1 & | & 5 \\ 0 & 0.25\left(\dfrac{1}{0.25}\right) & | & 0.50\left(\dfrac{1}{0.25}\right) \end{bmatrix} \rightarrow \begin{bmatrix} 1 & 1 & | & 5 \\ 0 & 1 & | & 2 \end{bmatrix} \rightarrow \begin{matrix} y = 2 & x + y = 5 \\ & x + 2 = 5 \\ & x = 3 \end{matrix}$

She needs 3 L of the 15% solution and 2 L of the 40% solution to get the required solution.

23. Let s be the time spent swimming, b be the time spent biking, and r be the time spent running.

$s + b + r = 12$; the total time was 12 hours.

$1.8s + 16.8b + 6.55r = 140.6$; the total distance was 140.6 mi

$s + b = 2r$ or $s + b - 2r = 0$; swim time + bike time was $2 \times$ run time.

$\begin{bmatrix} 1 & 1 & 1 & | & 12 \\ 1.8 & 16.8 & 6.55 & | & 140.6 \\ 1 & 1 & -2 & | & 0 \end{bmatrix} \begin{matrix} \text{add } (-1.8)\times \\ \text{row 1 to row 2} \end{matrix} \rightarrow \begin{bmatrix} 1 & 1 & 1 & | & 12 \\ 1.8 + & 16.8 + & 6.55 + & | & 140.6 + \\ (-1.8)(1) & (-1.8)(1) & (-1.8)(1) & | & (-1.8)(12) \\ 1 & 1 & -2 & | & 0 \end{bmatrix} \rightarrow \begin{bmatrix} 1 & 1 & 1 & | & 12 \\ 0 & 15 & 4.75 & | & 119 \\ 1 & 1 & -2 & | & 0 \end{bmatrix}$

$\begin{bmatrix} 1 & 1 & 1 & | & 12 \\ 0 & 15 & 4.75 & | & 119 \\ 1 & 1 & -2 & | & 0 \end{bmatrix} \begin{matrix} \text{add } (-1)\times \\ \text{row 1 to row 3} \end{matrix} \rightarrow \begin{bmatrix} 1 & 1 & 1 & | & 12 \\ 0 & 15 & 4.75 & | & 119 \\ 1 + & 1 + & -2 + & | & 0 + \\ (-1)(1) & (-1)(1) & (-1)(1) & | & (-1)(12) \end{bmatrix} \rightarrow \begin{bmatrix} 1 & 1 & 1 & | & 12 \\ 0 & 15 & 4.75 & | & 119 \\ 0 & 0 & -3 & | & -12 \end{bmatrix}$

$$\begin{bmatrix} 1 & 1 & 1 & | & 12 \\ 0 & 15 & 4.75 & | & 119 \\ 0 & 0 & -3 & | & -12 \end{bmatrix} \begin{array}{l} \text{Multiply row 3} \\ \text{by} \left(-\dfrac{1}{3}\right) \end{array} \rightarrow \begin{bmatrix} 1 & 1 & 1 & | & 12 \\ 0 & 15 & 4.75 & | & 119 \\ 0 & 0 & -3\left(-\dfrac{1}{3}\right) & | & -12\left(-\dfrac{1}{3}\right) \end{bmatrix} \rightarrow \begin{bmatrix} 1 & 1 & 1 & | & 12 \\ 0 & 15 & 4.75 & | & 119 \\ 0 & 0 & 1 & | & 4 \end{bmatrix}$$

$r = 4$ $15b + 4.75r = 119$ $s + b + r = 12$

$15b + 4.75(4) = 119$ $s + \dfrac{20}{3} + 4 = 12$

$15b + 19 = 119$

$15b = 100$ $s + \dfrac{32}{3} = 12$

$b = \dfrac{20}{3} = 6\dfrac{2}{3}$ $s = \dfrac{36}{3} - \dfrac{32}{3}$

$s = \dfrac{4}{3} = 1\dfrac{1}{3}$

It took him 4 hr to complete the run, $6\dfrac{2}{3}$ hr to complete the bike ride, and $1\dfrac{1}{3}$ hr to complete the swim.

25.   Let c be the number of cheeseburgers consumed, f be the number or medium french fry orders consumed and a be the number of baked apple pies consumed.

$330c + 450f + 260a = 1960$; calories $\begin{bmatrix} 330 & 450 & 260 & | & 1960 \\ 14 & 22 & 13 & | & 90 \\ 6 & 57 & 34 & | & 143 \end{bmatrix}$

$14c + 22f + 13a = 90$; fat

$6c + 57f + 34a = 143$; carbohydrates

$$\begin{bmatrix} 330 & 450 & 260 & | & 1960 \\ 14 & 22 & 13 & | & 90 \\ 6 & 57 & 34 & | & 143 \end{bmatrix} \begin{array}{l} \text{multiply row 1} \\ \text{by} \left(\dfrac{1}{330}\right) \end{array} \rightarrow \begin{bmatrix} 330\left(\dfrac{1}{330}\right) & 450\left(\dfrac{1}{330}\right) & 260\left(\dfrac{1}{330}\right) & | & 1960\left(\dfrac{1}{330}\right) \\ 14 & 22 & 13 & | & 90 \\ 6 & 57 & 34 & | & 143 \end{bmatrix}$$

$$\begin{bmatrix} 1 & 1.364 & 0.7879 & | & 5.939 \\ 14 & 22 & 13 & | & 90 \\ 6 & 57 & 34 & | & 143 \end{bmatrix} \begin{array}{l} \text{add } (-14) \times \\ \text{row 1 to row 2} \end{array} \rightarrow \begin{bmatrix} 1 & 1.364 & 0.7879 & | & 5.939 \\ 14+ & 22+ & 13+ & | & 90+ \\ (-14)(1) & (-14)(1.364) & (-14)(0.7879) & | & (-14)(5.939) \\ 6 & 57 & 34 & | & 143 \end{bmatrix}$$

$$\begin{bmatrix} 1 & 1.364 & 0.7879 & | & 5.939 \\ 0 & 2.904 & 1.969 & | & 6.854 \\ 6 & 57 & 34 & | & 143 \end{bmatrix} \begin{array}{l} \text{add } (-6) \times \\ \text{row 1 to row 3} \end{array} \rightarrow \begin{bmatrix} 1 & 1.364 & 0.7879 & | & 5.939 \\ 0 & 2.904 & 1.969 & | & 6.854 \\ 6+ & 57+ & 34+ & | & 143+ \\ (-6)(1) & (-6)(1.364) & (-6)(0.7879) & | & (-6)(5.939) \end{bmatrix}$$

$$\begin{bmatrix} 1 & 1.364 & 0.7879 & | & 5.940 \\ 0 & 2.904 & 1.969 & | & 6.854 \\ 0 & 48.82 & 29.27 & | & 107.4 \end{bmatrix} \begin{array}{l} \text{multiply row 2} \\ \text{by} \left(\dfrac{1}{2.904}\right) \end{array} \rightarrow \begin{bmatrix} 1 & 1.364 & 0.7879 & | & 5.939 \\ 0 & 2.904\left(\dfrac{1}{2.904}\right) & 1.969\left(\dfrac{1}{2.904}\right) & | & 6.854\left(\dfrac{1}{2.904}\right) \\ 0 & 48.83 & 29.27 & | & 107.4 \end{bmatrix}$$

$$\begin{bmatrix} 1 & 1.364 & 0.7879 & | & 5.939 \\ 0 & 1 & 0.6780 & | & 2.360 \\ 0 & 48.83 & 29.27 & | & 107.4 \end{bmatrix} \begin{array}{l} \text{add } (-48.82) \times \\ \text{row 2 to row 3} \end{array} \rightarrow \begin{bmatrix} 1 & 1.364 & 0.7879 & | & 5.939 \\ 0 & 1 & 0.6780 & | & 2.360 \\ 0 & 48.82+ & 29.27+ & | & 107.4+ \\ (-48.82)(1) & (-48.82)(0.6780) & | & (-48.82)(2.360) \end{bmatrix}$$

$$\begin{bmatrix} 1 & 1.364 & 0.7879 & | & 5.939 \\ 0 & 1 & 0.6780 & | & 2.360 \\ 0 & 0 & -3.830 & | & -7.850 \end{bmatrix} \begin{matrix} \text{Multiply row 3} \\ \text{by} \left(-\dfrac{1}{3.830}\right) \end{matrix} \rightarrow \begin{bmatrix} 1 & 1.364 & 0.7879 & | & 5.939 \\ 0 & 1 & 0.6780 & | & 2.360 \\ 0 & 0 & -3.830\left(-\dfrac{1}{3.830}\right) & | & -7.839\left(-\dfrac{1}{3.830}\right) \end{bmatrix}$$

$$\begin{bmatrix} 1 & 1.364 & 0.7879 & | & 5.939 \\ 0 & 1 & 0.6780 & | & 2.360 \\ 0 & 0 & 1 & | & 2.198 \end{bmatrix}$$

Continuous rounding results in rounding errors. The answers must be the nearest integer since only integer values of orders are allowed.

$a = 2$ $f + 0.6780a = 2.360$ $c + 1.364f + 0.7879a = 5.939$

$\quad\quad\quad f + 0.6780(2) = 2.360$ $c + 1.364(1) + 0.7879(2) = 5.940$

$\quad\quad\quad f + 1.356 = 2.360$ $c + 2.9398 = 5.940$

$\quad\quad\quad\quad\quad f = 1$ $c = 3$

The meal consisted of 3 cheeseburgers, 1 medium french fries, and 2 baked apple pies.

Exercises 4.5 Solving Systems of Linear Inequalities

1. $y > 2x - 1$

The border line will be dashed.

x	$y = 2x - 1$	(x, y)
0	$2(0) - 1 = -1$	$(0, -1)$
1	$2(1) - 1 = 1$	$(2, 1)$

Test point is $(0, 0)$.

$0 \overset{?}{>} 2(0) - 1$

$0 > -1$, shade the half-plane

containing $(0,0)$.

$y < -x + 3$

The border line will be dashed.

x	$y = -x + 3$	(x, y)
0	$-(0) + 3 = 3$	$(0, 3)$
1	$-(1) + 3 = 2$	$(1, 2)$

Test point is $(0, 0)$.

$0 \overset{?}{<} -(0) + 3$

$0 < 3$, shade the half-plane

containing $(0,0)$.

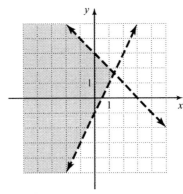

3. $y \leq \dfrac{1}{3}x + 3$

The border line is solid.

x	$y = \dfrac{1}{3}x + 3$	(x, y)
0	$\dfrac{1}{3}(0) + 3 = 3$	$(0, 3)$
3	$\dfrac{1}{3}(3) + 3 = 4$	$(3, 4)$

Test point is $(0, 0)$.

$0 \overset{?}{\leq} \dfrac{1}{3}(0) + 3$

$0 \leq 3$, shade the half-plane

containing $(0,0)$.

$y < -\dfrac{1}{2}x + 1$

The boundary line is dashed.

x	$y = -\dfrac{1}{2}x+1$	(x, y)
0	$-\dfrac{1}{2}(0)+1=1$	$(0,1)$
2	$-\dfrac{1}{2}(2)+1=0$	$(2,0)$

Test point is $(0,0)$.

$0 \overset{?}{<} -\dfrac{1}{2}(0)+1$

$0 < 1,$ shade the half-plane

containing $(0,0)$.

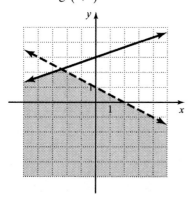

5.

$4x + 2y \geq -6$

$2y \geq -4x - 6$

$y \geq -2x - 3$

The boundary line is solid

x	$y = -2x-3$	(x, y)
-2	$-2(-2)-3=1$	$(-2,1)$
0	$-2(0)-3=-3$	$(0,-3)$

Test point is $(0,0)$.

$4(0)+2(0) \overset{?}{\geq} -6$

$0 \geq -6,$ shade the half plane

containing $(0,0)$.

$12x - 3y \geq -6$

$-3y \geq -12x - 6$

$y \leq 4x + 2$

The boundary line is solid.

x	$y = 4x+2$	(x, y)
-1	$4(-1)+2=-2$	$(-1,-2)$
0	$4(0)+2=2$	$(0,2)$

Test point is $(0,0)$.

$12(0)-3(0) \overset{?}{\geq} -6$

$0 \geq -6,$ shade the half-plane

containing $(0,0)$.

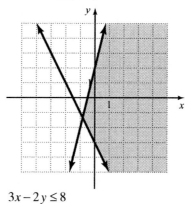

7. $3x - 2y \leq 8$

$-2y \leq -3x + 8$

$y \geq \dfrac{3}{2}x - 4$

The boundary line is solid.

x	$y = \dfrac{3}{2}x-4$	(x, y)
0	$\dfrac{3}{2}(0)-4=-4$	$(0,-4)$
2	$\dfrac{3}{2}(2)-4=-1$	$(2,-1)$

The test point is $(0,0)$.

$3(0)-2(0) \overset{?}{\leq} 8$

$0 \leq 8,$ shade the half-plane

containing $(0,0)$.

$-x - 3y > 0$

$-3y > x$

$y < -\dfrac{1}{3}x$

The boundary line is dashed.

x	$y = -\dfrac{1}{3}x$	(x, y)
0	$-\dfrac{1}{3}(0)=0$	$(0,0)$
3	$-\dfrac{1}{3}(3)=-1$	$(3,-1)$

Test point is $(-5,-5)$.

$-(-5)-3(-5) \overset{?}{>} 0$

$5 + 15 = 20 > 0$

Shade the half-plane containing $(-5,-5)$.

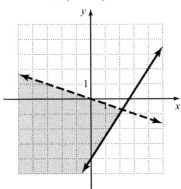

9. $4x+2y \le 4$

$2y \le -4x+4$

$y \le -2x+2$

The boundary line is solid.

x	$y=-2x+2$	(x,y)
0	$-2(0)+2=2$	$(0,2)$
1	$-2(1)+2=0$	$(1,0)$

Test point is $(0,0)$.

$4(0)+2(0)\overset{?}{\le}4$

$0 \le 4$, shade the half plane containing $(0,0.)$

$2x+y>-3$

$y>-2x-3$

The boundary line is dashed.

x	$y=-2x-3$	(x,y)
-1	$-2(-1)-3=-1$	$(-1,-1)$
0	$-2(0)-3=-3$	$(0,-3)$

Test point is $(0,0)$.

$2(0)+(0)\overset{?}{>}-3$

$0>-3$, shade the half-plane containing $(0,0)$.

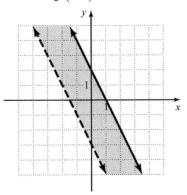

11. $3x-9y<18$

$-9y<-3x+18$

$y>\dfrac{1}{3}x-2$

The boundary line is dashed.

x	$y=\dfrac{1}{3}x-2$	(x,y)
0	$\dfrac{1}{3}(0)-2=-2$	$(0,-2)$
3	$\dfrac{1}{3}(3)-2=-1$	$(3,-1)$

Test point is $(0,0)$,

$3(0)-9(0)\overset{?}{<}18$

$0<18$, shade the half-plane containing (0.0).

$1.5x+0.5y>1.5$

$0.5y>-1.5x+1.5$

$y>-3x+3$

The boundary line is dashed.

x	$y=-3x+3$	(x,y)
0	$-3(0)+3=3$	$(0,3)$
1	$-3(1)+3=0$	$(1,0)$

Test point is $(0,0)$.

$1.5(0)+0.5(0)\overset{?}{>}1.5$

$0\not>1.5$

Shade the half-plane not containing $(0,0)$.

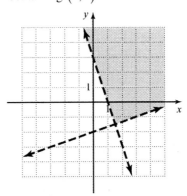

13. $y-x>1$

$y>x+1$

The boundary line is dashed.

x	$y=x+1$	(x,y)
0	$(0)+1=1$	$(0,1)$
1	$(1)+1=2$	$(1,2)$

Test point is $(0,0)$.

$0-0\overset{?}{>}1$

$0\not>1$, shade the half-plane not containing $(0,0)$.

$x\leq 4$

Boundary line is solid.

$x=4$	y	(x,y)
4	0	$(4,0)$
4	2	$(4,2)$

Test point is $(0,0)$.

$0\leq 4$, shade the half-plane containing $(0,0)$.

$y>0$

Boundary line is dashed.

x	$y=0$	(x,y)
-2	0	$(-2,0)$
2	0	$(2,0)$

Test point is $(0,5)$.

$5>0$, shade the half-plane containing $(0,5)$.

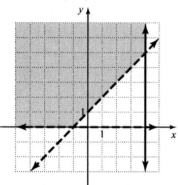

15. $-2x-y\geq 3$

$-y\geq 2x+3$

$y\leq -2x-3$

Boundary line is solid.

x	$y=-2x-3$	(x,y)
-1	$-2(-1)-3=-1$	$(-1,-1)$
0	$-2(0)-3=-3$	$(0,-3)$

Test point is $(0,0)$.

$-2(0)-(0)\overset{?}{\geq}3$

$0\not\geq 3$, shade the half-plane not containing $(0,0)$.

$x\geq -4$

The boundary line is solid

$x=-4$	y	(x,y)
-4	0	$(-4,0)$
-4	2	$(-4,2)$

Test point is $(0,0)$.

$0\geq -4$, shade the half-plane contining $(0,0)$.

$y\geq -2$

The boundary line is solid.

x	$y=-2$	(x,y)
0	-2	$(0,-2)$
2	-2	$(2,-2)$

Test point is $(0,0)$.

$0\geq -2$, shade the half-plane containing $(0,0)$.

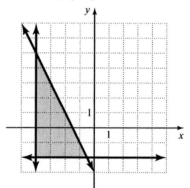

17. $3x-2y<2$

$-2y<-3x+2$

$y>\dfrac{3}{2}x-1$

Boundary line is dashed.

x	$y=\dfrac{3}{2}x-1$	(x,y)
0	$\dfrac{3}{2}(0)-1=-1$	$(0,-1)$
2	$\dfrac{3}{2}(2)-1=2$	$(2,2)$

Test point is $(0,0)$.

$3(0)-2(0)\overset{?}{<}2$

$0<2$, shade the half-plane containing $(0,0)$.

$x+3y<12$

$3y<-x+12$

$$y < -\frac{1}{3}x + 4$$

Boundary line is dashed.

x	$y = -\frac{1}{3}x + 4$	(x, y)
0	$-\frac{1}{3}(0) + 4 = 4$	$(0, 4)$
3	$-\frac{1}{3}(3) + 4 = 3$	$(3, 3)$

Test point is $(0, 0)$.

$$(0) + 3(0) \overset{?}{<} 12$$

$0 < 12$, shade the half-plane

containing $(0, 0)$.

$$x > -2$$

Boundary line is dashed.

$x = -2$	y	(x, y)
-2	0	$(-2, 0)$
-2	2	$(-2, 2)$

Test point is $(0, 0)$.

$0 > -2$, shade the half-plane

containing $(0, 0)$.

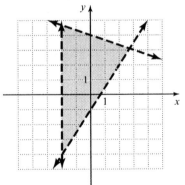

19. $$12x - 4y \geq 16$$
$$-4y \geq -12x + 16$$
$$y \leq 3x - 4$$

The boundary line is solid.

x	$y = 3x - 4$	(x, y)
0	$3(0) - 4 = -4$	$(0, -4)$
1	$3(1) - 4 = -1$	$(1, -1)$

Test point is $(0, 0)$.

$$12(0) - 4(0) \overset{?}{\geq} 16$$

$0 \not\geq 16$, shade the half-plane not

containing $(0, 0)$.

$$3x - 6y < -6$$
$$-6y < -3x - 6$$
$$y > \frac{1}{2}x + 1$$

The boundary line is dashed.

x	$y = \frac{1}{2}x + 1$	(x, y)
0	$\frac{1}{2}(0) + 1 = 1$	$(0, 1)$
2	$\frac{1}{2}(2) + 1 = 2$	$(2, 2)$

Test point is $(0, 0)$.

$$3(0) - 6(0) \overset{?}{<} -6$$

$0 \not< -6$, shade the half-plane not

containing $(0, 0)$.

$$y < 4$$

The boundary line is dashed.

x	$y = 4$	(x, y)
0	4	$(0, 4)$
2	4	$(2, 4)$

Test point is $(0, 0)$.

$0 < 4$, shade the half-plane

containing $(0, 0)$.

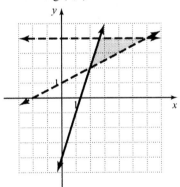

21. $$-x + y > -2$$
$$y > x - 2$$

The boundary line is dashed.

x	$y = x - 2$	(x, y)
0	$(0) - 2 = -2$	$(0, -2)$
2	$(2) - 2 = 0$	$(2, 0)$

Test point is $(0, 0)$.

$$-(0) + (0) \overset{?}{>} -2$$

$0 > -2$, shade the half-plane

containing $(0, 0)$.

$y > -x + 2$

The boundary line is dashed.

x	$y = -x + 2$	(x, y)
0	$-(0) + 2 = 2$	$(0, 2)$
2	$-(2) + 2 = 0$	$(2, 0)$

Test point is $(0, 0)$.

$(0) \overset{?}{<} -(0) + 2$

$0 < 2$, shade the half-plane

containing $(0, 0)$.

$2x - y > 1$

$-y > -2x + 1$

$y < 2x - 1$

The boundary line is dashed.

x	$y = 2x - 1$	(x, y)
0	$2(0) - 1 = -1$	$(0, -1)$
1	$2(1) - 1 = 1$	$(1, 1)$

Test point is $(0, 0)$.

$2(0) - (0) \overset{?}{>} 1$

$0 \not> 1$

Shade the half-plane not

containing $(0, 0)$.

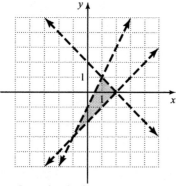

23.   a. Let x be the hours she works at the retail job
and y be the hours she works at the office job.
$x + y \geq 35 \quad x \leq 20 \quad y \leq 30$

b. $x + y \geq 35$

$y \geq -x + 35$

The boundary line is solid.

x	$y = -x + 35$	(x, y)
0	$-(0) + 35 = 35$	$(0, 35)$
35	$-(35) + 35 = 0$	$(35, 0)$

Test point is $(0, 0)$.

$(0) + (0) \overset{?}{\geq} 35$

$0 \not\geq 35$, shade the half-plane not

containing $(0, 0)$.

$x \leq 20$

The boundary line is solid.

$x = 20$	y	(x, y)
20	0	$(20, 0)$
20	20	$(20, 20)$

Test point is $(0, 0)$.

$0 \leq 20$, shade the half-plane

containing $(0, 0)$.

$y \leq 30$

The boundary line is solid.

x	$y = 30$	(x, y)
0	30	$(0, 30)$
20	30	$(20, 30)$

Test point is $(0, 0)$.

$0 \leq 30$, shade the half-plane

containing $(0, 0)$.

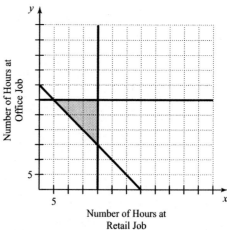

Number of Hours at
Office Job

Number of Hours at
Retail Job

c. She must work at between 20 and 30 hr at her
office job.

25.   a. Let l be the length of the lot and w be the width
of the lot. The perimeter is twice the width plus
twice the length.

$2l + 2w \leq 400$

$l \geq w + 25$

$w \geq 25$

$2l + 2w \leq 400$

$2w \leq -2l + 400$

$w \leq -l + 200$

The boundary line is solid.

l	$w = -l + 200$	(l, w)
0	$-(0) + 200 = 200$	$(0, 200)$
200	$-(200) + 200 = 0$	$(200, 0)$

Test point is $(0,0)$.

$2(0)+2(0)\overset{?}{\leq}400$

$0\leq400$, shade the half-plane

containing $(0,0)$.

$l\geq w+25$

$l-25\geq w$

$w\leq l-25$

The boundary line is solid.

l	$w=l-25$	(l,w)
25	$(25)-25=0$	$(25,0)$
200	$(200)-25=175$	$(200,175)$

Test point is $(0,0)$.

$0\overset{?}{\geq}0+25$

$0\ngeq25$, shade the half-plane not

containing $(0,0)$.

$w\geq25$

The boundary line is solid

l	$w=25$	(l,w)
25	25	$(25,25)$
200	25	$(200,25)$

Test point is $(0,0)$.

$0\ngeq25$, shade the half-plane not

containing the point $(0,0)$.

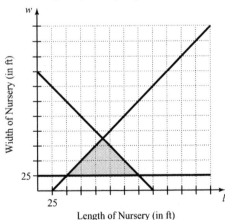

Length of Nursery (in ft)

c. The solution region represents all possible
dimensions for the nursery lot.

27. a. Let x be the number of half-page ads and y be
the number of full-page ads.
$150x+225y<15000$

$x>y$

$x\geq20$

b. $150x+225y<15000$

$225y<-150x+15000$

$y<-\dfrac{2}{3}x+\dfrac{200}{3}$

The boundary line is dashed.

x	$y=-\dfrac{2}{3}x+\dfrac{200}{3}$	(x,y)
0	$-\dfrac{2}{3}(0)+\dfrac{200}{3}$	$\left(0,66\dfrac{2}{3}\right)$
100	$-\dfrac{2}{3}(100)+\dfrac{200}{3}=0$	$(100,0)$

Test point is $(0,0)$.

$150(0)+225(0)\overset{?}{<}15000$

$0<15000$, shade the half-plane

containing $(0,0)$.

$x>y$

$y<x$

The boundary is dashed.

x	$y=x$	(x,y)
0	0	$(0,0)$
50	50	$(50,50)$

The test point is $(10,0)$.

$0<10$, shade the half-plane

containing $(10,0)$.

$x>20$

The boundary is dashed.

$x=20$	y	(x,y)
20	0	$(20,0)$
20	50	$(20,50)$

Test point is $(0,0)$.

$0\ngtr20$, shade the half-plane not

containing $(0,0)$.

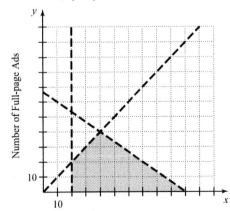

Number of Half-page Ads

29. a. Let x be the number of tables and y be the chairs.
$2x+1.5y\leq360$; assembly

$3x+y\leq400$; finishing and painting.

b. $2x + 1.5y \leq 360$

$1.5y \leq -2x + 360$

$y \leq -\dfrac{4}{3}x + 240$

The boundary line is solid.

x	$y = -\dfrac{4}{3}x + 240$	(x, y)
0	$-\dfrac{4}{3}(0) + 240 = 240$	$(0, 240)$
180	$-\dfrac{4}{3}(180) + 240 = 0$	$(180, 0)$

Test point is $(0, 0)$.

$2(0) + 1.5(0) \overset{?}{\leq} 360$

$0 \leq 360$, shade the half-plane

containing $(0, 0)$.

$3x + y \leq 400$

$y \leq -3x + 400$

The boundary line is solid.

x	$y = -3x + 400$	(x, y)
0	$-3(0) + 400 = 400$	$(0, 400)$
100	$-3(100) + 400 = 100$	$(100, 100)$

Test point is $(0, 0)$.

$3(0) + (0) \overset{?}{\leq} 400$

$0 \leq 400$, shade the half-plane

containing $(0, 0)$.

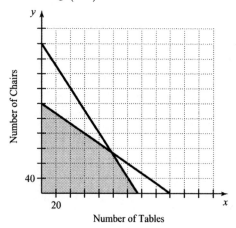

Chapter 4 Review Exercises

1. $4(1) - 3(2) \overset{?}{=} -2$

$4 - 6 \overset{?}{=} -2 \qquad -2 = -2$ True

$-(1) + 6(2) \overset{?}{=} 11$

$-1 + 12 \overset{?}{=} 11 \qquad 11 = 11$ True
A solution.

2. $3\left(-\dfrac{2}{3}\right) + 2(-4) \overset{?}{=} -10$

$-2 - 8 \overset{?}{=} -10 \qquad -10 = -10$ True

$9\left(-\dfrac{2}{3}\right) - 5(-4) \overset{?}{=} 14$

$-6 + 20 \overset{?}{=} 14 \qquad 14 = 14$ True
A solution.

3.

x	$y = x + 4$	(x, y)
-2	$(-2) + 4 = 2$	$(-2, 2)$
0	$(0) + 4 = 4$	$(0, 4)$

x	$y = 1 - 2x$	(x, y)
0	$1 - 2(0) = 1$	$(0, 1)$
1	$1 - 2(1) = -1$	$(1, -1)$

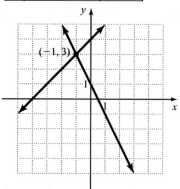

The solution is $(-1, 3)$.

4. $5y - 15 = 0$

$5y = 15$

$y = 3$

x	$y = 3$	(x, y)
0	3	$(0, 3)$
2	3	$(2, 3)$

$4x + 3y = 9$

$3y = -4x + 9$

$y = -\dfrac{4}{3}x + 3$

x	$y = -\dfrac{4}{3}x + 3$	(x, y)
0	$-\dfrac{4}{3}(0)x + 3 = 3$	$(0, 3)$
3	$-\dfrac{4}{3}(3) + 3 = -1$	$(3, -1)$

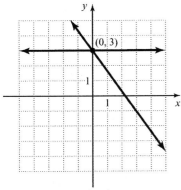

The solution is $(0, 3)$.

5. $2x - 4y = -8$

$-4y = -2x - 8 \qquad y = \dfrac{1}{2}x + 2$

x	$y = \dfrac{1}{2}x + 2$	(x, y)
0	$\dfrac{1}{2}(0) + 2 = 2$	$(0, 2)$
2	$\dfrac{1}{2}(2) + 2 = 3$	$(2, 3)$

$-x + 2y = -4$

$2y = x - 4$

$y = \dfrac{1}{2}x - 2$

x	$y = \dfrac{1}{2}x - 2$	(x, y)
-2	$\dfrac{1}{2}(-2) - 2 = -3$	$(-2, -3)$
0	$\dfrac{1}{2}(0) - 2 = -2$	$(0, -2)$

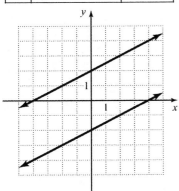

The lines are parallel. No solution.

6. $6x = 16 - 4y$

$6x - 16 = -4y$

$-\dfrac{3}{2}x + 4 = y$

$y = -\dfrac{3}{2}x + 4$

x	$y = -\dfrac{3}{2}x + 4$	(x, y)
0	$-\dfrac{3}{2}(0) + 4 = 4$	$(0, 4)$
2	$-\dfrac{3}{2}(2) + 4 = 1$	$(2, 1)$

$y = -\dfrac{3}{2}x + 4$

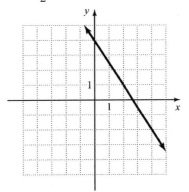

The lines have the same graph. There are infinitely many solutions.

7. $y = 3x + 7 \qquad\qquad y = 7x - 9$

$3x + 7 = 7x - 9$

$-4x = -16$

$x = 4$

$y = 3(4) + 7 = 12 + 7 = 19$

$(4, 19)$

8. $y = 8x - 10 \qquad\qquad x = \dfrac{1}{2}y - 1$

$y = 8\left(\dfrac{1}{2}y - 1\right) - 10$

$y = 4y - 8 - 10$

$-3y = -18$

$y = 6$

$x = \dfrac{1}{2}(6) - 1$

$x = 3 - 1 = 2$

$(2, 6)$

9. $4x + 2y = 10 \qquad y = -(2x + 5)$

$4x + 2(-2x - 5) = 10$

$4x - 4x - 10 = 10$

$-10 = 10$ False; no solution.

10. $5a - 3b = -16$ $6a = 2b$
                        $3a = b$

$5a - 3(3a) = -16$

$5a - 9a = -16$

$-4a = -16$

$a = 4$

$b = 3(4) = 12$

$a = 4,\ b = 12$

11. $x - 4y = 11$

$\dfrac{3x + 4y = 17}{}$

$4x\quad = 28$ $x = 7$

$(7) - 4y = 11$

$-4y = 4$ $y = -1$

$(7, -1)$

12. $2p + 5q = -8 \longrightarrow 2p + 5q = -8$

$2p - 3q = 8 \xrightarrow{\times(-1)} \dfrac{-2p + 3q = -8}{}$

$\qquad\qquad\qquad 8q = -16$

$q = -2$ $2p + 5(-2) = -8$

$\qquad\qquad 2p - 10 = -8$

$\qquad\qquad 2p = 2$

$\qquad\qquad p = 1$

$p = 1,\ q = -2$

13. $3s - 2t = 9 \xrightarrow{\times(-3)} -9s + 6t = -27$

$4s - 6t = 2 \longrightarrow \dfrac{4s - 6t = 2}{}$

$\qquad\qquad\qquad -5s = -25$

$s = 5$ $3(5) - 2t = 9$

$\qquad\qquad 15 - 2t = 9$

$\qquad\qquad -2t = -6$

$\qquad\qquad t = 3$

$s = 5,\ t = 3$

14. $1.5x + 2.5y = -3 \xrightarrow{\times(-4)} -6x - 10y = 12$

$6x + 10y = -12 \longrightarrow \dfrac{6x + 10y = -12}{}$

$\qquad\qquad\qquad\qquad 0 = 0$

There are infinitely many solutions.

15. $5(-2) + 2(3) + 2(0) \overset{?}{=} -4$

$-10 + 6 + 0 \overset{?}{=} -4$ $-4 = -4$ True

$2(-2) - 3(3) + (0) \overset{?}{=} -13$

$-4 - 9 + 0 \overset{?}{=} -13$ $-13 = -13$ True

$3(-2) + (3) + 4(0) \overset{?}{=} -3$

$-6 + 3 + 0 \overset{?}{=} -3$ $-3 = -3$ True

A solution.

16. $9\left(-\dfrac{1}{3}\right) + 8\left(-\dfrac{1}{4}\right) + 4\left(-\dfrac{1}{2}\right) \overset{?}{=} -7$

$-3 - 2 - 2 \overset{?}{=} -7$ $-7 = -7$ True

$6\left(-\dfrac{1}{3}\right) - 4\left(-\dfrac{1}{4}\right) - 2\left(-\dfrac{1}{2}\right) \overset{?}{=} -5$

$-2 + 1 + 1 \overset{?}{=} -5$ $0 = -5$ False

$2\left(-\dfrac{1}{4}\right) - 3\left(-\dfrac{1}{2}\right) \overset{?}{=} 1$

$-\dfrac{1}{2} + \dfrac{3}{2} = 1$ $1 = 1$ True

Not a solution.

17. $x - y + z = 1$

$\dfrac{3x + y - 2z = -3}{}$

$4x\qquad - z = -2$

$x - y + z = 1 \xrightarrow{\times 4} 4x - 4y + 4z = 4$

$x + 4y - z = 2 \longrightarrow \dfrac{x + 4y - z = 2}{}$

$\qquad\qquad\qquad 5x\qquad + 3z = 6$

$4x - z = -2 \xrightarrow{\times 3} 12x - 3z = -6$

$5x + 3z = 6 \longrightarrow \dfrac{5x + 3z = 6}{}$

$\qquad\qquad\qquad 17x\qquad = 0$

$x = 0$

$4(0) - z = -2$ $(0) - y + (2) = 1$

$z = 2$ $-y = -1$

$\qquad\qquad y = 1$

$(0, 1, 2)$

18. $4x + 3y - 6z = -4 \longrightarrow 4x + 3y - 6z = -4$

$x + y + z = 1 \xrightarrow{\times 6} \dfrac{6x + 6y + 6z = 6}{}$

$\qquad\qquad\qquad 10x + 9y\qquad = 2$

$10x + 9y = 2 \longrightarrow 10x + 9y = 2$

$2x + 9y = -2 \xrightarrow{\times(-1)} \dfrac{-2x - 9y = 2}{}$

$\qquad\qquad\qquad 8x\qquad = 4$

$x = \dfrac{1}{2}$

$10\left(\dfrac{1}{2}\right) + 9y = 2$ $\dfrac{1}{2} + \left(-\dfrac{1}{3}\right) + z = 1$

$5 + 9y = 2$ $\dfrac{3}{6} - \dfrac{2}{6} + z = \dfrac{6}{6}$

$9y = -3$ $\dfrac{1}{6} + z = \dfrac{6}{6}$

$y = -\dfrac{1}{3}$ $z = \dfrac{5}{6}$

$\left(\dfrac{1}{2}, -\dfrac{1}{3}, \dfrac{5}{6}\right)$

19.
$$3y - 4z = 4 \longrightarrow \qquad 3y - 4z = 4$$
$$-2x + 3y = 8 \xrightarrow{\times(-1)} 2x - 3y \quad = -8$$
$$\overline{\qquad\qquad 2x - 4z = -4}$$

$$3x - 6z = 5 \longrightarrow \qquad 3x - 6z = 5$$
$$2x - 4z = -4 \xrightarrow{\times\left(-\frac{3}{2}\right)} -3x + 6z = 6$$
$$\overline{\qquad\qquad 0 = 11 \text{ False}}$$

No solution.

20.
$$\frac{3}{4}x - \frac{2}{3}y \quad = -5 \xrightarrow{\times 24}$$
$$18x - 16y \quad = -120$$

$$\frac{1}{2}x + y - \frac{1}{4}z = 0 \xrightarrow{\times(-36)}$$
$$-18x - 36y + 9z = 0$$
$$\overline{\qquad -52y + 9z = -120}$$

$$-52y + 9z = -120 \longrightarrow \quad -52y + 9z = -120$$

$$\frac{1}{3}y + 3z = 13 \xrightarrow{\times(-3)} \quad -y - 9z = -39$$
$$\overline{\qquad -53y \quad = -159}$$

$$y = 3 \quad \frac{1}{3}(3) + 3z = 13 \quad \frac{3}{4}x - \frac{2}{3}(3) = -5$$
$$1 + 3z = 13 \qquad \frac{3}{4}x - 2 = -5$$
$$3z = 12 \qquad \frac{3}{4}x = -3$$
$$z = 4 \qquad x = -4$$

$$(-4, 3, 4)$$

21
$$\begin{bmatrix} 3 & -5 & \vline & 6 \\ 5 & -11 & \vline & 18 \end{bmatrix} \text{add } (-1) \times \text{row 2 to row 1}$$

$$\begin{bmatrix} 3 + (-1)(5) & -5 + (-1)(-11) & \vline & 6 + (-1)(18) \\ 5 & -11 & \vline & 18 \end{bmatrix}$$

$$\begin{bmatrix} -2 & 6 & \vline & -12 \\ 5 & -11 & \vline & 18 \end{bmatrix} \text{multiply row 1 by } -\frac{1}{2}$$

$$\begin{bmatrix} -2\left(-\frac{1}{2}\right) & 6\left(-\frac{1}{2}\right) & \vline & -12\left(-\frac{1}{2}\right) \\ 5 & -11 & \vline & 18 \end{bmatrix}$$

$$\begin{bmatrix} 1 & -3 & \vline & 6 \\ 5 & -11 & \vline & 18 \end{bmatrix} \text{add } (-5) \times \text{row 1 to row2}$$

$$\begin{bmatrix} 1 & -3 & \vline & 6 \\ 5 + (-5)(1) & -11 + (-5)(-3) & \vline & 18 + (-5)(6) \end{bmatrix}$$

$$\begin{bmatrix} 1 & -3 & \vline & 6 \\ 0 & 4 & \vline & -12 \end{bmatrix} \text{Multiply row 2 by } \left(\frac{1}{4}\right)$$

$$\begin{bmatrix} 1 & -3 & \vline & 6 \\ 0 & 4\left(\frac{1}{4}\right) & \vline & -12\left(\frac{1}{4}\right) \end{bmatrix}$$

$$\begin{bmatrix} 1 & -3 & \vline & 6 \\ 0 & 1 & \vline & -3 \end{bmatrix}$$

$$y = -3 \quad x - 3(-3) = 6$$
$$x + 9 = 6$$
$$x = -3$$

$$(-3, -3)$$

22.

$$\begin{bmatrix} 4 & -9 & 0 & \vline & -7 \\ \frac{2}{3} & -1 & 2 & \vline & 0 \\ 8 & 2 & 15 & \vline & 11 \end{bmatrix} \begin{array}{l} \text{Multiply row 1 by } \left(\frac{1}{4}\right) \\ \\ \text{Multiply row 2 by 3} \end{array} \rightarrow \begin{bmatrix} 4\left(\frac{1}{4}\right) & -9\left(\frac{1}{4}\right) & 0\left(\frac{1}{4}\right) & \vline & -7\left(\frac{1}{4}\right) \\ \frac{2}{3}(3) & -1(3) & 2(3) & \vline & 0(3) \\ 8 & 2 & 15 & \vline & 11 \end{bmatrix} \rightarrow \begin{bmatrix} 1 & -\frac{9}{4} & 0 & \vline & -\frac{7}{4} \\ 2 & -3 & 6 & \vline & 0 \\ 8 & 2 & 15 & \vline & 11 \end{bmatrix}$$

$$\begin{bmatrix} 1 & -\frac{9}{4} & 0 & \vline & -\frac{7}{4} \\ 2 & -3 & 6 & \vline & 0 \\ 8 & 2 & 15 & \vline & 11 \end{bmatrix} \begin{array}{l} \text{Add } (-2) \times \text{ row 1 to row 2} \rightarrow \\ \text{Add } (-8) \times \text{ row 1 to row 3} \end{array} \begin{bmatrix} 1 & -\frac{9}{4} & 0 & \vline & -\frac{7}{4} \\ 2 + (-2)(1) & -3 + (-2)\left(-\frac{9}{4}\right) & 6 + (-2)(0) & \vline & 0 + (-2)\left(-\frac{7}{4}\right) \\ 8 + (-8)(1) & 2 + (-8)\left(-\frac{9}{4}\right) & 15 + (-8)(0) & \vline & 11 + (-8)\left(-\frac{7}{4}\right) \end{bmatrix}$$

$$\begin{bmatrix} 1 & -\dfrac{9}{4} & 0 & \bigm| & -\dfrac{7}{4} \\ 0 & \dfrac{3}{2} & 6 & \bigm| & \dfrac{7}{2} \\ 0 & 20 & 15 & \bigm| & 25 \end{bmatrix} \begin{array}{l} \text{Multiply row 2 by } \dfrac{2}{3} \\[2mm] \text{Multiply row 3 by } \left(\dfrac{1}{5}\right) \end{array}$$

$$\begin{bmatrix} 1 & -\dfrac{9}{4} & 0 & \bigm| & -\dfrac{7}{4} \\ 0\left(\dfrac{2}{3}\right) & \dfrac{3}{2}\left(\dfrac{2}{3}\right) & 6\left(\dfrac{2}{3}\right) & \bigm| & \dfrac{7}{2}\left(\dfrac{2}{3}\right) \\ 0\left(\dfrac{1}{5}\right) & 20\left(\dfrac{1}{5}\right) & 15\left(\dfrac{1}{5}\right) & \bigm| & 25\left(\dfrac{1}{5}\right) \end{bmatrix} \rightarrow \begin{bmatrix} 1 & -\dfrac{9}{4} & 0 & \bigm| & -\dfrac{7}{4} \\ 0 & 1 & 4 & \bigm| & \dfrac{7}{3} \\ 0 & 4 & 3 & \bigm| & 5 \end{bmatrix}$$

$$\begin{bmatrix} 1 & -\dfrac{9}{4} & 0 & \bigm| & -\dfrac{7}{4} \\ 0 & 1 & 4 & \bigm| & \dfrac{7}{3} \\ 0 & 4 & 3 & \bigm| & 5 \end{bmatrix} \begin{array}{l} \text{add } (-4)\times \\ \text{row 2 to row 3} \rightarrow \end{array}$$

$$\begin{bmatrix} 1 & -\dfrac{9}{4} & 0 & \bigm| & -\dfrac{7}{4} \\ 0 & 1 & 4 & \bigm| & \dfrac{7}{3} \\ 0 & 4+(-4)(1) & 3+(-4)(4) & \bigm| & 5+(-4)\left(\dfrac{7}{3}\right) \end{bmatrix} \rightarrow \begin{bmatrix} 1 & -\dfrac{9}{4} & 0 & \bigm| & -\dfrac{7}{4} \\ 0 & 1 & 4 & \bigm| & \dfrac{7}{3} \\ 0 & 0 & -13 & \bigm| & -\dfrac{13}{3} \end{bmatrix}$$

$$\begin{bmatrix} 1 & -\dfrac{9}{4} & 0 & \bigm| & -\dfrac{7}{4} \\ 0 & 1 & 4 & \bigm| & \dfrac{7}{3} \\ 0 & 0 & -13 & \bigm| & -\dfrac{13}{3} \end{bmatrix} \begin{array}{l} \text{Multiply row 3} \\ \text{by } \left(-\dfrac{1}{13}\right) \end{array} \rightarrow$$

$$\begin{bmatrix} 1 & -\dfrac{9}{4} & 0 & \bigm| & -\dfrac{7}{4} \\ 0 & 1 & 4 & \bigm| & \dfrac{7}{3} \\ 0 & 0 & -13\left(-\dfrac{1}{13}\right) & \bigm| & -\dfrac{13}{3}\left(-\dfrac{1}{13}\right) \end{bmatrix} \rightarrow \begin{bmatrix} 1 & -\dfrac{9}{4} & 0 & \bigm| & -\dfrac{7}{4} \\ 0 & 1 & 4 & \bigm| & \dfrac{7}{3} \\ 0 & 0 & 1 & \bigm| & \dfrac{1}{3} \end{bmatrix}$$

$$\begin{bmatrix} 1 & -\dfrac{9}{4} & 0 & \bigm| & -\dfrac{7}{4} \\ 0 & 1 & 4 & \bigm| & \dfrac{7}{3} \\ 0 & 0 & 1 & \bigm| & \dfrac{1}{3} \end{bmatrix}$$

$$z = \frac{1}{3} \qquad y + 4z = \frac{7}{3} \qquad x - \frac{9}{4}y + (0)z = -\frac{7}{4}$$

$$y + 4\left(\frac{1}{3}\right) = \frac{7}{3} \qquad x - \frac{9}{4}(1) = -\frac{7}{4}$$

$$y + \frac{4}{3} = \frac{7}{3} \qquad x = \frac{2}{4}$$

$$y = 1 \qquad x = \frac{1}{2}$$

$$\left(\frac{1}{2}, 1, \frac{1}{3}\right)$$

23. $6x - 4y \le -12$

$-4y \le -6x - 12$

$y \ge \dfrac{3}{2}x + 3$

The boundary line is solid

x	$y = \dfrac{3}{2}x + 3$	(x, y)
-2	$\dfrac{3}{2}(-2) + 3 = 0$	$(-2, 0)$
0	$\dfrac{3}{2}(0) + 3 = 3$	$(0, 3)$

Test point is $(0, 0)$.

$6(0) - 4(0) \overset{?}{\le} -12$

$0 \not\le -12$, shade the half-plane not

containing $(0, 0)$.

$4x + 2y > 2$

$2y > -4x + 2$

$y > -2x + 1$

The boundary line is dashed.

x	$y = -2x + 1$	(x, y)
0	$-2(0) + 1 = 1$	$(0, 1)$
1	$-2(1) + 1 = -1$	$(1, -2)$

Test point is $(0, 0)$.

$4(0) + 2(0) \overset{?}{>} 2$

$0 \not> 2$

Shade the half-plane not

containing $(0, 0)$.

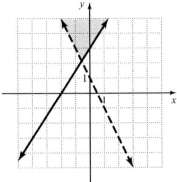

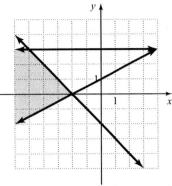

24.　$y \le -x - 2$

The boundary line is solid

x	$y = -x - 2$	(x, y)
0	$-(0) - 2 = -2$	$(0, -2)$
-2	$-(-2) - 2 = 0$	$(-2, 0)$

Test point is $(0, 0)$.

$0 \overset{?}{\le} -(0) - 2$

$0 \not\le -2$, shade the half-plane not

containing $(0, 0)$.

$y \ge \dfrac{1}{2}x + 1$

The boundary line is solid.

x	$y = \dfrac{1}{2}x + 1$	(x, y)
0	$\dfrac{1}{2}(0) + 1 = 1$	$(0, 1)$
2	$\dfrac{1}{2}(2) + 1 = 2$	$(2, 2)$

Test point is $(0, 0)$.

$0 \overset{?}{\ge} \dfrac{1}{2}(0) + 1$

$0 \not\ge 1$, shade the half-plane not

containing $(0, 0)$.

$y \le 3$

The boundary line is solid.

x	$y = 3$	(x, y)
0	3	$(0, 3)$
2	3	$(2, 3)$

Test point is $(0, 0)$.

$0 \le 3$, shade the half-plane

containing $(0, 0)$.

25.　Let p be the monthly income and m be the
monthly mortgage payment.

$p - m = 2185$

$m = 0.24p$

$p - (0.24p) = 2185$

$0.76p = 2185$

$p = 2875$

$m = 0.24(2875) = 690$

The family's monthly income is \$2875 and the
mortgage is \$690.

26.　Let f be the number of female students and m be
the number of male students.

$f + m = 9500$

$m + 1254 = f$

$(m + 1254) + m = 9500$

$2m + 1254 = 9500$

$2m = 8246$

$m = 4123$

$f = 4123 + 1254 = 5377$

There are 4123 male students and 5377 female
students attending the college.

27.　Let w be the width and l be the length of the soccer
field. The perimeter is twice the width plus twice
the length.

$2l + 2w = 400$

$w = l - 40$

$w - l = -40$

$-l + w = -40 \longrightarrow -l + w = -40$

$2l + 2w = 400 \xrightarrow{\times \frac{1}{2}} l + w = 200$

$\phantom{2l + 2w = 400 \xrightarrow{\times \frac{1}{2}}} 2w = 160$

$w = 80$ yd

$80 = l - 40$

120 yd $= l$

Area $=$ length $\times$ width

$A = lw = (120)(80) = 9600$ sq yd

The area of the soccer field is 9600 sq yd.

28.   Let d be the distance they travel and t be the time it takes the boy to catch his sister. The rate is in mph so time must be in hours.

$6t = d$; the boy

$3\left(t + \dfrac{10}{60}\right) = d$; the sister

$6t = 3\left(t + \dfrac{10}{60}\right)$

$6t = 3t + \dfrac{1}{2}$

$3t = \dfrac{1}{2}$

$t = \dfrac{1}{6}$

It takes the boy $\dfrac{1}{6}$ hr or 10 minutes to catch up to his sister.

29.   Let h be the hours for the service calls and t be the total charges.

$100 + 40h = t$; Parker Plumbing

$75 + 50h = t$; Plumbing Solutions

$100 + 40h = 75 + 50h$

$25 = 10h$

$\dfrac{25}{10} = h$

$h = 2\dfrac{1}{2}$

Both pluming services will charge the same amount in 2½ hr.

30.   Let $C(x)$ be the cost of producing x helmets and $R(x)$ be the revenue from selling x helmets.

$C(x) = 1200 + 1.20x$

$R(x) = 6x$

$1200 + 1.20x = 6x$

$1200 = 4.8x$

$250 = x$

$x = 250$

The manufacturer breaks even when 250 helmets are produced and sent.

31.   Let x be the number of employees on the department with 60% layoff and y be the number of employees in the department with 30% layoff.

$x + y = 180$

$0.60x + 0.30y = 0.50(180)$

$0.6x + 0.3y = 90 \longrightarrow 0.6x + 0.3y = 90$

$x + y = 180 \xrightarrow{\times(-0.3)} \underline{-0.3x - 0.3y = -54}$

$\hspace{3.5cm} 0.3x \hspace{1.2cm} = 36$

$x = 120$

$120 + y = 180$

$y = 60$

there were 120 employees in one department and 60 employees in the other before the layoffs.

32.   Let s be the speed of the swimmer in still water and c be the speed of the current.

$s + c = 2.1$

$\underline{s - c = 1.1}$

$2s \hspace{0.6cm} = 3.2$

$s = 1.6$

$1.6 + c = 2.1$

$c = 0.5$

The athlete swims at a rate of 1.6 mph in still water and the rate of the current is 0.5 mph.

33.   Let d be the number of tickets sold before 5:00 P.M. and n be the number of tickets sold after 5:00 P.M.

$4d = n$

$5.50d + 8.00n = 31725$

$5.5d + 8(4d) = 31725$

$5.5d + 32d = 31725$

$37.5d = 31725$

$d = 846$

$n = 4(846) = 3384$

The movie theater sold 846 tickets before 5:00 P.M. and 3384 tickets after 5:00 P.M.

34.   Let l be the amount of money invested in the low-risk fund and h be the amount invested in the high-risk fund.

$l = 2h$

$0.0525l - 0.015h = 234$

$0.0525(2h) - 0.015h = 234$

$0.105h - 0.015h = 234$

$0.09h = 234$

$h = 2600$

$l = 2(2600) = 5200$

The couple invested $5200 in the low-risk fund and $2600 in the high-risk fund.

35.   Let l be the amount of 45% ethanol added and h be the amount of 75% ethanol added.

$13\dfrac{1}{3}$ L of the 45% disinfectant should be mixed

with $6\dfrac{2}{3}$ L of the 75% disinfectant.

36.   Let b be the original price of the boots and w be the original price of the outerwear.

$0.5b + 0.3w = 165$; savings

$(b - 0.5b) + (w - 0.3w) = 285$; amount paid

$0.5b + 0.7w = 285 \longrightarrow \quad 0.5b + 0.7w = 285$

$0.5b + 0.3w = 165 \xrightarrow{\times(-1)} -0.5b - 0.3w = -165$

$$0.4w = 120$$

$w = 300$

$0.5b + 0.3(300) = 165$

$0.5b + 90 = 165$

$0.5b = 75$

$b = 150$

The original price of the boots was $150 and the original price of the outerwear was $300.

37. Let x be the number of 1-point baskets, y be the number of 2-point baskets and z be the number of 3-point baskets.

$x + 2y + 3z = 112$

$y = 10 + \dfrac{1}{2}(x + z)$

$x + y + z = 55$

$y = 10 + \dfrac{1}{2}(x + z) \xrightarrow{\times 2} 2y = 20 + x + z$

$-x + 2y - z = 20$

$l + h = 20$

$0.45l + 0.75h = 0.55(20)$

$0.45l + 0.75h = 11.0 \longrightarrow \quad 0.45l + 0.75h = 11.0$

$l + h = 20 \xrightarrow{\times(-0.45)} \quad -0.45l - 0.45h = -9.0$

$$0.30h = 2$$

$h = \dfrac{2}{0.3} = \dfrac{20}{3} = 6\dfrac{2}{3}$

$l + \dfrac{20}{3} = 20$

$l = \dfrac{60}{3} - \dfrac{20}{3} = \dfrac{40}{3} = 13\dfrac{1}{3}$

$x + y + z = 55$

$-x + 2y - z = 20$

$$3y = 75$$

$y = 25$

$x + 2y + 3z = 112$

$-x + 2y - z = 20$

$$4y + 2z = 132$$

$4(25) + 2z = 132 \qquad x + 25 + 16 = 55$

$100 + 2z = 132 \qquad x + 41 = 55$

$2z = 32 \qquad\qquad x = 14$

$z = 16$

1-point baskets: 14; 2-point baskets: 25; 3-point baskets: 16.

38. Let x be the number of 1-credit courses, y be the number of 2-credit courses and z be the number of 4-credit courses.

$x + y + z = 10$

$x + 2y + 4z = 32$

$y = \dfrac{2}{3}z$

$x + \dfrac{2}{3}z + z = 10 \qquad\quad x + 2\left(\dfrac{2}{3}z\right) + 4z = 32$

$x + \dfrac{5}{3}z = 10 \qquad\qquad x + \dfrac{4}{3}z + 4z = 32$

$$x + \dfrac{16}{3}z = 32$$

$x + \dfrac{16}{3}z = 32 \longrightarrow \quad x + \dfrac{16}{3}z = 32$

$x + \dfrac{5}{3}z = 10 \xrightarrow{\times(-1)} -x - \dfrac{5}{3}z = -10$

$$\dfrac{11}{3}z = 22$$

$z = 22\left(\dfrac{3}{11}\right) = 6 \quad x + \dfrac{5}{3}(6) = 10 \quad 0 + y + 6 = 10$

$x + 10 = 10 \qquad\quad y = 4$

$x = 0$

1 credit courses: 0; 2-credit courses: 4; 4-credit courses: 6

39. Let x be the number of 16-oz drinks, y be the number of 24-oz drinks and z be the number of 32-oz drinks sold.

$x + y + z = 465$

$0.99x + 1.09y + 1.19z = 515.45$

$z = y + 25$

$x + y + (y + 25) = 465$

$x + 2y = 440$

$0.99x + 1.09y + 1.19(y + 25) = 515.45$

$0.99x + 1.09y + 1.19y + 29.75 = 515.45$

$0.99x + 2.28y = 485.70 \longrightarrow$

$$0.99x + 2.28y = 485.70$$

$x + 2y = 440 \xrightarrow{\times(-0.99)} -0.99x - 1.98y = -435.60$

$$0.30y = 50.10$$

$y = 167$

$x + 2(167) = 440 \qquad 106 + 167 + z = 465$

$x + 334 = 440 \qquad\quad 273 + z = 465$

$x = 106 \qquad\qquad z = 192$

16-oz drinks: 106; 24-oz drinks: 167; 32-oz drinks: 192.

40. Let R be the average salary of a RN, L be the average salary of the LPN and A be the average salary of the medical assistant.

$R = 7800 + L \quad \longrightarrow \quad R - L = 7800$

$A = L - 11400 \quad \longrightarrow \quad A - L = -11400$

$L + A = 15700 + R \longrightarrow -R + L + A = 15700$

$-R + L + A = 15700$

$\underline{R - L \qquad = 7800}$

$\qquad A = 23500$

$23500 = L - 11400$

$34900 = L$

$R = 7800 + 34900 = 42700$

The average salary of a RN is \$42,700, of a LPN is \$34,900, and of a medical assistant is \$23,500.

41.   a. $2t + 3a \le 500$; assembly

$1.5t + 2a \le 300$; painting

b. $3a \le -2t + 500$

$a \le -\dfrac{2}{3}t + \dfrac{500}{3}$

The border line is solid.

t	$a = -\dfrac{2}{3}t + \dfrac{500}{3}$	(t,a)
0	$-\dfrac{2}{3}(0) + \dfrac{500}{3} = \dfrac{500}{3}$	$\left(0, 166\dfrac{2}{3}\right)$
250	$-\dfrac{2}{3}(250) + \dfrac{500}{3} = 0$	$(250, 0)$

Test point is $(0,0)$.

$2(0) + 3(0) \overset{?}{\le} 500$

$0 \le 500$, shade the half-plane

containing $(0,0)$.

$2a \le -1.5t + 300$

$a \le -0.75t + 150$

The boundary line is solid.

t	$a = -0.75t + 150$	(t,a)
0	$-0.75(0) + 150 = 150$	$(0,150)$
200	$-0.75(200) + 150 = 0$	$(200,0)$

Test point is $(0,0)$.

$1.5(0) + 2(0) \overset{?}{\le} 300$

$0 \le 300$, shade the half-plane

containing $(0,0)$.

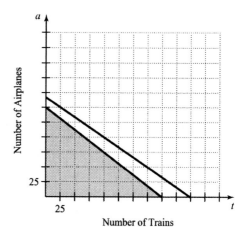

c.   The solution regions represents all the possible production units of trains and corresponding number of airplanes the company can assemble and paint each month.

42.   a.   Let x be the amount of money invested at 8% and y be the amount of money invested at 6%.

$x + y \le 12000$

$0.08y > 0.06x$

$y \ge 4500$

b. $y \le -x + 12000$

The boundary line is solid.

x	$y = -x + 12000$	(x, y)
0	$-(0) + 12000 = 12000$	$(0, 12000)$
12000	$-(12000) + 12000 = 0$	$(12000, 0)$

The test point is $(0,0)$.

$(0) + (0) \overset{?}{\le} 12000$

$0 \le 12000$, shade the half-plane

containing $(0,0)$.

$0.08y > 0.06x$

$y > \dfrac{3}{4}x$

The boundary line is dashed.

Test point is $(0, 12000)$,

$0.08(12000) \overset{?}{>} 0.06(0)$

$960 > 0$, shade the half-plane

containing $(0, 12000)$.

$y \ge 4500$

The boundary line is solid

x	$y = 4500$	(x, y)
0	4500	$(0, 4500)$
12000	4500	$(12000, 4500)$

Test point is $(0,0)$.

$0 \not\geq 4500$, shade the half-plane not containing $(0,0)$.

x	$y = \dfrac{3}{4}x$	(x, y)
0	$\dfrac{3}{4}(0) = 0$	$(0,0)$
12000	$\dfrac{3}{4}(12000) = 9000$	$(12000, 9000)$

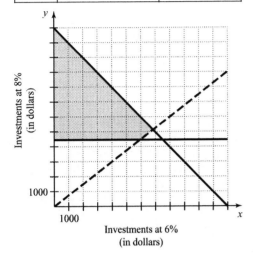

Chapter 4 Posttest

1. $8\left(\dfrac{1}{4}\right) + 2(-2) \overset{?}{=} 0$

$2 - 4 \overset{?}{=} 0$

$-2 = 0$ False
Not a solution

2.

x	$y = -2x + 3$	(x, y)
0	$-2(0) + 3 = 3$	$(0,3)$
2	$-2(2) + 3 = -1$	$(2,-1)$

$3x - 2y = 8$

$-2y = -3x + 8$

$y = \dfrac{3}{2}x - 4$

x	$y = \dfrac{3}{2}x - 4$	(x, y)
0	$\dfrac{3}{2}(0) - 4 = -4$	$(0,-4)$
2	$\dfrac{3}{2}(2) - 4 = -1$	$(2,-1)$

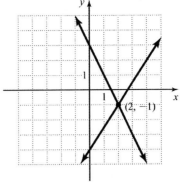

Intersection is $(2,-1)$.

3. $5x = 20$

$x = 4$ is a vertical line through $(4,0)$

$-4x - 6y = 8$

$-6y = 4x + 8$

$y = -\dfrac{2}{3}x - \dfrac{4}{3}$

x	$y = -\dfrac{2}{3}x - \dfrac{4}{3}$	(x, y)
-2	$-\dfrac{2}{3}(-2) - \dfrac{4}{3} = 0$	$(-2,0)$
4	$-\dfrac{2}{3}(4) - \dfrac{4}{3} = -4$	$(4,-4)$

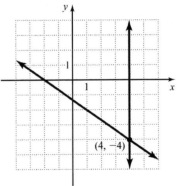

Intersection is $(4,-4)$.

4. $1.5x - 3y = 6$

$-3y = -1.5x + 6$

$y = 0.5x - 2$

x	$y = 0.5x - 2$	(x, y)
0	$0.5(0) - 2 = -2$	$(0,-2)$
2	$0.5(2) - 2 = -1$	$(2,-1)$

$-3x + 6y = -6$

$6y = 3x - 6$

$y = \dfrac{1}{2}x - 1$

x	$y=\dfrac{1}{2}x-1$	(x,y)
0	$\dfrac{1}{2}(0)-1=-1$	$(0,-1)$
2	$\dfrac{1}{2}(2)-1=0$	$(2,0)$

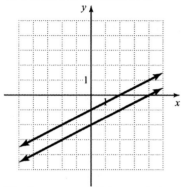

The lines are parallel, no solution.

5. $x=6\left(\dfrac{1}{3}x+3\right)-11$

$x=2x+18-11$

$-x=7$

$x=-7$

$y=\dfrac{1}{3}(-7)+3$

$y=-\dfrac{7}{3}+\dfrac{9}{3}=\dfrac{2}{3}$

$\left(-7,\dfrac{2}{3}\right)$

6. $5p-q=1$

$-q=-5p+1$

$q=5p-1$

$7p-2(5p-1)=-1$

$7p-10p+2=-1$

$-3p=-3$

$p=1$

$q=5(1)-1=4$

$p=1,\ q=4$

7. $8x=4y-24$

$x=0.5y-3$

$1.2(0.5y-3)-0.6y=-3.6$

$0.6y-3.6-0.6y=-3.6$

$-3.6=-3.6$

There are infinitely many solutions.

8. $2x-2y=5$

$\dfrac{5x+2y=9}{7x\quad=14}$

$x=2$

$2(2)-2y=5$

$4-2y=5$

$-2y=1$

$y=-\dfrac{1}{2}$

$\left(2,-\dfrac{1}{2}\right)$

9. $4x+5y=20 \xrightarrow{\times3} 12x+15y=60$

$6x-3y=-12\xrightarrow{\times(-2)}\dfrac{-12x+6y=24}{21y=84}$

$y=4$

$4x+5(4)=20$

$4x+20=20$

$4x=0$

$x=0$

$(0,4)$

10. $\dfrac{1}{4}u-3v=-4 \xrightarrow{\times8} 2u-24v=-32$

$\dfrac{2}{3}u-8v=-11\xrightarrow{\times(-3)}\dfrac{-2u+24v=33}{0=1\ \text{False}}$

No solution.

11. $3(-2)+4(-1)-8\left(\dfrac{1}{2}\right)\overset{?}{=}-14$

$-6-4-4\overset{?}{=}-14 \quad -14=-14\ \text{True}$

$2(-2)-3(-1)+6\left(\dfrac{1}{2}\right)\overset{?}{=}2$

$-4+3+3\overset{?}{=}2 \qquad 2=2\ \text{True}$

$(-2)+2(-1)-2\left(\dfrac{1}{2}\right)\overset{?}{=}-5$

$-2-2-1\overset{?}{=}-5 \qquad -5=-5\ \text{True}$

Yes, it is a solution.

12. $-2x-y+3z=5\xrightarrow{\times(-3)}6x+3y-9z=-15$

$4x-3y+z=29 \longrightarrow \dfrac{4x-3y+z=29}{10x\quad-8z=14}$

$-2x-y+3z=5\xrightarrow{\times2}-4x-2y+6z=10$

$3x+2y-4z=-9\longrightarrow \dfrac{3x+2y-4z=-9}{-x\quad+2z=1}$

$10x-8z=14\longrightarrow10x-8z=14$

$-x+2z=1\xrightarrow{\times4}\dfrac{-4x+8z=4}{6x\quad=18}$

$x=3$

$-(3)+2z=1$ $\qquad$ $-2(3)-y+3(2)=5$

$2z=4$ $\qquad$ $-6-y+6=5$

$z=2$ $\qquad$ $-y=5$

$\qquad\qquad$ $y=-5$

$(3,-5,2)$

$y=1$

$1.5x+3.5y=2$

$1.5x+3.5(1)=2$ $\qquad$ $1.4(1)-0.9z=-1.3$

$1.5x=-1.5$ $\qquad$ $-0.9z=-2.7$

$x=-1$ $\qquad$ $z=3$

$(-1,1,3)$

13. $1.4y-0.9z=-1.3\longrightarrow$

$\qquad\qquad$ $1.4y-0.9z=-1.3$

$-0.1x-0.2y+0.3z=0.8\xrightarrow{\times 3}$

$\qquad\qquad$ $\underline{-0.3x-0.6y+0.9z=2.4}$

$\qquad\qquad$ $-0.3x+0.8y\qquad=1.1$

$-0.3x+0.8y=1.1\xrightarrow{\times 5}-1.5x+4.0y=5.5$

$1.5x+3.5y=2\quad\longrightarrow\quad \underline{1.5x+3.5y=2}$

$\qquad\qquad\qquad\qquad 7.5y=7.5$

14. $\begin{bmatrix}2 & -4 & 5 & | & 7 \\ 1 & -3 & 2 & | & 5 \\ 3 & -1 & 1 & | & -6\end{bmatrix}$ interchange rows 1 and 2 $\begin{bmatrix}1 & -3 & 2 & | & 5 \\ 2 & -4 & 5 & | & 7 \\ 3 & -1 & 1 & | & -6\end{bmatrix}$

$\begin{bmatrix}1 & -3 & 2 & | & 5 \\ 2 & -4 & 5 & | & 7 \\ 3 & -1 & 1 & | & -6\end{bmatrix}$
add $(-2)\times$ row 1 to row 2
add $(-3)\times$ row 1 to row 3
$\rightarrow \begin{bmatrix}1 & -3 & 2 & | & 5 \\ 2+(-2)(1) & -4+(-2)(-3) & 5+(-2)(2) & | & 7+(-2)(5) \\ 3+(-3)(1) & -1+(-3)(-3) & 1+(-3)(2) & | & -6+(-3)(5)\end{bmatrix}=\begin{bmatrix}1 & -3 & 2 & | & 5 \\ 0 & 2 & 1 & | & -3 \\ 0 & 8 & -5 & | & -21\end{bmatrix}$

$\begin{bmatrix}1 & -3 & 2 & | & 5 \\ 0 & 2 & 1 & | & -3 \\ 0 & 8 & -5 & | & -21\end{bmatrix}$
multiply row 2 by $\left(\dfrac{1}{2}\right)$
add $(-4)\times$ row 2 to row 3
$\rightarrow \begin{bmatrix}1 & -3 & 2 & | & 5 \\ 0 & 2\left(\dfrac{1}{2}\right) & 1\left(\dfrac{1}{2}\right) & | & -3\left(\dfrac{1}{2}\right) \\ 0 & 8+(-4)(2) & -5+(-4)(1) & | & -21+(-4)(-3)\end{bmatrix}\rightarrow \begin{bmatrix}1 & -3 & 2 & | & 5 \\ 0 & 1 & \dfrac{1}{2} & | & -\dfrac{3}{2} \\ 0 & 0 & -9 & | & -9\end{bmatrix}$

$\begin{bmatrix}1 & -3 & 2 & | & 5 \\ 0 & 1 & \dfrac{1}{2} & | & -\dfrac{3}{2} \\ 0 & 0 & -9 & | & -9\end{bmatrix}$
Multiply row 3 by $\left(-\dfrac{1}{9}\right)$
$\rightarrow \begin{bmatrix}1 & -3 & 2 & | & 5 \\ 0 & 1 & \dfrac{1}{2} & | & -\dfrac{3}{2} \\ 0 & 0 & -9\left(-\dfrac{1}{9}\right) & | & -9\left(-\dfrac{1}{9}\right)\end{bmatrix}\rightarrow \begin{bmatrix}1 & -3 & 2 & | & 5 \\ 0 & 1 & \dfrac{1}{2} & | & -\dfrac{3}{2} \\ 0 & 0 & 1 & | & 1\end{bmatrix}$

$z=1$ $\qquad$ $y+\dfrac{1}{2}z=-\dfrac{3}{2}$ $\qquad$ $x-3y+2z=5$

$\qquad\qquad$ $y+\dfrac{1}{2}(1)=-\dfrac{3}{2}$ $\qquad$ $x-3(-2)+2(1)=5$

$\qquad\qquad\qquad$ $y=-\dfrac{4}{2}$ $\qquad$ $x+6+2=5$

$\qquad\qquad\qquad\qquad$ $x+8=5$

$\qquad\qquad\qquad$ $y=-2$ $\qquad$ $x=-3$

$(-3,-2,1)$

15.

$6x - 4y \geq -16$

$-4y \geq -6x - 16$

$y \leq \dfrac{3}{2}x + 4$ The boundry line is solid

x	$y = \dfrac{3}{2}x + 4$	(x, y)
-2	$\dfrac{3}{2}(-2) + 4 = 1$	$(-2, 1)$
0	$\dfrac{3}{2}(0) + 4 = 4$	$(0, 4)$

Test point is $(0, 0)$.

$6(0) - 4(0) \overset{?}{\geq} -16$

$0 \geq -16$, shade the half-plane containing $(0, 0)$.

$x + 2y > -2$

$2y > -x - 2$

$y > -\dfrac{1}{2}x - 1$ The boundary line is dashed.

x	$y = -\dfrac{1}{2}x - 1$	(x, y)
0	$-\dfrac{1}{2}(0) - 1 = -1$	$(0, -1)$
2	$-\dfrac{1}{2}(2) - 1 = -2$	$(2, -2)$

Test point is $(0, 0)$.

$(0) + 2(0) \overset{?}{>} -2$

$0 > -2$, shade the half-plane containing $(0, 0)$.

$x \leq 3$

The boundary line is solid.

$x = 3$	y	(x, y)
3	0	$(3, 0)$
3	2	$(3, 2)$

Test point is $(0, 0)$.

$0 \leq 3$, shade the half-plane
containing $(0, 0)$.

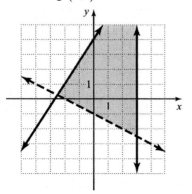

16.   Let l be the length of the field and w be the width of the field. Perimeter is twice the length plus twice the width.

$2l + 2w = 350$

$w = l - 55$

$2l + 2(l - 55) = 350$

$2l + 2l - 110 = 350$

$4l = 460$

$l = 115$

$w = 115 - 55$

$w = 60$

The length is 115 yd and the width is 60 yd.

17.   Let p be the rate of the airplane in still air and w be the rate of the wind.

$p - w = 468$

$\underline{p + w = 486}$

$2p \quad = 954$

$p = 477$

The rate of the airplane in still air was 477 mph.

18.   Let l represent the money invested in the low-risk fund and h represent the money invested in the high-risk fund.

$l + h = 8000 \xrightarrow{\times 0.024} 0.024l + 0.024h = 192$

$0.036l - 0.024h = -12 \longrightarrow$

$\qquad \underline{0.036l - 0.024h = -12}$

$\qquad 0.06l \qquad\quad = 180$

$l = 3000$

$3000 + h = 8000$

$h = 5000$

$3000 was invested in the low-risk fund and $5000 was invested in the high-risk fund.

19.   Let y be the number of servings of yogurt, b be the number of servings of bagels and j be the number of servings of orange juice.

$100y + 290b + 110j = 820$

$4y + 11b + 2j = 25$

$150y + 100b + 20j = 460$

$100y + 290b + 110j = 820 \longrightarrow$

$\qquad\qquad 100y + 290b + 110j = 820$

$4y + 11b + 2j = 25 \xrightarrow{\times(-55)}$

$\qquad \underline{-220y - 605b - 110j = -1375}$

$\qquad -120y - 315b \qquad = -555$

$100y + 290b + 110j = 820 \longrightarrow$

$\qquad\qquad 100y + 290b + 110j = 820$

$150y + 100b + 20j = 460 \xrightarrow{\times(-5.5)}$

$\qquad \underline{-825y - 550b - 110j = -2530}$

$\qquad -725y - 260b \qquad = -1710$

$-120y-315b=-555 \xrightarrow{\times\frac{1}{3}} -40y-105b=-185$

$-725y-260b=-1710 \xrightarrow{\times\left(-\frac{1}{5}\right)} 145y+52b=342$

$-40y-105b=-185 \xrightarrow{\times 29}$

$$-1160y-3045b=-5365$$

$145y+52b=342 \xrightarrow{\times 8}$ $\underline{\quad 1160y+416b=2736\quad}$

$$-2629b=-2629$$

$b=1$

$145y+52(1)=342 \qquad 4(2)+11(1)+2j=25$

$145y=290 \qquad\qquad 8+11+2j=25$

$y=2 \qquad\qquad\quad 2j=6$

$\qquad\qquad\qquad\qquad\quad j=3$

2 servings of yogurt, 1 plain bagel, and 3 servings of orange juice.

20. Let x be the hours the faster student drives per day and y be the hours the slower student drives per day..

a. $64x+60y \geq 300$

$x+y \leq 12$

$x>y$

b. $64x+60y \geq 300$

$60y \geq -64x+300$

$y \geq -\dfrac{16}{15}x+5$

The boundary line is solid.

x	$y=-\dfrac{16}{15}x+5$	(x,y)
0	$-\dfrac{16}{15}(0)+5=5$	$(0,5)$
3	$-\dfrac{16}{15}(3)+5=\dfrac{9}{5}$	$\left(3,\dfrac{9}{5}\right)$

Test point is $(0,0)$.

$64(0)+60(0)\overset{?}{\geq}300$

$0 \ngeq 300$, shade the half plane not containing $(0,0)$.

$x+y \leq 12$

$y \leq -x+12$

The boundary line is solid

x	$y=-x+12$	(x,y)
0	$-(0)+12=12$	$(0,12)$
12	$-(12)+12=0$	$(12,0)$

Test point is $(0,0)$.

$(0)+(0)\overset{?}{\leq}12$

$0 \leq 12$, shade the half-plane containing $(0,0)$.

$x>y$

$y<x$

The boundary line is dashed.

x	$y=x$	(x,y)
0	0	$(0,0)$
10	10	$(10,10)$

Test point is $(10,0)$.

$0<10$, shade the half-plane containing $(10,0)$.

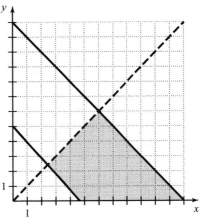

c. Answers may vary. Possible answers: $(6,4)$: the faster student drives 6 hr and the slower student drives 4 hr. $(5,3)$: the faster student drives 5 hr and the slower student drives 3 hr.

Cumulative Review Exercises

1. $9x-\dfrac{1}{2}(12-4x)=6x+14$

$9x-\dfrac{1}{2}(12)-\dfrac{1}{2}(-4x)=6x+14$

$9x-6+2x=6x+14$

$11x-6=6x+14$

$11x-6x-6=6x-6x+14$

$5x-6=14$

$5x-6+6=14+6$

$5x=20$

$\dfrac{5x}{5}=\dfrac{20}{5}$

$x=4$

2. $8 - |x - 5| = 3$

$8 - 8 - |x - 5| = 3 - 8$

$-|x - 5| = -5$

$-|x - 5|(-1) = -5(-1)$

$|x - 5| = 5$

$x - 5 = 5$ or $x - 5 = -5$

$x - 5 + 5 = 5 + 5$ $x - 5 + 5 = -5 + 5$

$x = 10$ $x = 0$

3. $-1 < 5 - 2x \le 7$

$-1 - 5 < 5 - 5 - 2x \le 7 - 5$

$-6 < -2x \le 2$

$\dfrac{-6}{-2} > \dfrac{-2x}{-2} \ge \dfrac{2}{-2}$

$3 > x \ge -1$

$-1 \le x < 3$

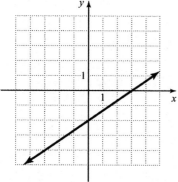

4. $4x - 6y = 12$

$-6y = -4x + 12$

$y = \dfrac{2}{3}x - 2$

x	$y = \dfrac{2}{3}x - 2$	(x, y)
-3	$\dfrac{2}{3}(-3) - 2 = -4$	$(-3, -4)$
0	$\dfrac{2}{3}(0) - 2 = -2$	$(0, -2)$
3	$\dfrac{2}{3}(3) - 2 = 0$	$(3, 0)$

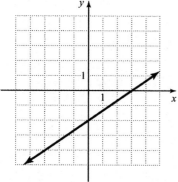

5. $12x + 3y = -9$

$3y = -12x - 9$

$y = -4x - 3$

$y = mx + b, \; m = -4$

Perpendicular lines have slopes that are negative

reciprocals. The needed slope is $\dfrac{1}{4}$.

$m = \dfrac{1}{4}$, passes through $(4, -1)$

$y - y_1 = m(x - x_1)$

$y - (-1) = \dfrac{1}{4}(x - 4)$

$y + 1 = \dfrac{1}{4}x - 1$

$y = \dfrac{1}{4}x - 2$

6. $g(x) = x^2 - 5x - 7$

$g(-2) = (-2)^2 - 5(-2) - 7$

$g(-2) = 4 + 10 - 7$

$g(-2) = 7$

7.   No, the graph fails the vertical line test. The y-axis crosses the graph more than once.

8.   Let h be the number of hours worked repairing the automobile.

$35h + 112 = 322$

$35h = 210$

$h = 6$

The customer was charged for 6 hr or labor.

9.   Let s be the weight registered by the scale.

$|2.43 - s| = 0.05$

$2.43 - s = 0.05$ or $2.43 - s = -0.05$

$-s = -2.38$ $-s = -2.48$

$s = 2.38$ $s = 2.48$

price $= 1.49s = 1.49(2.38) = 3.5462$

price $= 1.49s = 1.49(2.48) = 3.6952$

The customer could be charged between \$3.55 and \$3.70 for the purchase.

10.   Points are: $(1, 88)$ and $(3, 24)$

$m = \dfrac{v_2 - v_1}{t_2 - t_1} = \dfrac{24 - 88}{3 - 1} = \dfrac{-64}{2} = -32$

Using $(3, 24)$

$v - v_1 = m(t - t_1)$

$v - 24 = -32(t - 3)$

$v - 24 = -32t + 96$

$v = -32t + 120$

t	$v = -32t + 120$	(t, v)
0	$-32(0) + 120 = 120$	$(0, 120)$
5	$-32(5) + 120 = -40$	$(5, -40)$

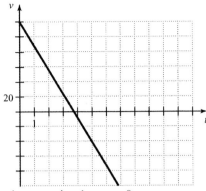

t-intercept is where $v = 0$.

$0 = -32t + 120$

$-120 = -32t$

$\dfrac{-120}{-32} = t$

$t = \dfrac{15}{4}$ $\left(\dfrac{15}{4}, 0\right)$

v- intercept is where $t = 0$.

$v = -32(0) + 120$

$v = 120$

$(0, 120)$

t-intercept : $\left(\dfrac{15}{4}, 0\right)$; v-intercept: (0, 120). The t-

intercept represents the time at which the object changes from an upward direction to a downward direction. The v-intercept represents the initial velocity of the object.

Chapter 5 Polynomials

Pretest

1. a. $6x^4, \ -2x, \ \dfrac{x^3}{4}, \ -x^6, \ 3x^2$

    b. $6, -2, ¼, -1, 3$

    c. $-x^6 + 6x^4 + \dfrac{x^3}{4} + 3x^2 - 2x$

    d. 6

    e. Leading term: $-x^6$;
        leading coefficient: -1.

2. $5n^3 - n^2 + \ 8n - 12$

    $\underline{-7n^3 + 4n^2 \qquad +9}$

    $-2n^3 + 3n^2 + 8n - 3$

3. $8x^4 - 3x^2 + 2x - \left(-10x^4 - x^2 + 9x + 1\right)$

    $8x^4 - 3x^2 + 2x + 10x^4 + x^2 - 9x - 1 =$

    $18x^4 - 2x^2 - 7x - 1$

4. $\left(\dfrac{1}{4}pq^2\right)8p^2 - \left(\dfrac{1}{4}pq^2\right)4pq + \left(\dfrac{1}{4}pq^2\right)16q^2$

    $2p^3q^2 - p^2q^3 + 4pq^4$

5. $6x^2 + 15xy - 2xy - 5y^2 =$

    $6x^2 + 13xy - 5y^2$

6. $(6n-1)(6n-1) = 36n^2 - 6n - 6n + 1$

    $36n^2 - 12n + 1$

7. $64a^2 - 24ab + 24ab - 9b^2$

    $64a^2 - 9b^2$

8. $u^3 - 2u^2 + 4u + 2u^2 - 4u + 8$

    $u^3 + 8$

9. $\begin{array}{r} 3x^3 - 2x^2 + x + \dfrac{-9}{2x+1} \\ 2x+1\overline{\smash{\big)}\,6x^4 - x^3 + 0x^2 + x - 9} \\ \underline{6x^4 + 3x^3} \\ -4x^3 + 0x^2 \\ \underline{-4x^3 - 2x^2} \\ 2x^2 + x \\ \underline{2x^2 + x} \\ -9 \end{array}$

10. $(x+4)(x-8)$

11. $3(-24) = -72$

    $18(-4) = -72 \quad 18 + (-4) = 14$

    $3x^2 + 18x - 4x - 24$

    $3x(x+6) - 4(x+6)$

    $(3x-4)(x+6)$

12. $2q\left(25p^2 - 20pq + 4q^2\right)$

    $2q\left((5p)^2 - 2(5p)(2q) + (2q)^2\right)$

    $2q(5p - 2q)^2$

13. $(6ab)^2 - (11)^2$

    $(6ab+11)(6ab-11)$

14. $9x^2(x-y) - 4(x-y)$

    $\left(9x^2 - 4\right)(x-y)$

    $\left((3x)^2 - (2)^2\right)(x-y)$

    $(3x+2)(3x-2)(x-y)$

15. $12t^2 - 18t = 0$

    $6t(2t - 3) = 0$

    $6t = 0 \quad 2t - 3 = 0$

    $t = 0 \qquad 2t = 3$

    $\qquad\qquad t = \dfrac{3}{2}$

16. $x^2 - 10x + 24 = 3$

    $x^2 - 10x + 21 = 0$

    $(x-7)(x-3) = 0$

    $x - 7 = 0 \quad x - 3 = 0$

    $x = 7 \qquad x = 3$

17. $0.25(100)^2 - 20(100) - 125 =$

    $0.25(10000) - 2000 - 125 =$

    $2500 - 2125 = 375$

    The profit is $375.

18. $(100+2x)(70+x)$

    $7000 + 100x + 140x + 2x^2$

    $2x^2 + 240x + 7000$

    The area is $\left(2x^2 + 240x + 7000\right)\text{m}^2$.

19. $a\left(T_1^4 - T_2^4\right) = a\left(T_1^2 - T_2^2\right)\left(T_1^2 + T_2^2\right) =$

    $a\left(T_1 - T_2\right)\left(T_1 + T_2\right)\left(T_1^2 + T_2^2\right)$

20. $64000(1+r)^2 = 81000$

    $(1+r)^2 = \dfrac{81}{64}$

    $r^2 + 2r + 1 = \dfrac{81}{64}$

    $r^2 + 2r - \dfrac{17}{64} = 0$

    $64r^2 + 128r - 17 = 0$

    $(8r-1)(8r+17) = 0$

$8r - 1 = 0$ $8r + 17 = 0$

$8r = 1$ $8r = -17$

$r = 0.125$ $r = -2.125$

The negative answer is meaningless. The average rate of return was 12.5%.

Exercises 5.1 Addition and Subtraction of Polynomials

1.   Polynomial.

3.   Not a polynomial, $\dfrac{4}{n}$ disqualifies it.

5.   Polynomial.

7.   Not a polynomial, n^{-1} disqualifies it.

9.   Terms: $5x^3,\ -x^2,\ -6x,\ 7$

    Coefficients: $5,\ -1,\ -6,\ 7$

11.   Terms: $4n,\ -\dfrac{n^2}{3}$

    Coefficients: $4,\ -\dfrac{1}{3}$

13.   Terms: $3a^2,\ -8ab,\ 5b^2$

    Coefficients: $3,\ -8,\ 5$

15.   Polynomial of degree 3.

17.   Binomial of degree 2.

19.   Trinomial of degree 4.

21.   Monomial of degree 5.

23. $-3x^2 + 9x + 2$;

    leading term: $-3x^2$;

    leading coefficient: -3.

25. $5x^5 + 8x^4 - 2x^3 - x + 10$;

    leading term: $5x^5$;

    leading coefficient: 5.

27. $-x^6 + 8x^4 - x^3 + 4x^2 + 5x - 11$;

    leading term: $-x^6$;

    leading coefficient: -1.

29. $-x^3 - 4x^2 y + 5xy^2 + y^3$;

31. $p^5 q^4 + 4p^4 + 2p^3 q + 3p^2 q^2 - pq^3$

33. $-5x^2 + 3x^2 + 10x - 8 - 1$

    $-2x^2 + 10x - 9$

35. $4n^3 - n^3 - 6n^2 + 7n^2 - 7n + 9n + 2 - 2$

    $3n^3 + n^2 + 2n$

37. $-6x^4 + \dfrac{1}{2}x^2 - \dfrac{2}{3}x^2 + \dfrac{3}{8} + \dfrac{3}{4}$

    $-6x^4 - \dfrac{1}{6}x^2 + \dfrac{9}{8}$

39.   a. $2(2)^2 - 7(2) + 6 = 2(4) - 14 + 6 =$

       $8 - 8 = 0$

    b. $2(-3)^2 - 7(-3) + 6 = 2(9) + 21 + 6 =$

       $18 + 27 = 45$

41.   a. $8\left(\dfrac{3}{2}\right)^3 - 4\left(\dfrac{3}{2}\right)^2 - 2\left(\dfrac{3}{2}\right) + 7 =$

       $8\left(\dfrac{27}{8}\right) - 4\left(\dfrac{9}{4}\right) - 3 + 7 =$

       $27 - 9 + 4 = 22$

    b. $8\left(-\dfrac{1}{2}\right)^3 - 4\left(-\dfrac{1}{2}\right)^2 - 2\left(-\dfrac{1}{2}\right) + 7 =$

       $8\left(-\dfrac{1}{8}\right) - 4\left(\dfrac{1}{4}\right) + 1 + 7 =$

       $-1 - 1 + 8 = 6$

43. $3x + 9 + 2x^2 - 4x + 1 =$

    $2x^2 + 3x - 4x + 9 + 1 = 2x^2 - x + 10$

45. $a^3 - 5a^2 + 3 - 5a^2 - a + 3 =$

    $a^3 - 5a^2 - 5a^2 - a + 3 + 3 = a^3 - 10a^2 - a + 6$

47. $3x^4 - 7x^3 + x^2 + 8x - 10 + 8x^3$

       $-1 + 10 - 9x - 7x^2 + x^4 =$

    $3x^4 + x^4 - 7x^3 + 8x^3 + x^2 - 7x^2$

       $+ 8x - 9x - 10 - 1 + 10 =$

    $4x^4 + x^3 - 6x^2 - x - 1$

49. $12p^5 - 2p^3 + 4p^2 - 11p -$

       $\left(13p^5 + p^4 + 2p^3 - 3p^2 - 11p - 1\right) =$

    $12p^5 - 2p^3 + 4p^2 - 11p$

       $-13p^5 - p^4 - 2p^3 + 3p^2 + 11p + 1 =$

    $12p^5 - 13p^5 - p^4 - 2p^3$

       $-2p^3 + 4p^2 + 3p^2 - 11p + 11p + 1 =$

    $-p^5 - p^4 - 4p^3 + 7p^2 + 1$

51. $x^2 + 5xy + 6y^2 + 9x^2 y - 2xy^2 -$

       $3xy + x^2 - y^2 + 2x^2 y - 12xy^2 =$

    $x^2 + x^2 + 9x^2 y + 2x^2 y + 5xy -$

       $3xy - 2xy^2 - 12xy^2 + 6y^2 - y^2 =$

    $2x^2 + 11x^2 y + 2xy - 14xy^2 + 5y^2$

53. $-y^3 - 3y^2 + 4y$

    $\dfrac{6y^3 + 8y^2 - 3y + 2}{5y^3 + 5y^2 + y + 2}$

55. $3p^4 - 2p^2 \quad\ -5 \quad\ \rightarrow \quad\ 3p^4 - 2p^2 \quad\quad -5$

    $\dfrac{-\left(p^2 - 10p + 21\right)}{} \quad \rightarrow \quad \dfrac{-p^2 + 10p - 21}{3p^4 - 3p^2 + 10p - 26}$

57. $-3x^2 - 3x + 12$

    $8x^2 - 4x - 13$

    $\dfrac{-5x^2 + 7x}{\qquad -1}$

59. $-x^3 + 10x^2 y - 14xy^2 + 16y^3$
$-\left(9y^3 - 11xy^2 + 2x^3\right)$

$-x^3 + 10x^2 y - 14xy^2 + 16y^3$
$\underline{-2x^3 + 11xy^2 - 9y^3}$
$-3x^3 + 10x^2 y - 3xy^2 + 7y^3$

61. $3x^2 - 7x + 5 - 5x + 8x^2 + 2 + 6x - 9x^2 =$
$3x^2 + 8x^2 - 9x^2 - 7x - 5x + 6x + 5 + 2 =$
$2x^2 - 6x + 7$

63. $12n^3 + 16 - 11n^3 + 9n^2 - 3n - 8 + 10n + 13 =$
$12n^3 - 11n^3 + 9n^2 - 3n + 10n + 16 - 8 + 13$
$n^3 + 9n^2 + 7n + 21$

65. $f(x) + g(x) = 2x^2 - 8 + 2x^2 + 7x + 5$
$= 2x^2 + 2x^2 + 7x - 8 + 5$
$= 4x^2 + 7x - 3$

$f(x) - g(x) = 2x^2 - 8 - \left(2x^2 + 7x + 5\right)$
$= 2x^2 - 8 - 2x^2 - 7x - 5$
$= 2x^2 - 2x^2 - 7x - 8 - 5$
$= -7x - 13$

67. $f(x) + g(x) = -5x^4 + 6x^2 - 3$
$\underline{4x^4 - 3x^3 + 2x^2 - x }$
$-x^4 - 3x^3 + 8x^2 - x - 3$
$f(x) - g(x) = -5x^4 + 6x^2 - 3$
$\underline{-\left(4x^4 - 3x^3 + 2x^2 - x\right)}$

$f(x) - g(x) = -5x^4 + 6x^2 - 3$
$\underline{-4x^4 + 3x^3 - 2x^2 + x }$
$-9x^4 + 3x^3 + 4x^2 + x - 3$

69.

Time, t (in sec)	$-16t^2 + 520$	Height (in ft)
0	$-16(0)^2 + 520$ $0 + 520$	520
1	$-16(1)^2 + 520$ $-16 + 520$	504
2	$-16(2)^2 + 520$ $-64 + 520$	456
3	$-16(3)^2 + 520$ $-144 + 520$	376

71. $18(100) + 3.5(100)^2 - 0.005(100)^3 =$
$1800 + 35000 - 5000 = 31800$
The factory's revenue in May was $31,800.

73. $8t^4 - 82t^3 + 245t^2 - 303t + 38387$
$\underline{25t^2 + 93t + 14783}$
$8t^4 - 82t^3 + 270t^2 - 210t + 53170$
($8t^4 - 82t^3 + 270t^2 - 210t + 53170$) thousand.

75. $4x^2 - x + 909 - \left(-24x^2 - 21x + 783\right) =$
$4x^2 - x + 909 + 24x^2 + 21x - 783 =$
$28x^2 + 20x + 126$
($28x^2 + 20x + 126$) thousand.

77. $R(x) = -0.005x^2 + 40x$
$C(x) = 12x + 10000$
$P(x) = R(x) - C(x)$
$P(x) = -0.005x^2 + 40x - 12x - 10000$
$P(x) = -0.005x^2 + 28x - 10000$

Exercises 5.2 Multiplication of Polynomials

1. $(6)(-5)n^3 \bullet n^3 = -30n^{3+3} = -30n^6$

3. $\left(-\dfrac{2}{3}\right)(-9)r \bullet r^3 \bullet t^2 \bullet t = 6r^{1+3}t^{2+1} = 6r^4 t^3$

5. $(10)(-1)(-2)x^5 \bullet x^3 \bullet x^4 = 20x^{5+3+4} = 20x^{12}$

7. $(-3)(2)p \bullet p^3 \bullet q \bullet q^2 \bullet r = -6p^{1+3}q^{1+2}r$
$= -6p^4 q^3 r$

9. $\left(-4ab^5\right) \bullet \left(-4ab^5\right) \bullet \left(-4ab^5\right) =$
$(-4)(-4)(-4)a \bullet a \bullet a \bullet b^5 \bullet b^5 \bullet b^5 =$
$-64a^{1+1+1}b^{5+5+5} = -64a^3 b^{15}$

11. $(-2x)(5) - (-2x)(4x) = -10x + 8x^2$
or $8x^2 - 10x$

13. $4n^2(6n) - 4n^2(-1) = 24n^3 + 4n^2$

15. $(-3x)x^2 - (-3x)4x + (-3x)5 =$
$-3x^3 + 12x^2 - 15x$

17. $\left(\dfrac{1}{2}n^3\right)12m^2 + \left(\dfrac{1}{2}n^3\right)8n = 6m^2 n^3 + 4n^4$

19. $\left(4x^2 y^4\right)\left(7x^5 - 4x^3 + 1\right) =$
$\left(4x^2 y^4\right)7x^5 - \left(4x^2 y^4\right)4x^3 + \left(4x^2 y^4\right) =$
$28x^7 y^4 - 16x^5 y^4 + 4x^2 y^4$

21. $\left(-2a^2 b^3\right)\left(-8a^3\right) + \left(-2a^2 b^3\right)3a^2 b -$
$\left(-2a^2 b^3\right)4ab^2 + \left(-2a^2 b^3\right)b^3 =$
$16a^5 b^3 - 6a^4 b^4 + 8a^3 b^5 - 2a^2 b^6$

23. $(2y)\bullet1+(2y)4y-(2y)4y^2+$
$\qquad\qquad (3y^2)y-(3y^2)2=$
$2y+8y^2-8y^3+3y^3-6y^2=$
$-5y^3+2y^2+2y$

25. $(6x^4)2x-(6x^4)1+(-4x^3)2x^2-(-4x^3)5+$
$\qquad\qquad (3)2x^5+(3)x^4-(3)8x^3=$
$12x^5-6x^4-8x^5+20x^3+6x^5+3x^4-24x^3=$
$10x^5-3x^4-4x^3$

27. $\left(\frac{1}{4}p^2\right)8p^2-\left(\frac{1}{4}p^2\right)12pq+\left(\frac{1}{4}p^2\right)4q^2+$
$\qquad\qquad (-q^2)3q^2-(-q^2)5pq+(-q^2)p^2=$
$2p^4-3p^3q+p^2q^2-3q^4+5pq^3-p^2q^2=$
$2p^4-3p^3q+5pq^3-3q^4$

29. $(x+2)(x+4)=$
$\quad$ F $\quad$ O $\quad$ I $\quad$ L
$x^2+4x+2x+8=x^2+6x+8$

31. $(n-6)(n-3)=$
$\quad$ F $\quad$ O $\quad$ I $\quad$ L
$n^2-3n-6n+18=n^2-9n+18$

33. $(5-a)(a+7)$
$\quad$ F $\quad$ O $\quad$ I $\quad$ L
$5a+35-a^2-7a=-a^2-2a+35$

35. $(y+7)^2=(y+7)(y+7)=$
$\quad$ F $\quad$ O $\quad$ I $\quad$ L
$y^2+7y+7y+49=y^2+14y+49$

37. $(2x-1)(x+4)=$
$\quad$ F $\quad$ O $\quad$ I $\quad$ L
$2x^2+8x-x-4=2x^2+7x-4$

39. $(3-2x)(2+3x)=$
$\quad$ F $\quad$ O $\quad$ I $\quad$ L
$6+9x-4x-6x^2=-6x^2+5x+6$

41. $(5x+3)(6x+5)=$
$\quad$ F $\quad$ O $\quad$ I $\quad$ L
$30x^2+25x+18x+15=30x^2+43x+15$

43. $(4x-9)^2=(4x-9)(4x-9)=$
$\quad$ F $\quad$ O $\quad$ I $\quad$ L
$16x^2-36x-36x+81=16x^2-72x+81$

45. $(a-b)(2a+3b)=$
$\quad$ F $\quad$ O $\quad$ I $\quad$ L
$2a^2+3ab-2ab-3b^2=2a^2+ab-3b^2$

47. $(9p+10q)(2p-q)=$
$\quad$ F $\quad$ O $\quad$ I $\quad$ L
$18p^2-9pq+20pq-10q^2=$
$18p^2+11pq-10q^2$

49. $(7x-11y)(8x-7y)=$
$\quad$ F $\quad$ O $\quad$ I $\quad$ L
$56x^2-49xy-88xy+77y^2=$
$56x^2-137xy+77y^2$

51. $\left(\frac{1}{2}x+6y\right)\left(\frac{2}{3}x+8y\right)=$
$\quad$ F $\quad$ O $\quad$ I $\quad$ L
$\frac{1}{3}x^2+4xy+4xy+48y^2=\frac{1}{3}x^2+8xy+48y^2$

53. $\quad n^2+3n+2$
$\qquad \underline{\quad n-1\quad}$
$\quad -n^2-3n-2$
$\quad \underline{n^3+3n^2+2n\quad}$
$\quad n^3+2n^2-n-2$

55. $\quad x^2-5x+6$
$\qquad \underline{\quad 3x+2\quad}$
$\quad 2x^2-10x+12$
$\underline{3x^3-15x^2+18x\quad}$
$3x^3-13x^2+8x+12$

57. $\quad 5x^2-10x+25$
$\qquad \underline{\quad \frac{1}{5}x^2-2\quad}$
$\quad -10x^2+20x-50$
$\underline{x^4-2x^3+5x^2\quad}$
$x^4-2x^3-5x^2+20x-50$

59. $\qquad 2x^3+x^2-6$
$\qquad\qquad \underline{\quad y-7x^2\quad}$
$\qquad -14x^5-7x^4+42x^2$
$\underline{2x^3y+x^2y-6y\qquad}$
$2x^3y+x^2y-6y-14x^5-7x^4+42x^2=$
$-14x^5-7x^4+42x^2+2x^3y+x^2y-6y$

61. $\qquad x^2-3x-4$
$\qquad \underline{\quad x^2+3x+4\quad}$
$\qquad 4x^2-12x-16$
$\qquad 3x^3-9x^2-12x$
$\underline{x^4-3x^3-4x^2\qquad}$
$x^4\qquad -9x^2-24x-16=$
$x^4-9x^2-24x-16$

63. $\left(x^3+4y^4\right)\left(3x^2+y\right)=$

    F   O   I   L

    $3x^5+x^3y+12x^2y^4+4y^5$

65. $\left(4p^2-3q^2\right)\left(3p^2+4q^2\right)=$

    F   O   I   L

    $12p^4+16p^2q^2-9p^2q^2-12q^4=$

    $12p^4+7p^2q^2-12q^4$

67. $(t-10)(t+10)=(t)^2-(10)^2=t^2-100$

69. $(x+8)^2=(x)^2+2(8)(x)+(8)^2=$

    $x^2+16x+64$

71. $(4n-3)(4n+3)=(4n)^2-(3)^2=16n^2-9$

73. $(2n-5)^2=(2n)^2+2(2n)(-5)+(-5)^2=$

    $4n^2-20n+25$

75. $\left(b-\dfrac{1}{3}a\right)^2=(b)^2+2(b)\left(-\dfrac{1}{3}a\right)+\left(-\dfrac{1}{3}a\right)^2=$

    $b^2-\dfrac{2}{3}ab+\dfrac{1}{9}a^2$ or $\dfrac{1}{9}a^2-\dfrac{2}{3}ab+b^2$

77. $(5x+y)(5x-y)=(5x)^2-(y)^2=25x^2-y^2$

79. $(11y-9x)(11y+9x)=(11y)^2-(9x)^2=$

    $121y^2-81x^2$

81. $(4p+7q)^2=(4p)^2+2(4p)(7q)+(7q)^2=$

    $16p^2+56pq+49q^2$

83. $\left(2x^2-9y^4\right)^2=$

    $\left(2x^2\right)^2+2\left(2x^2\right)\left(-9y^4\right)+\left(-9y^4\right)^2=$

    $4x^4-36x^2y^4+81y^8$

85. $\left(p^4-8q^2\right)\left(p^4+8q^2\right)=\left(p^4\right)^2-\left(8q^2\right)^2=$

    p^8-64q^4

87. $[(x+4)-y][(x+4)+y]=(x+4)^2-y^2=$

    $x^2+2(x)(4)+(4)^2-y^2=x^2+8x+16-y^2$

89. $[(1-a)-b]^2=$

    $(1-a)^2+2(1-a)(-b)+(-b)^2=$

    $1^2+2(1)(-a)+(-a)^2-2b+2ab+b^2=$

    $1-2a+a^2-2b+2ab+b^2=$

    $a^2+b^2-2a+2ab-2b+1$

91. $(x-3)(4x+1)(4x-1)=$

    $(x-3)\left((4x)^2-(1)^2\right)=(x-3)\left(16x^2-1\right)=$

    F   O   I   L

    $16x^3-x-48x^2+3=16x^3-48x^2-x+3$

93. $(2n-1)^3=(2n-1)(2n-1)^2=$

    $(2n-1)\left((2n)^2+2(2n)(-1)+(-1)^2\right)=$

    $(2n-1)\left(4n^2-4n+1\right)$

    $4n^2-4n+1$

    $\underline{\qquad 2n-1\qquad}$

    $-4n^2+4n-1$

    $\underline{8n^3-8n^2+2n\qquad}$

    $8n^3-12n^2+6n-1$

95. $(6a+b)(a-6b)(a+b)=$

    F   O   I   L

    $\left(6a^2-36ab+ab-6b^2\right)(a+b)=$

    $\left(6a^2-35ab-6b^2\right)(a+b)$

    $6a^2-35ab-6b^2$

    $\underline{\qquad a+b\qquad}$

    $6a^2b-35ab^2-6b^3$

    $\underline{6a^3-35a^2b-6ab^2\qquad}$

    $6a^3-29a^2b-41ab^2-6b^3$

97. $(x+2y)^3=(x+2y)(x+2y)^2=$

    $(x+2y)\left((x)^2+2(x)(2y)+(2y)^2\right)=$

    $(x+2y)\left(x^2+4xy+4y^2\right)$

    $x^2+4xy+4y^2$

    $\underline{\qquad x+2y\qquad}$

    $2x^2y+8xy^2+8y^3$

    $\underline{x^3+4x^2y+4xy^2\qquad}$

    $x^3+6x^2y+12xy^2+8y^3$

99. $(2x+3y)(2x-3y)\left(4x^2+9y^2\right)=$

    $\left((2x)^2-(3y)^2\right)\left(4x^2+9y^2\right)=$

    $\left(4x^2-9y^2\right)\left(4x^2+9y^2\right)=\left(4x^2\right)^2-\left(9y^2\right)^2=$

    $16x^4-81y^4$

101. $f(x)\bullet g(x)=\left(3x^2-1\right)(5x+2)=$

    F   O   I   L

    $15x^3+6x^2-5x-2$

103. $f(x)\bullet g(x)=\left(x^2+7x-3\right)\left(x^2-6x\right)=$

    x^2+7x-3

    $\underline{\qquad x^2-6x\qquad}$

    $-6x^3-42x^2+18x$

    $\underline{x^4+7x^3-3x^2\qquad}$

    $x^4+x^3-45x^2+18x$

105.   a. $f(x) = x^2 - 2x + 5$

$f(n-1) = (n-1)^2 - 2(n-1) + 5 =$

$n^2 - 2n + 1 - 2n + 2 + 5 = n^2 - 4n + 8$

b. $f(x) = x^2 - 2x + 5$

$f(2n+3x) = (2n+3)^2 - 2(2n+3) + 5 =$

$4n^2 + 12n + 9 - 4n - 6 + 5 =$

$4n^2 + 8n + 8$

107.   a. $f(x) = x^2 - x - 9$

$f(x-2) = (x-2)^2 - (x-2) - 9 =$

$x^2 - 4x + 4 - x + 2 - 9 = x^2 - 5x - 3$

b. $f(x-2) - f(x) =$

$x^2 - 5x - 3 - (x^2 - x - 9) =$

$x^2 - 5x - 3 - x^2 + x + 9 = -4x + 6$

c. $f(x+h) - f(x) =$

$(x+h)^2 - (x+h) - 9 - (x^2 - x - 9) =$

$x^2 + 2xh + h^2 - x - h - 9 - x^2 + x + 9 =$

$2xh + h^2 - h = h^2 + 2xh - h$

109. $p(V_2 - V_1) = pV_2 - pV_1$

111.   a. $(12+x)(6+x) =$

F   O   I   L

$72 + 12x + 6x + x^2 = x^2 + 18x + 72$

b. $x^2 + 18x + 72 - 72 = x^2 + 18x$

The size of her patio will increase by $(x^2 + 18x)$ sq

ft.

113.   a. Longest panel: $(x+0.1)$ in. by $(x+0.1)$ in.

Shortest panel : $(x-0.1)$ in. by $(x-0.1)$ in.

b. $(x+0.1)^2 - (x-0.1)^2 =$

$x^2 + 0.2x + 0.01 - (x^2 - 0.2x + 0.01) =$

$x^2 + 0.2x + 0.01 - x^2 + 0.2x - 0.01 = 0.4x$

The difference in area between the largest and
smallest possible panel is $0.4x$ sq in.

115.   Volume is length$\times$ width$\times$ height.

$(18-2x)(12-2x)x =$

$(216 - 36x - 24x + 4x^2)x =$

$x(4x^2 - 60x + 216) = 4x^3 - 60x^2 + 216x$

The volume of the box is $4x^3 - 60x^2 + 216x$ cu. in.

117.

$$0.2x^3 - x^2 + 2x + 67$$

$$\underline{10x^2 + 40x + 512}$$

$$102.4x^3 - 512x^2 + 1024x + 34304$$

$$8x^4 - 40x^3 + 80x^2 + 2680x$$

$$\underline{2x^5 - 10x^4 + 20x^{33} + 670x^2}$$

$$2x^5 - 2x^4 + 82.4x^3 + 238x^2 + 3704x + 34304$$

dollars.

Exercises 5.3 Division of Polynomials

1. $\dfrac{6x^4}{2x^3} = \dfrac{6}{2} \bullet \dfrac{x^4}{x^3} = 3x^{4-3} = 3x$

3. $\dfrac{20y^5}{-4y^3} = \dfrac{20}{-4} \bullet \dfrac{y^5}{y^3} = -5y^{5-3} = -5y^2$

5. $\dfrac{-9x^5 y^2}{-3xy} = \dfrac{-9}{-3} \bullet \dfrac{x^5}{x} \bullet \dfrac{y^2}{y} = 3x^{5-1} y^{2-1} = 3x^4 y$

7. $\dfrac{1}{3x}(6x^3 + 9x^2) = \dfrac{6x^3}{3x} + \dfrac{9x^2}{3x} = 2x^{3-1} + 3x^{2-1} =$

$2x^2 + 3x$

9. $\dfrac{24n^3}{-4} - \dfrac{10n^2}{-4} + \dfrac{4n}{-4} = -6n^3 + \dfrac{5}{2}n^2 - n$

11. $\dfrac{54a^5}{6a^3} - \dfrac{6a^4}{6a^3} + \dfrac{36a^3}{6a^3} = 9a^{5-3} - a^{4-3} + 6a^{3-3} =$

$9a^2 - a + 6$

13. $\dfrac{16t^4}{-2t^2} + \dfrac{10t^3}{-2t^2} - \dfrac{18t^2}{-2t^2} - \dfrac{8t}{-2t^2} =$

$-8t^{4-2} - 5t^{3-2} + 9t^{2-2} + \dfrac{4}{t^{2-1}} =$

$-8t^2 - 5t + 9 + \dfrac{4}{t}$

15. $\dfrac{8p^2}{4q^2} - \dfrac{16pq}{4q^2} + \dfrac{28q^2}{4q^2} = \dfrac{2p^2}{q^2} - \dfrac{4p}{q^{2-1}} + 7q^{2-2} =$

$\dfrac{2p^2}{q^2} - \dfrac{4p}{q} + 7$

17. $\dfrac{9x^3 y}{-3xy} + \dfrac{6x^2 y^2}{-3xy} - \dfrac{12xy^3}{-3xy} =$

$-3x^{3-1} y^{1-1} - 2x^{2-1} y^{2-1} + 4x^{1-1} y^{3-1} =$

$-3x^2 - 2xy + 4y^2$

19. $\dfrac{8a^4 b^3}{4a^2 b^2} - \dfrac{4a^3 b^2}{4a^2 b^2} + \dfrac{a^2 b}{4a^2 b^2} - \dfrac{12ab^2}{4a^2 b^2} =$

$2a^{4-2} b^{3-2} - a^{3-2} b^{2-2} + \dfrac{a^{2-2}}{4b^{2-1}} - \dfrac{3b^{2-2}}{a^{2-1}} =$

$2a^2 b - a + \dfrac{1}{4b} - \dfrac{3}{a}$

21.
$$x-2\overline{\smash)x^2-4x+4} \qquad \frac{x-2}{}$$

$$\underline{x^2-2x}$$
$$-2x+4$$
$$\underline{-2x+4}$$

23.
$$n+1\overline{\smash)n^3+5n^2-n-5} \qquad \frac{n^2+4n-5}{}$$

$$\underline{n^3+n^2}$$
$$4n^2\ -n$$
$$\underline{4n^2+4n}$$
$$-5n-5$$
$$\underline{-5n-5}$$

25.
$$-x+5\overline{\smash)3x^3-8x^2-39x+11} \qquad \frac{-3x^2-7x+4}{}$$

$$\underline{3x^3-15x^2}$$
$$7x^2-39x$$
$$\underline{7x^2-35x}$$
$$-4x+11$$
$$\underline{-4x+20}$$
$$-9$$

$$-3x^2-7x+4+\frac{-9}{5-x}$$

27.
$$5x+4\overline{\smash)5x^2-11x-12} \qquad \frac{x-3}{}$$

$$\underline{5x^2+4x}$$
$$-15x-12$$
$$\underline{-15x-12}$$

29.
$$3n+4\overline{\smash)-3n^3+5n^2+0n+12} \qquad \frac{-n^2+3n-4}{}$$

$$\underline{-3n^3-4n^2}$$
$$9n^2+0n$$
$$\underline{9n^2+12n}$$
$$-12n+12$$
$$\underline{-12n-16}$$
$$28$$

$$-n^2+3n-4+\frac{28}{3n+4}$$

31.
$$2x+3\overline{\smash)4x^4+0x^3-7x^2+x-3} \qquad \frac{2x^3-3x^2+x-1}{}$$

$$\underline{4x^4+6x^3}$$
$$-6x^3-7x^2$$
$$\underline{-6x^3-9x^2}$$
$$2x^2+x$$
$$\underline{2x^2+3x}$$
$$-2x-3$$
$$\underline{-2x-3}$$

33.
$$-3a+1\overline{\smash)6a^3+13a^2-5a-7} \qquad \frac{-2a^2-5a}{}$$

$$\underline{6a^3-2a^2}$$
$$15a^2-5a$$
$$\underline{15a^2-5a}$$
$$-7$$

$$-2a^2-5a+\frac{-7}{1-3a}$$

35.
$$4y-3\overline{\smash)4y^5-7y^4+7y^3-7y^2+7y-3} \qquad \frac{y^4-y^3+y^2-y+1}{}$$

$$\underline{4y^5-3y^4}$$
$$-4y^4+7y^3$$
$$\underline{-4y^4+3y^3}$$
$$4y^3-7y^2$$
$$\underline{4y^3-3y^2}$$
$$-4y^2+7y$$
$$\underline{-4y^2+3y}$$
$$4y-3$$
$$\underline{4y-3}$$

37.
$$2x+1\overline{\smash)8x^3+0x^2+0x+1} \qquad \frac{4x^2-2x+1}{}$$

$$\underline{8x^3+4x^2}$$
$$-4x^2+0x$$
$$\underline{-4x^2-2x}$$
$$2x+1$$
$$\underline{2x+1}$$

39.
$$x^2+0x+3\overline{\smash)x^4-x^3+5x^2-3x+6} \qquad \frac{x^2-x+2}{}$$

$$\underline{x^4+0x^3+3x^2}$$
$$-x^3+2x^2-3x$$
$$\underline{-x^3+0x^2-3x}$$
$$2x^2+0x+6$$
$$\underline{2x^2+0x+6}$$

41.

$$x^2 + 0x - 4 \overline{)2x^3 - x^2 + 0x + 5}$$
$$\underline{2x^3 + 0x^2 - 8x}$$
$$-x^2 + 8x + 5$$
$$\underline{-x^2 + 0x + 4}$$
$$8x + 1$$

quotient $2x - 1$

$$2x - 1 + \frac{8x + 1}{x^2 - 4}$$

43.

$$p^2 + 4 \overline{)p^4 - 0p^2 - 16}$$
$$\underline{p^4 + 4p^2}$$
$$-4p^2 - 16$$
$$\underline{-4p^2 - 16}$$

quotient $p^2 - 4$

45.

$$n^2 - 2n + 3 \overline{)n^3 + 0n^2 + 0n + 2}$$
$$\underline{n^3 - 2n^2 + 3n}$$
$$2n^2 - 3n + 2$$
$$\underline{2n^2 - 4n + 6}$$
$$n - 4$$

quotient $n + 2$

$$n + 2 + \frac{n - 4}{n^2 - 2n + 3}$$

47. $\dfrac{f(x)}{g(x)} = \dfrac{x^2 - 5x - 24}{x - 8}$

$$x - 8 \overline{)x^2 - 5x - 24}$$
$$\underline{x^2 - 8x}$$
$$3x - 24$$
$$\underline{3x - 24}$$

quotient $x + 3$

49. $\dfrac{f(x)}{g(x)} = \dfrac{4x^3 - 9x + 11}{2x + 3}$

$$2x + 3 \overline{)4x^3 + 0x^2 - 9x + 11}$$
$$\underline{4x^3 + 6x^2}$$
$$-6x^2 - 9x$$
$$\underline{-6x^2 - 9x}$$
$$11$$

quotient $2x^2 - 3x$

$$2x^2 - 3x + \frac{11}{2x + 3}$$

51. a. $\dfrac{7.95 + 0.05x}{x} = \dfrac{7.95}{x} + 0.05$

b. 5 hr = 300 min.

$$\frac{7.95}{300} + 0.05 = 0.0265 + 0.05 = 0.0765$$

The average cost for 5 hr of long-distance is $0.08 per min.

53. a. $\dfrac{30000(1 - r^3)}{1 - r} = \dfrac{30000 - 30000r^3}{1 - r}$

$$-r + 1 \overline{)-30000r^3 + 00000r^2 + 00000r + 30000}$$
$$\underline{-30000r^3 + 30000r^2}$$
$$-30000r^2 + 00000r$$
$$\underline{-30000r^2 + 30000r}$$
$$-30000r + 30000$$
$$\underline{-30000 + 30000}$$

quotient $30000r^2 + 30000r + 30000$

b. $30000(1.04)^2 + 30000(1.04) + 30000$

$32448 + 31200 + 30000 = 93648$

The employee will earn a total of $93,648 in three years.

Exercises 5.4 The Greatest Common Factor and Factoring by Grouping

1. $2a(a^2) + 2a(4) = 2a(a^2 + 4)$

3. $8(4) - 8(5a) + 8(3a^2) = 8(4 - 5a + 3a^2)$

5. $x^2(3x^2) + x^2(7x) - x^2(9) = x^2(3x^2 + 7x - 9)$

7. $4p(3p^4) - 4p(p^3) - 4p(6) =$
   $4p(3p^4 - p^3 - 6)$

9. $9x^2 - 28y^2$ is a prime polynomial.

11. $6y^2(x^2) + 6y^2(3xy) + 6y^2(6y^2) =$
    $6y^2(x^2 + 3xy + 6y^2)$

13. $9p^3q^2(-3p^3) + 9p^3q^2(-5p^2q^3) +$
    $\qquad 9p^3q^2(-4pq) + 9p^3q^2(8q^2) =$
    $9p^3q^2(-3p^3 - 5p^2q^3 - 4pq + 8q^2)$ or
    $-9p^3q^2(3p^3) - 9p^3q^2(5p^2q^3) -$
    $\qquad 9p^3q^2(4pq) - 9p^3q^2(-8q^2) =$
    $-9p^3q^2(3p^3 + 5p^2q^3 + 4pq - 8q^2)$

15. $ab(-a^2b) + ab(-3ab^3c) + ab(-c^2) =$
    $ab(-a^2b - 3ab^3c - c^2)$ or
    $-ab(a^2b) - ab(3ab^3c) - ab(c^2) =$
    $-ab(a^2b + 3ab^3c + c^2)$

17. $3x(x - 5) + 2(x - 5) = (x - 5)(3x + 2)$

19. $(2x - 3y)(3x) - (2x - 3y)(2y) =$
    $(2x - 3y)(3x - 2y)$

21. $x(x+y)^2 - y(x+y)^2 = (x+y)^2(x-y)$

23. $x^2(x+2y^2) - 3y(x+2y^2) + (x+2y^2) =$

$(x+2y^2)(x^2 - 3y + 1)$

25. $A = P(1+rt)$

$\dfrac{A}{(1+rt)} = \dfrac{P(1+rt)}{(1+rt)}$

$P = \dfrac{A}{(1+rt)}$

27. $2A = 2\left(\dfrac{1}{2}b_1h + \dfrac{1}{2}b_2h\right)$

$2A = \dfrac{2}{2}b_1h + \dfrac{2}{2}b_2h$

$2A = b_1h + b_2h$

$2A = h(b_1 + b_2)$

$\dfrac{2A}{(b_1 + b_2)} = \dfrac{h(b_1 + b_2)}{(b_1 + b_2)}$

$h = \dfrac{2A}{b_1 + b_2}$

29. $x(y-7) + 10(-1)(-7+y) =$

$x(y-7) - 10(y-7) = (y-7)(x-10)$

31. $4x(z-y) - (-1)(-y+z) =$

$4x(z-y) + (1)(z-y) = (z-y)(4x+1)$

33. $(2x-y) + 2x(-1)(-y+2x) =$

$(2x-y) - 2x(2x-y) = (2x-y)(1-2x)$ or

$(2x-y)(-2x+1)$

35. $a(b+5) + c(b+5) = (b+5)(a+c)$

37. $x(x-9) + 2(x-9) = (x-9)(x+2)$

39. $3y(3x-1) + 1(3x-1) = (3x-1)(3y+1)$

41. $2s(5t-3) - 5(5t-3) = (5t-3)(2s-5)$

43. $w(14u+15v) - 2x(14u+15v) =$

$(14u+15v)(w-2x)$

45. $2a(a-2b) + b(a-2b) = (a-2b)(2a+b)$

47. $3x(2x+y) - z(2x+y) = (2x+y)(3x-z)$

49. $x(x^2-y) - y(x^2-y) = (x^2-y)(x-y)$

51. $4c(3c^2+d^2) + 3d(3c^2+d^2) =$

$(3c^2+d^2)(4c+3d)$

53. $3a(b-2) + 4c(b-2) = (b-2)(3a+4c)$

55. $p^2(4-r) + q^3(-r+4) =$

$p^2(4-r) + q^3(4-r) = (4-r)(p^2+q^3)$

57.   a. $720 - 16t^2 = 16(45-t^2)$

b. $t=5$; $16(45-5^2) =$

$16(45-25) = 16(20) = 320$ The stone is 320 ft above the ground 5 sec after it is dropped.

59.   a. $l^2 - 25l = l(l-25)$

b.   In the expression: $l(l-25)$, $l-25$ represents the width of the pool.

$l - 25 = 25$; $l = 50$

The length of pool is 50 m.

61. $P + Pr + (P+Pr)r = (P+Pr) + (P+Pr)r =$

$P(1+r) + P(1+r)r = P(1+r) + Pr(1+r) =$

$(1+r)(P+Pr) = (1+r)P(1+r) = P(1+r)^2$

Exercises 5.5 Factoring Trinomials

1. $(x-1)(x-3)$

3. $(x+5)(x+7)$

5. $(x-2y)(x+4y)$

7.   Both factors of 12 have the same sign as the middle term: positive. Sum is 7: 4 and 3

$(x+3)(x+4)$

9.   Both factors of 35 have the same sign as the middle term: negative.

Sum is –12: –5 and –7. $(n-5)(n-7)$

11.   Two factors of 48 have different sign, one with largest absolute value is positive. Sum is 2: 8 and –6. $(t-6)(t+8)$

13.   Two factors of 54 have different sign, one with largest absolute value is negative. Sum is –3: 6 and –9. $(x+6)(x-9)$

15. $-y^2 - 7y + 18$ Two factors of 18 have same sign and differ by 7 since the two y factors have different sign. $(-y+2)(y+9)$. Or

$-1(y^2 + 7y - 18)$ Two factors of 18 have different sign, one with largest absolute value is positive. Sum is 7: 9 and –2 $-(y-2)(y+9)$.

17.   Both factors of 36 have the same sign as the middle term: positive. Sum is 12: 6 and 6.

$(x+6)(x+6) = (x+6)^2$

19.   Two factors of 12 have different sign, one with largest absolute value is negative. Sum –8. None exist. Prime polynomial.

21.   Both factors of 6 have the same sign as the middle term: negative. Sum is –5: –2 and –3.

$(x-3y)(x-2y)$

23.   Two factors of 15 have different sign, one with largest absolute value is negative. Sum is –2: –5 and 3 $(a+3b)(a-5b)$

25. Both factors of 4 have the same sign as the middle term: negative. Sum is –3. None exist. Prime polynomial.

27. Two factors of 30 have different sign, one with largest absolute value is negative. Sum is –1: 5 and –6. $(c+5d)(c-6d)$

29. 5 is a common factor. $5\left(p^2+4p+4\right)$

Both factors of 4 have the same sign as the middle term: positive. Sum is 4: 2 and 2.

$5(p+2)(p+2)=5(p+2)^2$

31. –1 is a common factor. $-\left(y^2-4y-21\right)$ Two factors of 21 have different sign, one with largest absolute value is negative. Sum is –4: –7 and 3

$-(y-7)(y+3)$

33. $2c$ is a common factor $2c\left(c^2-2c-48\right)$ Two factors of 48 have different sign, one with largest absolute value is negative. Sum is –2: –8 and 6

$2c(c-8)(c+6)$

35. $-q^2$ is a common factor. $-q^2\left(p^2+8p-20\right)$

Two factors of 20 have different sign, one with largest absolute value is positive. Sum is 8: 10 and –2. $-q^2(p+10)(p-2)$

37. $-2m^2n^2$ is a common factor $-2m^2n^2\left(n^2-6n+5\right)$

Both factors of 5 have the same sign as the middle term: negative. Sum is –6: –1 and –5.

$-2m^2n^2(n-5)(n-1)$

39. Two factors of 72 have different sign, one with largest absolute value is positive. Sum is 1: 9 and –8 $(ab-8)(ab+9)$

41. Two factors of 30 have different sign, one with largest absolute value is negative. Sum is –7: –10 and 3 $\left(x^2+3\right)\left(x^2-10\right)$

43. Two factors of 52 have different sign, one with largest absolute value is positive. Sum is 9: –4 and 13 $\left(y^3-4\right)\left(y^3+13\right)$

45. n is a common factor. $n\left(-n^8-12n^4+64\right)$ Two factors of 64 have the same sign. Since the two factors of $-n^8$ have opposite sign, the factors of 64 differ by 12: 4 and 16 $n\left(-n^4+4\right)\left(n^4+16\right)$ or $-n$ is a factor. $-n\left(n^8+12n^4-64\right)$ Two factors of 64 have different sign, one with largest absolute value is positive. Sum is 12: 16 and –4.

$-n\left(n^4-4\right)\left(n^4+16\right)$

47. Two factors of 63 have different sign, one with largest absolute value is negative. Sum is –2: 7 and –9 $\left(p^3q^2+7\right)\left(p^3q^2-9\right)$

49. First term must be $\dfrac{2x^2}{x}=2x$ and the second term must be $\dfrac{3}{3}=1$: $(2x+1)(x+3)$

51. First term must be $\dfrac{4x^2}{2x}=2x$ and the second term must be $\dfrac{-5}{-1}=5$: $(2x-1)(2x+5)$

53. First term must be $\dfrac{12x^2}{3x}=4x$ and the second term must be $\dfrac{18y^2}{-2y}=-9y$:

$(3x-2y)(4x-9y)$

55. 3 is prime and all terms are positive, so the factors must start $(3x+\ \ )(x+\ \ )$. Factors of 6 are 1 and 6, 6 and 1, 2 and 3, and 3 and 2. $(3x+2)(x+3)$. Middle term is $(3x)3+(x)2=11x$ Check.

57. 2 is prime and both factors of 18 must be the same as the middle term: negative so the factors must start out $(2a-\ \ )(a-\ \ )$. The factors of 18 are 1 and 18, 18 and 1, 2 and 9, 9 and 2, 3 and 6, and 6 and 3. $(2a-9)(a-2)$ Middle term is $(2a)(-2)+(-9)a=-13a$ Check.

59. ac product is –60. Two factors of –60 whose sum is 4 is 10 and –6.

$4t^2+10t-6t-15=2t(2t+5)-3(2t+5)=$ $(2t+5)(2t-3)$

61. ac product is –72. Two factors of –72 whose sum is –1 are 8 and –9.

$6n^2-9n+8n-12=3n(2n-3)+4(2n-3)=$ $(2n-3)(3n+4)$

63. ac product is –60. Two factors of –60 whose sum is –4 is –10 and 6.

$20-10m+6m-3m^2=$

$10(2-m)+3m(2-m)=(10+3m)(2-m)=$ $(-m+2)(3m+10)$ or $-(m-2)(3m+10)$

65. ac product is –40. Two factors of –40 whose sum is –14 do not exist. Prime polynomial.

67. ac product is 36. Two factors of 36 whose sum is 12 is 6 and 6.

$4p^2+6p+6p+9=$

$2p(2p+3)+3(2p+3)=(2p+3)(2p+3)=$ $(2p+3)^2$

69. ac product is 60. Two factors of 60 whose sum is –17 are –12 and –5.

$2x^2 - 12xy - 5xy + 30y^2 =$

$2x(x-6y) - 5y(x-6y) =$

$(x-6y)(2x-5y)$

71.   *ac* product is –168. Two factors of –168 whose sum is –2 are –14 and 12.

$8p^2 + 12pq - 14pq - 21q^2 =$

$4p(2p+3q) - 7q(2p+3q) =$

$(2p+3q)(4p-7q)$

73.   *ac* product is –36. Two factors of –36 whose sum is 5 are 9 and –4.

$6c^2 + 9cd - 4cd - 6d^2 =$

$3c(2c+3d) - 2d(2c+3d) =$

$(2c+3d)(3c-2d)$

75.   *ac* product is 24. Two factors of 24 whose sum is 17 do not exist. Prime Polynomial.

77.   5 is a common factor. $5(3n^2 - 10n - 8)$

ac product is –24. Two factors of –24 whose sum is –10 are –12 and 2.

$5(3n^2 - 12n + 2n - 8) =$

$5(3n(n-4) + 2(n-4)) = 5(n-4)(3n+2)$

79. $4y^2$ is a common factor. $4y^2(4x^2 + 4x + 1)$

ac product is 4. Two factors of 4 whose sum is 4 are 2 and 2. $4y^2(4x^2 + 2x + 2x + 1)$

$4y^2(2x(2x+1) + 1(2x+1)) =$

$4y^2(2x+1)(2x+1) = 4y^2(2x+1)^2$

81.   –2 is a common factor. $-2(4a^2 + 7ab - 36b^2)$ *ac* product is –144. Two factors of –144 whose sum is 7 are –9 and 16. $-2(4a^2 + 16ab - 9ab + 36b^2) =$

$-2(4a(a+4b) - 9b(a+4b)) =$

$-2(a+4b)(4a-9b)$

83. $3ab^2$ is a common factor. $3ab^2(10b^2 - ab - 3a^2)$

ac product is –30. Two factors of –30 whose sum is –1 are –6 and 5. $3ab^2(10b^2 - 6ab + 5ab - 3a^2) =$

$3ab^2(2b(5b-3a) + a(5b-3a)) =$

$3ab^2(5b-3a)(2b+a)$

85.   *ac* product is 300. Two factors of 300 whose sum is 40 are 30 and 10.

$12x^2y^2 + 10xy + 30xy + 25 =$

$2xy(6xy+5) + 5(6xy+5) =$

$(6xy+5)(2xy+5)$

87.   *ac* product is –120. Two factors of –120 whose sum is 26 are 30 and –4.

$5n^4 + 30n^2 - 4n^2 - 24 =$

$5n^2(n^2+6) - 4(n^2+6) =$

$(n^2+6)(5n^2-4)$

89.   *ac* product is 12. Two factors of 12 whose sum is –13 are –12 and –1.

$4a^4 - 12a^2b^3 - a^2b^3 + 3b^6 =$

$4a^2(a^2 - 3b^3) - b^3(a^2 - 3b^3) =$

$(a^2 - 3b^3)(4a^2 - b^3)$

91. x^2y is a common factor.

$x^2y(6x^2 + 23xy^2 + 20y^4)$ *ac* product is 120. Two factors of 120 whose sum is 23 are 15 and 8.

$x^2y(6x^2 + 15xy^2 + 8xy^2 + 20y^4) =$

$x^2y(3x(2x+5y^2) + 4y^2(2x+5y^2)) =$

$x^2y(2x+5y^2)(3x+4y^2)$

93.   a.   Two factors of 4000 whose sum is 140 are 40 and 100. $(x+40)(x+100)$

b.   The dimensions of the original ice-skating rink was 100 ft by 40 ft.

95.   a.   –16 is a common factor.

$-16(-12 + 4t + t^2) = -16(t^2 + 4t - 12) =$

$-16(t+6)(t-2)$

97.   *ac* product is –60. Two factors of –60 whose sum is –4 are –10 and 6.

$4n^2 - 4n - 15 = 4n^2 - 10n + 6n - 15 =$

$2n(2n-5) + 3(2n-5) = (2n-5)(2n+3)$

$(2n+3) - (2n-5) = 2n+3-2n+5 = 8$

Exercises 5.6 Special Factoring

1. $x^2 = (x)^2$; $9 = (3)^2$ and $2(x)(3) = 6x$

Perfect square trinomial.

3. $x^2 = (x)^2$; 18 is not a perfect square.

Neither.

5. $16x^2 = (4x)^2$; $25y^2 = (-5y)^2$ and

$2(4x)(-5y) = -40xy$

Perfect square trinomial.

7. $4x^2 = (2x)^2$ and $9y^2 = (3y)^2$

Difference of squares.

9. $9x^4 = (3x^2)^2$; $1 = (-1)^2$, $2(3x^2)(-1) \neq -4x^2$

Neither.

11. $16x^4 - y^4$: $16x^4 = (4x^2)^2$, $y^4 = (y^2)^2$

Difference of squares.

13. $25x^6 = \left(5x^3\right)^2$, $-y^4$ is not a perfect square.
Neither.

15. $(x)^2 - 2(6)(x) + (6)^2 = (x-6)^2$

17. $(y)^2 + 2y(9) + 9^2 = (y+9)^2$

19. $4a^2 - 20a + 25 = (2a)^2 - 2(2a)(5) + (5)^2 =$
$(2a-5)^2$

21. $-9n^2$ is not a perfect square. Prime Polynomial.

23. $(x)^2 - (4)^2 = (x-4)(x+4)$

25. $(11)^2 - (y)^2 = (11-y)(11+y)$

27. $(3x)^2 - (2)^2 = (3x-2)(3x+2)$

29. $(0.4r)^2 - (0.9)^2 = (0.4r-0.9)(0.4r+0.9)$

31. $(8x)^2 + 2(8x)(y) + (y)^2 = (8x+y)^2$

33. Not the difference of two squares. Prime polynomial.

35. $\left(\frac{1}{3}a\right)^2 - (2b)^2 = \left(\frac{1}{3}a - 2b\right)\left(\frac{1}{3}a + 2b\right)$

37. $\left(\frac{1}{2}u\right)^2 - 2\left(\frac{1}{2}u\right)(v) + (v)^2 = \left(\frac{1}{2}u - v\right)^2$

39. $(7)^2 + 2(7)(-4ab) + (-4ab)^2 = (7-4ab)^2$ or
$(4ab)^2 + 2(4ab)(-7) + (-7)^2 = (4ab-7)^2$

41. $(2u-v)^2 - (8)^2 = (2u-v-8)(2u-v+8)$

43. $(7)^2 - \left[2(x+y)\right]^2 =$
$(7 - 2(x+y))(7 + 2(x+y)) =$
$(7 - 2x - 2y)(7 + 2x + 2y)$

45. $\left(p^3\right)^2 - 2\left(p^3\right)(11) + (11)^2 = \left(p^3 - 11\right)^2$

47. $\left(3a^4\right)^2 + 2\left(3a^4\right)(8b) + (8b)^2 =$
$\left(3a^4 + 8b\right)^2$

49. $\left(2a^2\right)^2 - (15)^2 = \left(2a^2 - 15\right)\left(2a^2 + 15\right)$

51. $\left(7x^3\right)^2 - \left(12y^2\right)^2 =$
$\left(7x^3 - 12y^2\right)\left(7x^3 + 12y^2\right)$

53. $\left(10p^2q\right)^2 - (3r)^2 = \left(10p^2q - 3r\right)\left(10p^2q + 3r\right)$

55. $((3p+q)-(2p-q))((3p+q)+(2p-q)) =$
$(3p+q-2p+q)(3p+q+2p-q) =$
$(p+2q)(5p) = 5p(p+2q)$

57. $(x)^3 - (4)^3$ is the difference of cubes

59. $\left(x^2\right)^3 - 3(y)^3$ is neither.
$-\left(ab+4c^2\right)\left(a^2b^2 - 4abc^2 + 16c^4\right)$

61. $\left(y^4\right)^3 + (0.2x)^3$ is the sum of cubes.

63. $(x)^2 + (1)^3 = (x+1)\left(x^2 - (x)(1) + 1\right) =$
$(x+1)\left(x^2 - x + 1\right)$

65. $(p)^3 - (2)^2 = (p-2)\left(p^2 + (2)(p) + 2^2\right) =$
$(p-2)\left(p^2 + 2p + 4\right)$

67. $27t^2 - 2^2$ is a prime polynomial.

69. $\left(\frac{1}{2}\right)^3 - (a)^3 =$
$\left(\frac{1}{2} - a\right)\left(\left(\frac{1}{2}\right)^2 + \left(\frac{1}{2}\right)a + a^2\right) =$
$\left(\frac{1}{2} - a\right)\left(\frac{1}{4} + \frac{1}{2}a + a^2\right)$

71. $(5x)^3 + (y)^3 =$
$(5x+y)\left((5x)^2 - (5x)(y) + y^2\right) =$
$(5x+y)\left(25x^2 - 5xy + y^2\right)$

73. $(0.4b)^3 - (0.3a)^3 =$
$(0.4b - 0.3a)$
$\left((0.4b)^2 + (0.4b)(0.3a) + (0.3a)^2\right) =$
$(0.4b - 0.3a)\left(0.16b^2 + 0.12ab + 0.09a^2\right)$

75. $(3pq)^3 + (5)^3 =$
$(3pq+5)\left((3pq)^2 - (3pq)(5) + (5)^2\right) =$
$(3pq+5)\left(9p^2q^2 - 15pq + 25\right)$

77. $\left(a^2\right)^3 - (2)^3 =$
$\left(a^2 - 2\right)\left(\left(a^2\right)^2 + \left(a^2\right)(2) + (2)^2\right) =$
$\left(a^2 - 2\right)\left(a^4 + 2a^2 + 4\right)$

79. $\left(4x^3\right)^3 + (3y)^3 =$
$\left(4x^3 + 3y\right)\left(\left(4x^3\right)^2 - \left(4x^3\right)(3y) + (3y)^2\right) =$
$\left(4x^3 + 3y\right)\left(16x^6 - 12x^3y + 9y^2\right)$

81. $\left(2p^4\right)^3 - \left(q^3\right)^3 =$
$\left(2p^4 - q^3\right)\left(\left(2p^4\right)^2 + \left(2p^4\right)\left(q^3\right) + \left(q^3\right)^2\right) =$
$\left(2p^4 - q^3\right)\left(4p^8 + 2p^4q^3 + q^6\right)$

83. $-\left(a^3b^3 + 64c^6\right) = -\left((ab)^3 + \left(4c^2\right)^3\right) =$
$-\left(ab + 4c^2\right)\left((ab)^2 - (ab)\left(4c^2\right) + \left(4c^2\right)^2\right) =$

85. $(3)^3 - (a+1)^3 =$

$(3-(a+1))\big((3)^2 + 3(a+1) + (a+1)^2\big) =$

$(3-a-1)(9+3a+3+a^2+2a+1) =$

$(2-a)(a^2+5a+13)$

87. $((x-2)+(x+2))$

$\big((x-2)^2 - (x-2)(x+2) + (x+2)^2\big) =$

$(2x)\big(x^2-4x+4-(x^2-4)+x^2+4x+4\big) =$

$2x(x^2+12)$

89. Common factor is $3x^2$.

$3x^2(9x^2-6x+1) = 3x^2(3x-1)^2$

91. Common factor is $4xy$.

$4xy(4x^2-25y^2) = 4xy(2x-5y)(2x+5y)$

93. Common factor is $2uv^3$.

$2uv^3(27u^3+64v^3) = 2uv^3\left(\begin{array}{c}(3u)^3 - \\ +(4v)^3\end{array}\right) =$

$2uv^3(3u+4v)\big((3u)^2 - (3u)(4v) + (4v)^2\big) =$

$2uv^3(3u+4v)(9u^2-12uv+16v^2)$

95. Common factor is $2x$

$2x(16x^4-8x^2y^2+y^4) = 2x(4x^2-y^2)^2 =$

$2x(2x+y)(2x-y)(2x+y)(2x-y) =$

$2x(2x+y)^2(2x-y)^2$

97. Common factor is $-y^4$

$-y^4(x^8-256) = -y^4(x^4+16)(x^4-16) =$

$-y^4(x^4+16)(x^2+4)(x^2-4) =$

$-y^4(x^4+16)(x^2+4)(x+2)(x-2)$

99. Common factor is 3 $3(81p^4-16q^4) =$

$3(9p^2+4q^2)(9p^2-4q^2) =$

$3(9p^2+4q^2)(3p+2q)(3p-2q)$

101. Common factor is $y-z$

$x^2(y-z)+(-1)(y-z) =$

$(y-z)(x^2-1) = (y-z)(x+1)(x-1)$

103. Common factor is $v+w$

$(v+w)(u^3+8) = (v+w)(u+2)(u^2-2u+4)$

105. $y^4(4x^2-9) - z^4(4x^2-9) =$

$(y^4-z^4)(4x^2-9) =$

$(y^2-z^2)(y^2+z^2)(2x-3)(2x+3) =$

$(y-z)(y+z)(y^2+z^2)(2x-3)(2x+3)$

107. $(p-2q)^2 - 36 = (p-2q-6)(p-2q+6)$

109. $4c^2-(a+5b)^2 =$

$(2c-(a+5b))(2c+(a+5b)) =$

$(2c-a-5b)(2c+a+5b)$

111. $(x^{2n})^2 - 4^2 = (x^{2n}+4)(x^{2n}-4) =$

$(x^{2n}+4)\big((x^n)^2-2^2\big) =$

$(x^{2n}+4)(x^n+2)(x^n-2)$

113. $(t^{2a})^2 - (s)^2 = (t^{2a}-s)(t^{2a}+s)$

115. $\big((5a^n)^2 - (2b^m)^2\big) = (5a^n-2b^m)(5a^n+2b^m)$

117. Area of the matte is outside area − inside area.

$x^2-8^2 = (x-8)(x+8)$ sq in.

119. Common factor is 4.

$4(81-4t^2) = 4(9-2t)(9+2t)$

121. $10000\left(1+r+\dfrac{1}{4}r^2\right) = 10000\left(1+\dfrac{1}{2}r\right)^2 =$

$10000\left(1+\dfrac{r}{2}\right)^2$

123. Volume of a cube is side^3. $x^3+y^3 =$

$(x+y)(x^2-xy+y^2)$

Exercises 5.7 Solving Quadratic Equations by Factoring

1. $x+3=0$ or $x-4=0$

$x=-3$ $x=4$

3. $4n-3=0$ or $n-2=0$

$4n=3$ $n=2$

$n=\dfrac{3}{4}$

5. $2x+1=0$ or $2x+3=0$

$2x=-1$ $2x=-3$

$x=-\dfrac{1}{2}$ $x=-\dfrac{3}{2}$

7. $(3-p)(3-p)=0$

$3-p=0$

$-p=-3$

$p=3$

9. $x(x+5)=0$

$x=0$ or $x+5=0$

$x=-5$

11. $3n(2n-1)=0$

$3n=0$ or $2n-1=0$

$n=0$ $2n=1$

$n=\dfrac{1}{2}$

13. $(x+6)(x+2)=0$

$x+6=0$ or $x+2=0$

$x=-6$ $x=-2$

15. $(a-2)(a-1)=0$

$a-2=0$ or $a-1=0$

$a=2$ $a=1$

17. $(4+t)(9-t)=0$

$4+t=0$ or $9-t=0$

$t=-4$ $-t=-9$

                      $t=9$

19. $(2x+7)(x-1)=0$

$2x+7=0$ or $x-1=0$

$2x=-7$ $x=1$

$x=-\dfrac{7}{2}$

21. $(2r-5)(2r-5)=0$

$2r-5=0$

$2r=5$

$r=\dfrac{5}{2}$

23. $5(4x^2-9)=0$

$5(2x+3)(2x-3)=0$

$2x+3=0$ or $2x-3=0$

$2x=-3$ $2x=3$

$x=-\dfrac{3}{2}$ $x=\dfrac{3}{2}$

25. $2(3x^2+14x+15)=0$

$2(3x+5)(x+3)=0$

$3x+5=0$ or $x+3=0$

$3x=-5$ $x=-3$

$x=-\dfrac{5}{3}$

27. $r^2-49=0$

$(r+7)(r-7)=0$

$r+7=0$ or $r-7=0$

$r=-7$ $r=7$

29. $15x^2-9x=0$

$3x(5x-3)=0$

$3x=0$ or $5x-3=0$

$x=0$ $5x=3$

$x=\dfrac{3}{5}$

31. $p^2+4p-32=0$

$(p+8)(p-4)=0$

$p+8=0$ or $p-4=0$

$p=-8$ $p=4$

33. $6t^2-19t-36=0$

$(3t+4)(2t-9)=0$

$3t+4=0$ or $2t-9=0$

$3t=-4$ $2t=9$

$t=-\dfrac{4}{3}$ $t=\dfrac{9}{2}$

35. $3x^2-10x+3=0$

$(3x-1)(x-3)=0$

$3x-1=0$ or $x-3=0$

$3x=1$ $x=3$

$x=\dfrac{1}{3}$

37. $y^2-2y=8$

$y^2-2y-8=0$

$(y-4)(y+2)=0$

$y-4=0$ or $y+2=0$

$y=4$ $y=-2$

39. $3n^2+17n+20=0$

$(3n+5)(n+4)=0$

$3n+5=0$ or $n+4=0$

$3n=-5$ $n=-4$

$n=-\dfrac{5}{3}$

41. $6a^2-9a=2a-4$

$6a^2-11a+4=0$

$(2a-1)(3a-4)=0$

$2a-1=0$ or $3a-4=0$

$2a=1$ $3a=4$

$a=\dfrac{1}{2}$ $a=\dfrac{4}{3}$

43. $v^2-2v-24=-9$

$v^2-2v-15=0$

$(v-5)(v+3)=0$

$v-5=0$ or $v+3=0$

$v=5$ $v=-3$

45. $4x^2 - 1 = 3x$

$4x^2 - 3x - 1 = 0$

$(4x+1)(x-1) = 0$

$4x+1 = 0$ or $x-1 = 0$

$4x = -1$ $x = 1$

$x = -\dfrac{1}{4}$

47. $5t^2 - 13t + 6 = 3t^2 - 4t + 2$

$2t^2 - 9t + 4 = 0$

$(2t-1)(t-4) = 0$

$2t-1 = 0$ or $t-4 = 0$

$2t = 1$ $t = 4$

$t = \dfrac{1}{2}$

49. $x^2 - 4x + 12 - 3x = 0$

$x^2 - 7x + 12 = 0$

$(x-4)(x-3) = 0$

$x-4 = 0$ or $x-3 = 0$

$x = 4$ $x = 3$

51. $2r^2 + 2r + 3r - 18 = -6$

$2r^2 + 5r - 12 = 0$

$(r+4)(2r-3) = 0$

$r+4 = 0$ or $2r-3 = 0$

$r = -4$ $2r = 3$

$r = \dfrac{3}{2}$

53. $3x^2 - 18 + 7x = x^2 + 2x$

$2x^2 + 5x - 18 = 0$

$(2x+9)(x-2) = 0$

$2x+9 = 0$ or $x-2 = 0$

$2x = -9$ $x = 2$

$x = -\dfrac{9}{2}$

55. $x^2 - 10x + 28 = 4$

$x^2 - 10x + 24 = 0$

$(x-4)(x-6) = 0$

$x-4 = 0$ or $x-6 = 0$

$x = 4$ $x = 6$

57. $3x^2 + 4x = 9x + 2$

$3x^2 - 5x - 2 = 0$

$(3x+1)(x-2) = 0$

$3x+1 = 0$ or $x-2 = 0$

$3x = -1$ $x = 2$

$x = -\dfrac{1}{3}$

59. $5x^2 - 6x + 4 = x^2 - 13x + 1$

$4x^2 + 7x + 3 = 0$

$(4x+3)(x+1) = 0$

$4x+3 = 0$ or $x+1 = 0$

$4x = -3$ $x = -1$

$x = -\dfrac{3}{4}$

61. $h = 0 = 900 - 16t^2$

$16t^2 - 900 = 0$

$(4t-30)(4t+30) = 0$

$4t-30 = 0$ or $4x+30 = 0$

$4t = 30$ $4x = -30$

$t = \dfrac{30}{4} = \dfrac{15}{2}$ $x = -\dfrac{30}{4} = -\dfrac{15}{2}$

The negative answer makes no sense in this problem. The sandbag will hit the ground in $\dfrac{15}{2}$ or 7.5 sec.

63. $w(w+50) = 5000$

$w^2 + 50w = 5000$

$w^2 + 50w - 5000 = 0$

$(w-50)(w+100) = 0$

$w-50 = 0$ or $w+100 = 0$

$w = 50$ $w = -100$

The negative answer makes no sense in this problem. $w+50 = 100$. The soccer field is 50 yd by 100 yd.

65. $8000\left[(1+r)^2 - 1\right] = 1680$

$8000\left[1+2r+r^2 - 1\right] = 1680$

$8000\left[r^2 + 2r\right] = 1680$

$8000r^2 + 16000r - 1680 = 0$

$80\left(100r^2 + 200r - 21\right) = 0$

$80(10r-1)(10r+21) = 0$

$10r-1 = 0$ or $10r+21 = 0$

$10r = 1$ $10r = -21$

$r = \dfrac{1}{10}$ $r = -\dfrac{21}{10}$

The negative answer makes no sense in this problem. The average rate of return on the investment was 10%.

67. Use the Pythagorean Theorem.

$$15^2 = 12^2 + x^2$$

$$225 = 144 + x^2$$

$$x^2 - 81 = 0$$

$$(x-9)(x+9) = 0$$

$$x-9 = 0 \quad \text{or} \quad x+9 = 0$$

$$x = 9 \qquad\qquad x = -9$$

The negative answer makes no sense in this problem. The ladder should be placed 9 ft from the house.

69. Use the Pythagorean Theorem.

$$(x-3)^2 + x^2 = 15^2$$

$$x^2 - 6x + 9 + x^2 = 225$$

$$2x^2 - 6x - 216 = 0$$

$$2(x^2 - 3x - 108) = 0$$

$$2(x-12)(x+9) = 0$$

$$x - 12 = 0 \quad \text{or} \quad x + 9 = 0$$

$$x = 12 \qquad\qquad x = -9$$

The negative answer makes no sense in this problem. $x - 3 = 9$ The screen is 12 in by 9 in.

Chapter 5 Review Exercises

1. Polynomial.
2. Not a polynomial because of the negative exponent.
3. Terms: $3n$ and -1; coefficients: 3 and -1.
4. Terms x^5, $-4x^3$, $-x^2$, $\dfrac{x}{2}$; coefficients: 1, -4, -1, and $\dfrac{1}{2}$.
5. Binomial of degree 3.
6. Monomial of degree 2.
7. Polynomial of degree 4.
8. Trinomial of degree 5.
9. $-y^6 - 4y^4 + y^3 + 5y^2 - 3y + 10$; leading term: $-y^6$; leading coefficient -1.
10. $-\dfrac{x^3}{5} + 9x^2 - 2x + 7$; leading term $-\dfrac{x^3}{5}$; leading coefficient: $-\dfrac{1}{5}$.
11. $2n^3 - 7n^2 + 11n + 8$
12. $2x^4 - \dfrac{1}{4}x^4 + x^2 + 3x^2 - x - \dfrac{1}{2}x =$

$\dfrac{7}{4}x^4 + 4x^2 - \dfrac{3}{2}x$

13. a. $8(3)^2 - 16(3) - 3 = 8(9) - 48 - 3 =$

$72 - 51 = 21$

b. $8\left(-\dfrac{3}{4}\right)^2 - 16\left(-\dfrac{3}{4}\right) - 3 =$

$8\left(\dfrac{9}{16}\right) + 12 - 3 = \dfrac{9}{2} + 9 = \dfrac{9}{2} + \dfrac{18}{2} = \dfrac{27}{2}$

14. a. $-(2)^3 + 6(2)^2 + 5(2) - 9 =$

$-8 + 6(4) + 10 - 9 = -8 + 24 + 1 = 17$

b. $-(-2)^3 + 6(-2)^2 + 5(-2) - 9 =$

$-(-8) + 6(4) - 10 - 9 = 8 + 24 - 19 = 13$

15. $9y^2 + 2y - 13 + 17 + y - 10y^2 - 3y^3 =$

$-3y^3 + 9y^2 - 10y^2 + 2y + y - 13 + 17 =$

$-3y^3 - y^2 + 3y + 4$

16. $12n^5 + 3n^4 - 11n^2 - 6n - 5n^5 +$

$\qquad\qquad\qquad 2n - 3n^4 + 16n^2 - 1 =$

$12n^5 - 5n^5 + 3n^4 - 3n^4 - 11n^2 + 16n^2 -$

$\qquad\qquad\qquad\qquad 6n + 2n - 1 =$

$7n^5 + 5n^2 - 4n - 1$

17. $a^3 - \dfrac{2}{3}a - 15a^2 + 9 - \left(2a^3 - 10a^2 + \dfrac{1}{3}a - 3\right) =$

$a^3 - \dfrac{2}{3}a - 15a^2 + 9 - 2a^3 + 10a^2 - \dfrac{1}{3}a + 3 =$

$a^3 - 2a^3 - 15a^2 + 10a^2 - \dfrac{2}{3}a - \dfrac{1}{3}a + 9 + 3 =$

$-a^3 - 5a^2 - a + 12$

18. $4x^2 - 7x - 11 + 9x - x^2 + 2x^3 + 8x + 4 =$

$2x^3 + 4x^2 - x^2 - 7x + 9x + 8x - 11 + 4 =$

$2x^3 + 3x^2 + 10x - 7$

19. $7x^2 + 1 - 3x^2 + 5x - 2 - 2 - x - 4x^2 =$

$7x^2 - 3x^2 - 4x^2 + 5x - x + 1 - 2 - 2 =$

$4x - 3$

20. $8n^3 - 1 + 2n^3 + 3n^2 - 4n + 6 - 5n^3 + 3n^2 =$

$8n^3 + 2n^3 - 5n^3 + 3n^2 + 3n^2 - 4n - 1 + 6 =$

$5n^3 + 6n^2 - 4n + 5$

21. $(-3x^2)(2) - (-3x^2)(4x) = -6x^2 + 12x^3 =$

$12x^3 - 6x^2$

22. $\left(\dfrac{1}{3}ab^3\right)9a^2 - \left(\dfrac{1}{3}ab^3\right)18ab - \left(\dfrac{1}{3}ab^3\right)3b^2 =$

$3a^3b^3 - 6a^2b^4 - ab^5$

23. $(2x^2)2x - (2x^2)4 - (x)3x^2 + (x)8x + (x)5 =$

$4x^3 - 8x^2 - 3x^3 + 8x^2 + 5x =$

$4x^3 - 3x^3 - 8x^2 + 8x^2 + 5x = x^3 + 5x$

24. $(6b)6a^3 - (6b)a^2b^2 + (6b)b - (4a^2)5ab -$

$\qquad\qquad\qquad\qquad (4a^2)b^3 - b^2 =$

$36a^3b - 6a^2b^3 + 6b^2 - 20a^3b - 4a^2b^3 - b^2 =$

$36a^3b - 20a^3b - 6a^2b^3 - 4a^2b^3 + 6b^2 - b^2 =$

$16a^3b - 10a^2b^3 + 5b^2$

25. $(n-6)(n+10) =$

    F   O   I   L

$n^2 + 10n - 6n - 60 = n^2 + 4n - 60$

26. $(3t+1)(t+2) =$

    F   O   I   L

$3t^2 + 6t + t + 2 = 3t^2 + 7t + 2$

27. $(2x-7)(2x-5) =$

    F   O   I   L

$4x^2 - 10x - 14x + 35 = 4x^2 - 24x + 35$

28. $(4x+3y)(3x-4y) =$

     F   O   I   L

$12x^2 - 16xy + 9xy - 12y^2 =$

$12x^2 - 7xy - 12y^2$

29.
$$3p^2 - pq - 2q^2$$
$$\underline{ p^2 + q}$$
$$3p^2q - pq^2 - 2q^3$$
$$\underline{3p^4 - p^3q - 2p^2q^2 }$$
$$3p^4 - p^3q - 2p^2q^2 + 3p^2q - pq^2 - 2q^3 =$$
$$3p^4 - p^3q + 3p^2q - 2p^2q^2 - pq^2 - 2q^3$$

30.
$$u^4 + 4u^2v^2 + 16v^4$$
$$\underline{ u^2 - 4v^2}$$
$$-4u^4v^2 - 16u^2v^4 - 64v^6$$
$$\underline{u^6 + 4u^4v^2 + 16u^2v^4 }$$
$$u^6 - 64v^6 =$$
$$u^6 - 64v^6$$

31.
$$2x^2 + x - 3$$
$$\underline{ x^2 - 3x + 6}$$
$$12x^2 + 6x - 18$$
$$-6x^3 - 3x^2 + 9x$$
$$\underline{2x^4 + x^3 - 3x^2 }$$
$$2x^4 - 5x^3 + 6x^2 + 15x - 18$$

32.
$$2a^3 + a^2 - 3a - 4$$
$$\underline{ 3a^2 - 7a + 1}$$
$$2a^3 + a^2 - 3a - 4$$
$$-14a^4 - 7a^3 + 21a^2 + 28a$$
$$\underline{6a^5 + 3a^4 - 9a^3 - 12a^2 }$$
$$6a^5 - 11a^4 - 14a^3 + 10a^2 + 25a - 4$$

33. $(5x-3)(5x+3) = (5x)^2 - (3)^2 = 25x^2 - 9$

34. $(q+3p^2)(q-3p^2) = (q)^2 - (3p^2)^2 =$

$q^2 - 9p^4$

35. $(4n-7)^2 = (4n)^2 + 2(4n)(-7) + (-7)^2 =$

$16n^2 - 56n + 49$

36. $(9a+2b)^2 = (9a)^2 + 2(9a)(2b) + (2b)^2 =$

$81a^2 + 36ab + 4b^2$

37. $(2a+3)^2(2a+3) =$

$(4a^2 + 12a + 9)(2a+3) =$
$$4a^2 + 12a + 9$$
$$\underline{ 2a + 3}$$
$$12a^2 + 36a + 27$$
$$\underline{8a^3 + 24a^2 + 18a }$$
$$8a^3 + 36a^2 + 54a + 27$$

38. $(4x-y)(4x+y)(x+y) =$

$(16x^2 - y^2)(x+y) =$

    F   O   I   L

$16x^3 + 16x^2y - xy^2 - y^3 =$

$16x^3 + 16x^2y - xy^2 - y^3$

39. $\dfrac{32a^4}{8a} - \dfrac{16a^2}{8a} + \dfrac{24a}{8a} - \dfrac{4}{8a} =$

$4a^3 - 2a + 3 - \dfrac{1}{2a}$

40. $\dfrac{9p^3q^4}{-3p^2q} - \dfrac{3p^2q^3}{-3p^2q} + \dfrac{6pq^2}{-3p^2q} - \dfrac{q}{-3p^2q} =$

$-3pq^3 + q^2 - \dfrac{2q}{p} + \dfrac{1}{3p^2}$

41. $\dfrac{16xy^3z}{4xyz} - \dfrac{8xy^2z^2}{4xyz} + \dfrac{12x^2y^2z}{4xyz} =$

$4y^2 - 2yz + 3xy$

42.
$$\begin{array}{r} x+7 \\ 2x-5 \overline{\smash{)}2x^2 + 9x - 35} \\ \underline{2x^2 - 5x } \\ 14x - 35 \\ \underline{\underline{14x - 35}} \end{array}$$

43.
$$\begin{array}{r} 5x - 1 \\ x^2 + 0x + 2 \overline{\smash{)}5x^3 - x^2 + 10x + 2} \\ \underline{5x^3 + 0x^2 + 10x } \\ -x^2 + 0x + 2 \\ \underline{-x^2 + 0x - 2} \\ 4 \end{array}$$

$5x - 1 + \dfrac{4}{x^2 + 2}$

44.

$$5x-2\overline{)125x^3+0x^2+0x-8}$$ with quotient $25x^2+10x+4$

$$\underline{125x^3-50x^2}$$
$$50x^2+0x$$
$$\underline{50x^2-20x}$$
$$20x-8$$
$$\underline{20x-8}$$

45.

$$x-4\overline{)4x^4-18x^3+9x^2+0x-10}$$ with quotient $4x^3-2x^2+x+4$

$$\underline{4x^4-16x^3}$$
$$-2x^3+9x^2$$
$$\underline{-2x^3+8x^2}$$
$$x^2-0x$$
$$\underline{x^2-4x}$$
$$4x-10$$
$$\underline{4x-16}$$
$$6$$

$$4x^3-2x^2+x+4+\frac{6}{x-4}$$

46.

$$3x-1\overline{)9x^3+0x^2+2x-1}$$ with quotient $3x^2+x+1$

$$\underline{9x^3-3x^2}$$
$$3x^2+2x$$
$$\underline{3x^2-x}$$
$$3x-1$$
$$\underline{3x-1}$$

47. $9x^2y\left(\dfrac{36x^5y^3}{9x^2y}-\dfrac{27x^4y}{9x^2y}-\dfrac{9x^3y^2}{9x^2y}+\dfrac{18x^2y^4}{9x^2y}\right)=$

$9x^2y\left(4x^3y^2-3x^2-xy+2y^3\right)$

48. $2p(p-q)-(-1)(p-q)=(p-q)(2p+1)$

49. $x^2+7x+2xy+14y=$

$x(x+7)+2y(x+7)=(x+7)(x+2y)$

50. $2a^2-4a-3ab+6b=$

$2a(a-2)-3b(a-2)=(a-2)(2a-3b)$

51. $a(b-5)-8(b-5)=(b-5)(a-8)$

52. $3u^2(1+3v)-2w^2(1+3v)=$

$(1+3v)(3u^2-2w^2)$

53. $2S=2\left(\dfrac{1}{2}an+\dfrac{1}{2}bn\right)$

$2S=an+bn$

$2S=n(a+b)$

54. $T=k(x_1+x_2)$

$\dfrac{T}{x_1+x_2}=\dfrac{k(x_1+x_2)}{x_1+x_2}$

$k=\dfrac{T}{x_1+x_2}$

55. Two factors of 20 whose sum is –9 are –5 and –4.

$(x-5)(x-4)$

56. $-\left(p^2+5p-5\right)$ Two factors of –5 whose sum is +5

do not exist. Prime polynomial.

57. Two factors of 21 whose sum is 10 are 7 and 3.

$(a+7b)(a+3b)$

58. Common factor is $-4p^2q^2$.

$-4p^2q^2\left(p^2-p-12q^2\right)$. Two factors of 12 whose

sum is –1 are –4 and 3.

$-4p^2q^2(p+3q)(p-4q)$

59. Common factor is n. $n\left(n^4+14n^2-32\right)$ Two

factors of –32 whose sum is 14 are 16 and –2.

$n\left(n^2-2\right)\left(n^2+16\right)$

60. ac product is 196. Two factors of 196 whose sum

is –28   are –14 and –14.

$4a^2-14a-14a+49=$

$2a(2a-7)-7(2a-7)=(2a-7)(2a-7)=$

$(2a-7)^2$

61. ac product is –72. Two factors of –72 whose sum

is –38 do not exist. Prime polynomial.

62. Common factor is 2. $2\left(6u^2-5uv-6v^2\right)$

ac product is –36. Two factors of –36 whose sum

is –5 are –9 and 4.

$2\left(6u^2-9uv+4uv-6v^2\right)=$

$2\left(3u(2u-3v)+2v(2u-3v)\right)=$

$2(2u-3v)(3u+2v)$

63. Common factor is $-6xy$. $-6xy\left(5x^2+7x+2\right)$

ac product is 10. Two factors of 10 whose sum is

7 are 5 and 2.

$-6xy\left(5x^2+5x+2x+2\right)=$

$-6xy\left(5x(x+1)+2(x+1)\right)=$

$-6xy(x+1)(5x+2)$

64. ac product is –8. Two factors of –8 whose sum is

–2 are –4 and 2.

$$8p^6 - 4p^3q^2 + 2p^3q^2 - q^4 =$$
$$4p^3\left(2p^3 - q^2\right) + q^2\left(2p^3 - q^2\right) =$$
$$\left(2p^3 - q^2\right)\left(4p^3 + q^2\right)$$

65. $(2n)^2 + 2(2n)(-11) + (-11)^2 = (2n-11)^2$

66. $(3a)^2 + 2(3a)(5b) + (5b)^2 = (3a+5b)^2$

67. $(10y)^2 - (7x)^2 = (10y - 7x)(10y + 7x)$

68. Common factor is 3.
$$3\left((u)^3 + (3)^3\right) = 3(u+3)\left(u^2 - 3u + 9\right)$$

69. $(4c)^3 - (3d)^3 =$
$$(4c - 3d)\left((4c)^2 + (4c)(3d) + (3d)^2\right) =$$
$$(4c - 3d)\left(16c^2 + 12cd + 9d^2\right)$$

70. Common factor is 3.
$$3\left(4x^6y^4 - 4x^3y^2 + 1\right) =$$
$$3\left(\left(2x^3y^2\right)^2 + 2\left(2x^3y^2\right)(-1) + (-1)^2\right) =$$
$$3\left(2x^3y^2 - 1\right)^2$$

71. $((x+y)+z)((x+y)-z) =$
$$(x+y+z)(x+y-z)$$

72. $(1)^3 + (3a+1)^3 =$
$$(1 + (3a+1))\left(1^2 - 1(3a+1) + (3a+1)^2\right) =$$
$$(3a+2)\left(1 - 3a - 1 + 9a^2 + 6a + 1\right) =$$
$$(3a+2)\left(9a^2 + 3a + 1\right)$$

73. Common factor is 2. $2\left(16u^{2n} - v^{2m}\right)$
$$2\left(\left(4u^n\right)^2 - \left(v^m\right)^2\right) = 2\left(4u^n + v^m\right)\left(4u^n - v^m\right)$$

74. $x^2(x-1) + 9(-1)(x-1) =$
$$(x-1)\left(x^2 - 9\right) = (x-1)(x+3)(x-3)$$

75. $x+1=0$ or $5x-4=0$
$x = -1$ $5x = 4$
$$x = \frac{4}{5}$$

76. $(n-8)(n+8) = 0$
$n-8=0$ or $n+8=0$
$n = 8$ $n = -8$

77. $5y^2 - 15y = 0$
$5y(y-3) = 0$
$5y = 0$ or $y - 3 = 0$
                  $y = 3$
$y = 0$

78. $(2+t)(4-3t) = 0$
$2+t=0$ or $4-3t=0$
$t = -2$ $-3t = -4$
$$t = \frac{4}{3}$$

79. $12k^2 - 60k + 75 = 0$
$3\left(4k^2 - 20k + 25\right) = 0$
$3(2k-5)^2 = 0$
$(2k-5)^2 = 0$
$2k - 5 = \pm\sqrt{0} = 0$
$2k = 5$
$$k = \frac{5}{2}$$

80. $6r^2 - 21r + 18 = 0$
$3\left(2r^2 - 7r + 6\right) = 0$
$3(2r-3)(r-2) = 0$
$2r-3=0$ or $r-2=0$
$2r = 3$ $r = 2$
$$r = \frac{3}{2}$$

81. $9a^2 + 12a = -4$
$9a^2 + 12a + 4 = 0$
$(3a+2)^2 = 0$
$3a + 2 = \pm\sqrt{0} = 0$
$3a = -2$
$$a = -\frac{2}{3}$$

82. $9x^2 + 15x - 12x - 20 = 5x^2 - 13$
$4x^2 + 3x - 7 = 0$
$(4x+7)(x-1) =$
$4x+7=0$ or $x-1=0$
$4x = -7$ $x = 1$
$$x = -\frac{7}{4}$$

83. In 2000 $x = 1$.
$$21(1)^3 - 117(1)^2 + 263(1) + 2757 = 2924$$
The average amount awarded in 2000 was $2924.

84. $P(x) = R(x) - C(x) =$
$0.25x - (0.1x + 1500) =$
$0.25x - 0.1x - 1500 = 0.15x - 1500$
$P(x) = 0.15x - 1500$ dollars.

85. $R = xp = x\left(250 - \dfrac{1}{4}x\right)$

$R = 250x - \dfrac{1}{4}x^2$

86. Area is length × width
$A = (6+x)(14-x) = 84 - 6x + 14x - x^2$
$A = \left(-x^2 + 8x + 84\right)$ sq ft.

87. $\dfrac{2000(1-r)(1+r)}{1-r} = 2000(1+r) =$
$2000 + 2000r$

88. a. $0.85p + 1.7q = 0.85(p + 2q)$

b. $0.85(30 + 2(45)) = 0.85(30 + 90) =$

$0.85(120) = 102$ The total purchase price was

$102.

c. $30 + 2(45) = 30 + 90 = 120$.
$120 - 102 = 18$. The customer saved $18. with the
discount.

89. a. Two factors of 720 that add to 58 are 18 and
40. $(x+18)(x+40)$

b. $x = 0$ $(0)^2 + 58(0) + 720 = 720$ The original

dog run had an area of 720 sq ft.

90. Common factor is –4.
$-4\left(4t^2 - 15t - 25\right) = -4(4t+5)(t-5)$

91. Common factor is 4π.
$4\pi\left(r_2^2 - r_1^2\right) = 4\pi\left(r_2 - r_1\right)\left(r_2 + r_1\right)$

92. $(x)^2 + 2(x)(2y) + (2y)^2 = (x+2y)^2$

93. $R = 200x - 2x^2 = 5000$

$2x^2 - 200x + 5000 = 0$

$2\left(x^2 - 100x + 2500\right) = 0$

$2(x-50)^2 = 0$

$(x-50)^2 = 0$

$x - 50 = \pm\sqrt{0} = 0$

$x = 50$
50 DVD's must be sold per day to generate revenue
of $5000.

94. $(40 - 2x)(30 - 2x) = 336$

$1200 - 140x + 4x^2 = 336$

$4x^2 - 140x + 864 = 0$

$4\left(x^2 - 35x + 216\right) = 0$

$4(x-8)(x-27) = 0$

$x - 8 = 0$ or $x - 27 = 0$

$x = 8$ $x = 27$

$30 - 2(8) = 14$ $40 - 2(8) = 24$

$30 - 2(27) = -24$ $40 - 2(27) = -14$

Negative answers make no sense in this problem.
An 8-in. by 8-in. square should be cut from each
corner.

95. Use the Pythagorean theorem.
$8^2 + 15^2 = d^2$

$64 + 225 = d^2$

$289 = d^2$

$d = \pm\sqrt{289} = \pm 17$

Negative answers make no sense in this problem.
The technician used 17 ft. of wire.

96. $x^2 + (x+150)^2 = 750^2$

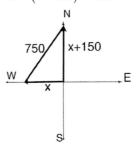

$x^2 + x^2 + 300x + 22500 = 562500$

$2x^2 + 300x - 540000 = 0$

$2\left(x^2 + 150x - 270000\right) = 0$

$2(x - 450)(x + 600) = 0$

$x - 450 = 0$ or $x + 600 = 0$

$x = 450$ $x = -600$

Negative answers make no sense in this problem.
$x + 150 = 450 + 150 = 600$ The slower airplane
flew 450 mi. and the faster airplane flew 600 mi.

Chapter 5 Posttest

1. a. $1, 5n^3, -4n^5, -n^4, -\dfrac{n}{3}$

b. $1, 5, -4, -1, -\dfrac{1}{3}$

c. $-4n^5 - n^4 + 5n^3 - \dfrac{n}{3} + 1$

d. 5

e. Leading term: $-4n^5$; leading coefficient –4.

2. $2x^4 + 6x^3 - x^2 - 3x + 8$
$\underline{3x^4 - 5x^3 + x^2 - 4x}$
$5x^4 + x^3 - 7x + 8$
$5x^4 + x^3 - 7x + 8$

3. $8y^2 - 10y^3 + y - 14 - \left(4y - 9y^3 + 7y^2 - 11\right) =$
$8y^2 - 10y^3 + y - 14 - 4y + 9y^3 - 7y^2 + 11 =$
$-10y^3 + 9y^3 + 8y^2 - 7y^2 + y - 4y - 14 + 11 =$
$-y^3 + y^2 - 3y - 3$

4. $\left(-\dfrac{2}{3}x^2y^3\right)(12x^3y)+\left(-\dfrac{2}{3}x^2y^3\right)(9xy)-$

$\quad \left(-\dfrac{2}{3}x^2y^3\right)(6y)-\left(-\dfrac{2}{3}x^2y^3\right)(15y^2)=$

$-8x^5y^4-6x^3y^4+4x^2y^4+10x^2y^5$

5. $(2a-7b)(7a+2b)=$

   F   O   I   L

$14a^2+4ab-49ab-14b^2=$

$14a^2-45ab-14b^2$

6. $(5-3p)^2=(5)^2+2(5)(-3p)+(-3p)^2=$

$25-30p+9p^2=9p^2-30p+25$

7. $(4u-9v)(4u+9v)=(4u)^2-(9v)^2=$

$16u^2-81v^2$

8. $2x^2+5x-2$

$\underline{-x^2-3x+1}$

$2x^2+5x-2$

$-6x^3-15x^2+6x$

$\underline{-2x^4-5x^3+2x^2}$

$-2x^4-11x^3-11x^2+11x-2$

9. $3x^3+x^2-3x-1$

$3x-1\overline{\smash{)}9x^4+0x^3-10x^2+0x+1}$

$\underline{9x^4-3x^3}$

$3x^3-10x^2$

$\underline{3x^3-x^2}$

$-9x^2+0x$

$\underline{-9x^2+3x}$

$-3x+1$

$\underline{\underline{-3x+1}}$

10. *ac* product is –280. Two factors of –280 whose sum is –6 are 14 and –20.

$8x^2+14x-20x-35=$

$2x(4x+7)-5(4x+7)=(4x+7)(2x-5)$

11. Common factor is $-6ab$.

$-6ab\left(a^2b^2+6ab+8\right)$ Two factors of 8 that add to

6 are 4 and 2. $-6ab(ab+2)(ab+4)$

12. $(9p)^2-(10q)^2=(9p+10q)(9p-10q)$

13. $(4)^3-(n)^3=(4-n)\left(4^2+4n+n^2\right)=$

$(4-n)\left(16+4n+n^2\right)$

14. $x^2(x+y)-4z^2(y+x)=$

$(x+y)\left(x^2-4z^2\right)=(x+y)(x+2z)(x-2z)$

15. $4r^2=16$

$r^2=4$

$r=\pm\sqrt{4}=\pm2$

16. $2x^2+x-15=6$

$2x^2+x-21=0$

$(2x+7)(x-3)=0$

$2x+7=0\quad$ or $\quad x-3=0$

$2x=-7x=3$

$x=-\dfrac{7}{2}$

17. In 2000, $x=1$.

$-\dfrac{5}{6}(1)^3+3(1)^2-\dfrac{1}{6}(1)+432=$

$-\dfrac{5}{6}+3-\dfrac{1}{6}+432=434$

The average size of a farm in 2000 was 434 acres.

18. a. After 2 years:

$1000(1+r)^2=1000\left(1+2r+r^2\right)=$

$\left(1000r^2+2000r+1000\right)$ dollars

After 3 years:

$1000(1+r)^3=1000(1+r)(1+r)^2=$

$1000\left(1+2r+r^2\right)(1+r)=$

$1000\left(1+2r+r^2+r+2r^2+r^3\right)=$

$1000\left(1+3r+3r^2+r^3\right)=$

$\left(1000r^3+3000r^2+3000r+1000\right)$ dollars

b. $1000r^3+3000r^2+3000r+1000-$

$(1000r^2+2000r+1000)=$

$1000r^3+3000r^2+3000r+1000-$

$1000r^2-2000r-1000=$

$\left(1000r^3+2000r^2+1000r\right)$ dollars

19. Common factor is –16.

$-16\left(t^2+3t-10\right)=-16(t+5)(t-2)$

20. Use the Pythagorean theorem.

$20^2=x^2+16^2$

$x^2=20^2-16^2$

$x^2=400-256=144$

$x=\pm\sqrt{144}=\pm12$

The negative answer makes no sense in this problem. The ladder should be placed 12 ft. from the building.

Cumulative Review Exercises

1. $6a^4c\left(2^{1(-3)}a^{2(-3)}b^{-1(-3)}c^{1(-3)}\right) =$

$6a^4c\left(2^{-3}a^{-6}b^{3}c^{-3}\right) = \dfrac{6a^4c\left(b^3\right)}{2^3a^6c^3} =$

$\dfrac{6b^3}{8a^{6-4}c^{3-1}} = \dfrac{3b^3}{4a^2c^2}$

2. $5x - 3x + 7 = \dfrac{12}{2} - \dfrac{4x}{2} + 11$

$2x + 7 = 6 - 2x + 11$

$2x + 7 = 17 - 2x$

$2x + 2x + 7 - 7 = 17 - 2x + 2x - 7$

$4x = 10$

$\dfrac{4x}{4} = \dfrac{10}{4}$

$x = \dfrac{5}{2}$

3. $2x + 3 \le 9$ or $2x + 3 \ge -9$

   $2x \le 6$ $2x \ge -12$

   $x \le 3$ $x \ge -6$

   $-6 \le x \le 3$

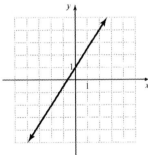

4. $-4y = -6x - 4$

   $y = \dfrac{-6x}{-4} - \dfrac{4}{-4}$

   $y = \dfrac{3}{2}x + 1$

x	$y = \dfrac{3}{2}x + 1$	(x, y)
0	$\dfrac{3}{2}(0) + 1 = 1$	$(0,1)$
2	$\dfrac{3}{2}(2) + 1 = 4$	$(2,4)$

5. Corresponding line is

   $2x - y = 1$

   $-y = -2x + 1$

   $y = 2x - 1$

x	$y = 2x - 1$	(x, y)
0	$2(0) - 1 = -1$	$(0,-1)$
2	$2(2) - 1 = 3$	$(2,3)$

   Boundary line is dashed. Test point is (0, 0).

   $2(0) - 0 \overset{?}{>} 1$

   $0 > 1$ False, shade the region not containing $(0,0)$.

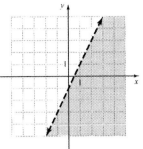

6. $2x - y + 3z = -3 \longrightarrow 2x - y + 3z = -3$

   $x - 2y - z = -2 \xrightarrow{\times 3} \underline{3x - 6y - 3z = -6}$

   $\hphantom{x - 2y - z = -2} \quad 5x - 7y \hphantom{- 3z} = -9$

   $4x + 5y - 2z = 16 \longrightarrow 4x + 5y - 2z = 16$

   $x - 2y - z = -2 \xrightarrow{\times(-2)} \underline{-2x + 4y + 2z = 4}$

   $\hphantom{x - 2y - z = -2} \quad 2x + 9y \hphantom{2z} = 20$

   $5x - 7y = -9 \xrightarrow{\times 2} \quad 10x - 14y = -18$

   $2x + 9y = 20 \xrightarrow{\times(-5)} \underline{-10x - 45y = -100}$

   $\hphantom{2x + 9y = 20 \times(-5)} \quad -59y = -118$

   $y = 2$

   $2x + 9(2) = 20$

   $2x + 18 = 20$

   $2x = 2$

   $x = 1$

   $2(1) - (2) + 3z = -3$

   $3z = -3$

   $z = -1$

   $(1, 2, -1)$

7. Corresponding equation is

   $y = 1 - x$

x	$y = 1 - x$	(x, y)
0	$1 - 0 = 1$	$(0,1)$
2	$1 - 2 = -1$	$(2,-1)$

   The boundary line is dashed. Test point is $(0,0)$.

   $0 \overset{?}{<} 1 - 0$; $0 < 1$ True, shade the

   region containing $(0,0)$.

   Corresponding equation is $y = \dfrac{1}{3}x - 3$

x	$y = \dfrac{1}{3}x - 3$	(x, y)
0	$\dfrac{1}{3}(0) - 3 = -3$	$(0,-3)$
3	$\dfrac{1}{3}(3) - 3 = -2$	$(3,-2)$

The boundary line is solid. Test point is $(0,0)$.

$0 \overset{?}{\geq} \dfrac{1}{3}(0) - 3; \quad 0 \geq -3$ True, shade the

region containing $(0,0)$.

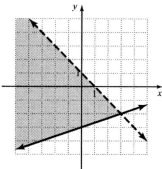

8.   Let x be the amount invested at 5% and y be the amount invested at 6%.

$x + y = 15000$

$0.05x + 0.06y \geq 875$

$x = 15000 - y$

$0.05(15000 - y) + 0.06y \geq 875$

$750 - 0.05y + 0.06y \geq 875$

$0.01y \geq 125$

$y \geq 12500$

$15000 - x = y$

$15000 - x \geq 12500$

$-x \geq -2500$

$x \leq 2500$

They should invest at most \$2500 in the account earning 5% interest and at least \$12500 in the account earning 6% interest.

9. $b = 0.08h + 4.00$

10.   Let h be the number of hardcover books sold and p be the number of paperbacks sold.

$p + h = 548 \xrightarrow{\times(-2.50)}$

$\qquad\qquad -2.50p - 2.50h = -1370$

$2.50p + 6.00h = 2007 \longrightarrow$

$\qquad\qquad \underline{2.50p + 6.00h = 2007}$

$\qquad\qquad\qquad 3.50h = 637$

$h = 182$

$p + 182 = 548$

$p = 366$

The store sold 366 paperback books and 182 hardcover books.

Chapter 6 Rational Expressions and Equations

Pretest

1. a. The expression is undefined when the denominator has a value of 0.

$$x^2 - 3x = 0$$

$$x(x-3) = 0$$

$$x = 0 \quad x - 3 = 0$$

$$x = 3$$

b. The expression is undefined when the denominator has a value of 0.

$$n^2 + 9n + 14 = 0$$

$$(n+7)(n+2) = 0$$

$$n + 7 = 0 \quad n + 2 = 0$$

$$n = -7 \quad n = -2$$

2. $$\frac{\cancel{A}(6a^2 - 9b + ab^2)}{\cancel{A}(3ab)} = \frac{6a^2 - 9b + ab^2}{3ab}$$

3. $$\frac{2p-1}{(1+2p)(1-2p)} = \frac{-1\cancel{(1-2p)}}{(1+2p)\cancel{(1-2p)}} =$$

$$-\frac{1}{2p+1}$$

4. $$\frac{(y-7)\cancel{(y+5)}}{(2y+3)\cancel{(y+5)}} = \frac{y-7}{2y+3}$$

5. $$\frac{\cancel{8}\,\cancel{x}\,\cancel{x}}{\cancel{4}\,(x-4)} \bullet \frac{-1\cancel{(x-4)}}{\cancel{x}\,\cancel{x}\,(3x-y)} = -\frac{2}{3x-y}$$

6. $$\frac{(t+1)\cancel{(t+1)}}{t\cancel{(t-2)}} \bullet \frac{\cancel{(t-9)}\cancel{(t-2)}}{\cancel{(t-9)}\cancel{(t+1)}} = \frac{t+1}{t}$$

7. $$\frac{\cancel{(p-3q)}\cancel{(p+3q)}}{q\cancel{(p+3q)}} \times \frac{1}{(p+8q)\cancel{(p-3q)}} =$$

$$\frac{1}{q(p+8q)}$$

8. $$\frac{(4n+3)\cancel{(n-4)}}{\cancel{(n-4)}\cancel{(n^2+4n+16)}} \times \frac{\cancel{n^2+4n+16}}{(4n-3)(2n+3)} =$$

$$\frac{4n+3}{(4n-3)(2n+3)}$$

9. $$\frac{2}{9y^2} + \frac{1}{3y(y-2)}; \ LCD = 9y^2(y-2)$$

$$\frac{2(y-2)}{9y^2(y-2)} + \frac{3y}{(3y)(3y)(y-2)} =$$

10. $$\frac{2y-4+3y}{9y^2(y-2)} = \frac{5y-4}{9y^2(y-2)}$$

$$\frac{r-3}{(r+1)(r-1)} - \frac{r+1}{-1(r-1)}$$

$$LCD = (r-1)(r+1)$$

$$\frac{r-3}{(r+1)(r-1)} - \frac{(r+1)(r+1)}{-1(r+1)(r-1)} =$$

$$\frac{r-3+r^2+2r+1}{(r+1)(r-1)} = \frac{r^2+3r-2}{r^2-1}$$

11. $$\frac{5}{(x-4)(x+3)} + \frac{x}{(x+3)(x-2)}$$

$$LCD = (x-4)(x+3)(x-2)$$

$$\frac{5(x-2)}{(x-4)(x+3)(x-2)} + \frac{x(x-4)}{(x-4)(x+3)(x-2)} =$$

$$\frac{5x-10+x^2-4x}{(x-4)(x+3)(x-2)} = \frac{x^2+x-10}{(x-4)(x+3)(x-2)}$$

12. $$\frac{2p+3}{(2p-3)^2} - \frac{p}{(2p-3)(p+1)}$$

$$LCD = (2p-3)^2(p+1)$$

$$\frac{(2p+3)(p+1)}{(2p-3)^2(p+1)} - \frac{p(2p-3)}{(2p-3)(2p-3)(p+1)} =$$

$$\frac{2p^2+5p+3-(2p^2-3p)}{(2p-3)^2(p+1)} = \frac{8p+3}{(2p-3)^2(p+1)}$$

13. a. $$LCD = 3x^2y^2$$

$$\frac{3x^2y^2\left(\frac{3}{x^2} - \frac{1}{3y^2}\right)}{3x^2y^2\left(\frac{3}{x} + \frac{1}{y}\right)} = \frac{\frac{9x^2y^2}{x^2} - \frac{3x^2y^2}{3y^2}}{\frac{9x^2y^2}{x} + \frac{3x^2y^2}{y}} =$$

$$\frac{9y^2-x^2}{9xy^2+3x^2y} = \frac{\cancel{(3y+x)}(3y-x)}{3xy\cancel{(3y+x)}} = \frac{3y-x}{3xy}$$

b. $$LCD = (x+6)(x-4)$$

$$\frac{\left(\frac{(x+5)(x-5)}{x+6}\right)(x+6)(x-4)}{\left(\frac{-(x-5)}{(x+6)(x-4)}\right)(x+6)(x-4)} =$$

$$\frac{(x+5)(x-5)(x-4)}{-(x-5)} = -(x+5)(x-4)$$

14. $$\frac{3}{x+2} - \frac{1}{x+8} = \frac{12}{(x+2)(x+8)}$$

$$LCD = (x+2)(x+8)$$

$$\frac{3(x+2)(x+8)}{x+2} - \frac{1(x+2)(x+8)}{x+8} =$$
$$\frac{12(x+2)(x+8)}{(x+2)(x+8)}$$

$3(x+8)-1(x+2)=12$

$3x+24-x-2=12$

$2x+22=12$

$2x=-10$

$x=-5$

15. $LCD = (n+1)(n+4)$

$$\frac{2(n+1)(n+4)}{n+1} + \frac{2(n+1)(n+4)}{n+4} =$$
$$-1(n+1)(n+4)$$

$2(n+4)+2(n+1)=-(n^2+5n+4)$

$2n+8+2n+2=-n^2-5n-4$

$n^2+9n+14=0$

$(n+7)(n+2)=0$

$n+7=0 \quad n+2=0$

$n=-7 \quad n=-2$

16. $4(y-1)=y^2$

$4y-4=y^2$

$y^2-4y+4=0$

$(y-2)^2=0$

$y-2=\pm\sqrt{0}=0$

$y=2$

17. $y=\dfrac{k}{x}$

$2.4=\dfrac{k}{25}$

$2.4(25)=k$

$k=60$

$y=\dfrac{60}{x}$

18.   Let s be the speed of the car.
Distance = rate $\times$ time.

$$\text{time} = \frac{\text{distance}}{\text{rate}}$$

$$\frac{150}{r} = \frac{120}{r-12}$$

$150(r-12)=120r$

$150r-1800=120r$

$30r=1800$

$r=60, \quad r-12=48$

The average speed of the car was 60 mph and the average speed of the train was 48 mph.

19.   Let t be the time it takes to fill the prescriptions if the two technicians work together.

	Rate of work	Time Worked	Part of Task
Experienced	$1 \div 6$	t	$t(1 \div 6)$
In-experienced	$1 \div 9$	t	$t(1 \div 9)$

$$t\left(\frac{1}{6}\right)+t\left(\frac{1}{9}\right)=1$$

$$\frac{6t}{36}+\frac{4t}{36}=1$$

$$\frac{10t}{36}=1$$

$$t=\frac{36}{10}=\frac{18}{5}=3\frac{3}{5}$$

Working together, it would take the technicians

$3\dfrac{3}{5}$ hr or (3 hr and 36 min) to fill the prescriptions.

20. $d=kF$

$3=k(12)$

$$k=\frac{3}{12}=\frac{1}{4}$$

$$d=\frac{1}{4}F$$

$$d=\frac{1}{4}(30)=\frac{15}{2}=7\frac{1}{2}$$

The spring will stretch 7½ in.

Exercises 6.1 Multiplication and Division of Rational Expressions

1.   Expressions are undefined when the denominator is zero or when $x=0$.

3.   Expressions are only undefined when the denominator is zero, $\dfrac{2n-1}{4}$ is defined for all real numbers.

5.   Expressions are undefined when the denominator is zero or when $6x-3=0$.

$6x=3; \quad x=\dfrac{1}{2}$

7.   Expressions are undefined when the denominator is zero or when

$n^2-8n+12=0$

$(n-6)(n-2)=0$

$n-6=0 \quad \text{or} \quad n-2=0$

$n=6 \qquad\qquad n=2$

9.   Expressions are undefined when the denominator is zero or when $x^2-9=0$.

$$(x-3)(x+3)=0$$
$$x-3=0 \quad \text{or} \quad x+3=0$$
$$x=3 \qquad\qquad x=-3$$

11. Expressions are undefined when the denominator is zero or when $2x^2+x-3=0$.

$$(x-1)(2x+3)=0$$
$$x-1=0 \quad \text{or} \quad 2x+3=0$$
$$x=1 \qquad\qquad 2x=-3$$
$$\qquad\qquad\qquad x=-\frac{3}{2}$$

13. $\dfrac{\cancel{x}(2)}{\cancel{x}(3x-4)}\overset{?}{=}\dfrac{2}{3x-4}$

$\dfrac{2}{3x-4}=\dfrac{2}{3x-4}$; equivalent

15. $\dfrac{n^2+1}{(n+1)(n-1)}\overset{?}{=}\dfrac{n+1}{n-1}$

Not equivalent.

17. $\dfrac{(x-2)(2x-3)}{(8+x)(2-x)}\overset{?}{=}\dfrac{(x-2)(2x-3)}{(8+x)(-1)(-2+x)}=$

$\dfrac{\cancel{(x-2)}(2x-3)}{(8+x)(-1)\cancel{(x-2)}}=-\dfrac{2x-3}{x+8}\neq\dfrac{2x-3}{x+8}$

Not equivalent.

19. $\dfrac{\cancel{3ab}(8a^2)}{\cancel{3ab}(b^2)}=\dfrac{8a^2}{b^2}$

21. $\dfrac{\cancel{2x}(3x^2-2)}{\cancel{2x}(x)}=\dfrac{3x^2-2}{x}$

23. $\dfrac{\cancel{4}(-3p^2q)}{\cancel{4}(2p+q)}=-\dfrac{3p^2q}{2p+q}$

25. $\dfrac{a-7}{a-7}=1$

27. $\dfrac{-(2y-5)}{5y-2}$ Cannot be simplified.

29. $\dfrac{3\cancel{(3n^2-1)}}{-4\cancel{(3n^2-1)}}=-\dfrac{3}{4}$

31. $\dfrac{(x-4)\cancel{(x+4)}}{4\cancel{(x+4)}}=\dfrac{x-4}{4}$

33. $\dfrac{\cancel{(n-3)}(n-3)}{\cancel{(n-3)}(n+4)}=\dfrac{n-3}{n+4}$

35. $\dfrac{(r-3)(r-5)}{-3(r^2-r-20)}=\dfrac{(r-3)\cancel{(r-5)}}{-3\cancel{(r-5)}(r+4)}=$

$-\dfrac{r-3}{3(r+4)}$

37. $\dfrac{(2x+3y)\cancel{(x+9y)}}{\cancel{(x+9y)}(3x-5y)}=\dfrac{2x+3y}{3x-5y}$

39. $\dfrac{2b(a+7)-6(a+7)}{a^2b(2b-6)}=\dfrac{\cancel{(2b-6)}(a+7)}{a^2b\cancel{(2b-6)}}=$

$\dfrac{a+7}{a^2b}$

41. $\dfrac{\cancel{(4-y)}(16+4y+y^2)}{\cancel{(4-y)}(4+y)}=\dfrac{y^2+4y+16}{y+4}$

43. $\dfrac{\left(6x^3y\right)(x)}{3y}\cdot\dfrac{\cancel{(3y)}(\cancel{3})(y)}{\left(6x^3y\right)(\cancel{3})}=xy$

45. $\dfrac{4\cancel{(2y-1)}}{6y(y-2)}\cdot\dfrac{3y}{2y-1}=\dfrac{\overset{2}{\cancel{4}}}{\underset{2}{\cancel{6}}(y-2)}=\dfrac{2}{y-2}$

47. $\dfrac{(p-5)\cancel{(p+6)}}{p^2\cancel{(p-2)}}\cdot\dfrac{2\cancel{p}\cancel{(p-2)}}{(p+6)\cancel{(p+6)}}=\dfrac{2(p-5)}{p(p+6)}$

49. $\dfrac{x(x-2y)}{-(x^2-4y^2)}\cdot\dfrac{(x+2y)(x-y)}{x^2+y^2}=$

$\dfrac{x\cancel{(x-2y)}}{-(x+2y)\cancel{(x-2y)}}\cdot\dfrac{\cancel{(x+2y)}(x-y)}{x^2+y^2}=$

$-\dfrac{x(x-y)}{x^2+y^2}$

51. $\dfrac{\cancel{(r-4)}(r-3)}{\cancel{(r-4)}\cancel{(r+5)}}\cdot\dfrac{\cancel{(r+5)}(r+5)}{-(r^2+5r-24)}=$

$\dfrac{\cancel{(r-3)}(r+5)}{-\cancel{(r-3)}(r+8)}=-\dfrac{r+5}{r+8}$

53. $\dfrac{\cancel{(2n+3)}\cancel{(n+4)}}{\cancel{(n+4)}\cancel{(n-1)}}\cdot\dfrac{(n-8)\cancel{(n-1)}}{(3n-2)\cancel{(2n+3)}}=$

$\dfrac{n-8}{3n-2}$

55. $\dfrac{\cancel{(x-2)}\cancel{(x+2)}}{\cancel{(x-2)}\cancel{(x-8)}}\cdot\dfrac{-\cancel{(x-8)}}{\cancel{(x+2)}(x^2-2x+4)}=$

$-\dfrac{1}{x^2-2x+4}$

57. $\dfrac{\cancel{(2x+7y)}(2x-7y)}{x\cancel{(2x+7y)}(2x+7y)}\cdot\dfrac{6xy(2+x)}{(2x)(x+2)+7y(x+2)}=$

$$\frac{2x-7y}{\cancel{k}(2x+7y)}\bullet\frac{6\cancel{k}y\cancel{(x+2)}}{\cancel{(x+2)}(2x+7y)}=\frac{6y(2x-7y)}{(2x+7y)^2}$$

59. $$\frac{\overset{4}{\cancel{32}}\overset{x^2}{\cancel{x^4}}}{\underset{3}{\cancel{9}}\,xy^2}\bullet\frac{\overset{5}{\cancel{15}}\,\cancel{y^4}}{\underset{3}{24}\,\cancel{x^4}\,\cancel{y^4}}=\frac{20\overset{x}{\cancel{x^2}}}{9\cancel{k}y^3}=\frac{20x}{9y^3}$$

61. $$\frac{2\cancel{(2t-5)}}{\underset{4t}{\cancel{12t^2}}}\bullet\frac{\cancel{3t}(2t+3)}{\cancel{2t-5}}=\frac{\cancel{2}(2t+3)}{\underset{2}{\cancel{4}}t}=\frac{2t+3}{2t}$$

63. $$\frac{\cancel{6}\,\cancel{(a-2)}}{3\underset{a}{\cancel{a^2}}\,\cancel{(a+3)}}\bullet\frac{\cancel{(a+3)}\,\cancel{(a-2)}}{\cancel{(a-2)}\cancel{(a-2)}}=\frac{1}{3a}$$

65. $$\frac{(p+4q)\cancel{(p-4q)}}{q(p-8q)\cancel{(p-8q)}}\bullet\frac{\cancel{(p-8q)}(p+4q)}{-2\cancel{(p-4q)}}=$$
$$-\frac{(p+4q)^2}{2q(p-8q)}$$

67. $$\frac{\cancel{(3x-1)}\,\cancel{(x+4)}}{\cancel{(x+4)}\cancel{(x+9)}}\bullet\frac{\cancel{(x+9)}(2x-3)}{(2x+3)\cancel{(3x-1)}}=\frac{2x-3}{2x+3}$$

69. $$\frac{3\cancel{(t^2+4t+16)}}{1}\bullet\frac{2(t+4)\cancel{(t-4)}}{\cancel{(t-4)}\cancel{(t^2+4t+16)}}=$$
$$\frac{6(t+4)}{1}=6(t+4)$$

71. $$\frac{(2p+q)(2p-q)}{-(8p^3-q^3)}\bullet\frac{(p-3q)(4p+9q)}{2p(p-3q)+q(p-3q)}=$$
$$\frac{\cancel{(2p+q)}\,\cancel{(2p-q)}}{-\cancel{(2p-q)}(4p^2+2pq+q^2)}\bullet\frac{\cancel{(p-3q)}(4p+9q)}{\cancel{(p-3q)}\cancel{(2p+q)}}=$$
$$-\frac{4p+9q}{4p^2+2pq+q^2}$$

73. $$\frac{(x+5)\cancel{(x-5)}}{\cancel{x-4}}\bullet\frac{(x-6)\cancel{(x-4)}}{\cancel{(x-5)}(x+3)}\bullet\frac{x+3}{(x+5)(x+5)}=$$
$$\frac{\cancel{(x+5)}(x-6)\cancel{(x+3)}}{\cancel{(x+3)}\cancel{(x+5)}(x+5)}=\frac{x-6}{x+5}$$

75. $$f(x)\bullet g(x)=\frac{x-4}{\cancel{k}(x+1)}\bullet\frac{2\cancel{k}}{x+1}=\frac{2(x-4)}{(x+1)^2}$$
$$f(x)\div g(x)=f(x)\bullet\frac{1}{g(x)}=$$
$$\frac{x-4}{x\cancel{(x+1)}}\bullet\frac{\cancel{x+1}}{2x}=\frac{x-4}{2x^2}$$

77. $$f(x)\bullet g(x)=\frac{(x-3)\cancel{(x-4)}}{x+3}\bullet\frac{-(x-3)\cancel{(x+3)}}{x-4}=$$
$$-(x-3)^2$$
$$f(x)\div g(x)=f(x)\bullet\frac{1}{g(x)}=$$
$$\frac{\cancel{(x-3)}(x-4)}{x+3}\bullet\frac{x-4}{-\cancel{(x-3)}(x+3)}=-\frac{(x-4)^2}{(x+3)^2}$$

79. Expressions are undefined when the denominator is zero or when $100-p=0$.
$p=100$. The expression is undefined for cleaning 100% of the pollutants.

81. $$\frac{a(1-r^3)}{1-r}=\frac{a\cancel{(1-r)}(1+r+r^2)}{\cancel{1-r}}=a(r^2+r+1)$$

83. $$\frac{V^2}{\underset{R}{\cancel{R^2}}}\bullet\frac{\cancel{R}}{1}=\frac{V^2}{R}$$

85. $$\frac{1}{100+i}\bullet\frac{i}{1}=\frac{i}{100+i}$$

Exercises 6.2 Addition and Subtraction of Rational Expressions

1. $$\frac{n-10+3n+2}{4n^2}=\frac{4n-8}{4n^2}=\frac{\cancel{4}(n-2)}{\cancel{4}n^2}=\frac{n-2}{n^2}$$

3. $$\frac{4n-15-(2n-3)}{n-6}=\frac{4n-15-2n+3}{n-6}=$$
$$\frac{2n-12}{n-6}=\frac{2\cancel{(n-6)}}{\cancel{n-6}}=2$$

5. $$\frac{3y-2x-(4y-3x)}{x^2-y^2}=\frac{3y-2x-4y+3x}{x^2-y^2}=$$
$$\frac{x-y}{\cancel{(x-y)}(x+y)}=\frac{1}{x+y}$$

7. $$\frac{y^2-3+7+y-y^2}{y^2-y-12}=\frac{y+4}{(y+3)(y-4)}$$

9. $$8x^2y^3=2\bullet2\bullet2\bullet x^2\bullet y^3$$
$$6x^3y^2=2\bullet3\bullet x^3\bullet y^2$$
$$LCD=2\bullet2\bullet2\bullet3\bullet x^3\bullet y^3=24x^3y^3$$
$$\frac{3}{8x^2y^3}\bullet\frac{3x}{3x}=\frac{9x}{24x^3y^3}$$
$$\frac{1}{6x^3y^2}\bullet\frac{4y}{4y}=\frac{4y}{24x^3y^3}$$

11. $$LCD=(n-2)(n-1)$$
$$\frac{n}{n-2}\bullet\frac{n-1}{n-1}=\frac{n(n-1)}{(n-2)(n-1)}$$

$$\frac{7}{n-1}\bullet\frac{n-2}{n-2}=\frac{7(n-2)}{(n-2)(n-1)}$$

13. $2t^2+12t=2t(t+6)$

$3t^3+18t^2=3t^2(t+6)$

$\text{LCD}=6t^2(t+6)$

$$\frac{3}{2t(t+6)}\bullet\frac{3t}{3t}=\frac{9t}{6t^2(t+6)}$$

$$\frac{4}{3t^2(t+6)}\bullet\frac{2}{2}=\frac{8}{6t^2(t+6)}$$

15. $p^2-9q^2=(p+3q)(p-3q)$

$\text{LCD}=(p+3q)(p-3q)$

$$\frac{2p-q}{(p+3q)(p-3q)}$$

$$\frac{3}{(p-3q)}\bullet\frac{(p+3q)}{(p+3q)}=\frac{3(p+3q)}{(p+3q)(p-3q)}$$

17. $n^2-6n+8=(n-4)(n-2)$

$n^2+4n-12=(n+6)(n-2)$

$\text{LCD}=(n-4)(n-2)(n+6)$

$$\frac{2n}{(n-2)(n-4)}\bullet\frac{n+6}{n+6}=\frac{2n(n+6)}{(n-2)(n-4)(n+6)}$$

$$\frac{3n}{(n-2)(n+6)}\bullet\frac{n-4}{n-4}=\frac{3n(n-4)}{(n-2)(n-4)(n+6)}$$

19. $3n^2+5n-2=(3n-1)(n+2)$

$n^2-n-6=(n+2)(n-3)$

$3n^2-10n+3=(3n-1)(n-3)$

$\text{LCD}=(3n-1)(n+2)(n-3)$

$$\frac{1}{(3n-1)(n+2)}\bullet\frac{n-3}{n-3}=\frac{n-3}{(3n-1)(n+2)(n-3)}$$

$$\frac{n}{(n+2)(n-3)}\bullet\frac{3n-1}{3n-1}=\frac{n(3n-1)}{(3n-1)(n+2)(n-3)}$$

$$\frac{n-4}{(3n-1)(n-3)}\bullet\frac{n+2}{n+2}=\frac{(n-4)(n+2)}{(3n-1)(n+2)(n-3)}$$

21. $\text{LCD}=24x^2y^2$

$$\frac{1}{8x^2y}\bullet\frac{3y}{3y}+\frac{1}{12xy^2}\bullet\frac{2x}{2x}=$$

$$\frac{3y}{24x^2y^2}+\frac{2x}{24x^2y^2}=\frac{3y+2x}{24x^2y^2}$$

23. $\text{LCD}=p$

$$\frac{3}{p}-\frac{4p}{1}\bullet\frac{p}{p}=\frac{3}{p}-\frac{4p^2}{p}=\frac{3-4p^2}{p}$$

25. $\text{LCD}=(n+4)(n+1)$

$$\frac{n}{n+4}\bullet\frac{n+1}{n+1}+\frac{2}{n+1}\bullet\frac{n+4}{n+4}=$$

$$\frac{n^2+n}{(n+4)(n+1)}+\frac{2n+8}{(n+4)(n+1)}=$$

$$\frac{n^2+3n+8}{(n+4)(n+1)}$$

27. $\text{LCD}=(x-2y)(2x-y)$

$$\frac{5}{x-2y}\bullet\frac{2x-y}{2x-y}+\frac{2}{2x-y}\bullet\frac{x-2y}{x-2y}=$$

$$\frac{10x-5y}{(x-2y)(2x-y)}+\frac{2x-4y}{(x-2y)(2x-y)}=$$

$$\frac{12x-9y}{(x-2y)(2x-y)}=\frac{3(4x-3y)}{(x-2y)(2x-y)}$$

29. $\text{LCD}=a-3$

$$\frac{7a}{a-3}+\frac{5a+6}{3-a}\bullet\frac{-1}{-1}=\frac{7a}{a-3}+\frac{-5a-6}{a-3}=$$

$$\frac{7a-5a-6}{a-3}=\frac{2a-6}{a-3}=\frac{2(a-3)}{a-3}=2$$

31. $$\frac{1}{-2(r-2)}+\frac{7}{3r(r-2)}=$$

$$\frac{1}{-2(r-2)}\bullet\frac{-3r}{-3r}+\frac{7}{3r(r-2)}\bullet\frac{2}{2}=\frac{-3r+14}{6r(r-2)}$$

33. $$\frac{4t-1}{(t-4)(t+4)}+\frac{2}{-(t-4)}=$$

$$\frac{4t-1}{(t-4)(t+4)}+\frac{-2}{(t-4)}\bullet\frac{(t+4)}{(t+4)}=$$

$$\frac{4t-1-2t-8}{(t+4)(t-4)}=\frac{2t-9}{(t+4)(t-4)}$$

35. $$\frac{n^2-4}{(n-3)(n-7)}-\frac{4}{n-7}\bullet\frac{n-3}{n-3}=$$

$$\frac{n^2-4-4n+12}{(n-3)(n-7)}=\frac{n^2-4n+8}{(n-3)(n-7)}$$

37. $$\frac{6}{(u+5v)(u+6v)}+\frac{3}{(u+6v)(u-4v)}=$$

$$\frac{6}{(u+5v)(u+6v)}\bullet\frac{u-4v}{u-4v}+$$

$$\frac{3}{(u+6v)(u-4v)}\bullet\frac{u+5v}{u+5v}=$$

$$\frac{6u-24v+3u+15v}{(u+5v)(u+6v)(u-4v)}=$$

$$\frac{9u-9v}{(u+5v)(u+6v)(u-4v)}=$$

$$\frac{9(u-v)}{(u+5v)(u+6v)(u-4v)}$$

39. $\dfrac{4}{(x-3)(x+1)} - \dfrac{x}{(x+2)(x+1)} =$

$\dfrac{4}{(x-3)(x+1)} \cdot \dfrac{x+2}{x+2} - \dfrac{x}{(x+2)(x+1)} \cdot \dfrac{x-3}{x-3} =$

$\dfrac{4x+8-x^2+3x}{(x-3)(x+2)(x+1)} = \dfrac{8+7x-x^2}{(x-3)(x+2)(x+1)} =$

$\dfrac{(8-x)\cancel{(1+x)}}{(x-3)(x+2)\cancel{(x+1)}} = \dfrac{8-x}{(x-3)(x+2)}$

41. $\dfrac{-2x}{(2x-3)(x+4)} + \dfrac{3x}{(x+4)(3x+1)} =$

$\dfrac{-2x}{(2x-3)(x+4)} \cdot \dfrac{3x+1}{3x+1} + \dfrac{3x}{(x+4)(3x+1)} \cdot \dfrac{2x-3}{2x-3}$

$\dfrac{-6x^2-2x+6x^2-9x}{(2x-3)(x+4)(3x+1)} =$

$\dfrac{-11x}{(2x-3)(x+4)(3x+1)} =$

$-\dfrac{11x}{(2x-3)(x+4)(3x+1)}$

43. $\dfrac{4x+3}{(a+4)(a-2)} - \dfrac{3a-2}{(a-2)^2} =$

$\dfrac{4a+3}{(a+4)(a-2)} \cdot \dfrac{a-2}{a-2} - \dfrac{3a-2}{(a-2)^2} \cdot \dfrac{a+4}{a+4} =$

$\dfrac{4a^2-5a-6-(3a^2+10a-8)}{(a+4)(a-2)^2} =$

$\dfrac{a^2-15a+2}{(a+4)(a-2)^2}$

45. $\dfrac{1-x}{3x^2(2x-5)(x+1)} + \dfrac{1}{2x(x^2-1)} =$

$\dfrac{1-x}{3x^2(2x-5)(x+1)} \cdot \dfrac{2(x-1)}{2(x-1)} +$

$\dfrac{1}{2x(x-1)(x+1)} \cdot \dfrac{3x(2x-5)}{3x(2x-5)} =$

$\dfrac{(1-x)(2x-2)+6x^2-15x}{6x^2(2x-5)(x+1)(x-1)} =$

$\dfrac{-2x^2+4x-2+6x^2-15x}{6x^2(2x-5)(x+1)(x-1)} =$

$\dfrac{4x^2-11x-2}{6x^2(2x-5)(x+1)(x-1)}$

47. $\dfrac{4}{(v-3)(v+3)} - \dfrac{2}{v+1} + \dfrac{v-6}{(v-3)(v+1)} =$

$\dfrac{4}{(v-3)(v+3)} \cdot \dfrac{v+1}{v+1} - \dfrac{2}{v+1} \cdot \dfrac{(v-3)(v+3)}{(v-3)(v+3)} +$

$\dfrac{v-6}{(v-3)(v+1)} \cdot \dfrac{v+3}{v+3} =$

$\dfrac{4v+4-2(v^2-9)+v^2-3v-18}{(v-3)(v+3)(v+1)} =$

$\dfrac{4v+4-2v^2+18+v^2-3v-18}{(v-3)(v+3)(v+1)} =$

$\dfrac{-v^2+v+4}{(v-3)(v+3)(v+1)}$

49. $\dfrac{3}{2(x+4)} - \dfrac{4x}{(2x-1)^2} - \dfrac{x+7}{-(2x-1)(x+4)} =$

$\dfrac{3}{2(x+4)} \cdot \dfrac{(2x-1)^2}{(2x-1)^2} - \dfrac{4x}{(2x-1)^2} \cdot \dfrac{2(x+4)}{2(x+4)} +$

$\dfrac{x+7}{(2x-1)(x+4)} \cdot \dfrac{2(2x-1)}{2(2x-1)} =$

$\dfrac{3(4x^2-4x+1)-8x(x+4)+2(2x^2+13x-7)}{2(x+4)(2x-1)^2} =$

$\dfrac{12x^2-12x+3-8x^2-32x+4x^2+26x-14}{2(x+4)(2x-1)^2} =$

$\dfrac{8x^2-18x-11}{2(x+4)(2x-1)^2}$

51. $f(x)+g(x) = \dfrac{8}{(x+6)(x+4)} + \dfrac{2}{(x+4)(x-9)} =$

$\dfrac{8}{(x+6)(x+4)} \cdot \dfrac{x-9}{x-9} + \dfrac{2}{(x+4)(x-9)} \cdot \dfrac{x+6}{x+6} =$

$\dfrac{8x-72+2x+12}{(x+6)(x+4)(x-9)} = \dfrac{10x-60}{(x+6)(x+4)(x-9)} =$

$\dfrac{10(x-6)}{(x+6)(x+4)(x-9)}$

$f(x)-g(x) = \dfrac{8}{(x+6)(x+4)} - \dfrac{2}{(x+4)(x-9)} =$

$\dfrac{8}{(x+6)(x+4)} \cdot \dfrac{x-9}{x-9} - \dfrac{2}{(x+4)(x-9)} \cdot \dfrac{x+6}{x+6} =$

$\dfrac{8x-72-2x-12}{(x+6)(x+4)(x-9)} = \dfrac{6x-84}{(x+6)(x+4)(x-9)} =$

$\dfrac{6(x-14)}{(x+6)(x+4)(x-9)}$

53. $f(x)+g(x) = \dfrac{x+4}{3x(x-4)} + \dfrac{-2}{x^2} =$

$$\frac{x+4}{3x(x-4)}\cdot\frac{x}{x}+\frac{-2}{x^2}\cdot\frac{3(x-4)}{3(x-4)}=$$

$$\frac{x^2+4x-6x+24}{3x^2(x-4)}=\frac{x^2-2x+24}{3x^2(x-4)}$$

$$f(x)-g(x)=\frac{x+4}{3x(x-4)}-\frac{-2}{x^2}=$$

$$\frac{x+4}{3x(x-4)}\cdot\frac{x}{x}+\frac{2}{x^2}\cdot\frac{3(x-4)}{3(x-4)}=\frac{x^2+4x+6x-24}{3x^2(x-4)}$$

$$\frac{x^2+10x-24}{3x^2(x-4)}=\frac{(x+12)(x-2)}{3x^2(x-4)}$$

55. $\dfrac{V_1}{\pi r^2}-\dfrac{V_2}{\pi r^2}=\dfrac{V_1-V_2}{\pi r^2}$

57. $100\left(\dfrac{S_1}{S_0}-1\left(\dfrac{S_0}{S_0}\right)\right)=100\left(\dfrac{S_1-S_0}{S_0}\right)=$

$$\frac{100(S_1-S_0)}{S_0}$$

59. $\dfrac{1}{C_1}+\dfrac{1}{C_2}=\dfrac{1}{C_1}\cdot\dfrac{C_2}{C_2}+\dfrac{1}{C_2}\cdot\dfrac{C_1}{C_1}=\dfrac{C_2+C_1}{C_1C_2}$

61. $\dfrac{m}{s+w}+\dfrac{m}{s-w}=$

$$\frac{m}{s+w}\cdot\frac{s-w}{s-w}+\frac{m}{s-w}\cdot\frac{s+w}{s+w}=$$

$$\frac{ms-mw+ms+mw}{(s+w)(s-w)}=\frac{2ms}{(s+w)(s-w)}$$

63. $\text{time}=\dfrac{\text{distance}}{\text{rate}}$

$$\frac{4}{r}+\frac{4}{2r}=\frac{4}{r}\cdot\frac{2}{2}+\frac{4}{2r}=\frac{8+4}{2r}=\frac{12}{2r}=\frac{6}{r}$$

The whole trip took $\dfrac{6}{r}$ hr.

Exercises 6.3 Complex Rational Expressions

1. $\dfrac{\frac{12}{3}}{\frac{3}{5n}}=\dfrac{12}{1}\div\dfrac{3}{5n}=\dfrac{12}{1}\cdot\dfrac{5n}{3}=20n$

3. $\dfrac{\frac{6}{x}}{4x^2}=\dfrac{6}{x}\div4x^2=\dfrac{6}{x}\cdot\dfrac{1}{4x^2}=\dfrac{3}{2x^3}$

5. $\dfrac{\frac{a+2}{2a^2}}{\frac{a+2}{4a}}=\dfrac{a+2}{2a^2}\div\dfrac{a+2}{4a}=\dfrac{a+2}{2a^2}\cdot\dfrac{4a}{a+2}=\dfrac{2}{a}$

7. $\dfrac{\frac{10r^2}{3r-2}}{\frac{25r^3}{3r-2}}=\dfrac{10r^2}{3r-2}\div\dfrac{25r^3}{3r-2}=\dfrac{10r^2}{3r-2}\cdot\dfrac{3r-2}{25r^3}=\dfrac{2}{5r}$

9. $\dfrac{\frac{s^2-16}{4s^3}}{\frac{4-s}{3s}}=\dfrac{(s+4)(s-4)}{4s^3}\div\dfrac{-(s-4)}{3s}=$

$$\frac{(s+4)(s-4)}{4s^3}\cdot\frac{3s}{-(s-4)}=-\frac{3(s+4)}{4s^2}$$

11. $\dfrac{\frac{4n-8}{5n+15}}{\frac{2n-4}{n-5}}=\dfrac{4n-8}{5n+15}\div\dfrac{2n-4}{n-5}=$

$$\frac{4(n-2)}{5(n+3)}\cdot\frac{n-5}{2(n-2)}=\frac{2(n-5)}{5(n+3)}$$

13. $\dfrac{\left(\frac{3}{n}\right)\cdot n}{\left(1-\frac{1}{n}\right)\cdot n}=\dfrac{3}{n-1}$

15. $\dfrac{\left(1+\frac{2}{t}\right)\cdot t^2}{\left(1-\frac{4}{t^2}\right)\cdot t^2}=\dfrac{t^2+2t}{t^2-4}=\dfrac{t(t+2)}{(t-2)(t+2)}=\dfrac{t}{t-2}$

17. $\dfrac{\left(\frac{p-12}{p}+p\right)\cdot p}{\left(\frac{p+4}{1}\right)\cdot p}=\dfrac{p-12+p^2}{p(p+4)}=$

$$\frac{(p+4)(p-3)}{p(p+4)}=\frac{p-3}{p}$$

19. $\dfrac{(2x-y)(2x+y)}{-x(2x-y)}=-\dfrac{2x+y}{x}$

$$\frac{\left(\frac{4}{y}-\frac{y}{x^2}\right)\cdot x^2y}{\left(\frac{1}{x}-\frac{2}{y}\right)\cdot x^2y}=\frac{4x^2-y^2}{xy-2x^2}=$$

21. $\dfrac{\left(\frac{3}{4n^3}-\frac{1}{2n^2}\right)\cdot12n^3}{\left(\frac{4}{3n^2}+\frac{1}{2n}\right)\cdot12n^3}=\dfrac{9-6n}{16n+6n^2}=\dfrac{3(3-2n)}{2n(8+3n)}$

23. $\dfrac{\left(2-\frac{11}{x}+\frac{12}{x^2}\right)\cdot x^2}{\left(1-\frac{2}{x}-\frac{8}{x^2}\right)\cdot x^2}=\dfrac{2x^2-11x+12}{x^2-2x-8}=$

$$\frac{(2x-3)\cancel{(x-4)}}{\cancel{(x-4)}(x+2)}=\frac{2x-3}{x+2}$$

25. $$\frac{\left(\dfrac{a}{b^2}-\dfrac{b}{a^2}\right)\bullet a^3b^3}{\left(\dfrac{3}{a^3}-\dfrac{3}{b^3}\right)\bullet a^3b^3}=\frac{a^4b-ab^4}{3b^3-3a^3}=\frac{ab\left(a^3-b^3\right)}{-3\left(a^3-b^3\right)}=-\frac{ab}{3}$$

27. $$\frac{\left(\dfrac{6}{x-y}+\dfrac{9}{x+y}\right)\bullet(x+y)(x-y)}{\left(\dfrac{9}{x-y}-\dfrac{6}{x+y}\right)\bullet(x+y)(x-y)}=$$

$$\frac{6(x+y)+9(x-y)}{9(x+y)-6(x-y)}=\frac{6x+6y+9x-9y}{9x+9y-6x+6y}=$$

$$\frac{15x-3y}{3x+15y}=\frac{\cancel{3}(5x-y)}{\cancel{3}(x+5y)}=\frac{5x-y}{x+5y}$$

29. $$\frac{\left(\dfrac{2}{(x-2)(x-1)}-\dfrac{2}{-1(x-2)}\right)}{\left(\dfrac{4}{(x+2)(x-2)}+\dfrac{4}{(x+2)(x-1)}\right)}\bullet$$

$$\frac{(x-2)(x-1)(x+2)}{(x-2)(x-1)(x+2)}=$$

$$\frac{2(x+2)+2(x-1)(x+2)}{4(x-1)+4(x-2)}=$$

$$\frac{2x+4+2\left(x^2-x-2\right)}{4x-4+4x-8}=\frac{2x+4+2x^2+2x-4}{8x-12}=$$

$$\frac{2x^2+4x}{4(2x-3)}=\frac{\cancel{2}x(x+2)}{\cancel{4}(2x-3)}=\frac{x(x+2)}{2(2x-3)}$$

31. $$\frac{\left(\dfrac{\cancel{(2n+5)}(n-4)}{-(3n-2)\cancel{(2n+5)}}\right)\bullet(3n-2)(n+4)}{\left(\dfrac{(n-4)(n-4)}{(3n-2)(n+4)}\right)\bullet(3n-2)(n+4)}=$$

$$\frac{-\cancel{(n-4)}(n+4)}{\cancel{(n-4)}(n-4)}=-\frac{n+4}{n-4}$$

33. $$\frac{\left(\dfrac{1}{x}+\dfrac{1}{x^2}\right)\bullet x^2}{\left(\dfrac{3}{x}\right)\bullet x^2}=\frac{x+1}{3x}$$

35. $$\frac{\left(\dfrac{1}{a^3}\right)\bullet a^3b}{\left(\dfrac{1}{a}+\dfrac{1}{b}\right)\bullet a^3b}=\frac{b}{a^2b+a^3}=\frac{b}{a^2(a+b)}$$

37. $$\frac{\left(\dfrac{F}{1}\right)\bullet g}{\left(\dfrac{w}{g}\right)\bullet g}=\frac{gF}{w}$$

39. $$\frac{\left(\dfrac{f}{1}\right)\bullet S}{\left(1+\dfrac{v}{S}\right)\bullet S}=\frac{Sf}{S+v}$$

41. a. $$\frac{\left(\dfrac{2d}{1}\right)\bullet(rR)}{\left(\dfrac{d}{r}+\dfrac{d}{R}\right)\bullet(rR)}=\frac{2drR}{dR+dr}=$$

$$\frac{2\cancel{d}rR}{\cancel{d}(R+r)}=\frac{2rR}{R+r}$$

b. $$\frac{2rR}{R+r}=\frac{2(40)(60)}{60+40}=\frac{4800}{100}=48$$

Her average speed was 48 mph.

43. $$\frac{\left(\dfrac{V}{1}\right)\bullet R(R-2)}{\left(\dfrac{1}{R}+\dfrac{1}{R-2}\right)\bullet R(R-2)}=\frac{VR(R-2)}{R-2+R}=$$

$$\frac{VR(R-2)}{2R-2}$$

Exercises 6.4 Solving Rational Equations

1. $$\left(\frac{x}{10}+\frac{3}{5}\right)\bullet 20=\left(\frac{x}{20}\right)\bullet 20$$ Check

$$2x+12=x$$

$$x=-12$$

$$\frac{-12}{10}+\frac{3}{5}\overset{?}{=}\frac{-12}{20}$$

$$\frac{-6}{5}+\frac{3}{5}\overset{?}{=}\frac{-3}{5}$$

$$-\frac{3}{5}=-\frac{3}{5}\quad\text{True}$$

3. $$\left(\frac{r}{8}+\frac{r-4}{12}\right)\bullet 24=\left(\frac{r}{24}\right)\bullet 24$$ Check

$$3r+2(r-4)=r$$

$$3r+2r-8=r$$

$$5r-8=r$$

$$4r=8$$

$$r=2$$

$$\frac{2}{8}+\frac{2-4}{12}\overset{?}{=}\frac{2}{24}$$

$$\frac{1}{4}-\frac{2}{12}\overset{?}{=}\frac{1}{12}$$

$$\frac{3}{12}-\frac{2}{12}\overset{?}{=}\frac{1}{12}$$

$$\frac{1}{12}=\frac{1}{12}\quad\text{True}$$

5. $\left(\dfrac{x+5}{x}-\dfrac{2}{3}\right)\bullet 3x=0\bullet 3x$ Check

$3(x+5)-2x=0$ $\dfrac{-15+5}{-15}-\dfrac{2}{3}\overset{?}{=}0$

$3x+15-2x=0$ $\dfrac{-10}{-15}-\dfrac{2}{3}\overset{?}{=}0;\quad \dfrac{2}{3}-\dfrac{2}{3}\overset{?}{=}0$

$x=-15$ $0=0$ True

7. Cross product method.   Check

$7r=2(r+20)$ $\dfrac{7}{8+20}\overset{?}{=}\dfrac{2}{8}$

$7r=2r+40$ $\dfrac{7}{28}\overset{?}{=}\dfrac{1}{4}$

$5r=40$

$r=8$ $\dfrac{1}{4}=\dfrac{1}{4}$ True

9. $\left(\dfrac{2}{p}-\dfrac{3p+1}{4p}\right)\bullet 4p=-1\bullet(4p)$

$8-(3p+1)=-4p$

$8-3p-1=-4p$

$-3p+7=-4p$

$p=-7$

Check $\dfrac{2}{-7}-\dfrac{3(-7)+1}{4(-7)}\overset{?}{=}-1$

$-\dfrac{2}{7}-\dfrac{-20}{-28}\overset{?}{=}-1$

$-\dfrac{2}{7}-\dfrac{5}{7}\overset{?}{=}-1;\quad -1=-1$ True

11. $\left(\dfrac{8}{a-1}-4\right)\bullet(a-1)=\dfrac{2a}{a-1}\bullet(a-1)$

$8-4(a-1)=2a$ Check $\dfrac{8}{2-1}-4\overset{?}{=}\dfrac{2(2)}{2-1}$

$8-4a+4=2a$

$-4a+12=2a$ $8-4\overset{?}{=}\dfrac{4}{1};\quad 4=4$ True

$-6a=-12$

$a=2$

13. Cross product method   Check

$1(x+5)=5(x+5)$ $\dfrac{1}{-5+5}\overset{?}{=}\dfrac{5}{-5+5}$

$x+5=5x+25$

$-4x=20$ $\dfrac{1}{0}$ is undefined.

$x=-5$

-5 is not a solution

No solution

15. $\left(\dfrac{2}{n}+n\right)\bullet n=3\bullet n$ Check $n=1$

$2+n^2=3n$ $\dfrac{2}{1}+1\overset{?}{=}3$

$n^2-3n+2=0$ $3=3$ True

$(n-2)(n-1)=0$ Check $n=2$

$n-2=0\quad n-1=0$ $\dfrac{2}{2}+2\overset{?}{=}3$

$n=2\qquad n=1$

            $3=3$ True

17. Cross product method. Check $a=6$

$a^2=36$ $\dfrac{6}{4}\overset{?}{=}\dfrac{9}{6}$

$a^2-36=0$

$(a-6)(a+6)=0$ $\dfrac{3}{2}=\dfrac{3}{2}$ True

$a-6=0\quad a+6=0$

$a=6\qquad a=-6$

Check $a=-6$

$\dfrac{-6}{4}\overset{?}{=}\dfrac{9}{-6}$

$-\dfrac{3}{2}=-\dfrac{3}{2}$ True

19. $\left(\dfrac{t}{t-1}-\dfrac{t^2}{t-1}\right)\bullet(t-1)=5\bullet(t-1)$

$t-t^2=5t-5$

$-t^2-4t+5=0$ Check $t=1$

$(-t-5)(t-1)=0$ $\dfrac{1}{1-1}-\dfrac{1^2}{1-1}\overset{?}{=}5$

$-t-5=0\quad t-1=0$

$-t=5\qquad t=1$ $\dfrac{1}{0}$ is undefined.

$t=-5$

            $t=1$ is not a solution

Check $t=-5$

$\dfrac{-5}{-5-1}-\dfrac{(-5)^2}{-5-1}\overset{?}{=}5$

$\dfrac{-5}{-6}-\dfrac{25}{-6}\overset{?}{=}5;\quad \dfrac{5}{6}+\dfrac{25}{6}\overset{?}{=}5$

$\dfrac{30}{6}\overset{?}{=}5;\qquad 5=5$ True

21. $\left(4+\dfrac{7}{p}\right)\bullet p^2=\left(\dfrac{15}{p^2}\right)\bullet p^2$

$4p^2+7p=15$ Check $p=-3$

$4p^2+7p-15=0$ $4+\dfrac{7}{-3}\overset{?}{=}\dfrac{15}{(-3)^2}$

$(p+3)(4p-5)=0$

$p+3=0\quad 4p-5=0$ $\dfrac{12}{3}-\dfrac{7}{3}\overset{?}{=}\dfrac{15}{9}$

$p=-3\qquad 4p=5$

      $p=\dfrac{5}{4}$ $\dfrac{5}{3}=\dfrac{5}{3}$ True

Check $p = \frac{5}{4}$; $4 + \dfrac{7}{\frac{5}{4}} \stackrel{?}{=} \dfrac{15}{\left(\frac{5}{4}\right)^2}$

$4 + \dfrac{7}{1} \bullet \dfrac{4}{5} \stackrel{?}{=} \dfrac{\overset{3}{\cancel{15}}}{1} \bullet \dfrac{16}{\underset{5}{\cancel{25}}}$; $\dfrac{20}{5} + \dfrac{28}{5} \stackrel{?}{=} \dfrac{48}{5}$

$\dfrac{48}{5} = \dfrac{48}{5}$ True

23. $\left(\dfrac{r+7}{2} + \dfrac{4}{r}\right) \bullet 2r = \dfrac{1}{2} \bullet 2r$

$r(r+7) + 8 = r$ Check $r = -4$

$r^2 + 7r + 8 = r$ $\dfrac{-4+7}{2} + \dfrac{4}{-4} \stackrel{?}{=} \dfrac{1}{2}$

$r^2 + 6r + 8 = 0$ $\dfrac{3}{2} - \dfrac{2}{2} \stackrel{?}{=} \dfrac{1}{2}$

$(r+4)(r+2) = 0$

$r+4 = 0$ $r+2 = 0$ $\dfrac{1}{2} = \dfrac{1}{2}$ True

$r = -4$ $r = -2$

Check $r = -2$

$\dfrac{-2+7}{2} + \dfrac{4}{-2} \stackrel{?}{=} \dfrac{1}{2}$

$\dfrac{5}{2} - \dfrac{4}{2} \stackrel{?}{=} \dfrac{1}{2}$; $\dfrac{1}{2} = \dfrac{1}{2}$ True

25. $\left(\dfrac{1}{x} + \dfrac{2}{x+10}\right) \bullet x(x+10) = \left(\dfrac{x}{x+10}\right) \bullet x(x+10)$

$x + 10 + 2x = x^2$ Check $x = -2$

$x^2 - 3x - 10 = 0$ $\dfrac{1}{-2} + \dfrac{2}{-2+10} \stackrel{?}{=} \dfrac{-2}{-2+10}$

$(x-5)(x+2) = 0$

$x-5 = 0$ $x+2 = 0$ $\dfrac{-4}{8} + \dfrac{2}{8} \stackrel{?}{=} \dfrac{-2}{8}$

$x = 5$ $x = -2$ $\dfrac{-2}{8} = \dfrac{-2}{8}$ True

Check $x = 5$

$\dfrac{1}{5} + \dfrac{2}{5+10} \stackrel{?}{=} \dfrac{5}{5+10}$

$\dfrac{3}{15} + \dfrac{2}{15} \stackrel{?}{=} \dfrac{5}{15}$; $\dfrac{5}{15} = \dfrac{5}{15}$ True

27. Cross product method   Check $n = -8$

$6(n-2) = 10(n+2)$ $\dfrac{6}{-8+2} \stackrel{?}{=} \dfrac{10}{-8-2}$

$6n - 12 = 10n + 20$

$-4n = 32$ $\dfrac{6}{-6} \stackrel{?}{=} \dfrac{10}{-10}$

$n = -8$ $-1 = -1$ True

29. Cross product method

$1(a+8) = 4(a+1)$

$a + 8 = 4a + 4$

$-3a = -4$ $a = \dfrac{4}{3}$

Check $a = \dfrac{4}{3}$; $\dfrac{1}{\frac{4}{3}+1} \stackrel{?}{=} \dfrac{4}{\frac{4}{3}+8}$

$\dfrac{1}{\frac{7}{3}} \stackrel{?}{=} \dfrac{4}{\frac{28}{3}}$; $\dfrac{1}{1} \bullet \dfrac{3}{7} \stackrel{?}{=} \dfrac{4}{1} \bullet \dfrac{3}{28}$; $\dfrac{3}{7} = \dfrac{3}{7}$ True

31. $\left(\dfrac{3-7r}{(r-3)(r+3)} - \dfrac{r}{-(r-3)}\right) \bullet (r+3)(r-3) =$

$\left(\dfrac{10}{r+3}\right) \bullet (r+3)(r-3)$

$3 - 7r + r(r+3) = 10(r-3)$

$3 - 7r + r^2 + 3r = 10r - 30$

$r^2 - 14r + 33 = 0$

$(r-11)(r-3) = 0$

$r-11 = 0$ $r-3 = 0$

$r = 11$ $r = 3$

Check $r = 3$

$\dfrac{3-7(3)}{3^2-9} - \dfrac{3}{3-3} \stackrel{?}{=} \dfrac{10}{3+3}$

$\dfrac{3}{0}$ is undefined. $r = 3$ is not a solution.

Check $r = 11$

$\dfrac{3-7(11)}{11^2-9} - \dfrac{11}{3-11} \stackrel{?}{=} \dfrac{10}{11+3}$

$\dfrac{3-77}{121-9} - \dfrac{11}{-8} \stackrel{?}{=} \dfrac{10}{14}$

$\dfrac{-74}{112} + \dfrac{11}{8} \stackrel{?}{=} \dfrac{5}{7}$; $\dfrac{-37}{56} + \dfrac{77}{56} \stackrel{?}{=} \dfrac{40}{56}$

$\dfrac{40}{56} = \dfrac{40}{56}$ True

33. $\left(\dfrac{x}{x-1} - 1\right) \bullet (x-1)(x-5) =$

$\left(-\dfrac{7}{x-5}\right) \bullet (x-1)(x-5)$

$x(x-5) - (x-1)(x-5) = -7(x-1)$

$x^2 - 5x - x^2 + 6x - 5 = -7x + 7$

$x - 5 = -7x + 7$; $8x = 12$

$x = \dfrac{12}{8} = \dfrac{3}{2}$

Check $x = \dfrac{3}{2}$ $\dfrac{\frac{3}{2}}{\frac{3}{2}-1} - 1 \stackrel{?}{=} -\dfrac{7}{\frac{3}{2}-5}$

$\dfrac{\frac{3}{2} \bullet \frac{2}{1}}{\left(\frac{3}{2}-1\right) \bullet \frac{2}{1}} - 1 \stackrel{?}{=} -\dfrac{7 \bullet \frac{2}{1}}{\left(\frac{3}{2}-5\right) \bullet \frac{2}{1}}$

$$\frac{3}{3-2}-1 \overset{?}{=} -\frac{14}{3-10}$$

$$3-1 \overset{?}{=} -(-2); \quad 2=2 \text{ True}$$

35. Cross product method.

$$x(x-7)=6(3)$$

$$x^2-7x=18$$

$$x^2-7x-18=0$$

$$(x-9)(x+2)=0$$

$$x-9=0 \quad x+2=0$$

$$x=9 \qquad x=-2$$

Check $x=-2$ Check $x=9$

$$\frac{-2}{3}\overset{?}{=}\frac{6}{-2-7} \qquad \frac{9}{3}\overset{?}{=}\frac{6}{9-7}$$

$$-\frac{2}{3}\overset{?}{=}\frac{6}{-9} \qquad\qquad 3\overset{?}{=}\frac{6}{2}$$

$$-\frac{2}{3}=-\frac{2}{3} \text{ True} \qquad 3=3 \text{ True}$$

37. Cross product method.

$$(t-4)(t+6)=(-3)8$$

$$t^2+2t-24=-24$$

$$t^2+2t=0$$

$$t(t+2)=0$$

$$t=0 \quad t+2=0$$

$$t=-2$$

Check $t=0$ Check $x=-2$

$$\frac{0-4}{8}\overset{?}{=}\frac{-3}{0+6} \qquad \frac{-2-4}{8}\overset{?}{=}\frac{-3}{-2+6}$$

$$\frac{-4}{8}\overset{?}{=}\frac{-3}{6} \qquad\qquad \frac{-6}{8}\overset{?}{=}\frac{-3}{4}$$

$$\frac{-1}{2}=\frac{-1}{2} \text{ True} \qquad \frac{-3}{4}=\frac{-3}{4} \text{ True}$$

39. $$\left(\frac{x}{x+5}-\frac{3}{x+4}\right)\bullet(x+5)(x+4)=$$

$$\left(\frac{7x+1}{(x+5)(x+4)}\right)\bullet(x+5)(x+4)$$

$$x(x+4)-3(x+5)=7x+1$$

$$x^2+4x-3x-15=7x+1$$

$$x^2-6x-16=0$$

$$(x+2)(x-8)=0$$

$$x+2=0 \quad x-8=0$$

$$x=-2 \qquad x=8$$

Check $x=-2$

$$\frac{-2}{-2+5}-\frac{3}{-2+4}\overset{?}{=}\frac{7(-2)+1}{(-2)^2+9(-2)+20}$$

$$\frac{-2}{3}-\frac{3}{2}\overset{?}{=}\frac{-13}{4-18+20}$$

$$\frac{-4}{6}-\frac{9}{6}\overset{?}{=}\frac{-13}{6}; \qquad \frac{-13}{6}=\frac{-13}{6} \text{ True}$$

Check $x=8$

$$\frac{8}{8+5}-\frac{3}{8+4}\overset{?}{=}\frac{7(8)+1}{8^2+9(8)+20}$$

$$\frac{8}{13}-\frac{3}{12}\overset{?}{=}\frac{56+1}{64+72+20}$$

$$\frac{96}{156}-\frac{39}{156}\overset{?}{=}\frac{57}{156}$$

$$\frac{57}{156}=\frac{57}{156} \text{ True}$$

41. $$\left(\frac{n-1}{n(n-2)}-\frac{n}{4(n-2)}\right)\bullet 4n(n-2)=$$

$$0\bullet 4n(n-2)$$

$$4(n-1)-n^2=0 \quad \text{Check } n=2$$

$$4n-4-n^2=0 \qquad \frac{2-1}{2^2-2(2)}-\frac{2}{4(2)-8}\overset{?}{=}0$$

$$n^2-4n+4=0$$

$$(n-2)(n-2)=0 \quad \frac{1}{0} \text{ and } \frac{2}{0} \text{ are undefined.}$$

$$n-2=0$$

$$\qquad\qquad n=2 \text{ is not a solution.}$$

$$n=2$$

No solution

43. $$\frac{-8}{(y+1)(y-1)}=-\frac{(y+5)}{y(y+1)}$$

$$\frac{-8}{(y+1)(y-1)}\bullet(y)(y+1)(y-1)=$$

$$-\frac{(y+5)}{y(y+1)}\bullet(y)(y+1)(y-1)$$

$$-8y=-(y+5)(y-1)$$

$$-8y=-y^2-4y+5$$

$$y^2-4y-5=0$$

$$(y+1)(y-5)=0$$

$$y+1=0 \quad y-5=0$$

$$y=-1 \qquad y=5$$

Check $y=-1$

$$-\frac{8}{(-1)^2-1}\overset{?}{=}-\frac{-1+5}{(-1)^2+(-1)}$$

$$-\frac{8}{0} \text{ and } \frac{4}{0} \text{ are undefined.}$$

$$y=-1 \text{ is not a solution}$$

Check $y=5$

$$-\frac{8}{5^2-1}\overset{?}{=}-\frac{5+5}{5^2+5}$$

$$\frac{-8}{24} \overset{?}{=} \frac{-10}{30}$$

$$\frac{-1}{3} = \frac{-1}{3} \text{ True}$$

45. $$\frac{2y}{(y-3)(y+3)} + \frac{y-1}{-2(y-3)} = 1$$

$$\frac{2y}{(y-3)(y+3)} \bullet 2(y-3)(y+3) + \frac{y-1}{-2(y-3)}$$

$$\bullet 2(y-3)(y+3) = 1 \bullet 2(y-3)(y+3)$$

$$4y - (y-1)(y+3) = 2(y-3)(y+3)$$

$$4y - (y^2 + 2y - 3) = 2(y^2 - 9)$$

$$4y - y^2 - 2y + 3 = 2y^2 - 18$$

$$-3y^2 + 2y + 21 = 0$$

$$3y^2 - 2y - 21 = 0$$

$$(3y+7)(y-3) = 0$$

$$3y + 7 = 0 \quad y - 3 = 0$$

$$3y = -7 \quad y = 3$$

$$y = -\frac{7}{3}$$

Check $y = 3$

$$\frac{2(3)}{3^2 - 9} + \frac{3-1}{6-2(3)} \overset{?}{=} 1$$

$$\frac{6}{0} + \frac{2}{0} \overset{?}{=} 1 \qquad \frac{6}{0} \text{ and } \frac{2}{0} \text{ are both undefined.}$$

$x = 3$ is not a solution.

Check $y = -\dfrac{7}{3}$

$$\frac{2\left(-\frac{7}{3}\right)}{\left(-\frac{7}{3}\right)^2 - 9} + \frac{-\frac{7}{3} - 1}{6 - 2\left(-\frac{7}{3}\right)} \overset{?}{=} 1$$

$$\frac{-\frac{14}{3}}{\frac{49}{9} - 9} + \frac{-\frac{7}{3} - 1}{6 + \frac{14}{3}} \overset{?}{=} 1$$

$$\frac{-\frac{14}{3} \bullet 9}{\left(\frac{49}{9} - 9\right) \bullet 9} + \frac{\left(-\frac{7}{3} - 1\right) \bullet 3}{\left(6 + \frac{14}{3}\right) \bullet 3} \overset{?}{=} 1$$

$$\frac{-14(3)}{49 - 81} + \frac{-7 - 3}{18 + 14} \overset{?}{=} 1$$

$$\frac{-42}{-32} + \frac{-10}{32} \overset{?}{=} 1$$

$$\frac{32}{32} \overset{?}{=} 1$$

$$1 = 1 \text{ True}$$

47. Cross product method

$$Pt = W$$

$$\frac{Pt}{P} = \frac{W}{P}$$

$$t = \frac{W}{P}$$

49. $$\frac{I_2}{I_1} \bullet I_1 = \frac{a^2}{b^2} \bullet I_1$$

$$I_2 = \frac{a^2 I_1}{b^2}$$

51. $$\frac{1}{R}(RR_1 R_2) = \frac{1}{R_1}(RR_1 R_2) + \frac{1}{R_2}(RR_1 R_2)$$

$$R_1 R_2 = RR_2 + RR_1$$

$$R_1 R_2 - RR_1 = RR_2$$

$$R_1(R_2 - R) = RR_2$$

$$\frac{R_1(R_2 - R)}{R_2 - R} = \frac{RR_2}{R_2 - R}$$

$$R_1 = \frac{RR_2}{R_2 - R}$$

53. Cross product method.

$$V(m_1 + m_2) = m_1 v_1 + m_2 v_2$$

$$Vm_1 + Vm_2 = m_1 v_1 + m_2 v_2$$

$$Vm_1 - m_1 v_1 = m_2 v_2 - Vm_2$$

$$m_1(V - v_1) = m_2 v_2 - Vm_2$$

$$\frac{m_1(V - v_1)}{V - v_1} = \frac{m_2 v_2 - Vm_2}{V - v_1}$$

$$m_1 = \frac{m_2 v_2 - Vm_2}{V - v_1} = \frac{m_2(v_2 - V)}{V - v_1}$$

55. $$\frac{x+9}{x-1} = \frac{3}{2} \quad \text{Cross product method}$$

$$2(x+9) = 3(x-1)$$

$$2x + 18 = 3x - 3$$

$$-x = -21$$

$$x = 21$$

57. $$\frac{2}{x-1} - \frac{4}{x+5} = -2$$

$$\frac{2}{x-1} \bullet (x-1)(x+5) - \frac{4}{x+5} \bullet (x-1)(x+5)$$

$$= -2 \bullet (x-1)(x+5)$$

$$2(x+5) - 4(x-1) = -2(x^2 + 4x - 5)$$

$$2x + 10 - 4x + 4 = -2x^2 - 8x + 10$$

$$2x^2 + 6x + 4 = 0$$

$$2(x+1)(x+2) = 0$$

$$x + 1 = 0 \quad x + 2 = 0$$

$$x = -1 \quad x = -2$$

59. $\dfrac{x+3}{4}=\dfrac{x}{x-6}$ Cross product method

$\dfrac{x+3}{4}=\dfrac{x}{x-6}$

$(x+3)(x-6)=4x$

$x^2-3x-18=4x$

$x^2-7x-18=0$

$(x-9)(x+2)=0$

$x-9=0 \quad x+2=0$

$x=9 \qquad x=-2$

61. $\dfrac{124}{150}=\dfrac{x}{1128}$

$\dfrac{124}{150}\bullet 1128=\dfrac{x}{1128}\bullet 1128$

$\dfrac{124\bullet 1128}{150}=x$

$x=932.48$

Approximately 932 employees are satisfied with their benefits package.

63. Let x be the speed of the wind.

$\text{time}=\dfrac{\text{distance}}{\text{rate}}$

$\dfrac{1125}{420+x}=\dfrac{975}{420-x}$ Cross product method

$1125(420-x)=975(420+x)$

$472500-1125x=409500+975x$

$63000=2100x$

$x=30$

The speed of the wind was 30 mph.

65. Let x be the rate she walked during her cardio workout.

$\text{time}=\dfrac{\text{distance}}{\text{rate}} \qquad \dfrac{5}{2x}+\dfrac{1}{x}=70$

$\dfrac{5}{2x}\bullet 2x+\dfrac{1}{x}\bullet 2x=70\bullet 2x$

$5+2=140x$

$7=140x$

$x=\dfrac{7}{140}=\dfrac{1}{20}\dfrac{\text{mi}}{\text{min}}\times\dfrac{60\text{ min}}{\text{hr}}=\dfrac{60}{20}\dfrac{\text{mi}}{\text{hr}}=3\dfrac{\text{mi}}{\text{hr}}$

$2x=2\bullet 3=6$

She ran at a rate of 6 mph during her cardio workout.

67. Let x be the rate the team rows in still water.

$\text{time}=\dfrac{\text{distance}}{\text{rate}}$

$\dfrac{12}{x-1}+\dfrac{12}{x+1}=1\dfrac{16}{60}$

$\dfrac{12}{x-1}+\dfrac{12}{x+1}=\dfrac{76}{60}=\dfrac{19}{15}$

$\dfrac{12}{x-1}\bullet 15(x-1)(x+1)+\dfrac{12}{x+1}\bullet$

$\qquad 15(x-1)(x+1)=\dfrac{19}{15}\bullet 15(x-1)(x+1)$

$180(x+1)+180(x-1)=19(x-1)(x+1)$

$180x+180+180x-180=19x^2-19$

$19x^2-360x-19=0$

$(19x+1)(x-19)=0$

$19x+1=0 \quad x-19=0$

$19x=-1 \qquad x=19$

$x=-\dfrac{1}{19}$

The negative answer makes no sense in this problem The team rows at a rate of 19 mph in still water.

69.

	Rate of work	Time Worked	Part of Task
One crew	$1\div 9$	t	$t(1\div 9)$
Another crew	$1\div 6$	t	$t(1\div 6)$

$\dfrac{t}{9}+\dfrac{t}{6}=1$

$\dfrac{t}{9}\bullet 18+\dfrac{t}{6}\bullet 18=1\bullet 18$

$2t+3t=18$

$5t=18$

$t=\dfrac{18}{5}=3\dfrac{3}{5}=3.6$

Working together, it would take $3\dfrac{3}{5}$ hr (or 3 hr and 36 min) to prepare the field.

71.

	Rate of work	Time Worked	Part of Task
One worker	$1\div 3$	$\dfrac{4}{3}$	$\dfrac{4}{3}(1\div 3)$
Other worker	$1\div x$	$\dfrac{4}{3}$	$\dfrac{4}{3}(1\div x)$

$\dfrac{4}{3}\left(\dfrac{1}{3}\right)+\dfrac{4}{3}\left(\dfrac{1}{x}\right)=1$

$\dfrac{4}{9}+\dfrac{4}{3x}=1$

$\dfrac{4}{9}\bullet 9x+\dfrac{4}{3x}\bullet 9x=1\bullet 9x$

$$4x + 12 = 9x$$
$$-5x = -12$$
$$x = \frac{12}{5} = 2\frac{2}{5}$$

It takes the other worker $2\frac{2}{5}$ hr (or 2 hr and 24 min) to load the truck working alone.

73.   a. $\dfrac{1}{f} \bullet r_1 r_2 f = (n-1)\left(\dfrac{1}{r_1} - \dfrac{1}{r_2}\right) \bullet r_1 r_2 f$

$$r_1 r_2 = (n-1)(r_2 f - r_1 f)$$
$$r_1 r_2 = n(r_2 f - r_1 f) - (r_2 f - r_1 f)$$
$$r_1 r_2 + r_2 f - r_1 f = n(r_2 f - r_1 f)$$
$$\frac{r_1 r_2 + r_2 f - r_1 f}{r_2 f - r_1 f} = \frac{n(r_2 f - r_1 f)}{r_2 f - r_1 f}$$
$$n = \frac{r_1 r_2 + r_2 f - r_1 f}{r_2 f - r_1 f}$$
$$n = \frac{r_1 r_2 - r_1 f + r_2 f}{f(r_2 - r_1)}$$

   b. $n = \dfrac{r_1 r_2 - r_1 f + r_2 f}{f(r_2 - r_1)}$

$$n = \frac{(2.5)(3) - (2.5)(30) + (3)(30)}{30(3 - 2.5)}$$
$$n = \frac{7.5 - 75 + 90}{30(0.5)} = \frac{22.5}{15} = 1.5$$

Exercises 6.5 Variation

1.   Decreases; inverse variation.
3.   Increases; direct variation.
5.   Increases; direct variation.
7.   Decreases; inverse variation.
9. $y = kx$

$$48 = k(16)$$
$$k = \frac{48}{16} = 3$$
$$y = 3x$$

11. $y = kx$

$$6 = k(36)$$
$$k = \frac{6}{36} = \frac{1}{6}$$
$$y = \frac{1}{6}x$$

13. $y = kx \qquad 3 = k\dfrac{1}{3}$

$$k = 3\left(\frac{3}{1}\right) = 9$$

15. $y = 9x$
       $y = kx$

$$0.9 = k(0.6)$$
$$k = \frac{0.9}{0.6} = \frac{3}{2}$$
$$y = \frac{3}{2}x$$

17. $y = \dfrac{k}{x} \qquad 13 = \dfrac{k}{3}$

$$k = 13(3) = 39$$
$$y = \frac{39}{x}$$

19. $y = \dfrac{k}{x} \qquad 1.8 = \dfrac{k}{15}$

$$k = 1.8(15) = 27$$
$$y = \frac{27}{x}$$

21. $y = \dfrac{k}{x} \qquad 0.7 = \dfrac{k}{0.4}$

$$k = 0.7(0.4) = 0.28 = \frac{28}{100} = \frac{7}{25}$$
$$y = \frac{\frac{7}{25}}{x} = \frac{7}{25x}$$

23. $y = \dfrac{k}{x} \qquad 27 = \dfrac{k}{\frac{2}{3}}$

$$k = 27\left(\frac{2}{3}\right) = 18$$
$$y = \frac{18}{x}$$

25. $y = kxz \qquad 160 = k(10)(4)$

$$160 = k(40)$$
$$k = \frac{160}{40} = 4$$
$$y = 4xz$$

27. $y = kxz \qquad 360 = k(25)(12)$

$$360 = k(300)$$
$$k = \frac{360}{300} = \frac{6}{5}$$
$$y = \frac{6}{5}xz$$

29. $y = kxz \qquad 63 = k(4.2)(5)$

$$63 = k(21)$$
$$k = \frac{63}{21} = 3$$
$$y = 3xz$$

31. $y = kxz \qquad 4.5 = k(0.6)(0.3)$

$4.5 = k(0.18)$

$k = \dfrac{4.5}{0.18} = 25$

$y = 25xz$

33. $y = \dfrac{kx}{z^2} \qquad 20 = \dfrac{k(4)}{(5)^2}$

$20 = \dfrac{k(4)}{25}$

$k = 20\left(\dfrac{25}{4}\right) = 125$

$y = \dfrac{125x}{z^2}$

35. $y = \dfrac{k}{xz^2} \qquad 100 = \dfrac{k}{(20)(0.5)^2}$

$100 = \dfrac{k}{(20)(0.25)} = \dfrac{k}{5}$

$100 = \dfrac{k}{5}$

$k = 100(5) = 500$

$y = \dfrac{500}{xz^2}$

37. $y = \dfrac{kxw}{z^2} \qquad 130 = \dfrac{k(13)(16)}{(0.4)^2}$

$130 = \dfrac{k(208)}{0.16} = k(1300)$

$130 = k(1300)$

$k = \dfrac{130}{1300} = \dfrac{1}{10}$

$y = \dfrac{\dfrac{1}{10}xw}{z^2}$

$y = \dfrac{xw}{10z^2}$

39. a. $A = ki \qquad 1080 = k(36000)$

$k = \dfrac{1080}{36000} = \dfrac{3}{100} = 0.03$

$A = \dfrac{3}{100}i \text{ or } A = 0.03i$

The constant of variation represents the income tax rate, which is 3%.

b. $A = 0.03i$

$A = 0.03(26500) = 795$ A person will pay \$795 in income tax.

41. $w = \dfrac{k}{f}$

$5.1 = \dfrac{k}{300}$

$k = 5.1(300) = 1530$

$w = \dfrac{1530}{f}$

$w = \dfrac{1530}{500} = 3.06$

The wavelength of the 500 Hz sound is 3.06m.

43. $E = kmv^2$

$113.6 = k(0.142)(40)^2$

$113.6 = k(227.2)$

$k = \dfrac{113.6}{227.2} = \dfrac{1}{2}$

$E = \dfrac{1}{2}mv^2$

$E = \dfrac{1}{2}(0.142)(20)^2 = 28.4$

The baseball has an energy of 28.4 J.

45. $I = \dfrac{k}{d^2}$

$21.6 = \dfrac{k}{2^2}$

$k = 21.6(2^2) = 86.4$

$I = \dfrac{86.4}{d^2}$

$I = \dfrac{86.4}{4^2} = \dfrac{86.4}{16} = 5.4$

The illumination 4 m above the table is 5.4 lumens per sq m.

Chapter 6 Review Exercises

1. Undefined when $2x - 1 = 0$

$2x = 1$

$x = \dfrac{1}{2}$

2. Undefined when $n^2 - 6n + 8 = 0$

$(n-4)(n-2) = 0$

$n - 4 = 0 \quad n - 2 = 0$

$n = 4 \qquad n = 2$

3. $\dfrac{1-t}{5-t} \overset{?}{=} \dfrac{t-1}{t-5}$

$\dfrac{\cancel{(-1)}(-1+t)}{\cancel{(-1)}(-5+t)} \overset{?}{=} \dfrac{t-1}{t-5}$

$\dfrac{t-1}{t-5}=\dfrac{t-1}{t-5}$ true, they are equivalent.

4. $\dfrac{4p^4+6p}{2p^3-3p^2}\overset{?}{=}\dfrac{2p^2+2}{1-p}$

$\dfrac{2p\left(2p^3+3\right)}{p^2\left(2p-3\right)}\overset{?}{=}\dfrac{2\left(p^2+1\right)}{\left(-1\right)\left(p-1\right)}$

$\dfrac{2\left(2p^3+3\right)}{p\left(2p-3\right)}\neq\dfrac{-2\left(p^2+1\right)}{p-1}$ Not equivalent.

5. $\dfrac{\cancel{3xy}\left(2x^2y\right)}{\cancel{3xy}\left(3x-4y\right)}=\dfrac{2x^2y}{3x-4y}$

6. $\dfrac{-1\cancel{\left(6n-2\right)}}{2\cancel{\left(6n-2\right)}}=-\dfrac{1}{2}$

7. $\dfrac{\left(a-2b\right)\cancel{\left(a+2b\right)}}{5\cancel{\left(a+2b\right)}}=\dfrac{a-2b}{5}$

8. $\dfrac{r^3+1}{r^2+1}=\dfrac{\left(r+1\right)\left(r^2-r+1\right)}{r^2+1}$
    Cannot be simplified.

9. $\dfrac{\left(x+8\right)\cancel{\left(x+2\right)}}{\cancel{\left(x+2\right)}\left(x-7\right)}=\dfrac{x+8}{x-7}$

10. $\dfrac{\left(2t-1\right)\left(2t-1\right)}{-\left(6t^2+13t-8\right)}=\dfrac{\left(2t-1\right)\left(2t-1\right)}{-\left(2t-1\right)\left(3t+8\right)}=-\dfrac{2t-1}{3t+8}$

11. $\dfrac{\cancel{16}\,\cancel{u}^{u^2}\,v}{\cancel{12}\,\cancel{v}^{v}}\cdot\dfrac{9u\,\cancel{v}^{v}}{2\cancel{u}}=\dfrac{\cancel{4}\cdot\cancel{9}\,u^3v^2}{\cancel{2}\cdot\cancel{3}}=6u^3v^2$

12. $\dfrac{\cancel{20}^{5}\,pq}{\cancel{8}\,\cancel{q}^{2\,q^2}}\cdot\dfrac{\cancel{p}\,\cancel{q}}{25\,\cancel{p}^{p^2}}=\dfrac{\cancel{5}\,\cancel{p}\,\cancel{q}}{\cancel{50}^{10}\,\cancel{q}^{q}\,\cancel{p}^{p}}=\dfrac{1}{10pq}$

13. $\dfrac{\cancel{6}^{3}\,\cancel{a}\left(b-2\right)}{\cancel{6}\,\cancel{a}^{2\,a}}\cdot\dfrac{a\cancel{b}\left(7a-1\right)}{\cancel{b}^{b}\cancel{\left(b-2\right)}}=\dfrac{3\cancel{a}\left(7a-1\right)}{2\cancel{a}b}=$
     $\dfrac{3\left(7a-1\right)}{2b}$

14. $\dfrac{\cancel{6}\cancel{\left(y-5\right)}}{\cancel{y}^{y}\left(y-4\right)}\cdot\dfrac{y-4}{-3\cancel{\left(y-5\right)}}=-\dfrac{1}{3y}$

15. $\dfrac{\cancel{\left(x-2\right)}\cancel{\left(x+2\right)}}{\cancel{\left(x-5\right)}\cancel{\left(x+2\right)}}\cdot\dfrac{2\cancel{\left(x-5\right)}\left(x+5\right)}{x^2\cancel{\left(x-2\right)}}=\dfrac{2\left(x+5\right)}{x^2}$

16. $\dfrac{-\cancel{\left(r+3\right)}\cancel{\left(r-1\right)}}{\cancel{\left(r+3\right)}\cancel{\left(r-3\right)}}\cdot\dfrac{\left(r+10\right)\cancel{\left(r-3\right)}}{\cancel{\left(r-1\right)}\left(r^2+r+1\right)}=-\dfrac{r+10}{r^2+r+1}$

17. $\dfrac{\cancel{\left(2x-5\right)}\cancel{\left(x-4\right)}}{\left(x-4\right)\cancel{\left(x-4\right)}}\cdot\dfrac{1}{\cancel{\left(2x-5\right)}\left(2x+3\right)}=$
     $\dfrac{1}{\left(x-4\right)\left(2x+3\right)}$

18. $\dfrac{\cancel{\left(3n+4\right)}\cancel{\left(n+1\right)}}{\cancel{\left(n-6\right)}\cancel{\left(n+1\right)}}\cdot\dfrac{\left(n+9\right)\cancel{\left(n-6\right)}}{\cancel{\left(3n+4\right)}\left(3n+4\right)}=\dfrac{n+9}{3n+4}$

19. $\dfrac{x-1}{x^3+x^2}=\dfrac{x-1}{x^2\left(x+1\right)}$

$\dfrac{2}{x^2+2x+1}=\dfrac{2}{\left(x+1\right)\left(x+1\right)}$

LCD $=x^2\left(x+1\right)^2$

$\dfrac{x-1}{x^2\left(x+1\right)}\cdot\dfrac{\left(x+1\right)}{\left(x+1\right)}=\dfrac{\left(x-1\right)\left(x+1\right)}{x^2\left(x+1\right)^2}$

$\dfrac{2}{\left(x+1\right)\left(x+1\right)}\cdot\dfrac{x^2}{x^2}=\dfrac{2x^2}{x^2\left(x+1\right)^2}$

20. $\dfrac{x+5}{x^2-16x+48}=\dfrac{x+5}{\left(x-4\right)\left(x-12\right)}$

$\dfrac{2x-3}{x^2-10x-24}=\dfrac{2x-3}{\left(x+2\right)\left(x-12\right)}$

LCD $=\left(x-4\right)\left(x+2\right)\left(x-12\right)$

$\dfrac{x+5}{\left(x-4\right)\left(x-12\right)}\cdot\dfrac{x+2}{x+2}=\dfrac{\left(x+5\right)\left(x+2\right)}{\left(x-4\right)\left(x+2\right)\left(x-12\right)}$

$\dfrac{2x-3}{\left(x+2\right)\left(x-12\right)}\cdot\dfrac{x-4}{x-4}=\dfrac{\left(2x-3\right)\left(x-4\right)}{\left(x-4\right)\left(x+2\right)\left(x-12\right)}$

21. $\dfrac{8}{3x^2y}+\dfrac{4}{3x^2y}=\dfrac{12}{3x^2y}=\dfrac{4}{x^2y}$

22. $\dfrac{2n+9}{n+6}-\dfrac{n+3}{n+6}=\dfrac{2n+9-n-3}{n+6}=\dfrac{n+6}{n+6}=1$

23. LCD $=\left(p-5\right)\left(p-4\right)$

$\dfrac{6}{p-5}\cdot\dfrac{\left(p-4\right)}{\left(p-4\right)}-\dfrac{8}{p-4}\cdot\dfrac{\left(p-5\right)}{\left(p-5\right)}=$

$\dfrac{6p-24-8p+40}{\left(p-5\right)\left(p-4\right)}=\dfrac{-2p+16}{\left(p-5\right)\left(p-4\right)}$

24. $\dfrac{a-4}{8a^2-16a}=\dfrac{a-4}{8a\left(a-2\right)}$

$\dfrac{2}{4a^3-8a^2}=\dfrac{2}{4a^2\left(a-2\right)}$

LCD $=8a^2\left(a-2\right)$

$\dfrac{a-4}{8a\left(a-2\right)}\cdot\dfrac{a}{a}+\dfrac{2}{4a^2\left(a-2\right)}\cdot\dfrac{2}{2}=$

$$\frac{a^2-4a+4}{8a^2(a-2)}=\frac{(a-2)\,(a-2)}{8a^2\,(a-2)}=\frac{a-2}{8a^2}$$

25. $$\frac{t^2-6t}{18-3t-t^2}=\frac{t^2-6t}{-(t+6)(t-3)}$$

$$\text{LCD}=(t+6)(t-3)$$

$$\frac{1}{t-3}\bullet\frac{(t+6)}{(t+6)}-\frac{t^2-6t}{-(t+6)(t-3)}=$$

$$\frac{t+6+t^2-6t}{(t+6)(t-3)}=\frac{t^2-5t+6}{(t+6)(t-3)}=$$

$$\frac{(t-3)(t-2)}{(t+6)\,(t-3)}=\frac{t-2}{t+6}$$

26. $$\frac{5y-1}{y^2-4}=\frac{5y-1}{(y-2)(y+2)}$$

$$\frac{2}{2-y}=-\frac{2}{y-2}$$

$$\text{LCD}=(y-2)(y+2)$$

$$\frac{5y-1}{(y-2)(y+2)}+\frac{-2}{y-2}\bullet\frac{(y+2)}{(y+2)}=$$

$$\frac{5y-1-2y-4}{(y-2)(y+2)}=\frac{3y-5}{(y-2)(y+2)}$$

27. $$\frac{2x}{x^2+2x-3}=\frac{2x}{(x+3)(x-1)}$$

$$\frac{1}{x^2-2x+1}=\frac{1}{(x-1)^2}$$

$$\text{LCD}=(x+3)(x-1)^2$$

$$\frac{2x}{(x+3)(x-1)}\bullet\frac{(x-1)}{(x-1)}+\frac{1}{(x-1)^2}\bullet\frac{(x+3)}{(x+3)}=$$

$$\frac{2x^2-2x+x+3}{(x+3)(x-1)^2}=\frac{2x^2-x+3}{(x+3)(x-1)^2}$$

28. $$\frac{u+1}{2u^2+11u+12}=\frac{u+1}{(2u+3)(u+4)}$$

$$\frac{1-u}{u^2-5u-36}=\frac{1-u}{(u+4)(u-9)}$$

$$\text{LCD}=(2u+3)(u+4)(u-9)$$

$$\frac{u+1}{(2u+3)(u+4)}\bullet\frac{(u-9)}{(u-9)}-$$

$$\frac{-(u-1)}{(u+4)(u-9)}\bullet\frac{(2u+3)}{(2u+3)}=$$

$$\frac{u^2-8u-9+2u^2+u-3}{(2u+3)(u+4)(u-9)}=$$

$$\frac{3u^2-7u-12}{(2u+3)(u+4)(u-9)}$$

29. $$\frac{\dfrac{36x^3}{x-4}\bullet2(x-4)}{\dfrac{18x}{2(x-4)}\bullet2(x-4)}=\frac{72x^3}{18x}=4x^2$$

30. $$\frac{\left(\dfrac{1}{x^2}-9\right)\bullet x^2}{\left(\dfrac{1}{x}-3\right)\bullet x^2}=\frac{1-9x^2}{x-3x^2}=$$

$$\frac{(1-3x)(1+3x)}{x(1-3x)}=\frac{3x+1}{x}$$

31. $$\frac{\left(1-\dfrac{4}{p}-\dfrac{5}{p^2}\right)\bullet p^2}{\left(1+\dfrac{2}{p}+\dfrac{1}{p^2}\right)\bullet p^2}=\frac{p^2-4p-5}{p^2+2p+1}=$$

$$\frac{(p-5)(p+1)}{(p+1)(p+1)}=\frac{p-5}{p+1}$$

32. $$\frac{\left(\dfrac{3}{x+3}+\dfrac{6}{x-1}\right)\bullet(x-1)(x+3)}{\left(\dfrac{3}{x-1}-\dfrac{6}{x+3}\right)\bullet(x-1)(x+3)}=$$

$$\frac{3(x-1)+6(x+3)}{3(x+3)-6(x-1)}=\frac{3x-3+6x+18}{3x+9-6x+6}=$$

$$\frac{9x+15}{-3x+15}=\frac{3(3x+5)}{3(-x+5)}=\frac{3x+5}{-x+5}$$

33. $$\frac{\dfrac{(r-6)(r-2)}{(2r-1)(r-6)}}{\dfrac{(r-2)(r-2)}{(3r+4)(2r-1)}}=$$

$$\frac{\dfrac{(r-2)}{(2r-1)}\bullet(3r+4)(2r-1)}{\dfrac{(r-2)(r-2)}{(3r+4)(2r-1)}\bullet(3r+4)(2r-1)}=$$

$$\frac{(r-2)(3r+4)}{(r-2)(r-2)}=\frac{3r+4}{r-2}$$

34. $$\frac{\left(2x^{-2}+x^{-1}\right)\bullet x^3}{\left(x^{-3}\right)\bullet x^3}=\frac{2x+x^2}{x^0}=2x+x^2$$

35. $$\frac{y+1}{3}\bullet24-\frac{y}{8}\bullet24=\frac{2y-1}{24}\bullet24$$

$$(y+1)\bullet8-y\bullet3=2y-1$$

$$8y+8-3y=2y-1$$

$$5y+8=2y-1$$
$$3y=-9$$
$$y=-3$$

36. $$\frac{a-12}{4a}\bullet 4a+\frac{3}{a}\bullet 4a=1\bullet 4a$$
$$a-12+12=4a$$
$$0=3a$$
$$a=0$$
$$\frac{0-12}{4(0)}\text{ and }\frac{3}{0}\text{ are undefined.}$$
$a=0$ is not a solution.
No solution.

37. $$\frac{t+7}{t-1}\bullet(t-1)+6(t-1)=\frac{2t}{-1(t-1)}(t-1)$$
$$t+7+6(t-1)=-2t$$
$$t+7+6t-6=-2t$$
$$9t+1=0$$
$$9t=-1$$
$$t=-\frac{1}{9}$$

38.   Cross product method.
$$5(x-2)=4(x+3)$$
$$5x-10=4x+12$$
$$x=22$$

39. $$\frac{n+1}{n^2}\bullet n^2-\frac{3}{n}\bullet n^2+1\bullet n^2=0\bullet n^2$$
$$n+1-3n+n^2=0$$
$$n^2-2n+1=0$$
$$(n-1)(n-1)=0$$
$$n-1=0$$
$$n=1$$

40. $$\frac{10}{r(r+2)}\bullet r(r+2)+\frac{r}{r+2}\bullet r(r+2)=\frac{5}{r}\bullet r(r+2)$$
$$10+r^2=5(r+2)$$
$$10+r^2=5r+10$$
$$r^2-5r=0$$
$$r(r-5)=0$$
$$r=0 \quad r-5=0$$
$$r=5$$
$$\frac{10}{0^2+2(0)}\text{ and }\frac{5}{0}\text{ are undefined when }r=0$$
$r=0$ is not a solution
$$r=5$$

41.   Cross product method.
$$x(x-4)=1(x+6)$$

$$x^2-4x=x+6$$
$$x^2-5x-6=0$$
$$(x-6)(x+1)=0$$
$$x-6=0 \quad x+1=0$$
$$x=6 \qquad x=-1$$

42. $$\frac{p-5}{(p+1)^2}\bullet(p+1)^2-\frac{7}{p+1}\bullet(p+1)^2=$$
$$\frac{p}{p+1}\bullet(p+1)^2$$
$$p-5-7(p+1)=p(p+1)$$
$$p-5-7p-7=p^2+p$$
$$p^2+7p+12=0$$
$$(p+3)(p+4)=0$$
$$p+3=0 \quad p+4=0$$
$$p=-3 \qquad p=-4$$

43. $$F\bullet r=\frac{mv^2}{r}\bullet r$$
$$Fr=mv^2$$
$$\frac{Fr}{v^2}=\frac{mv^2}{v^2}$$
$$m=\frac{Fr}{v^2}$$

44. $$R\bullet(R_1+R_2)=\frac{R_1R_2}{(R_1+R_2)}\bullet(R_1+R_2)$$
$$RR_1+RR_2=R_1R_2$$
$$RR_2-R_1R_2=-RR_1 \quad\text{or}\quad RR_1=R_1R_2-RR_2$$
$$R_2(R-R_1)=-RR_1 \qquad\qquad RR_1=R_2(R_1-R)$$
$$R_2=-\frac{RR_1}{R-R_1} \qquad\qquad R_2=\frac{RR_1}{R_1-R}$$

45. $$y=kx \quad 1.6=k(4)$$
$$\frac{1.6}{4}=k$$
$$k=0.4$$
$$y=0.4x$$

46. $$y=\frac{k}{x} \quad \frac{1}{2}=\frac{k}{3}$$
$$2k=3; \quad k=\frac{3}{2}$$
$$y=\frac{\frac{3}{2}}{x}=\frac{3}{2}\bullet\left(\frac{1}{x}\right)$$
$$y=\frac{3}{2x}$$

47. $$y=kxz \quad 144=k(4)(6)$$
$$144=24k$$

$k = \dfrac{144}{24} = 6$

$y = 6xz$

48. $y = \dfrac{kx^2}{z^2} \qquad 2 = \dfrac{k(5)^2}{(10)^2}$

$2 = \dfrac{25k}{100}$

$2 = \dfrac{k}{4}$

$k = 8$

$y = \dfrac{8x^2}{z^2}$

49. $\dfrac{1500 + 2x}{x}$ is undefined when $x = 0$.

50. $1 \bullet \dfrac{T_2}{T_2} - \dfrac{T_1}{T_2} = \dfrac{T_2 - T_1}{T_2}$

51. $V\left(\dfrac{1}{R_1} \bullet \dfrac{R_2}{R_2} + \dfrac{1}{R_2} \bullet \dfrac{R_1}{R_1} \right)$

$V\left(\dfrac{R_2}{R_1 R_2} + \dfrac{R_1}{R_1 R_2} \right)$

$V\left(\dfrac{R_2 + R_1}{R_1 R_2} \right)$

52. $\dfrac{1 \bullet pq}{\left(\dfrac{1}{p} + \dfrac{1}{q} \right) \bullet pq} = \dfrac{pq}{q + p}$

53. $\dfrac{1 \text{ in}}{5 \text{ mi}} = \dfrac{8 \text{ in}}{x \text{ mi}}$ or $\dfrac{5 \text{ mi}}{1 \text{ in}} = \dfrac{x \text{ mi}}{8 \text{ in}}$

Cross product method

$1x = 40$

The actual distance between the cities is 40 mi.

54. Let x be the speed of the current.

$\text{time} = \dfrac{\text{distance}}{\text{rate}}$

$\dfrac{108}{34 + x} = \dfrac{96}{34 - x}$

Cross product method

$108(34 - x) = 96(34 + x)$

$3672 - 108x = 3264 + 96x$

$-204x = -408$

$x = \dfrac{-408}{-204} = 2$

The speed of the current is 2 km per hr.

55. Let x be the speed on the way back to school.

$\text{time} = \dfrac{\text{distance}}{\text{rate}}$

$\dfrac{294}{x} + \dfrac{294}{\dfrac{3}{2}x} = 11\dfrac{40}{60} = 11\dfrac{2}{3} = \dfrac{35}{3}$

$\dfrac{294}{x} + \dfrac{294}{\dfrac{3}{2}x} = \dfrac{35}{3}$

$\dfrac{294}{x} + \dfrac{294}{1}\left(\dfrac{2}{3x} \right) = \dfrac{35}{3}$

$\dfrac{294}{x} + \dfrac{196}{x} = \dfrac{35}{3}$

$\dfrac{294}{x} \bullet 3x + \dfrac{196}{x} \bullet 3x = \dfrac{35}{3} \bullet 3x$

$882 + 588 = 35x$

$1470 = 35x$

$x = \dfrac{1470}{35} = 42$

$\dfrac{3}{2}(42) = 63$

Her average speed was 63 mph on the drive home and was 42 mph on the way back to school.

56.

	Rate of work	Time Worked	Part of Task
One clerk	$1 \div 16$	t	$t(1 \div 16)$
Another clerk	$1 \div 12$	t	$t(1 \div 12)$

$t\left(\dfrac{1}{16} \right) + t\left(\dfrac{1}{12} \right) = 1$

$\dfrac{t}{16} + \dfrac{t}{12} = 1$

$\dfrac{t}{16} \bullet 48 + \dfrac{t}{12} \bullet 48 = 1 \bullet 48$

$3t + 4t = 48$

$7t = 48$

$t = \dfrac{48}{7} = 6\dfrac{6}{7}$

Working together, it will take $6\dfrac{6}{7}$ hr to complete the job.

57. $v = kt$

$19.6 = k(2)$

$k = \dfrac{19.6}{2} = 9.8$

$v = 9.8t$

$v = 9.8(5) = 49$

Its velocity after 5 sec is 49 m per sec.

58. $A = \dfrac{k}{d}$ $8 = \dfrac{k}{12.5}$

$8(12.5) = k$

$k = 100$

$A = \dfrac{100}{d}$

$A = \dfrac{100}{10} = 10$

The accommodation is 10 diopters.

Chapter 6 Posttest

1.   a.   The expression is undefined when $4x - 2x^2 = 0$

$2x(2 - x) = 0$

$2x = 0 \quad 2 - x = 0$

$x = 0 \qquad x = 2$

b.   The expression is undefined when

$n^2 - 8n + 16 = 0$

$(n - 4)(n - 4) = 0$

$n - 4 = 0$

$n = 4$

2. $\dfrac{2\cancel{y}\left(4y - 2xy^2 + 3x^2\right)}{2\cancel{y}\left(6xy\right)} = \dfrac{4y - 2xy^2 + 3x^2}{6xy}$

3. $\dfrac{-1\cancel{(3a - 2)}}{\cancel{(3a - 2)}\,(3a + 2)} = -\dfrac{1}{3a + 2}$

4. $\dfrac{(3n - 2)\,\cancel{(n - 2)}}{(n + 8)\,\cancel{(n - 2)}} = \dfrac{3n - 2}{n + 8}$

5. $\dfrac{\cancel{6}\,p\cancel{q^2}}{\cancel{2}\,\cancel{(p - 6q)}} \cdot \dfrac{\cancel{(p - 6q)}\,(p + 6q)}{\cancel{p}\cancel{q^2}\,(3pq - 1)} = \dfrac{p + 6q}{3pq - 1}$

6. $\dfrac{y\cancel{(y + 3)}}{(y + 2)\,\cancel{(y + 2)}} \cdot \dfrac{\cancel{(y + 2)}\,\cancel{(y - 9)}}{\cancel{(y + 3)}\,\cancel{(y - 9)}} = \dfrac{y}{y + 2}$

7. $\dfrac{(a - 5b)\,\cancel{(a - 4b)}}{1} \cdot \dfrac{a\,\cancel{(a + 4b)}}{\cancel{(a - 4b)}\,\cancel{(a + 4b)}} = a(a - 5b)$

8. $\dfrac{\left(x^2 - 3xy + 9y^2\right)}{(3x - 1y)(2x + 5y)} \cdot \dfrac{(2x + 5y)\,(x + 3y)}{(x + 3y)\left(x^2 - 3xy + 9y^2\right)} =$

$\dfrac{\cancel{\left(x^2 - 3xy + 9y^2\right)}}{(3x - 1y)\,\cancel{(2x + 5y)}} \cdot \dfrac{\cancel{(2x + 5y)}}{\cancel{\left(x^2 - 3xy + 9y^2\right)}} = \dfrac{1}{3x - y}$

9. $\dfrac{1}{6r^3} + \dfrac{1}{4r^2(r - 3)} =$

$\dfrac{1}{6r^3} \cdot \dfrac{2(r - 3)}{2(r - 3)} + \dfrac{1}{4r^2(r - 3)} \cdot \dfrac{3r}{3r} =$

$\dfrac{2r - 6 + 3r}{12r^3(r - 3)} = \dfrac{5r - 6}{12r^3(r - 3)}$

10. $\dfrac{1}{2t - 1} - \dfrac{3t - 11}{-\left(4t^2 - 1\right)} =$

$\dfrac{1}{2t - 1} + \dfrac{3t - 11}{(2t - 1)(2t + 1)} =$

$\dfrac{1}{2t - 1} \cdot \dfrac{2t + 1}{2t + 1} + \dfrac{3t - 11}{(2t - 1)(2t + 1)} =$

$\dfrac{2t + 1 + 3t - 11}{(2t + 1)(2t - 1)} = \dfrac{5t - 10}{(2t + 1)(2t - 1)} =$

$\dfrac{5(t - 2)}{(2t + 1)(2t - 1)}$

11. $\dfrac{n}{(n - 4)(n - 2)} + \dfrac{3}{(n - 2)(n + 1)} =$

$\dfrac{n}{(n - 4)(n - 2)} \cdot \dfrac{n + 1}{n + 1} + \dfrac{3}{(n - 2)(n + 1)} \cdot \dfrac{n - 4}{n - 4} =$

$\dfrac{n^2 + n + 3n - 12}{(n - 4)(n - 2)(n + 1)} = \dfrac{n^2 + 4n - 12}{(n - 4)(n - 2)(n + 1)} =$

$\dfrac{\cancel{(n - 2)}\,(n + 6)}{(n - 4)\,\cancel{(n - 2)}\,(n + 1)} = \dfrac{n + 6}{(n - 4)(n + 1)}$

12. $\dfrac{3y - 2}{(3y + 2)^2} - \dfrac{y}{(3y + 2)(y - 3)} =$

$\dfrac{3y - 2}{(3y + 2)^2} \cdot \dfrac{y - 3}{y - 3} - \dfrac{y}{(3y + 2)(y - 3)} \cdot \dfrac{3y + 2}{3y + 2} =$

$\dfrac{3y^2 - 11y + 6 - 3y^2 - 2y}{(3y + 2)^2(y - 3)} = \dfrac{-13y + 6}{(3y + 2)^2(y - 3)}$

13.   a. $\dfrac{\left(\dfrac{1}{x^2} - 4\right) \cdot x^2}{\left(\dfrac{3}{x} + 6\right) \cdot x^2} = \dfrac{1 - 4x^2}{3x - 6x^2} =$

$\dfrac{\cancel{(1 + 2x)}\,(1 - 2x)}{3x\,\cancel{(1 + 2x)}} = \dfrac{1 - 2x}{3x}$

b. $\dfrac{\left(\dfrac{8}{a^2} - \dfrac{6}{a} + 1\right) \cdot a^2}{\left(\dfrac{4}{a^2} - \dfrac{5}{a} + 1\right) \cdot a^2} = \dfrac{8 - 6a + a^2}{4 - 5a + a^2} =$

$\dfrac{a^2 - 6a + 8}{a^2 - 5a + 4} = \dfrac{\cancel{(a - 4)}\,(a - 2)}{\cancel{(a - 4)}\,(a - 1)} = \dfrac{a - 2}{a - 1}$

14. $\dfrac{3}{n - 9} + \dfrac{1}{n + 2} = \dfrac{n^2}{(n - 9)(n + 2)}$

$$\frac{3}{n-9} \bullet (n-9)(n+2) + \frac{1}{n+2} \bullet (n-9)(n+2) =$$

$$\frac{n^2}{(n-9)(n+2)} \bullet (n-9)(n+2)$$

$$3(n+2) + (n-9) = n^2$$

$$3n + 6 + n - 9 = n^2$$

$$n^2 - 4n + 3 = 0$$

$$(n-1)(n-3) = -$$

$$n - 1 = 0 \qquad n - 3 = 0$$

$$n = 1 \qquad n = 3$$

15. $$\frac{x-1}{x+2} \bullet (x-5)(x+2) - 1 \bullet (x-5)(x+2) =$$

$$\frac{2}{x-5} \bullet (x-5)(x+2)$$

$$(x-1)(x-5) - (x-5)(x+2) = 2(x+2)$$

$$x^2 - 6x + 5 - x^2 + 3x + 10 = 2x + 4$$

$$-3x + 15 = 2x + 4$$

$$-5x = -11$$

$$x = \frac{11}{5}$$

16. Cross product method.

$$2(2) = (y+4)(y+7)$$

$$4 = y^2 + 11y + 28$$

$$y^2 + 11y + 24 = 0$$

$$(y+8)(y+3) = 0$$

$$y + 8 = 0 \qquad y + 3 = 0$$

$$y = -8 \qquad y = -3$$

17. $$y = kxz$$

$$18.2 = k(1.4)(65)$$

$$18.2 = 91k$$

$$k = \frac{18.2}{91} = 0.2$$

$$y = 0.2xz$$

18. Let x be the speed of the river's current.

$$\text{time} = \frac{\text{distance}}{\text{rate}}$$

$$\frac{174}{40+x} = \frac{146}{40-x}$$

Cross product method

$$174(40-x) = 146(40+x)$$

$$6960 - 174x = 5840 + 146x$$

$$1120 = 320x$$

$$x = \frac{1120}{320} = 3.5$$

The speed of the river's current is 3.5 km per hr.

19. 2 hr 40 min $= 2\frac{40}{60} = 2\frac{2}{3}$ hr.

	Rate of work	Time Worked	Part of Task
One gardener	$\frac{1}{6}$	$2\frac{2}{3}$	$\frac{1}{6}\left(2\frac{2}{3}\right)$
Second gardener	$\frac{1}{x}$	$2\frac{2}{3}$	$\frac{1}{x}\left(2\frac{2}{3}\right)$

$$\frac{1}{6}\left(2\frac{2}{3}\right) + \frac{1}{x}\left(2\frac{2}{3}\right) = 1$$

$$\frac{1}{6}\left(\frac{8}{3}\right) + \frac{1}{x}\left(\frac{8}{3}\right) = 1$$

$$\frac{4}{9} + \frac{8}{3x} = 1$$

$$\frac{4}{9} \bullet 9x + \frac{8}{3x} \bullet 9x = 1 \bullet 9x$$

$$4x + 24 = 9x$$

$$24 = 5x$$

$$x = \frac{24}{5} = 4\frac{4}{5}$$

It would take the second gardener $4\frac{4}{5}$ hr (or 4 hr and 48 min) to mow the lawn working alone.

20. Let A be the measure of the exterior angle and s be the number of sides of the regular polygon. (An octagon has 8 sides and a dodecagon has 12 sides.)

$$A = \frac{k}{s}; \qquad 45 = \frac{k}{8}$$

$$k = (8)(45) = 360$$

$$A = \frac{360}{s}$$

$$A = \frac{360}{12} = 30$$

The measure of each exterior angle of a regular dodecagon is 30 degrees.

Cumulative Review Exercises

1. $$\left(2xy^2\right)^2 \left(4x^3 y\right)^{-2} = 4x^2 y^4 \bullet \frac{1}{16x^6 y^2} =$$

$$\frac{y^{4-2}}{4x^{6-2}} = \frac{y^2}{4x^4}$$

2. $$8 - 3 + 9n = 12 - 7n$$

$$5 + 9n = 12 - 7n$$

$$16n = 7$$

$$n = \frac{7}{16}$$

3. $m = \dfrac{y_2 - y_1}{x_2 - x_1} = \dfrac{4 - 5}{2 - (-1)} = \dfrac{-1}{3} = -\dfrac{1}{3}$

4. $6x = 3y - 3$

$6x + 3 = 3y$

$y = \dfrac{6x + 3}{3} = 2x + 1$

x	$y = 2x + 1$	(x, y)
0	$2(0) + 1 = 1$	$(0, 1)$
2	$2(2) + 1 = 5$	$(2, 5)$

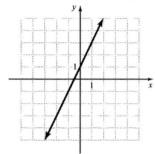

5. $2x - y + z = 3$

$x + 3y - z = -10$

$3x + 2y = -7$

$x + 3y - z = -10 \xrightarrow{\times 4} 4x + 12y - 4z = -40$

$x + 2y + 4z = 7 \longrightarrow \underline{\quad\quad x + 2y + 4z = 7}$

$5x + 14y \quad\quad = -33$

$3x + 2y = -7 \xrightarrow{\times(-7)} -21x - 14y = 49$

$5x + 14y = -33 \longrightarrow \underline{\quad 5x + 14y = -33}$

$-16x \quad\quad = 16$

$x = -1$

$3(-1) + 2y = -7 \quad\quad 2(-1) - (-2) + z = 3$

$-3 + 2y = -7 \quad\quad\quad -2 + 2 + z = 3$

$2y = -4 \quad\quad\quad\quad\quad z = 3$

$y = -2 \quad\quad\quad\quad\quad (-1, -2, 3)$

6. $-(5 - x^2)(x^2 - x + 1) = (x^2 - 5)(x^2 - x + 1)$

$ x^2 - x + 1$

$ \underline{x^2 - 5}$

$ -5x^2 + 5x - 5$

$\underline{x^4 - x^3 + x^2}$

$x^4 - x^3 - 4x^2 + 5x - 5$

7. $\dfrac{4(\cancel{x^2 - 3x + 9})}{3(9 - x^2)} \cdot \dfrac{1}{(x + 3)(\cancel{x^2 - 3x + 9})} =$

$\dfrac{4}{3(3 + x)(3 - x)(x + 3)} = \dfrac{4}{(x + 3)^2(3 - x)}$

8. Let h be the amount of money invested in the high-risk fund and l be the amount of money invested in the low-risk fund.

$l = 3h$

$0.09l - 0.04h = 2760$

$0.09(3h) - 0.04h = 2760$

$0.27h - 0.04h = 2760$

$0.23h = 2760$

$h = \dfrac{2760}{0.23} = 12000$

$l = 3(12000) = 36000$

She invested \$12,000 in the high-risk fund and \$36,000 in the low risk fund.

9. Use the Pythagorean theorem.

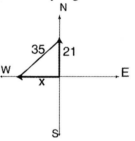

$35^2 = x^2 + 21^2$

$1225 = x^2 + 441$

$x^2 = 784$

$x = \sqrt{784} = 28$

$\text{rate} = \dfrac{\text{distance}}{\text{time}}$

$\text{rate} = \dfrac{28}{0.5} = 56$

The speed of the westbound train is 56 mph.

10. Let x be the weight of one case of cola

$|x - 288| \le 0.5$

$-0.5 \le x - 288 \le 0.5$

$-0.5 + 288 \le x - 288 + 288 \le 0.5 + 288$

$287.5 \le x \le 288.5$

The maximum amount of cola in each case is 288.5 oz and the minimum amount of cola in each case is 287.5 oz.

CHAPTER 7 RADICAL EXPRESSIONS AND EQUATIONS

Chapter 7 Pretest

1. a. $2\sqrt{36} = 2\sqrt{(6)^2} = 2(6) = 12$

    b. $\sqrt[3]{-64} = \sqrt[3]{(-4)^3} = -4$

2. $\sqrt{100u^2v^4} = \sqrt{10^2 u^2 \left(v^2\right)^2} = 10uv^2$

3. $\left(81x^4\right)^{\frac{3}{4}} = \left(\sqrt[4]{81x^4}\right)^3 = \left(\sqrt[4]{3^4 x^4}\right)^3 =$

    $(3x)^3 = 3^3 x^3 = 27x^3$

4. a. $\dfrac{8p^{\frac{2}{3}}}{\left(36p^{\frac{4}{3}}\right)^{\frac{1}{2}}} = \dfrac{8p^{\frac{2}{3}}}{36^{\frac{1}{2}} p^{\frac{4}{3}\cdot\frac{1}{2}}} = \dfrac{8p^{\frac{2}{3}}}{6p^{\frac{2}{3}}} = \dfrac{8}{6} = \dfrac{4}{3}$

    b. $\sqrt[6]{x^2 y^4} = \left(x^2 y^4\right)^{\frac{1}{6}} = x^{\frac{2}{6}} y^{\frac{4}{6}} = x^{\frac{1}{3}} y^{\frac{2}{3}} =$

    $\left(xy^2\right)^{\frac{1}{3}} = \sqrt[3]{xy^2}$

5. $\sqrt{6a} \bullet \sqrt{7b} = \sqrt{(6a)(7b)} = \sqrt{42ab}$

6. $\dfrac{\sqrt[3]{18r^2}}{\sqrt[3]{3r}} = \sqrt[3]{\dfrac{18r^2}{3r}} = \sqrt[3]{6r}$

7. $\sqrt{147x^5 y^4} = \sqrt{49 \bullet 3 \bullet x^4 \bullet x \bullet y^4} =$

    $\sqrt{49x^4 y^4}\sqrt{3x} = 7x^2 y^2 \sqrt{3x}$

8. $\sqrt{\dfrac{2p}{25q^8}} = \dfrac{\sqrt{2p}}{\sqrt{25q^8}} = \dfrac{\sqrt{2p}}{5q^4}$

9. $3\sqrt{12} - 5\sqrt{3} + \sqrt{108} =$

    $3\sqrt{4 \bullet 3} - 5\sqrt{3} + \sqrt{36 \bullet 3} =$

    $3 \bullet 2\sqrt{3} - 5\sqrt{3} + 6\sqrt{3} = (6 - 5 + 6)\sqrt{3} = 7\sqrt{3}$

10. $\left(\sqrt{x} - 8\right)\left(2\sqrt{x} + 1\right)$

       F   O   I   L

    $2\left(\sqrt{x}\right)^2 + \sqrt{x} - 16\sqrt{x} - 8 = 2x - 15\sqrt{x} - 8$

11. $\dfrac{\sqrt{2x}}{\sqrt{27y}} \bullet \dfrac{\sqrt{3y}}{\sqrt{3y}} = \dfrac{\sqrt{6xy}}{\sqrt{81y^2}} = \dfrac{\sqrt{6xy}}{9y}$

12. $\dfrac{\sqrt{n}}{\sqrt{n} + \sqrt{3}} \bullet \dfrac{\left(\sqrt{n} - \sqrt{3}\right)}{\left(\sqrt{n} - \sqrt{3}\right)} =$

    $\dfrac{\left(\sqrt{n}\right)^2 - \sqrt{3}\sqrt{n}}{\left(\sqrt{n}\right)^2 - \left(\sqrt{3}\right)^2} = \dfrac{n - \sqrt{3n}}{n - 3}$

13. $\sqrt{x+4} - 9 = -3$ Check $x = 32$

    $\sqrt{x+4} = 6$ $\sqrt{32+4} - 9 \overset{?}{=} -3$

    $\left(\sqrt{x+4}\right)^2 = 6^2$ $\sqrt{36} - 9 \overset{?}{=} -3$

    $x + 4 = 36$ $6 - 9 \overset{?}{=} -3$

    $x = 32$ $-3 = -3$ True

14. $\left(\sqrt{x^2 - 2}\right)^2 = \left(\sqrt{9x - 10}\right)^2$ Check $x = 8$

    $x^2 - 2 = 9x - 10$ $\sqrt{8^2 - 2} = \sqrt{9(8) - 10}$

    $x^2 - 9x + 8 = 0$ $\sqrt{64 - 2} = \sqrt{72 - 10}$

    $(x-8)(x-1) = 0$ $\sqrt{62} = \sqrt{62}$ True

    $x - 8 = 0$ $x - 1 = 0$

    $x = 8$ $x = 1$

    Check $x = 1$

    $\sqrt{1^2 - 2} = \sqrt{1 - 2} = \sqrt{-1}$

    $\sqrt{-1}$ is not a real number.

    $x = 1$ is not a solution

15. $\sqrt{2x} = \sqrt{x+7} - 1$

    $\left(\sqrt{2x}\right)^2 = \left(\sqrt{x+7} - 1\right)^2$

    $2x = (x+7) - 2\sqrt{x+7} + 1$

    $x - 8 = -2\sqrt{x+7}$

    $(x-8)^2 = \left(-2\sqrt{x+7}\right)^2$

    $x^2 - 16x + 64 = 4(x+7)$

    $x^2 - 16x + 64 = 4x + 28$

    $x^2 - 20x + 36 = 0$

    $(x-18)(x-2) = 0$

    $x - 18 = 0$ $x - 2 = 0$

    $x = 18$ $x = 2$

    Check $x = 18$ Check $x = 2$

    $\sqrt{2(18)} - \sqrt{18+7} \overset{?}{=} -1$ $\sqrt{2(2)} - \sqrt{2+7} \overset{?}{=} -1$

    $\sqrt{36} - \sqrt{25} \overset{?}{=} -1$ $\sqrt{4} - \sqrt{9} \overset{?}{=} -1$

    $6 - 5 \overset{?}{=} -1$ $2 - 3 \overset{?}{=} -1$

    $1 = -1$ False $x = 18$ $-1 = -1$ True

    is not a solution

16. $\left(5 - \left(\sqrt{9}\right)\left(\sqrt{-1}\right)\right)\left(4 - \left(\sqrt{25}\right)\left(\sqrt{-1}\right)\right) =$

    $(5 - 3i)(4 - 5i) =$

       F   O   I   L

    $20 - 25i - 12i + 15i^2 = 20 - 37i + 15(-1) =$

    $20 - 37i - 15 = 5 - 37i$

17. $\dfrac{1+2i}{1-2i} \bullet \dfrac{1+2i}{1+2i} = \dfrac{1+4i+4i^2}{1-4i^2} = \dfrac{1+4i-4}{1+4} =$

$\dfrac{-3+4i}{5} = -\dfrac{3}{5} + \dfrac{4i}{5}$

18. a. $\sqrt{\dfrac{h-d}{16}} = \dfrac{\sqrt{h-d}}{\sqrt{16}} = \dfrac{\sqrt{h-d}}{4}$

b. $\dfrac{\sqrt{h-d}}{4} = \dfrac{\sqrt{200-125}}{4} = \dfrac{\sqrt{75}}{4} =$

$\dfrac{\sqrt{25\bullet 3}}{4} = \dfrac{5\sqrt{3}}{4} = 2.16506...$

It takes the stone $\dfrac{5\sqrt{3}}{4}$ sec, or approximately 2.2

sec to be 125 ft above the ground.

19. Use the Pythagorean theorem. Let x be the length
of the diagonal.

$x^2 = 50^2 + 94^2 = 2500 + 8836 = 11336$

$x = \sqrt{11336} = \sqrt{4 \bullet 2834} = 2\sqrt{2834}$

$x = 106.4706...$

The diagonal of the court is $2\sqrt{2834}$ ft or about
106.5 ft.

20. $\dfrac{f}{120} = \dfrac{120\sqrt{p}}{120}$

$\dfrac{f}{120} = \sqrt{p}$

$\left(\dfrac{f}{120}\right)^2 = \left(\sqrt{p}\right)^2$

$p = \dfrac{f^2}{14400}$

Exercises 7.1 Radical Expressions and Rational Exponents

1. $\sqrt{64} = \sqrt{8^2} = 8$

3. $-\sqrt{100} = -\sqrt{10^2} = -10$

5. $\sqrt{-36}$ is not a real number

7. $2\sqrt{16} = 2\sqrt{4^2} = 2(4) = 8$

9. $\sqrt[3]{27} = \sqrt[3]{3^3} = 3$

11. $5\sqrt[3]{-8} = 5\sqrt[3]{(-2)^3} = 5(-2) = -10$

13. $\sqrt[4]{256} = \sqrt[4]{4^4} = 4$

15. $8\sqrt[5]{-1} = 8\sqrt[5]{(-1)^5} = 8(-1) = -8$

17. $\sqrt{\dfrac{9}{16}} = \dfrac{\sqrt{9}}{\sqrt{16}} = \dfrac{\sqrt{3^2}}{\sqrt{4^2}} = \dfrac{3}{4}$

19. $\sqrt[3]{-\dfrac{8}{125}} = \dfrac{\sqrt[3]{-8}}{\sqrt[3]{125}} = \dfrac{\sqrt[3]{(-2)^3}}{\sqrt[3]{5^3}} = \dfrac{-2}{5} = -\dfrac{2}{5}$

21. $\sqrt{0.04} = \sqrt{(0.2)^2} = 0.2$

23. $\sqrt{21} = 4.58257... \approx 4.583$

25. $\sqrt{46} = 6.78232... \approx 6.782$

27. $\sqrt{14.25} = 3.77491... \approx 3.775$

29. $\sqrt[3]{112} = 4.82028... \approx 4.820$

31. $\sqrt[5]{150} = 2.72406... \approx 2.724$

33. $\sqrt{x^8} = \sqrt{(x^4)^2} = x^4$

35. $\sqrt{16a^6} = \sqrt{(4a^3)^2} = 4a^3$

37. $9\sqrt{p^8q^4} = 9\sqrt{(p^4q^2)^2} = 9p^4q^2$

39. $\dfrac{1}{3}\sqrt{36x^{10}y^2} = \dfrac{1}{3}\sqrt{(6x^5y)^2} = \dfrac{1}{3}(6x^5y) = 2x^5y$

41. $\sqrt[3]{-125u^9} = \sqrt[3]{(-5u^3)^3} = -5u^3$

43. $2\sqrt[3]{216u^3v^{12}} = 2\sqrt[3]{(6uv^4)^3} = 2(6uv^4) = 12uv^4$

45. $\sqrt[4]{16t^{12}} = \sqrt[4]{(2t^3)^4} = 2t^3$

47. $\sqrt[5]{p^5q^{15}} = \sqrt[5]{(pq^3)^5} = pq^3$

49. $16^{\frac{1}{2}} = \sqrt{16} = \sqrt{4^2} = 4$

51. $-16^{\frac{1}{2}} = -\sqrt{16} = -\sqrt{4^2} = -4$

53. $(-64)^{\frac{1}{3}} = \sqrt[3]{-64} = \sqrt[3]{(-4)^3} = -4$

55. $6x^{\frac{1}{4}} = 6\sqrt[4]{x}$

57. $\left(36a^2\right)^{\frac{1}{2}} = \sqrt{36a^2} = \sqrt{(6a)^2} = 6a$

59. $\left(-216u^6\right)^{\frac{1}{3}} = \sqrt[3]{-216u^6} = \sqrt[3]{(-6u^2)^3} = -6u^2$

61. $27^{\frac{4}{3}} = \left(\sqrt[3]{27}\right)^4 = \left(\sqrt[3]{3^3}\right)^4 = (3^4) = 81$

63. $-16^{\frac{3}{2}} = -\left(\sqrt{16}\right)^3 = -\left(\sqrt{4^2}\right)^3 = -(4)^3 = -64$

65. $\left(-27y^3\right)^{\frac{2}{3}} = \left(\sqrt[3]{-27y^3}\right)^2 = \left(\sqrt[3]{(-3y)^3}\right)^2 =$

$(-3y)^2 = 9y^2$

67. $-81^{-\frac{3}{4}} = -\dfrac{1}{81^{\frac{3}{4}}} = -\dfrac{1}{\left(\sqrt[4]{81}\right)^3} = -\dfrac{1}{\left(\sqrt[4]{3^4}\right)^3} =$

$-\dfrac{1}{3^3} = -\dfrac{1}{27}$

69. $\left(\dfrac{x^{10}}{4}\right)^{-\frac{1}{2}} = \left(\dfrac{4}{x^{10}}\right)^{\frac{1}{2}} = \sqrt{\dfrac{4}{x^{10}}} = \dfrac{\sqrt{4}}{\sqrt{x^{10}}} = \dfrac{\sqrt{2^2}}{\sqrt{(x^5)^2}} = \dfrac{2}{x^5}$

71. $16 \bullet 16^{\frac{1}{2}} = 16^1 \bullet 16^{\frac{1}{2}} = 16^{\frac{3}{2}} = \left(\sqrt{16}\right)^3 =$

$$\left(\sqrt{4^2}\right)^3 = 4^3 = 64$$

5. $\sqrt[3]{x} \cdot \sqrt[6]{x} = x^{\frac{1}{3}} \cdot x^{\frac{1}{6}} = x^{\frac{1}{3}+\frac{1}{6}} = x^{\frac{1}{2}} = \sqrt{x}$

7. $\sqrt[3]{p} \cdot \sqrt[4]{q}$ cannot be simplified.

73. $\dfrac{6^{\frac{3}{5}}}{6^{\frac{2}{5}}} = 6^{\frac{3}{5}-\frac{2}{5}} = 6^{\frac{1}{5}} = \sqrt[5]{6}$

9. $\dfrac{\sqrt[3]{x}}{\sqrt[4]{x}} = \dfrac{x^{\frac{1}{3}}}{x^{\frac{1}{4}}} = x^{\frac{1}{3}-\frac{1}{4}} = x^{\frac{1}{12}} = \sqrt[12]{x}$

75. $\left(\dfrac{1}{2}\right)^{\frac{3}{2}}\left(\dfrac{1}{2}\right)^{-\frac{1}{2}} = \left(\dfrac{1}{2}\right)^{\frac{3}{2}+\frac{-1}{2}} = \left(\dfrac{1}{2}\right)^{\frac{2}{2}} = \left(\dfrac{1}{2}\right)^{1} = \dfrac{1}{2}$

11. $\sqrt{\sqrt{y}} = \left(y^{\frac{1}{2}}\right)^{\frac{1}{2}} = y^{\frac{1}{2}\cdot\frac{1}{2}} = y^{\frac{1}{4}} = \sqrt[4]{y}$

77. $\left(9^{\frac{3}{4}}\right)^{\frac{2}{3}} = 9^{\frac{3}{4}\cdot\frac{2}{3}} = 9^{\frac{1}{2}} = \sqrt{9} = \sqrt{3^2} = 3$

13. $\sqrt[4]{x^8 y^2} = x^{\frac{8}{4}} y^{\frac{2}{4}} = x^2 y^{\frac{1}{2}} = x^2 \sqrt{y}$

79. $4n^{\frac{2}{5}} n^{\frac{1}{5}} = 4n^{\frac{2}{5}+\frac{1}{5}} = 4n^{\frac{3}{5}} = 4\sqrt[5]{n^3}$

15. $\sqrt[6]{x^4} \cdot \sqrt[3]{x} = x^{\frac{4}{6}} \cdot x^{\frac{1}{3}} = x^{\frac{2}{3}+\frac{1}{3}} = x^1 = x$

81. $\left(y^{-4}\right)^{\frac{-1}{8}} = y^{(-4)\cdot\frac{-1}{8}} = y^{\frac{4}{8}} = y^{\frac{1}{2}} = \sqrt{y}$

17. $\dfrac{\sqrt[3]{y^2}}{\sqrt[9]{y^3}} = \dfrac{y^{\frac{2}{3}}}{y^{\frac{3}{9}}} = y^{\frac{2}{3}-\frac{1}{3}} = y^{\frac{1}{3}} = \sqrt[3]{y}$

83. $\left(4x^2\right)^{-\frac{1}{2}} = \dfrac{1}{\left(4x^2\right)^{\frac{1}{2}}} = \dfrac{1}{\sqrt{4x^2}} = \dfrac{1}{\sqrt{(2x)^2}} = \dfrac{1}{2x}$

19. $\sqrt[4]{p^2} \cdot \sqrt{q} = p^{\frac{2}{4}} \cdot q^{\frac{1}{2}} = p^{\frac{1}{2}} \cdot q^{\frac{1}{2}} = (pq)^{\frac{1}{2}} = \sqrt{pq}$

21. $\sqrt{6} \cdot \sqrt{5} = \sqrt{6 \cdot 5} = \sqrt{30}$

85. $\dfrac{5r^{\frac{3}{4}}}{r^{\frac{1}{2}}} = 5r^{\frac{3}{4}-\frac{1}{2}} = 5r^{\frac{1}{4}} = 5\sqrt[4]{r}$

23. $\sqrt{3x} \cdot \sqrt{2y} = \sqrt{3x \cdot 2y} = \sqrt{6xy}$

25. $\sqrt[3]{4a^2} \cdot \sqrt[3]{9b} = \sqrt[3]{4a^2 \cdot 9b} = \sqrt[3]{36a^2 b}$

87. $\left(\dfrac{a^2}{b^6}\right)^{\frac{1}{3}} = \sqrt[3]{\dfrac{a^2}{b^6}} = \dfrac{\sqrt[3]{a^2}}{\sqrt[3]{(b^2)^3}} = \dfrac{\sqrt[3]{a^2}}{b^2}$

27. $\sqrt[4]{3n} \cdot \sqrt[4]{7n^2} = \sqrt[4]{3n \cdot 7n^2} = \sqrt[4]{21n^3}$

29. $\sqrt{\dfrac{x}{2}} \cdot \sqrt{\dfrac{6}{y}} = \sqrt{\dfrac{x}{2} \cdot \dfrac{6}{y}} = \sqrt{\dfrac{3x}{y}}$

89. $3x\left(16x^8\right)^{\frac{1}{2}} = 3x\sqrt{16x^8} = 3x\sqrt{\left(4x^4\right)^2}$

$$= 3x\left(4x^4\right) = 12x^5$$

31. $\sqrt{24} = \sqrt{4 \cdot 6} = \sqrt{4} \cdot \sqrt{6} = 2\sqrt{6}$

33. $-3\sqrt{80} = -3\sqrt{16 \cdot 5} = -3\sqrt{16} \cdot \sqrt{5} =$

$$-3 \cdot 4\sqrt{5} = -12\sqrt{5}$$

91. $\dfrac{\left(2p^{\frac{1}{6}}\right)^6}{16p^3} = \dfrac{2^6 p^{\frac{6}{6}}}{16p^3} = \dfrac{64p}{16p^3} = \dfrac{4}{p^2}$

35. $\sqrt[3]{81} = \sqrt[3]{27 \cdot 3} = \sqrt[3]{27} \cdot \sqrt[3]{3} = 3\sqrt[3]{3}$

37. $\sqrt[4]{96} = \sqrt[4]{16 \cdot 6} = \sqrt[4]{16} \cdot \sqrt[4]{6} = 2\sqrt[4]{6}$

39. $\sqrt[5]{64} = \sqrt[5]{32 \cdot 2} = \sqrt[5]{32} \cdot \sqrt[5]{2} = 2\sqrt[5]{2}$

93. $t = \dfrac{1}{4}\sqrt{s} = \dfrac{1}{4}\sqrt{100} = \dfrac{1}{4}(10) = \dfrac{5}{2} = 2.5$

41. $6\sqrt{x^7} = 6\sqrt{x^6 \cdot x} = 6\sqrt{x^6} \cdot \sqrt{x} = 6x^3\sqrt{x}$

It takes the stone $\dfrac{5}{2}$, or 2.5 sec to reach the ground.

43. $\sqrt{20y} = \sqrt{4 \cdot 5y} = \sqrt{4} \cdot \sqrt{5y} = 2\sqrt{5y}$

95. a. $s = \sqrt{A} = \sqrt{25} = 5$ The length of the side of the frame is 5 in.

45. $\sqrt{200r^4} = \sqrt{100r^4 \cdot 2} = \sqrt{100r^4} \cdot \sqrt{2} = 10r^2\sqrt{2}$

b. A 1 in. border top, bottom and each side will leave $5 - 2(1) = 3$ in. A 3-in. by 3-in. photograph fits in the frame.

47. $\sqrt{54x^5 y^7} = \sqrt{9x^4 y^6 \cdot 6xy} =$

$$\sqrt{9x^4 y^6} \cdot \sqrt{6xy} = 3x^2 y^3 \sqrt{6xy}$$

97. a. $8000(0.5)^{\frac{t}{3}} = 8000\sqrt[3]{0.5^t}$

49. $\sqrt[3]{32n^5} = \sqrt[3]{8n^3 \cdot 4n^2} = \sqrt[3]{8n^3} \cdot \sqrt[3]{4n^2} = 2n\sqrt[3]{4n^2}$

b. $8000(0.5)^{\frac{6}{3}} = 8000(0.5)^2 = 8000(0.25) = 2000$

51. $\sqrt[5]{64n^8} = \sqrt[5]{32n^5 \cdot 2n^3} = \sqrt[5]{32n^5} \cdot \sqrt[5]{2n^3} = 2n\sqrt[5]{2n^3}$

The value of the equipment 6 yr after it was purchased is $2000.

53. $\sqrt[3]{72x^7 y^9} = \sqrt[3]{8x^6 y^9 \cdot 9x} = \sqrt[3]{8x^6 y^9} \cdot \sqrt[3]{9x} =$

$$2x^2 y^3 \sqrt[3]{9x}$$

Exercises 7.2 Simplifying Radical Expressions

55. $\sqrt[4]{64x^5 y^{10}} = \sqrt[4]{16x^4 y^8 \cdot 4xy^2} =$

$$\sqrt[4]{16x^4 y^8} \cdot \sqrt[4]{4xy^2} = 2xy^2 \sqrt[4]{4xy^2}$$

1. $\sqrt[6]{n^2} = n^{\frac{2}{6}} = n^{\frac{1}{3}} = \sqrt[3]{n}$

57. $\dfrac{\sqrt{90}}{\sqrt{10}} = \sqrt{\dfrac{90}{10}} = \sqrt{9} = 3$

3. $\sqrt[8]{16} = \sqrt[8]{2^4} = 2^{\frac{4}{8}} = 2^{\frac{1}{2}} = \sqrt{2}$

59. $\dfrac{\sqrt{30n}}{\sqrt{6}} = \sqrt{\dfrac{30n}{6}} = \sqrt{5n}$

61. $\dfrac{\sqrt{12x^3 y}}{\sqrt{3x}} = \sqrt{\dfrac{12x^3 y}{3x}} = \sqrt{4x^2 y} = 2x\sqrt{y}$

63. $\dfrac{\sqrt[3]{16u^2}}{\sqrt[3]{4u}} = \sqrt[3]{\dfrac{16u^2}{4u}} = \sqrt[3]{4u}$

65. $\dfrac{\sqrt[4]{24a^3 b^2}}{\sqrt[4]{4a^2 b}} = \sqrt[4]{\dfrac{24a^3 b^2}{4a^2 b}} = \sqrt[4]{6ab}$

67. $\sqrt{\dfrac{25}{16}} = \dfrac{\sqrt{25}}{\sqrt{16}} = \dfrac{5}{4}$

69. $\sqrt{\dfrac{7}{81}} = \dfrac{\sqrt{7}}{\sqrt{81}} = \dfrac{\sqrt{7}}{9}$

71. $\sqrt{\dfrac{2}{n^6}} = \dfrac{\sqrt{2}}{\sqrt{n^6}} = \dfrac{\sqrt{2}}{n^3}$

73. $\sqrt{\dfrac{7a}{121}} = \dfrac{\sqrt{7a}}{\sqrt{121}} = \dfrac{\sqrt{7a}}{11}$

75. $\sqrt{\dfrac{a}{9b^4}} = \dfrac{\sqrt{a}}{\sqrt{9b^4}} = \dfrac{\sqrt{a}}{3b^2}$

77. $\sqrt{\dfrac{9u}{25v^2}} = \dfrac{\sqrt{9u}}{\sqrt{25v^2}} = \dfrac{3\sqrt{u}}{5v}$

79. $\sqrt[3]{\dfrac{27a^2}{64}} = \dfrac{\sqrt[3]{27a^2}}{\sqrt[3]{64}} = \dfrac{3\sqrt[3]{a^2}}{4}$

81. $\sqrt[3]{\dfrac{9a}{8b^6 c^9}} = \dfrac{\sqrt[3]{9a}}{\sqrt[3]{8b^6 c^9}} = \dfrac{\sqrt[3]{9a}}{2b^2 c^3}$

83. $\sqrt[4]{\dfrac{2a^4 b^3}{81c^8}} = \dfrac{\sqrt[4]{2a^4 b^3}}{\sqrt[4]{81c^8}} = \dfrac{a\sqrt[4]{2b^3}}{3c^2}$

85. $\sqrt{\dfrac{13a^4 b}{9c^6 d^2}} = \dfrac{\sqrt{13a^4 b}}{\sqrt{9c^6 d^2}} = \dfrac{a^2 \sqrt{13b}}{3c^3 d}$

87. $d = \sqrt{(x_2 - x_1)^2 + (y_2 - y_1)^2} =$

$\sqrt{(4-10)^2 + (-3-3)^2} = \sqrt{(-6)^2 + (-6)^2} =$

$\sqrt{72} = \sqrt{36 \bullet 2} = 6\sqrt{2}$

89. $d = \sqrt{(x_2 - x_1)^2 + (y_2 - y_1)^2} =$

$\sqrt{(6-12)^2 + (12-15)^2} = \sqrt{(-6)^2 + (-3)^2} =$

$\sqrt{36+9} = \sqrt{45} = \sqrt{9 \bullet 5} = 3\sqrt{5}$

91. $d = \sqrt{(x_2 - x_1)^2 + (y_2 - y_1)^2} =$

$\sqrt{(-8-(-4))^2 + (0-(-3))^2} =$

$\sqrt{(-4)^2 + (3)^2} = \sqrt{16+9} = \sqrt{25} = 5$

93. $\sqrt{64d} = \sqrt{64} \bullet \sqrt{d} = 8\sqrt{d}$

95. $w = \sqrt{d^2 - l^2} = \sqrt{42^2 - 30^2} = \sqrt{1764 - 900} =$

$\sqrt{864} = \sqrt{144 \bullet 6} = 12\sqrt{6} = 29.3938....$

The width of the screen is $12\sqrt{6}$ or approximately 29 in.

97. $d = \sqrt{68^2 + 24^2} = \sqrt{4624 + 576} = \sqrt{5200} =$

$\sqrt{400 \bullet 13} = 20\sqrt{13} = 72.1110...$

The length of the string let out is $20\sqrt{13}$ ft, or about 72.1 ft.

99. a. The second college is located at (48,20).

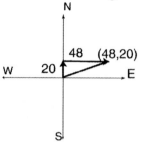

b. $d = \sqrt{48^2 + 20^2} = \sqrt{2304 + 400} = \sqrt{2704} = 52$
The second college is 52 mi from her home.

Exercises 7.3 Addition and Subtraction of Radical Expressions

1. $4\sqrt{3} + \sqrt{3} = (4+1)\sqrt{3} = 5\sqrt{3}$

3. $3\sqrt[3]{2} - 6\sqrt[3]{2} = (3-6)\sqrt[3]{2} = -3\sqrt[3]{2}$

5. $4\sqrt{2} - 2\sqrt{7}$ cannot be simplified.

7. $-8\sqrt{y} - 12\sqrt{y} = (-8-12)\sqrt{y} = -20\sqrt{y}$

9. $7\sqrt{x} + 4\sqrt[3]{x}$ cannot be simplified.

11. $-11\sqrt{n} + 2\sqrt{n} + 9\sqrt{n} = (-11+2+9)\sqrt{n} = 0$

13. $12\sqrt[4]{p} - 5\sqrt[4]{p} + \sqrt[4]{p} = (12-5+1)\sqrt[4]{p} = 8\sqrt[4]{p}$

15. $9y\sqrt{3x} + 4y\sqrt{3x} = (9y + 4y)\sqrt{3x} = 13y\sqrt{3x}$

17. $-7\sqrt{2r-1} + 3\sqrt{2r-1} = (-7+3)\sqrt{2r-1} =$

$-4\sqrt{2r-1}$

19. $\sqrt{x^2 - 9} + \sqrt{x^2 - 9} = (1+1)\sqrt{x^2 - 9} =$

$2\sqrt{x^2 - 9}$

21. $\sqrt{6} + \sqrt{24} = \sqrt{6} + \sqrt{4 \bullet 6} = \sqrt{6} + 2\sqrt{6} =$

$(1+2)\sqrt{6} = 3\sqrt{6}$

23. $\sqrt{72} - \sqrt{8} = \sqrt{36 \bullet 2} - \sqrt{4 \bullet 2} = 6\sqrt{2} - 2\sqrt{2} =$

$(6-2)\sqrt{2} = 4\sqrt{2}$

25. $3\sqrt{18} - 4\sqrt{2} + \sqrt{50} =$

$3\sqrt{9 \bullet 2} - 4\sqrt{2} + \sqrt{25 \bullet 2} =$

$9\sqrt{2} - 4\sqrt{2} + 5\sqrt{2} = (9-4+5)\sqrt{2} = 10\sqrt{2}$

27. $-5\sqrt[3]{24} + \sqrt[3]{-81} + 9\sqrt[3]{3} =$

$-5\sqrt[3]{8 \cdot 3} + \sqrt[3]{(-27) \cdot 3} + 9\sqrt[3]{3}$

$= -10\sqrt[3]{3} - 3\sqrt[3]{3} + 9\sqrt[3]{3}$

$= (-10 - 3 + 9)\sqrt[3]{3} = -4\sqrt[3]{3}$

29. $\sqrt{54x^3} - x\sqrt{150x} = \sqrt{9x^2 \cdot 6x} - x\sqrt{25 \cdot 6x} =$

$3x\sqrt{6x} - 5x\sqrt{6x} = (3x - 5x)\sqrt{6x} = -2x\sqrt{6x}$

31. $\dfrac{1}{4}\sqrt{128n^5} + \sqrt{242n} =$

$\dfrac{1}{4}\sqrt{64n^4 \cdot 2n} + \sqrt{121 \cdot 2n} =$

$\dfrac{8n^2}{4}\sqrt{2n} + 11\sqrt{2n} = (2n^2 + 11)\sqrt{2n}$

33. $-4y\sqrt{xy^3} + 7x\sqrt{x^3 y} =$

$-4y\sqrt{y^2 \cdot xy} + 7x\sqrt{x^2 \cdot xy} =$

$-4y^2\sqrt{xy} + 7x^2\sqrt{xy} = (-4y^2 + 7x^2)\sqrt{xy}$

35. $\sqrt[3]{-125p^9} + p\sqrt[3]{-8p^6} = -5p^3 + p(-2p^2) =$

$-5p^3 - 2p^3 = -7p^3$

37. $5\sqrt[4]{48ab^3} - 2\sqrt[4]{3a^5 b^3} =$

$5\sqrt[4]{16 \cdot 3ab^3} - 2\sqrt[4]{a^4 \cdot 3ab^3} =$

$10\sqrt[4]{3ab^3} - 2a\sqrt[4]{3ab^3} = (10 - 2a)\sqrt[4]{3ab^3}$

39. $2\sqrt{125} + \dfrac{1}{6}\sqrt{144} - \dfrac{3}{4}\sqrt{80} =$

$2\sqrt{25 \cdot 5} + \dfrac{1}{6}(12) - \dfrac{3}{4}\sqrt{16 \cdot 5} =$

$10\sqrt{5} + 2 - \dfrac{3}{4}(4)\sqrt{5} = 10\sqrt{5} + 2 - 3\sqrt{5} =$

$(10 - 3)\sqrt{5} + 2 = 7\sqrt{5} + 2$

41. $\dfrac{3}{5}\sqrt[3]{-125} - \dfrac{1}{4}\sqrt[3]{48} + \dfrac{1}{2}\sqrt[3]{162} =$

$\dfrac{3}{5}(-5) - \dfrac{1}{4}\sqrt[3]{8 \cdot 6} + \dfrac{1}{2}\sqrt[3]{27 \cdot 6} =$

$-3 - \dfrac{1}{4}(2)\sqrt[3]{6} + \dfrac{1}{2}(3)\sqrt[3]{6} =$

$-3 + \left(-\dfrac{1}{2} + \dfrac{3}{2}\right)\sqrt[3]{6} = -3 + \dfrac{2}{2}\sqrt[3]{6} = \sqrt[3]{6} - 3$

43. $f(x) + g(x) = 5x\sqrt{20x} + 3\sqrt{5x^3} =$

$5x\sqrt{4 \cdot 5x} + 3\sqrt{x^2 \cdot 5x} = 10x\sqrt{5x} + 3x\sqrt{5x} =$

$(10x + 3x)\sqrt{5x} = 13x\sqrt{5x}$

$f(x) - g(x) = 5x\sqrt{20x} - 3\sqrt{5x^3} =$

$5x\sqrt{4 \cdot 5x} - 3\sqrt{x^2 \cdot 5x} = 10x\sqrt{5x} - 3x\sqrt{5x} =$

$(10x - 3x)\sqrt{5x} = 7x\sqrt{5x}$

45. $f(x) + g(x) = 2x\sqrt[4]{64x} + \left(-\sqrt[4]{4x^5}\right) =$

$2x\sqrt[4]{16 \cdot 4x} - \sqrt[4]{x^4 \cdot 4x} = 4x\sqrt[4]{4x} - x\sqrt[4]{4x} =$

$(4x - x)\sqrt[4]{4x} = 3x\sqrt[4]{4x}$

$f(x) - g(x) = 2x\sqrt[4]{64x} - \left(-\sqrt[4]{4x^5}\right) =$

$2x\sqrt[4]{16 \cdot 4x} + \sqrt[4]{x^4 \cdot 4x} = 4x\sqrt[4]{4x} + x\sqrt[4]{4x} =$

$(4x + x)\sqrt[4]{4x} = 5x\sqrt[4]{4x}$

47. $\sqrt{64(80)} - \sqrt{64(20)} = \sqrt{5120} - \sqrt{1280} =$

$\sqrt{1024 \cdot 5} - \sqrt{256 \cdot 5} = 32\sqrt{5} - 16\sqrt{5} =$

$(32 - 16)\sqrt{5} = 16\sqrt{5} = 35.7770...$

The difference in velocity is $16\sqrt{5}$ ft per sec or about 35.8 ft per sec.

49. $\sqrt{128} - \sqrt{72} = \sqrt{64 \cdot 2} - \sqrt{36 \cdot 2} =$

$8\sqrt{2} - 6\sqrt{2} = (8 - 6)\sqrt{2} = 2\sqrt{2} = 2.82842....$

The side of the larger tile is $2\sqrt{2}$ in. or about 2.8 in. longer than the smaller tile.

51. a. $l = \sqrt{b^2 + h^2} = \sqrt{4^2 + 2^2} = \sqrt{16 + 4}$

$= \sqrt{20} = \sqrt{4 \cdot 5} = 2\sqrt{5}$

The length of the ramp is $2\sqrt{5}$ ft.

b. $\sqrt{(4 + 2)^2 + 2^2} - 2\sqrt{5} =$

$\sqrt{6^2 + 2^2} - 2\sqrt{5} = \sqrt{36 + 4} - 2\sqrt{5} =$

$\sqrt{40} - 2\sqrt{5} = 6.32455... - 4.47213... =$

1.8524...

The length of the ramp increases by approximately 1.9 ft.

Exercises 7.4 Multiplication and Division of Radical Expressions

1. $\sqrt{12} \cdot \sqrt{8} = \sqrt{12 \cdot 8} = \sqrt{96} = \sqrt{16 \cdot 6} = 4\sqrt{6}$

3. $(-4\sqrt{3})(\sqrt{7}) = -4\sqrt{3 \cdot 7} = -4\sqrt{21}$

5. $5\sqrt[3]{6}(3\sqrt[3]{9}) = 15\sqrt[3]{6 \cdot 9} = 15\sqrt[3]{54} =$

$15\sqrt[3]{27 \cdot 2} = 15 \cdot 3\sqrt[3]{2} = 45\sqrt[3]{2}$

7. $(2\sqrt{10x})(7\sqrt{5x^5}) = 14\sqrt{10x \cdot 5x^5} =$

$14\sqrt{50x^6} = 14\sqrt{25x^6 \cdot 2} = 14 \cdot 5x^3\sqrt{2} =$

$70x^3\sqrt{2}$

9. $(8\sqrt{ab^3})(-2\sqrt{a^3 b}) = -16\sqrt{ab^3 \cdot a^3 b} =$

$-16\sqrt{a^4 b^4} = -16a^2 b^2$

11. $\sqrt[3]{12x^2 y} \cdot \sqrt[3]{-16xy^4} = \sqrt[3]{12x^2 y \cdot (-16xy^4)} =$

$\sqrt[3]{-192x^3 y^5} = \sqrt[3]{-64x^3 y^3 (3y^2)} = -4xy\sqrt[3]{3y^2}$

13. $\sqrt{2}\left(\sqrt{8}-4\right)=\sqrt{2}\bullet\sqrt{8}-4\sqrt{2}=$

$\sqrt{2\bullet8}-4\sqrt{2}=\sqrt{16}-4\sqrt{2}=4-4\sqrt{2}$

15. $\sqrt{6}\left(2\sqrt{3}+\sqrt{12}\right)=2\sqrt{6}\bullet\sqrt{3}+\sqrt{6}\sqrt{12}=$

$2\sqrt{18}+\sqrt{72}=2\sqrt{9\bullet2}+\sqrt{36\bullet2}=$

$6\sqrt{2}+6\sqrt{2}=12\sqrt{2}$

17. $-2\sqrt{3}\left(2\sqrt{5}-6\sqrt{3}\right)=$

$-4\sqrt{3}\bullet\sqrt{5}+12\sqrt{3}\sqrt{3}=-4\sqrt{15}+12\sqrt{9}=$

$-4\sqrt{15}+12\bullet3=-4\sqrt{15}+36$

19. $\sqrt[3]{4}\left(5\sqrt[3]{12}+2\sqrt[3]{3}\right)=5\sqrt[3]{4}\bullet\sqrt[3]{12}+2\sqrt[3]{4}\bullet\sqrt[3]{3}=$

$5\sqrt[3]{48}+2\sqrt[3]{12}=5\sqrt[3]{8\bullet6}+2\sqrt[3]{12}=$

$5\bullet2\sqrt[3]{6}+2\sqrt[3]{12}=10\sqrt[3]{6}+2\sqrt[3]{12}$

21. $\sqrt{x}\left(\sqrt{x^3}+\sqrt{2x}\right)=\sqrt{x}\bullet\sqrt{x^3}+\sqrt{x}\bullet\sqrt{2x}=$

$\sqrt{x^4}+\sqrt{2x^2}=x^2+x\sqrt{2}$

23. $\sqrt[4]{a^2}\left(3\sqrt[4]{2a^3}-\sqrt[4]{10a^2}\right)=$

$3\sqrt[4]{a^2}\bullet\sqrt[4]{2a^3}-\sqrt[4]{a^2}\bullet\sqrt[4]{10a^2}=3\sqrt[4]{2a^5}-\sqrt[4]{10a^4}$

$=3\sqrt[4]{a^4\bullet2a}-a\sqrt[4]{10}=3a\sqrt[4]{2a}-a\sqrt[4]{10}$

25. $\left(\sqrt{2}-3\right)\left(\sqrt{2}+4\right)$

$\quad$ F $\qquad$ O $\quad$ I $\quad$ L

$\sqrt{2}\bullet\sqrt{2}+4\sqrt{2}-3\sqrt{2}-12=$

$\left(\sqrt{2}\right)^2+(4-3)\sqrt{2}-12=$

$2+\sqrt{2}-12=-10+\sqrt{2}$

27. $\left(2-4\sqrt{3}\right)\left(4+3\sqrt{3}\right)$

$\quad$ F $\qquad$ 0 $\quad$ I $\quad$ L

$8+6\sqrt{3}-16\sqrt{3}-12\left(\sqrt{3}\right)^2$

$8-10\sqrt{3}-36=-28-10\sqrt{3}$

29. $\left(\sqrt{8}+\sqrt{3}\right)\left(\sqrt{2}+\sqrt{12}\right)=$

$\qquad$ F $\qquad$ 0 $\qquad$ I $\qquad$ L

$\sqrt{8}\bullet\sqrt{2}+\sqrt{8}\bullet\sqrt{12}+\sqrt{3}\bullet\sqrt{2}+\sqrt{3}\bullet\sqrt{12}=$

$\sqrt{16}+\sqrt{96}+\sqrt{6}+\sqrt{36}=$

$4+\sqrt{16\bullet6}+\sqrt{6}+6=10+4\sqrt{6}+\sqrt{6}=$

$10+5\sqrt{6}$

31. $\left(2\sqrt{r}-4\right)\left(8\sqrt{r}+6\right)=$

$\quad$ F $\qquad$ 0 $\quad$ I $\quad$ L

$16\left(\sqrt{r}\right)^2+12\sqrt{r}-32\sqrt{r}-24=$

$16r-20\sqrt{r}-24$

33. $\left(\sqrt{6}+\sqrt{2}\right)\left(\sqrt{6}-\sqrt{2}\right)=\left(\sqrt{6}\right)^2-\left(\sqrt{2}\right)^2=6-2=4$

35. $\left(\sqrt{x}-8\right)\left(\sqrt{x}+8\right)=\left(\sqrt{x}\right)^2-8^2=x-64$

37. $\left(\sqrt{5x}+\sqrt{y}\right)\left(\sqrt{5x}-\sqrt{y}\right)=$

$\left(\sqrt{5x}\right)^2-\left(\sqrt{y}\right)^2=5x-y$

39. $\left(\sqrt{x-1}-5\right)\left(\sqrt{x-1}+5\right)=\left(\sqrt{x-1}\right)^2-5^2=$

$x-1-25=x-26$

41. $\left(3\sqrt{x}-2\right)^2=\left(3\sqrt{x}\right)^2-2\left(3\sqrt{x}\right)(2)+2^2=$

$9x-12\sqrt{x}+4$

43. $\left(\sqrt{6a}+4\right)^2=\left(\sqrt{6a}\right)^2+2\left(\sqrt{6a}\right)(4)+4^2=$

$6a+8\sqrt{6a}+16$

45. $\left(1-\sqrt{n+7}\right)^2=$

$1^2-2(1)\left(\sqrt{n+7}\right)+\left(\sqrt{n+7}\right)^2=$

$1-2\sqrt{n+7}+n+7=n-2\sqrt{n+7}+8$

47. $-\dfrac{\sqrt{32}}{4\sqrt{2}}=-\dfrac{1}{4}\sqrt{\dfrac{32}{2}}=-\dfrac{1}{4}\sqrt{16}=-\dfrac{4}{4}=-1$

49. $\dfrac{\sqrt{84x^3}}{\sqrt{7x}}=\sqrt{\dfrac{84x^3}{7x}}=\sqrt{12x^2}=\sqrt{4x^2\bullet3}=2x\sqrt{3}$

51. $-\dfrac{n\sqrt{60n^7}}{2\sqrt{5n^3}}=-\dfrac{n}{2}\sqrt{\dfrac{60n^7}{5n^3}}=-\dfrac{n}{2}\sqrt{12n^4}=$

$-\dfrac{n}{2}\sqrt{4n^4\bullet3}=-\dfrac{n}{2}\left(2n^2\right)\sqrt{3}=-n^3\sqrt{3}$

53. $\dfrac{\sqrt[4]{128r^{10}}}{6r\sqrt[4]{4r^3}}=\dfrac{1}{6r}\sqrt[4]{\dfrac{128r^{10}}{4r^3}}=\dfrac{1}{6r}\sqrt[4]{32r^7}=$

$\dfrac{1}{6r}\sqrt[4]{16r^4\bullet2r^3}=\dfrac{2r}{6r}\sqrt[4]{2r^3}=\dfrac{\sqrt[4]{2r^3}}{3}$

55. $\sqrt{\dfrac{5a}{16}}=\dfrac{\sqrt{5a}}{\sqrt{16}}=\dfrac{\sqrt{5a}}{4}$

57. $\sqrt{\dfrac{12x}{y^6}}=\dfrac{\sqrt{12x}}{\sqrt{y^6}}=\dfrac{\sqrt{4\bullet3x}}{y^3}=\dfrac{2\sqrt{3x}}{y^3}$

59. $\sqrt[3]{\dfrac{54}{n^9}}=\dfrac{\sqrt[3]{54}}{\sqrt[3]{n^9}}=\dfrac{\sqrt[3]{27\bullet2}}{n^3}=\dfrac{3\sqrt[3]{2}}{n^3}$

61. $\sqrt{\dfrac{32a^5}{9b^8}}=\dfrac{\sqrt{32a^5}}{\sqrt{9b^8}}=\dfrac{\sqrt{16a^4\bullet2a}}{3b^4}=\dfrac{4a^2\sqrt{2a}}{3b^4}$

63. $\dfrac{4}{\sqrt{5}}\bullet\dfrac{\sqrt{5}}{\sqrt{5}}=\dfrac{4\sqrt{5}}{5}$

65. $\dfrac{\sqrt{y}}{\sqrt{40}}=\dfrac{\sqrt{y}}{2\sqrt{10}}\bullet\dfrac{\sqrt{10}}{\sqrt{10}}=\dfrac{\sqrt{10y}}{2\bullet10}=\dfrac{\sqrt{10y}}{20}$

67. $\dfrac{\sqrt{3a}}{\sqrt{18}}=\dfrac{\sqrt{3a}}{3\sqrt{2}}\bullet\dfrac{\sqrt{2}}{\sqrt{2}}=\dfrac{\sqrt{6a}}{3\bullet2}=\dfrac{\sqrt{6a}}{6}$

69. $\dfrac{\sqrt{9u}}{6\sqrt{v}}=\dfrac{3\sqrt{u}}{6\sqrt{v}}=\dfrac{\sqrt{u}}{2\sqrt{v}}\bullet\dfrac{\sqrt{v}}{\sqrt{v}}=\dfrac{\sqrt{uv}}{2v}$

71. $\dfrac{\sqrt{25x^4}}{\sqrt{3y}}=\dfrac{5x^2}{\sqrt{3y}}\bullet\dfrac{\sqrt{3y}}{\sqrt{3y}}=\dfrac{5x^2\sqrt{3y}}{3y}$

73. $\dfrac{\sqrt{10xy}}{\sqrt{9z}}=\dfrac{\sqrt{10xy}}{3\sqrt{z}}\bullet\dfrac{\sqrt{z}}{\sqrt{z}}=\dfrac{\sqrt{10xyz}}{3z}$

75. $\dfrac{\sqrt[3]{9x}}{\sqrt[3]{2y^2}}\bullet\dfrac{\sqrt[3]{4y}}{\sqrt[3]{4y}}=\dfrac{\sqrt[3]{36xy}}{\sqrt[3]{8y^3}}=\dfrac{\sqrt[3]{36xy}}{2y}$

77. $\sqrt{\dfrac{11}{x}}=\dfrac{\sqrt{11}}{\sqrt{x}}\bullet\dfrac{\sqrt{x}}{\sqrt{x}}=\dfrac{\sqrt{11x}}{x}$

79. $\sqrt{\dfrac{7x}{3y}}=\dfrac{\sqrt{7x}}{\sqrt{3y}}\bullet\dfrac{\sqrt{3y}}{\sqrt{3y}}=\dfrac{\sqrt{21xy}}{3y}$

81. $\sqrt{\dfrac{5x^3}{48y^3}}=\dfrac{\sqrt{5x^3}}{\sqrt{48y^3}}=\dfrac{x\sqrt{5x}}{4y\sqrt{3y}}\bullet\dfrac{\sqrt{3y}}{\sqrt{3y}}=$

$\dfrac{x\sqrt{15xy}}{4y\bullet 3y}=\dfrac{x\sqrt{15xy}}{12y^2}$

83. $\sqrt[3]{\dfrac{a^2b}{32c^4}}=\dfrac{\sqrt[3]{a^2b}}{\sqrt[3]{32c^4}}=\dfrac{\sqrt[3]{a^2b}}{\sqrt[3]{8c^3\bullet 4c}}=$

$\dfrac{\sqrt[3]{a^2b}}{2c\sqrt[3]{4c}}\bullet\dfrac{\sqrt[3]{2c^2}}{\sqrt[3]{2c^2}}=\dfrac{\sqrt[3]{2a^2bc^2}}{2c\sqrt[3]{8c^3}}=$

$\dfrac{\sqrt[3]{2a^2bc^2}}{2c\bullet 2c}=\dfrac{\sqrt[3]{2a^2bc^2}}{4c^2}$

85. $\dfrac{2-\sqrt{3}}{\sqrt{6}}\bullet\dfrac{\sqrt{6}}{\sqrt{6}}=\dfrac{2\sqrt{6}-\sqrt{18}}{6}=$

$\dfrac{2\sqrt{6}-\sqrt{9\bullet 2}}{6}=\dfrac{2\sqrt{6}-3\sqrt{2}}{6}$

87. $\dfrac{\sqrt{a}-\sqrt{b}}{\sqrt{b}}\bullet\dfrac{\sqrt{b}}{\sqrt{b}}=\dfrac{\sqrt{a}\bullet\sqrt{b}-\left(\sqrt{b}\right)^2}{\left(\sqrt{b}\right)^2}=\dfrac{\sqrt{ab}-b}{b}$

89. $\dfrac{\sqrt{5}+10\sqrt{t}}{\sqrt{15t}}\bullet\dfrac{\sqrt{15t}}{\sqrt{15t}}=\dfrac{\sqrt{5}\bullet\sqrt{15t}+10\sqrt{t}\bullet\sqrt{15t}}{\left(\sqrt{15t}\right)^2}$

$\dfrac{\sqrt{75t}+10\sqrt{15t^2}}{15t}=\dfrac{\sqrt{25\bullet 3t}+10\sqrt{t^2\bullet 15}}{15t}=$

$\dfrac{5\sqrt{3t}+10t\sqrt{15}}{15t}=\dfrac{5\left(\sqrt{3t}+2t\sqrt{15}\right)}{15t}=\dfrac{\sqrt{3t}+2t\sqrt{15}}{3t}$

91. $\dfrac{\sqrt[3]{x}-4}{\sqrt[3]{x^2}}\bullet\dfrac{\sqrt[3]{x}}{\sqrt[3]{x}}=\dfrac{\sqrt[3]{x\bullet x}-4\sqrt[3]{x}}{\sqrt[3]{x^3}}=\dfrac{\sqrt[3]{x^2}-4\sqrt[3]{x}}{x}=$

93. $\dfrac{1}{2+\sqrt{2}}\bullet\dfrac{2-\sqrt{2}}{2-\sqrt{2}}=\dfrac{2-\sqrt{2}}{2^2-\left(\sqrt{2}\right)^2}=\dfrac{2-\sqrt{2}}{4-2}=\dfrac{2-\sqrt{2}}{2}$

95. $\dfrac{6}{\sqrt{2}-\sqrt{5}}\bullet\dfrac{\sqrt{2}+\sqrt{5}}{\sqrt{2}+\sqrt{5}}=\dfrac{6\left(\sqrt{2}+\sqrt{5}\right)}{\left(\sqrt{2}\right)^2-\left(\sqrt{5}\right)^2}=\dfrac{6\left(\sqrt{2}+\sqrt{5}\right)}{2-5}$

$=\dfrac{6\left(\sqrt{2}+\sqrt{5}\right)}{-3}=-2\left(\sqrt{2}+\sqrt{5}\right)=-2\sqrt{2}-2\sqrt{5}$

97. $\dfrac{8}{2+\sqrt{2x}}\bullet\dfrac{2-\sqrt{2x}}{2-\sqrt{2x}}=\dfrac{8\left(2-\sqrt{2x}\right)}{\left(2\right)^2-\left(\sqrt{2x}\right)^2}=$

$\dfrac{8\left(2-\sqrt{2x}\right)}{4-2x}=\dfrac{8\left(2-\sqrt{2x}\right)}{2\left(2-x\right)}=$

$\dfrac{4\left(2-\sqrt{2x}\right)}{2-x}=\dfrac{8-4\sqrt{2x}}{2-x}$

99. $\dfrac{\sqrt{x}}{\sqrt{x}+y}\bullet\dfrac{\sqrt{x}-y}{\sqrt{x}-y}=\dfrac{\left(\sqrt{x}\right)^2-y\sqrt{x}}{\left(\sqrt{x}\right)^2-y^2}=\dfrac{x-y\sqrt{x}}{x-y^2}$

101. $\dfrac{\sqrt{a}+3}{\sqrt{a}-\sqrt{2}}\bullet\dfrac{\sqrt{a}+\sqrt{2}}{\sqrt{a}+\sqrt{2}}=$

$\dfrac{\left(\sqrt{a}\right)^2+\sqrt{a}\bullet\sqrt{2}+3\bullet\sqrt{a}+3\bullet\sqrt{2}}{\left(\sqrt{a}\right)^2-\left(\sqrt{2}\right)^2}=$

$\dfrac{a+\sqrt{2a}+3\sqrt{a}+3\sqrt{2}}{a-2}$

103. $\dfrac{\sqrt{x}-\sqrt{y}}{\sqrt{x}+\sqrt{y}}\bullet\dfrac{\sqrt{x}-\sqrt{y}}{\sqrt{x}-\sqrt{y}}=$

$\dfrac{\left(\sqrt{x}\right)^2-2\sqrt{x}\bullet\sqrt{y}+\left(\sqrt{y}\right)^2}{\left(\sqrt{x}\right)^2-\left(\sqrt{y}\right)^2}=\dfrac{x-2\sqrt{xy}+y}{x-y}$

105. $\dfrac{2\sqrt{a}+3\sqrt{b}}{3\sqrt{a}-2\sqrt{b}}\bullet\dfrac{3\sqrt{a}+2\sqrt{b}}{3\sqrt{a}+2\sqrt{b}}=$

$\dfrac{6\left(\sqrt{a}\right)^2+4\sqrt{ab}+9\sqrt{ab}+6\left(\sqrt{b}\right)^2}{\left(3\sqrt{a}\right)^2-\left(2\sqrt{b}\right)^2}=$

$\dfrac{6a+13\sqrt{ab}+6b}{9a-4b}$

107. $f\left(x\right)\bullet g\left(x\right)=\left(3x\sqrt{2x}\right)\bullet\left(\dfrac{1}{3}\sqrt{6x}\right)=$

$\dfrac{3x}{3}\sqrt{12x^2}=x\sqrt{4x^2\bullet 3}=2x^2\sqrt{3}$

$\dfrac{f\left(x\right)}{g\left(x\right)}=\dfrac{3x\sqrt{2x}}{\dfrac{1}{3}\sqrt{6x}}=9x\sqrt{\dfrac{2x}{6x}}=9x\sqrt{\dfrac{1}{3}}=$

$9x\dfrac{1}{\sqrt{3}}\bullet\dfrac{\sqrt{3}}{\sqrt{3}}=9x\dfrac{\sqrt{3}}{3}=3x\sqrt{3}$

109. $f(x) \bullet g(x) = (\sqrt{x}+1) \bullet (\sqrt{x}-1) =$

$(\sqrt{x})^2 - 1^2 = x - 1$

$\dfrac{f(x)}{g(x)} = \dfrac{\sqrt{x}+1}{\sqrt{x}-1} \bullet \dfrac{\sqrt{x}+1}{\sqrt{x}+1} =$

$\dfrac{(\sqrt{x})^2 + 2\sqrt{x} + 1^2}{(\sqrt{x})^2 - 1^2} = \dfrac{x + 2\sqrt{x} + 1}{x - 1}$

111. a. Area of a triangle is half the base times the height. The base is a.

$A = \left(\dfrac{1}{2}a\right)\left(\dfrac{\sqrt{3}}{2}a\right) = \dfrac{\sqrt{3}}{4}a^2$

b. $A = \dfrac{\sqrt{3}}{4}(8)^2 = \dfrac{64\sqrt{3}}{4} = 16\sqrt{3}$ sq in.

113. $2\pi \dfrac{\sqrt{L}}{\sqrt{32}} \bullet \dfrac{\sqrt{2}}{\sqrt{2}} = 2\pi \dfrac{\sqrt{2L}}{\sqrt{64}} = \dfrac{2\pi\sqrt{2L}}{8} = \dfrac{\pi\sqrt{2L}}{4}$

115. $\dfrac{\sqrt{A}}{\sqrt{4\pi}} \bullet \dfrac{\sqrt{\pi}}{\sqrt{\pi}} = \dfrac{\sqrt{\pi A}}{\sqrt{4\pi^2}} = \dfrac{\sqrt{\pi A}}{2\pi}$

Exercises 7.5 Solving Radical Equations

1. $(\sqrt{3n})^2 = 6^2$

$3n = 36$

$n = 12$

3. $(\sqrt{x+6})^2 = 3^2$

$x + 6 = 9$

$x = 3$

5. $(\sqrt{5x-6})^2 = 2^2$

$5x - 6 = 4$

$5x = 10$

$x = 2$

7. $(\sqrt[3]{3y+10})^3 = (-2)^3$

$3y + 10 = -8$

$3y = -18$

$y = -6$

9. $\sqrt{x} + 9 = 8$

$\sqrt{x} = -1$

$\sqrt{x} \geq 0$, no solution.

11. $\sqrt{x} - 20 = -9$

$\sqrt{x} = 11$

$(\sqrt{x})^2 = 11^2$

$x = 121$

13. $14 - \sqrt[3]{x} = 11$

$3 = \sqrt[3]{x}$

$(3)^3 = (\sqrt[3]{x})^3$

$x = 27$

15. $\sqrt{6x} + 17 = 29$

$\sqrt{6x} = 12$

$(\sqrt{6x})^2 = 12^2$

$6x = 144; \quad x = 24$

17. $\sqrt{2y-1} - 8 = 5$

$\sqrt{2y-1} = 13$

$(\sqrt{2y-1})^2 = 13^2$

$2y - 1 = 169$

$2y = 170; \quad y = 85$

19. $14 - \sqrt{4a+9} = 13$

$-\sqrt{4a+9} = -1$

$(-\sqrt{4a+9})^2 = (-1)^2$

$4a + 9 = 1$

$4a = -8; \quad a = -2$

21. $\sqrt{5x-1} - \sqrt{3x+11} = 0$

$\sqrt{5x-1} = \sqrt{3x+11}$

$(\sqrt{5x-1})^2 = (\sqrt{3x+11})^2$

$5x - 1 = 3x + 11$

$2x = 12; \quad x = 6$

23. $(2\sqrt{x-3})^2 = (\sqrt{7x+15})^2$

$4(x-3) = 7x + 15$

$4x - 12 = 7x + 15$

$-3x = 27$

$x = -9$

$\sqrt{x-3} = \sqrt{-12}$, not a real number.

No solution.

25. $(\sqrt[3]{3y-19})^3 = (\sqrt[3]{6y+26})^3$

$3y - 19 = 6y + 26$

$-3y = 45; \quad y = -15$

27. $(\sqrt{a^2+7})^2 = (\sqrt{5a+1})^2$

$a^2 + 7 = 5a + 1$

$a^2 - 5a + 6 = 0$

$(a-2)(a-3) = 0$

$a - 2 = 0 \quad a - 3 = 0$

$a = 2 \qquad a = 3$

Check $a = 2$ Check $a = 3$

$\sqrt{2^2+7} \overset{?}{=} \sqrt{5(2)+1}$ $\sqrt{3^2+7} \overset{?}{=} \sqrt{5(3)+1}$

$\sqrt{11} = \sqrt{11}$ True $\sqrt{16} = \sqrt{16}$ True

29. $\sqrt[3]{a^2-6} + \sqrt[3]{1-4a} = 0$

$\sqrt[3]{a^2-6} = -\sqrt[3]{1-4a}$

$\left(\sqrt[3]{a^2-6}\right)^3 = \left(-\sqrt[3]{1-4a}\right)^3$

$a^2 - 6 = -(1-4a)$

$a^2 - 6 = -1 + 4a$

$a^2 - 4a - 5 = 0$

$(a-5)(a+1) = 0$

$a - 5 = 0 \quad a + 1 = 0$

$a = 5 \qquad a = -1$

Check $a = 5$ Check $a = -1$

$\sqrt[3]{5^2-6} + \sqrt[3]{1-4(5)} \overset{?}{=} 0$ $\sqrt[3]{(-1)^2-6} + \sqrt[3]{1-4(-1)} \overset{?}{=} 0$

$\sqrt[3]{19} + \sqrt[3]{-19} \overset{?}{=} 0$ $\sqrt[3]{-5} + \sqrt[3]{5} \overset{?}{=} 0$

$\sqrt[3]{19} - \sqrt[3]{19} \overset{?}{=} 0$ $-\sqrt[3]{5} + \sqrt[3]{5} \overset{?}{=} 0$

$0 = 0$ True $0 = 0$ True

31. $\left(\sqrt{2x+8}\right)^2 = (-x)^2$

$2x + 8 = x^2$

$x^2 - 2x - 8 = 0$

$(x-4)(x+2) = 0$

$x - 4 = 0 \quad x + 2 = 0$

$x = 4 \qquad x = -2$

Check $x = 4$ Check $x = -2$

$\sqrt{2(4)+8} \overset{?}{=} -4$ $\sqrt{2(-2)+8} \overset{?}{=} -(-2)$

$\sqrt{16} \overset{?}{=} -4$ $\sqrt{4} \overset{?}{=} 2$

$4 = -4$ False $2 = 2$ True

$x = 4$ is not
a solution.

33. $2n - \sqrt{6-5n} = 0$

$2n = \sqrt{6-5n}$

$(2n)^2 = \left(\sqrt{6-5n}\right)^2$

$4n^2 = 6 - 5n$

$4n^2 + 5n - 6 = 0$

$(4n-3)(n+2) = 0$

$4n - 3 = 0 \quad n + 2 = 0$

$4n = 3 \qquad n = -2$

$n = \dfrac{3}{4}$

Check $n = \dfrac{3}{4}$

$2\left(\dfrac{3}{4}\right) - \sqrt{6-5\left(\dfrac{3}{4}\right)} = 0$

$\dfrac{3}{2} - \sqrt{\dfrac{24}{4} - \dfrac{15}{4}} \overset{?}{=} 0$

$\dfrac{3}{2} - \sqrt{\dfrac{9}{4}} \overset{?}{=} 0$

$\dfrac{3}{2} - \dfrac{3}{2} \overset{?}{=} 0$

$0 = 0$ True

Check $n = -2$

$2(-2) - \sqrt{6-5(-2)} \overset{?}{=} 0$

$-4 - \sqrt{16} \overset{?}{=} 0$

$-4 - 4 \overset{?}{=} 0$

$-8 = 0$ False, $n = -2$
is not a solution.

35. $(x-2)^2 = \left(\sqrt{4x-11}\right)^2$

$x^2 - 4x + 4 = 4x - 11$

$x^2 - 8x + 15 = 0$

$(x-5)(x-3) = 0$

$x - 5 = 0 \quad x - 3 = 0$

$x = 5 \qquad x = 3$

Check $x = 3$ Check $x = 5$

$3 - 2 \overset{?}{=} \sqrt{4(3)-11}$ $5 - 2 \overset{?}{=} \sqrt{4(5)-11}$

$1 = \sqrt{1}$ $3 = \sqrt{9}$

$1 = 1$ True $3 = 3$ True

37. $\sqrt{3t+1} - 1 = 2t$

$\sqrt{3t+1} = 2t + 1$

$\left(\sqrt{3t+1}\right)^2 = (2t+1)^2$

$3t + 1 = 4t^2 + 4t + 1$

$4t^2 + t = 0$

$t(4t+1) = 0$

$t = 0 \quad 4t + 1 = 0$

$\qquad\quad 4t = -1$

$\qquad\quad t = -\dfrac{1}{4}$

Check $t = 0$ Check $t = -\dfrac{1}{4}$

$\sqrt{3(0)+1} - 1 \overset{?}{=} 2(0)$ $\sqrt{3\left(-\dfrac{1}{4}\right)+1} - 1 \overset{?}{=} 2\left(-\dfrac{1}{4}\right)$

$\sqrt{1} - 1 \overset{?}{=} 0$ $\sqrt{\dfrac{1}{4}} - 1 \overset{?}{=} -\dfrac{1}{2}$

$1 - 1 \overset{?}{=} 0$ $\dfrac{1}{2} - 1 \overset{?}{=} -\dfrac{1}{2}$

$0 = 0$ True $-\dfrac{1}{2} = -\dfrac{1}{2}$ True

39. $\sqrt{3n} + \sqrt{n-2} = 4$

$\sqrt{n-2} = 4 - \sqrt{3n}$

$$\left(\sqrt{n-2}\right)^2 = \left(4-\sqrt{3n}\right)^2$$

$$n-2 = 16-8\sqrt{3n}+3n$$

$$8\sqrt{3n} = 18+2n$$

$$4\sqrt{3n} = 9+n$$

$$\left(4\sqrt{3n}\right)^2 = \left(9+n\right)^2$$

$$16(3n) = 81+18n+n^2$$

$$n^2-30n+81 = 0$$

$$(n-27)(n-3) = 0$$

$$n-27 = 0 \quad n-3 = 0$$

$$n = 27 \qquad n = 3$$

Check $n = 3$ Check $n = 27$

$$\sqrt{3(3)}+\sqrt{3-2} \overset{?}{=} 4 \quad \sqrt{3(27)}+\sqrt{27-2} \overset{?}{=} 4$$

$$\sqrt{9}+\sqrt{1} \overset{?}{=} 4 \qquad \sqrt{81}+\sqrt{25} \overset{?}{=} 4$$

$$3+1 = 4 \qquad\qquad 9+5 \overset{?}{=} 4$$

$$4 = 4 \text{ True} \qquad\quad 14 = 4 \text{ False, } n = 27$$

is not a solution

41. $\sqrt{x-2}+1 = -\sqrt{x+3}$

$$\left(\sqrt{x-2}+1\right)^2 = \left(-\sqrt{x+3}\right)^2$$

$$x-2+2\sqrt{x-2}+1 = x+3$$

$$2\sqrt{x-2} = 4$$

$$\sqrt{x-2} = 2 \qquad\qquad \text{Check } x = 6$$

$$\left(\sqrt{x-2}\right)^2 = 2^2 \qquad \sqrt{6-2}+1 \overset{?}{=} -\sqrt{6+3}$$

$$x-2 = 4 \qquad\qquad \sqrt{4}+1 \overset{?}{=} -\sqrt{9}$$

$$x = 6 \qquad\qquad\qquad 2+1 \overset{?}{=} -3$$

$$\qquad\qquad\qquad\qquad 3 = -3 \text{ False, no solution}$$

43. $\left(\sqrt{x+5}-2\right)^2 = \left(\sqrt{x-1}\right)^2$

$$x+5-4\sqrt{x+5}+4 = x-1$$

$$10 = 4\sqrt{x+5}$$

$$5 = 2\sqrt{x+5}$$

$$5^2 = \left(2\sqrt{x+5}\right)^2$$

$$25 = 4(x+5)$$

$$25 = 4x+20$$

$$-4x = -5$$

$$x = \frac{5}{4}$$

Check $x = \dfrac{5}{4}$

$$\sqrt{\frac{5}{4}+5}-2 \overset{?}{=} \sqrt{\frac{5}{4}-1}$$

$$\sqrt{\frac{25}{4}}-2 \overset{?}{=} \sqrt{\frac{1}{4}}$$

$$\frac{5}{2}-\frac{4}{2} \overset{?}{=} \frac{1}{2}$$

$$\frac{1}{2} = \frac{1}{2} \text{ True}$$

45. $\sqrt{2y+3}-\sqrt{3y+7} = -1$

$$\sqrt{2y+3} = \sqrt{3y+7}-1$$

$$\left(\sqrt{2y+3}\right)^2 = \left(\sqrt{3y+7}-1\right)^2$$

$$2y+3 = 3y+7-2\sqrt{3y+7}+1$$

$$2\sqrt{3y+7} = y+5$$

$$\left(2\sqrt{3y+7}\right)^2 = (y+5)^2$$

$$4(3y+7) = y^2+10y+25$$

$$12y+28 = y^2+10y+25$$

$$y^2-2y-3 = 0$$

$$(y-3)(y+1) = 0$$

$$y-3 = 0 \quad y+1 = 0$$

$$y = 3 \qquad y = -1$$

Check $y = 3$

$$\sqrt{2(3)+3}-\sqrt{3(3)+7} \overset{?}{=} -1$$

$$\sqrt{9}-\sqrt{16} \overset{?}{=} -1$$

$$3-4 \overset{?}{=} -1$$

$$-1 = -1 \text{ True}$$

Check $y = -1$

$$\sqrt{2(-1)+3}-\sqrt{3(-1)+7} \overset{?}{=} -1$$

$$\sqrt{1}-\sqrt{4} \overset{?}{=} -1$$

$$1-2 \overset{?}{=} -1$$

$$-1 = -1 \text{ True}$$

47. $\left(\sqrt[3]{x^3+8}\right)^3 = (x+2)^3$

$$x^3+8 = x^3+6x^2+12x+8$$

$$6x^2+12x = 0$$

$$6x(x+2) = 0$$

$$6x = 0 \quad x+2 = 0$$

$$x = 0 \qquad x = -2$$

Check $x = 0$ Check $x = -2$

$\sqrt[3]{(0)^3 + 8} \overset{?}{=} 0 + 2$ $\sqrt[3]{(-2)^3 + 8} \overset{?}{=} -2 + 2$

$\sqrt[3]{8} \overset{?}{=} 2$ $\sqrt[3]{0} \overset{?}{=} 0$

$2 = 2$ True $0 = 0$ True

49. $900 = \sqrt{8000h + h^2}$

$900^2 = \left(\sqrt{8000h + h^2}\right)^2$

$810000 = 8000h + h^2$

$h^2 + 8000h - 810000 = 0$

$(h - 100)(h + 8100) = 0$

$h - 100 = 0 \quad h + 8100 = 0$

$h = 100 \qquad h = -8100$

The negative answer makes no sense in this application. The satellite is 100 mi above the Earth's surface.

51.   a. $S = \sqrt{30fL}$

$S^2 = \left(\sqrt{30fL}\right)^2$

$S^2 = 30fL$

$L = \dfrac{S^2}{30f}$

b. $L = \dfrac{30^2}{30(0.5)} = \dfrac{900}{15} = 60$

The length of the skid marks is 60 ft.

53. $15^2 = 12^2 + d^2$

$d^2 = 15^2 - 12^2$

$d = \sqrt{15^2 - 12^2} = \sqrt{225 - 144} = \sqrt{81} = 9$

The painter must place the ladder 9 ft from the side of the house.

Exercises 7.6 Complex Numbers

1. $\sqrt{-4} = \sqrt{(-1)(4)} = \sqrt{4}\sqrt{-1} = 2i$

3. $\sqrt{-\dfrac{1}{16}} = \sqrt{\left(\dfrac{1}{16}\right)(-1)} = \dfrac{\sqrt{1}}{\sqrt{16}}\sqrt{-1} = \dfrac{1}{4}i$

5. $\sqrt{-3} = \sqrt{(-1)3} = \sqrt{-1}\sqrt{3} = i\sqrt{3}$

7. $\sqrt{-18} = \sqrt{(9)(-1)(2)} = \sqrt{9}\sqrt{-1}\sqrt{2} = 3i\sqrt{2}$

9. $\sqrt{-500} = \sqrt{(100)(-1)(5)} =$

$\sqrt{100}\sqrt{-1}\sqrt{5} = 10i\sqrt{5}$

11. $-\sqrt{-9} = -\sqrt{(9)(-1)} = -\sqrt{9}\sqrt{-1} = -3i$

13. $6\sqrt{\dfrac{-5}{16}} = 6\dfrac{\sqrt{(-1)(5)}}{\sqrt{16}} = 6\dfrac{i\sqrt{5}}{4} = \dfrac{3i\sqrt{5}}{2}$

15. $-\dfrac{1}{4}\sqrt{-12} = -\dfrac{1}{4}\sqrt{(4)(-1)(3)} =$

$-\dfrac{1}{4}\sqrt{4}\sqrt{-1}\sqrt{3} = -\dfrac{1}{4}2i\sqrt{3} = -\dfrac{i\sqrt{3}}{2}$

17. $(1 + 12i) + 8i = 1 + 12i + 8i =$

$1 + (12 + 8)i = 1 + 20i$

19. $(3 - 15i) + (2 + 9i) = 3 - 15i + 2 + 9i =$

$(3 + 2) + (-15 + 9)i = 5 - 6i$

21. $(7 - i) - (7 + 5i) = 7 - i - 7 - 5i =$

$(7 - 7) + (-1 - 5)i = -6i$

23. $(-8 - 6i) - (-1 - 3i) = -8 - 6i + 1 + 3i =$

$(-8 + 1) + (-6 + 3)i = -7 - 3i$

25. $16 - \left(18 + \sqrt{-4}\right) = 16 - 18 - 2i = -2 - 2i$

27. $\left(10 - 3\sqrt{-16}\right) + \left(2 - \sqrt{-25}\right) =$

$(10 - 3(4i)) + (2 - 5i) = 10 - 12i + 2 - 5i =$

$(10 + 2) + (-12 - 5)i = 12 - 17i$

29. $(5i)(2i) = 10i^2 = -10$

31. $\left(i\sqrt{3}\right)\left(-3i\sqrt{3}\right) = -3i^2\left(\sqrt{3}\right)^2 = 3(3) = 9$

33. $7i \bullet 9i = 7 \bullet 9i^2 = -63$

35. $-2i(14i) = -28i^2 = 28$

37. $3i(1 - i) = 3i - 3i^2 = 3i + 3 = 3 + 3i$

39. $-i(12 + 7i) = -12i - 7i^2 = -12i + 7 = 7 - 12i$

41. $\sqrt{-9}\left(7 + \sqrt{-16}\right) = 3i(7 + 4i) = 21i + 12i^2 =$

$21i - 12 = -12 + 21i$

43. $-\sqrt{2}\left(\sqrt{8} - \sqrt{-18}\right) = -\sqrt{2}\left(2\sqrt{2} - 3i\sqrt{2}\right) =$

$-2\left(\sqrt{2}\right)^2 + 3i\left(\sqrt{2}\right)^2 = -4 + 6i$

45. $(4 + 2i)(2 + 3i) =$

F   O   I   L

$8 + 12i + 4i + 6i^2 = 8 + 16i - 6 = 2 + 16i$

47. $(10 - i)(4 + 6i) =$

F   O   I   L

$40 + 60i - 4i - 6i^2 = 40 + 56i + 6 = 46 + 56i$

49. $(7i - 7)(3 - 5i) =$

F   O   I   L

$21i - 35i^2 - 21 + 35i = 56i + 35 - 21 =$

$14 + 56i$

51. $(-4 - 2i)(2 - 4i) =$

F   O   I   L

$-8 + 16i - 4i + 8i^2 = -8 + 12i - 8 = -16 + 12i$

53. $(6 + 5i)(6 - 5i) = (6)^2 - (5i)^2 = 36 - 25i^2 =$

$36 + 25 = 61$

55. $(3+2i)^2 = (3)^2 + 2(3)(2i) + (2i)^2 =$
$9 + 12i + 4i^2 = 9 + 12i - 4 = 5 + 12i$

57. $(2-3i)^2 = (2)^2 - (2)(2)(3i) + (3i)^2 =$
$4 - 12i + 9i^2 = 4 - 12i - 9 = -5 - 12i$

59. $\left(\sqrt{-1} + \sqrt{2}\right)\left(\sqrt{-9} - \sqrt{8}\right) =$

$\left(i + \sqrt{2}\right)\left(3i - 2\sqrt{2}\right) =$

F   O   I   L

$3i^2 - 2i\sqrt{2} + 3i\sqrt{2} - 2\left(\sqrt{2}\right)^2 =$

$-3 + i\sqrt{2} - 4 = -7 + i\sqrt{2}$

61.
Complex Number	Conjugate	Product
$1+10i$	$1-10i$	$1^2 - (10i)^2 =$
		$1 - 100i^2 =$
		$1 + 100 = 101$

63.
Complex Number	Conjugate	Product
$4-3i$	$4+3i$	$4^2 - (3i)^2 =$
		$16 - 9i^2 =$
		$16 + 9 = 25$

65.
Complex Number	Conjugate	Product
$-9+6i$	$-9-6i$	$(-9)^2 - (6i)^2 =$
		$81 - 36i^2 =$
		$81 + 36 = 117$

67.
Complex Number	Conjugate	Product
$8i$	$-8i$	$-(8i)^2 =$
		$-64i^2 = 64$

69.
Complex Number	Conjugate	Product
$-11i$	$+11i$	$-(11i)^2 =$
		$-121i^2 = 121$

71. $\dfrac{7}{4+i} \cdot \dfrac{4-i}{4-i} = \dfrac{7(4-i)}{(4+i)(4-i)} =$

$\dfrac{28 - 7i}{16 - i^2} = \dfrac{28 - 7i}{17} = \dfrac{28}{17} - \dfrac{7}{17}i$

73. $\dfrac{-3}{1-5i} \cdot \dfrac{1+5i}{1+5i} = \dfrac{-3(1+5i)}{(1-5i)(1+5i)} =$

$\dfrac{-3 - 15i}{1^2 - 25i^2} = \dfrac{-3 - 15i}{26} = -\dfrac{3}{26} - \dfrac{15}{26}i$

75. $\dfrac{5}{4i} \cdot \dfrac{-4i}{-4i} = \dfrac{-20i}{-16i^2} = \dfrac{-20i}{16} = -\dfrac{5}{4}i$

77. $-\dfrac{2}{\sqrt{-49}} = \dfrac{-2}{7i} \cdot \dfrac{-7i}{-7i} = \dfrac{14i}{-49i^2} = \dfrac{14i}{49} = \dfrac{2}{7}i$

79. $\dfrac{4-3i}{i} \cdot \dfrac{-i}{-i} = \dfrac{-4i + 3i^2}{-i^2} = \dfrac{-3 - 4i}{1} = -3 - 4i$

81. $\dfrac{3+5i}{1+i} \cdot \dfrac{1-i}{1-i} = \dfrac{3 + 2i - 5i^2}{1 - i^2} = \dfrac{3 + 2i + 5}{1 + 1} =$

$\dfrac{8 + 2i}{2} = 4 + i$

83. $\dfrac{6+3i}{2-2i} \cdot \dfrac{2+2i}{2+2i} = \dfrac{12 + 18i + 6i^2}{4 - 4i^2} =$

$\dfrac{12 + 18i - 6}{4 + 4} = \dfrac{6 + 18i}{8} = \dfrac{6}{8} + \dfrac{18}{8}i = \dfrac{3}{4} + \dfrac{9}{4}i$

85. $\dfrac{2 - \sqrt{-16}}{5 - \sqrt{-100}} = \dfrac{2 - 4i}{5 - 10i} \cdot \dfrac{5 + 10i}{5 + 10i} =$

$\dfrac{10 + 20i - 20i - 40i^2}{25 - 100i^2} =$

$\dfrac{10 + 40}{25 + 100} = \dfrac{50}{125} = \dfrac{2}{5}$

87. $\dfrac{8 - \sqrt{-36}}{6 + \sqrt{-64}} = \dfrac{8 - 6i}{6 + 8i} \cdot \dfrac{6 - 8i}{6 - 8i} =$

$\dfrac{48 - 100i + 48i^2}{36 - 64i^2} = \dfrac{48 - 100i - 48}{100} =$

$\dfrac{-100i}{100} = -i$

89. $i^{18} = i^{16} \cdot i^2 = \left(i^4\right)^4 i^2 = (1)^4 i^2 = i^2 = -1$

91. $i^{35} = i^{32} \cdot i^3 = \left(i^4\right)^8 \cdot i^2 \cdot i = (1)^8 (-1)i = -i$

93. $i^{12} \cdot i^9 = i^{21} = i^{20} \cdot i = \left(i^4\right)^5 i = (1)^5 i = i$

95. $\dfrac{i^{38}}{i^{19}} = i^{19} = i^{16} \cdot i^3 = \left(i^4\right)^4 \cdot i^2 \cdot i =$

$(1)^4 (-1)i = -i$

97. $(3+9i) + (5-8i) = (3+5) + (9-8)i = 8+i$
The total impedance is $(8+i)$ ohms.

99. $V = IZ = (8+5i)(9+3i) = 72 + 69i + 15i^2 =$
$72 + 69i - 15 = 57 + 69i$
The voltage is $(57 + 69i)$ volts.

Chapter 7 Review Exercises

1. $-6\sqrt{121} = -6\sqrt{11^2} = -6(11) = -66$

2. $2\sqrt[3]{-125} = 2\sqrt[3]{(-5)^3} = 2(-5) = -10$

3. $\sqrt{\dfrac{1}{9}} = \dfrac{\sqrt{1}}{\sqrt{9}} = \dfrac{1}{3}$

4. $\sqrt{0.36} = \sqrt{(0.6)^2} = 0.6$

5. $\sqrt{81y^8} = \sqrt{(9y^4)^2} = 9y^4$

6. $-\sqrt{49a^6b^2} = -\sqrt{(7a^3b)^2} = -7a^3b$

7. $\sqrt[3]{-216x^9} = \sqrt[3]{(-6x^3)^3} = -6x^3$

8. $\sqrt[5]{243p^{15}} = \sqrt[5]{(3p^3)^5} = 3p^3$

9. $-64^{\frac{1}{2}} = -\sqrt{64} = -\sqrt{8^2} = -8$

10. $7x^{\frac{1}{3}} = 7\sqrt[3]{x}$

11. $-(16n^4)^{\frac{3}{4}} = -\left(\sqrt[4]{16n^4}\right)^3 =$

$-\left(\sqrt[4]{(2n)^4}\right)^3 = -(2n)^3 = -2^3n^3 = -8n^3$

12. $8^{-\frac{2}{3}} = \frac{1}{8^{\frac{2}{3}}} = \frac{1}{\left(\sqrt[3]{8}\right)^2} = \frac{1}{\left(\sqrt[3]{2^3}\right)^2} = \frac{1}{2^2} = \frac{1}{4}$

13. $x^{\frac{1}{4}} \bullet x^{\frac{1}{2}} = x^{\frac{1}{4}+\frac{1}{2}} = x^{\frac{3}{4}} = \sqrt[4]{x^3}$

14. $\frac{r^{\frac{2}{3}}}{6r^{\frac{1}{6}}} = \frac{1}{6}r^{\frac{2}{3}-\frac{1}{6}} = \frac{1}{6}r^{\frac{1}{2}} = \frac{1}{6}\sqrt{r} = \frac{\sqrt{r}}{6}$

15. $(25y^2)^{-\frac{1}{2}} = \frac{1}{(25y^2)^{\frac{1}{2}}} = \frac{1}{\sqrt{25y^2}} =$

$\frac{1}{\sqrt{(5y)^2}} = \frac{1}{5y}$

16. $\frac{3a^{\frac{2}{3}}}{\left(6a^{\frac{1}{6}}\right)^2} = \frac{3a^{\frac{2}{3}}}{36a^{\frac{1}{3}}} = \frac{a^{\frac{2}{3}-\frac{1}{3}}}{12} = \frac{a^{\frac{1}{3}}}{12} = \frac{\sqrt[3]{a}}{12}$

17. $\sqrt[8]{x^2} = x^{\frac{2}{8}} = x^{\frac{1}{4}} = \sqrt[4]{x}$

18. $\sqrt[6]{n^4} \bullet \sqrt[3]{n} = n^{\frac{4}{6}} \bullet n^{\frac{1}{3}} = n^{\frac{2}{3}+\frac{1}{3}} = n^1 = n$

19. $\sqrt{\sqrt[4]{y^2}} = \left(y^{\frac{2}{4}}\right)^{\frac{1}{2}} = y^{\frac{2}{4}\bullet\frac{1}{2}} = y^{\frac{1}{4}} = \sqrt[4]{y}$

20. $\sqrt[6]{p^3q^6} = (p^3q^6)^{\frac{1}{6}} = p^{\frac{3}{6}}q^{\frac{6}{6}} = p^{\frac{1}{2}}q = q\sqrt{p}$

21. $\frac{\sqrt[3]{a^2}}{\sqrt{a}} = \frac{a^{\frac{2}{3}}}{a^{\frac{1}{2}}} = a^{\frac{2}{3}-\frac{1}{2}} = a^{\frac{1}{6}} = \sqrt[6]{a}$

22. $\sqrt[4]{x^2} \bullet \sqrt[10]{y^5} = x^{\frac{2}{4}}y^{\frac{5}{10}} = x^{\frac{1}{2}}y^{\frac{1}{2}} = (xy)^{\frac{1}{2}} = \sqrt{xy}$

23. $\sqrt{10r} \bullet \sqrt{3s} = \sqrt{10r \bullet 3s} = \sqrt{30rs}$

24. $\sqrt[3]{4p} \bullet \sqrt[3]{7pq^2} = \sqrt[3]{4p \bullet 7pq^2} = \sqrt[3]{28p^2q^2}$

25. $\sqrt{300n^3} = \sqrt{100n^2 \bullet 3n} =$

$\sqrt{100n^2} \bullet \sqrt{3n} = 10n\sqrt{3n}$

26. $\sqrt{45x^5y^4} = \sqrt{9x^4y^4 \bullet 5x} = \sqrt{9x^4y^4} \bullet \sqrt{5x} =$

$3x^2y^2\sqrt{5x}$

27. $\sqrt[3]{128t^7} = \sqrt[3]{64t^6 \bullet 2t} =$

$\sqrt[3]{64t^6} \bullet \sqrt[3]{2t} = 4t^2\sqrt[3]{2t}$

28. $\sqrt[4]{96a^5b^{10}} = \sqrt[4]{16a^4b^8 \bullet 6ab^2} =$

$\sqrt[4]{16a^4b^8} \bullet \sqrt[4]{6ab^2} = 2ab^2\sqrt[4]{6ab^2}$

29. $\frac{\sqrt{35a}}{\sqrt{7}} = \sqrt{\frac{35a}{7}} = \sqrt{5a}$

30. $\frac{\sqrt[3]{12p^2q^2}}{\sqrt[3]{6pq^2}} = \sqrt[3]{\frac{12p^2q^2}{6pq^2}} = \sqrt[3]{2p}$

31. $\sqrt{\frac{n}{25}} = \frac{\sqrt{n}}{\sqrt{25}} = \frac{\sqrt{n}}{5}$

32. $\sqrt{\frac{6}{49y^4}} = \frac{\sqrt{6}}{\sqrt{49y^4}} = \frac{\sqrt{6}}{7y^2}$

33. $\sqrt[3]{\frac{64u^2}{125v^9}} = \frac{\sqrt[3]{64u^2}}{\sqrt[3]{125v^9}} = \frac{4\sqrt[3]{u^2}}{5v^3}$

34. $\sqrt[4]{\frac{4p^4q^3}{81r^4s^8}} = \frac{\sqrt[4]{4p^4q^3}}{\sqrt[4]{81r^4s^8}} = \frac{p\sqrt[4]{4q^3}}{3rs^2}$

35. $9\sqrt{x} - 5\sqrt{x} = (9-5)(\sqrt{x}) = 4\sqrt{x}$

36. $3\sqrt[3]{q^2} + 8\sqrt[3]{q^2} = (3+8)\sqrt[3]{q^2} = 11\sqrt[3]{q^2}$

37. $\sqrt{48} + \sqrt{27} = \sqrt{16 \bullet 3} + \sqrt{9 \bullet 3} =$

$4\sqrt{3} + 3\sqrt{3} = (4+3)\sqrt{3} = 7\sqrt{3}$

38. $-\sqrt{96} - 5\sqrt{6} + 3\sqrt{54} =$

$-\sqrt{16 \bullet 6} - 5\sqrt{6} + 3\sqrt{9 \bullet 6} =$

$-4\sqrt{6} - 5\sqrt{6} + 9\sqrt{6} = (-4-5+9)\sqrt{6} = 0$

39. $6\sqrt[3]{56a^4} - \sqrt[3]{189a} = 6\sqrt[3]{8a^3 \bullet 7a} - \sqrt[3]{27 \bullet 7a} =$

$12a\sqrt[3]{7a} - 3\sqrt[3]{7a} = (12a-3)\sqrt[3]{7a}$

40. $\frac{1}{3}\sqrt[3]{27p^5q} + 2p\sqrt[3]{p^2q} =$

$\frac{1}{3}\sqrt[3]{37p^3 \bullet p^2q} + 2p\sqrt[3]{p^2q} =$

$\frac{3p}{3}\sqrt[3]{p^2q} + 2p\sqrt[3]{p^2q} =$

$(p+2p)\sqrt[3]{p^2q} = 3p\sqrt[3]{p^2q}$

41. $\left(-2\sqrt{3a}\right)\left(3\sqrt{6a}\right) = -6\sqrt{3a \bullet 6a} =$

$-6\sqrt{18a^2} = -6\sqrt{9a^2 \bullet 2} = -6(3a)\sqrt{2} =$

$-18a\sqrt{2}$

42. $\sqrt{5}\left(4\sqrt{10}-2\sqrt{5}\right)=4\sqrt{10\bullet 5}-2\sqrt{5\bullet 5}=$

$4\sqrt{50}-2\sqrt{25}=4\sqrt{25\bullet 2}-2\bullet 5=$

$4\bullet 5\sqrt{2}-10=20\sqrt{2}-10$

43. $\sqrt[3]{2n}\left(\sqrt[3]{n^2}-\sqrt[3]{4}\right)=\sqrt[3]{2n^3}-\sqrt[3]{8n}=$

$n\sqrt[3]{2}-2\sqrt[3]{n}$

44. $\left(4\sqrt{t}-5\right)\left(\sqrt{t}-3\right)=$

    F   O   I   L

$4\left(\sqrt{t}\right)^2-12\sqrt{t}-5\sqrt{t}+15=4t-17\sqrt{t}+15$

45. $\left(\sqrt{6}-\sqrt{x}\right)\left(\sqrt{6}+\sqrt{x}\right)=$

$\left(\sqrt{6}\right)^2-\left(\sqrt{x}\right)^2=6-x$

46. $\left(\sqrt{2y}-1\right)^2=\left(\sqrt{2y}\right)^2-2\sqrt{2y}+1=$

$2y-2\sqrt{2y}+1$

47. $\dfrac{\sqrt{72n^3}}{4\sqrt{6}}=\dfrac{1}{4}\sqrt{\dfrac{72n^3}{6}}=\dfrac{1}{4}\sqrt{12n^3}=$

$\dfrac{1}{4}\sqrt{4n^2\bullet 3n}=\dfrac{2n}{4}\sqrt{3n}=\dfrac{n\sqrt{3n}}{2}$

48. $\sqrt{\dfrac{32a}{9b^4}}=\dfrac{\sqrt{16\bullet 2a}}{\sqrt{9b^4}}=\dfrac{4\sqrt{2a}}{3b^2}$

49. $\dfrac{1}{\sqrt{8}}\bullet\dfrac{\sqrt{2}}{\sqrt{2}}=\dfrac{\sqrt{2}}{\sqrt{16}}=\dfrac{\sqrt{2}}{4}$

50. $\dfrac{\sqrt{16x}}{2\sqrt{y}}=\dfrac{4\sqrt{x}}{2\sqrt{y}}\bullet\dfrac{\sqrt{y}}{\sqrt{y}}=\dfrac{2\sqrt{xy}}{y}$

51. $\sqrt{\dfrac{14p^2}{3q}}=\dfrac{\sqrt{14p^2}}{\sqrt{3q}}\bullet\dfrac{\sqrt{3q}}{\sqrt{3q}}=\dfrac{\sqrt{42p^2q}}{\sqrt{9q^2}}=$

$\dfrac{p\sqrt{42q}}{3q}$

52. $\sqrt[3]{\dfrac{5v}{54u^5}}=\dfrac{\sqrt[3]{5v}}{\sqrt[3]{27u^3\bullet 2u^2}}=\dfrac{\sqrt[3]{5v}}{3u\sqrt[3]{2u^2}}\bullet\dfrac{\sqrt[3]{4u}}{\sqrt[3]{4u}}=$

$\dfrac{\sqrt[3]{20uv}}{3u\sqrt[3]{8u^3}}=\dfrac{\sqrt[3]{20uv}}{6u^2}$

53. $\dfrac{\sqrt{10}-3}{\sqrt{5}}\bullet\dfrac{\sqrt{5}}{\sqrt{5}}=\dfrac{\sqrt{50}-3\sqrt{5}}{5}=\dfrac{5\sqrt{2}-3\sqrt{5}}{5}$

54. $\dfrac{2\sqrt{6a}+\sqrt{2}}{\sqrt{2a}}\bullet\dfrac{\sqrt{2a}}{\sqrt{2a}}=\dfrac{2\sqrt{12a^2}+\sqrt{4a}}{2a}=$

$\dfrac{2(2a)\sqrt{3}+2\sqrt{a}}{2a}=\dfrac{2\left(2a\sqrt{3}+\sqrt{a}\right)}{2a}=$

$\dfrac{2a\sqrt{3}+\sqrt{a}}{a}$

55. $\dfrac{4}{\sqrt{3}-1}\bullet\dfrac{\sqrt{3}+1}{\sqrt{3}+1}=\dfrac{4\left(\sqrt{3}+1\right)}{\left(\sqrt{3}\right)^2-1^2}=\dfrac{4\left(\sqrt{3}+1\right)}{2}=$

$2\left(\sqrt{3}+1\right)=2\sqrt{3}+2$

56. $\dfrac{\sqrt{x}+2}{\sqrt{x}-\sqrt{5}}\bullet\dfrac{\sqrt{x}+\sqrt{5}}{\sqrt{x}+\sqrt{5}}=$

$\dfrac{\left(\sqrt{x}\right)^2+\sqrt{5x}+2\sqrt{x}+2\sqrt{5}}{\left(\sqrt{x}\right)^2-\left(\sqrt{5}\right)^2}=$

$\dfrac{x+\sqrt{5x}+2\sqrt{x}+2\sqrt{5}}{x-5}$

57. $\left(\sqrt{x+8}\right)^2=4^2$

$x+8=16$

$x=8$

58. $\sqrt{n}-2=3$

$\sqrt{n}=5$

$\left(\sqrt{n}\right)^2=5^2$

$n=25$

59. $\sqrt{3n-4}+1=-2$ Check $n=\dfrac{13}{3}$

$\sqrt{3n-4}=-3$

$\left(\sqrt{3n-4}\right)=(-3)^2$ $\sqrt{3\dfrac{13}{3}-4}+1\overset{?}{=}-2$

$3n-4=9$ $\sqrt{9}+1\overset{?}{=}-2$

$3n=13$ $3+1\overset{?}{=}-2$

$n=\dfrac{13}{3}$ $4=-2$ False, No solution.

Note: The solution could have been halted with the second step since $\sqrt{3n-4}\ge 0$ and cannot be a negative number.

60. $\left(\sqrt{x^2-7}\right)^2=\left(\sqrt{5x+7}\right)^2$

$x^2-7=5x+7$

$x^2-5x-14=0$

$(x+2)(x-7)=0$

$x+2=0$ $x-7=0$

$x=-2$ $x=7$

Check $x=-2$

$\sqrt{(-2)^2-7}=\sqrt{-3}$, not a real number.

$x=-2$ is not a solution.

Check $x=7$

$\sqrt{7^2-7}\overset{?}{=}\sqrt{5(7)+7}$

$\sqrt{42}=\sqrt{42}$ True

61. $\left(\sqrt[3]{2x-3}\right)^3 = (-2)^3$

$2x-3 = -8$

$2x = -5$

$x = -\dfrac{5}{2}$

62. $\left(\sqrt{x+5}+1\right)^2 = \left(\sqrt{3x+4}\right)^2$

$x+5+2\sqrt{x+5}+1 = 3x+4$

$2\sqrt{x+5} = 2x-2$

$\sqrt{x+5} = x-1$

$\left(\sqrt{x+5}\right)^2 = (x-1)^2$

$x+5 = x^2-2x+1$

$x^2-3x-4 = 0$

$(x-4)(x+1) = 0$

$x-4 = 0 \qquad x+1 = 0$

$x = 4 \qquad\quad x = -1$

Check $x = 4$

$\sqrt{4+5}+1 \overset{?}{=} \sqrt{3(4)+4}$

$\sqrt{9}+1 \overset{?}{=} \sqrt{16}$

$3+1 \overset{?}{=} 4$

$4 = 4$ True

Check $x = -1$

$\sqrt{-1+5}+1 \overset{?}{=} \sqrt{3(-1)+4}$

$\sqrt{4}+1 \overset{?}{=} \sqrt{1}$

$2+1 \overset{?}{=} 1$

$3 = 1$ False, $x = -1$, is not a solution

63. $\sqrt{-36} = \sqrt{36(-1)} = \sqrt{36} \bullet \sqrt{-1} = 6i$

64. $\sqrt{-125} = \sqrt{(25)(-1)(5)} = \sqrt{25} \bullet \sqrt{-1} \bullet \sqrt{5} =$

$5i\sqrt{5}$

65. $(6-4i)+(2+9i) = (6+2)+(-4+9)i =$

$8+5i$

66. $\left(\sqrt{-4}-3\right)-\left(\sqrt{-16}-7\right) = 2i-3-4i+7 =$

$(-3+7)+(2-4)i = 4-2i$

67. $\sqrt{-81} \bullet \sqrt{-1} = 9i \bullet i = 9i^2 = -9$

68. $-2i(5i+1) = -10i^2-2i =$

$-10(-1)-2i = 10-2i$

69. $(3-3i)(8+3i)$

$\quad$ F $\quad$ O $\quad$ I $\quad$ L

$24+9i-24i-9i^2 = 24-15i+9 = 33-15i$

70. $(5-i)^2 = 5^2-2(5)i+i^2 =$

$25-10i-1 = 24-10i$

71. $\dfrac{-1}{4-4i} \bullet \dfrac{4+4i}{4+4i} = \dfrac{-(4+4i)}{4^2-(4i)^2} = \dfrac{-4(1+i)}{16-16i^2} =$

$\dfrac{-4(1+i)}{16+16} = \dfrac{-4(1+i)}{32} = \dfrac{-(1+i)}{8} = -\dfrac{1}{8}-\dfrac{1}{8}i$

72. $\dfrac{3-4i}{6-2i} \bullet \dfrac{6+2i}{6+2i} = \dfrac{18-18i-8i^2}{36-4i^2} =$

$\dfrac{18-18i+8}{36+4} = \dfrac{26-18i}{40} = \dfrac{26}{40}-\dfrac{18}{40}i$

$= \dfrac{13}{20}-\dfrac{9}{20}i$

73. $i^{38} = i^{36} \bullet i^2 = \left(i^4\right)^9(-1) = (1)^9(-1) = -1$

74. $i^{53} = i^{52} \bullet i = \left(i^4\right)^{13} \bullet i = (1)^{13} \bullet i = i$

75. a. $N(2)^{\frac{t}{20}} = N\sqrt[20]{2^t}$

b. $N = 10, \ t = 60$

$10(2)^{\frac{60}{20}} = 10(2)^3 = 10(8) = 80$

80 bacteria are present after 1 hr.

76. $\sqrt{64R} = \sqrt{8^2 R} = 8\sqrt{R}$

77. a. $v = \sqrt{2ad}, \ a = 2, \ d = 50$

$v = \sqrt{2(2)(50)} = \sqrt{2(100)} =$

$10\sqrt{2} = 14.14213...$

The velocity of the car is $10\sqrt{2}$ m per sec or about 14.1 m per sec.

b. $\sqrt{2(4)(50)}-\sqrt{2(2)(50)} = \sqrt{400}-\sqrt{200} =$

$20-\sqrt{100 \bullet 2} = 20-10\sqrt{2} = 5.85876...$

The velocity is $\left(20-10\sqrt{2}\right)$ m per sec or about 5.9 m per sec.

78. $\sqrt{\dfrac{k}{I}} = \dfrac{\sqrt{k}}{\sqrt{I}} \bullet \dfrac{\sqrt{I}}{\sqrt{I}} = \dfrac{\sqrt{kI}}{I}$

79. $2\pi\sqrt{\dfrac{m}{k}} = 2\pi\dfrac{\sqrt{m}}{\sqrt{k}} \bullet \dfrac{\sqrt{k}}{\sqrt{k}} =$

$2\pi\dfrac{\sqrt{mk}}{k} = \dfrac{2\pi\sqrt{mk}}{k}$

80. $d^2 = 8^2+4^2$

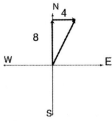

$d^2 = 64 + 16 = 80$

$d = \sqrt{80} = \sqrt{16 \bullet 5} = 4\sqrt{5} = 8.94427...$

The office building is $4\sqrt{5}$ or approximately 8.9 mi from her home.

81. $24^2 = s^2 + 20^2$

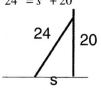

$576 = s^2 + 400$

$s^2 = 176$

$s = \sqrt{176} = \sqrt{16 \bullet 11} = 4\sqrt{11} = 13.2664...$

The wire needs to be anchored to the ground at $4\sqrt{11}$ ft or approximately 13.3 ft from the pole.

82. $13.5 = 18 - 0.5\sqrt{x-4}$

$-4.5 = -0.5\sqrt{x-4}$

$\sqrt{x-4} = 9$

$\left(\sqrt{x-4}\right)^2 = 9^2$

$x - 4 = 81$

$x = 85$

85 bottles per week are demanded.

Chapter 7 Posttest

1.   a. $-3\sqrt{81} = -3\sqrt{9^2} = -3(9) = -27$

     b. $\sqrt[3]{-216} = \sqrt[3]{(-6)^3} = -6$

2. $\sqrt{144a^6b^2} = \sqrt{\left(12a^3b\right)^2} = 12a^3b$

3. $\left(32x^{10}\right)^{\frac{2}{5}} = \left(\sqrt[5]{32x^{10}}\right)^2 =$

     $\left(\sqrt[5]{\left(2x^2\right)^5}\right)^2 = \left(2x^2\right)^2 = 4x^4$

4.   a. $\dfrac{\left(16p^{\frac{1}{3}}\right)^{\frac{3}{2}}}{8p^{\frac{1}{3}}} = \dfrac{16^{\frac{3}{2}} p^{\frac{1}{2}}}{8p^{\frac{1}{3}}} = \dfrac{\left(\sqrt{16}\right)^3 p^{\frac{1}{2}-\frac{1}{3}}}{8} =$

     $\dfrac{4^3 p^{\frac{1}{6}}}{8} = \dfrac{64\sqrt[6]{p}}{8} = 8\sqrt[6]{p}$

b. $\sqrt[8]{x^6 y^2} = \left(x^6 y^2\right)^{\frac{1}{8}} = x^{\frac{6}{8}} y^{\frac{2}{8}} = x^{\frac{3}{4}} y^{\frac{1}{4}} =$

     $\left(x^3 y\right)^{\frac{1}{4}} = \sqrt[4]{x^3 y}$

5. $\sqrt[3]{5p^2} \bullet \sqrt[3]{4q} = \sqrt[3]{5p^2 \bullet 4q} = \sqrt[3]{20p^2 q}$

6. $\dfrac{\sqrt{56n}}{\sqrt{7n}} = \sqrt{\dfrac{56n}{7n}} = \sqrt{8} = \sqrt{4 \bullet 2} = 2\sqrt{2}$

7. $\sqrt{117x^3 y^7} = \sqrt{9x^2 y^6 \bullet 13xy} =$

     $\sqrt{\left(3xy^3\right)^2 \bullet 13xy} = 3xy^3 \sqrt{13xy}$

8. $\sqrt{\dfrac{6u}{49v^6}} = \dfrac{\sqrt{6u}}{\sqrt{49v^6}} = \dfrac{\sqrt{6u}}{\sqrt{\left(7v^3\right)^2}} = \dfrac{\sqrt{6u}}{7v^3}$

9. $-4\sqrt{24} + 2\sqrt{54} - 7\sqrt{6} =$

     $-4\sqrt{4 \bullet 6} + 2\sqrt{9 \bullet 6} - 7\sqrt{6} =$

     $-8\sqrt{6} + 6\sqrt{6} - 7\sqrt{6} =$

     $(-8 + 6 - 7)\sqrt{6} = -9\sqrt{6}$

10. $\left(4\sqrt{2} + 3\right)\left(2\sqrt{2} - 5\right) =$

     F   O   I   L

     $8\left(\sqrt{2}\right)^2 - 20\sqrt{2} + 6\sqrt{2} - 15 =$

     $16 - 14\sqrt{2} - 15 = 1 - 14\sqrt{2}$

11. $\dfrac{\sqrt{3a}}{\sqrt{50b}} \bullet \dfrac{\sqrt{2b}}{\sqrt{2b}} = \dfrac{\sqrt{6ab}}{\sqrt{100b^2}} = \dfrac{\sqrt{6ab}}{\sqrt{\left(10b\right)^2}} = \dfrac{\sqrt{6ab}}{10b}$

12. $\dfrac{\sqrt{x}}{\sqrt{x} - \sqrt{y}} \bullet \dfrac{\sqrt{x} + \sqrt{y}}{\sqrt{x} + \sqrt{y}} = \dfrac{\left(\sqrt{x}\right)^2 + \sqrt{xy}}{\left(\sqrt{x}\right)^2 - \left(\sqrt{y}\right)^2} =$

     $\dfrac{x + \sqrt{xy}}{x - y}$

13. $\sqrt{2x-1} + 9 = 5$ Check $x = \dfrac{17}{2}$

     $\sqrt{2x-1} = -4$

     $\left(\sqrt{2x-1}\right)^2 = (-4)^2$ $\sqrt{2\left(\dfrac{17}{2}\right) - 1} + 9 \overset{?}{=} 5$

     $2x - 1 = 16$ $\sqrt{16} + 9 \overset{?}{=} 5$

     $2x = 17$

     $x = \dfrac{17}{2}$ $4 + 9 \overset{?}{=} 5$

                                    $13 = 5$ False,

                                    no solution.

The same conclusion could have been reached at the end of the second step since $\sqrt{2x-1} \geq 0$ and cannot be negative.

14. $\left(\sqrt{8-3x}\right)^2 = \left(\sqrt{6-x^2}\right)^2$

     $8 - 3x = 6 - x^2$

$x^2 - 3x + 2 = 0$

$(x-1)(x-2) = 0$

$x - 1 = 0 \quad x - 2 = 0$

$x = 1 \qquad x = 2$

Check $x = 1$ Check $x = 2$

$\sqrt{8 - 3(1)} \stackrel{?}{=} \sqrt{6 - 1^2}$ $\sqrt{8 - 3(2)} \stackrel{?}{=} \sqrt{6 - 2^2}$

$\sqrt{5} = \sqrt{5}$ True $\sqrt{2} = \sqrt{2}$ True

15. $\sqrt{x+3} + \sqrt{2x+5} = 2$

$\sqrt{x+3} = 2 - \sqrt{2x+5}$

$\left(\sqrt{x+3}\right)^2 = \left(2 - \sqrt{2x+5}\right)^2$

$x + 3 = 4 - 4\sqrt{2x+5} + 2x + 5$

$4\sqrt{2x+5} = x + 6$

$\left(4\sqrt{2x+5}\right)^2 = (x+6)^2$

$16(2x+5) = x^2 + 12x + 36$

$32x + 80 = x^2 + 12x + 36$

$x^2 - 20x - 44 = 0$

$(x-22)(x+2) = 0$

$x - 22 = 0 \quad x + 2 = 0$

$x = 22 \qquad x = -2$

Check $x = 22$

$\sqrt{22+3} + \sqrt{2 \cdot 22 + 5} \stackrel{?}{=} 2$ Check $x = -2$

$\sqrt{25} + \sqrt{49} \stackrel{?}{=} 2$ $\sqrt{-2+3} + \sqrt{2(-2)+5} \stackrel{?}{=} 2$

$5 + 7 \stackrel{?}{=} 2$ $\sqrt{1} + \sqrt{1} \stackrel{?}{=} 2$

$12 = 2$ False, $x = 22$ $2 = 2$ True

is not a solution.

16. $\left(3 + \sqrt{-49}\right)\left(1 - \sqrt{-16}\right) = (3+7i)(1-4i) =$

    F   O   I   L

$3 - 12i + 7i - 28i^2 = 3 - 5i + 28 = 31 - 5i$

17. $\dfrac{3-5i}{2+3i} \cdot \dfrac{2-3i}{2-3i} = \dfrac{6 - 19i + 15i^2}{4 - 9i^2} =$

$\dfrac{6 - 19i - 15}{4 + 9} = \dfrac{-9 - 19i}{13} = -\dfrac{9}{13} - \dfrac{19}{13}i$

18.   a. $\sqrt{\dfrac{S}{4\pi}} = \dfrac{\sqrt{S}}{\sqrt{4\pi}} \cdot \dfrac{\sqrt{\pi}}{\sqrt{\pi}} = \dfrac{\sqrt{\pi S}}{\sqrt{4\pi^2}} = \dfrac{\sqrt{\pi S}}{2\pi}$

    b. $\dfrac{\sqrt{\pi(512)}}{2\pi} = \dfrac{\sqrt{256 \cdot 2\pi}}{2\pi} = \dfrac{16\sqrt{2\pi}}{2\pi} = \dfrac{8\sqrt{2\pi}}{\pi}$

The radius of the beach ball is $\dfrac{8\sqrt{2\pi}}{\pi}$ in.

19. $\sqrt{8000(200) + (200)^2} =$

$\sqrt{1600000 + 40000} = \sqrt{1640000} =$

$\sqrt{40000 \cdot 41} = 200\sqrt{41} = 1280.624...$

The distance to the horizon is $200\sqrt{41}$ mi or about 1280.6 mi.

20. $20 = 32 - \sqrt{x-5}$

$\sqrt{x-5} = 12$

$\left(\sqrt{x-5}\right)^2 = 12^2$

$x - 5 = 144$

$x = 149$

The daily demand is 149 units.

Cumulative Review Exercises

1. $2(3x-4) > 9x + 7$

$6x - 8 > 9x + 7$

$-3x > 15$

$x < -5$

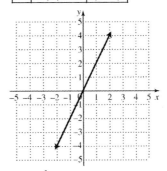

2. $4x = 2y$

$y = 2x$

x	$y = 2x$	(x, y)
0	$2(0) = 0$	$(0,0)$
2	$2(2) = 4$	$(2,4)$

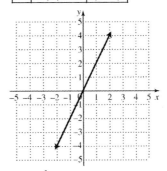

3. $y < -\dfrac{1}{2}x + 3$

Boundary line is dashed.

x	$y = -\dfrac{1}{2}x + 3$	(x, y)
0	$-\dfrac{1}{2}(0) + 3 = 3$	$(0,3)$
2	$-\dfrac{1}{2}(2) + 3 = 2$	$(2,2)$

Test point is (0,0). $0 \stackrel{?}{<} -\dfrac{1}{2}(0) + 3; \;\; 0 < 3$

Shade the region containing (0,0).

$y \geq x - 2$

The boundary line is solid.

x	$y = x - 2$	(x, y)
0	$(0) - 2 = -2$	$(0, -2)$
2	$2 - 2 = 0$	$(2, 0)$

Test point is $(0,0)$. $0 \overset{?}{\geq} 0 - 2;$ $0 > -2$
Shade the region containing $(0,0)$.

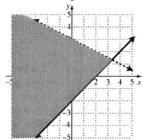

4. $7x^2 - 4x - 9 - (5x^2 - x - 6) =$

$7x^2 - 4x - 9 - 5x^2 + x + 6 =$

$7x^2 - 5x^2 - 4x + x - 9 + 6 =$

$2x^2 - 3x - 3$

5. $x^3 - 2x^2 - 4x + 8 = x^2(x - 2) - 4(x - 2) =$

$(x - 2)(x^2 - 4) = (x - 2)(x - 2)(x + 2) =$

$(x - 2)^2(x + 2)$

6. $3(x - 1)^2 = 12$

$(x - 1)^2 = 4$

$x^2 - 2x + 1 = 4$

$x^2 - 2x - 3 = 0$

$(x + 1)(x - 3) = 0$

$x + 1 = 0 \quad x - 3 = 0$

$x = -1 \quad x = 3$

7. $\dfrac{3}{(x-1)(x-1)} + \dfrac{2}{-(x^2 + 3x - 4)} =$

$\dfrac{3}{(x-1)(x-1)} + \dfrac{-2}{(x-1)(x+4)} =$

$\dfrac{3}{(x-1)^2} \cdot \dfrac{(x+4)}{(x+4)} + \dfrac{-2}{(x-1)(x+4)} \cdot \dfrac{(x-1)}{(x-1)} =$

$\dfrac{3x + 12 - 2x + 2}{(x-1)^2(x+4)} = \dfrac{x + 14}{(x-1)^2(x+4)}$

8. a. $h = $ hours, $p = $ pay (h, p)

$(20, 110)$ and $(25, 137.5)$

$m = \dfrac{p_2 - p_1}{h_2 - h_1} = \dfrac{137.5 - 110}{25 - 20} = \dfrac{27.5}{5} = 5.5$

$p - p_1 = m(h - h_1)$

$p - 110 = 5.5(h - 20)$

$p - 110 = 5.5h - 110$

$p = 5.5h$

b. The slope represents the employee's hourly rate which is \$5.50.

9. $h = -16t^2 + 24t + 250 = 115$

$-16t^2 + 24t + 135 = 0$

$16t^2 - 24t - 135 = 0$

$(4t - 15)(4t + 9)$

$4t - 15 = 0 \quad 4t + 9 = 0$

$4t = 15 \quad 4t = -9$

$t = \dfrac{15}{4} \quad t = -\dfrac{9}{4}$

The negative answer makes no sense in this problem The object will be 115 ft above the ground in $\dfrac{15}{4}$ sec or 3.75 sec after it is thrown.

10. $t = \dfrac{k}{n}$

$50 = \dfrac{k}{2}$

$k = 100$

$t = \dfrac{100}{n}$

$t = \dfrac{100}{8} = 12.5$

It will take 8 painters 12.5 hr to paint the house.

CHAPTER 8 QUADRATIC EQUATIONS, FUNCTIONS AND INEQUALITIES

Chapter 8 Pretest

1. $3x^2 + 17 = 5$

   $3x^2 = -12$

   $x^2 = -4$

   $x = \pm\sqrt{-4} = \pm\sqrt{4(-1)} = \pm 2i$

   $x = 2i \quad x = -2i$

2. $4a^2 + 12a = 7$

   $4\left(a^2 + 3a\right) = 7$

   $4\left(a^2 + 3a + \left(\dfrac{3}{2}\right)^2\right) = 7 + 4\left(\dfrac{3}{2}\right)^2$

   $4\left(a + \dfrac{3}{2}\right)^2 = 7 + 4\left(\dfrac{9}{4}\right) = 7 + 9 = 16$

   $4\left(a + \dfrac{3}{2}\right)^2 = 16$

   $\left(a + \dfrac{3}{2}\right)^2 = 4$

   $a + \dfrac{3}{2} = \pm\sqrt{4} = \pm 2$

   $a = 2 - \dfrac{3}{2} = \dfrac{4}{2} - \dfrac{3}{2} = \dfrac{1}{2}$

   $a = -2 - \dfrac{3}{2} = -\dfrac{4}{2} - \dfrac{3}{2} = -\dfrac{7}{2}$

3. $2x^2 - 6x + 3 = 0$

   $a = 2 \quad b = -6 \quad c = 3$

   $x = \dfrac{-(-6) \pm \sqrt{(-6)^2 - 4(2)(3)}}{2(2)}$

   $x = \dfrac{6 \pm \sqrt{36 - 24}}{4} = \dfrac{6 \pm \sqrt{12}}{4} = \dfrac{6 \pm 2\sqrt{3}}{4}$

   $x = \dfrac{2(3 \pm \sqrt{3})}{4} \quad x = \dfrac{3 + \sqrt{3}}{2}, \quad x = \dfrac{3 - \sqrt{3}}{2}$

4. $3x^2 + 5x - 1 = 0$

   $a = 3 \quad b = 5 \quad c = -1$

   $b^2 - 4ac = (5)^2 - 4(3)(-1) = 25 + 12 = 37.$

   37 is positive, not a perfect square.

   Two real solutions.

5. $6(2n - 3)^2 = 48$

   $(2n - 3)^2 = 8$

   $2n - 3 = \pm\sqrt{8} = \pm 2\sqrt{2}$

   $2n = 3 \pm 2\sqrt{2}$

$n = \dfrac{3 + 2\sqrt{2}}{2}, \quad x = \dfrac{3 - 2\sqrt{2}}{2}$

6. $x^2 - 4x + 12 = 0$

   $a = 1 \quad b = -4 \quad c = 12$

   $x = \dfrac{-(-4) \pm \sqrt{(-4)^2 - 4(1)(12)}}{2(1)}$

   $x = \dfrac{4 \pm \sqrt{16 - 48}}{2} = \dfrac{4 \pm \sqrt{-32}}{2} = \dfrac{4 \pm 4i\sqrt{2}}{2}$

   $x = 2 + 2i\sqrt{2}, \quad x = 2 - 2i\sqrt{2}$

7. $3x^2 + 15x + 16 = x$

   $3x^2 + 14x + 16 = 0$

   $(x + 2)(3x + 8) = 0$

   $x + 2 = 0 \quad 3x + 8 = 0$

   $x = -2 \quad 3x = -8$

   $x = -\dfrac{8}{3}$

8. $2x^2 + 2x = 1 - 6x$

   $2x^2 + 8x - 1 = 0$

   $a = 2 \quad b = 8 \quad c = -1$

   $x = \dfrac{-(8) \pm \sqrt{(8)^2 - 4(2)(-1)}}{2(2)}$

   $x = \dfrac{-8 \pm \sqrt{64 + 8}}{4} = \dfrac{-8 \pm \sqrt{72}}{4}$

   $x = \dfrac{-8 \pm 6\sqrt{2}}{4} = \dfrac{-4 \pm 3\sqrt{2}}{2}$

   $x = \dfrac{-4 + 3\sqrt{2}}{2}, x = \dfrac{-4 - 3\sqrt{2}}{2}$

9. $5x^2 - 10x + 9 = 3$

   $5x^2 - 10x + 6 = 0$

   $a = 5 \quad b = -10 \quad c = 6$

   $x = \dfrac{-(-10) \pm \sqrt{(-10)^2 - 4(5)(6)}}{2(5)}$

   $x = \dfrac{10 \pm \sqrt{100 - 120}}{10} = \dfrac{10 \pm \sqrt{-20}}{10}$

   $x = \dfrac{10 \pm \sqrt{4(5)(-1)}}{10} = \dfrac{10 \pm 2i\sqrt{5}}{10}$

   $x = \dfrac{5 + i\sqrt{5}}{5}, \quad x = \dfrac{5 - i\sqrt{5}}{5}$

10. $0.04x^2 - 0.12x + 0.09 = 0$

    $100\left(0.04x^2 - 0.12x + 0.09\right) = 100(0)$

    $4x^2 - 12x + 9 = 0$

    $(2x - 3)^2 = 0$

$2x - 3 = \pm\sqrt{0} = 0$

$2x = 3$

$x = \dfrac{3}{2}$

11. $x^4 - x^2 - 72 = 0$

Let $u = x^2$

$\left(x^2\right)^2 - \left(x^2\right) - 72 = 0$

$u^2 - u - 72 = 0$

$(u - 9)(u + 8) = 0$

$u - 9 = 0 \quad u + 8 = 0$

$u = 9 \qquad u = -8$

$x^2 = 9 \qquad x^2 = -8$

$x = \pm\sqrt{9} \qquad x = \pm\sqrt{-8} = \pm\sqrt{4(-1)(2)}$

$x = \pm 3 \qquad\qquad x = \pm 2i\sqrt{2}$

12. $x = -\dfrac{3}{2}, \quad x = 4$

$2x = -3 \qquad x - 4 = 0$

$2x + 3 = 0$

$(2x + 3)(x - 4) = 0$

$2x^2 - 5x - 12 = 0$

13. $f(x) = x^2 - 4x + 3$

$a = 1 \qquad b = -4$

$x = -\dfrac{b}{2a} = -\dfrac{-4}{2(1)} = 2$

$f(2) = (2)^2 - 4(2) + 3 = 4 - 8 + 3 = -1$

Vertex: $(2, -1)$

Axis of symmetry: $x = 2$

$f(0) = (0)^2 - 4(0) + 3 = 0$

y-intercept: $(0, 3)$

$x^2 - 4x + 3 = 0$

$(x - 3)(x - 1) = 0$

$x - 3 = 0 \quad x - 1 = 0$

$x = 3 \qquad x = 1$

x-intercepts: $(3, 0)$ and $(1, 0)$

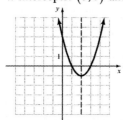

14. $f(x) = 12 - x - x^2$

$a = -1 \qquad b = -1$

$x = -\dfrac{b}{2a} = -\dfrac{-1}{2(-1)} = -\dfrac{1}{2}$

$f\left(-\dfrac{1}{2}\right) = 12 - \left(-\dfrac{1}{2}\right) - \left(-\dfrac{1}{2}\right)^2 =$

$\dfrac{48}{4} + \dfrac{2}{4} - \dfrac{1}{4} = \dfrac{49}{4}$

Vertex: $\left(-\dfrac{1}{2}, \dfrac{49}{4}\right)$

Axis of symmetry: $x = -\dfrac{1}{2}$

$f(0) = 12 - (0) - (0)^2 = 12$

y-intercept: $(0, 12)$

$12 - x - x^2 = 0$

$(4 + x)(3 - x) = 0$

$4 + x = 0 \quad 3 - x = 0$

$x = -4 \qquad x = 3$

x-intercepts: $(-4, 0)$ and $(3, 0)$

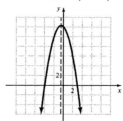

15.

x	$f(x) = \dfrac{1}{2}x^2 + x - 4$	(x, y)
-4	$\dfrac{1}{2}(-4)^2 + (-4) - 4 = 0$	$(-4, 0)$
-2	$\dfrac{1}{2}(-2)^2 + (-2) - 4 = -4$	$(-2, -4)$
0	$\dfrac{1}{2}(0)^2 + (0) - 4 = -4$	$(0, -4)$
2	$\dfrac{1}{2}(2)^2 + (2) - 4 = 0$	$(2, 0)$
4	$\dfrac{1}{2}(4)^2 + (4) - 4 = 8$	$(4, 8)$

$x = -\dfrac{b}{2a} = -\dfrac{1}{2\left(\dfrac{1}{2}\right)} = -\dfrac{1}{1} = -1$

$f(-1) = \dfrac{1}{2}(-1)^2 + (-1) - 4 = -\dfrac{9}{2}$

Vertex: $\left(-1, -\dfrac{9}{2}\right)$

Domain: $(-\infty, \infty)$ Range: $\left[-\dfrac{9}{2}, \infty\right)$

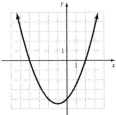

16. $x^2 - 6x + 8 > 0$

$x^2 - 6x + 8 = 0$

$(x-4)(x-2) = 0$

$x - 4 = 0 \quad x - 2 = 0$

$x = 4 \qquad x = 2$

Inter-val	Test Value	$x^2 - 6x + 8 > 0$	Conclu-sion
$x < 2$	-6	$(-6)^2 - 6(-6) + 8 =$ 80	$80 > 0$
$2 \le x \le 4$	3	$(3)^2 - 6(3) + 8 =$ -1	$-1 \le 0$
$4 < x$	6	$(6)^2 - 6(6) + 8 =$ 8	$8 > 0$

$\xleftarrow{\hspace{1cm}} \begin{array}{ccccccccccccc} & & & & & & &) & & (& & & \\ -5 & -4 & -3 & -2 & -1 & 0 & 1 & 2 & 3 & 4 & 5 & 6 & 7 \end{array} \xrightarrow{\hspace{1cm}}$

$(-\infty, 2) \cup (4, \infty)$

17. $h = -16t^2 + 20t = -50$

$-16t^2 + 20t + 50 = 0$

$8t^2 - 10t - 25 = 0$

$(4t + 5)(2t - 5) = 0$

$4t + 5 = 0 \quad 2t - 5 = 0$

$4t = -5 \quad 2t = 5$

$t = -\dfrac{5}{4} \qquad t = \dfrac{5}{2}$

The negative answer makes no sense in this problem. The object is 50 ft below the point of release $\dfrac{5}{2}$ sec, or 2.5 sec, after it is tossed upward.

18. $time = \dfrac{distance}{rate}$

Let x be the speed of the current.

$\dfrac{6}{9+x} = \dfrac{6}{9-x} - 0.5$

$\dfrac{6}{9+x} \bullet (9-x)(9+x) = \dfrac{6}{9-x} \bullet (9-x)(9+x)$
$\qquad\qquad\qquad\qquad - 0.5 \bullet (9-x)(9+x)$

$54 - 6x = 54 + 6x - 0.5(81 - x^2)$

$54 - 6x = 54 + 6x - 40.5 + 0.5x^2$

$0.5x^2 + 12x - 40.5 = 0$

$x^2 + 24x - 81 = 0$

$(x+27)(x-3) = 0$

$x + 27 = 0 \quad x - 3 = 0$

$x = -27 \qquad x = 3$

The negative answer makes no sense in this problem. The speed of the current is 3 mph.

19.   Let $r =$ the radius of the total planting area.

$\pi r^2 = 157$

$3.14 r^2 = 157$

$r^2 = 50$

$r = \pm\sqrt{50} = 7.071...$

The radius of the planting area is approximately 6.1 ft. The maximum planting area is $(3.14)(6.1)^2 =$ 116.8 sq ft.

20. $R(x) = 55x - 0.5x^2 \ge 1200$

$-0.5x^2 + 55x - 1200 \ge 0$

$0.5x^2 - 55x + 1200 \le 0$

$x^2 - 110x + 2400 = 0$

$(x - 80)(x - 30) = 0$

$x - 80 = 0 \quad x - 30 = 0$

$x = 80 \qquad x = 30$

Inter-val	Test Value	$55x - 0.5x^2$ ≥ 1200	Conclu-sion
$x < 30$	0	$55(0) - 0.5(0)^2$ $= 0$	$0 < 1200$
$30 \le x$ ≤ 80	50	$55(50) - 0.5(50)^2$ $= 1500$	$1500 \ge 1200$
$80 < x$	90	$55(90) - 0.5(90)^2$ $= 900$	$900 \le 1200$

The company must sell between and including 30 and 80 bottles for revenue of at least $1200.

Exercises 8.1 Solving Quadratic Equations By Completing The Square

1. $x^2 = 16$

$x = \pm 4$

$x = 4, \ x = -4$

3. $y^2 = 24$

$y = \pm\sqrt{24} = \pm 2\sqrt{6}$

$y = 2\sqrt{6}, \ y = -2\sqrt{6}$

5. $a^2 + 25 = 0$

$a^2 = -25$

$a = \pm\sqrt{-25} = \pm 5i$

$a = 5i, \ a = -5i$

7. $4n^2 - 8 = 0$

$4n^2 = 8$

$n^2 = 2$

$n = \pm\sqrt{2}$

$n = \sqrt{2}, \ n = -\sqrt{2}$

9. $\frac{1}{6}y^2 = 12$

$y^2 = 72$

$y = \pm\sqrt{72} = \pm 6\sqrt{2}$

$y = 6\sqrt{2}, \ y = -6\sqrt{2}$

11. $3x^2 + 6 = 21$

$3x^2 = 15$

$x^2 = 5$

$x = \pm\sqrt{5}$

$x = \sqrt{5}, \ x = -\sqrt{5}$

13. $8 - 9n^2 = 14$

$-9n^2 = 6$

$n^2 = -\frac{6}{9}$

$n = \pm\sqrt{-\frac{6}{9}} = \pm\frac{\sqrt{-6}}{\sqrt{9}} = \pm\frac{i\sqrt{6}}{3}$

$n = \frac{i\sqrt{6}}{3}, \ n = -\frac{i\sqrt{6}}{3}$

15. $(x-1)^2 = 48$

$x - 1 = \pm\sqrt{48} = \pm 4\sqrt{3}$

$x = 1 \pm 4\sqrt{3}$

$x = 1 + 4\sqrt{3}, \ x = 1 - 4\sqrt{3}$

17. $(2n+5)^2 = 75$

$2n + 5 = \pm\sqrt{75} = \pm 5\sqrt{3}$

$2n = -5 \pm 5\sqrt{3}$

$n = \frac{-5 \pm 5\sqrt{3}}{2}$

$n = \frac{-5 + 5\sqrt{3}}{2}, \ n = \frac{-5 - 5\sqrt{3}}{2}$

19. $(4a-3)^2 + 9 = 1$

$(4a-3)^2 = -8$

$4a - 3 = \pm\sqrt{-8} = \pm 2i\sqrt{2}$

$4a = 3 \pm 2i\sqrt{2}$

$a = \frac{3 \pm 2i\sqrt{2}}{4}$

$a = \frac{3 + 2i\sqrt{2}}{4}, \ a = \frac{3 - 2i\sqrt{2}}{4}$

21. $16(x+4)^2 = 81$

$(x+4)^2 = \frac{81}{16}$

$x + 4 = \pm\sqrt{\frac{81}{16}} = \pm\frac{\sqrt{81}}{\sqrt{16}} = \pm\frac{9}{4}$

$x = -4 \pm \frac{9}{4} = -\frac{16}{4} \pm \frac{9}{4}$

$x = -\frac{7}{4}, \ x = -\frac{25}{4}$

23. $x^2 - 6x + 9 = 80$

$(x-3)^2 = 80$

$x - 3 = \pm\sqrt{80} = \pm 4\sqrt{5}$

$x = 3 \pm 4\sqrt{5}$

$x = 3 + 4\sqrt{5}, \ x = 3 - 4\sqrt{5}$

25. $4p^2 + 12p + 9 = 32$

$(2p+3)^2 = 32$

$2p + 3 = \pm\sqrt{32} = \pm 4\sqrt{2}$

$2p = -3 \pm 4\sqrt{2}$

$p = \frac{-3 \pm 4\sqrt{2}}{2}$

$p = \frac{-3 + 4\sqrt{2}}{2}, \ p = \frac{-3 - 4\sqrt{2}}{2}$

27. $(3n-2)(3n+2) = -52$

$9n^2 - 4 = -52$

$9n^2 = -48$

$n^2 = \frac{-48}{9}$

$n = \pm\sqrt{\frac{-48}{9}} = \pm\frac{\sqrt{-48}}{\sqrt{9}} = \pm\frac{4i\sqrt{3}}{3}$

$n = \frac{4i\sqrt{3}}{3}, \ n = -\frac{4i\sqrt{3}}{3}$

29. $2x - 1 = \frac{18}{2x-1}$

$(2x-1)^2 = 18$

$2x - 1 = \pm\sqrt{18} = \pm 3\sqrt{2}$

$2x = 1 \pm 3\sqrt{2}$

$x = \frac{1 \pm 3\sqrt{2}}{2}$

$x = \frac{1 + 3\sqrt{2}}{2}, \ x = \frac{1 - 3\sqrt{2}}{2}$

31. $V = \pi r^2 h$

$\frac{V}{\pi h} = \frac{\pi r^2 h}{\pi h}$

$$r^2 = \frac{V}{\pi h}$$

$$r = \pm\sqrt{\frac{V}{\pi h}}$$

r is a radius and always positive.

$$r = \sqrt{\frac{V}{\pi h}} = \frac{\sqrt{V}}{\sqrt{\pi h}} \bullet \frac{\sqrt{\pi h}}{\sqrt{\pi h}} = \frac{\sqrt{\pi V h}}{\pi h}$$

33. $$F = \frac{mv^2}{r}$$

$$Fr = mv^2$$

$$\frac{Fr}{m} = v^2$$

$$v = \pm\sqrt{\frac{Fr}{m}} = \pm\frac{\sqrt{Fr}}{\sqrt{m}} \bullet \frac{\sqrt{m}}{\sqrt{m}} = \pm\frac{\sqrt{Frm}}{m}$$

35. $$x^2 - 12x + \left[\left(\frac{-12}{2}\right)^2\right] = x^2 - 12x + 36$$

37. $$n^2 + 7n + \left[\left(\frac{7}{2}\right)^2\right] = n^2 + 7n + \frac{49}{4}$$

39. $$t^2 - \frac{4}{3}t + \left[\left(\frac{1}{2} \bullet \frac{-4}{3}\right)^2\right] = t^2 - \frac{4}{3}t + \left[\left(\frac{-2}{3}\right)^2\right] =$$

$$t^2 - \frac{4}{3}t + \frac{4}{9}$$

41. $$x^2 - 8x + \left(\frac{1}{2} \bullet 8\right)^2 = 0 + \left(\frac{1}{2} \bullet 8\right)^2$$

$$x^2 - 8x + 16 = 16$$

$$(x-4)^2 = 16$$

$$x - 4 = \pm\sqrt{16}$$

$$x - 4 = \pm 4$$

$$x = 4 \pm 4$$

$$x = 0, \ x = 8$$

43. $$n^2 - 3n = 4$$

$$n^2 - 3n + \left(\frac{-3}{2}\right)^2 = 4 + \left(\frac{-3}{2}\right)^2$$

$$n^2 - 3n + \frac{9}{4} = \frac{16}{4} + \frac{9}{4}$$

$$\left(n - \frac{3}{2}\right)^2 = \frac{25}{4}$$

$$n - \frac{3}{2} = \pm\sqrt{\frac{25}{4}}$$

$$n - \frac{3}{2} = \pm\frac{5}{2}$$

$$n = \frac{3}{2} \pm \frac{5}{2}$$

$$n = 4, \ n = -1$$

45. $$x^2 + 4x - 2 = 0$$

$$x^2 + 4x = 2$$

$$x^2 + 4x + \left(\frac{4}{2}\right)^2 = 2 + \left(\frac{4}{2}\right)^2$$

$$x^2 + 4x + 4 = 2 + 4$$

$$(x+2)^2 = 6$$

$$x + 2 = \pm\sqrt{6}$$

$$x = -2 \pm \sqrt{6}$$

$$x = -2 + \sqrt{6}, \ x = -2 - \sqrt{6}$$

47. $$a^2 + 7a = 3a - 4$$

$$a^2 + 4a = -4$$

$$a^2 + 4a + \left(\frac{4}{2}\right)^2 = -4 + \left(\frac{4}{2}\right)^2$$

$$a^2 + 4a + 4 = -4 + 4$$

$$(a+2)^2 = 0$$

$$a + 2 = \pm\sqrt{0}$$

$$a = -2$$

49. $$x^2 - 9x + 4 = x - 25$$

$$x^2 - 10x = -29$$

$$x^2 - 10x + \left(\frac{-10}{2}\right)^2 = -29 + \left(\frac{-10}{2}\right)^2$$

$$x^2 - 10x + 25 = -29 + 25$$

$$(x-5)^2 = -4$$

$$x - 5 = \pm\sqrt{-4}$$

$$x = 5 \pm 2i$$

$$x = 5 + 2i, \ x = 5 - 2i$$

51. $$2n^2 - 8n = -24$$

$$2(n^2 - 4n) = 2(-12)$$

$$n^2 - 4n = -12$$

$$n^2 - 4n + \left(\frac{-4}{2}\right)^2 = -12 + \left(\frac{-4}{2}\right)^2$$

$$n^2 - 4n + 4 = -12 + 4$$

$$(n-2)^2 = -8$$

$$n - 2 = \pm\sqrt{-8}$$

$$n = 2 \pm 2i\sqrt{2}$$

$$n = 2 + 2i\sqrt{2}, \ n = 2 - 2i\sqrt{2}$$

53. $$3x^2 - 12x - 84 = 0$$

$$3(x^2 - 4x - 28) = 0$$

$$x^2 - 4x - 28 = 0$$

$$x^2 - 4x = 28$$

$$x^2 - 4x + \left(\frac{-4}{2}\right)^2 = 28 + \left(\frac{-4}{2}\right)^2$$

$$x^2 - 4x + 4 = 28 + 4$$

$$(x-2)^2 = 32$$

$$x - 2 = \pm\sqrt{32}$$

$$x = 2 \pm 4\sqrt{2}$$

$$x = 2 + 4\sqrt{2}, \ x = 2 - 4\sqrt{2}$$

55. $$4a^2 + 20a - 12 = 0$$

$$4(a^2 + 5a - 3) = 0$$

$$a^2 + 5a - 3 = 0$$

$$a^2 + 5a = 3$$

$$a^2 + 5a + \left(\frac{5}{2}\right)^2 = 3 + \left(\frac{5}{2}\right)^2$$

$$a^2 + 5a + \frac{25}{4} = \frac{12}{4} + \frac{25}{4}$$

$$\left(a + \frac{5}{2}\right)^2 = \frac{37}{4}$$

$$a + \frac{5}{2} = \pm\sqrt{\frac{37}{4}}$$

$$a + \frac{5}{2} = \pm\frac{\sqrt{37}}{2}$$

$$a = -\frac{5}{2} \pm \frac{\sqrt{37}}{2}$$

$$a = \frac{-5 + \sqrt{37}}{2}, \ a = \frac{-5 - \sqrt{37}}{2}$$

57. $$3y^2 - 9y + 15 = 0$$

$$3(y^2 - 3y + 5) = 0$$

$$y^2 - 3y + 5 = 0$$

$$y^2 - 3y = -5$$

$$y^2 - 3y + \left(\frac{-3}{2}\right)^2 = -5 + \left(\frac{-3}{2}\right)^2$$

$$y^2 - 3y + \frac{9}{4} = \frac{-20}{4} + \frac{9}{4}$$

$$\left(y - \frac{3}{2}\right)^2 = \frac{-11}{4}$$

$$y - \frac{3}{2} = \pm\sqrt{\frac{-11}{4}}$$

$$y - \frac{3}{2} = \pm\frac{i\sqrt{11}}{2}$$

$$y = \frac{3 + i\sqrt{11}}{2}, \ y = \frac{3 - i\sqrt{11}}{2}$$

59. $$x^2 - \frac{4}{3}x - 4 = 0$$

$$x^2 - \frac{4}{3}x = 4$$

$$x^2 - \frac{4}{3}x + \left(\frac{1}{2} \bullet \frac{-4}{3}\right)^2 = 4 + \left(\frac{1}{2} \bullet \frac{-4}{3}\right)^2$$

$$x^2 - \frac{4}{3}x + \left(\frac{-2}{3}\right)^2 = 4 + \left(\frac{-2}{3}\right)^2$$

$$x^2 - \frac{4}{3}x + \frac{4}{9} = \frac{36}{9} + \frac{4}{9}$$

$$\left(x - \frac{2}{3}\right)^2 = \frac{40}{9}$$

$$x - \frac{2}{3} = \pm\sqrt{\frac{40}{9}} = \pm\frac{2\sqrt{10}}{3}$$

$$x = \frac{2}{3} \pm \frac{2\sqrt{10}}{3}$$

$$x = \frac{2 + 2\sqrt{10}}{3}, \ x = \frac{2 - 2\sqrt{10}}{3}$$

61. $$4y^2 + 11y + 6 = 0$$

$$4y^2 + 11y = -6$$

$$\frac{4y^2 + 11y}{4} = \frac{-6}{4}$$

$$y^2 + \frac{11}{4}y = \frac{-3}{2}$$

$$y^2 + \frac{11}{4}y + \left(\frac{1}{2} \bullet \frac{11}{4}\right)^2 = \frac{-3}{2} + \left(\frac{1}{2} \bullet \frac{11}{4}\right)^2$$

$$y^2 + \frac{11}{4}y + \frac{121}{64} = \frac{-3}{2} + \frac{121}{64}$$

$$\left(y + \frac{11}{8}\right)^2 = \frac{-96}{64} + \frac{121}{64}$$

$$\left(y + \frac{11}{8}\right)^2 = \frac{25}{64}$$

$$y + \frac{11}{8} = \pm\sqrt{\frac{25}{64}}$$

$$y + \frac{11}{8} = \pm\frac{5}{8}$$

$$y = -\frac{11}{8} \pm \frac{5}{8}$$

$$y = -2, \ y = -\frac{6}{8} = -\frac{3}{4}$$

63. $$2p^2 + 7p = 6p - 8$$

$$2p^2 + p = -8$$

$$\frac{2p^2 + p}{2} = \frac{-8}{2}$$

$$p^2 + \frac{1}{2}p = -4$$

$$p^2 + \frac{1}{2}p + \left(\frac{1}{2} \cdot \frac{1}{2}\right)^2 = -4 + \left(\frac{1}{2} \cdot \frac{1}{2}\right)^2$$

$$p^2 + \frac{1}{2}p + \frac{1}{16} = -\frac{64}{16} + \frac{1}{16}$$

$$\left(p + \frac{1}{4}\right)^2 = \frac{-63}{16}$$

$$p + \frac{1}{4} = \pm\sqrt{\frac{-63}{16}}$$

$$p + \frac{1}{4} = \pm\frac{3i\sqrt{7}}{4}$$

$$p = -\frac{1}{4} \pm \frac{3i\sqrt{7}}{4}$$

$$p = \frac{-1 + 3i\sqrt{7}}{4}, \quad p = \frac{-1 - 3i\sqrt{7}}{4}$$

65. $$x^2 - 9 = 4x - 6$$

$$x^2 - 4x = 3$$

$$x^2 - 4x + \left(\frac{-4}{2}\right)^2 = 3 + \left(\frac{-4}{2}\right)^2$$

$$x^2 - 4x + 4 = 3 + 4$$

$$(x - 2)^2 = 7$$

$$x - 2 = \pm\sqrt{7}$$

$$x = +2 + \sqrt{7}, \quad x = +2 - \sqrt{7}$$

67. $$4x^2 = x^2 - 6x + 6$$

$$3x^2 + 6x - 6 = 0$$

$$3(x^2 + 2x - 2) = 0$$

$$x^2 + 2x - 2 = 0$$

$$x^2 + 2x = 2$$

$$x^2 + 2x + \left(\frac{2}{2}\right)^2 = 2 + \left(\frac{2}{2}\right)^2$$

$$x^2 + 2x + 1 = 2 + 1$$

$$(x + 1)^2 = 3$$

$$x + 1 = \pm\sqrt{3}$$

$$x = -1 + \sqrt{3}, \quad x = -1 - \sqrt{3}$$

69. $$A = \pi r^2$$

$$78.5 = 3.14 r^2$$

$$r^2 = \frac{78.5}{3.14} = 25$$

$$r = \pm\sqrt{25}$$

$$r = 5, \quad r = -5$$

The negative answer makes no sense in this problem. The team is searching 5 mi from the last know location of the hikers.

71. $$1102.50 = 1000(1 + r)^2$$

$$(1 + r)^2 = \frac{1102.50}{1000}$$

$$(1 + r)^2 = 1.1025$$

$$1 + r = \pm\sqrt{1.1025}$$

$$1 + r = \pm 1.05$$

$$r = -1 \pm 1.05$$

$$r = -2.05, \quad r = 0.05$$

The negative answer makes no sense on this problem. The interest rate is 5%.

73. a. $$1000 = -16t^2 + 2000$$

$$-16t^2 + 2000 = 1000$$

$$-16t^2 = -1000$$

$$t^2 = \frac{1000}{16}$$

$$t = \sqrt{\frac{1000}{16}} = \frac{10\sqrt{10}}{4} = \frac{5\sqrt{10}}{2} = 7.9056\ldots$$

The sandbag will be 1000 ft above the ground in approximately 7.9 sec after it is dropped.

b. $$h = -16(2 \bullet 7.9)^2 + 2000 = -1994.24 \ne 0$$

$$0 = -16t^2 + 2000$$

$$16t^2 = 2000$$

$$t^2 = \frac{2000}{16}$$

$$t = \sqrt{\frac{2000}{16}} = \frac{20\sqrt{5}}{4} = 5\sqrt{5} = 11.1803\ldots$$

No, the sandbag will reach the ground in approximately 11.2 sec which is not equal to 2(7.9) or about 15.8 sec.

75. a. $$A = lw, \quad l = w + 10$$

$$A = (w + 10)w$$

$$144 = w^2 + 10w$$

$$w^2 + 10w = 144$$

$$w^2 + 10w + \left(\frac{10}{2}\right)^2 = 144 + \left(\frac{10}{2}\right)^2$$

$$w^2 + 10w + 25 = 144 + 25$$

$$(w + 5)^2 = 169$$

$$w + 5 = \pm\sqrt{169}$$

$$w = -5 \pm 13$$

$$w = 8, \quad w = -18$$

The negative answer makes no sense in this problem. The width is 8 ft. and the length is 8 + 10 or 18 ft.

b. Fencing $$= 2w + l = 2(8) + 18 = 34\text{ft.}$$

cost $$= 34(14.95) = 508.30$$

It will cost $508.30 to enclose the patio.

Exercises 8.2 Solving Quadratic Equations by Using the Quadratic Formula

1. $x^2 + 3x + 2 = 0$

$a = 1 \qquad b = 3 \qquad c = 2$

$x = \dfrac{-(3) \pm \sqrt{(3)^2 - 4(1)(2)}}{2(1)} = \dfrac{-3 \pm \sqrt{9-8}}{2} =$

$x = \dfrac{-3 \pm \sqrt{1}}{2} = \dfrac{-3 \pm 1}{2}$

$x = -2,\ x = -1$

3. $x^2 - 6x - 1 = 0$

$a = 1 \qquad b = -6 \qquad c = -1$

$x = \dfrac{-(-6) \pm \sqrt{(-6)^2 - 4(1)(-1)}}{2(1)}$

$x = \dfrac{6 \pm \sqrt{36+4}}{2} = \dfrac{6 \pm \sqrt{40}}{2} = \dfrac{6 \pm 2\sqrt{10}}{2}$

$x = 3 \pm \sqrt{10}$

$x = 3 + \sqrt{10},\ x = 3 - \sqrt{10}$

5. $x^2 = x + 11$

$x^2 - x - 11 = 0$

$a = 1 \qquad b = -1 \qquad c = -11$

$x = \dfrac{-(-1) \pm \sqrt{(-1)^2 - 4(1)(-11)}}{2(1)}$

$x = \dfrac{1 \pm \sqrt{1+44}}{2} = \dfrac{1 \pm \sqrt{45}}{2} = \dfrac{1 \pm 3\sqrt{5}}{2}$

$x = \dfrac{1 + 3\sqrt{5}}{2},\ x = \dfrac{1 - 3\sqrt{5}}{2}$

7. $x^2 - 4x + 13 = 8$

$x^2 - 4x + 5 = 0$

$a = 1 \qquad b = -4 \qquad c = 5$

$x = \dfrac{-(-4) \pm \sqrt{(-4)^2 - 4(1)(5)}}{2(1)}$

$x = \dfrac{4 \pm \sqrt{16-20}}{2} = \dfrac{4 \pm \sqrt{-4}}{2} = \dfrac{4 \pm 2i}{2}$

$x = 2 + i,\ x = 2 - i$

9. $3x^2 + 6x = 7$

$3x^2 + 6x - 7 = 0$

$a = 3 \qquad b = 6 \qquad c = -7$

$x = \dfrac{-(6) \pm \sqrt{(6)^2 - 4(3)(-7)}}{2(3)}$

$x = \dfrac{-6 \pm \sqrt{36+84}}{6} = \dfrac{-6 \pm \sqrt{120}}{6} = \dfrac{-6 \pm 2\sqrt{30}}{6}$

$x = \dfrac{2\left(-3 \pm \sqrt{30}\right)}{6}$

$x = \dfrac{-3 + \sqrt{30}}{3},\ x = \dfrac{-3 - \sqrt{30}}{3}$

11. $6t^2 - 8t = 3t - 4$

$6t^2 - 11t + 4 = 0$

$a = 6 \qquad b = -11 \qquad c = 4$

$t = \dfrac{-(-11) \pm \sqrt{(-11)^2 - 4(6)(4)}}{2(6)}$

$t = \dfrac{11 \pm \sqrt{121-96}}{12} = \dfrac{11 \pm \sqrt{25}}{12} = \dfrac{11 \pm 5}{12}$

$t = \dfrac{16}{12} = \dfrac{4}{3},\quad t = \dfrac{6}{12} = \dfrac{1}{2}$

13. $2x^2 + 8x + 9 = 0$

$a = 2 \qquad b = 8 \qquad c = 9$

$x = \dfrac{-(8) \pm \sqrt{(8)^2 - 4(2)(9)}}{2(2)}$

$x = \dfrac{-8 \pm \sqrt{64-72}}{4} = \dfrac{-8 \pm \sqrt{-8}}{4}$

$x = \dfrac{-8 \pm 2i\sqrt{2}}{4} = \dfrac{2\left(-4 \pm i\sqrt{2}\right)}{4}$

$x = \dfrac{-4 + i\sqrt{2}}{2},\ x = \dfrac{-4 - i\sqrt{2}}{2}$

15. $1 - 5x^2 = 4x^2 + 6x$

$-9x^2 - 6x + 1 = 0$

$a = -9 \qquad b = -6 \qquad c = 1$

$x = \dfrac{-(-6) \pm \sqrt{(-6)^2 - 4(-9)(1)}}{2(-9)}$

$x = \dfrac{6 \pm \sqrt{36+36}}{-18} = \dfrac{6 \pm \sqrt{72}}{-18} = \dfrac{6 \pm 6\sqrt{2}}{-18}$

$x = \dfrac{6\left(1 \pm \sqrt{2}\right)}{-18} = \dfrac{-\left(1 \pm \sqrt{2}\right)}{3}$

$x = \dfrac{-1 - \sqrt{2}}{3},\ x = \dfrac{-1 + \sqrt{2}}{3}$

17. $2y^2 - 9y + 10 = 1 + 3y - 2y^2$

$4y^2 - 12y + 9 = 0$

$a = 4 \qquad b = -12 \qquad c = 9$

$y = \dfrac{-(-12) \pm \sqrt{(-12)^2 - 4(4)(9)}}{2(4)} =$

$y = \dfrac{12 \pm \sqrt{144-144}}{8} = \dfrac{12 \pm \sqrt{0}}{8}$

$y = \dfrac{12}{8} = \dfrac{3}{2}$

19.

$$\frac{x^2}{4} - \frac{x}{2} = -3$$

$$\frac{x^2}{4} - \frac{x}{2} + 3 = 0$$

$$4\left(\frac{x^2}{4} - \frac{x}{2} + 3\right) = 4(0)$$

$$x^2 - 2x + 12 = 0$$

$$a = 1 \qquad b = -2 \qquad c = 12$$

$$x = \frac{-(-2) \pm \sqrt{(-2)^2 - 4(1)(12)}}{2(1)}$$

$$x = \frac{2 \pm \sqrt{4 - 48}}{2} = \frac{2 \pm \sqrt{-44}}{2}$$

$$x = \frac{2 \pm 2i\sqrt{11}}{2}$$

$$x = 1 + i\sqrt{11} \quad x = 1 - i\sqrt{11}$$

21.

$$\frac{1}{2}x^2 + \frac{2}{3}x - \frac{5}{6} = 0$$

$$6\left(\frac{1}{2}x^2 + \frac{2}{3}x - \frac{5}{6}\right) = 6(0)$$

$$3x^3 + 4x - 5 = 0$$

$$a = 3 \qquad b = 4 \qquad c = -5$$

$$x = \frac{-(4) \pm \sqrt{(4)^2 - 4(3)(-5)}}{2(3)}$$

$$x = \frac{-4 \pm \sqrt{16 + 60}}{6} = \frac{-4 \pm \sqrt{76}}{6}$$

$$x = \frac{-4 \pm 2\sqrt{19}}{6} = \frac{2(-2 \pm \sqrt{19})}{6}$$

$$x = \frac{-2 + \sqrt{19}}{3}, \quad x = \frac{-2 - \sqrt{19}}{3}$$

23.

$$0.2x^2 + x + 0.8 = 0$$

$$5(0.2x^2 + x + 0.8) = 5(0)$$

$$x^2 + 5x + 4 = 0$$

$$a = 1 \qquad b = 5 \qquad c = 4$$

$$x = \frac{-(5) \pm \sqrt{(5)^2 - 4(1)(4)}}{2(1)}$$

$$x = \frac{-5 \pm \sqrt{25 - 16}}{2} = \frac{-5 \pm \sqrt{9}}{2} = \frac{-5 \pm 3}{2}$$

$$x = \frac{-8}{2} = -4, \quad x = \frac{-2}{2} = -1$$

25.

$$0.03x^2 - 0.12x + 0.24 = 0$$

$$100(0.03x^2 - 0.12x + 0.24) = 100(0)$$

$$3x^2 - 12x + 24 = 0$$

$$3(x^2 - 4x + 8) = 0$$

$$x^2 - 4x + 8 = 0$$

$$a = 1 \qquad b = -4 \qquad c = 8$$

$$x = \frac{-(-4) \pm \sqrt{(-4)^2 - 4(1)(8)}}{2(1)}$$

$$x = \frac{4 \pm \sqrt{16 - 32}}{2} = \frac{4 \pm \sqrt{-16}}{2} = \frac{4 \pm 4i}{2}$$

$$x = 2 + 2i, \quad x = 2 - 2i$$

27.

$$(x + 6)(x + 2) = 8$$

$$x^2 + 8x + 12 = 8$$

$$x^2 + 8x + 4 = 0$$

$$a = 1 \qquad b = 8 \qquad c = 4$$

$$x = \frac{-(8) \pm \sqrt{(8)^2 - 4(1)(4)}}{2(1)}$$

$$x = \frac{-8 \pm \sqrt{64 - 16}}{2} = \frac{-8 \pm \sqrt{48}}{2} = \frac{-8 \pm 4\sqrt{3}}{2}$$

$$x = \frac{2(-4 \pm 2\sqrt{3})}{2} = -4 \pm 2\sqrt{3}$$

$$x = -4 + 2\sqrt{3}, \quad x = -4 - 2\sqrt{3}$$

29.

$$(2x - 3)^2 = 8(x + 1)$$

$$4x^2 - 12x + 9 = 8x + 8$$

$$4x^2 - 20x + 1 = 0$$

$$a = 4 \qquad b = -20 \qquad c = 1$$

$$x = \frac{-(-20) \pm \sqrt{(-20)^2 - 4(4)(1)}}{2(4)}$$

$$x = \frac{20 \pm \sqrt{400 - 16}}{8} = \frac{20 \pm \sqrt{384}}{8}$$

$$x = \frac{20 \pm 8\sqrt{6}}{8} = \frac{4(5 \pm 2\sqrt{6})}{8}$$

$$x = \frac{5 + 2\sqrt{6}}{2}, \quad x = \frac{5 - 2\sqrt{6}}{2}$$

31.

$$1.4x^2 - 2.7x - 0.1 = 0$$

$$a = 1.4 \qquad b = -2.7 \qquad c = -0.1$$

$$x = \frac{-(-2.7) \pm \sqrt{(-2.7)^2 - 4(1.4)(-0.1)}}{2(1.4)}$$

$$x = \frac{2.7 \pm \sqrt{7.29 + 0.56}}{2.8} = \frac{2.7 \pm \sqrt{7.85}}{2.8}$$

$$x = \frac{2.7 \pm 2.8017...}{2.8}$$

$$x = 1.9649... \approx 1.965$$

$$x = -0.03635... \approx -0.036$$

33.

$$0.003x^2 + 0.23x + 1.124 = 0$$

$$a = 0.003 \qquad b = 0.23 \qquad c = 1.124$$

$$x = \frac{-(0.23) \pm \sqrt{(0.23)^2 - 4(0.003)(1.124)}}{2(0.003)}$$

$$x = \frac{-0.23 \pm \sqrt{0.0529 - 0.013488}}{0.006}$$

$$x = \frac{-0.23 \pm \sqrt{0.039412}}{0.006}$$

$$x = \frac{-0.23 \pm 0.198524....}{0.006}$$

$$x = -5.2459... \approx -5.246$$

$$x = -71.4207... \approx -71.421$$

35. $x^2 + 2x + 4 = 0$

$a = 1 \qquad b = 2 \qquad c = 4$

$(2)^2 - 4(1)(4) = 4 - 16 = -12$

Two complex solutions (containing i).

37. $4x^2 - 12x = -9$

$4x^2 - 12x + 9 = 0$

$a = 4 \qquad b = -12 \qquad c = 9$

$(-12)^2 - 4(4)(9) = 144 - 144 = 0$

One real solution.

39. $6x^2 = 2 - 5x$

$6x^2 + 5x - 2 = 0$

$a = 6 \qquad b = 5 \qquad c = -2$

$(5)^2 - 4(6)(-2) = 25 + 48 = 73$

Two real solutions.

41. $7x^2 - x + 3 = 0$

$a = 7 \qquad b = -1 \qquad c = 3$

$(-1)^2 - 4(7)(3) = 1 - 84 = -83$

Two complex solutions (containing i).

43. $3x^2 + 10 = 0$

$3x^2 + 0x + 10 = 0$

$a = 3 \qquad b = 0 \qquad c = 10$

$(0)^2 - 4(3)(10) = -120$

Two complex solutions (containing i).

45. $300 = -16t^2 - 20t + 800$

$16t^2 + 20t - 500 = 0$

$4(4t^2 + 5t - 125) = 0$

$4t^2 + 5t - 125 = 0$

$a = 4 \qquad b = 5 \qquad c = -125$

$$t = \frac{-(5) \pm \sqrt{(5)^2 - 4(4)(-125)}}{2(4)}$$

$$t = \frac{-5 \pm \sqrt{25 + 2000}}{8} = \frac{-5 \pm \sqrt{2025}}{8}$$

$$t = \frac{-5 \pm 45}{8}$$

$t = 5, \quad t = -6.25$

The negative answer makes no sense in this problem. The stone is 300 ft above the ground 5 sec after it is thrown downward.

47.   length $= 36 - 2x$

width $= 20 - 2x$

Area $= (36 - 2x)(20 - 2x)$

$465 = 720 - 112x + 4x^2$

$4x^2 - 112x + 255 = 0$

$a = 4 \qquad b = -112 \qquad c = 255$

$$x = \frac{-(-112) \pm \sqrt{(-112)^2 - 4(4)(255)}}{2(4)} =$$

$$x = \frac{112 \pm \sqrt{12544 - 4080}}{8} = \frac{112 \pm \sqrt{8464}}{8}$$

$$x = \frac{112 \pm 92}{8}$$

$x = 25.5, \quad x = 2.5$

25.5 in cannot be cut from 20 in and that answer is discarded. Squares measuring 2.5 in by 2.5 in should be cut from each corner.

49. $x(300 - 5x) = 3520$

$300x - 5x^2 = 3520$

$-5x^2 + 300x - 3520 = 0$

$-5(x^2 - 60x + 704) = 0$

$x^2 - 60x + 704 = 0$

$a = 1 \qquad b = -60 \qquad c = 704$

$$x = \frac{-(-60) \pm \sqrt{(-60)^2 - 4(1)(704)}}{2(1)}$$

$$x = \frac{60 \pm \sqrt{3600 - 2816}}{2}$$

$$x = \frac{60 \pm \sqrt{784}}{2} = \frac{60 \pm 28}{2}$$

$x = 16 \qquad\qquad x = 44$

$300 - 5x = \qquad 300 - 5x =$

$300 - 5(16) = \quad 300 - 5(44) =$

$220 \qquad\qquad 80$

44 tickets will have a ticket price of only $80. 16 tickets has a ticket price of $220.

The company must sell 16 tickets to generate revenue of $3520.

51. $215 = -\dfrac{1}{2}t^2 + 64t + 29$

$-\dfrac{1}{2}t^2 + 64t - 186 = 0$

$a = -\dfrac{1}{2}$ $b = 64$ $c = -186$

$t = \dfrac{-(64) \pm \sqrt{(64)^2 - 4\left(-\dfrac{1}{2}\right)(-186)}}{2\left(-\dfrac{1}{2}\right)}$

$t = \dfrac{-64 \pm \sqrt{4096 - 372}}{-1} = -\left(-64 \pm \sqrt{3724}\right)$

$t = 64 \pm 61.0245...$

$t = 2.97541...,\ \ t = 125.0245...$

The solution $x = 125$ is discarded.
There were approximately 215,000 reports of identity theft in the year 2003.

Exercises 8.3 More on Quadratic Equations

1. $\quad 2 - \dfrac{3}{x} + \dfrac{1}{x^2} = 0$

$x^2\left(2 - \dfrac{3}{x} + \dfrac{1}{x^2}\right) = x^2(0)$

$2x^2 - 3x + 1 = 0$

$(2x - 1)(x - 1) = 0$

$2x - 1 = 0 \quad x - 1 = 0$

$2x = 1 \qquad x = 1$

$x = \dfrac{1}{2}$

Check $x = \dfrac{1}{2}$

$2 - \dfrac{3}{\frac{1}{2}} + \dfrac{1}{\left(\frac{1}{2}\right)^2} \overset{?}{=} 0$

Check $x = 1$

$2 - \dfrac{3}{1} + \dfrac{1}{(1)^2} \overset{?}{=} 0$

$2 - 3\left(\dfrac{2}{1}\right) + 1\left(\dfrac{4}{1}\right) \overset{?}{=} 0$

$2 - 3 + 1 \overset{?}{=} 0$

$0 = 0$ True

$2 - 6 + 4 \overset{?}{=} 0$

$0 = 0$ True

3. $\quad \dfrac{3}{p - 1} + \dfrac{4}{p - 4} = 1$

$\dfrac{3(p-1)(p-4)}{p - 1} + \dfrac{4(p-1)(p-4)}{p - 4}$
$\qquad = 1(p-1)(p-4)$

$3(p - 4) + 4(p - 1) = (p - 1)(p - 4)$

$3p - 12 + 4p - 4 = p^2 - 5p + 4$

$p^2 - 12p + 20 = 0$

$(p - 2)(p - 10) = 0$

$p - 2 = 0 \quad p - 10 = 0$

$p = 2 \qquad p = 10$

Check $p = 2$

$\dfrac{3}{2 - 1} + \dfrac{4}{2 - 4} \overset{?}{=} 1$

$\dfrac{3}{1} + \dfrac{4}{-2} \overset{?}{=} 1$

$3 - 2 \overset{?}{=} 1$

$1 = 1$ True

Check $p = 10$

$\dfrac{3}{10 - 1} + \dfrac{4}{10 - 4} \overset{?}{=} 1$

$\dfrac{3}{9} + \dfrac{4}{6} \overset{?}{=} 1$

$\dfrac{1}{3} + \dfrac{2}{3} \overset{?}{=} 1$

$1 = 1$ True

5. $\quad$ Let $u = n^2$

$\left(n^2\right)^2 - 8\left(n^2\right) + 12 = 0$

$u^2 - 8u + 12 = 0$

$(u - 6)(u - 2) = 0$

$u - 6 = 0 \quad u - 2 = 0$

$u = 6 \qquad u = 2$

$n^2 = 6 \qquad n^2 = 2$

$n = \pm\sqrt{6} \quad n = \pm\sqrt{2}$

Check $n = \sqrt{6}$

$\left(\sqrt{6}\right)^4 - 8\left(\sqrt{6}\right)^2$
$\qquad + 12 \overset{?}{=} 0$

$36 - 8(6) + 12 \overset{?}{=} 0$

$36 - 48 + 12 \overset{?}{=} 0$

$0 = 0$ True

Check $n = -\sqrt{6}$

$\left(-\sqrt{6}\right)^4 - 8\left(-\sqrt{6}\right)^2$
$\qquad + 12 \overset{?}{=} 0$

$36 - 8(6) + 12 \overset{?}{=} 0$

$36 - 48 + 12 \overset{?}{=} 0$

$0 = 0$ True

Check $n = \sqrt{2}$

$\left(\sqrt{2}\right)^4 - 8\left(\sqrt{2}\right)^2 + 12 \overset{?}{=} 0$

$4 - 8(2) + 12 \overset{?}{=} 0$

$4 - 16 + 12 \overset{?}{=} 0$

$0 = 0$ True

Check $n = -\sqrt{2}$

$\left(-\sqrt{2}\right)^4 - 8\left(-\sqrt{2}\right)^2 + 12 \overset{?}{=} 0$

$4 - 8(2) + 12 \overset{?}{=} 0$

$4 - 16 + 12 \overset{?}{=} 0$

$0 = 0$ True

7. $\quad 3x^4 + 11x^2 - 3 = -x^4$

$4x^4 + 11x^2 - 3 = 0$

Let $u = x^2$

$4\left(x^2\right)^2 + 11\left(x^2\right) - 3 = 0$

$4u^2 + 11u - 3 = 0$

$(4u - 1)(u + 3) = 0$

$4u - 1 = 0 \quad u + 3 = 0$

$4u = 1 \qquad u = -3$

$u = \dfrac{1}{4}$

$x^2 = \dfrac{1}{4} \qquad x^2 = -3$

$x = \pm\sqrt{\dfrac{1}{4}}$ $\quad x = \pm\sqrt{-3}$

$\qquad\qquad\quad\ x = \pm i\sqrt{3}$

$$x = \pm\frac{1}{2}$$

Check $x = \frac{1}{2}$

$$3\left(\frac{1}{2}\right)^4 + 11\left(\frac{1}{2}\right)^2 - 3 \overset{?}{=} -\left(\frac{1}{2}\right)^4$$

$$\frac{3}{16} + \frac{11}{4} - 3 \overset{?}{=} -\frac{1}{16}$$

$$\frac{3}{16} + \frac{44}{16} - \frac{48}{16} \overset{?}{=} -\frac{1}{16}$$

$$-\frac{1}{16} = -\frac{1}{16} \text{ True}$$

Check $x = -\frac{1}{2}$

$$3\left(-\frac{1}{2}\right)^4 + 11\left(-\frac{1}{2}\right)^2 - 3 \overset{?}{=} -\left(-\frac{1}{2}\right)^4$$

$$\frac{3}{16} + \frac{11}{4} - 3 \overset{?}{=} -\frac{1}{16}$$

$$\frac{3}{16} + \frac{44}{16} - \frac{48}{16} \overset{?}{=} -\frac{1}{16}$$

$$-\frac{1}{16} = -\frac{1}{16} \text{ True}$$

Check $x = i\sqrt{3}$

$$3\left(i\sqrt{3}\right)^4 + 11\left(i\sqrt{3}\right)^2 - 3 \overset{?}{=} -\left(i\sqrt{3}\right)^4$$

$$3\left(9i^4\right) + 11\left(3i^2\right) - 3 \overset{?}{=} -\left(9i^4\right)$$

$$27 - 33 - 3 \overset{?}{=} -9$$

$$-9 = -9 \text{ True}$$

Check $x = -i\sqrt{3}$

$$3\left(-i\sqrt{3}\right)^4 + 11\left(-i\sqrt{3}\right)^2 - 3 \overset{?}{=} -\left(-i\sqrt{3}\right)^4$$

$$3\left(9i^4\right) + 11\left(3i^2\right) - 3 \overset{?}{=} -\left(9i^4\right)$$

$$27 - 33 - 3 \overset{?}{=} -9$$

$$-9 = -9 \text{ True}$$

9. Let $u = \sqrt{h}$

$$\left(\sqrt{h}\right)^2 - 4\left(\sqrt{h}\right) + 4 = 0$$

$$u^2 - 4u + 4 = 0$$

$$(u-2)^2 = 0$$

$$u - 2 = 0$$

$$u = 2 \qquad \text{Check } h = 4$$

$$2 = \sqrt{h} \qquad 4 - 4\sqrt{4} + 4 \overset{?}{=} 0$$

$$2^2 = \left(\sqrt{h}\right)^2 \qquad 4 - 8 + 4 \overset{?}{=} 0$$

$$h = 4 \qquad 0 = 0 \text{ True}$$

11. Let $u = x^{\frac{1}{4}}$

$$\left(x^{\frac{1}{4}}\right)^2 + 4\left(x^{\frac{1}{4}}\right) - 32 = 0$$

$$u^2 + 4u - 32 = 0$$

$$(u-4)(u+8) = 0$$

$$u - 4 = 0 \quad u + 8 = 0$$

$$u = 4 \qquad u = -8$$

$$x^{\frac{1}{4}} = 4 \qquad x^{\frac{1}{4}} = -8$$

$$x = (4)^4 \quad x = (-8)^4$$

$$x = 256 \quad x = 4096$$

Check $x = 256$

$$256^{\frac{1}{2}} + 4(256)^{\frac{1}{4}} - 32 \overset{?}{=} 0$$

$$16 + 4(4) - 32 \overset{?}{=} 0$$

$$16 + 16 - 32 \overset{?}{=} 0$$

$$0 = 0 \text{ True}$$

Check $x = 4096$

$$4096^{\frac{1}{2}} + 4(4096)^{\frac{1}{4}} - 32 \overset{?}{=} 0$$

$$64 + 4(8) - 32 \overset{?}{=} 0$$

$$64 + 32 - 32 \overset{?}{=} 0$$

$$64 = 0 \text{ False}$$

$x = 4096$ is not a solution.

13. Let $u = t^{\frac{1}{3}}$

$$\left(t^{\frac{1}{3}}\right)^2 + 3\left(t^{\frac{1}{3}}\right) + 2 = 0$$

$$u^2 + 3u + 2 = 0 \qquad t^{\frac{1}{3}} = -2 \quad t^{\frac{1}{3}} = -1$$

$$(u+2)(u+1) = 0 \qquad t = (-2)^3 \quad t = (-1)^3$$

$$u + 2 = 0 \quad u + 1 = 0 \qquad t = -8 \qquad t = -1$$

$$u = -2 \qquad u = -1$$

Check $t = -8$ $\qquad\qquad$ Check $t = -1$

$$(-8)^{\frac{2}{3}} + 3(-8)^{\frac{1}{3}} + 2 \overset{?}{=} 0 \quad (-1)^{\frac{2}{3}} + 3(-1)^{\frac{1}{3}} + 2 \overset{?}{=} 0$$

$$(-2)^2 + 3(-2) + 2 \overset{?}{=} 0 \quad (-1)^2 + 3(-1) + 2 \overset{?}{=} 0$$

$$4 - 6 + 2 \overset{?}{=} 0 \qquad\qquad 1 - 3 + 2 \overset{?}{=} 0$$

$$0 = 0 \text{ True} \qquad\qquad 0 = 0 \text{ True}$$

15. Let $u = n - 3$

$$(n-3)^2 - 5(n-3) + 6 = 0$$

$$u^2 - 5u + 6 = 0$$

$$(u-3)(u-2) = 0$$

$u-3=0 \quad u-2=0$

$u=3 \qquad u=2$

$n-3=3 \quad n-3=2$

$n=6 \qquad n=5$

Check $n=6$ $\qquad$ Check $n=5$

$(6-3)^2-5(6-3)+6\overset{?}{=}0 \quad (5-3)^2-5(5-3)+6\overset{?}{=}0$

$3^2-5(3)+6\overset{?}{=}0 \qquad 2^2-5(2)+6\overset{?}{=}0$

$9-15+6\overset{?}{=}0 \qquad 4-10+6\overset{?}{=}0$

$0=0$ True $\qquad 0=0$ True

17. Let $u=\sqrt{2x+4}$

$\left(\sqrt{2x+4}\right)^2+2\left(\sqrt{2x+4}\right)=24$

$u^2+2u=24$

$u^2+2u-24=0$

$(u+6)(u-4)=0$

$u+6=0 \quad u-4=0$

$u=-6 \qquad u=4$

$\sqrt{2x+4}=-6 \qquad \sqrt{2x+4}=4$

$\left(\sqrt{2x+4}\right)^2=(-6)^2 \quad \left(\sqrt{2x+4}\right)^2=4^2$

$2x+4=36 \qquad 2x+4=16$

$2x=32 \qquad 2x=12$

$x=16 \qquad x=6$

$\qquad$ Check $x=16$

$(2\bullet16+4)+2\sqrt{2\bullet16+4}\overset{?}{=}24$

$(36)+2\sqrt{36}\overset{?}{=}24$

$36+12\overset{?}{=}24$

$48=24$ False

$x=16$ is not a solution

Check $x=6$

$(2\bullet6+4)+2\sqrt{2\bullet6+4}\overset{?}{=}24$

$(16)+2\sqrt{16}\overset{?}{=}24$

$16+8\overset{?}{=}24$

$24=24$ True

19. $x=7 \qquad x=2$

$x-7=0 \quad x-2=0$

$(x-7)(x-2)=0$

$x^2=9x+14=0$

21. $y=-4 \qquad y=9$

$y+4=0 \quad y-9=0$

$(y+4)(y-9)=0$

$y^2-5y-36=0$

23. $t=\dfrac{2}{3} \qquad t=-2$

$3t=2 \qquad\quad t+2=0$

$3t-2=0$

$(3t-2)(t+2)=0$

$3t^2+4t-4=0$

25. $n=-\dfrac{3}{2} \quad n=-\dfrac{4}{3}$

$2n=-3 \qquad 3n=-4$

$2n+3=0 \quad 3n+4=0$

$(2n+3)(3n+4)=0$

$6n^2+17n+12=0$

27. $x=4$

$x-4=0$

$(x-4)^2=0$

$x^2-8x+16=0$

29. $t=\sqrt{2} \qquad t=-\sqrt{2}$

$t-\sqrt{2}=0 \quad t+\sqrt{2}=0$

$\left(t-\sqrt{2}\right)\left(t+\sqrt{2}\right)=0$

$t^2-2=0$

31. $x=3i \qquad x=-3i$

$x-3i=0 \quad x+3i=0$

$(x-3i)(x+3i)=0$

$x^2-9i^2=0$

$x^2+9=0$

33. $BMI=\dfrac{W}{H^2}$

$20=\dfrac{52}{H^2}$

$20H^2=52$

$H^2=\dfrac{52}{20}=2.6$

$H=\sqrt{2.6}=1.61245...$

The person's height is approximately 1.6 m.

35. $\text{time}=\dfrac{\text{distance}}{\text{rate}}$

Time going to work + time going home = 1

$\dfrac{15}{r}+\dfrac{15}{r-8}=1$

$\dfrac{15}{r}\bullet(r)(r-8)+\dfrac{15}{r-8}\bullet(r)(r-8)=1\bullet(r)(r-8)$

$15(r-8)+15(r)=r^2-8r$

$15r-120+15r=r^2-8r$

$r^2-38r+120=0$

$$a = 1 \qquad b = -38 \qquad c = 120$$

$$r = \frac{-(-38) \pm \sqrt{(-38)^2 - 4(1)(120)}}{2(1)}$$

$$r = \frac{38 \pm \sqrt{1444 - 480}}{2} = \frac{38 \pm \sqrt{964}}{2}$$

$$r = \frac{38 \pm 2\sqrt{241}}{2} = 19 \pm \sqrt{241} = 19 \pm 15.5241...$$

$$r = 34.5241... , \quad r = 3.4758...$$

$$r - 8 = 26.5241... , \quad r - 8 = -4.5241...$$

The negative answer makes no sense in this problem. She drives to work at an average speed of about 35 mph and she drives home at an average speed of about 27 mph.

37. Let L equal the time the large pipe takes to empty the pool alone.

$$\text{time} = \frac{\text{work}}{\text{rate}}$$

Work done by large pipe in one hour + the work done by the small pipe in one hour = work done in one hour by both pipes.

	Rate of work	Time Worked	Part of Task
Large pipe	$\dfrac{1}{L}$	1	$\dfrac{1}{L}$
small pipe	$\dfrac{1}{L+1.5}$	1	$\dfrac{1}{L+1.5}$

$$\frac{1}{L} + \frac{1}{L+1.5} = \frac{1}{2}$$

$$\frac{1}{L} \bullet 2L(L+1.5) + \frac{1}{L+1.5} \bullet 2L(L+1.5)$$

$$= \frac{1}{2} \bullet 2L(L+1.5)$$

$$2(1.5+L) + 2L = L^2 + 1.5L$$

$$3 + 2L + 2L = L^2 + 1.5L$$

$$L^2 - 2.5L - 3 = 0$$

$$a = 1 \qquad b = -2.5 \qquad c = -3$$

$$L = \frac{-(-2.5) \pm \sqrt{(-2.5)^2 - 4(1)(-3)}}{2(1)}$$

$$L = \frac{2.5 \pm \sqrt{6.25 + 12}}{2} = \frac{2.5 \pm \sqrt{18.25}}{2}$$

$$L = \frac{2.5 \pm 4.27200...}{2}$$

$$L = 3.38600... , \quad L = -0.88600...$$

$$L + 1.5 = 3.38600... + 1.5 = 4.88600...$$

The negative answer makes no sense in this problem. If only one drain is open, it takes the large drain 3.4 hour and the small drain 4.9 hr to empty the pool.

Exercises 8.4 Graphing Quadratic Functions

1.

x	$y = f(x) = 2x^2$	(x, y)
-2	$2(-2)^2 = 8$	$(-2, 8)$
-1	$2(-1)^2 = 2$	$(-1, 2)$
0	$2(0)^2 = 0$	$(0, 0)$
1	$2(1)^2 = 2$	$(1, 2)$
2	$2(2)^2 = 8$	$(2, 8)$

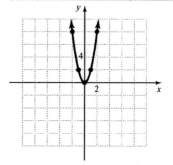

3.

x	$y = f(x) = \dfrac{1}{2}x^2$	(x, y)
-4	$\dfrac{1}{2}(-4)^2 = 8$	$(-4, 8)$
-2	$\dfrac{1}{2}(-2)^2 = 2$	$(-2, 2)$
0	$\dfrac{1}{2}(0)^2 = 0$	$(0, 0)$
2	$\dfrac{1}{2}(2)^2 = 2$	$(2, 2)$
4	$\dfrac{1}{2}(4)^2 = 8$	$(4, 8)$

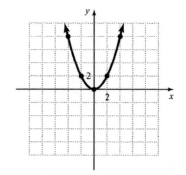

5.

x	$f(x) = 2 - x^2$	(x, y)
-3	$2 - (-3)^2 = -7$	$(-3, -7)$
-2	$2 - (-2)^2 = -2$	$(-2, -2)$
-1	$2 - (-1)^2 = -1$	$(-1, -1)$
0	$2 - (0)^2 = 2$	$(0, 2)$
1	$2 - (1)^2 = 1$	$(1, 1)$
2	$2 - (2)^2 = -2$	$(2, -2)$
3	$2 - (3)^2 = -7$	$(3, -7)$

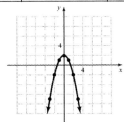

7. $f(x) = x^2 - 8x$

$a = 1 \qquad b = -8$

$-\dfrac{b}{2a} = -\dfrac{-8}{2(1)} = 4$

$f(4) = (4)^2 - 8(4) = -16$

Vertex: $(4, -16)$

Axis of symmetry: $x = 4$

$f(0) = (0)^2 - 8(0) = 0$

y-intercept: $(0, 0)$

$x^2 - 8x = 0$

$x(x - 8) = 0$

$x = 0 \quad x - 8 = 0$

$\qquad\qquad x = 8$

x-intercepts: $(0,0)$ and $(8,0)$

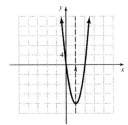

9. $f(x) = x^2 - 2x - 3$

$a = 1 \qquad b = -2$

$-\dfrac{b}{2a} = -\dfrac{-2}{2(1)} = 1$

$f(1) = (1)^2 - 2(1) - 3 = -4$

Vertex: $(1, -4)$

Axis of symmetry: $x = 1$

$x^2 - 2x - 3 = 0$

$(x - 3)(x + 1) = 0$

$x - 3 = 0 \quad x + 1 = 0$

$x = 3 \qquad x = -1$

x-intercepts: $(-1, 0)$ and $(3, 0)$

$f(0) = (0)^2 - 2(0) - 3 = -3$

y-intercept: $(0, -3)$

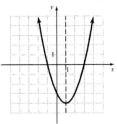

11. $f(x) = -x^2 + 4x + 12$

$a = 1 \qquad b = 4$

$-\dfrac{b}{2a} = -\dfrac{4}{2(-1)} = 2$

$f(2) = -(2)^2 + 4(2) + 12 = 16$

Vertex: $(2, 16)$

Axis of symmetry: $x = 2$

$f(0) = -(0)^2 + 4(0) + 12 = 12$

y-intercept: $(0, 12)$

$-x^2 + 4x + 12 = 0$

$(x + 2)(-x + 6) = 0$

$x + 2 = 0 \quad -x + 6 = 0$

$x = -2 \qquad x = 6$

x-intercepts: $(-2, 0)$ and $(6, 0)$

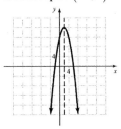

13. $f(x) = x^2 - 1$

$a = 1 \qquad b = 0$

$-\dfrac{b}{2a} = -\dfrac{0}{2(1)} = 0$

$f(0) = (0)^2 - 1 = -1$

Vertex: $(0, -1)$

Axis of symmetry: $x = 0$

$f(0) = (0)^2 - 1 = -1$

y-intercept: $(0,-1)$

$x^2-1=0$

$(x+1)(x-1)=0$

$x+1=0 \quad x-1=0$

$x=-1 \qquad x=1$

x-intercepts: $(-1,0)$ and $(1,0)$

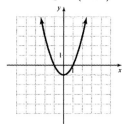

$-x^2+6x-9=0$

$x^2-6x+9=0$

$(x-3)^2=0$

$x-3=\pm\sqrt{0}=0$

$x=3$

x-intercept: $(3,0)$

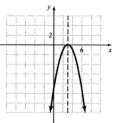

15. $f(x)=(x+1)^2$

$f(x)=x^2+2x+1$

$a=1 \quad b=2$

$-\dfrac{b}{2a}=-\dfrac{2}{2(1)}=-1$

$f(-1)=(-1+1)^2=0$

Vertex: $(-1,0)$

Axis of symmetry: $x=-1$

$(x+1)^2=0$

$x+1=\sqrt{0}=0$

$x=-1$

x-intercept: $(-1,0)$

$f(0)=(0+1)^2=1$

y-intercept: $(0,1)$

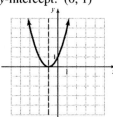

17. $f(x)=-x^2+6x-9$

$a=-1 \quad b=6$

$-\dfrac{b}{2a}=-\dfrac{6}{2(-1)}=3$

$f(3)=-(3)^2+6(3)-9=0$

Vertex: $(3,0)$

Axis of symmetry: $x=3$

$f(0)=-(0)^2+6(0)-9=-9$

y-intercept: $(0,-9)$

19. $f(x)=x^2-3x-10$

$a=1 \quad b=-3$

$-\dfrac{b}{2a}=-\dfrac{-3}{2(1)}=\dfrac{3}{2}$

$f\left(\dfrac{3}{2}\right)=\left(\dfrac{3}{2}\right)^2-3\left(\dfrac{3}{2}\right)-10=-\dfrac{49}{4}$

Vertex: $\left(\dfrac{3}{2},-\dfrac{49}{4}\right)$

Axis of symmetry: $x=\dfrac{3}{2}$

$f(0)=(0)^2-3(0)-10=-10$

y-intercept: $(0,-10)$

$x^2-3x-10=0$

$(x-5)(x+2)=0$

$x-5=0 \quad x+2=0$

$x=5 \qquad x=-2$

x-intercepts: $(5,0)$ and $(-2,0)$

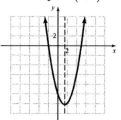

21.

Function	Opens	Maximum Minimum	Number of x-intercepts	Number of y-intercepts
$f(x) = x^2 + 5$	$a > 0$ Upward	$a > 0$ Minimum	$x^2 + 5 = 0$ $x^2 = -5$ No real solutions 0	$f(0) = 5$ 1
$f(x) = 1 - 4x + 4x^2$	$a > 0$ Upward	$a > 0$ Minimum	$b^2 - 4ac =$ $(-4)^2 - 4(4)(1) = 0$ 1	$f(0) =$ $1 - 4(0) + 4(0)^2 = 1$ 1
$f(x) = 2 - 3x^2$	$a < 0$ Downward	$a < 0$ Maximum	$b^2 - 4ac =$ $0^2 - 4(-3)(2) = 24$ Two real solutions 2	$f(0) =$ $2 - 3(0)^2 = 2$ 1
$f(x) = -2x^2 - 5x - 8$	$a < 0$ Downward	$a < 0$ Maximum	$b^2 - 4ac =$ $(-5)^2 - 4(-2)(-8) =$ -39 No real solutions 0	$f(0) =$ $-2(0)^2 - 5(0) - 8 = -8$ 1
$f(x) = 4x^2 - 4x - 1$	$a > 0$ Upward	$a > 0$ Minimum	$b^2 - 4ac =$ $(-4)^2 - 4(4)(-1) = 32$ Two real solutions 2	$f(0) =$ $4(0)^2 - 4(0) - 1 = -1$ 1

23.

x	$f(x) = 2x^2 - 1$	(x, y)
-2	$2(-2)^2 - 1 = 7$	$(-2, 7)$
-1	$2(-1)^2 - 1 = 1$	$(-1, 1)$
0	$2(0)^2 - 1 = -1$	$(0, -1)$
1	$2(1)^2 - 1 = 1$	$(1, 1)$
2	$2(2)^2 - 1 = 7$	$(2, 7)$

$-\dfrac{b}{2a} = -\dfrac{0}{2(2)} = 0 \quad f(0) = 2(0)^2 - 1 = -1$

Vertex: $(0, -1)$

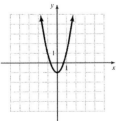

Domain: $(-\infty, \infty)$ Range: $[-1, \infty)$

25.

x	$g(x) = -3x^2 + 6x - 2$	(x, y)
-1	$-3(-1)^2 + 6(-1) - 2 = -11$	$(-1, -11)$
0	$-3(0)^2 + 6(0) - 2 = -2$	$(0, -2)$
1	$-3(1)^2 + 6(1) - 2 = 1$	$(1, 1)$
2	$-3(2)^2 + 6(2) - 2 = -2$	$(2, -2)$
3	$-3(3)^2 + 6(3) - 2 = -11$	$(3, -11)$

$-\dfrac{b}{2a} = -\dfrac{6}{2(-3)} = 1 \quad f(1) = -3(1)^2 + 6(1) - 2 = 1$

Vertex: $(1, 1)$

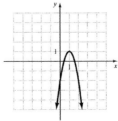

Domain: $(-\infty, \infty)$ Range: $(-\infty, 1]$

27.

x	$f(x) = 0.5x^2 + 2$	(x, y)
-2	$0.5(-2)^2 + 2 = 4$	$(-2, 4)$
-1	$0.5(-1)^2 + 2 = 2.5$	$(-1, 2.5)$
0	$0.5(0)^2 + 2 = 2$	$(0, 2)$
1	$0.5(1)^2 + 2 = 2.5$	$(1, 2.5)$
2	$0.5(2)^2 + 2 = 4$	$(2, 4)$

$$-\frac{b}{2a} = -\frac{0}{2(0.5)} = 0$$

$$f(0) = 0.5(0)^2 + 2 = 2$$

Vertex: $(0, 2)$

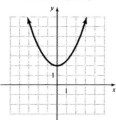

Domain: $(-\infty, \infty)$ Range: $[2, \infty)$

29.

x	$f(x) = x^2 - 3x - 4$	(x, y)
-2	$(-2)^2 - 3(-2) - 4 = 6$	$(-2, 6)$
-1	$(-1)^2 - 3(-1) - 4 = 0$	$(-1, 0)$
0	$(0)^2 - 3(0) - 4 = -4$	$(0, -4)$
1	$(1)^2 - 3(1) - 4 = -6$	$(1, -6)$
2	$(2)^2 - 3(2) - 4 = -6$	$(2, -6)$
3	$(3)^2 - 3(3) - 4 = -4$	$(3, -4)$
4	$(4)^2 - 3(4) - 4 = 0$	$(4, 0)$

$$-\frac{b}{2a} = -\frac{-3}{2(1)} = \frac{3}{2}$$

$$f\left(\frac{3}{2}\right) = \left(\frac{3}{2}\right)^2 - 3\left(\frac{3}{2}\right) - 4 = -\frac{25}{4}$$

Vertex: $\left(\frac{3}{2}, -\frac{25}{4}\right)$

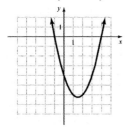

Domain: $(-\infty, \infty)$ Range: $\left[-\frac{25}{4}, \infty\right)$

31.

x	$f(x) = -2x^2 + 2x - 3$	(x, y)
-2	$-2(-2)^2 + 2(-2) - 3 = -15$	$(-2, -15)$
-1	$-2(-1)^2 + 2(-1) - 3 = -7$	$(-1, -7)$
0	$-2(0)^2 + 2(0) - 3 = -3$	$(0, -3)$
1	$-2(1)^2 + 2(1) - 3 = -3$	$(1, -3)$
2	$-2(2)^2 + 2(2) - 3 = -7$	$(2, -7)$

$$-\frac{b}{2a} = -\frac{2}{2(-2)} = \frac{1}{2}$$

$$f\left(\frac{1}{2}\right) = -2\left(\frac{1}{2}\right)^2 + 2\left(\frac{1}{2}\right) - 3 = -\frac{5}{2}$$

Vertex: $\left(\frac{1}{2}, -\frac{5}{2}\right)$

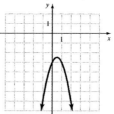

Domain: $(-\infty, \infty)$ Range: $\left(-\infty, -\frac{5}{2}\right]$

33. $f(x) = x^2 + 0.2x - 1$

Vertex: $(-0.1, 1.01)$

x-intercepts: $(-1.10, 0)$ and $(0.90, 0)$

y-intercept: $(0, -1)$

35. $f(x) = -0.15x^2 - x + 0.5$

Vertex: $(-3.33, 2.17)$

x-intercepts: $(-7.13, 0)$ and $(0.47, 0)$

y-intercept: $(0, 0.5)$

37. $f(x) = 5x^2 + 3x + 7$

Vertex: $(-0.30, 6.55)$

x-intercepts: none

y-intercept: $(0, 7)$

39.   a. $s = -16t^2 + 48t + 280$

$$-\frac{b}{2a} = -\frac{48}{2(-16)} = \frac{3}{2}$$

$$f\left(\frac{3}{2}\right) = -16\left(-\frac{3}{2}\right)^2 + 48\left(\frac{3}{2}\right) + 280 =$$

$$-16\left(\frac{9}{4}\right) + 72 + 280 = -36 + 352 = 316$$

Vertex: $\left(\frac{3}{2}, 316\right)$

b.

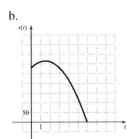

c. At $\dfrac{3}{2}$ sec (or 1.5 sec) after it is thrown, the stone reaches its maximum height of 316 ft.

41. a. $2l + 2w = 150$

$2l = 150 - 2w$

$l = \dfrac{150 - 2w}{2} = 75 - w$

b. $A = lw; \quad l = 75 - w$

$A(w) = (75 - w)w = 75w - w^2$

c.

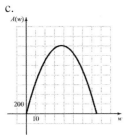

d. $-\dfrac{b}{2a} = -\dfrac{75}{2(-1)} = 37.5$

$w = A(37.5) = 75(37.5) - (37.5)^2 =$

$2812.5 - 1406.25 = 1406.25$

Vertex: $(37.5, 1406.25)$

$l = 75 - w = 75 - 37.5 = 37.5$

An exercise yard measuring 37.5 ft by 37.5 ft will produce a maximum area of 1406.25 sq ft.

43. a. $C(x) = 0.005x^2 - x + 100$

$-\dfrac{b}{2a} = -\dfrac{-1}{2(0.005)} = \dfrac{1}{0.010} = 100$

100 units must be produced in order to minimize the cost.

b. $C(100) = 0.005(100)^2 - (100) + 100 =$

$C(100) = 0.005(10000) = 50$ The minimum daily cost is $50.

Exercises 8.5 Solving Quadratic and Rational Inequalities

1. $x^2 - x > 0$

$x^2 - x = 0$

$x(x - 1) = 0$

$x = 0 \quad x - 1 = 0; \quad x = 1$

Inter-val	Test Value	$x^2 - x > 0$	Conclu-sion
$x < 0$	-5	$(-5)^2 - (-5) = 30$	$30 > 0$
$0 \le x \le 1$	$.5$	$(.5)^2 - (.5) = -.25$	$-.25 \le 0$
$1 < x$	2	$(2)^2 - (2) = 2$	$2 > 0$

$(-\infty, 0) \cup (1, \infty)$

3. $x^2 < 4$

$x^2 - 4 < 0$

$x^2 - 4 = 0$

$(x + 2)(x - 2) = 0$

$x + 2 = 0 \quad x - 2 = 0$

$x = -2 \quad\quad x = 2$

Inter-val	Test Value	$x^2 < 4$	Conclu-sion
$x \le -2$	-5	$(-5)^2 = 25$	$25 \ge 4$
$-2 < x < 2$	0	$(0)^2 = 0$	$0 < 4$
$2 \le x$	4	$(4)^2 = 16$	$16 \ge 4$

$(-2, 2)$

5. $x^2 - x - 2 \le 10$

$x^2 - x - 2 = 10$

$x^2 - x - 12 = 0$

$(x + 3)(x - 4) = 0$

$x + 3 = 0 \quad x - 4 = 0$

$x = -3 \quad\quad x = 4$

Inter-val	Test Value	$x^2 - x - 2 \le 10$	Conclu-sion
$x < 3$	-5	$(-5)^2 - (-5) - 2$ $= 28$	$28 > 0$
$-3 < x < 4$	0	$(0)^2 - (0) - 2$ $= -2$	$0 \le 10$
$4 < x$	5	$(5)^2 - (5) - 2$ $= 18$	$18 > 10$

$[-3, 4]$

7. $x^2 + 6x + 9 \ge 0$

$x^2 + 6x + 9 = 0$

$(x + 3)^2 = 0$

$x + 3 = 0$

$x = -3$

Inter-val	Test Value	$x^2+6x+9\geq 0$	Conclu-sion
$x<-3$	-5	$(-5)^2+6(-5)+9$ $=4$	$4\geq 0$
$x=-3$	-3	$(-3)^2+6(-3)+9$ $=0$	$0\geq 0$
$-3<x$	5	$(5)^2+6(5)+9$ $=64$	$64\geq 0$

$(-\infty,\infty)$

9. $6+x-x^2\leq 0$

$x^2-x-6\geq 0$

$x^2-x-6=0$

$(x-3)(x+2)=0$

$x-3=0 \quad x+2=0$

$x=3 \qquad x=-2$

Inter-val	Test Value	$6+x-x^2\leq 0$	Conclu-sion
$x\leq -2$	-3	$6+(-3)-(-3)^2$ $=-6$	$-6\leq 0$
$-2<x<3$	0	$6+(0)-(0)^2$ $=6$	$6>0$
$3\leq x$	6	$6+(4)-(4)^2$ $=-6$	$-6\leq 0$

$(-\infty,-2]\cup[3,\infty)$

11. $x^2+5x+4<0$

$x^2+5x+4=0$

$(x+4)(x+1)=0$

$x+4=0 \quad x+1=0$

$x=-4 \qquad x=-1$

Inter-val	Test Value	$x^2+5x+4<0$	Conclu-sion
$x\leq -4$	-5	$(-5)^2+5(-5)+4$ $=10$	$10\geq 0$
$-4<x<-1$	-2	$(-2)^2+5(-1)+4$ $=-2$	$-2<0$
$-1\leq x$	0	$(0)^2+5(0)+4$ $=4$	$4\geq 0$

$(-4,-1)$

13. $2x^2-3x+1\geq 0$

$2x^2-3x+1=0$

$(2x-1)(x-1)=0$

$2x-1=0 \quad x-1=0$

$2x=1 \qquad x=1$

$x=\dfrac{1}{2}$

Inter-val	Test Value	$2x^2-3x+1\geq 0$	Conclu-sion
$x\leq\dfrac{1}{2}$	0	$2(0)^2-3(0)+1$ $=1$	$1\geq 0$
$\dfrac{1}{2}<x<1$	$\dfrac{3}{4}$	$2\left(\dfrac{3}{4}\right)^2-3\left(\dfrac{3}{4}\right)+1$ $=-\dfrac{1}{8}$	$-\dfrac{1}{8}<0$
$1\leq x$	2	$2(2)^2-3(2)+1$ $=3$	$3\geq 0$

$\left(-\infty,\dfrac{1}{2}\right]\cup[1,\infty)$

15. $1-4x^2\leq 0$

$1-4x^2=0$

$(1-2x)(1+2x)=0$

$1-2x=0 \quad 1+2x=0$

$-2x=-1 \quad 2x=-1$

$x=\dfrac{1}{2} \qquad x=-\dfrac{1}{2}$

Inter-val	Test Value	$1-4x^2\leq 0$	Conclu-sion
$x\leq -\dfrac{1}{2}$	-1	$1-4(-1)^2=-3$	$-3\leq 0$
$-\dfrac{1}{2}<x<\dfrac{1}{2}$	0	$1-4(0)^2=1$	$1>0$
$\dfrac{1}{2}\leq x$	1	$1-4(1)^2=-3$	$-3\leq 0$

$\left(-\infty,-\dfrac{1}{2}\right]\cup\left[\dfrac{1}{2},\infty\right)$

17. $3>6x^2-7x$

$6x^2-7x-3=0$

$(3x+1)(2x-3)=0$

$3x+1=0 \quad 2x-3=0$

$3x=-1 \quad 2x=3$

$x=-\dfrac{1}{3} \quad x=\dfrac{3}{2}$

Inter-val	Test Value	$3>6x^2-7x$	Conclu-sion
$x\le-\dfrac{1}{3}$	-1	$6(-1)^2-$ $7(-1)=13$	$3\le13$
$-\dfrac{1}{3}<x<\dfrac{3}{2}$	0	$6(0)^2-7(0)$ $=0$	$3>0$
$\dfrac{3}{2}\le x$	2	$6(2)^2-7(2)$ $=10$	$3\le10$

$\left(-\dfrac{1}{3},\dfrac{3}{2}\right)$

19. $\dfrac{x}{x+2}\le0$

$\dfrac{x}{x+2}$ is undefined at $x=-2$

$\dfrac{x}{x+2}=0$ when $x=0$

Inter-val	Test Value	$\dfrac{x}{x+2}\le0$	Conclu-sion
$x<-2$	-3	$\dfrac{-3}{-3+2}=3$	$3>0$
$-2<x\le0$	-1	$\dfrac{-1}{-1+2}=-\dfrac{1}{2}$	$-\dfrac{1}{2}\le0$
$0<x$	1	$\dfrac{1}{1+2}=\dfrac{1}{3}$	$\dfrac{1}{3}>0$

$(-2,0]$

21. $\dfrac{1}{6-x}<0$

$\dfrac{1}{6-x}$ is undefined when $x=6$

Inter-val	Test value	$\dfrac{1}{6-x}<0$	Conclusion
$x<6$	0	$\dfrac{1}{6-0}=\dfrac{1}{6}$	$\dfrac{1}{6}\ge0$
$x>6$	7	$\dfrac{1}{6-7}=-1$	$-1<0$

$(6,\infty)$

23. $\dfrac{x+3}{x-3}>2$ $\quad$ $\dfrac{x+3}{x-3}$ is undefined when $x=3$

$\dfrac{x+3}{x-3}=2$

$x+3=2(x-3)$

$x+3=2x-6$

$x=9$

Inter-val	Test value	$\dfrac{x+3}{x-2}>2$	Conclu-sion
$x<3$	0	$\dfrac{0+3}{0-2}=-\dfrac{3}{2}$	$-\dfrac{3}{2}\le2$
$3<x<9$	5	$\dfrac{5+3}{5-2}=\dfrac{8}{3}$	$\dfrac{8}{3}>2$
$x\ge9$	10	$\dfrac{10+3}{10-2}=\dfrac{13}{9}$	$\dfrac{13}{9}\le2$

$(3,9)$

25. $\dfrac{2x-1}{x+4}\ge0$

$\dfrac{2x-1}{x+4}$ is undefined when $x=-4$

$\dfrac{2x-1}{x+4}=0$ when $2x-1=0$ or $x=\dfrac{1}{2}$

Inter-val	Test value	$\dfrac{2x-1}{x+4}\ge0$	Conclu-sion
$x<-4$	-5	$\dfrac{2(-5)-1}{-5+4}=11$	$11\ge0$
$-4<x<\dfrac{1}{2}$	0	$\dfrac{2(0)-1}{0+4}=-\dfrac{1}{4}$	$-\dfrac{1}{4}<0$
$\dfrac{1}{2}\le x$	1	$\dfrac{2(1)-1}{1+4}=\dfrac{1}{5}$	$\dfrac{1}{5}\ge0$

$(-\infty,-4)\cup\left[\dfrac{1}{2},\infty\right)$

27. $\dfrac{2x-1}{2x+5}\le2$

$\dfrac{2x-1}{2x+5}$ is undefined when $2x+5=0$

$2x=-5,\quad x=-\dfrac{5}{2}$

$\dfrac{2x-1}{2x+5}=2$

$2x-1=2(2x+5)$

$2x-1=4x+10$

$-2x=11$

$x=-\dfrac{11}{2}$

Inter-val	Test value	$\dfrac{2x-1}{2x+5}\le 2$	Conclu-sion
$x\le -\dfrac{11}{2}$	-6	$\dfrac{2(-6)-1}{2(-6)+5}$ $=\dfrac{11}{7}$	$\dfrac{11}{7}\le 2$
$-\dfrac{11}{2}<x<-\dfrac{5}{2}$	-4	$\dfrac{2(-4)-1}{-4+5}=3$	$3>2$
$-\dfrac{5}{2}<x$	0	$\dfrac{2(0)-1}{0+5}=-\dfrac{1}{5}$	$-\dfrac{1}{5}\le 2$

$$\left(-\infty,-\frac{11}{2}\right]\cup\left(-\frac{5}{2},\infty\right)$$

29. $h(t)=-16t^2+48t>0$

$-16t^2+48t=0$

$-16t(t-3)=0$

$-16t=0 \quad t-3=0$

$t=0 \qquad t=3$

Inter-val	Test value	$-16t^2+48t>0$	Conclu-sion
$x\le 0$	-1	$-16(-1)^2+48(-1)$ $=-64$	$-64\le 0$
$0<x<3$	1	$-16(1)^2+48(1)$ $=32$	$32>0$
$3\le x$	4	$-16(4)^2+48(4)$ $=-64$	$-64\le 0$

The penny is above the point of release between, but not including, 0 sec and 3 sec.

31. $C(x)=2x^2-60x+900<500$

$2x^2-60x+900=500$

$2x^2-60x+400=0$

$x^2-30x+200=0$

$(x-10)(x-20)=0$

$x-10=0 \quad x-20=0$

$x=10 \qquad x=20$

Inter-val	Test value	$2x^2-60x$ $+900<500$	Conclu-sion
$x\le 10$	9	$2(9)^2-60(9)$ $+900=522$	$522\ge 500$
$10<x<20$	15	$2(15)^2-60(15)$ $+900=450$	$450<500$
$20\ge x$	21	$2(21)^2-60(21)$ $+900=522$	$522\ge 500$

Producing between, but not including, 10 and 20 end tables per week will keep the cost under $500.

33. Let $l=$ the length and $w=$ the width.

$2l+2w=90$

$2w=90-2l$

$w=\dfrac{90-2l}{2}=45-l$

Area $A=lw=l(45-l)$

$A=45l-l^2$

$45l-l^2>450$

$l^2-45l+450=0$

$(l-15)(l-30)=0$

$l-15=0 \quad l-30=0$

$l=15 \qquad l=30$

Inter-val	Test value	$45l-l^2>450$	Conclu-sion
$x\le 15$	10	$45(10)-(10)^2$ $=350$	$350\le 450$
$15<x<30$	20	$45(20)-(20)^2$ $=500$	$500>450$
$30\le x$	40	$45(40)-(40)^2$ $=200$	$200\le 450$

The area will exceed 450 sq ft for any length between, but not including, 15 ft and 30 ft.

35. $C(x)=\dfrac{864+2x}{x}<8$

$\dfrac{864+2x}{x}$ is undefined when $x=0$

$\dfrac{864+2x}{x}=8$

$864+2x=8x$

$864=6x$

$x=144$

x is units sold so $x>0$

Inter-val	Test value	$\dfrac{864+2x}{x}<8$	Conclu-sion
$0<x\le 144$	90	$\dfrac{864+2(90)}{144}=\dfrac{58}{5}$	$8\ge\dfrac{58}{5}$
$144<x$	288	$\dfrac{864+2(288)}{288}=5$	$5<8$

The average cost will be less than $8 if more than 144 units are sold.

Chapter Review Exercises

1. $x^2 - 81 = 0$

$x^2 = 81$

$\sqrt{x^2} = \pm\sqrt{81}$

$x = \pm 9$

$x = 9, \ x = -9$

2. $3n^2 - 7 = 8$

$3n^2 = 15$

$n^2 = 5$

$\sqrt{n^2} = \pm\sqrt{5}$

$n = \pm\sqrt{5}$

$n = \sqrt{5} \quad n = -\sqrt{5}$

3. $4(a-5)^2 = 1$

$(a-5)^2 = \dfrac{1}{4}$

$\sqrt{(a-5)^2} = \pm\sqrt{\dfrac{1}{4}}$

$a - 5 = \pm\dfrac{1}{2}$

$a = 5 \pm \dfrac{1}{2}$

$a = \dfrac{11}{2} \quad a = \dfrac{9}{2}$

4. $(2x+1)^2 + 10 = 6$

$(2x+1)^2 = -4$

$\sqrt{(2x+1)^2} = \pm\sqrt{-4}$

$2x + 1 = \pm 2i$

$2x = -1 \pm 2i$

$x = \dfrac{-1 \pm 2i}{2}$

$x = \dfrac{-1+2i}{2} \quad x = \dfrac{-1-2i}{2}$

5. $x^2 + 8x + 16 = 2$

$(x+4)^2 = 2$

$\sqrt{(x+4)^2} = \pm\sqrt{2}$

$x + 4 = \pm\sqrt{2}$

$x = -4 \pm \sqrt{2}$

$x = -4 + \sqrt{2} \quad x = -4 - \sqrt{2}$

6. $(n-5)(n+5) = -33$

$n^2 - 25 = -33$

$n^2 = -8$

$\sqrt{n^2} = \pm\sqrt{-8}$

$n = \pm 2i\sqrt{2}$

$n = 2i\sqrt{2} \quad n = -2i\sqrt{2}$

7. $x^2 + 10x + \left[\left(\dfrac{10}{2}\right)^2\right] = x^2 + 10x + [25]$

8. $n^2 - 9n + \left[\left(\dfrac{-9}{2}\right)^2\right] = n^2 - 9n + \left[\dfrac{81}{4}\right]$

9. $x^2 - 6x + 2 = 0$

$x^2 - 6x = -2$

$x^2 - 6x + \left(\dfrac{6}{2}\right)^2 = -2 + \left(\dfrac{6}{2}\right)^2$

$x^2 - 6x + 9 = -2 + 9$

$(x-3)^2 = 7$

$x - 3 = \pm\sqrt{7}$

$x = 3 \pm \sqrt{7}$

$x = 3 + \sqrt{7} \quad x = 3 - \sqrt{7}$

10. $a^2 + a - 3 = 0$

$a^2 + a = 3$

$a^2 + a + \left(\dfrac{1}{2}\right)^2 = 3 + \left(\dfrac{1}{2}\right)^2$

$a^2 + a + \dfrac{1}{4} = 3 + \dfrac{1}{4}$

$\left(a + \dfrac{1}{2}\right)^2 = \dfrac{13}{4}$

$\sqrt{\left(a + \dfrac{1}{2}\right)^2} = \pm\sqrt{\dfrac{13}{4}}$

$a + \dfrac{1}{2} = \pm\dfrac{\sqrt{13}}{2}$

$a = -\dfrac{1}{2} \pm \dfrac{\sqrt{13}}{2}$

$a = \dfrac{-1+\sqrt{13}}{2} \quad a = \dfrac{-1-\sqrt{13}}{2}$

11. $2n^2 + 2n + 9 = 3 - 4n$

$2n^2 + 6n = -6$

$n^2 + 3n = -3$

$n^2 + 3n + \left(\dfrac{3}{2}\right)^2 = -3 + \left(\dfrac{3}{2}\right)^2$

$n^2 + 3n + \dfrac{9}{4} = -3 + \dfrac{9}{4}$

$\left(n + \dfrac{3}{2}\right)^2 = -\dfrac{3}{4}$

$$\sqrt{\left(n+\frac{3}{2}\right)^2} = \pm\sqrt{-\frac{3}{4}}$$

$$n+\frac{3}{2} = \pm\frac{i\sqrt{3}}{2}$$

$$n = -\frac{3}{2}\pm\frac{i\sqrt{3}}{2}$$

$$n = \frac{-3+i\sqrt{3}}{3} \quad n = \frac{-3-i\sqrt{3}}{2}$$

12. $3x^2 - 2x - 9 = 0$

$$3x^2 - 2x = 9$$

$$3\left(x^{2-}\frac{2}{3}x\right) = 9$$

$$x^2 - \frac{2}{3}x + \left(\frac{1}{2}\bullet\frac{-2}{3}\right)^2 = 3 + \left(\frac{1}{2}\bullet\frac{-2}{3}\right)^2$$

$$x^2 - \frac{2}{3}x + \left(-\frac{1}{3}\right)^2 = 3 + \left(-\frac{1}{3}\right)^2$$

$$x^2 - \frac{2}{3}x + \frac{1}{9} = 3 + \frac{1}{9}$$

$$\left(x-\frac{1}{3}\right)^2 = \frac{28}{9}$$

$$\sqrt{\left(x-\frac{1}{3}\right)^2} = \pm\sqrt{\frac{28}{9}}$$

$$x-\frac{1}{3} = \pm\frac{2\sqrt{7}}{3}$$

$$x = \frac{1}{3}\pm\frac{2\sqrt{7}}{3}$$

$$x = \frac{1+2\sqrt{7}}{3} \quad x = \frac{1-2\sqrt{7}}{3}$$

13. $x^2 + 7x + 6 = 0$

$a = 1 \qquad b = 7 \qquad c = 6$

$$x = \frac{-(7)\pm\sqrt{(7)^2-4(1)(6)}}{2(1)}$$

$$x = \frac{-7\pm\sqrt{49-24}}{2} = \frac{-7\pm\sqrt{25}}{2} = \frac{-7\pm5}{2}$$

$$x = \frac{-2}{2} = -1 \quad x = \frac{-12}{2} = -6$$

14. $x^2 - 4x + 5 = 0$

$a = 1 \qquad b = -4 \qquad c = 5$

$$x = \frac{-(-4)\pm\sqrt{(-4)^2-4(1)(5)}}{2(1)}$$

$$x = \frac{4\pm\sqrt{16-20}}{2} = \frac{4\pm\sqrt{-4}}{2} = \frac{4\pm2i}{2}$$

$$x = \frac{4+2i}{2} = 2+i \quad x = \frac{4-2i}{2} = 2-i$$

15. $3x^2 - 13x = 5 - 7x$

$$3x^2 - 6x - 5 = 0$$

$a = 3 \qquad b = -6 \qquad c = -5$

$$x = \frac{-(-6)\pm\sqrt{(-6)^2-4(3)(-5)}}{2(3)}$$

$$x = \frac{6\pm\sqrt{36+60}}{6} = \frac{6\pm\sqrt{96}}{6} = \frac{6\pm4\sqrt{6}}{6}$$

$$x = \frac{6+4\sqrt{6}}{6} = \frac{3+2\sqrt{6}}{3}$$

$$x = \frac{6-4\sqrt{6}}{6} = \frac{3-2\sqrt{6}}{3}$$

16. $4x^2 + 12x = -9$

$$4x^2 + 12x + 9 = 0$$

$a = 4 \qquad b = 12 \qquad c = 9$

$$x = \frac{-(12)\pm\sqrt{(12)^2-4(4)(9)}}{2(4)}$$

$$x = \frac{-12\pm\sqrt{144-144}}{8} = \frac{-12\pm\sqrt{0}}{8}$$

$$x = -\frac{12}{8} = -\frac{3}{2}$$

17. $\frac{1}{3}x^2 + \frac{3}{2}x + 1 = 0$

$$6\left(\frac{1}{3}x^2 + \frac{3}{2}x + 1\right) = 6(0)$$

$$2x^2 + 9x + 6 = 0$$

$a = 2 \qquad b = 9 \qquad c = 6$

$$x = \frac{-(9)\pm\sqrt{(9)^2-4(2)(6)}}{2(2)}$$

$$x = \frac{-9\pm\sqrt{81-48}}{4} = \frac{-9\pm\sqrt{33}}{4}$$

$$x = \frac{-9+\sqrt{33}}{4} \quad x = \frac{-9-\sqrt{33}}{4}$$

18. $0.01x^2 + 0.1x^2 + 0.34 = 0$

$$100\left(0.01x^2 + 0.1x^2 + 0.34\right) = 100(0)$$

$$x^2 + 10x + 34 = 0$$

$a = 1 \qquad b = 10 \qquad c = 34$

$$x = \frac{-(10)\pm\sqrt{(10)^2-4(1)(34)}}{2(1)}$$

$$x = \frac{-10\pm\sqrt{100-136}}{2} = \frac{-10\pm\sqrt{-36}}{2}$$

$$x = \frac{-10\pm6i}{2}$$

$$x = \frac{-10+6i}{2} = -5+3i$$

$$x = \frac{-10-6i}{2} = -5-3i$$

19. $2x^2 - x = 2x - 5$

$2x^2 - 3x + 5 = 0$

$a = 2 \qquad b = -3 \qquad c = 5$

$b^2 - 4ac = (-3)^2 - 4(2)(5) = 9 - 40 = -31$

Two complex solutions (containing i).

20. $4x^2 + 9x - 3 = 0$

$a = 4 \qquad b = 9 \qquad c = -3$

$b^2 - 4ac = (9)^2 - 4(4)(-3) = 81 + 48 = 129$

Two real solutions.

21. $\dfrac{2}{n-3} + \dfrac{1}{n-1} = -1$

$\dfrac{2}{n-3} \bullet (n-3)(n-1) + \dfrac{1}{n-1} \bullet (n-3)(n-1)$
$\qquad\qquad\qquad = -1 \bullet (n-3)(n-1)$

$2(n-1) + 1(n-3) = -1(n^2 - 4n + 3)$

$2n - 2 + n - 3 = -n^2 + 4n - 3$

$n^2 - n - 2 = 0$

$(n-2)(n+1) = 0$

$n - 2 = 0 \quad n + 1 = 0$

$n = 2 \qquad n = -1$

Check $n = 2$ Check $n = -1$

$\dfrac{2}{2-3} + \dfrac{1}{2-1} \overset{?}{=} -1 \qquad \dfrac{2}{-1-3} + \dfrac{1}{-1-1} \overset{?}{=} -1$

$-2 + 1 \overset{?}{=} -1 \qquad\qquad -\dfrac{1}{2} - \dfrac{1}{2} \overset{?}{=} -1$

$-1 = -1$ True $-1 = -1$ True

22. $x^4 - 2x^2 - 24 = 0$

Let $u = x^2$

$\left(x^2\right)^2 - 2\left(x^2\right) - 24 = 0$

$u^2 - 2u - 24 = 0$

$(u-6)(u+4) = 0$

$u - 6 = 0 \quad u + 4 = 0$

$u = 6 \qquad u = -4$

$x^2 = 6 \qquad x^2 = -4$

$x = \pm\sqrt{6} \quad x = \pm\sqrt{-4}$

$\qquad\qquad\quad x = \pm 2i$

Check $x = \sqrt{6}$ Check $x = -\sqrt{6}$

$\left(\sqrt{6}\right)^4 - 2\left(\sqrt{6}\right)^2 - 24 \overset{?}{=} 0 \qquad \left(-\sqrt{6}\right)^4 - 2\left(-\sqrt{6}\right)^2$

$36 - 12 - 24 \overset{?}{=} 0 \qquad\qquad\qquad -24 \overset{?}{=} 0$

$0 = 0$ True

$\qquad\qquad\qquad 36 - 12 - 24 \overset{?}{=} 0$

$\qquad\qquad\qquad\qquad 0 = 0$ True

Check $x = 2i$ Check $x = -2i$

$(2i)^4 - 2(2i)^2 - 24 \overset{?}{=} 0 \qquad (-2i)^4 - 2(-2i)^2 - 24 \overset{?}{=} 0$

$16 + 8 - 24 \overset{?}{=} 0 \qquad\qquad 16 + 8 - 24 \overset{?}{=} 0$

$0 = 0$ True $\qquad\qquad\qquad 0 = 0$ True

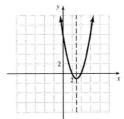

23. $x - 7\sqrt{x} + 12 = 0$

Let $u = \sqrt{x}$

$\left(\sqrt{x}\right)^2 - 7\sqrt{x} + 12 = 0$

$u^2 - 7u + 12 = 0$

$(u-4)(u-3) = 0$

$u - 4 = 0 \qquad u - 3 = 0$

$u = 4 \qquad\qquad u = 3$

$\sqrt{x} = 4 \qquad\quad \sqrt{x} = 3$

$\left(\sqrt{x}\right)^2 = 4^2 \quad \left(\sqrt{x}\right)^2 = (3)^2$

$x = 16 \qquad\qquad x = 9$

Check $x = 16$ Check $x = 9$

$(16) - 7\sqrt{16} + 12 \overset{?}{=} 0 \qquad (9) - 7\sqrt{9} + 12 \overset{?}{=} 0$

$16 - 28 + 12 \overset{?}{=} 0 \qquad\qquad 9 - 21 + 12 \overset{?}{=} 0$

$0 = 0$ True $\qquad\qquad\qquad 0 = 0$ True

24. $(p-1)^2 + 3(p-1) + 2 = 0$

Let $u = (p-1)$

$u^2 + 3u + 2 = 0$

$(u+1)(u+2) = 0$

$u + 1 = 0 \qquad u + 2 = 0$

$u = -1 \qquad\quad u = -2$

$p - 1 = -1 \quad p - 1 = -2$

$p = 0 \qquad\quad p = -1$

Check $p = 0$

$$((0)-1)^2 + 3((0)-1) + 2 \overset{?}{=} 0$$

$$1 - 3 + 2 \overset{?}{=} 0$$

$0 = 0$ True

Check $p = -1$

$$((-1)-1)^2 + 3((-1)-1) + 2 \overset{?}{=} 0$$

$$4 - 6 + 2 \overset{?}{=} 0$$

$0 = 0$ True

25. $x = \dfrac{5}{2}$ $x = -3$

$2x = 5$ $x + 3 = 0$

$2x - 5 = 0$

$(2x - 5)(x + 3) = 0$

$2x^2 + x - 15 = 0$

26. $n = -7$

$n + 7 = 0$

$(n + 7)^2 = 0^2$

$n^2 + 14n + 49 = 0$

27. $f(x) = x^2 - 6x + 5$

$$-\frac{b}{2a} = -\frac{-6}{2(1)} = 3$$

$$f(3) = (3)^2 - 6(3) + 5 = -4$$

Vertex: $(3, -4)$

Axis of symmetry: $x = 3$

$x^2 - 6x + 5 = 0$

$(x - 5)(x - 1) = 0$

$x - 5 = 0$ $x - 1 = 0$

$x = 5$ $x = 1$

x-intercepts: $(1, 0)$ and $(5, 0)$

$$f(0) = (0)^2 - 6(0) + 5 = 5$$

y-intercept: $(0, 5)$

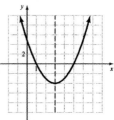

28. $f(x) = 3 + 2x - x^2$

$$-\frac{b}{2a} = -\frac{2}{2(-1)} = 1$$

$$f(1) = 3 + 2(1) - (1)^2 = 4$$

Vertex: $(1, 4)$

Axis of symmetry: $x = 1$

$3 + 2x - x^2 = 0$

$(3 - x)(1 + x) = 0$

$3 - x = 0$ $1 + x = 0$

$x = 3$ $x = -1$

x-intercepts: $(-1, 0)$ and $(3, 0)$

$$f(0) = 3 + 2(0) - (0)^2 = 3$$

y-intercept: $(0, 3)$

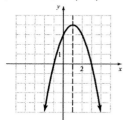

29. $f(x) = x^2 + 8x + 16$

$$-\frac{b}{2a} = -\frac{8}{2(1)} = -4$$

$$f(-4) = (-4)^2 + 8(-4) + 16 = 0$$

Vertex: $(-4, 0)$

Axis of symmetry: $x = -4$

$x^2 + 8x + 16 = 0$

$(x + 4)^2 = 0$

$x + 4 = 0$

$x = -4$

x-intercept: $(-4, 0)$

$$f(0) = (0)^2 + 8(0) + 16 = 16$$

y-intercept: $(0, 16)$

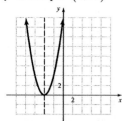

30. $f(x) = x^2 - 5x - 6$

$$-\frac{b}{2a} = -\frac{-5}{2(1)} = \frac{5}{2}$$

$$f\left(\frac{5}{2}\right) = \left(\frac{5}{2}\right)^2 - 5\left(\frac{5}{2}\right) - 6 = -\frac{49}{4}$$

Vertex: $\left(\dfrac{5}{2}, -\dfrac{49}{4}\right)$

Axis of symmetry: $x = \dfrac{5}{2}$

$x^2 - 5x - 6 = 0$

$(x+1)(x-6) = 0$

$x+1 = 0 \quad x-6 = 0$

$x = -1 \quad\quad x = 6$

x-intercepts: $(-1,0)$ and $(6,0)$

$f(0) = (0)^2 - 5(0) - 6 = -6$

y-intercept: $(0,-6)$

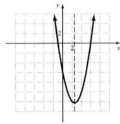

31.

Function	Opens	Maximum Minimum
$f(x) = x^2 + 9$	$a > 0$ Upward	$a > 0$ Minimum

Number of x-intercepts	Number of y-intercepts
$x^2 + 9 = 0$ $x^2 = -9$ No real solutions 0	$f(0) = 9$ 1

32.

Function	Opens	Maximum Minimum
$f(x) = 1 + 3x - 2x^2$	$a < 0$ Downward	$a < 0$ Maximum

Number of x-intercepts	Number of y-intercepts
$b^2 - 4ac =$ $3^2 - 4(-2)(1) = 17$ Two real solutions 2	$f(0) =$ $1 + 3(0) - 2(0)^2 = 1$ 1

33.

x	$f(x) = 3x - 4x^2$	(x, y)
-1	$3(-1) - 4(-1)^2 = -7$	$(-1, -7)$
-0.5	$3(-0.5) - 4(-0.5)^2$ $= -2.5$	$(-.5, -2.5)$
-0.25	$3(-0.25) - 4(-0.25)^2$ $= -1$	$(-2.5, -1)$
0	$3(0) - 4(0)^2 = 0$	$(0, 0)$
0.25	$3(0.25) - 4(0.25)^2 = 0.5$	$(0.25, 0.5)$
0.5	$3(0.5) - 4(0.5)^2 = 0.5$	$(0.5, 0.5)$
1	$3(1) - 4(1)^2 = -1$	$(1, -1)$

$-\dfrac{b}{2a} = -\dfrac{3}{2(-4)} = \dfrac{3}{8}$

$f\left(\dfrac{3}{8}\right) = 3\left(\dfrac{3}{8}\right) - 4\left(\dfrac{3}{8}\right)^2 = \dfrac{9}{16}$

Vertex: $\left(-\dfrac{3}{8}, \dfrac{9}{16}\right)$

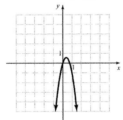

Domain: $(-\infty, \infty)$ Range: $\left(-\infty, \dfrac{9}{16}\right]$

34.

x	$f(x) = 2x^2 - x - 1$	(x, y)
-2	$2(-2)^2 - (-2) - 1 = 9$	$(-2, 9)$
-1	$2(-1)^2 - (-1) - 1 = 2$	$(-1, 2)$
0	$2(0)^2 - (0) - 1 = -1$	$(0, -1)$
1	$2(1)^2 - (1) - 1 = 0$	$(1, 0)$
2	$2(2)^2 - (2) - 1 = 5$	$(2, 5)$

$-\dfrac{b}{2a} = -\dfrac{-1}{2(2)} = \dfrac{1}{4}$

$f\left(\dfrac{1}{4}\right) = 2\left(\dfrac{1}{4}\right)^2 - \left(\dfrac{1}{4}\right) - 1 = -\dfrac{9}{8}$

Vertex: $\left(\dfrac{1}{4}, -\dfrac{9}{8}\right)$

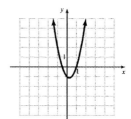

Domain: $(-\infty,\infty)$ Range: $\left[-\dfrac{9}{8},\infty\right)$

35. $x^2-4x<12$

$x^2-4x=12$

$x^2-4x-12=0$

$(x+2)(x-6)=0$

$x+2=0 \quad x-6=0$

$x=-2 \quad x=6$

Inter-val	Test Value	$x^2-4x<12$	Conclu-sion
$x\le -2$	-3	$(-3)^2-4(-3)=$ 21	$21\ge 12$
$-2<x<6$	0	$(0)^2-4(0)=$ 0	$0<12$
$6\le x$	7	$(7)^2-4(7)=21$	$21\ge 12$

$(-2,6)$

36. $10+3x-x^2\le 0$

$10+3x-x^2=0$

$(5-x)(2+x)=0$

$5-x=0 \quad 2+x=0$

$x=5 \quad\quad x=-2$

Inter-val	Test Value	$10+3x-x^2\le 0$	Conclu-sion
$x\le -2$	-3	$10+3(-3)-(-3)^2$ $=-8$	$-8\le 0$
$-2<x<5$	0	$10+3(0)-(0)^2$ $=10$	$0<10$
$5\le x$	6	$10+3(6)-(6)^2$ $5=-8$	$-8\le 0$

$(-\infty,-2]\cup[5,\infty)$

37. $2x^2-9x-4\ge -8$

$2x^2-9x-4=-8$

$2x^2-9x+4=0$

$(2x-1)(x-4)=0$

$2x-1=0 \quad x-4=0$

$2x=1 \quad\quad x=4$

$x=\dfrac{1}{2}$

Inter-val	Test Value	$2x^2-9x-4\ge -8$	Conclu-sion
$x\le\dfrac{1}{2}$	0	$2(0)^2-9(0)-4$ $=-4$	$-4\ge -8$
$\dfrac{1}{2}<x<4$	2	$2(2)^2-9(2)-4$ $=-14$	$-14<-8$
$4\le x$	5	$2(5)^2-9(5)-4$ $=1$	$1\ge -8$

$\left(-\infty,\dfrac{1}{2}\right]\cup[4,\infty)$

38. $3>4x^2-4x$

$4x^2-4x-3=0$

$(2x+1)(2x-3)=0$

$2x+1=0 \quad 2x-3=0$

$2x=-1 \quad\quad 2x=3$

$x=-\dfrac{1}{2} \quad\quad x=\dfrac{3}{2}$

Inter-val	Test Value	$3>4x^2-4x$	Conclu-sion
$x\le -\dfrac{1}{2}$	-1	$4(-1)^2-4(-1)$ $=8$	$3\le 8$
$-\dfrac{1}{2}<x<\dfrac{3}{2}$	0	$4(0)^2-4(0)$ $=0$	$3>0$
$\dfrac{3}{2}\le x$	3	$4(3)^2-4(3)$ $=24$	$3\le 24$

$\left(-\dfrac{1}{2},\dfrac{3}{2}\right)$

39. $\dfrac{x+3}{x-5}>-3$

$\dfrac{x+3}{x-5}$ is undefined when $x=5$

$\dfrac{x+3}{x-5}=-3$

$x+3=-3(x-5)$

$x+3=-3x+15$

$4x=12$

$x=3$

Inter-val	Test Value	$\dfrac{x+3}{x-5}>-3$	Conclu-sion
$x<3$	0	$\dfrac{0+3}{0-5}=-\dfrac{3}{5}$	$-\dfrac{3}{5}>-3$
$3\le x<5$	4	$\dfrac{4+3}{4-5}=-7$	$-7\le-3$
$5<x$	6	$\dfrac{6+3}{6-5}=9$	$9>-3$

$(-\infty,3)\cup(5,\infty)$ ⟵―+―+―+―)―+―(―+―+―+―+―⟶
$\qquad\qquad\qquad\quad$ −1 0 1 2 3 4 5 6 7 8 9 10 11

40. $\dfrac{4x-12}{3x}\le0$

$\dfrac{4x-12}{3x}$ is undefined when $x=0$

$\dfrac{4x-12}{3x}=0$

$4x-12=0$

$4x=12$

$x=3$

Inter-val	Test Value	$\dfrac{4x-12}{3x}\le0$	Conclu-sion
$x<0$	-1	$\dfrac{4(-1)-12}{3(-1)}=\dfrac{16}{3}$	$\dfrac{16}{3}>0$
$0<x\le3$	2	$\dfrac{4(2)-12}{3(2)}=-\dfrac{2}{3}$	$-\dfrac{2}{3}\le0$
$3<x$	6	$\dfrac{4(6)-12}{2(6)}=\dfrac{2}{3}$	$\dfrac{2}{3}>0$

$(0,3]$ ⟵―+―+―+―+―+―+―(―+―+―+―]―+―+―⟶
$\qquad\quad$ −6 −5 −4 −3 −2 −1 0 1 2 3 4 5 6

41. $s=16t^2$

$400=16t^2$

$25=t^2$

$\sqrt{t^2}=\pm\sqrt{25}$

$t=\pm5$

$t=5\quad t=-5$

The negative answer makes no sense in this problem. It will take 5 sec for the object to fall 400 ft.

42. $(3d)^2+d^2=10^2$

$9d^2+d^2=100$

$10d^2=100$

$d^2=10$

$\sqrt{d^2}=\pm\sqrt{10}$

$d=\sqrt{10}\qquad d$ is a distance and must be non-negative

$3d=3\sqrt{10}=9.4868...$

The ladder reaches approximately 9.5 ft up the side of the house.

43. 30 min is 0.5 hr. Let r be the rate of the train traveling west. Distance = rate × time.

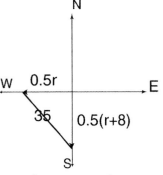

$(0.5r)^2+(0.5(r+8))^2=35^2$

$0.25r^2+(0.5r+4)^2=1225$

$0.25r^2+0.25r^2+4r+16=1225$

$0.5r^2+4r-1209=0$

$a=0.5\qquad b=4\qquad c=-1209$

$r=\dfrac{-(4)\pm\sqrt{(4)^2-4(0.5)(-1209)}}{2(0.5)}$

$r=\dfrac{-4\pm\sqrt{16+2418}}{1}=-4\pm\sqrt{2434}$

$r=-4\pm49.3355...$

$r=45.3355...\qquad r=-53.3355...$

$r+8=53.3355...\quad r+8=-45.3355...$

The negative answer makes no sense in this problem. The speed of the train traveling South is 53 mph and the speed of the train traveling west is 45 mph.

44. $A=5000\left[(1+r)^2-1\right]$

$1100=5000\left[(1+r)^2-1\right]$

$\dfrac{1100}{5000}=(1+r)^2-1$

$\dfrac{11}{50}=1+2r+r^2-1$

$r^2+2r-\dfrac{11}{50}=0$

$50\left(r^2+2r-\dfrac{11}{50}\right)=50(0)$

$50r^2+100r-11=0$

$a=50\qquad b=100\qquad c=-11$

$r=\dfrac{-(100)\pm\sqrt{(100)^2-4(50)(-11)}}{2(50)}$

$r=\dfrac{-100\pm\sqrt{10000+2200}}{100}$

$r = \dfrac{-100 \pm \sqrt{12200}}{100} = \dfrac{-100 \pm 110.4536...}{100}$

$r = -1 \pm 1.1045...$

$r = -2.1045...$ $r = 0.1045...$

The negative answer makes no sense in this problem. The average rate of return was about 10.5%

45.   The length of the base will be $40 - 2x$ and the width will be $25 - 2x$. Area is length × width.

$A = (40 - 2x)(25 - 2x) = 700$

$1000 - 130x + 4x^2 = 700$

$4x^2 - 130x + 300 = 0$

$2(2x^2 - 65x + 150) = 0$

$2x^2 - 65x + 150 = 0$

$a = 2$ $b = -65$ $c = 150$

$x = \dfrac{-(-65) \pm \sqrt{(-65)^2 - 4(2)(150)}}{2(2)}$

$x = \dfrac{65 \pm \sqrt{4225 - 1200}}{4} = \dfrac{65 \pm \sqrt{3025}}{4}$

$x = \dfrac{65 \pm 55}{4}$

$x = \dfrac{120}{4} = 30$ $x = \dfrac{10}{4} = \dfrac{5}{2}$

Two thirty inch squares cannot be cut from the original piece of cardboard. $\dfrac{5}{2}$ in by $\dfrac{5}{2}$ in squares should be cut from each corner.

46. $R(x) = 100x - 2x^2 = 1250$

$2x^2 - 100x + 1250 = 0$

$2(x^2 - 50x + 625) = 0$

$x^2 - 50x + 625 = 0$

$(x - 25)^2 = 0$

$x - 25 = 0$

$x = 25$

He needs to sell 25 cases per week.

47. $S = 7n^2 + 8n + 131 = 218$

$7n^2 + 8n - 87 = 0$

$a = 7$ $b = 8$ $c = -87$

$n = \dfrac{-(8) \pm \sqrt{(8)^2 - 4(7)(-87)}}{2(7)}$

$n = \dfrac{-8 \pm \sqrt{64 + 2436}}{14} = \dfrac{-8 \pm \sqrt{2500}}{14}$

$n = \dfrac{-8 \pm 50}{14}$

$n = \dfrac{-58}{14} = -\dfrac{29}{7}$ $n = \dfrac{42}{14} = 3$

The negative answer makes no sense in this problem 1999 + 3 = 2002 There were 218 stores in 2002.

48. $A = 0.009x^2 + 0.05x + 0.6 = 1.2$

$0.009x^2 + 0.05x - 0.6 = 0$

$a = 0.009$ $b = 0.05$ $c = -0.6$

$x = \dfrac{-(0.05) \pm \sqrt{(0.05)^2 - 4(0.009)(-0.6)}}{2(0.009)}$

$x = \dfrac{-0.05 \pm \sqrt{0.0025 + 0.0216}}{0.018}$

$x = \dfrac{-0.05 \pm \sqrt{0.0241}}{0.018} = \dfrac{-0.05 \pm 0.15524...}{0.018}$

$x = \dfrac{0.10524...}{0.018} = 5.846...$

$x = \dfrac{-0.20524...}{0.018} = -11.402....$

The negative answer makes no sense in this problem. 1995 + 6 = 2001. There were approximately 1.2 million sales associates in 2001.

49.   6 min is $\dfrac{6}{60} = \dfrac{1}{10}$ hr.   time $= \dfrac{\text{distance}}{\text{rate}}$

$\dfrac{8}{r} = \dfrac{8}{r + 2} + \dfrac{1}{10}$

$\dfrac{8}{r} \bullet 10r(r + 2) = \dfrac{8}{r + 2} \bullet 10r(r + 2)$

$+ \dfrac{1}{10} \bullet 10r(r + 2)$

$80(r + 2) = 80r + r(r + 2)$

$80r + 160 = 80r + r^2 + 2r$

$r^2 + 2r - 160 = 0$

$a = 1$ $b = 2$ $c = -160$

$r = \dfrac{-(2) \pm \sqrt{(2)^2 - 4(1)(-160)}}{2(1)}$

$r = \dfrac{-2 \pm \sqrt{4 + 640}}{2} = \dfrac{-2 \pm \sqrt{644}}{2}$

$r = \dfrac{-2 \pm 25.3771...}{2}$

$r = \dfrac{23.3771...}{2} = 11.6885...$

$r = \dfrac{-27.3771...}{2} = -13.6885...$

The negative answer makes no sense in this problem. $x + 2 = 13.6885...$ She bicycled to school at a rate of 13.7 mph.

50.   Let t be the time it takes the newer printing press to complete the job alone. In one hour the newer printer completes $\dfrac{1}{t}$ of the job, the older printer

completes $\dfrac{1}{t+5}$ and together they complete $\dfrac{1}{2}$ of the job.

$$\dfrac{1}{t+5}+\dfrac{1}{t}=\dfrac{1}{2}$$

$$\dfrac{1}{t+5}\bullet(t+5)(t)(2)+\dfrac{1}{t}\bullet(t+5)(t)(2)=$$

$$\dfrac{1}{2}\bullet(t+5)(t)(2)$$

$$2t+2(t+5)=t(t+5)$$

$$2t+2t+10=t^2+5t$$

$$t^2+t-10=0$$

$$a=1 \qquad b=1 \qquad c=-10$$

$$t=\dfrac{-(1)\pm\sqrt{(1)^2-4(1)(-10)}}{2(1)}$$

$$t=\dfrac{-1\pm\sqrt{1+40}}{2}=\dfrac{-1\pm\sqrt{41}}{2}$$

$$t=\dfrac{-1\pm6.4031...}{2}$$

$$t=\dfrac{-7.4031}{2}=-3.701... \quad t+5=1.298...$$

$$t=\dfrac{5.4031...}{2}=2.701.. \quad t+5=7.701...$$

The negative answer makes no sense in this problem. Working alone, it takes the newer printing press about 2.7 hr and the older printing press about 7.7 hr to complete the job.

51. a. perimeter $=2l+2w=300$

$$2w=300-2l$$

$$w=\dfrac{300-2l}{2}=150-l$$

b. $Area=lw$

$$A(l)=l(150-l)=150l-l^2$$

c.

x	$A(l)=150l-l^2$	(x,y)
25	$150(25)-(025)^2=3125$	$(25,3125)$
50	$150(50)-(50)^2=5000$	$(50,5000)$
75	$150(75)-(75)^2=5625$	$(75,5625)$
100	$150(100)-(100)^2=5000$	$(100,5000)$
125	$150(125)-(125)^2=3125$	$(125,3125)$

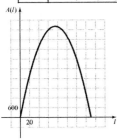

d. $a=-1 \qquad b=150$

Vertex is where $l=-\dfrac{b}{2a}=-\dfrac{150}{2(-1)}=75$

$$w=150-l=150-75=75$$

$$A(75)=150l-l^2=150(75)-(75)^2$$

$$A(75)=11250-5625=5625$$

A park measuring 75 ft by 75 ft will produce a maximum area of 5625 sq ft.

52. a. $C(x)=-0.05x^2-2x+100$

x	$C(x)=0.05x^2-2x+100$	(x,y)
0	$0.05(0)^2-2(0)+100=100$	$(0,100)$
10	$0.05(10)^2-2(10)+100=85$	$(10,85)$
20	$0.05(20)^2-2(20)+100=80$	$(20,80)$
30	$0.05(30)^2-2(30)+100=85$	$(30,85)$
40	$0.05(40)^2-2(40)+100=100$	$(40,100)$

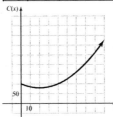

b. Vertex is where $x=-\dfrac{b}{2a}$

$$a=0.05 \quad b=-2$$

$$x=-\dfrac{b}{2a}=-\dfrac{-2}{2(0.05)}=20$$

20 units must be fabricated per day in order to minimize the cost.

c. $C(20)=0.05(20)^2-2(20)+100$

$$C(20)=0.05(400)-40+100$$

$$C(20)=20-40+100=80$$

The minimum cost is $80.

53. $h(t)=-16t^2+80t+4$

$$40=-16t^2+80t+4$$

$$16t^2-80t+36=0$$

$$4(4t^2-20t+9)=0$$

$$4t^2-20t+9=0$$

$$(2t-1)(2t-9)=0$$

$$2t-1=0 \quad 2t-9=0$$

$$2t=1 \qquad 2t=9$$

$$t=\dfrac{1}{2} \qquad t=\dfrac{9}{2}$$

The baseball is 40 ft above the ground at $\dfrac{1}{2}$ sec and $\dfrac{9}{2}$ sec.

54.   Perimeter is $2l + 2w = 44$

$2l = 44 - 2w$

$l = 22 - w$

Area is lw

$A = (22 - w)w$

$120 \leq 22w - w^2$

$120 = 22w - w^2$

$w^2 - 22w + 120 = 0$

$(w - 12)(w - 10) = 0$

$w - 12 = 0 \quad w - 10 = 0$

$w = 12 \qquad w = 10$

Interval	Test Value	$120 \leq 22w - w^2$	Conclusion
$x < 10$	9	$22(9) - (9)^2$ $= 117$	$120 > 117$
$10 \leq x \leq 12$	11	$22(11) - (11)^2$ $= 121$	$120 \leq 121$
$12 < x$	13	$22(13) - (13)^2$ $= 117$	$120 > 117$

Any width between and including 10 ft and 12 ft will produce an area of at least 120 sq ft.

Chapter 8 Posttest

1. $5n^2 - 11 = 29$

$5n^2 = 40$

$n^2 = 8$

$\sqrt{n^2} = \sqrt{8}$

$n = \pm 2\sqrt{2}$

$n = 2\sqrt{2} \quad n = -2\sqrt{2}$

2. $3p^2 - 6p = -24$

$3(p^2 - 2p) = -24$

$p^2 - 2p = -8$

$p^2 - 2p + \left(\dfrac{-2}{2}\right)^2 = -8 + \left(\dfrac{-2}{2}\right)^2$

$p^2 - 2p + 1 = -8 + 1$

$(p - 1)^2 = -7$

$p - 1 = \pm\sqrt{-7}$

$p = 1 \pm i\sqrt{7}$

$p = 1 + i\sqrt{7} \quad p = 1 - i\sqrt{7}$

3. $4x^2 + 4x - 3 = 0$

$a = 4 \qquad b = 4 \qquad c = -3$

$x = \dfrac{-(4) \pm \sqrt{(4)^2 - 4(4)(-3)}}{2(4)}$

$x = \dfrac{-4 \pm \sqrt{16 + 48}}{8} = \dfrac{-4 \pm \sqrt{64}}{8} = \dfrac{-4 \pm 8}{8}$

$x = \dfrac{-4 + 8}{8} = \dfrac{4}{8} = \dfrac{1}{2}$

$x = \dfrac{-4 - 8}{8} = \dfrac{-12}{8} = -\dfrac{3}{2}$

4. $2x^2 + 7x + 9 = 0$

$a = 2 \quad b = 7 \quad c = 9$

$b^2 - 4ac = (7)^2 - 4(2)(9) = -23$

Two complex solutions (containing i).

5. $5(3n + 2)^2 - 90 = 0$

$5(3n + 2)^2 = 90$

$(3n + 2)^2 = 18$

$3n + 2 = \pm\sqrt{18} = \pm 3\sqrt{2}$

$3n = -2 \pm 3\sqrt{2}$

$n = \dfrac{-2 \pm 3\sqrt{2}}{3}$

$n = \dfrac{-2 + 3\sqrt{2}}{3} \quad n = \dfrac{-2 - 3\sqrt{2}}{3}$

6. $x^2 + 8x = 6$

$x^2 + 8x - 6 = 0$

$a = 1 \qquad b = 8 \qquad c = -6$

$x = \dfrac{-(8) \pm \sqrt{(8)^2 - 4(1)(-6)}}{2(1)}$

$x = \dfrac{-8 \pm \sqrt{64 + 24}}{2} = \dfrac{-8 \pm \sqrt{88}}{2}$

$x = \dfrac{-8 \pm 2\sqrt{22}}{2} = -4 \pm \sqrt{22}$

$x = -4 + \sqrt{22} \quad x = -4 - \sqrt{22}$

7. $x^2 - x - 2 = 4x - 13$

$x^2 - 5x + 11 = 0$

$a = 1 \qquad b = -5 \qquad c = 11$

$x = \dfrac{-(-5) \pm \sqrt{(-5)^2 - 4(1)(11)}}{2(1)}$

$x = \dfrac{5 \pm \sqrt{25 - 44}}{2} = \dfrac{5 \pm \sqrt{-19}}{2}$

$x = \dfrac{5 + i\sqrt{19}}{2} \quad x = \dfrac{5 - i\sqrt{19}}{2}$

$x^2 + 3x - 18 = 0$

$(x+6)(x-3) = 0$

8. $4x^2 + 3x = 7 + 6x$

$4x^2 - 3x - 7 = 0$

$(x+1)(4x-7) = 0$

$x+1=0 \quad 4x-7=0$

$x=-1 \quad\quad 4x=7$

$$x = \frac{7}{4}$$

9. $2x^2 - 12x + 20 = 1$

$2x^2 - 12x + 19 = 0$

$a = 2 \quad\quad b = -12 \quad\quad c = 19$

$$x = \frac{-(-12) \pm \sqrt{(-12)^2 - 4(2)(19)}}{2(2)}$$

$$x = \frac{12 \pm \sqrt{144 - 152}}{4} = \frac{12 \pm \sqrt{-8}}{4}$$

$$x = \frac{12 \pm 2i\sqrt{2}}{4} = \frac{2\left(6 \pm i\sqrt{2}\right)}{4}$$

$$x = \frac{6 + i\sqrt{2}}{2} \quad x = \frac{6 - i\sqrt{2}}{2}$$

10. $\dfrac{1}{2}x^2 + x - 2 = 0$

$a = \dfrac{1}{2} \quad\quad b = 1 \quad\quad c = -2$

$$x = \frac{-(1) \pm \sqrt{(1)^2 - 4\left(\frac{1}{2}\right)(-2)}}{2\left(\frac{1}{2}\right)}$$

$$x = \frac{-1 \pm \sqrt{1+4}}{1} \quad x = -1 \pm \sqrt{5}$$

$x = -1 + \sqrt{5} \quad x = -1 - \sqrt{5}$

11. $x^{\frac{1}{2}} - 2x^{\frac{1}{4}} = -1$

$x^{\frac{1}{2}} - 2x^{\frac{1}{4}} + 1 = 0$

Let $u = x^{\frac{1}{4}}$

$$\left(x^{\frac{1}{4}}\right)^2 - 2\left(x^{\frac{1}{4}}\right) + 1 = 0$$

$u^2 - 2u + 1 = 0$

$(u-1)^2 = 0$

$u - 1 = 0$

$u = 1$

$x^{\frac{1}{4}} = 1$

$$\left(x^{\frac{1}{4}}\right)^4 = 1^4$$

$x = 1$

12. $n = \dfrac{1}{2} \quad\quad n = \dfrac{2}{3}$

$2n = 1 \quad\quad 3n = 2$

$2n - 1 = 0 \quad 3n - 2 = 0$

$(2n-1)(3n-2) = 0$

$6n^2 - 7n + 2 = 0$

13. $f(x) = x^2 - 6x + 8$

$$-\frac{b}{2a} = -\frac{-6}{2(1)} = 3$$

$f(3) = (3)^2 - 6(3) + 8 = -1$

Vertex: $(3, -1)$

Axis of symmetry: $x = 3$

$x^2 - 6x + 8 = 0$

$(x-2)(x-4) = 0$

$x - 2 = 0 \quad x - 4 = 0$

$x = 2 \quad\quad x = 4$

x-intercepts: $(2, 0)$ and $(4, 0)$.

$f(0) = (0)^2 - 6(0) + 8 = 8$

y-intercept $(0, 8)$.

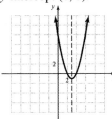

14. $f(x) = -x^2 + 3x + 10$

$$-\frac{b}{2a} = -\frac{3}{2(-1)} = \frac{3}{2}$$

$$f\left(\frac{3}{2}\right) = -\left(\frac{3}{2}\right)^2 + 3\left(\frac{3}{2}\right) + 10 = \frac{49}{4}$$

Vertex: $\left(\dfrac{3}{2}, \dfrac{49}{4}\right)$

Axis of symmetry: $x = \dfrac{3}{2}$

$-x^2 + 3x + 10 = 0$

$(-x-2)(x-5) = 0$

$-x - 2 = 0 \quad x - 5 = 0$

$x = -2 \quad\quad x = 5$

x-intercepts: $(-2, 0)$ and $(5, 0)$.

$f(0) = -(0)^2 + 3(0) + 10 = 10$

y-intercept $(0, 10)$

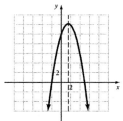

15.

x	$f(x) = 2x^2 - 4x - 1$	(x, y)
-1	$2(-1)^2 - 4(-1) - 1 = 5$	$(-1, 5)$
0	$2(0)^2 - 4(0) - 1 = -1$	$(0, -1)$
1	$2(1)^2 - 4(1) - 1 = -3$	$(1, -3)$
2	$2(2)^2 - 4(2) - 1 = -1$	$(2, -1)$
3	$2(3)^2 - 4(3) - 1 = 5$	$(3, 5)$

$$-\frac{b}{2a} = -\frac{-4}{2(2)} = \frac{4}{4} = 1$$

$$f(1) = 2(1)^2 - 4(1) - 1 = -3$$

Vertex: $(1, -3)$

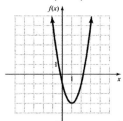

Domain: $(-\infty, \infty)$ Range: $[-3, \infty)$

16. $-x^2 - 3x + 18 < 0$

$-x^2 - 3x + 18 = 0$

$x + 6 = 0 \quad x - 3 = 0$

$x = -6 \quad\quad x = 3$

$x^2 + 3x - 18 = 0$

$(x + 6)(x - 3) = 0$

Inter-val	Test Value	$-x^2 - 3x + 18 < 0$	Conclu-sion
$x < -6$	-7	$-(-7)^2 - 3(-7) + 18$ $= -10$	$-10 < 0$
$-6 \le x \le 3$	0	$-(0)^2 - 3(0) + 18$ $= 18$	$18 \ge 0$
$3 < x$	4	$-(4)^2 - 3(4) + 18$ $= -10$	$-10 < 0$

$(-\infty, -6) \cup (3, \infty)$

$\longleftarrow \!\!\!+\!\!+\!\!+\!\!+\!\!+\!\!+\!\!+\!\!+\!\!+\!\!+\!\!+\!\!\longrightarrow$
$\quad -8\,-7\,-6\,-5\,-4\,-3\,-2\,-1\ \ 0\ \ 1\ \ 2\ \ 3\ \ 4$

17. Let r be the average speed of the airplane flying south.

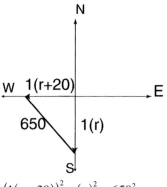

$(1(r+20))^2 + (r)^2 = 650^2$

$r^2 + 40r + 400 + r^2 = 422500$

$2r^2 + 40r - 422100 = 0$

$2(r^2 + 20r - 211050) = 0$

$r^2 + 20r - 211050 = 0$

$a = 1 \qquad b = 20 \qquad c = -211050$

$$r = \frac{-(20) \pm \sqrt{(20)^2 - 4(1)(-211050)}}{2(1)}$$

$$r = \frac{-20 \pm \sqrt{400 + 844200}}{2} = \frac{-20 \pm \sqrt{844600}}{2}$$

$$r = \frac{-20 \pm 919.0212..}{2} =$$

$$r = \frac{-20 - 919.0212..}{2} = r = \frac{-939.0212..}{2}$$

$r = -469.51... \quad r + 20 = -449.51...$

$$r = \frac{-20 + 919.0212...}{2} = \frac{899.0212...}{2}$$

$r = 449.510... \quad r + 20 = 469.510...$

The negative answer makes no sense in this problem. The average speed of the airplane flying west is approximately 470 mph and the average speed of the airplane flying south is approximately 450 mph.

18. Let t be the time it takes the senior clerk to process the applications alone. In one hour the senior clerk completes $\frac{1}{t}$ of the job, the junior clerk completes $\frac{1}{t+3}$ and together they complete $\frac{1}{2}$ of the job.

$$\frac{1}{t} + \frac{1}{t+3} = \frac{1}{2}$$

$$\frac{1}{t} \bullet 2t(t+3) + \frac{1}{t+3} \bullet 2t(t+3) = \frac{1}{2} \bullet 2t(t+3)$$

$2(t+3) + 2t = t(t+3)$

$2t + 6 + 2t = t^2 + 3t$

$t^2 - t - 6 = 0$

$(t - 3)(t + 2) = 0$

$t - 3 = 0 \quad t + 2 = 0$

$t = 3 \qquad t = -2$

$t + 3 = 6 \quad t + 3 = 1$

The negative answer makes no sense in this problem. Working alone, the senior clerk can process the applications in 3 hr and the junior clerk can process the applications in 6 hr.

19. $h(t) = -16t^2 + 96t + 3$

$a = -16 \quad b = 96$

Vertex is where $t = -\dfrac{b}{2a} = -\dfrac{96}{2(-16)} = 3$

$h(3) = -16(3)^2 + 96(3) + 3 =$

$-16(9) + 288 + 3 = -144 + 288 + 3 = 147$

The rocket will reach its maximum height of 147 ft in 3 sec.

20. $C(x) = 0.025x^2 - 8x + 800 < 320$

$0.025x^2 - 8x + 800 = 320$

$0.025x^2 - 8x + 480 = 0$

$a = 0.025 \qquad b = -8 \qquad c = 480$

$x = \dfrac{-(-8) \pm \sqrt{(-8)^2 - 4(0.025)(480)}}{2(0.025)}$

$x = \dfrac{8 \pm \sqrt{64 - 48}}{0.05} = \dfrac{8 \pm \sqrt{16}}{0.05} = \dfrac{8 \pm 4}{0.05}$

$x = \dfrac{8 + 4}{0.05} = \dfrac{12}{0.05} = 240 \quad x = \dfrac{8 - 4}{0.05} = \dfrac{4}{0.05} = 80$

Interval	Test Value	$0.025x^2 - 8x$ $+800 < 320$	Conclusion
$x \le 80$	60	$0.025(60)^2$ $-8(60) + 800 = 410$	$410 \ge 320$
$80 < x$ 240	100	$0.025(100)^2$ $-8(100) + 800 = 250$	$250 < 320$
$240 \le x$	260	$0.025(260)^2 -$ $8(260) + 800 = 410$	$410 \ge 320$

The factory can produce between, but not including 80 and 240 units each day.

Cumulative Review Exercises

1. $4n^5 \left(2n^3\right)^{-1} = \dfrac{4n^5}{2n^3} = 2n^{5-3} = 2n^2$

2. $|2x - 3| + 1 = 7$

$|2x - 3| = 6$

$2x - 3 = 6 \quad 2x - 3 = -6$

$2x = 9 \qquad 2x = -3$

$x = \dfrac{9}{2} \qquad x = -\dfrac{3}{2}$

3. $x + 4y - 8 = 0$

$4y = -x + 8$

$y = \dfrac{-x + 8}{4}$

x	$y = \dfrac{-x+8}{4}$	(x, y)
0	$\dfrac{-(0)+8}{4} = 2$	$(0, 2)$
4	$\dfrac{-(4)+8}{4} = 1$	$(4, 1)$

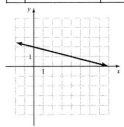

4. Every first element has a unique second element. Yes, the relation represents a function.

5. $\begin{array}{r} a^2 + 2a + 4 \\ \underline{a - 2} \\ -2a^2 - 4a - 8 \\ \underline{a^3 + 2a^2 + 4a} \\ a^3 \qquad\qquad -8 \\ a^3 - 8 \end{array}$

6. $2x^2 y^4 - 12x^3 y^3 + 16x^4 y^2 =$

$2x^2 y^2 \left(y^2 - 6xy + 8x^2\right) =$

$2x^2 y^2 (y - 2x)(y - 4x)$

7. $6x^2 - 2x = -1$

$6x^2 - 2x + 1 = 0$

$a = 6 \qquad b = -2 \qquad c = 1$

$x = \dfrac{-(-2) \pm \sqrt{(-2)^2 - 4(6)(1)}}{2(6)}$

$x = \dfrac{2 \pm \sqrt{4 - 24}}{12} = \dfrac{2 \pm \sqrt{-20}}{12} = \dfrac{2 \pm 2i\sqrt{5}}{12}$

$x = \dfrac{2\left(1 \pm i\sqrt{5}\right)}{12}$

$x = \dfrac{1 + i\sqrt{5}}{6} \qquad x = \dfrac{1 - i\sqrt{5}}{6}$

8. $\sqrt{27} - 3\sqrt{18} + 7\sqrt{3} =$

$\sqrt{9 \cdot 3} - 3\sqrt{9 \cdot 2} + 7\sqrt{3} =$

$3\sqrt{3} - 9\sqrt{2} + 7\sqrt{3} = 10\sqrt{3} - 9\sqrt{2}$

9.   a. Perimeter $= 2 \times$ length $+ 2 \times$ width

$2l + 2w < 1000$

b. The boundary line is dashed.

$2l + 2w = 1000$

$2w = 1000 - 2l$

$w = 500 - l$

l	$w = 500 - l$	(l, w)
0	$500 - (0) = 500$	$(0, 500)$
500	$500 - (500) = 0$	$(500, 0)$

Test point is (0, 0).

$2(0) + 2(0) \overset{?}{<} 1000$

$0 < 1000$ True.

Shade the region containing $(0, 0)$

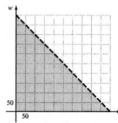

c. Answers may vary. Possible answers are 300 ft by 150 ft, 400 ft by 50 ft, or 200 ft. by 250 ft.

10.   a. Using the points (m, B):

$(120, 13.50), \quad (248, 19.90)$

$slope = \dfrac{B_2 - B_1}{m_2 - m_1} = \dfrac{19.90 - 13.50}{248 - 120}$

$slope = \dfrac{6.40}{128} = 0.05$

$B - B_1 = slope(m - m_1)$

$B - 13.50 = 0.05(m - 120)$

$B - 13.50 = 0.05m - 6.00$

$B = 0.05m + 7.5$

b. The slope is 0.05. It represents the per-minute fee for long-distance calls.

c. The y-intercept is (0, 7.5). It represents the flat monthly fee that the phone service charges.

CHAPTER 9 EXPONENTIAL AND LOGARITHMIC FUNCTIONS

Chapter 9 Pretest

1. $f(x) = 2x - 1$ $g(x) = 2x^2 + 5x - 3$

    a. $(f + g)(x) = 2x - 1 + 2x^2 + 5x - 3 =$

    $2x^2 + 7x - 4$

    b. $(f - g)(x) = (2x - 1) - (2x^2 + 5x - 3) =$

    $2x - 1 - 2x^2 - 5x + 3$

    $-2x^2 - 3x + 2$

    c. $(f \bullet g)(x) = (2x - 1)(2x^2 + 5x - 3) =$

    $4x^3 + 10x^2 - 6x - 2x^2 - 5x + 3 =$

    $4x^3 + 8x^2 - 11x + 3$

    d. $\left(\dfrac{f}{g}\right)(x) = \dfrac{2x - 1}{2x^2 + 5x - 3} = \dfrac{2x - 1}{(x + 3)(2x - 1)} =$

    $\dfrac{1}{x + 3}, \quad x \neq -3, \dfrac{1}{2}$

2. $f(x) = \dfrac{5}{x}$ $g(x) = 3x - 4$

    a. $(f \circ g)(x) = \dfrac{5}{3x - 4}; \quad x \neq \dfrac{4}{3}$

    b. $(g \circ f)(x) = 3\left(\dfrac{5}{x}\right) - 4 = \dfrac{15}{x} - 4; \quad x \neq 0$

    c. $(f \circ g)(3) = \dfrac{5}{3(3) - 4} = \dfrac{5}{5} = 1$

    d. $(g \circ f)(-5) = \dfrac{15}{(-5)} - 4 = -3 - 4 = -7$

3. Yes, it is a one-to-one function as each y-value in the range corresponds to exactly one x-value in the domain.

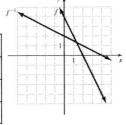

(x, y) in f	(x, y) in f^{-1}
$(0, 4)$	$(4, 0)$
$(1, 2)$	$(2, 1)$
$(3, -2)$	$(-2, 3)$

4. $f(x) = 3x - 7$

    $y = 3x - 7$ Substitute y for $f(x)$

    $x = 3y - 7$ Interchange x and y

    $x + 7 = 3y$

    $y = \dfrac{x + 7}{3}$

$f^{-1}(x) = \dfrac{x + 7}{3}$

5. a. $f(x) = 2^{x-5}$ $f(3) = 2^{3-5} = 2^{-2} = \dfrac{1}{2^2} = \dfrac{1}{4}$

    b. $f(x) = -e^{-x}$

    $f(-2) = -e^{-(-2)} = -e^2 = -7.3890... = -7.389$

6. a. $\log_7 (1) = \log_7 \left(7^0\right) = 0$

    b. $\log_9 \left(\dfrac{1}{81}\right) = \log_9 \left(\dfrac{1}{9^2}\right) = \log_9 \left(9^{-2}\right) = -2$

7. a. $f(x) = 2^x + 1$

x	$f(x) = 2^x + 1$	(x, y)
-3	$2^{-3} + 1 = \dfrac{9}{8}$	$\left(-3, \dfrac{9}{8}\right)$
-2	$2^{-2} + 1 = \dfrac{5}{4}$	$\left(-2, \dfrac{5}{4}\right)$
-1	$2^{-1} + 1 = \dfrac{3}{2}$	$\left(-1, \dfrac{3}{2}\right)$
0	$2^0 + 1 = 2$	$(0, 2)$
1	$2^1 + 1 = 3$	$(1, 3)$
2	$2^2 + 1 = 5$	$(2, 5)$
3	$2^3 + 1 = 9$	$(3, 9)$

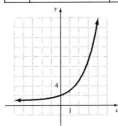

b. $f(x) = -\log_4(x)$

$y = -\log_4 x$

$-y = \log_4 x$

$4^{-y} = x$

y	$x = 4^{-y}$	(x, y)
-3	$4^{-(-3)} = 4^3 = 64$	$(64, -3)$
-2	$4^{-(-2)} = 4^2 = 16$	$(16, -2)$
-1	$4^{-(-1)} = 4$	$(4, -1)$
0	$4^{-(0)} = 1$	$(1, 0)$
1	$4^{-(1)} = \dfrac{1}{4}$	$\left(\dfrac{1}{4}, 1\right)$
2	$4^{-(2)} = \dfrac{1}{4^2} = \dfrac{1}{16}$	$\left(\dfrac{1}{16}, 2\right)$
3	$4^{-(3)} = \dfrac{1}{4^3} = \dfrac{1}{64}$	$\left(\dfrac{1}{64}, 3\right)$

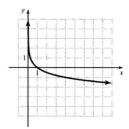

8.   a. $\log_6\left(6^5\right)=5$

b. $\log_4 1=\log_4\left(4^0\right)=0$

9.   a. $\log\dfrac{1}{10}=\log_{10}10^{-1}=-1$

b. $\ln e^5=\log_e e^5=5$

10. $\log_3 8=\dfrac{\log 8}{\log 3}=\dfrac{\ln 8}{\ln 3}=1.89278...=1.8928$

11.   a. $\log_5\left(5x^2\right)=\log_5 5+\log_5 x^2=$

$1+2\log_5 x$

b. $\log_8\dfrac{3x^3}{y}=\log_8 3x^3-\log_8 y=$

$\log_8 3+\log_8 x^3-\log_8 y=$

$\log_8 3+3\log_8 x-\log_8 y$

12.   a. $3\log_7 2+\log_7 5=\log_7 2^3+\log_7 5=$

$\log_7\left(2^3\bullet 5\right)=\log_7 40$

b. $4\log_6 x-2\log_6\left(x+2\right)=$

$\log_6 x^4-\log_6\left(x+2\right)^2=\log_6\left(\dfrac{x^4}{\left(x+2\right)^2}\right)$

13. $5^x=25$

$5^x=5^2$

$x=2$

14. $4^{x+1}=32^x$

$\left(2^2\right)^{x+1}=\left(2^5\right)^x$

$2^{2(x+1)}=2^{5x}$

$2(x+1)=5x$

$2x+2=5x$

$-3x=-2$

$x=\dfrac{2}{3}$

15. $\log_x\dfrac{1}{2}=-1$

$\dfrac{1}{2}=x^{-1}$

$\dfrac{1}{2}=\dfrac{1}{x}$

$x=2$

16. $\log_2\left(x-4\right)=3$

$x-4=2^3=8$

$x=12$

17. $\log_2 x+\log_2\left(x+6\right)=4$

$\log_2\left(x(x+6)\right)=4$

$x(x+6)=2^4$

$x^2+6x=16$

$x^2+6x-16=0$

$\left(x+8\right)\left(x-2\right)=0$

$x+8=0\quad x-2=0$

$x=-8\qquad x=2$

Check $x=-8$

$\log_2\left(-8\right)+\log_2\left(-8+6\right)\overset{?}{=}4$

$\log_2 x$ is only defined for $x>0$

-8 is not a solution.

Check for $x=2$

$\log_2 2+\log_2\left(2+6\right)\overset{?}{=}4$

$1+\log_2 8\overset{?}{=}4$

$1+\log_2 2^3\overset{?}{=}4$

$1+3\overset{?}{=}4;\quad 4=4$ True

18. $C(x)=P(1.04)^x$

$C(x)=3.89(1.04)^5=3.89(1.21665...)$

$C(x)=4.7327....$

A gallon of milk will cost about \$4.73 in 5 yr.

19. $\ln\left(r+1\right)=k$

$\ln\left(r+1\right)=0.045$

$r+1=e^{0.045}=1.04602...$

$r=0.04602...$

The effective annual interest rate is approximately 4.6%.

20. $C=C_0 e^{-0.21t}$

$12=100e^{-0.21t}$

$\dfrac{12}{100}=e^{-0.21t}$

$0.12=e^{-0.21t}$

$\ln\left(0.12\right)=-0.21t$

$\dfrac{\ln\left(0.12\right)}{-0.21}=t$

$t=\dfrac{-2.12026...}{-0.21}=10.096...$

It will take about 10.1 days for 100 mg of gallium-67 to decay to 12 mg.

Exercises 9.1 The Algebra of Functions and Inverse Functions

1. $f(x) = 2x+3 \quad g(x) = 4x^2-9$

$(f+g)(x) = 2x+3+4x^2-9 = 4x^2+2x-6$

$(f-g)(x) = 2x+3-(4x^2-9) =$

$2x+3-4x^2+9 = -4x^2+2x+12$

$(f \bullet g)(x) = (2x+3)(4x^2-9) =$

$8x^3-18x+12x^2-27 =$

$8x^3+12x^2-18x-27$

$\left(\dfrac{f}{g}\right)(x) = \dfrac{2x+3}{4x^2-9} = \dfrac{2x+3}{(2x+3)(2x-3)} =$

$\dfrac{1}{2x-3}; \quad x \ne -\dfrac{3}{2},\dfrac{3}{2}$

3. $f(x) = 3x^2+11x+6, \quad g(x) = 2x^2+5x-3$

$(f+g)(x) = 3x^2+11x+6+2x^2+5x-3 =$

$5x^2+16x+3$

$(f-g)(x) = 3x^2+11x+6-(2x^2+5x-3) =$

$3x^2+11x+6-2x^2-5x+3 = x^2+6x+9$

$(f \bullet g)(x) = (3x^2+11x+6)(2x^2+5x-3) =$

$\begin{array}{r} 3x^2+11x+6 \\ 2x^2+5x-3 \\ \hline -9x^2-33x-18 \\ 15x^3+55x^2+30x \\ 6x^4+22x^3+12x^2 \quad\quad \\ \hline 6x^4+37x^3+58x^2-3x-18 \end{array}$

$\left(\dfrac{f}{g}\right)(x) = \dfrac{3x^2+11x+6}{2x^2+5x-3} = \dfrac{(3x+2)(x+3)}{(x+3)(2x-1)} =$

$\dfrac{3x+2}{2x-1}; \quad x \ne -3,\dfrac{1}{2}$

5. $f(x) = \dfrac{1}{x+3}; \quad g(x) = \dfrac{3}{x-1}$

$(f+g)(x) = \dfrac{1}{x+3}+\dfrac{3}{x-1} =$

$\dfrac{1}{x+3} \bullet \dfrac{x-1}{x-1} + \dfrac{3}{x-1} \bullet \dfrac{x+3}{x+3} =$

$\dfrac{x-1+3(x+3)}{(x+3)(x-1)} = \dfrac{x-1+3x+9}{(x+3)(x-1)} =$

$\dfrac{4x+8}{(x+3)(x-1)} = \dfrac{4(x+2)}{(x+3)(x-1)}; \quad x \ne -3,1$

$(f-g)(x) = \dfrac{1}{x+3}-\dfrac{3}{x-1} =$

$\dfrac{1}{x+3} \bullet \dfrac{x-1}{x-1} - \dfrac{3}{x-1} \bullet \dfrac{x+3}{x+3} =$

$\dfrac{x-1-3(x+3)}{(x+3)(x-1)} = \dfrac{x-1-3x-9}{(x+3)(x-1)} =$

$\dfrac{-2x-10}{(x+3)(x-1)} = \dfrac{-2(x+5)}{(x+3)(x-1)}; \quad x \ne -3,1$

$(f \bullet g)(x) = \left(\dfrac{1}{x+3}\right)\left(\dfrac{3}{x-1}\right) =$

$\dfrac{3}{(x+3)(x-1)}; \quad x \ne -3,1$

$\left(\dfrac{f}{g}\right)(x) = \dfrac{\frac{1}{x+3}}{\frac{3}{x-1}} = \dfrac{1}{x+3} \bullet \dfrac{x-1}{3} =$

$\dfrac{x-1}{3(x+3)}; \quad x \ne -3,1$

7. $f(x) = 2\sqrt{x}; \quad g(x) = 4\sqrt{x}-1$

$(f+g)(x) = 2\sqrt{x}+4\sqrt{x}-1 = 6\sqrt{x}-1$

$(f-g)(x) = 2\sqrt{x}-(4\sqrt{x}-1) =$

$2\sqrt{x}-4\sqrt{x}+1 = -2\sqrt{x}+1$

$(f \bullet g)(x) = (2\sqrt{x})(4\sqrt{x}-1) =$

$8(\sqrt{x})^2-2\sqrt{x} = 8x-2\sqrt{x}$

$\left(\dfrac{f}{g}\right)(x) = \dfrac{2\sqrt{x}}{4\sqrt{x}-1} = \dfrac{2\sqrt{x}}{4\sqrt{x}-1} \bullet \dfrac{4\sqrt{x}+1}{4\sqrt{x}+1} =$

$\dfrac{8(\sqrt{x})^2+2\sqrt{x}}{16(\sqrt{x})^2-1} = \dfrac{8x+2\sqrt{x}}{16x-1}; \quad x \ne \dfrac{1}{16}$

9. $(f+g)(3) = (3^2-3(3)-4)+(1-(3)^2) =$

$9-9-4+1-9 = -12$

11. $(f-g)(-1) =$

$((-1)^2-3(-1)-4)-(1-(-1)^2) =$

$1+3-4-(1-1) = 4-4-0 = 0$

13. $(f \bullet g)(2) = ((2)^2-3(2)-4)(1-(2)^2) =$

$(4-6-4)(1-4) = (-6)(-3) = 18$

15. $\left(\dfrac{g}{f}\right)(5) = \dfrac{1-(5)^2}{(5)^2-3(5)-4} = \dfrac{1-25}{25-15-4}$

$= \dfrac{-24}{6} = -4$

17. $f(x) = 2x - 4; \ g(x) = \dfrac{1}{2}x - 5$

   a. $(f \circ g)(x) = 2\left(\dfrac{1}{2}x - 5\right) - 4 =$

   $x - 10 - 4 = x - 14$

   b. $(g \circ f)(x) = \dfrac{1}{2}(2x - 4) - 5 =$

   $x - 2 - 5 = x - 7$

   c. $(f \circ g)(3) = (3) - 14 = -11$

   d. $(g \circ f)(-1) = (-1) - 7 = -8$

19. $f(x) = x - 1; \ g(x) = x^2 + 4x - 10$

   a. $(f \circ g)(x) = (x^2 + 4x - 10) - 1 = x^2 + 4x - 11$

   b. $(g \circ f)(x) = (x - 1)^2 + 4(x - 1) - 10 =$

   $x^2 - 2x + 1 + 4x - 4 - 10 = x^2 + 2x - 13$

   c. $(f \circ g)(1) = (1)^2 + 4(1) - 11 = 1 + 4 - 11 = -6$

   d. $(g \circ f)(-1) = (-1)^2 + 2(-1) - 13 =$

   $1 - 2 - 13 = -14$

21. $f(x) = \dfrac{3}{x}; \ g(x) = 2x + 5$

   a. $(f \circ g)(x) = \dfrac{3}{2x + 5}; \ x \neq -\dfrac{5}{2}$

   b. $(g \circ f)(x) = 2\left(\dfrac{3}{x}\right) + 5 = \dfrac{6}{x} + 5; \ x \neq 0$

   c. $(f \circ g)\left(\dfrac{1}{2}\right) = \dfrac{3}{2\left(\dfrac{1}{2}\right) + 5} = \dfrac{3}{1 + 5} = \dfrac{3}{6} = \dfrac{1}{2}$

   d. $(g \circ f)(-2) = \dfrac{6}{(-2)} + 5 = -3 + 5 = 2$

23. $f(x) = -\sqrt{x}; \ g(x) = 1 - 4x$

   a. $(f \circ g)(x) = -\sqrt{1 - 4x}; \ x \leq \dfrac{1}{4}$

   b. $(g \circ f)(x) = 1 - 4\left(-\sqrt{x}\right) = 1 + 4\sqrt{x}; \ x \geq 0$

   d. $(f \circ g)(-6) = -\sqrt{1 - 4(-6)} =$

   $-\sqrt{1 + 24} = -\sqrt{25} = -5$

   d. $(g \circ f)(16) = 1 + 4\sqrt{(16)} =$

   $1 + 4(4) = 1 + 16 = 17$

25.   One-to-one function.
27.   One-to-one function.
29.   Not a one-to-one function.
31.   One-to-one function.
33.   The function has the point $(3, 2)$. The only choice
      with the point $(2, 3)$ is choice c.

35.   The function has the point $(3, -5)$. The only
      choice with the point $(-5, 3)$ is choice a.

37. $f^{-1}: \{(5, -4), (3, -2), (1, 0), (-1, 2), (-3, 4)\}$

39. $g^{-1}: \left\{ \begin{array}{l} (-3, -27), (-2, -8), (-1, -1), (0, 0), \\ (1, 1), (2, 8), (3, 27) \end{array} \right\}$

41. $y = 4x$ Substitute y for $f(x)$

   $x = 4y$ Interchange x and y

   $y = \dfrac{1}{4}x$

   $f^{-1}(x) = \dfrac{1}{4}x$

43. $y = \dfrac{1}{4}x$ Substitute y for $g(x)$

   $x = \dfrac{1}{4}y$ Interchange x and y

   $y = 4x$

   $g^{-1}(x) = 4x$

45. $y = -x - 5$ Substitute y for $f(x)$

   $x = -y - 5$ Interchange x and y

   $y = -x - 5$

   $f^{-1}(x) = -x - 5$

47. $y = 5x + 2$ Substitute y for $f(x)$

   $x = 5y + 2$ Interchange x and y

   $x - 2 = 5y$

   $y = \dfrac{x - 2}{5}$

   $f^{-1}(x) = \dfrac{x - 2}{5}$

49. $y = \dfrac{1}{2}x - 3$ Substitute y for $g(x)$

   $x = \dfrac{1}{2}y - 3$ Interchange x and y

   $x + 3 = \dfrac{1}{2}y$

   $2(x + 3) = y$

   $g^{-1}(x) = 2x + 6$

51. $y = x^3 - 4$ Substitute y for $f(x)$

   $x = y^3 - 4$ Interchange x and y

   $x + 4 = y^3$

   $y = \sqrt[3]{x + 4}$

   $f^{-1}(x) = \sqrt[3]{x + 4}$

53. $y = \dfrac{3}{x+4}$ Substitute y for $h(x)$

$x = \dfrac{3}{y+4}$ Interchange x and y

$x(y+4) = 3$

$y+4 = \dfrac{3}{x}$

$y = \dfrac{3}{x} - 4 = \dfrac{3}{x} - \dfrac{4x}{x}$

$h^{-1}(x) = \dfrac{3-4x}{x}$

55. $y = \dfrac{x}{2x-1}$ Substitute y for $f(x)$

$x = \dfrac{y}{2y-1}$ Interchange x and y

$2xy - x = y$ or $2xy - x = y$

$2xy - y = x$ $-x = y - 2xy$

$y(2x-1) = x$ $-x = y(1-2x)$

$y = \dfrac{x}{2x-1}$ $\dfrac{-x}{1-2x} = y$

$f^{-1}(x) = \dfrac{x}{2x-1}$ or $f^{-1}(x) = -\dfrac{x}{1-2x}$

57. $y = \sqrt[3]{x+4}$ Substitute y for $f(x)$

$x = \sqrt[3]{y+4}$ Interchange x and y

$x^3 = \left(\sqrt[3]{y+4}\right)^3$

$x^3 = y + 4$

$x^3 - 4 = y$

$f^{-1}(x) = x^3 - 4$

59. $(f \circ g)(x) = f(g(x)) = f(3x+1) =$

$\dfrac{(3x+1)-1}{3} = \dfrac{3x+1-1}{3} = \dfrac{3x}{3} = x$

$(g \circ f)(x) = g(f(x)) = g\left(\dfrac{x-1}{3}\right) =$

$3\left(\dfrac{(x-1)}{3}\right) + 1 = x - 1 + 1 = x$

$(f \circ g)(x) = x = (g \circ f)(x)$, the functions
are inverses of one other.

61. $(p \circ q)(x) = p(q(x)) = p\left(\dfrac{1}{5}x+2\right) =$

$5\left(\dfrac{1}{5}x+2\right) - 10 = x + 10 - 10 = x$

$(q \circ p)(x) = q(p(x)) = q(5x-10) =$

$\dfrac{1}{5}(5x-10) + 2 = x - 2 + 2 = x$

$(p \circ q)(x) = x = (q \circ p)(x)$, the functions
are inverses of one other.

63. $(f \circ g)(x) = f(g(x)) = f\left(\dfrac{x+1}{4}\right) =$

$-4\left(\dfrac{x+1}{4}\right) - 1 = -(x+1) - 1 =$

$-x - 1 - 1 = -x - 2;$ $(f \circ g)(x) \neq x$

$(g \circ f)(x) = g(f(x)) = g(-4x-1) =$

$\dfrac{(-4x-1)+1}{4} = \dfrac{-4x-1+1}{4} = \dfrac{-4x}{4} = -x$

$(g \circ f)(x) \neq x$

$(f \circ g)(x) \neq x \neq (g \circ f)(x)$, the functions
are not inverses of one another.

65. $(g \circ h)(x) = g(h(x)) = g\left(\sqrt[3]{x}-5\right) =$

$\left(\left(\sqrt[3]{x}-5\right)+5\right)^3 = \left(\sqrt[3]{x}-5+5\right)^3 = \left(\sqrt[3]{x}\right)^3 = x$

$(h \circ g)(x) = h(g(x)) = h\left((x+5)^3\right) =$

$\sqrt[3]{(x+5)^3} - 5 = x + 5 - 5 = x$

$(g \circ h)(x) = x = (h \circ g)(x)$, the functions
are inverses of one other.

67. $(p \circ q)(x) = p(q(x)) = p(2x^3+7) =$

$\sqrt[3]{2(2x^3+7)-7} = \sqrt[3]{4x^3+14-7}$

$= \sqrt[3]{4x^3+7} \neq x$

$(q \circ p)(x) = q(p(x)) = q\left(\sqrt[3]{2x-7}\right) =$

$2\left(\sqrt[3]{2x-7}\right)^3 + 7 = 2(2x-7) + 7 =$

$4x - 14 + 7 = 4x - 7 \neq x$

$(p \circ q)(x) \neq x \neq (q \circ p)(x)$, the functions
are not inverses of one other.

69. $(f \circ g)(x) = f(g(x)) = f\left(\dfrac{2}{x+3}\right) = \dfrac{2}{\dfrac{2}{x+3}} - 3$

$= \dfrac{2}{1} \cdot \dfrac{x+3}{2} - 3 = \dfrac{2(x+3)}{2} - 3 = x + 3 - 3 = x$

$(g \circ f)(x) = g(f(x)) = g\left(\dfrac{2}{x} - 3\right) =$

$\dfrac{2}{\left(\dfrac{2}{x}-3\right)+3} = \dfrac{2}{\dfrac{2}{x}-3+3} = \dfrac{2}{\dfrac{2}{x}} = \dfrac{2}{1} \cdot \dfrac{x}{2} = x$

$(f \circ g)(x) = x = (g \circ f)(x)$, the functions
are inverses of one other.

71. $(-3,0)$ and $(0,3)$ are on the function,
$(0,-3)$ and $(3,0)$ are on the inverse
function.

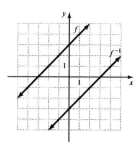

73. $(0,4)$, $(1,3)$, $(2,0)$ and $(3,-5)$
       are on the function,
       $(4,0)$, $(3,1)$, $(0,2)$ and $(-5,3)$
       are on the inverse function.

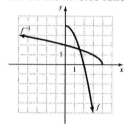

75.   a. $C(x) = 4.2x + 1000$; $x(d) = 500d$
       $(C \circ d)(x) = 4.2(500d) + 1000$

       $= 2100d + 1000$
       It represents the plant's weekly cost for d days of operation.
       b. $(C \circ d)(5) = 2100(5) + 1000 =$
       $10500 + 1000 = 11500$
       The weekly cost is $11,500.

77.   a. $S(n) = 180n - 360$

       $y = 180n - 360$ Substitute y for $S(n)$

       $n = 180y - 360$ Interchange n and y

       $n + 360 = 180y$

       $\dfrac{n + 360}{180} = y$

       $S^{-1}(n) = \dfrac{n + 360}{180}$

       b.   The inverse function can be used to calculate the number of sides of a polygon if the sum of the interior angles is known.
       c. $S^{-1}(540) = \dfrac{540 + 360}{180} = \dfrac{900}{180} = 5$
       The polygon has five sides.

79.   a. $B(t) = 0.05t + 4.5$

       b. $y = 0.05t + 4.5$ Substitute y for $B(t)$

       $t = 0.05y + 4.5$ Interchange t and y

       $t - 4.5 = 0.05y$

       $\dfrac{t - 4.5}{0.05} = y$

$$y = \frac{1}{0.05}t - \frac{4.5}{0.05}$$
$$B^{-1}(t) = 20t - 90$$

c. The inverse can be used to determine the number of minutes of long-distance calling.

Exercises 9.2 Exponential Functions

1.   Polynomial function; x has an integer exponent.

3.   Radical function; the exponent $\dfrac{1}{2}$ is $\sqrt{}$.

5.   Exponential function, it has a variable in the exponent.

7.   Polynomial function; x has an integer exponent.

9. $f(x) = 2^x$

       a. $f(-3) = 2^{-3} = \dfrac{1}{2^3} = \dfrac{1}{8}$

       b. $f(0) = 2^0 = 1$

       c. $f(4) = 2^4 = 16$

11. $g(x) = \left(\dfrac{1}{9}\right)^x$

       a. $g\left(-\dfrac{1}{2}\right) = \left(\dfrac{1}{9}\right)^{-\frac{1}{2}} = \left(\dfrac{9}{1}\right)^{\frac{1}{2}} = 9^{\frac{1}{2}} = \sqrt{9} = 3$

       b. $g\left(\dfrac{1}{2}\right) = \left(\dfrac{1}{9}\right)^{\frac{1}{2}} = \sqrt{\dfrac{1}{9}} = \dfrac{\sqrt{1}}{\sqrt{9}} = \dfrac{1}{3}$

       c. $g(2) = \left(\dfrac{1}{9}\right)^2 = \dfrac{1^2}{9^2} = \dfrac{1}{81}$

13. $f(x) = 3^{x-4}$

       a. $f(1) = 3^{1-4} = 3^{-3} = \dfrac{1}{3^3} = \dfrac{1}{27}$

       b. $f(3) = 3^{3-4} = 3^{-1} = \dfrac{1}{3}$

       c. $f(6) = 3^{6-4} = 3^2 = 9$

15. $h(x) = -2^x + 3$

       a. $h(-3) = -2^{-3} + 3 = -\dfrac{1}{2^3} + 3$

       $= -\dfrac{1}{8} + \dfrac{24}{8} = \dfrac{23}{8}$

       b. $h(0) = -2^0 + 3 = -1 + 3 = 2$

       c. $h(4) = -2^4 + 3 = -16 + 3 = -13$

17. $f(x) = -e^x$

       a. $f(-5) = -e^{-5} = -0.00673\ldots = -0.007$

       b. $f(1) = -e^1 = -2.71828\ldots = -2.718$

19. $g(x) = e^{-2x}$

a. $g(2) = e^{-2(2)} = e^{-4} = 0.01831... = 0.018$

b. $g\left(-\dfrac{1}{2}\right) = e^{-2\left(-\frac{1}{2}\right)} = e^{1} = 2.7182... = 2.718$

21. $f(x) = e^{3x-2}$

a. $f\left(-\dfrac{1}{3}\right) = e^{3\left(-\frac{1}{3}\right)-2} = e^{-1-2} = e^{-3}$

$= 0.0497... = 0.050$

b. $f(0) = e^{3(0)-2} = e^{-2} = 0.13533... = 0.135$

23. $f(x) = 3^{x}$

x	$f(x) = 3^{x}$	(x, y)
-3	$(3)^{-3} = \dfrac{1}{3^{3}} = \dfrac{1}{27}$	$\left(-3, \dfrac{1}{27}\right)$
-2	$(3)^{-2} = \dfrac{1}{3^{2}} = \dfrac{1}{9}$	$\left(-2, \dfrac{1}{9}\right)$
-1	$(3)^{-1} = \dfrac{1}{3}$	$\left(-1, \dfrac{1}{3}\right)$
0	$(3)^{0} = 1$	$(0, 1)$
1	$(3)^{1} = 3$	$(1, 3)$
2	$(3)^{2} = 9$	$(2, 9)$
3	$(3)^{3} = 27$	$(3, 27)$

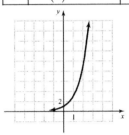

25. $f(x) = \left(\dfrac{1}{2}\right)^{x}$

x	$f(x) = \left(\dfrac{1}{2}\right)^{x}$	(x, y)
-3	$\left(\dfrac{1}{2}\right)^{-3} = 2^{3} = 8$	$(-3, 8)$
-2	$\left(\dfrac{1}{2}\right)^{-2} = 2^{2} = 4$	$(-2, 4)$
-1	$\left(\dfrac{1}{2}\right)^{-1} = 2$	$(-1, 2)$
0	$\left(\dfrac{1}{2}\right)^{0} = 1$	$(0, 1)$
1	$\left(\dfrac{1}{2}\right)^{1} = \dfrac{1}{2}$	$\left(1, \dfrac{1}{2}\right)$

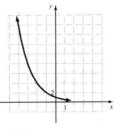

27. $f(x) = -2^{x}$

x	$f(x) = -2^{x}$	(x, y)
-3	$-2^{-3} = -\dfrac{1}{2^{3}} = -\dfrac{1}{8}$	$\left(-3, -\dfrac{1}{8}\right)$
-2	$-2^{-2} = -\dfrac{1}{2^{2}} = -\dfrac{1}{4}$	$\left(-2, -\dfrac{1}{4}\right)$
-1	$-2^{-1} = -\dfrac{1}{2}$	$\left(-1, -\dfrac{1}{2}\right)$
0	$-2^{0} = -1$	$(0, -1)$
1	$-2^{1} = -2$	$(1, -2)$
2	$-2^{2} = -4$	$(2, -4)$
3	$-2^{3} = -8$	$(3, -8)$

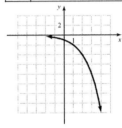

29. $f(x) = 2^{x-2}$

x	$f(x) = 2^{x-2}$	(x, y)
-1	$2^{-1-2} = 2^{-3} = \dfrac{1}{2^{3}} = \dfrac{1}{8}$	$\left(-1, \dfrac{1}{8}\right)$
0	$2^{0-2} = 2^{-2} = \dfrac{1}{2^{2}} = \dfrac{1}{4}$	$\left(0, \dfrac{1}{4}\right)$
1	$2^{1-2} = 2^{-1} = \dfrac{1}{2}$	$\left(1, \dfrac{1}{2}\right)$
2	$2^{2-2} = 2^{0} = 1$	$(2, 1)$
3	$2^{3-2} = 2^{1} = 2$	$(3, 2)$
4	$2^{4-2} = 2^{2} = 4$	$(4, 4)$
5	$2^{5-2} = 2^{3} = 8$	$(5, 8)$

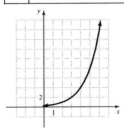

31    $f(x) = \left(\dfrac{1}{3}\right)^x + 2$

x	$f(x) = \left(\dfrac{1}{3}\right)^x + 2$	(x, y)
-3	$\left(\dfrac{1}{3}\right)^{-3} + 2 = 3^3 + 2 =$ $27 + 2 = 29$	$(-3, 29)$
-2	$\left(\dfrac{1}{3}\right)^{-2} + 2 = 3^2 + 2 =$ $9 + 2 = 11$	$(-2, 11)$
-1	$\left(\dfrac{1}{3}\right)^{-1} + 2 = 3 + 2 = 5$	$(-1, 5)$
0	$\left(\dfrac{1}{3}\right)^{0} + 2 = 1 + 2 = 3$	$(0, 3)$
1	$\left(\dfrac{1}{3}\right)^{1} + 2 = \dfrac{1}{3} + 2 =$ $\dfrac{7}{3}$	$\left(1, \dfrac{7}{3}\right)$
2	$\left(\dfrac{1}{3}\right)^{2} + 2 = \dfrac{1}{9} + 2 =$ $\dfrac{19}{9}$	$\left(2, \dfrac{19}{9}\right)$
3	$\left(\dfrac{1}{3}\right)^{3} + 2 = \dfrac{1}{27} + 2 =$ $\dfrac{55}{27}$	$\left(3, \dfrac{55}{27}\right)$

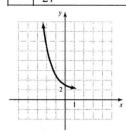

33. $5^x = 25$
$5^x = 5^2$
$x = 2$

35. $2^x = \dfrac{1}{32}$
$2^x = \dfrac{1}{2^5}$
$2^x = 2^{-5}$
$x = -5$

37. $36 = 6^{-x}$
$6^2 = 6^{-x}$
$2 = -x; \quad x = -2$

39. $8^x = 16$
$\left(2^3\right)^x = 2^4$
$2^{3x} = 2^4$
$3x = 4$
$x = \dfrac{4}{3}$

41. $4^{x+1} = 64$
$4^{x+1} = 4^3$
$x + 1 = 3$
$x = 2$

43. $7^{x-4} = 1$
$7^{x-4} = 7^0$
$x - 4 = 0$
$x = 4$

45. $16^{x+1} = 32$
$\left(2^4\right)^{x+1} = 2^5$
$2^{4(x+1)} = 2^5$
$4(x+1) = 5$
$4x + 4 = 5$
$4x = 1$
$x = \dfrac{1}{4}$

47. $9^{-x+3} = \dfrac{1}{27}$
$\left(3^2\right)^{-x+3} = \dfrac{1}{3^3}$
$3^{2(-x+3)} = 3^{-3}$
$2(-x+3) = -3$
$-2x + 6 = -3$
$-2x = -9$
$x = \dfrac{9}{2}$

49. $100^{x-5} = 100000^x$
$\left(10^2\right)^{x-5} = \left(10^5\right)^x$
$10^{2(x-5)} = 10^{5x}$
$2(x-5) = 5x$
$2x - 10 = 5x$
$-3x = 10$
$x = -\dfrac{10}{3}$

51. $64^{x-2} = 128^{x-3}$
$\left(2^6\right)^{x-2} = \left(2^7\right)^{x-3}$
$2^{6(x-2)} = 2^{7(x-3)}$

$6(x-2)=7(x-3)$

$6x-12=7x-21$

$-x=-9$

$x=9$

53. $S(n)=28000(1.04)^n$

$s(2)=28000(1.04)^2=$

$28000(1.0816)=30284.8$

The employee's salary will be \$30,284.80.

55. a. $C(m)=40(0.95)^m$

$C(12)=40(0.95)^{12}=$

$40(0.54036...)=21.6144...$

The concentration will be approximately 21.6 parts per million after 1 yr.

b. $C(0)=40(0.95)^0=40(1)=40$

The initial concentration of pollutants was 40 parts per million.

57. $A=P\left(1+\dfrac{r}{n}\right)^{nt}$

$A=8000\left(1+\dfrac{0.06}{12}\right)^{12(5)}=8000(1.005)^{60}=$

$8000(1.348850...)=10790.801...$

The amount in the account after 5 yr will be \$10,790.80.

59. $C(t)=50e^{-0.125t}$

$C(8)=50e^{-0.125(8)}=50e^{-1}=$

$50(0.36787...)=18.393...$

The concentration after 8 hr is approximately 18 mg/L.

61. $N=N_0(2)^{2h}$

$1280=10(2)^{2h}$

$128=(2)^{2h}$

$2^7=2^{2h}$

$7=2h$

$h=\dfrac{7}{2}=3.5$

1280 bacteria will be present in 3.5 hr.

Exercises 9.3 Logarithmic Functions

1. $\log_3 81=4 \quad 3^4=81$

3. $\log_{\frac{1}{2}}\dfrac{1}{32}=5 \quad \left(\dfrac{1}{2}\right)^5=\dfrac{1}{32}$

5. $\log_5 \dfrac{1}{25}=-2 \quad 5^{-2}=\dfrac{1}{25}$

7. $\log_{\frac{1}{4}} 4=-1 \quad \left(\dfrac{1}{4}\right)^{-1}=4$

9. $\log_{16} 2=\dfrac{1}{4} \quad 16^{\frac{1}{4}}=2$

11. $\log_{10}\sqrt{10}=\dfrac{1}{2} \quad 10^{\frac{1}{2}}=\sqrt{10}$

13. $3^5=243 \quad \log_3 243=5$

15. $\left(\dfrac{1}{4}\right)^1=\dfrac{1}{4} \quad \log_{\frac{1}{4}}\left(\dfrac{1}{4}\right)=1$

17. $2^{-4}=\dfrac{1}{16} \quad \log_2 \dfrac{1}{16}=-4$

19. $\left(\dfrac{1}{3}\right)^{-4}=81 \quad \log_{\frac{1}{3}} 81=-4$

21. $49^{\frac{1}{2}}=7 \quad \log_{49} 7=\dfrac{1}{2}$

23. $11^{\frac{1}{5}}=\sqrt[5]{11} \quad \log_{11}\sqrt[5]{11}=\dfrac{1}{5}$

25. $\log_5 125=\log_5 5^3=3$

27. $\log_3 9=\log_3 3^2=2$

29. $\log_6 6=\log_6 6^1=1$

31. $\log_{\frac{1}{2}}\dfrac{1}{16}=\log_{\frac{1}{2}}\dfrac{1}{2^4}=\log_{\frac{1}{2}}\left(\dfrac{1}{2}\right)^4=4$

33. $\log_4 \dfrac{1}{64}=\log_4 \dfrac{1}{4^3}=\log_4 4^{-3}=-3$

35. $\log_{\frac{1}{4}} 16=\log_{\frac{1}{4}} 4^2=$

$\log_{\frac{1}{4}}\dfrac{1}{4^{-2}}=\log_{\frac{1}{4}}\left(\dfrac{1}{4}\right)^{-2}=-2$

37. $\log_9 1=\log_9 9^0=0$

39. $\log_{27} 3=\log_{27}\sqrt[3]{27}=\log_{27} 27^{\frac{1}{3}}=\dfrac{1}{3}$

41. $\log_{\frac{1}{16}}\dfrac{1}{2}=\log_{\frac{1}{16}}\sqrt[4]{\dfrac{1}{16}}=\log_{\frac{1}{16}}\left(\dfrac{1}{16}\right)^{\frac{1}{4}}=\dfrac{1}{4}$

43. $\log_{36}\dfrac{1}{6}=\log_{36}\dfrac{1}{\sqrt{36}}=\log_{36}\dfrac{1}{36^{\frac{1}{2}}}=$

$\log_{36} 36^{-\frac{1}{2}}=-\dfrac{1}{2}$

45. $\log_3 x=3 \quad 3^3=x \quad x=27$

47. $\log_6 x=-2 \quad 6^{-2}=x \quad x=\dfrac{1}{6^2}=\dfrac{1}{36}$

49. $\log_{\frac{2}{3}} x=-1 \quad \left(\dfrac{2}{3}\right)^{-1}=x \quad x=\dfrac{3}{2}$

51. $\log_4 x=\dfrac{1}{2} \quad 4^{\frac{1}{2}}=x \quad x=\sqrt{4}=2$

53. $\log_x 216 = 3$ $x^3 = 216$ $x = \sqrt[3]{216} = 6$

55. $\log_x 2 = \dfrac{1}{3}$ $x^{\frac{1}{3}} = 2$ $x = 2^3 = 8$

57. $\log_x \dfrac{9}{16} = 2$ $x^2 = \dfrac{9}{16}$ $x = \sqrt{\dfrac{9}{16}} = \dfrac{3}{4}$

59. $\log_x 7 = -1$ $x^{-1} = 7$ $\left(x^{-1}\right)^{-1} = (7)^{-1}$

$x = 7^{-1}$ $x = \dfrac{1}{7}$

61. $\log_4 8 = x$ $4^x = 8$ $\left(2^2\right)^x = 2^3$

$2^{2x} = 2^3$ $2x = 3$ $x = \dfrac{3}{2}$

63. $\log_{27} 81 = x$ $27^x = 81$ $\left(3^3\right)^x = 3^4$

$3^{3x} = 3^4$ $3x = 4$ $x = \dfrac{4}{3}$

65. $\log_{\frac{1}{3}} 81 = x$ $\left(\dfrac{1}{3}\right)^x = 81$ $\left(3^{-1}\right)^x = 3^4$

$3^{-x} = 3^4$ $-x = 4$ $x = -4$

67. $y = \log_3(x)$

$x = 3^y$

y	$x = 3^y$	(x, y)
-2	$3^{-2} = \dfrac{1}{3^2} = \dfrac{1}{9}$	$\left(\dfrac{1}{9}, -2\right)$
-1	$3^{-1} = \dfrac{1}{3}$	$\left(\dfrac{1}{3}, -1\right)$
0	$3^0 = 1$	$(1, 0)$
1	$3^1 = 3$	$(3, 1)$
2	$3^2 = 9$	$(9, 2)$

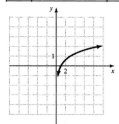

69. $y = \log_{\frac{1}{3}} x$

$\left(\dfrac{1}{3}\right)^y = x$

y	$x = \left(\dfrac{1}{3}\right)^y$	(x, y)
-3	$\left(\dfrac{1}{3}\right)^{-3} = 3^3 = 27$	$(27, -3)$
-2	$\left(\dfrac{1}{3}\right)^{-2} = 3^2 = 9$	$(9, -2)$
-1	$\left(\dfrac{1}{3}\right)^{-1} = 3$	$(3, -1)$
0	$\left(\dfrac{1}{3}\right)^0 = 1$	$(1, 0)$
1	$\left(\dfrac{1}{3}\right)^1 = \dfrac{1}{3}$	$\left(\dfrac{1}{3}, 1\right)$
2	$\left(\dfrac{1}{3}\right)^2 = \dfrac{1}{3^2} = \dfrac{1}{9}$	$\left(\dfrac{1}{9}, 2\right)$
3	$\left(\dfrac{1}{3}\right)^3 = \dfrac{1}{3^3} = \dfrac{1}{27}$	$\left(\dfrac{1}{27}, 3\right)$

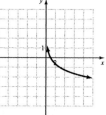

71. $y = -\log_3 x$

$-y = \log_3 x$

$3^{-y} = x$

$x = 3^{-y}$

y	$x = 3^{-y}$	(x, y)
-3	$3^{-(-3)} = 3^3 = 27$	$(27, -3)$
-2	$3^{-(-2)} = 3^2 = 9$	$(9, -2)$
-1	$3^{-(-1)} = 3^1 = 3$	$(3, -1)$
0	$3^{-0} = 1$	$(1, 0)$
1	$3^{-1} = \dfrac{1}{3}$	$\left(\dfrac{1}{3}, 1\right)$
2	$3^{-2} = \dfrac{1}{3^2} = \dfrac{1}{9}$	$\left(\dfrac{1}{9}, 2\right)$
3	$3^{-3} = \dfrac{1}{3^3} = \dfrac{1}{27}$	$\left(\dfrac{1}{27}, 3\right)$

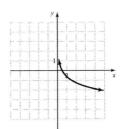

73. $P = 10\log_{10}\left(\dfrac{W_2}{W_1}\right) = 10\log_{10}\left(\dfrac{100}{10^{-2}}\right)$

$P = 10\log_{10}\left(\dfrac{10^2}{10^{-2}}\right) = 10\log_{10}\left(10^4\right)$

$P = 10(4) = 40$

The power gain is 40 dB.

75. $h = \log_2\left(\dfrac{N}{N_0}\right) = \log_2\left(\dfrac{512}{8}\right) = \log_2\left(64\right)$

$h = \log_2\left(2^6\right) = 6$

The population reaches 512 bacteria in 6 hr.

77. $\log_2 i = -t$

$\log_2 i = -3 \quad 2^{-3} = i \quad i = \dfrac{1}{2^3} = \dfrac{1}{8}$

The amount of the current is $\dfrac{1}{8}$ amp.

79. $t = N + \log_2 N = 64 + \log_2 64$

$t = 64 + \log_2 2^6 = 64 + 6 = 70$

It takes the computer 70 picoseconds to carry out 64 computations.

81. a. $\log_{36} x = \dfrac{1}{2} \quad 35^{\frac{1}{2}} = x \quad x = \sqrt{36} = 6$

The length of the side of the fence is 6 ft.
b. The base represents the area enclosed by the fence.

Exercises 9.4 Properties of Logarithms

1. $\log_2\left(16 \bullet 5\right) = \log_2 16 + \log_2 5 =$

$\log_2 2^4 + \log_2 5 = 4 + \log_2 5$

3. $\log_6 \dfrac{7}{36} = \log_6 7 - \log_6 36 =$

$\log_6 7 - \log_6 6^2 = \log_6 7 - 2$

5. $\log_3 8x = \log_3 8 + \log_3 x$

7. $\log_n uv = \log_n u + \log_n v$

9. $\log_b\left[a(b-1)\right] = \log_b a + \log_b (b-1)$

11. $\log_4 \dfrac{64}{n} = \log_4 64 - \log_4 n =$

$\log_4 4^3 - \log_4 n = 3 - \log_4 n$

13. $\log_7 \dfrac{v}{u} = \log_7 v - \log_7 u$

15. $\log_a \dfrac{b-a}{b+a} = \log_a\left(b-a\right) - \log_a\left(b+a\right)$

17. $\log_2 5 + \log_2 7 = \log_2\left(5 \bullet 7\right) = \log_2 35$

19. $\log_7 10 - \log_7 2 = \log_7 \dfrac{10}{2} = \log_7 5$

21. $1 + \log_x 6 = \log_x x^1 + \log_x 6 = \log_x 6x$

23. $1 - \log_b 16 = \log_b b^1 - \log_b 16 = \log_b \dfrac{b}{16}$

25. $\log_5 2 + \log_5\left(x-5\right) =$

$\log_5 2(x-5) = \log_5\left(2x-10\right)$

27. $\log_n x + \log_n z = \log_n xz$

29. $\log_5 k - \log_5 n = \log_5 \dfrac{k}{n}$

31. $\log_{10}\left(a+b\right) - \log_{10}\left(a-b\right) = \log_{10} \dfrac{a+b}{a-b}$

33. $\log_6 8^2 = 2\log_6 8$

35. $\log_3 x^4 = 4\log_3 x$

37. $\log_a \sqrt[5]{b} = \log_a b^{\frac{1}{5}} = \dfrac{1}{5}\log_a b$

39. $\log_4 a^{-1} = (-1)\log_4 a = -\log_4 a$

41. Since $\log_b b^x = x \quad \log_5 5^4 = 4$

43. Since $\log_b b^x = x \quad \log_2 2^{\frac{1}{2}} = \dfrac{1}{2}$

45. Since $\log_b b^x = x \quad \log_x x^{-3} = -3$

47. Since $b^{\log_b x} = x, \quad 8^{\log_8 15} = 15$

49. Since $b^{\log_b x} = x, \quad 9^{\log_9 x} = x$

51. Since $b^{\log_b x} = x, \quad x^{\log_x 10} = 10$

53. $2\log_2 6 + \log_2 3 = \log_2\left(6^2 \bullet 3\right) = \log_2 108$

55. $4\log_7 2 - 3\log_7 4 = \log_7 2^4 - \log_7 4^3 =$

$\log_7 \dfrac{2^4}{4^3} = \log_7 \dfrac{16}{64} = \log_7 \dfrac{1}{4}$

57. $-\log_4 x + 6\log_4 y = \log_4 x^{-1} + \log_4 y^6 =$

$\log_4\left(x^{-1} \bullet y^6\right) = \log_4 \dfrac{y^6}{x}$

59. $2\log_b 3 + 3\log_b 2 - \log_b 9 =$

$\log_b 3^2 + \log_b 2^3 - \log_b 9 = \log_b\left(\dfrac{3^2 \bullet 2^3}{9}\right) =$

$\log_b\left(\dfrac{9 \bullet 8}{9}\right) = \log_b 8$

61. $\dfrac{1}{2}\left(\log_4 x - 2\log_4 y\right) = \dfrac{1}{2}\log_4 x - \log_4 y =$

$$\log_4 x^{\frac{1}{2}} - \log_4 y = \log_4 \frac{x^{\frac{1}{2}}}{y} = \log_4 \frac{\sqrt{x}}{y}$$

63. $2\log_5 x + \log_5 (x-1) =$

$$\log_5 x^2 + \log_5 (x-1) = \log_5 x^2 (x-1) =$$

$$\log_5 (x^3 - x^2)$$

65. $\frac{1}{3}\left[\log_6 (x^2 - y^2) - \log_6 (x+y)\right] =$

$$\frac{1}{3}\log_6 \frac{x^2 - y^2}{x+y} = \frac{1}{3}\log_6 \frac{(x-y)(x+y)}{x+y} =$$

$$\frac{1}{3}\log_6 (x-y) = \log_6 (x-y)^{\frac{1}{3}} = \log_6 \sqrt[3]{x-y}$$

67. $-\log_2 z + 4\log_2 x - 5\log_2 y =$

$$-\log_2 z + \log_2 x^4 - \log_2 y^5 =$$

$$\log_2 x^4 - \log_2 y^5 - \log_2 z = \log_2 \frac{x^4}{y^5 z}$$

69. $\frac{1}{4}\log_5 a - 8\log_5 b + \frac{3}{4}\log_5 c =$

$$\log_5 a^{\frac{1}{4}} - \log_5 b^8 + \log_5 c^{\frac{3}{4}} =$$

$$\log_5 \frac{a^{\frac{1}{4}}(c^3)^{\frac{1}{4}}}{b^8} = \log_5 \frac{\sqrt[4]{ac^3}}{b^8}$$

71. $\log_6 3y^2 = \log_6 3 + \log_6 y^2 = \log_6 3 + 2\log_6 y$

73. $\log_x x^3 y^2 = \log_x x^3 + 2\log_x y = 3 + 2\log_x y$

75. $\log_2 4x^2 y^5 = \log_2 4 + \log_2 x^2 + \log_2 y^5 =$

$$\log_2 2^2 + 2\log_2 x + 5\log_2 y =$$

$$2 + 2\log_2 x + 5\log_2 y$$

77. $\log_8 \sqrt{10x} = \log_8 (10x)^{\frac{1}{2}} = \frac{1}{2}\log_8 10x =$

$$\frac{1}{2}[\log_8 10 + \log_8 x] = \frac{1}{2}\log_8 10 + \frac{1}{2}\log_8 x$$

79. $\log_4 \frac{x^2}{y} = \log_4 x^2 - \log_4 y = 2\log_4 x - \log_4 y$

81. $\log_7 \sqrt[4]{\frac{u^3}{v}} = \log_7 \left(\frac{u^3}{v}\right)^{\frac{1}{4}} = \frac{1}{4}\log_7 \frac{u^3}{v} =$

$$\frac{1}{4}[\log_7 u^3 - \log_y v] = \frac{1}{4}[3\log_7 u - \log_y v] =$$

$$\frac{3}{4}\log_7 u - \frac{1}{4}\log_7 v$$

83. $\log_c \frac{a^2 c^4}{b^3} = \log_c a^2 + \log_c c^4 - \log_c b^3 =$

$$2\log_c a + 4 - 3\log_c b$$

85. $\log_6 \frac{x^3}{(x-y)^2} = \log_6 x^3 - \log_6 (x-y)^2 =$

$3\log_6 x - 2\log_6 (x-y)$

87. $\log_a x^2 \sqrt[5]{y^3 z^2} = \log_a x^2 + \log_a (y^3 z^2)^{\frac{1}{5}} =$

$$2\log_a x + \frac{1}{5}\log_a (y^3 z^2) =$$

$$2\log_a x + \frac{1}{5}\left[\log_a y^3 + \log_a z^2\right] =$$

$$2\log_a x + \frac{1}{5}[3\log_a y + 2\log_a z] =$$

$$2\log_a x + \frac{3}{5}\log_a y + \frac{2}{5}\log_a z$$

89. $M = \log_{10} I = \log_{10} 10^{8.3} = 8.3$

The magnitude of the earthquake was 8.3.

91. $S = 10\log_{10}\left(\frac{P}{P_0}\right)^2 = 2 \cdot 10\log_{10}\frac{P}{P_0} =$

$$20[\log_{10} P - \log_{10} P_0] =$$

$$20\log_{10} P - 20\log_{10} P_0$$

93. a. $\log_{10} C = \log_{10} C_0 + 0.2t \log_{10} \frac{1}{2} =$

$$\log_{10} C = \log_{10} C_0 + \log_{10}\left(\frac{1}{2}\right)^{0.2t}$$

$$\log_{10} C = \log_{10}\left[C_0\left(\frac{1}{2}\right)^{0.2t}\right]$$

$$C = 10^{\log_{10}\left[C_0\left(\frac{1}{2}\right)^{0.2t}\right]} = C_0\left(\frac{1}{2}\right)^{0.2t}$$

$$C = C_0\left(\frac{1}{2}\right)^{0.2t}$$

b. $C = 50\left(\frac{1}{2}\right)^{0.2(10)} = 50\left(\frac{1}{2}\right)^2 =$

$$50\left(\frac{1}{4}\right) = 12.5$$

12.5 g will remain after 10 yr.

Exercises 9.5 Common Logarithms, Natural Logarithms, and Change of Base

1. $\log 4 = 0.60205... \approx 0.6021$

3. $\log 18 = 1.25527... \approx 1.2553$

5. $\log\left(\frac{2}{3}\right) = -0.17609... \approx -0.1761$

7. $\log 1.3 = 0.11394... \approx 0.1139$

9. $\ln 3 = 1.09861... \approx 1.0986$

11. $\ln 17 = 2.83321... \approx 2.8332$

13. $\ln\left(\frac{5}{8}\right) = -0.47000 \approx -0.4700$

15. $\ln 1.2 = 0.18232... \approx 0.1823$

17. $\log 1,000,000 = \log 10^6 = 6$

19. $\log\left(\dfrac{1}{1000}\right) = \log\left(\dfrac{1}{10^3}\right) = \log\left(10^{-3}\right) = -3$

21. $\log(0.01) = \log\left(10^{-2}\right) = -2$

23. $\log \sqrt[4]{1000} = \log \sqrt[4]{10^3} = \log 10^{\frac{3}{4}} = \dfrac{3}{4}$

25. $\log 10^x = x$

27. $\ln e^4 = 4$

29. $\ln \dfrac{1}{e} = \ln e^{-1} = -1$

31. $\ln \sqrt{e} = \ln e^{\frac{1}{2}} = \dfrac{1}{2}$

33. $\ln e^b = b$

35. $10^{\log 6} = 6$

37. $e^{\ln 3} = 3$

39. $\log_2 7 = \dfrac{\ln 7}{\ln 2}$ or $\dfrac{\log 7}{\log 2} = 2.80735... \approx 2.8074$

41. $\log_6 21 = \dfrac{\ln 21}{\ln 6}$ or $\dfrac{\log 21}{\log 6} =$

    $1.69918... \approx 1.6992$

43. $\log_{\frac{1}{2}} 11 = \dfrac{\ln 11}{\ln \frac{1}{2}}$ or $\dfrac{\log 11}{\log \frac{1}{2}} =$

    $-3.45943... \approx -3.4594$

45. $\log_3 \dfrac{1}{2} = \dfrac{\ln \frac{1}{2}}{\ln 3}$ or $\dfrac{\log \frac{1}{2}}{\log 3} =$

    $-0.63092... \approx -0.6309$

47. $\log_5 3.6 = \dfrac{\ln 3.6}{\ln 5}$ or $\dfrac{\log 3.6}{\log 5} =$

    $0.79588... \approx 0.7959$

49. $\log_7 0.023 = \dfrac{\ln 0.023}{\ln 7}$ or $\dfrac{\log 0.023}{\log 7} =$

    $-1.938558... \approx -1.9386$

51. $pH = -\log\left[H^+\right] = -\log\left[3.2 \times 10^{-13}\right] =$

    $-\left(\log[3.2] + \log\left[10^{-13}\right]\right) =$

    $-(0.5051499... - 13) = -(-12.49485)... \approx 12.5$

    The pH of household bleach is approximately 12.5.

53. $R(x) = 1.45 + 2\log(x+1) =$

    $1.45 + 2\log(5+1) = 1.45 + 2\log(6) =$

    $1.45 + 2(0.7781...) = 1.45 + 1.5563... =$

    $3.006...$

    The company's revenue was approximately $3 million in the year 2005.

55. $kd = -\left(\ln I - \ln I_0\right)$

    $kd = -\left(\ln \dfrac{I}{I_0}\right)$

    $-kd = \ln \dfrac{I}{I_0}$

    $e^{-kd} = \dfrac{I}{I_0}$

    $I = I_0 e^{-kd}$

57. $\log_2 60 = \dfrac{\ln 60}{\ln 2}$ or $\dfrac{\log 60}{\log 2} = 5.90689... \approx 5.9$

    The population will grow to 60 bacteria in approximately 5.9 hr.

Exercises 9.6 Exponential and Logarithmic Equations

1. $x = \log_3 18 = \dfrac{\ln 18}{\ln 3}$ or $\dfrac{\log 18}{\log 3} =$

    $2.63092... \approx 2.6309$

3. $x = \log_{\frac{1}{2}} 9 = \dfrac{\ln 9}{\ln \frac{1}{2}}$ or $\dfrac{\log 9}{\log \frac{1}{2}} =$

    $-3.16992... \approx -3.1699$

5. $x = \log_4 \dfrac{3}{4} = \dfrac{\ln \frac{3}{4}}{\ln 4}$ or $\dfrac{\log \frac{3}{4}}{\log 4} =$

    $-0.20751... \approx -0.2075$

7. $x = \log_{5.4} 0.0034 = \dfrac{\ln 0.0034}{\ln 5.4}$ or $\dfrac{\log 0.0034}{\log 5.4} =$

    $-3.37048... \approx -3.3705$

9. $3x = \log_2 4.6$

    $x = \dfrac{1}{3}\log_2 4.6 = \left(\dfrac{1}{3}\right)\dfrac{\ln 4.6}{\ln 2}$ or $\left(\dfrac{1}{3}\right)\dfrac{\log 4.6}{\log 2} =$

    $\left(\dfrac{1}{3}\right)(2.201633...) = 0.73387... \approx 0.7339$

11. $100^x = 55$

    $\left(10^2\right)^x = 55$

    $10^{2x} = 55$

    $2x = \log 55$

    $x = \left(\dfrac{1}{2}\right)1.74036... = 0.87018... \approx 0.8702$

13. $x + 4 = \log_3 38 = \dfrac{\ln 38}{\ln 3}$ or $\dfrac{\log 38}{\log 3} =$

    $x + 4 = 3.31107... \approx 3.3111$

    $x = -4 + 3.3111 = -0.6889$

15. $2x-3=\log_5 43 = \dfrac{\ln 43}{\ln 5}$ or $\dfrac{\log 43}{\log 5}$

$2x-3=2.33696...\approx 2.3370$

$2x-3=2.3370$

$2x=5.3370$

$x=2.6685$

17. $0.25x=\ln(3.1)=1.13140...\approx 1.1314$

$x=\dfrac{1.1314}{0.25}=4.5256$

19. $x+10=3^4$

$x=3^4-10=81-10=71$

21. $4x-3=5^1$

$4x=5+3=8$

$x=\dfrac{8}{4}=2$

23. $x+1=2^{-3}=\dfrac{1}{8}$

$x=\dfrac{1}{8}-1=-\dfrac{7}{8}$

25. $x^2-21=10^2=100$

$x^2=100+21=121$

$x=\pm\sqrt{121}=\pm 11$

$x=11,\ \ x=-11$

27. $\log_4 x+\log_4 6=2$

$\log_4 6x=2$

$6x=4^2$

$x=\dfrac{16}{6}=\dfrac{8}{3}$

29. $\log_3 x-\log_3 7=2$

$\log_3 \dfrac{x}{7}=2$

$\dfrac{x}{7}=3^2=9$

$x=7(9)=63$

31. $\log_2 x+\log_2(x-3)=2$

$\log_2 x(x-3)=2$

$x(x-3)=2^2$

$x^2-3x=4$

$x^2-3x-4=0$

$(x-4)(x+1)=0$

$x-4=0\ \ \ x+1=0$

$x=4\ \ \ \ \ \ \ x=-1$

Check $x=-1$

$\log_2(-1)+\log_2(-1-3)\overset{?}{=}2$

Logarithm of values ≤ 0 is undefined. $x=-1$ is not a solution.

Check $x=4$

$\log_2(4)+\log_2(4-3)\overset{?}{=}2$

$\log_2 2^2+\log_2 1\overset{?}{=}2$

$2+0=2$ True

33. $\log_2(x+2)+\log_2(x-5)=3$

$\log_2(x+2)(x-5)=3$

$(x+2)(x-5)=2^3$

$x^2-3x-10=8$

$x^2-3x-18=0$

$(x-6)(x+3)=0$

$x-6=0\ \ \ x+3=0$

$x=6\ \ \ \ \ \ \ x=-3$

Check $x=6$

$\log_2(6+2)+\log_2(6-5)\overset{?}{=}3$

$\log_2 8+\log_2 1\overset{?}{=}3$

$\log_2 2^3+\log_2 2^0\overset{?}{=}3$

$3+0=3$ True

Check $x=-3$

$\log_2(-3+2)+\log_2(-3-5)\overset{?}{=}3$

$\log_2(-1)+\log_2(-8)\overset{?}{=}3$

Logarithms of values ≤ 0 are undefined. $x=-3$ is not a solution.

35. $\log_4(2x-1)+\log_4(6x-1)=2$

$\log_4\left[(2x-1)(6x-1)\right]=2$

$(2x-1)(6x-1)=4^2$

$12x^2-8x+1=16$

$12x^2-8x-15=0$

$(2x-3)(6x+5)=0$

$2x-3=0\ \ \ 6x+5=0$

$2x=3\ \ \ \ \ \ \ 6x=-5$

$x=\dfrac{3}{2}\ \ \ \ \ \ \ x=-\dfrac{5}{6}$

Check $x = \dfrac{3}{2}$

$\log_4\left(2\left(\dfrac{3}{2}\right)-1\right)+\log_4\left(6\left(\dfrac{3}{2}\right)-1\right)\overset{?}{=}2$

$\log_4 2 + \log_4 8 \overset{?}{=} 2$

$\log_4(2 \bullet 8)\overset{?}{=}2$

$\log_4 16\overset{?}{=}2$

$\log_4 4^2\overset{?}{=}2$

$2 = 2$ True

Check $x = -\dfrac{5}{6}$

$\log_4\left(2\left(-\dfrac{5}{6}\right)-1\right)+\log_4\left(6\left(-\dfrac{5}{6}\right)-1\right)\overset{?}{=}2$

$\log_4\left(-\dfrac{8}{3}\right)+\log_4(-6)\overset{?}{=}2$

Logarithms of values ≤ 0 are undefined .

$-\dfrac{5}{6}$ is not a solution.

37. $\log_3(7x)-\log_3(x-1)=2$

$\log_3\dfrac{7x}{x-1}=2$

$\dfrac{7x}{x-1}=3^2$

$7x=9(x-1)$

$7x=9x-9$

$-2x=-9$

$x=\dfrac{9}{2}$

39. $\log_2(3x+7)-\log_2(x-1)=3$

$\log_2\dfrac{3x+7}{x-1}=3$

$\dfrac{3x+7}{x-1}=2^3$

$3x+7=8(x-1)$

$3x+7=8x-8$

$-5x=-15$

$x=3$

41. $\log_8 x+\log_8(x+1)=\dfrac{1}{3}$

$\log_8\left[x(x+1)\right]=\dfrac{1}{3}$

$x(x+1)=8^{\frac{1}{3}}=\sqrt[3]{8}=2$

$x^2+x=2$

$x^2+x-2=0$

$(x-1)(x+2)=0$

$x-1=0 \quad x+2=0$

$x=1 \qquad x=-2$

Check $x=1$

$\log_8 1+\log_8(1+1)\overset{?}{=}\dfrac{1}{3}$

$\log_8 8^0+\log_8 2\overset{?}{=}\dfrac{1}{3}$

$0+\log_8 8^{\frac{1}{3}}\overset{?}{=}\dfrac{1}{3}$

$\dfrac{1}{3}=\dfrac{1}{3}$ True

Check $x=-2$

$\log_8(-2)+\log_8(-2+1)\overset{?}{=}\dfrac{1}{3}$

$\log_8(-2)+\log_8(-1)\overset{?}{=}\dfrac{1}{3}$

Logarithms of values ≤ 0 are undefined.

$x=-2$ is not a solution.

43. $\log_2(3x-8)-\log_2(x+4)=-1$

$\log_2\dfrac{3x-8}{x+4}=-1$

$\dfrac{3x-8}{x+4}=2^{-1}=\dfrac{1}{2}$

$2(3x-8)=1(x+4)$

$6x-16=x+4$

$5x=20$

$x=4$

45. $P=284(1.007)^t=350$

$(1.007^t)=\dfrac{350}{284}$

$t=\log_{1.007}\dfrac{350}{284}=\dfrac{\ln\dfrac{350}{284}}{\ln 1.007}=29.955...$ or

$t=\dfrac{\log\dfrac{350}{284}}{\log 1.007}=29.955...$

The population will be 350 million people in the year 2030.

47. $A=P\left(1+\dfrac{r}{n}\right)^{nt}$

$2000=1000\left(1+\dfrac{0.05}{4}\right)^{4t}$

$(1.0125)^{4t}=2$

$4t=\log_{1.0125}2=\dfrac{\ln 2}{\ln 1.0125}=55.797...$ or

$$4t = \frac{\log 2}{\log 1.0125} = 55.797...$$

$$t = \frac{55.797..}{4} = 13.949...$$

It will take approximately 14 yr for the amount in the account to double.

49. $pH = -\log\left[H^+\right] = 7.4$

$\log\left[H^+\right] = -7.4$

$H^+ = 10^{-7.4} = 3.9810...\times 10^{-8}$

The concentration of hydrogen ions in blood is about 4.0×10^{-8}.

51.   a. $C = 300e^{0.2x}$

$$\frac{C}{300} = e^{0.2x}$$

$$\ln\left(\frac{C}{300}\right) = 0.2x$$

$$x = \frac{1}{0.2}\ln\left(\frac{C}{300}\right) = 5\ln\left(\frac{C}{300}\right)$$

b. $x = 5\ln\left(\frac{1000}{300}\right) = 5(1.2039...) = 6.019...$

The circulation reached 1,000,000 in about 6 yr after it was reached.

53.   a. $A = 12000e^{r(0)} = 12000e^0 =$

$12000(1) = 12000$

The initial investment was \$12,000; the initial investment was the amount in the account when $t = 0$.

b. $31814 = 12000e^{r(15)}$

$$e^{15r} = \frac{31814}{12000}$$

$$15r = \ln\left(\frac{31814}{12000}\right) = 0.9749997...$$

$$r = \frac{0.9749997...}{15} = 0.06499...$$

The annual interest rate is about 6.5%.

55. $R = 1.7 + 2.3\ln(x+1) = 7$

$2.3\ln(x+1) = 7 - 1.7 = 5.3$

$$\ln(x+1) = \frac{5.3}{2.3}$$

$x+1 = e^{\frac{5.3}{2.3}} = 10.0176...$

$x = 9.0176...$

The company's revenue reached \$7 million 9 months after the action figures were on the market.

Chapter 9 Review Exercises

1. $(f+g)(x) = 5 - 6x + x - 3 = -5x + 2$

$(f-g)(x) = 5 - 6x - (x-3) =$

$5 - 6x - x + 3 = -7x + 8$

$(f \bullet g)(x) = (5-6x)(x-3) =$

$-6x^2 + 23x - 15$

$\left(\dfrac{f}{g}\right)(x) = \dfrac{5-6x}{x-3}; \ x \neq 3$

2. $(f+g)(x) = 3x^2 + 1 + 2x^2 - 4x = 5x^2 - 4x + 1$

$(f-g)(x) = 3x^2 + 1 - (2x^2 - 4x) =$

$3x^2 + 1 - 2x^2 + 4x = x^2 + 4x + 1$

$(f \bullet g)(x) = (3x^2 + 1)(2x^2 - 4x) =$

$6x^4 - 12x^3 + 2x^2 - 4x$

$\left(\dfrac{f}{g}\right)(x) = \dfrac{3x^2 + 1}{2x^2 - 4x}; \ x \neq 0, 2$

3. $(f+g)(x) = \dfrac{2}{x-3} + \dfrac{3}{x^2 - 9} =$

$$\frac{2}{x-3} + \frac{3}{(x+3)(x-3)} =$$

$$\frac{2}{x-3} \bullet \frac{(x+3)}{(x+3)} + \frac{3}{(x+3)(x-3)} =$$

$$\frac{2x+6+3}{(x+3)(x-3)} = \frac{2x+9}{(x+3)(x-3)}; \ x \neq 3, -3$$

$(f-g)(x) = \dfrac{2}{x-3} - \dfrac{3}{x^2 - 9} =$

$$\frac{2}{x-3} - \frac{3}{(x+3)(x-3)} =$$

$$\frac{2}{x-3} \bullet \frac{(x+3)}{(x+3)} - \frac{3}{(x+3)(x-3)} =$$

$$\frac{2x+6-3}{(x+3)(x-3)} = \frac{2x+3}{(x+3)(x-3)}; \ x \neq 3, -3$$

$(f \bullet g)(x) = \left(\dfrac{2}{x-3}\right)\left(\dfrac{3}{x^2 - 9}\right) =$

$$\frac{6}{(x-3)(x^2-9)}$$

$\left(\dfrac{f}{g}\right)(x) = \dfrac{\dfrac{2}{x-3}}{\dfrac{3}{x^2-9}} = \dfrac{\dfrac{2}{x-3}}{\dfrac{3}{(x+3)(x-3)}} =$

$$\frac{\dfrac{2}{x-3}\bullet(x+3)(x-3)}{\dfrac{3}{(x+3)(x-3)}\bullet(x+3)(x-3)}=$$

$$\frac{2(x+3)}{3};\ x\neq3,-3$$

4. $(f+g)(x)=7\sqrt{x}+2+\sqrt{x}-2=8\sqrt{x}$

$(f-g)(x)=7\sqrt{x}+2-\left(\sqrt{x}-2\right)=$

$7\sqrt{x}+2-\sqrt{x}+2=6\sqrt{x}+4$

$(f\bullet g)(x)=\left(7\sqrt{x}+2\right)\left(\sqrt{x}-2\right)=$

$7\left(\sqrt{x}\right)^{2}-12\sqrt{x}-4=7x-12\sqrt{x}-4$

$\left(\dfrac{f}{g}\right)(x)=\dfrac{7\sqrt{x}+2}{\sqrt{x}-2}\bullet\dfrac{\sqrt{x}+2}{\sqrt{x}+2}=$

$\dfrac{7\left(\sqrt{x}\right)^{2}+16\sqrt{x}+4}{\left(\sqrt{x}\right)^{2}-4}=\dfrac{7x+16\sqrt{x}+4}{x-4};\ x\neq4$

5. $(f+g)(-2)=\left[(-2)^{2}-6(-2)+5\right]+$
$$\left[(-2)^{2}-(-2)\right]=$$
$21+6=27$

6. $(f-g)(3)=\left[(3)^{2}-6(3)+5\right]-$
$$\left[(3)^{2}-(3)\right]=$$
$-4-6=-10$

7. $(f\bullet g)(1)=\left[(1)^{2}-6(1)+5\right]\bullet\left[(1)^{2}-(1)\right]=$
$0\bullet0=0$

8. $\left(\dfrac{f}{g}\right)(-4)=\dfrac{(-4)^{2}-6(-4)+5}{(-4)^{2}-(-4)}=\dfrac{45}{20}=\dfrac{9}{4}$

9. a. $f(x)=x+2;\ g(x)=x^{2}-5x+9$

$(f\circ g)(x)=f\left[g(x)\right]=\left[x^{2}-5x+9\right]+2=$

$x^{2}-5x+11$

b. $(g\circ f)(x)=g\left[f(x)\right]=$

$[x+2]^{2}-5[x+2]+9=$

$x^{2}+4x+4-5x-10+9=x^{2}-x+3$

c. $(f\circ g)(0)=(0)^{2}-5(0)+11=11$

d. $(g\circ f)(-2)=(-2)^{2}-(-2)+3=9$

10. a. $f(x)=\sqrt{x};\ g(x)=2x-9$

$(f\circ g)(x)=f\left[g(x)\right]=\sqrt{2x-9}$

b. $(g\circ f)(x)=g\left[f(x)\right]=2\left(\sqrt{x}\right)-9=$

$2\sqrt{x}-9$

c. $(f\circ g)(9)=\sqrt{2(9)-9}=\sqrt{9}=3$

d. $(g\circ f)(5)=2\sqrt{5}-9$

11. Not one-to-one. It fails the horizontal line test.
The line $y=2$ intersects the graph twice.

12. One-to-one. No horizontal line intersects the graph
more than once.

13. $f(x)=8x+3$

$y=8x+3$; substitute y for $f(x)$

$x=8y+3$; interchange x and y.

$x-3=8y$

$\dfrac{x-3}{8}=y$

$f^{-1}(x)=\dfrac{x-3}{8}$

14. $f(x)=\dfrac{1}{6}x-1$

$y=\dfrac{1}{6}x-1$; substitute y for $f(x)$

$x=\dfrac{1}{6}y-1$; interchange x and y.

$x+1=\dfrac{1}{6}y$

$6(x+1)=y$

$f^{-1}(x)=6x+6$

15. $f(x)=x^{3}-5$

$y=x^{3}-5$; substitute y for $f(x)$

$x=y^{3}-5$; interchange x and y.

$x+5=y^{3}$

$(x+5)^{\frac{1}{3}}=\left(y^{3}\right)^{\frac{1}{3}}$

$\sqrt[3]{x+5}=y$

$f^{-1}(x)=\sqrt[3]{x+5}$

16. $f(x)=\sqrt[3]{x+10}$

$y=\sqrt[3]{x+10}$; substitute y for $f(x)$

$x=\sqrt[3]{y+10}$; interchange x and y.

$x=(y+10)^{\frac{1}{3}}$

$[x]^{3}=\left[(y+10)^{\frac{1}{3}}\right]^{3}$

$x^{3}=y+10$

$x^{3}-10=y$

$f^{-1}(x)=x^{3}-10$

17. $f(x)=\dfrac{2}{x+3}$

$$y = \frac{2}{x+3}; \text{ substitute } y \text{ for } f(x)$$

$$x = \frac{2}{y+3}; \text{ interchange } x \text{ and } y.$$

$$x(y+3) = 2$$

$$xy + 3x = 2$$

$$xy = 2 - 3x$$

$$y = \frac{2-3x}{x}$$

$$f^{-1}(x) = \frac{2-3x}{x}$$

18. $f(x) = \dfrac{x}{3x+1}$

$$y = \frac{x}{3x+1}; \text{ substitute } y \text{ for } f(x)$$

$$x = \frac{y}{3y+1}; \text{ interchange } x \text{ and } y.$$

$$x(3y+1) = y$$

$$3xy + x = y$$

$$x = y - 3xy$$

$$x = y(1-3x)$$

$$\frac{x}{1-3x} = y$$

$$f^{-1}(x) = \frac{x}{1-3x}$$

19. $f(x) = \dfrac{2}{3}x + 2; \quad g(x) = \dfrac{3}{2}x - 3$

$$(f \circ g)(x) = f[g(x)] = \frac{2}{3}\left[\frac{3}{2}x - 3\right] + 2 =$$

$$[x-2] + 2 = x$$

$$(g \circ f)(x) = g[f(x)] = \frac{3}{2}\left[\frac{2}{3}x + 2\right] - 3 =$$

$$[x+3] - 3 = x$$

$(f \circ g)(x) = x = (g \circ f)(x)$; the functions are inverses of each other.

20. $f(x) = \dfrac{6}{x} - 4; \quad g(x) = \dfrac{6}{x} + 4$

$$(f \circ g)(x) = f[g(x)] = \frac{6}{\left[\dfrac{6}{x}+4\right]} - 4 =$$

$$\frac{6 \bullet x}{\left(\dfrac{6}{x}+4\right)\bullet x} - 4 = \frac{6x}{6+4x} - 4 =$$

$$\frac{6x}{2(3+2x)} - 4 \bullet \frac{3+2x}{3+2x} = \frac{3x}{3+2x} - \frac{12+8x}{3+2x} =$$

$$\frac{-5x-12}{3+2x} \neq x$$

$$(g \circ f)(x) = g[f(x)] = \frac{6}{\left[\dfrac{6}{x}-4\right]} + 4 =$$

$$\frac{6 \bullet x}{\left(\dfrac{6}{x}-4\right)\bullet x} + 4 = \frac{6x}{6-4x} + 4 =$$

$$\frac{6x}{2(3-2x)} + 4 \bullet \frac{3-2x}{3-2x} = \frac{3x}{3-2x} + \frac{12-8x}{3-2x} =$$

$$\frac{-5x+12}{3-2x} \neq x$$

$(f \circ g)(x) \neq x \neq (g \circ f)(x)$; the functions are not inverses of each other.

21. $(-2,3)$ and $(0,-3)$ are on the function, $(3,-2)$ and $(-3,0)$ are on the inverse function.

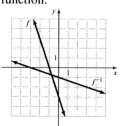

22. $(0,2)$, $(-1,3)$, and $(-4,4)$ are on the function. $(2,0)$, $(3,-1)$, and $(4,-4)$ are on the inverse function.

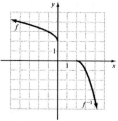

23. $f(x) = -3^x$

$$f(-3) = -3^{-3} = -\frac{1}{3^3} = -\frac{1}{27}$$

24. $f(x) = \left(\dfrac{1}{4}\right)^{-x}$

$$f(2) = \left(\frac{1}{4}\right)^{-2} = \frac{1^{-2}}{4^{-2}} = \frac{4^2}{1^2} = 16$$

25. $g(x) = 2^{x+3}$

$$g(-1) = 2^{-1+3} = 2^2 = 4$$

26. $g(x) = 9^x - 5$

$$g\left(\frac{3}{2}\right) = 9^{\frac{3}{2}} - 5 = \left(\sqrt{9}\right)^3 - 5 =$$

$$3^3 - 5 = 27 - 5 = 22$$

27. $f(x) = e^{2x}$

$$f\left(\frac{1}{2}\right) = e^{2\left(\frac{1}{2}\right)} = e^1 = 2.7182818.. \approx 2.7183$$

28. $h(x) = e^{-x+1}$

$$h(3) = e^{-3+1} = e^{-2} = 0.135335... \approx 0.1353$$

29. $f(x) = (3)^{-x}$

x	$f(x) = (3)^{-x}$	(x, y)
-3	$(3)^{-(-3)} = 3^3 = 27$	$(-3, 27)$
-2	$(3)^{-(-2)} = 3^2 = 9$	$(-2, 9)$
-1	$(3)^{-(-1)} = 3$	$(-1, 3)$
0	$(3)^{-0} = 1$	$(0, 1)$
1	$(3)^{-1} = \frac{1}{3}$	$\left(1, \frac{1}{3}\right)$
2	$(3)^{-2} = \frac{1}{9}$	$\left(2, \frac{1}{9}\right)$
3	$(3)^{-3} = \frac{1}{27}$	$\left(3, \frac{1}{27}\right)$

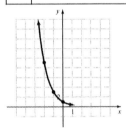

30. $f(x) = 2^x + 1$

x	$f(x) = 2^x + 1$	(x, y)
-3	$2^{-3} + 1 = \frac{1}{2^3} + 1 = \frac{1}{8} + 1 = \frac{9}{8}$	$\left(-3, \frac{9}{8}\right)$
-2	$2^{-2} + 1 = \frac{1}{2^2} + 1 = \frac{1}{4} + 1 = \frac{5}{4}$	$\left(-2, \frac{5}{4}\right)$
-1	$2^{-1} + 1 = \frac{1}{2} + 1 = \frac{3}{2}$	$\left(-1, \frac{3}{2}\right)$
0	$2^0 + 1 = 1 + 1 = 2$	$(0, 2)$
1	$2^1 + 1 = 2 + 1 = 3$	$(1, 3)$
2	$2^2 + 1 = 4 + 1 = 5$	$(2, 5)$
3	$2^3 + 1 = 8 + 1 = 9$	$(3, 9)$

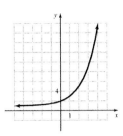

31. $4^x = 32$

$$(2^2)^x = 2^5$$
$$2^{2x} = 2^5$$
$$2x = 5$$
$$x = \frac{5}{2}$$

32. $27^x = \frac{1}{9}$

$$(3^3)^x = \frac{1}{3^2}$$
$$3^{3x} = 3^{-2}$$
$$3x = -2$$
$$x = -\frac{2}{3}$$

33. $2^{x-3} = 16$

$$2^{x-3} = 2^4$$
$$x - 3 = 4$$
$$x = 7$$

34. $25^{x+2} = 125^{3-x}$

$$(5^2)^{x+2} = (5^3)^{3-x}$$
$$5^{2(x+2)} = 5^{3(3-x)}$$
$$2(x+2) = 3(3-x)$$
$$2x + 4 = 9 - 3x$$
$$5x = 5$$
$$x = 1$$

35. $\log_6 216 = 3$

$$6^3 = 216$$

36. $\log_{\frac{1}{3}} 9 = -2$

$$\left(\frac{1}{3}\right)^{-2} = 9$$

37. $5^{-2} = \frac{1}{25}$

$$\log_5 \frac{1}{25} = -2$$

38. $81^{\frac{1}{4}} = 3$

$$\log_{81} 3 = \frac{1}{4}$$

39. $\log_8 8^1 = 1$

40. $\log_{\frac{1}{2}}\left(\dfrac{1}{32}\right) = \log_{\frac{1}{2}}\left(\dfrac{1}{2^5}\right) = \log_{\frac{1}{2}}\left(\dfrac{1}{2}\right)^5 = 5$

41. $\log_6 1 = 0$

42. $\log_{16} 2 = \log_{16} 16^{\frac{1}{4}} = \dfrac{1}{4}$

43. $\log_4 x = 3$

        $x = 4^3 = 64$

44. $\log_2 x = -6$

        $x = 2^{-6}$

        $x = \dfrac{1}{2^6} = \dfrac{1}{64}$

45. $\log_x 7 = -1$

        $x^{-1} = 7$

        $\left(x^{-1}\right)^{-1} = (7)^{-1}$

        $x = \dfrac{1}{7}$

46. $\log_x \dfrac{4}{9} = 2$

        $x^2 = \dfrac{4}{9}$

        $x = \pm\sqrt{\dfrac{4}{9}} = \pm\dfrac{2}{3}$

        Logarithms are only defined for values > 0.

        $x = +\dfrac{2}{3}$

47. $\log_4 64 = x$

        $\log_4 4^3 = x$

        $x = 3$

48. $\log_{\frac{1}{2}} 4 = x$

        $x = \log_{\frac{1}{2}} 2^2$

        $x = \log_{\frac{1}{2}}\left(\dfrac{1}{2}\right)^{-2} = -2$

49. $f(x) = -\log_4 x$

        $y = -\log_4 x$

        $-y = \log_4 x$

        $4^{-y} = x$

        $x = 4^{-y}$

y	$x = 4^{-y}$	(x, y)
-3	$4^{-(-3)} = 4^3 = 64$	$(64, -3)$
-2	$4^{-(-2)} = 4^2 = 16$	$(16, -2)$
-1	$4^{-(-1)} = 4^1 = 4$	$(4, -1)$
0	$4^{-0} = 1$	$(1, 0)$
1	$4^{-1} = \dfrac{1}{4}$	$\left(\dfrac{1}{4}, 1\right)$
2	$4^{-2} = \dfrac{1}{4^2} = \dfrac{1}{16}$	$\left(\dfrac{1}{16}, 2\right)$
3	$4^{-3} = \dfrac{1}{4^3} = \dfrac{1}{64}$	$\left(\dfrac{1}{64}, 3\right)$

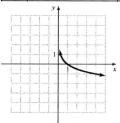

50. $f(x) = \log_x x$

        $y = \log_2 x$

        $x = 2^y$

y	$x = 2^y$	(x, y)
-2	$2^{-2} = \dfrac{1}{2^2} = \dfrac{1}{4}$	$\left(\dfrac{1}{4}, -2\right)$
-1	$2^{-1} = \dfrac{1}{2}$	$\left(\dfrac{1}{2}, -1\right)$
0	$2^0 = 1$	$(1, 0)$
1	$2^1 = 2$	$(2, 1)$
2	$2^2 = 4$	$(4, 2)$

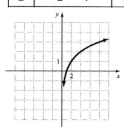

51. $\log_3 27x = \log_3 27 + \log_3 x =$

        $\log_3 3^3 + \log_3 x = 3 + \log_3 x$

52. $\log_6 \dfrac{6}{a} = \log_6 6 - \log_6 a = 1 - \log_6 a$

53. $\log_n \dfrac{x}{x-5} = \log_n x - \log_n (x-5)$

54. $\log_9 \left[u(u+1)\right] = \log_9 u + \log_9 (u+1)$

55. $\log_5 x^3 y = \log_5 x^3 + \log_5 y = 3\log_5 x + \log_5 y$

56. $\log_2 \sqrt[5]{x^2 y^3} = \log_2 \left(x^2 y^3\right)^{\frac{1}{5}} = \frac{1}{5} \log_2 x^2 y^3 =$

$\frac{1}{5}\left(\log_2 x^2 + \log_2 y^3\right) =$

$\frac{1}{5}\left(2\log_2 x + 3\log_2 y\right) =$

$\frac{2}{5}\log_2 x + \frac{3}{5}\log_2 y$

57. $\log_3 \frac{x^2 z^3}{y^2} = \log_3 x^2 + \log_3 z^3 - \log_3 y^2 =$

$2\log_3 x + 3\log_3 z - 2\log_3 y$

58. $\log_b \frac{b^2}{\left(a-b\right)^4} = \log_b b^2 - \log_b \left(a-b\right)^4 =$

$2 - 4\log_b \left(a-b\right)$

59. $\log_4 10 + \log_4 n = \log_4 \left(10n\right)$

60. $\log_9 x - \log_9 5 = \log_9 \frac{x}{5}$

61. $\log_3 a + 2\log_3 b = \log_3 a + \log_3 b^2$

$= \log_3 \left(ab^2\right)$

62. $5\log_b a - 4\log_b c = \log_b a^5 - \log_b c^4 =$

$\log_b \left(\frac{a^5}{c^4}\right)$

63. $\frac{1}{4}\left(3\log_6 x - 8\log_6 y\right) = \frac{3}{4}\log_6 x - \frac{8}{4}\log_6 y =$

$\log_6 x^{\frac{3}{4}} - \log_6 y^2 = \log_6 \frac{x^{\frac{3}{4}}}{y^2} = \log_6 \frac{\sqrt[4]{x^3}}{y^2}$

64. $2\log_a x - \log_a y - 4\log_a z =$

$\log_a x^2 - \log_a y - \log_a z^4 = \log_a \frac{x^2}{yz^4}$

65. Since $\log_b b^x = x$, $\log_8 8^3 = 3$

66. Since $\log_b b^x = x$, $\log_x x^{-\frac{1}{3}} = -\frac{1}{3}$

67. Since $b^{\log_b x} = x$, $5^{\log_5 y} = y$

68. Since $b^{\log_b x} = x$, $a^{\log_a 14} = 14$

69. $\log 23 = 1.36172... \approx 1.3617$

70. $\log 9.4 = 0.97312... \approx 0.9731$

71. $\ln 48 = 3.87120... \approx 3.8712$

72. $\ln \frac{2}{3} = -0.40546... -0.4055$

73. $\log 0.1 = \log \frac{1}{10} = \log 10^{-1} = -1$

74. $\log \sqrt[4]{1000} = \log \sqrt[4]{10^3} = \log 10^{\frac{3}{4}} = \frac{3}{4}$

75. $\ln e^{100} = 100$

76. $\ln \frac{1}{e^{-y}} = \ln e^{-y} = -y$

77. $\log_5 121 = \frac{\log 121}{\log 5}$ or $\frac{\ln 121}{\ln 5} = 2.97979... \approx$

2.9798

78. $\log_9 6.1 = \frac{\log 6.1}{\log 9}$ or $\frac{\ln 6.1}{\ln 9} = 0.82298.. \approx$

0.8230

79. $7^x = 72$

$x = \log_7 72 = \frac{\log 72}{\log 7}$ or $\frac{\ln 72}{\ln 7} = 2.19777 \approx$

2.1978

80. $6^{2x} = 0.58$

$2x = \log_6 0.58 = \frac{\log 0.58}{\log 6}$ or $\frac{\ln 0.58}{\ln 6}$

$2x = -0.30401...$

$x = \frac{-0.30401...}{2} = -0.15200... \approx -0.1520$

81. $2^{x-5} = 20$

$x - 5 = \log_2 20 = \frac{\log 20}{\log 2}$ or $\frac{\ln 20}{\ln 2}$

$x - 5 = 4.32192...$

$x = 4.32192... + 5 = 9.32192... \approx 9.3219$

82. $3^{2x+3} = 63$

$2x + 3 = \log_3 63 = \frac{\log 63}{\log 3}$ or $\frac{\ln 63}{\ln 3}$

$2x + 3 = 3.77124$

$2x = 0.77124...$

$x = 0.38562... \approx 0.3856$

83. $\log_7 \left(x+8\right) = 0$

$x + 8 = 7^0$

$x + 8 = 1$

$x = -7$

84. $\log_2 12 - \log_2 x = -3$

$\log_2 \frac{12}{x} = -3$

$\frac{12}{x} = 2^{-3} = \frac{1}{8}$

$8(12) = 1(x)$

$x = 96$

85. $\log_6 x + \log_6 \left(x-5\right) = 2$

$\log_6 \left[x\left(x-5\right)\right] = 2$

$x\left(x-5\right) = 6^2 = 36$

$x^2 - 5x - 36 = 0$

$$(x+4)(x-9)=0$$

$$x+4=0 \quad x-9=0$$

$$x=-4 \qquad x=9$$

Check $x=-4$

$$\log_6 -4 + \log_6(-4-5) \overset{?}{=} 2$$

Logarithms of values ≤ 0 are undefined.

$x=-4$ is not a solution.

Check $x=9$

$$\log_6 9 + \log_6(9-5) \overset{?}{=} 2$$

$$\log_6 \left[9(4)\right] \overset{?}{=} 2$$

$$\log_6 36 \overset{?}{=} 2$$

$$\log_6 6^2 \overset{?}{=} 2$$

$2=2$ True

86. $\log_5(x+2) + \log_5(x+6) = 1$

$$\log_5\left[(x+2)(x+6)\right] = 1$$

$$(x+2)(x+6) = 5^1$$

$$x^2 + 8x + 12 = 5$$

$$x^2 + 8x + 7 = 0$$

$$(x+7)(x+1) = 0$$

$$x+7=0 \quad x+1=0$$

$$x=-7 \qquad x=-1$$

Check $x=-7$

$$\log_5(-7+2) + \log_5(-7+6) \overset{?}{=} 1$$

Logarithms of values ≤ 0 are undefined.

$x=-7$ is not a solution.

Check $x=-1$

$$\log_5(-1+2) + \log_5(-1+6) \overset{?}{=} 1$$

$$\log_5(1) + \log_5(5) \overset{?}{=} 1$$

$$\log_5 5^0 + \log_5 5^1 \overset{?}{=} 1$$

$0+1=1$ True

87. $\log_4(x-3) - \log_4 x = -1$

$$\log_4 \left(\frac{x-3}{x}\right) = -1$$

$$\frac{x-3}{x} = 4^{-1} = \frac{1}{4}$$

$$4(x-3) = x(1)$$

$$4x - 12 = x$$

$$3x = 12$$

$$x = 4$$

88. $\log_3(2x-1) - \log_3(x-4) = 2$

$$\log_3\left(\frac{2x-1}{x-4}\right) = 2$$

$$\frac{2x-1}{x-4} = 3^2 = 9$$

$$2x-1 = 9(x-4)$$

$$2x-1 = 9x - 36$$

$$35 = 7x$$

$$x = 5$$

89.   a. $f(c) = 2500 + c; \quad c(s) = 0.008s$

$$(f \circ c)(s) = f\left[c(s)\right] = 2500 + (0.008s)$$

$$(f \circ c)(s) = 0.008s + 2500$$

It represents the agent's total monthly salary if his sales totaled s dollars.

b. $(f \circ c)(s) = 0.008s + 2500; \quad s = 400000$

$$(f \circ c)(s) = 0.008(400000) + 2500$$

$$(f \circ c)(s) = 3200 + 2500 = 5700$$

The agent's salary is $5,700.

90.   a. $P(x) = 10x - 150$

$y = 10x - 150;$ substitute y for $P(x)$

$x = 10y - 150;$ interchange x and y.

$$x + 150 = 10y$$

$$y = \frac{x+150}{10}$$

$$P^{-1}(x) = \frac{x}{10} + 15$$

b.   The inverse can be used to determine the number of jeans the company must sell in order to make a certain profit.

c. $P^{-1}(x) = \frac{x}{10} + 15$

$$P^{-1}(1200) = \frac{1200}{10} + 15 = 120 + 15$$

$$P^{-1}(x) = 135$$

135 pairs of jeans must be sold in order to make a weekly profit of $1200.

91.   a. $A = P\left(1 + \frac{r}{n}\right)^{nt} = 6500\left(1 + \frac{0.054}{2}\right)^{2(5)}$

$$A = 6500(1 + 0.027)^{10} = 6500(1.027)^{10}$$

$$A = 6500(1.305282...) = 8484.3346...$$

The amount in the account after 5 yr will be $8484.33.

b. $2(6500) = (6500)\left(1 + \frac{0.054}{2}\right)^{2t}$

$$\left(1 + \frac{0.054}{2}\right)^{2t} = 2$$

$(1.027)^{2t} = 2$

$2t = \log_{1.027} 2 = \dfrac{\log 2}{\log 1.027}$ or $\dfrac{\ln 2}{\ln 1.027}$

$2t = 26.01715...;\quad t = 13.0085...$

It will take about 13 yr for this investment to double.

92. a. $A = A_0 e^{-0.0231t}$

$A = 36e^{-0.0231(60)} = 36e^{-1.386} = 36(0.25007...)$

$A = 9.0026...$

9 mg remain after 60 yr.

b. $\dfrac{1}{2}A_0 = A_0 e^{-0.0231t}$

$e^{-0.0231t} = \dfrac{1}{2} = 0.5$

$-0.0231t = \ln(0.5)$

$t = \dfrac{\ln(0.5)}{-0.0231} = \dfrac{-0.693147...}{-0.0231} = 30.006...$

The half-life of cesium-137 is about 30 yr.

93. $t = \dfrac{2}{3}\log_2 \dfrac{N}{N_0}$

$t = \dfrac{2}{3}\log_2 \dfrac{384}{6} = \dfrac{2}{3}\log_2 64$

$t = \dfrac{2}{3}\log_2 2^6 = \dfrac{2}{3}(6) = 4$

384 bacterial will be in the colony in 4 hr.

94. $t = 15\log_4 \dfrac{v}{v_0} = 15\log_4 \dfrac{24}{3}$

$t = 15\log_4 8 = 15\dfrac{\log 8}{\log 4}$ or $15\dfrac{\ln 8}{\ln 4}$

$t = 15(1.5) = 22.5$

It will take 22.5 yr for the stamp to have a value of $24.

95. $s = \log \dfrac{10^{90}}{(x+1)^{16}} = \log 10^{90} - \log(x+1)^{16}$

$s = 90\log 10 - 16\log(x+1)$

$s = 90 - 16\log(x+1)$

96. $\ln(T-A) = \ln(98.6-A) - kt\ln e$

$\ln(T-A) - \ln(98.6-A) = -kt\ln e = -kt$

$\ln\left(\dfrac{T-A}{98.6-A}\right) = -kt$

$\dfrac{T-A}{98.6-A} = e^{-kt}$

$T-A = (98.6-A)e^{-kt}$

97. $\text{pH} = -\log\left[\text{H}^+\right]$

$\text{pH} = -\log\left[2.5\times 10^{-7}\right] = -\left[\log 2.5 + \log 10^{-7}\right]$

$\text{pH} = -\left[0.3979400... + (-7)\right] = -\left[-6.602059...\right]$

$\text{pH} = 6.602059...$

The pH of milk is about 6.6

98. $t = \dfrac{\ln x}{r} = \dfrac{\ln 3}{0.044} = \dfrac{1.09861...}{0.044} = 24.9684...$

It will take approximately 25 yr for the investment to triple.

99. $V = A(0.85)^t$

$15000 = 28500(0.85)^t$

$\dfrac{15000}{28500} = (0.85)^t$

$t = \log_{0.85}\dfrac{15000}{28500} = \dfrac{\log \dfrac{15000}{28500}}{\log 0.85}$ or $\dfrac{\ln \dfrac{15000}{28500}}{\ln 0.85}$

$t = 3.9494...$

The value will depreciate to $15,000 about 4 yr after it is purchased.

100. $A = Pe^{rt}$

$12300 = 8000e^{0.048t}$

$e^{0.048t} = \dfrac{12300}{8000} = 1.5375$

$0.048t = \ln(1.5375)$

$t = \dfrac{\ln(1.5375)}{0.048} = \dfrac{0.430157...}{0.048} = 8.9616...$

It will take approximately 9 yr for the amount in the account to grow to $12,300.

Chapter 9 Posttest

1. $f(x) = 3x^2 - 4x - 4;\quad g(x) = 3x^2 + 2x$

a. $(f+g)(x) = 3x^2 - 4x - 4 + 3x^2 + 2x =$

$6x^2 - 2x - 4$

b. $(f-g)(x) = 3x^2 - 4x - 4 - (3x^2 + 2x) =$

$3x^2 - 4x - 4 - 3x^2 - 2x = -6x - 4$

c. $(f \cdot g)(x) = (3x^2 - 4x - 4) \cdot (3x^2 + 2x) =$

$\begin{array}{r} 3x^2 - 4x - 4 \\ \underline{3x^2 + 2x} \\ 6x^3 - 8x^2 - 8x \\ \underline{9x^4 - 12x^3 - 12x^2\quad\quad} \\ 9x^4 - 6x^3 - 20x^2 - 8x \end{array}$

d. $\left(\dfrac{f}{g}\right)(x)=\dfrac{3x^2-4x-4}{3x^2+2x}=\dfrac{(3x+2)(x-2)}{x(3x+2)}=$

$\dfrac{x-2}{x};\ x\neq-\dfrac{2}{3},0$

2. $f(x)=\sqrt{x};\ g(x)=2x+5$

   a. $(f\circ g)(x)=f(g(x))=f(2x+5)=\sqrt{2x+5}$

   b. $(g\circ f)(x)=g(f(x))=g(\sqrt{x})=$

       $2\sqrt{x}+5$

   c. $(f\circ g)(2)=f(g(2))=f(2(2)+5)=$

       $\sqrt{2(2)+5}=\sqrt{9}=3$

   d. $(g\circ f)(16)=g(f(16))=g(\sqrt{16})=$

       $2\sqrt{16}+5=2(4)+5=13$

3.   Yes, it is a one-to-one function as each y-value in
      the range corresponds to exactly one x-value in the
      domain.
      The function has values:
      $(2,0),(1,1),(-2,2)$ and $(-5,2.5)$
      The inverse function has values:
      $(0,2),(1,1),(2,-2)$ and $(2.5,-5)$

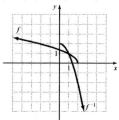

4. $f(x)=\dfrac{1}{x-7}$

      $y=\dfrac{1}{x-7};\ $ substitute y for $f(x)$

      $x=\dfrac{1}{y-7};\ $ interchange x and y.

      $x(y-7)=1$

      $xy-7x=1$

      $xy=7x+1$

      $y=\dfrac{7x+1}{x}$

      $f^{-1}(x)=\dfrac{7x+1}{x}$

5.   a. $f(x)=3^x-2$

          $f(-2)=3^{-2}-2=\dfrac{1}{3^2}-2$

          $f(-2)=\dfrac{1}{9}-\dfrac{18}{9}=-\dfrac{17}{9}$

   b. $f(x)=e^{x+2}$

       $f(5)=e^{5+2}=e^7=1096.63315...$

       $f(5)=1096.6332$

6.   a. $\log_9 1=\log_9 9^0=0$

   b. $\log_4\dfrac{1}{2}=\log_4 1-\log_4 2=$

       $\log_4 4^0-\log_4\sqrt{4}=0-\log_4 4^{\frac{1}{2}}=$

       $0-\dfrac{1}{2}=-\dfrac{1}{2}$

7.   a. $f(x)=-\left(\dfrac{1}{2}\right)^{-x}$

x	$f(x)=-\left(\dfrac{1}{2}\right)^{-x}$	(x,y)
-2	$-\left(\dfrac{1}{2}\right)^{-(-2)}=-\dfrac{1}{4}$	$\left(-2,-\dfrac{1}{4}\right)$
-1	$-\left(\dfrac{1}{2}\right)^{-(-1)}=-\dfrac{1}{2}$	$\left(-1,-\dfrac{1}{2}\right)$
0	$-\left(\dfrac{1}{2}\right)^{-0}=-1$	$(0,-1)$
1	$-\left(\dfrac{1}{2}\right)^{-1}=-2$	$(1,-2)$
2	$-\left(\dfrac{1}{2}\right)^{-2}=-4$	$(2,-4)$

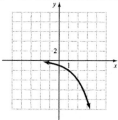

   b. $f(x)=-\log_3 x$

x	$f(x)=-\log_3 x$	(x,y)
$\dfrac{1}{9}$	$-\log_3\dfrac{1}{9}=2$	$\left(\dfrac{1}{9},2\right)$
$\dfrac{1}{3}$	$-\log_3\dfrac{1}{3}=1$	$\left(\dfrac{1}{3},1\right)$
1	$-\log_3 1=0$	$(1,0)$
3	$-\log_3 3=-1$	$(3,-1)$
9	$-\log_3 9=-2$	$(9,-2)$

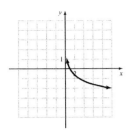

8. a. $\log_3\left(9x^4\right) = \log_3 9 + \log_3 x^4 =$

$\log_3 3^2 + 4\log_3 x = 2 + 4\log_3 x$

b. $\log_6 \dfrac{x^5}{6y^2} = \log_6 x^5 - \log_6 6 - \log_6 y^2 =$

$5\log_6 x - \log_6 6^1 - 2\log_6 y =$

$5\log_6 x - 2\log_6 y - 1$

9. a. $2\log_5 n + 5\log_5 2 = \log_5 n^2 + \log_5 2^5 =$

$\log_5\left(n^2 \cdot 2^5\right) = \log_5\left(32n^2\right)$

b. $3\log_b\left(a-2\right) - 4\log_b\left(a+2\right) =$

$\log_b\left(a-2\right)^3 - \log_b\left(a+2\right)^4 = \log_b \dfrac{\left(a-2\right)^3}{\left(a+2\right)^4}$

10. a. Since $\log_a a^x = x$, $\log_9 9^7 = 7$

b. Since $a^{\log_a x} = x$, $6^{\log_6 x} = x$

11. a. $\log\sqrt{1000} = \log\sqrt{10^3} = \log 10^{\frac{3}{2}} = \dfrac{3}{2}$

b. $\ln \dfrac{1}{e^5} = \ln e^{-5} = -5$

12. $\log_5 42 = \dfrac{\log 42}{\log 5}$ or $\dfrac{\ln 42}{\ln 5} = 2.32234...$

$\log_5 42 = 2.3223$

13. $7^x = 49$; $7^x = 7^2$; $x = 2$

14. $27^{2x-3} = \left(\dfrac{1}{3}\right)^{x-5}$

$\left(3^3\right)^{2x-3} = \left(3^{-1}\right)^{x-5}$

$3^{3(2x-3)} = 3^{-1(x-5)}$

$3(2x-3) = -(x-5)$

$6x-9 = -x+5$

$7x = 14$

$x = 2$

15. $\log_x 4 = -2$

$x^{-2} = 4$; $\dfrac{1}{x^2} = 4$

$1 = 4x^2$; $x^2 = \dfrac{1}{4}$

$x = \pm\sqrt{\dfrac{1}{4}} = \pm\dfrac{1}{2}$

Check $x = -\dfrac{1}{2}$

$\log_{-\frac{1}{2}} 4 \overset{?}{=} -2$

The base of logarithms > 0

$-\dfrac{1}{2}$ is not a solution

Check $x = \dfrac{1}{2}$

$\log_{\frac{1}{2}} 4 \overset{?}{=} -2$

$\log_{\frac{1}{2}} 2^2 \overset{?}{=} -2$

$\log_{\frac{1}{2}}\left(\dfrac{1}{2}\right)^{-2} \overset{?}{=} -2$

$-2 = -2$ True

16. $\log_5\left(2x+3\right) = 2$

$2x+3 = 5^2 = 25$

$2x = 22$

$x = 11$

17. $\log_2\left(x+3\right) + \log_2\left(x-4\right) = 3$

$\log_2\left(x+3\right)\left(x-4\right) = 3$

$\left(x+3\right)\left(x-4\right) = 2^3$

$x^2 - x - 12 = 8$

$x^2 - x - 20 = 0$

$\left(x-5\right)\left(x+4\right) = 0$

$x-5 = 0 \quad x+4 = 0$

$x = 5 \qquad x = -4$

Check $x = -4$

$\log_2\left(-4+3\right) + \log_2\left(-4-4\right) \overset{?}{=} 3$

$\log_2\left(-1\right) + \log_2\left(-8\right) \overset{?}{=} 3$

Logarithms of values ≤ 0 are undefined.

$x = -4$ is not a solution.

Check $x = 5$

$\log_2\left(5+3\right) + \log_2\left(5-4\right) \overset{?}{=} 3$

$\log_2 8 + \log_2 1 \overset{?}{=} 3$

$\log_2 2^3 + \log_2 2^0 \overset{?}{=} 3$

$3 + 0 = 3$ True

18. $P(t) = 1020(1.014)^t$

$t = 2009 - 2001 = 8$

$P(8) = 1020(1.014)^8 = 1020(1.117644...)$

$P(8) = 1139.997...$

The population of India in the year 2009 will be approximately 1140 million people.

19. $L = 10\left(\log I + 12\right)$

$10\left(\log I + 12\right) = 60$

$\log I + 12 = \dfrac{60}{10}$

$\log I + 12 = 6$

$\log I = 6 - 12$

$\log I = -6$

$I = 10^{-6}$

The intensity is $10^{-6} \; \dfrac{W}{m^2}$.

20. $C = 20e^{-0.125t}$

$5 = 20e^{-0.125t}$

$e^{-0.125t} = \dfrac{5}{20}$

$e^{-0.125t} = 0.25$

$-0.125t = \ln 0.25$

$t = \dfrac{\ln 0.25}{-0.125} = 11.09035...$

It takes about 11 hr for the concentration to decrease to 5 mg/L.

Cumulative Review Exercises

1. $3(2x-7) - 4x = -\dfrac{1}{3}(9x+12) - 8$

$6x - 21 - 4x = -3x - 4 - 8$

$2x - 21 = -3x - 12$

$5x = 9$

$x = \dfrac{9}{5}$

2. $|5x - 1| > 9$

$5x - 1 > 9 \quad 5x - 1 < -9$

$5x > 10 \qquad 5x < -8$

$x > 2 \qquad\quad x < -\dfrac{8}{5}$

$\left(-\infty, -\dfrac{8}{5}\right) \cup (2, \infty)$

3. $m = \dfrac{y_2 - y_1}{x_2 - x_1} = \dfrac{7-1}{-2-4} = \dfrac{6}{-6} = -1$

Using $(4, 1)$

$y - y_1 = m(x - x_1)$

$y - 1 = -1(x - 4)$; point-slope form

$y - 1 = -x + 4$

$y = -x + 5$; slope-intercept form

4. $81x^4 y^4 - 16 = (9x^2 y^2 - 4)(9x^2 y^2 + 4) =$

$(3xy + 2)(3xy - 2)(9x^2 y^2 + 4)$

5. $2x^2 + 4x - 5 = 0$

$a = 2 \qquad b = 4 \qquad c = -5$

$x = \dfrac{-(4) \pm \sqrt{(4)^2 - 4(2)(-5)}}{2(2)}$

$x = \dfrac{-4 \pm \sqrt{16 + 40}}{4} = \dfrac{-4 \pm \sqrt{56}}{4}$

$x = \dfrac{-4 \pm 2\sqrt{14}}{4} = \dfrac{2\left(-2 \pm \sqrt{14}\right)}{4}$

$x = \dfrac{-2 + \sqrt{14}}{2} \qquad x = \dfrac{-2 - \sqrt{14}}{2}$

6. $\left(4 - \sqrt{-16}\right)\left(7 - \sqrt{-1}\right) = (4 - 4i)(7 - i) =$

$28 - 32i + 4i^2 = 28 - 32i + 4(-1) = 24 - 32i$

7. $\log_4(x + 3) - \log_4 x = 2$

$\log_4 \dfrac{x + 3}{x} = 2$

$\dfrac{x + 3}{x} = 4^2 = 16$

$x + 3 = 16x$

$3 = 15x$

$x = \dfrac{1}{5}$

8. $W = 35.74 + 0.6215T - 35.75V^{0.16} + 0.4275TV^{0.16}$

$V = 18, T = 40$

$W = 35.74 + 0.6215(40) - 35.75(18)^{0.16}$

$\qquad\qquad\qquad\qquad + 0.4275(40)(18)^{0.16}$

$W = 35.74 + 24.86 - 35.75(1.58797...)$

$\qquad\qquad\qquad\qquad + 17.1(1.58797...)$

$W = 60.60 - 56.77009... + 27.15436...$

$W = 30.98427....$

The wind chill temperature is approximately 31°F.

9.   Let h be the amount invested in the high-risk fund and l be the amount invested in the low-risk fund.

$l + h = 15000 \xrightarrow{\;\times 2\;} 2l + 2h = 30000$

$0.06l - 0.02h = 100 \xrightarrow{\;\times 100\;} 6l - 2h = 10000$

$\qquad\qquad\qquad\qquad\qquad\quad 8l \qquad\quad = 40000$

$l = 5000$

$5000 + h = 15000$

$h = 10000$

5000 was invested in the low-risk fund and $10,000$ was invested in the high-risk fund.

10. $s(t) = -16t^2 + 96t + 6$

$a = -16, \quad b = 96$

$-\dfrac{b}{2a} = -\dfrac{96}{2(-16)} = -\dfrac{96}{-32} = 3$

$a < 0$, the point is a maximum.

It takes the rocket 3 sec to reach its maximum height.

CHAPTER 10 CONIC SECTIONS

Chapter 10 Pretest.

1. $y = 3x^2 - 12x + 23$

   $y = 3(x^2 - 4x) + 23$

   $y = 3\left(x^2 - 4x + \left(\dfrac{-4}{2}\right)^2\right) + 23 - 3\left(\dfrac{-4}{2}\right)^2$

   $y = 3(x^2 - 4x + 4) + 23 - 3(4)$

   $y = 3(x - 2)^2 + 11$ Vertex: $(2, 11)$

2.   a. $d = \sqrt{(x_2 - x_1)^2 + (y_2 - y_1)^2}$

   $d = \sqrt{(-7 - (-5))^2 + (13 - 9)^2}$

   $d = \sqrt{(-2)^2 + (4)^2} = \sqrt{4 + 16} = \sqrt{20} = 2\sqrt{5}$

   b. $d = \sqrt{(x_2 - x_1)^2 + (y_2 - y_1)^2}$

   $d = \sqrt{(0.8 - 1.2)^2 + (-0.7 - (-1))^2}$

   $d = \sqrt{(-0.4)^2 + (0.3)^2} = \sqrt{0.16 + 0.09}$

   $d = \sqrt{0.25} = 0.5$

3.   a. $\left(\dfrac{11 + (-3)}{2}, \dfrac{-6 + 10}{2}\right) = \left(\dfrac{8}{2}, \dfrac{4}{2}\right) = (4, 2)$

   b. $\left(\dfrac{1 + 0}{2}, \dfrac{-4 + 1}{2}\right) = \left(\dfrac{1}{2}, \dfrac{-3}{2}\right) = \left(\dfrac{1}{2}, -\dfrac{3}{2}\right)$

4. $(x - 7)^2 + (y - (-3))^2 = \left(\sqrt{10}\right)^2$

   $(x - 7)^2 + (y + 3)^2 = 10$

5. $x^2 + y^2 - 2x - 5 = 0$

   $x^2 - 2x + y^2 = 5$

   $x^2 - 2x + \left(\dfrac{-2}{2}\right)^2 + y^2 = 5 + \left(\dfrac{-2}{2}\right)^2$

   $x^2 - 2x + 1 + y^2 = 5 + 1$

   $(x - 1)^2 + (y - 0)^2 = 6$

   Center: $(1, 0)$, radius $= \sqrt{6}$

6. $x = -2(y + 1)^2 + 3$

   $x = -2(y - (-1))^2 + 3$

   $h = 3,\ k = -1$

   Vertex: $(3, -1)$

   Axis of symmetry: $y = -1$

y	$x = -2(y+1)^2 + 3$	(x, y)
-3	$-2(-3+1)^2 + 3 = -5$	$(-5, -3)$
-2	$-2(-2+1)^2 + 3 = 1$	$(1, -2)$
-1	$-2(-1+1)^2 + 3 = 3$	$(3, -1)$
0	$-2(0+1)^2 + 3 = 1$	$(1, 0)$
1	$-2(1+1)^2 + 3 = -5$	$(-5, 1)$

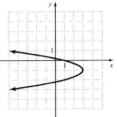

7. $x^2 + y^2 = 81$

   $(x - 0)^2 + (y - 0)^2 = 9^2$

   Center: $(0, 0)$ radius: 9

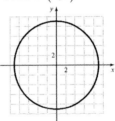

8. $(x + 2)^2 + (y - 1)^2 = 16$

   $(x - (-2))^2 + (y - 1)^2 = 4^2$

   Center: $(-2, 1)$ radius: 4

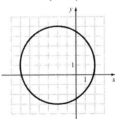

9. $\dfrac{x^2}{9} + y^2 = 1$

   $\dfrac{x^2}{3^2} + \dfrac{y^2}{1^2} = 1$

   $a = 3,\ b = 1$

   x-intercepts: $(\pm 3, 0)$ or $(3, 0)$ and $(-3, 0)$

   y-intercepts: $(0, \pm 1)$ or $(0, 1)$ and $(0, -1)$

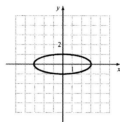

10. $12x^2 + 3y^2 = 48$

$$\frac{12x^2}{48} + \frac{3y^2}{48} = \frac{48}{48}$$

$$\frac{x^2}{4} + \frac{y^2}{16} = 1$$

$$\frac{x^2}{2^2} + \frac{y^2}{4^2} = 1$$

$a = 2, \ b = 4$

x-intercepts are $(\pm 2,0)$ or $(2,0)$ and $(-2,0)$

y-intercepts are $(0,\pm 4)$ or $(0,4)$ and $(0,-4)$

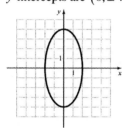

11. $\dfrac{y^2}{25} - \dfrac{x^2}{9} = 1$

$$\frac{y^2}{5^2} - \frac{x^2}{3^2} = 1$$

$a = 3, \ b = 5$

y-intercepts are $(0,\pm 5)$ or

$(0,5)$ and $(0,-5)$

Equations of asymptotes are

$$y = \pm \frac{5}{3}x \text{ or } y = \frac{5}{3}x \text{ and } y = -\frac{5}{3}x$$

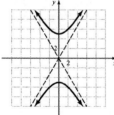

12. $x^2 - 4y^2 = 16$

$$\frac{x^2}{16} - \frac{4y^2}{16} = \frac{16}{16}$$

$$\frac{x^2}{16} - \frac{y^2}{4} = 1$$

$$\frac{x^2}{4^2} - \frac{y^2}{2^2} = 1$$

$a = 4, \ b = 2$

x-intercepts are $(\pm 4,0)$ or

$(4,0)$ and $(-4,0)$

Equations of asymptotes are

$$y = \pm \frac{2}{4}x \text{ or } y = \frac{1}{2}x \text{ and } y = -\frac{1}{2}x$$

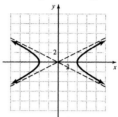

13. $x^2 + y^2 = 9; \quad x = y - 3$

$$(y-3)^2 + y^2 = 9$$

$$y^2 - 6y + 9 + y^2 = 9$$

$$2y^2 - 6y = 0$$

$$2y(y-3) = 0$$

$2y = 0 \qquad\qquad$ or $\quad y - 3 = 0$

$y = 0 \qquad\qquad\qquad\quad y = 3$

$x = y - 3 = 0 - 3 \qquad x = y - 3 = 3 - 3$

$x = -3 \qquad\qquad\qquad x = 0$

$(-3,0)$ and $(0,3)$

14. $y = x^2 - 2; \quad y = -x^2 - 6$

$$x^2 - 2 = -x^2 - 6$$

$$2x^2 = -4$$

$$x^2 = -2; \quad x = \pm\sqrt{-2} = \pm i\sqrt{2}$$

$$y = x^2 - 2$$

$$y = -2 - 2 = -4$$

$$\left(-i\sqrt{2}, -4\right) \text{ and } \left(i\sqrt{2}, -4\right)$$

15. $4x^2 + 2y^2 = 26$

$$\underline{5x^2 - 2y^2 = 28}$$

$$9x^2 \qquad\quad = 54$$

$$x^2 = 6$$

$$x = \pm\sqrt{6}$$

$$4x^2 + 2y^2 = 26$$

$$4(6) + 2y^2 = 26$$

$$24 + 2y^2 = 26$$

$$2y^2 = 2$$

$$y^2 = 1$$

$$y = \pm\sqrt{1} = \pm 1$$

$$\left(\sqrt{6},1\right), \ \left(-\sqrt{6},1\right), \ \left(\sqrt{6},-1\right), \ \left(-\sqrt{6},-1\right)$$

16. $x^2 - 9y^2 < 36$

Boundary line is dashed.

$x^2 - 9y^2 = 36$

$\dfrac{x^2}{36} - \dfrac{9y^2}{36} = \dfrac{36}{36}$

$\dfrac{x^2}{36} - \dfrac{y^2}{4} = 1$

$\dfrac{x^2}{6^2} - \dfrac{y^2}{2^2} = 1$

$a = 6, \ b = 2$

x-intercepts are $(\pm 6, 0)$ or

$(6,0)$ and $(-6,0)$

Equations of asymptotes are

$y = \pm \dfrac{2}{6} x$ or $y = \dfrac{1}{3} x$ and $y = -\dfrac{1}{3} x$

Test point is $(0,0)$

$(0)^2 + 9(0)^2 \overset{?}{<} 36$

$0 + 0 < 36$ True. Shade the region

containing $(0,0)$.

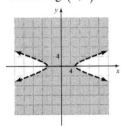

17. $x^2 + (y+3)^2 \le 4$

Boundary line is solid.

$(x-0)^2 + (y-(-3))^2 = 4$

Center: $(0,-3)$, radius $= 2$

Test point is $(0,0)$

$(0)^2 + (0+3)^2 \overset{?}{\le} 4$

$9 \le 4$ False, shade the region not

containing the point $(0,0)$.

$8x^2 + 32y^2 \ge 128$

Boundary line is solid.

$8x^2 + 32y^2 = 128$

$\dfrac{8x^2}{128} + \dfrac{32y^2}{128} = \dfrac{128}{128}$

$\dfrac{x^2}{16} + \dfrac{y^2}{4} = 1$

$\dfrac{x^2}{4^2} + \dfrac{y^2}{2^2} = 1$

$a = 4, \ b = 2$

x-intercepts: $(\pm 4, 0)$ or $(4,0)$ and $(-4,0)$

y-intercepts: $(0, \pm 2)$ or $(0,2)$ and $(0,-2)$

Test point is $(0,0)$.

$8(0)^2 + 32(0)^2 \ge 128$

$0 + 0 \ge 128$ False. Shade the region not

containing the point $(0,0)$.

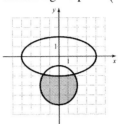

18. The parabola has vertex at $(0,0)$ and is of

the form $x = k(y-0)^2 + 0$. $x = ky^2$ It

passes through the point $\left(2, \dfrac{15}{2}\right)$.

$x = ky^2$

$2 = k\left(\dfrac{15}{2}\right)^2$

$2 = \dfrac{225}{4} k$

$k = 2\left(\dfrac{4}{225}\right) = \dfrac{8}{225}$

$x = \dfrac{8}{225} y^2$

19. $\dfrac{x^2}{354^2} + \dfrac{y^2}{181^2} = 1$

The maximum distance from the sun to the comet (sun to farthest vertex) is 658 million miles($r + r + s$) in the diagram below. That is the distance from the sun to the center of the ellipse plus the distance from the center of the ellipse to the vertex. The distance from the center of the ellipse to the vertex is $a = r + s = 354$ million miles. The distance from the sun to the center is $r = 658 - 354 = 304$ million miles. The distance from the sun (focus) to the nearest vertex is $s = 354 - r = 354 - 304 = 50$.

The minimum distance to the sun is about 50 million miles.

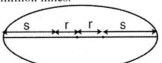

20. $x^2 + y^2 \le 1000^2$ or $x^2 + y^2 = 1,000,000$

Boundary line is solid

$x^2 + y^2 = 1000^2$

Center: $(0,0)$ radius $= 1000$

Test point is $(0,0)$.

$0^2 + 0^2 \overset{?}{\le} 1000^2$

$0 \le 1000^2$ True. Shade the region

containing the point $(0,0)$.

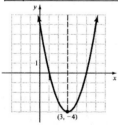

Exercises 10.1 Introduction to Conics: The Parabola

1. $y = (x-3)^2 - 4$

$h = 3,\ k = -4$

Vertex: $(3,-4)$; axis of symmetry: $x = 3$

x	$y = (x-3)^2 - 4$	(x,y)
0	$(0-3)^2 - 4 = 5$	$(0,5)$
1	$(1-3)^2 - 4 = 0$	$(1,0)$
2	$(2-3)^2 - 4 = -3$	$(2,-3)$
3	$(3-3)^2 - 4 = -4$	$(3,-4)$
4	$(4-3)^2 - 4 = -3$	$(4,-3)$
5	$(5-3)^2 - 4 = 0$	$(5,0)$
6	$(6-3)^2 - 4 = 5$	$(6,5)$

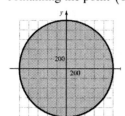

3      $y = -\dfrac{1}{2}(x+2)^2 - 5$

$y = -\dfrac{1}{2}\left(x-(-2)\right)^2 + (-5)$

$h = -2,\ k = -5$

Vertex: $(-2,-5)$

Axis of symmetry: $x = -2$

x	$y = -\dfrac{1}{2}(x+2)^2 - 5$	(x,y)
-5	$-\dfrac{1}{2}(-5+2)^2 - 5 = -\dfrac{19}{2}$	$\left(-5, -\dfrac{19}{2}\right)$
-4	$-\dfrac{1}{2}(-4+2)^2 - 5 = -7$	$(-4,-7)$
-3	$-\dfrac{1}{2}(-3+2)^2 - 5 = -\dfrac{11}{2}$	$\left(-3, -\dfrac{11}{2}\right)$
-2	$-\dfrac{1}{2}(-2+2)^2 - 5 = -5$	$(-2,-5)$
-1	$-\dfrac{1}{2}(-1+2)^2 - 5 = -\dfrac{11}{2}$	$\left(-1, -\dfrac{11}{2}\right)$
0	$-\dfrac{1}{2}(0+2)^2 - 5 = -7$	$(0,-7)$
1	$-\dfrac{1}{2}(1+2)^2 - 5 = -\dfrac{19}{2}$	$\left(1, -\dfrac{19}{2}\right)$

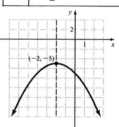

5      $x = 4(y-1)^2$

$x = 4(y-1) + 0$

$h = 0;\ k = 1$

Vertex: $(0,1)$

Axis of symmetry: $y = 1$

y	$x = 4(y^2 - 1)$	(x,y)
3	$4(3-1)^2 = 16$	$(16,3)$
2	$4(2-1)^2 = 4$	$(4,2)$
1	$4(1-1)^2 = 0$	$(0,1)$
0	$4(0-1)^2 = 4$	$(4,0)$
-1	$4(-1-1)^2 = 16$	$(16,-1)$

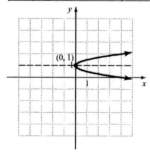

7. $x = -y^2 + 2y + 2$

$x = -\left(y^2 - 2y + \left(\dfrac{-2}{2}\right)^2\right) + 2 + \left(\dfrac{-2}{2}\right)^2$

$x = -(y-1)^2 + 3$

$h = 3, \ k = 1$

Vertex: $(3, 1)$

Axis of symmetry: $y = 1$

y	$x = -y^2 + 2y + 2$	(x, y)
-2	$-(-2)^2 + 2(-2) + 2 = -6$	$(-6, -2)$
-1	$-(-1)^2 + 2(-1) + 2 = -1$	$(-1, -1)$
0	$-(0)^2 + 2(0) + 2 = 2$	$(2, 0)$
1	$-(1)^2 + 2(1) + 2 = 3$	$(3, 1)$
2	$-(2)^2 + 2(2) + 2 = 2$	$(2, 2)$
3	$-(3)^2 + 2(3) + 2 = -1$	$(-1, 3)$
4	$-(4)^2 + 2(4) + 2 = -6$	$(-6, 4)$

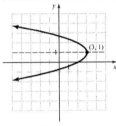

9. $y = -2x^2 + 12x - 10$

$y = -2(x^2 - 6x) - 10$

$y = -2\left(x^2 - 6x + \left(\dfrac{-6}{2}\right)^2\right) - 10 + 2\left(\dfrac{-6}{2}\right)^2$

$y = -2(x-3)^2 + 8$

$h = 3, \ k = 8$

Vertex: $(3, 8)$

Axis of symmetry: $x = 3$

x	$y = -2x^2 + 12x - 10$	(x, y)
0	$-2(0)^2 + 12(0) - 10 = -10$	$(0, -10)$
1	$-2(1)^2 + 12(1) - 10 = 0$	$(1, 0)$
2	$-2(2)^2 + 12(2) - 10 = 6$	$(2, 6)$
3	$-2(3)^2 + 12(3) - 10 = 8$	$(3, 8)$
4	$-2(4)^2 + 12(4) - 10 = 6$	$(4, 6)$
5	$-2(5)^2 + 12(5) - 10 = 0$	$(5, 0)$
6	$-2(6)^2 + 12(6) - 10 = -10$	$(6, -10)$

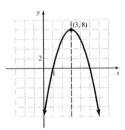

11. $x = 3y^2 + 12y + 10$

$x = 3(y^2 + 4y) + 10$

$x = 3\left(y^2 + 4y + \left(\dfrac{4}{2}\right)^2\right) + 10 - 3\left(\dfrac{4}{2}\right)^2$

$x = 3(y+2)^2 - 2$

$x = 3(y - (-2))^2 - 2$

$h = -2, \ k = -2$

Vertex: $(-2, -2)$

Axis of symmetry: $y = -2$

y	$x = 3y^2 + 12y + 10$	(x, y)
1	$3(1)^2 + 12(1) + 10 = 25$	$(25, 1)$
0	$3(0)^2 + 12(0) + 10 = 10$	$(10, 0)$
-1	$3(-1)^2 + 12(-1) + 10 = 1$	$(-1, 1)$
-2	$3(-2)^2 + 12(-2) + 10 = -2$	$(-2, -2)$
-3	$3(-3)^2 + 12(-3) + 10 = 1$	$(1, -3)$
-4	$3(-4)^2 + 12(-4) + 10 = 10$	$(10, -4)$

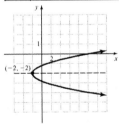

13. $y = x^2 - x + 1$

$y = x^2 - x + \left(\dfrac{-1}{2}\right)^2 + 1 - \left(\dfrac{-1}{2}\right)^2$

$y = \left(x - \dfrac{1}{2}\right)^2 + \dfrac{3}{4}$

$h = \dfrac{1}{2}, \ k = \dfrac{3}{4}$

Vertex: $\left(\dfrac{1}{2}, \dfrac{3}{4}\right)$

15. $y = 5x^2 - 50x + 57$

$y = 5(x^2 - 10x) + 57$

$$y = 5\left(x^2 - 10x + \left(\frac{-10}{2}\right)^2\right) + 57 - 5\left(\frac{-10}{2}\right)^2$$

$$y = 5\left(x^2 - 10x + 25\right) + 57 - 5 \bullet 25$$

$$y = 5\left(x - 5\right)^2 - 68$$

$$h = 5, \ k = -68$$

Vertex: $(5, -68)$

17. $x = -2y^2 - 32y - 95$

$$x = -2\left(y^2 + 16y\right) - 95$$

$$x = -2\left(y^2 + 16y + \left(\frac{16}{2}\right)^2\right) - 95 - (-2)\left(\frac{16}{2}\right)^2$$

$$x = -2\left(y + 8\right)^2 - 95 + 128$$

$$x = -2\left(y + 8\right)^2 + 33$$

$$x = -2\left(y - (-8)\right)^2 + 33$$

$$h = 33, k = -8$$

Vertex: $(33, -8)$

19. $x = 3y^2 + 9y + 11$

$$x = 3\left(y^2 + 3y\right) + 11$$

$$x = 3\left(y^2 + 3y + \left(\frac{3}{2}\right)^2\right) + 11 - 3\left(\frac{3}{2}\right)^2$$

$$x = 3\left(y + \frac{3}{2}\right)^2 + 11 - \frac{27}{4}$$

$$x = 3\left(y - \left(-\frac{3}{2}\right)\right)^2 + \frac{17}{4}$$

$$h = \frac{17}{4}, \ k = -\frac{3}{2}$$

Vertex: $\left(\frac{17}{4}, -\frac{3}{2}\right)$

21. $h = -2, \ k = 7$

$$y = a\left(x - (-2)\right)^2 + 7$$

$$y = a\left(x + 2\right)^2 + 7$$

Passes through $(3, 12)$

$$12 = a\left(3 + 2\right)^2 + 7$$

$$5 = a\left(5\right)^2$$

$$5 = 25a$$

$$a = \frac{5}{25} = \frac{1}{5}$$

$$y = \frac{1}{5}(x + 2)^2 + 7$$

23. $h = 4, \ k = 0$

$$x = a\left(y - 0\right)^2 + 4$$

Passes through $(0, 1)$

$$0 = a\left(1 - 0\right)^2 + 4$$

$$-4 = a(1)$$

$$a = -4$$

$$x = -4\left(y - 0\right)^2 + 4$$

$$x = -4y^2 + 4$$

25. $R = -\left(x - 40\right)^2 + 1600$

$$h = 40, \ k = 1600$$

Vertex: $(40, 1600)$

(40, 1600); it shows that the company will have a maximum revenue of \$1600 when 40 bottles of perfume are sold.

27.   a.   Perimeter $= 2l + 2w = 500$

$$2l = 500 - 2w$$

$$l = \frac{500 - 2w}{2} = 250 - w$$

Area $= A = lw = \left(250 - w\right)w$

$$A = -w^2 + 250w$$

$$A = -\left(w^2 - 250w\right)$$

$$A = -\left(w^2 - 250w + \left(\frac{-250}{2}\right)^2\right) + \left(\frac{-250}{2}\right)^2$$

$$A = -\left(w^2 - 250w + 15625\right) + 15625$$

$$A = -\left(w - 125\right)^2 + 15,625$$

Vertex: $(125, 15,625)$

$l = 250 - w = 250 - 125 = 125$

Dimensions of 125 ft by 125 ft will produce a field with a maximum area of 15,625 sq ft.

29.   The vertex is at $(0, 0)$ and

passes through $(6, 20)$.

The parabola is of the form

$$x = a\left(y - k\right)^2 + h; \quad h = 0, \ k = 0$$

$$x = ay^2$$

$(6, 20)$ is on the parabola.

$$6 = a\left(20\right)^2 = 400a$$

$$a = \frac{6}{400} = \frac{3}{200}$$

$$x = \frac{3}{200}y^2$$

Exercises 10.2 The Circle

1. $d = \sqrt{\left(x_2 - x_1\right)^2 + \left(y_2 - y_1\right)^2}$

$$d = \sqrt{\left(9 - 3\right)^2 + \left(10 - 2\right)^2} = \sqrt{\left(6\right)^2 + \left(8\right)^2}$$

$d = \sqrt{36+64} = \sqrt{100} = 10$ units

3. $d = \sqrt{\left(x_2 - x_1\right)^2 + \left(y_2 - y_1\right)^2}$

$d = \sqrt{\left(-1-1\right)^2 + \left(2-6\right)^2} = \sqrt{\left(-2\right)^2 + \left(-4\right)^2}$

$d = \sqrt{4+16} = \sqrt{20} = 2\sqrt{5}$

$d = 4.4721... \approx 4.5$ units

5. $d = \sqrt{\left(x_2 - x_1\right)^2 + \left(y_2 - y_1\right)^2}$

$d = \sqrt{\left(5-8\right)^2 + \left(-6-\left(-4\right)\right)^2}$

$d = \sqrt{\left(-3\right)^2 + \left(-2\right)^2}$

$d = \sqrt{9+4} = \sqrt{13} = 3.6055... \approx 3.6$ units

7. $d = \sqrt{\left(x_2 - x_1\right)^2 + \left(y_2 - y_1\right)^2}$

$d = \sqrt{\left(-1.2-\left(-3.2\right)\right)^2 + \left(-5.3-1.7\right)^2}$

$d = \sqrt{\left(2\right)^2 + \left(-7\right)^2} = \sqrt{4+49} = \sqrt{53}$

$d = 7.2801... \approx 7.3$ units

9. $d = \sqrt{\left(x_2 - x_1\right)^2 + \left(y_2 - y_1\right)^2}$

$d = \sqrt{\left(\dfrac{1}{2} - \dfrac{1}{4}\right)^2 + \left(\dfrac{2}{3} - \dfrac{1}{3}\right)^2} = \sqrt{\left(\dfrac{1}{4}\right)^2 + \left(\dfrac{1}{3}\right)^2}$

$d = \sqrt{\dfrac{1}{16} + \dfrac{1}{9}} = \sqrt{\dfrac{9}{144} + \dfrac{16}{144}} =$

$d = \sqrt{\dfrac{25}{144}} = \dfrac{5}{12}$ units

11. $d = \sqrt{\left(x_2 - x_1\right)^2 + \left(y_2 - y_1\right)^2}$

$d = \sqrt{\left(\sqrt{3}-\left(-4\sqrt{3}\right)\right)^2 + \left(-3\sqrt{2}-\left(-2\sqrt{2}\right)\right)^2}$

$d = \sqrt{\left(5\sqrt{3}\right)^2 + \left(-\sqrt{2}\right)^2} = \sqrt{25 \bullet 3 + 2} = \sqrt{77}$

$d = 8.7749... \approx 8.8$ units

13. $\left(\dfrac{5+7}{2}, \dfrac{9+1}{2}\right) = \left(\dfrac{12}{2}, \dfrac{10}{2}\right) = (6,5)$

15. $\left(\dfrac{3+\left(-12\right)}{2}, \dfrac{11+\left(-1\right)}{2}\right) = \left(\dfrac{-9}{2}, \dfrac{10}{2}\right) =$

$\left(-\dfrac{9}{2}, 5\right)$

17. $\left(\dfrac{-8+\left(-13\right)}{2}, \dfrac{-11+\left(-2\right)}{2}\right) = \left(-\dfrac{21}{2}, -\dfrac{13}{2}\right)$

19. $\left(\dfrac{3.4+0.6}{2}, \dfrac{-1.1+\left(-3.9\right)}{2}\right) = \left(\dfrac{4}{2}, \dfrac{-5}{2}\right) =$

$(2,-2.5)$

21. $\left(\dfrac{\dfrac{3}{4}+\left(-\dfrac{1}{3}\right)}{2}, \dfrac{-\dfrac{2}{5}+\dfrac{1}{2}}{2}\right) = \left(\dfrac{\dfrac{9}{12}-\dfrac{4}{12}}{2}, \dfrac{-\dfrac{4}{10}+\dfrac{5}{10}}{2}\right)$

$= \left(\dfrac{\dfrac{5}{12}}{2}, \dfrac{\dfrac{1}{10}}{2}\right) = \left(\dfrac{\dfrac{5}{12} \bullet \dfrac{1}{2}}{2 \bullet \dfrac{1}{2}}, \dfrac{\dfrac{1}{10} \bullet \dfrac{1}{2}}{2 \bullet \dfrac{1}{2}}\right) = \left(\dfrac{5}{24}, \dfrac{1}{20}\right)$

23. $\left(\dfrac{-7\sqrt{3}+7\sqrt{3}}{2}, \dfrac{5\sqrt{6}+3\sqrt{6}}{2}\right) = \left(\dfrac{0}{2}, \dfrac{8\sqrt{6}}{2}\right) =$

$\left(0, 4\sqrt{6}\right)$

25. $x^2 + y^2 = 36$

$\left(x-0\right)^2 + \left(y-0\right)^2 = 6^2 \quad h = 0, \ k = 0$

Center: $(0,0)$, radius: 6

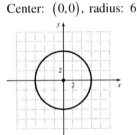

27. $\left(x-3\right)^2 + \left(y-2\right)^2 = 1 \quad h = 3, \ k = 2$

Center: $(3,2)$ radius: 1

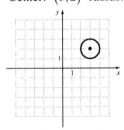

29. $\left(x+2\right)^2 + \left(y-4\right)^2 = 25$

$\left(x-\left(-2\right)\right)^2 + \left(y-4\right)^2 = 5^2 \quad h = -2, \ k = 4$

Center: $(-2,4)$ radius: 5

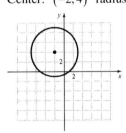

31. $x^2 + y^2 - 2y = 8$

$x^2 + y^2 - 2y + \left(\dfrac{-2}{2}\right)^2 = 8 + \left(\dfrac{-2}{2}\right)^2$

$$x^2+y^2-2y+1=8+1$$
$$(x-0)^2+(y-1)^2=9=3^2 \quad h=0, \ k=1$$
Center: $(0,1)$ radius: 3

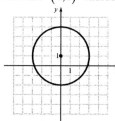

33. $x^2+y^2+2x+2y-23=0$
$$x^2+2x+y^2+2y=23$$
$$x^2+2x+\left(\frac{2}{2}\right)^2+y^2+2y+\left(\frac{2}{2}\right)^2=$$
$$23+\left(\frac{2}{2}\right)^2+\left(\frac{2}{2}\right)^2$$
$$x^2+2x+1+y^2+2y+1=23+1+1$$
$$(x+1)^2+(y+1)^2=25$$
$$(x-(-1))^2+(y-(-1))^2=5^2$$
$$h=-1, \ k=-1$$
Center: $(-1,-1)$ radius: 5

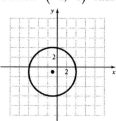

35. $x^2+y^2-8x-6y+16=0$
$$x^2-8x+y^2-6y=-16$$
$$x^2-8x+\left(\frac{-8}{2}\right)^2+y^2-6y+\left(\frac{-6}{2}\right)^2=$$
$$-16+\left(\frac{-8}{2}\right)^2+\left(\frac{-6}{2}\right)^2$$
$$x^2-8x+16+y^2-6y+9=-16+16+9$$
$$(x-4)^2+(y-3)^2=9=3^2 \quad h=4, \ k=3$$
Center: $(4,3)$ radius: 3

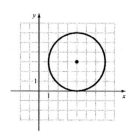

37. $(x-(-7))^2+(y-2)^2=9^2$
$$(x+7)^2+(y-2)^2=81$$

39. $(x-0)^2+(y-4)^2=\left(\sqrt{5}\right)^2$
$$x^2+(y-4)^2=5$$

41. The distance from the center to the point on the circle is the radius.
$$r=\sqrt{(-1-3)^2+(9-5)^2}=\sqrt{(-4)^2+(4)^2}$$
$$r=\sqrt{16+16}=\sqrt{32}$$
$$r^2=\left(\sqrt{32}\right)^2=32$$
$$(x-3)^2+(y-5)^2=32$$

43. The midpoint of the diameter is the center.
$$\left(\frac{-6+2}{2},\frac{1+11}{2}\right)=\left(\frac{-4}{2},\frac{12}{2}\right)=(-2,6)$$
The distance from the center to the endpoint of the diameter is the radius. Using (2, 11),
$$r=\sqrt{(2-(-2))^2+(11-6)^2}=\sqrt{(4)^2+(5)^2}$$
$$r=\sqrt{16+25}=\sqrt{41}$$
$$(x-(-2))^2+(y-6)^2=\left(\sqrt{41}\right)^2$$
$$(x+2)^2+(y-6)^2=41$$

45. $x^2+y^2+3x+4y=0$
$$x^2+3x+y^2+4y=0$$
$$x^2+3x+\left(\frac{3}{2}\right)^2+y^2+4y+\left(\frac{4}{2}\right)^2=$$
$$\left(\frac{3}{2}\right)^2+\left(\frac{4}{2}\right)^2$$
$$x^2+3x+\frac{9}{4}+y^2+4y+4=\frac{9}{4}+4$$
$$\left(x+\frac{3}{2}\right)^2+(y+2)^2=\frac{9}{4}+\frac{16}{4}=\frac{25}{4}$$
$$\left(x-\left(-\frac{3}{2}\right)\right)^2+(y-(-2))^2=\left(\frac{5}{2}\right)^2$$
$$h=-\frac{3}{2}, \ k=-2$$
Center: $\left(-\frac{3}{2},-2\right)$ radius: $\frac{5}{2}$

47. $x^2+y^2-10x+6y-4=0$
$$x^2-10x+y^2+6y=4$$
$$x^2-10x+\left(\frac{-10}{2}\right)^2+y^2+6y+\left(\frac{6}{2}\right)^2=$$
$$4+\left(\frac{-10}{2}\right)^2+\left(\frac{6}{2}\right)^2$$

$x^2 - 10x + 25 + y^2 + 6y + 9 = 4 + 25 + 9$

$(x-5)^2 + (y+3)^2 = 38$

$(x-5)^2 + (y-(-3))^2 = \left(\sqrt{38}\right)^2$

$h = 5, \quad k = -3$

Center: $(5, -3)$ radius: $\sqrt{38}$

49. $3x^2 + 3y^2 - 12x - 24 = 0$

$3\left(x^2 + y^2 - 4x - 8\right) = 0$

$x^2 + y^2 - 4x - 8 = 0$

$x^2 - 4x + y^2 = 8$

$x^2 - 4x + \left(\frac{-4}{2}\right)^2 + y^2 = 8 + \left(\frac{-4}{2}\right)^2$

$x^2 - 4x + 4 + y^2 = 8 + 4$

$(x-2)^2 + (y-0)^2 = 12 \quad h = 2, \quad k = 0$

Center: $(2, 0)$ radius: $\sqrt{12} = 2\sqrt{3}$

51. The distance is from $(11, 8)$ to $(-1, -1)$.

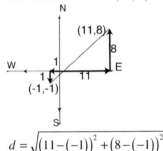

$d = \sqrt{(11-(-1))^2 + (8-(-1))^2}$

$d = \sqrt{(12)^2 + (9)^2} = \sqrt{144 + 81} = \sqrt{225} = 15$

The distance between her home and her office is 15 mi.

53. a. Midpoint of $\overline{AC}$ is D

$A: (2,1) \quad C: (6,5)$

$\left(\frac{2+6}{2}, \frac{1+5}{2}\right) = \left(\frac{8}{2}, \frac{6}{2}\right) = (4,3) \quad D: (4,3)$

b. Slope of $\overline{BD}$ $B: (1,6) \quad D: (4,3)$

$m_{\overline{BD}} = \frac{y_2 - y_1}{x_2 - x_1} = \frac{3-6}{4-1} = \frac{-3}{3} = -1$

Slope of $\overline{AC}$ $A: (2,1) \quad C: (6,5)$

$m_{\overline{AC}} = \frac{y_2 - y_1}{x_2 - x_1} = \frac{5-1}{6-2} = \frac{4}{4} = 1$

The slope of $\overline{BD}$ is -1 and the slope of $\overline{AC}$ is $+1$. Since the slopes are negative reciprocals $\overline{BD}$ is perpendicular to the base $\overline{AC}$ and is the altitude of the triangle.

c. Area $= \frac{1}{2}$ base $\times$ height.

Area $= \frac{1}{2}\left(\text{length of } \overline{AC}\right)\left(\text{length of } \overline{BD}\right)$.

length of $\overline{AC} = \sqrt{(6-2)^2 + (5-1)^2} =$

$\sqrt{(4)^2 + (4)^2} = \sqrt{16+16} = \sqrt{32} = 4\sqrt{2}$

length of $\overline{BD} = \sqrt{(4-1)^2 + (3-6)^2}$

$\sqrt{(3)^2 + (-3)^2} = \sqrt{9+9} = \sqrt{18} = 3\sqrt{2}$

Area $\frac{1}{2}\left(4\sqrt{2}\right)\left(3\sqrt{2}\right) = \frac{1}{2} \cdot 12 \cdot 2 = 12$

The area of triangle ABC is 12 sq units.

55. Half the diameter of 6 mi. is 3 mi.

$(x-0)^2 + (y-0)^2 = (3)^2$

$x^2 + y^2 = 9$

57. a. Center: $(-8, 15)$ radius: 36

$(x-(-8))^2 + (y-15)^2 = 36^2$

$(x+8)^2 + (y-15)^2 = 1296$

b. The distance from the center of the circle $(-8,15)$ to the apartment at $(15,-3)$

is $d = \sqrt{(15-(-8))^2 + (-3-15)^2}$

$d = \sqrt{(23)^2 + (-18)^2} = \sqrt{529 + 324} = \sqrt{853}$

$d = 29.2061...$

Yes, since $\sqrt{853} \approx 29.2 < 36$.

Exercises 10.3 The Ellipse and the Hyperbola

1. $\frac{x^2}{16} + \frac{y^2}{4} = 1 \quad \frac{x^2}{4^2} + \frac{y^2}{2^2} = 1 \quad a = 4, \quad b = 2$

x-intercepts: $(\pm 4, 0)$ or $(4,0)$ and $(-4,0)$

y-intercepts: $(0, \pm 2)$ or $(0,2)$ and $(0,-2)$

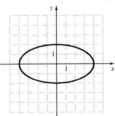

3. $\frac{x^2}{36} + \frac{y^2}{81} = 1 \quad \frac{x^2}{6^2} + \frac{y^2}{9^2} = 1 \quad a = 6 \quad b = 9$

x-intercepts: $(\pm 6, 0)$ or $(6,0)$ and $(-6,0)$

y-intercepts: $(0, \pm 9)$ or $(0,9)$ and $(0,-9)$

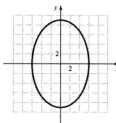

5. $64x^2 + 16y^2 = 64$

$$\frac{64x^2}{64} + \frac{16y^2}{64} = \frac{64}{64}$$

$$\frac{x^2}{1} + \frac{y^2}{4} = 1 \quad \frac{x^2}{1^2} + \frac{y^2}{2^2} = 1 \quad a = 1 \quad b = 2$$

x-intercepts: $(\pm 1, 0)$ or $(1, 0)$ and $(-1, 0)$

y-intercepts: $(0, \pm 2)$ or $(0, 2)$ and $(0, -2)$

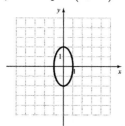

7. $x^2 + 4y^2 = 100$

$$\frac{x^2}{100} + \frac{4y^2}{100} = \frac{100}{100}$$

$$\frac{x^2}{100} + \frac{y^2}{25} = 1 \quad \frac{x^2}{10^2} + \frac{y^2}{5^2} = 1 \quad a = 10 \quad b = 5$$

x-intercepts: $(\pm 10, 0)$ or $(10, 0)$ and $(-10, 0)$

y-intercepts: $(0, \pm 5)$ or $(0, 5)$ and $(0, -5)$

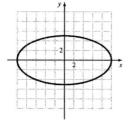

9. $2x^2 + 8y^2 = 128$

$$\frac{2x^2}{128} + \frac{8y^2}{128} = \frac{128}{128}$$

$$\frac{x^2}{64} + \frac{y^2}{16} = 1 \quad \frac{x^2}{8^2} + \frac{y^2}{4^2} = 1 \quad a = 8 \quad b = 4$$

x-intercepts: $(\pm 8, 0)$ or $(8, 0)$ and $(-8, 0)$

y-intercepts: $(0, \pm 4)$ or $(0, 4)$ and $(0, -4)$

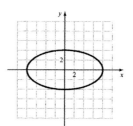

11. $\dfrac{x^2}{64} - \dfrac{y^2}{9} = 1 \quad \dfrac{x^2}{8^2} - \dfrac{y^2}{3^2} = 1 \quad a = 8 \quad b = 3$

x-intercepts: $(\pm 8, 0)$ or $(8, 0)$ and $(-8, 0)$

Equation of asymptotes are

$$y = \frac{3}{8}x \text{ and } y = -\frac{3}{8}x$$

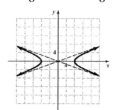

13. $\dfrac{y^2}{81} - \dfrac{x^2}{36} = 1 \quad \dfrac{y^2}{9^2} - \dfrac{x^2}{6^2} = 1 \quad a = 6 \quad b = 9$

y-intercepts: $(0, \pm 9)$ or $(0, 9)$ and $(0, -9)$

Equation of asymptotes are $y = \dfrac{9}{6}x = \dfrac{3}{2}x$

and $y = -\dfrac{3}{2}x$

15. $x^2 - 9y^2 = 225$

$$\frac{x^2}{225} - \frac{9y^2}{225} = \frac{225}{225}$$

$$\frac{x^2}{225} - \frac{y^2}{25} = 1 \quad \frac{x^2}{15^2} - \frac{y^2}{5^2} = 1 \quad a = 15 \quad b = 5$$

x-intercepts: $(\pm 15, 0)$ or $(15, 0)$ and $(-15, 0)$

Equation of asymptotes are

$$y = \frac{5}{15}x = \frac{1}{3}x \text{ and } y = -\frac{1}{3}x$$

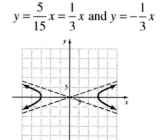

17. $3y^2 - 12x^2 = 108$

$\dfrac{3y^2}{108} - \dfrac{12x^2}{108} = \dfrac{108}{108}$

$\dfrac{y^2}{36} - \dfrac{x^2}{9} = 1 \quad \dfrac{y^2}{6^2} - \dfrac{x^2}{3^2} = 1 \quad a = 3 \quad b = 6$

y-intercepts: $(0, \pm 6)$ or $(0, 6)$ and $(0, -6)$

Equation of asymptotes are

$y = \dfrac{6}{3}x = 2x$ and $y = -2x$

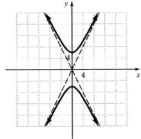

19. $8x^2 + 8y^2 = 32$

$\dfrac{8x^2}{8} + \dfrac{8y^2}{8} = \dfrac{32}{8}$

$x^2 + y^2 = 4$ Circle

21. $x^2 - 2y = 10$

$2y = x^2 - 10$

$y = \dfrac{1}{2}x^2 - 5$, Parabola

23. $10y^2 - 12x^2 = 120$

$\dfrac{10y^2}{120} - \dfrac{12x^2}{120} = \dfrac{120}{120}$

$\dfrac{y^2}{12} - \dfrac{x^2}{10} = 1$ Hyperbola

25. $a = 11, \; b = 3$

$\dfrac{x^2}{a^2} + \dfrac{y^2}{b^2} = 1 \quad \dfrac{x^2}{11^2} + \dfrac{y^2}{3^2} = 1 \quad \dfrac{x^2}{121} + \dfrac{y^2}{9} = 1$

27. $a = \sqrt{7}, \; b = 2\sqrt{2}$

$\dfrac{x^2}{a^2} + \dfrac{y^2}{b^2} = 1 \quad \dfrac{x^2}{\left(\sqrt{7}\right)^2} + \dfrac{y^2}{\left(2\sqrt{2}\right)^2} = 1$

$\dfrac{x^2}{7} + \dfrac{y^2}{4 \bullet 2} = 1 \quad \dfrac{x^2}{7} + \dfrac{y^2}{8} = 1$

29. $a = 4 \quad \dfrac{b}{a} = \dfrac{1}{4} = \dfrac{b}{4} \quad b = 1$

$\dfrac{x^2}{a^2} - \dfrac{y^2}{b^2} = 1 \quad \dfrac{x^2}{4^2} - \dfrac{y^2}{1^2} = 1 \quad \dfrac{x^2}{16} - y^2 = 1$

31. a. $\dfrac{x^2}{8100} + \dfrac{y^2}{5625} = 1 \quad \dfrac{x^2}{90^2} + \dfrac{y^2}{75^2} = 1$

$a = 90 \quad 2a = 180 \quad b = 75 \quad 2b = 150$

The length is 180 m and the width is 150 m.

b. Yes $\quad 135 < 180 < 185$

33. a. $A = 25\pi\left(R^2 - r^2\right) = 100\pi$

$\dfrac{25\pi\left(R^2 - r^2\right)}{100\pi} = \dfrac{100\pi}{100\pi}$

$\dfrac{R^2 - r^2}{4} = \dfrac{R^2}{4} - \dfrac{r^2}{4} = 1 \quad a = 2 \quad b = 2$

R-intercepts: $(0, \pm 2)$ or $(0, 2)$ and $(0, -2)$

Equation of asymptotes are

$y = \dfrac{2}{2}x = x$ and $y = -x$

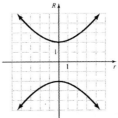

b. In Quadrant I, both the r- and R-coordinates of each point on the graph are nonnegative. Neither radius can be negative.

35. $2a = 6, \; a = 3 \quad 2b = 4 \quad b = 2$

$\dfrac{x^2}{a^2} + \dfrac{y^2}{b^2} = 1 \quad \dfrac{x^2}{3^2} + \dfrac{y^2}{2^2} = 1 \quad \dfrac{x^2}{9} + \dfrac{y^2}{4} = 1$

Exercises 10.4 Solving Nonlinear Systems of Equations

1. $y = x^2 - 2 \quad y = 2x + 1$

$x^2 - 2 = 2x + 1$

$x^2 - 2x - 3 = 0$

$(x - 3)(x + 1) = 0$

$x - 3 = 0 \quad$ or $\quad x + 1 = 0$

$x = 3 \qquad\qquad x = -1$

$y = (3)^2 - 2 = 9 - 2 = 7$

$y = (-1)^2 - 2 = 1 - 2 = -1$

$(-1, -1), (3, 7)$

3. $x^2 + y^2 = 12 \quad x = y^2 - 6$

$y^2 = x + 6$

$x^2 + x + 6 = 12$

$x^2 + x - 6 = 0$

$(x - 2)(x + 3) = 0$

$x - 2 = 0 \qquad\qquad x + 3 = 0$

$x = 2 \qquad\qquad x = -3$

$$y^2 = 2 + 6 = 8 \qquad y^2 = -3 + 6 = 3$$
$$y = \pm\sqrt{8} = \pm 2\sqrt{2} \qquad y = \pm\sqrt{3}$$
$$\left(2, 2\sqrt{2}\right), \left(2, -2\sqrt{2}\right), \left(-3, \sqrt{3}\right), \left(-3, -\sqrt{3}\right)$$

5.
$$y = x^2 - 5 \quad y = -x^2 + 11$$
$$x^2 - 5 = -x^2 + 11$$
$$2x^2 = 16$$
$$x^2 = 8$$
$$x = \pm\sqrt{8} = \pm 2\sqrt{2}$$
$$y = x^2 - 5 = 8 - 5 = 3$$
$$\left(2\sqrt{2}, 3\right)\left(-2\sqrt{2}, 3\right)$$

7.
$$x^2 + y^2 = 16 \quad x - y = 4$$
$$x = y + 4$$
$$(y + 4)^2 + y^2 = 16$$
$$y^2 + 8y + 16 + y^2 = 16$$
$$2y^2 + 8y = 0$$
$$2y(y + 4) = 0$$
$$2y = 0 \qquad y + 4 = 0$$
$$y = 0 \qquad y = -4$$
$$x = y + 4$$
$$x = 0 + 4 = 4 \qquad x = -4 + 4 = 0$$
$$(4, 0), (0, -4)$$

9.
$$x = 2y^2 - y - 3 \quad y = \frac{1}{4}x$$
$$x = 4y = 2y^2 - y - 3$$
$$2y^2 - 5y - 3 = 0$$
$$(2y + 1)(y - 3) = 0$$
$$2y + 1 = 0 \qquad y - 3 = 0$$
$$2y = -1 \qquad y = 3$$
$$y = -\frac{1}{2}$$
$$x = 4y = 4\left(-\frac{1}{2}\right) = -2$$
$$x = 4y = 4(3) = 12$$
$$\left(-2, -\frac{1}{2}\right), (12, 3)$$

11.
$$x^2 + y^2 = 32 \quad y = x^2 - 2$$
$$x^2 = y + 2$$
$$(y + 2) + y^2 = 32$$
$$y^2 + y - 30 = 0$$
$$(y - 5)(y + 6) = 0$$
$$y - 5 = 0 \qquad y + 6 = 0$$
$$y = 5 \qquad y = -6$$

$$x^2 = y + 2$$
$$x^2 = 5 + 2 \qquad x^2 = -6 + 2$$
$$x^2 = 7 \qquad x^2 = -4$$
$$x = \pm\sqrt{7} \qquad x = \pm\sqrt{-4} = \pm 2i$$
$$\left(\sqrt{7}, 5\right)\left(-\sqrt{7}, 5\right), (2i, -6), (-2i, -6)$$

13.
$$-x^2 + 2y^2 = -8$$
$$\underline{x^2 + 3y^2 = 18}$$
$$5y^2 = 10$$
$$y^2 = 2$$
$$y = \pm\sqrt{2}$$
$$x^2 + 3y^2 = 18 \quad y^2 = 2$$
$$x^2 + 3(2) = 18$$
$$x^2 + 6 = 18$$
$$x^2 = 12$$
$$x = \pm\sqrt{12} = \pm 2\sqrt{3}$$
$$\left(2\sqrt{3}, \sqrt{2}\right), \left(-2\sqrt{3}, \sqrt{2}\right)$$
$$\left(2\sqrt{3}, -\sqrt{2}\right), \left(-2\sqrt{3}, -\sqrt{2}\right)$$

15.
$$3x^2 + y^2 = 24 \longrightarrow 3x^2 + y^2 = 24$$
$$x^2 + y^2 = 16 \xrightarrow{\times(-1)} -x^2 - y^2 = -16$$
$$\overline{\qquad\qquad 2x^2 \qquad = 8}$$
$$x^2 = 4$$
$$x = \pm\sqrt{4} = \pm 2$$
$$x^2 + y^2 = 16$$
$$4 + y^2 = 16$$
$$y^2 = 12$$
$$y = \pm\sqrt{12} = \pm 2\sqrt{3}$$
$$\left(2, 2\sqrt{3}\right), \left(-2, 2\sqrt{3}\right), \left(2, -2\sqrt{3}\right), \left(-2, -2\sqrt{3}\right)$$

17.
$$5x^2 + 6y^2 = 24 \longrightarrow 5x^2 + 6y^2 = 24$$
$$5x^2 + 5y^2 = 25 \xrightarrow{\times(-1)} -5x^2 - 5y^2 = -25$$
$$\overline{\qquad\qquad\qquad y^2 = -1}$$
$$y = \pm\sqrt{-1} = \pm i$$
$$5x^2 + 5y^2 = 25$$
$$5x^2 + 5(-1) = 25$$
$$5x^2 = 30$$
$$x^2 = 6$$
$$x = \pm\sqrt{6}$$
$$\left(\sqrt{6}, i\right), \left(\sqrt{6}, -i\right), \left(-\sqrt{6}, i\right), \left(-\sqrt{6}, -i\right)$$

19.

$$5x^2 - 3y^2 = 35 \xrightarrow{\hspace{1cm}} 5x^2 - 3y^2 = 35$$
$$3x^2 - 3y^2 = 3 \xrightarrow{\times(-1)} \underline{-3x^2 + 3y^2 = -3}$$
$$2x^2 \qquad\quad = 32$$

$$x^2 = 16$$
$$x = \pm\sqrt{16} = \pm 4$$
$$3x^2 - 3y^2 = 3$$
$$3(16) - 3y^2 = 3$$
$$48 - 3y^2 = 3$$
$$-3y^2 = -45$$
$$y^2 = 15$$
$$y = \pm\sqrt{15}$$
$$\left(4, \sqrt{15}\right), \left(-4, \sqrt{15}\right), \left(4, -\sqrt{15}\right), \left(-4, -\sqrt{15}\right)$$

21.

$$6x^2 + 6y^2 = 96 \xrightarrow{\times\left(-\frac{1}{6}\right)} -x^2 - y^2 = -16$$
$$x^2 + 9y^2 = 144 \xrightarrow{\hspace{1cm}} \underline{x^2 + 9y^2 = 144}$$
$$8y^2 = 128$$

$$y^2 = 16$$
$$y = \pm\sqrt{16} = \pm 4$$
$$x^2 + 9y^2 = 144$$
$$x^2 + 9(16) = 144$$
$$x^2 + 144 = 144$$
$$x^2 = 0$$
$$x = 0$$
$$(0, 4), (0, -4)$$

23.

$$\frac{x^2}{4} + \frac{y^2}{16} = 1 \xrightarrow{\times 16} 4x^2 + y^2 = 16$$
$$\frac{x^2}{2} + \frac{y^2}{24} = 1 \xrightarrow{\times(-24)} \underline{-12x^2 - y^2 = -24}$$
$$-8x^2 \qquad = -8$$

$$x^2 = 1$$
$$x = \pm\sqrt{1} = \pm 1$$
$$4x^2 + y^2 = 16$$
$$4(1) + y^2 = 16$$
$$y^2 = 12$$
$$y = \pm\sqrt{12} = \pm 2\sqrt{3}$$
$$\left(1, 2\sqrt{3}\right), \left(-1, 2\sqrt{3}\right), \left(1, -2\sqrt{3}\right), \left(-1, -2\sqrt{3}\right)$$

25.

$$\frac{y^2}{8} - \frac{x^2}{4} = 1 \xrightarrow{\times 8} y^2 - 2x^2 = 8$$
$$\frac{y^2}{11} + \frac{x^2}{11} = 1 \xrightarrow{\times 22} \underline{2y^2 + 2x^2 = 22}$$
$$3y^2 \qquad = 30$$

$$y^2 = 10; \quad y = \pm\sqrt{10}$$
$$y^2 - 2x^2 = 8$$
$$10 - 2x^2 = 8$$
$$-2x^2 = -2$$
$$x^2 = 1; \quad x = \pm\sqrt{1} = \pm 1$$
$$\left(1, \sqrt{10}\right), \left(-1, \sqrt{10}\right), \left(1, -\sqrt{10}\right), \left(-1, -\sqrt{10}\right)$$

27.

$$(x-4)^2 + y^2 = 4 \rightarrow x^2 - 8x + 16 + y^2 = 4$$
$$x^2 - 8x + y^2 = -12$$
$$(x+2)^2 + y^2 = 16 \rightarrow x^2 + 4x + 4 + y^2 = 16$$
$$x^2 + 4x + y^2 = 12$$
$$x^2 - 8x + y^2 = -12 \xrightarrow{\times(-1)} -x^2 + 8x - y^2 = 12$$
$$x^2 + 4x + y^2 = 12 \xrightarrow{\hspace{1cm}} \underline{x^2 + 4x + y^2 = 12}$$
$$12x \qquad = 24$$

$$x = 2$$
$$(x+2)^2 + y^2 = 16$$
$$(2+2)^2 + y^2 = 16$$
$$16 + y^2 = 16$$
$$y^2 = 0; \quad y = 0$$
$$(2, 0)$$

29.

$$R = 0.25x^2 - 100x = 75x$$
$$0.25x^2 - 175x = 0$$
$$0.25x(x - 700) = 0$$
$$0.25x = 0 \qquad x - 700 = 0$$
$$x = 0 \qquad\quad x = 700$$

They will have the same revenue if they sell 0 or 700 organizers.

31.

$$x^2 + 2y^2 = 7 \xrightarrow{\hspace{1cm}} x^2 + 2y^2 = 7$$
$$x^2 - 3y^2 = 2 \xrightarrow{\times(-1)} \underline{-x^2 + 3y^2 = -2}$$
$$5y^2 = 5$$

$$y^2 = 1; \quad y = \pm 1$$
$$x^2 + 2y^2 = 7$$
$$x^2 + 2(1) = 7$$
$$x^2 = 5; \quad x = \pm\sqrt{5}$$

The comet travelling in the hyperbolic path travels in only one half of the hyperbola.

$x = +\sqrt{5}$ only. The paths will intersect at $\left(\sqrt{5}, 1\right)$ and $\left(\sqrt{5}, -1\right)$.

33.

$$x = y + 3$$
$$x^2 - y^2 = 75$$
$$(y+3)^2 - y^2 = 75$$

$y^2 + 6y + 9 - y^2 = 75$

$6y = 66$

$y = 11; \quad x = y + 3 = 11 + 3 = 14$

The smaller square has dimensions 11 in. by 11 in., in contrast to 14 in. by 14 in. for the larger square.

Exercises 10.5 Solving Nonlinear Inequalities and Nonlinear Systems of Inequalities

1. $x^2 + y^2 > 16$

The boundary line is dashed.

$x^2 + y^2 = 16$

$(x-0)^2 + (y-0)^2 = 4^2$

Circle: center: $(0,0)$ radius $= 4$

Test point is $(0,0)$

$0^2 + 0^2 \overset{?}{>} 16$

$0 > 16$ False, shade the region not

containing $(0,0)$.

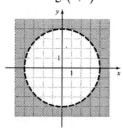

3. $(x-1)^2 + (y+1)^2 \le 25$

The boundary line is solid.

$(x-1)^2 + (y-(-1))^2 = 5^2$

Circle: center: $(1,-1)$ radius $= 5$

Test point is $(0,0)$

$(0-1)^2 + (0+1)^2 \overset{?}{\le} 25$

$1 + 1 \overset{?}{\le} 25; \quad 2 \le 25$ True, shade the region

containing the point $(0,0)$.

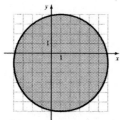

5. $y > -x^2 + 5x - 4$

The boundary line is dashed.

$y = -(x^2 - 5x) - 4$

$y = -\left(x^2 - 5x + \left(\dfrac{-5}{2}\right)^2\right) - 4 + \left(\dfrac{-5}{2}\right)^2$

$y = -\left(x^2 - 5x + \dfrac{25}{4}\right) - \dfrac{16}{4} + \dfrac{25}{4}$

$y = -\left(x - \dfrac{5}{2}\right)^2 + \dfrac{9}{4}$

Parabola opening down with vertex: $\left(\dfrac{5}{2}, \dfrac{9}{4}\right)$

x	$y = -\left(x - \dfrac{5}{2}\right)^2 + \dfrac{9}{4}$	(x, y)
0	$-\left(0 - \dfrac{5}{2}\right)^2 + \dfrac{9}{4} = -4$	$(0, -4)$
1	$-\left(1 - \dfrac{5}{2}\right)^2 + \dfrac{9}{4} = 0$	$(1, 0)$
2	$-\left(2 - \dfrac{5}{2}\right)^2 + \dfrac{9}{4} = 2$	$(2, 2)$
3	$-\left(3 - \dfrac{5}{2}\right)^2 + \dfrac{9}{4} = 2$	$(3, 2)$
4	$-\left(4 - \dfrac{5}{2}\right)^2 + \dfrac{9}{4} = 0$	$(4, 0)$
5	$-\left(5 - \dfrac{5}{2}\right)^2 + \dfrac{9}{4} = -4$	$(5, -4)$

Test point is $(0,0)$.

$0 \overset{?}{>} -(0)^2 + 5(0) - 4$

$0 \overset{?}{>} 0 + 0 - 4$

$0 > -4$ True, shade the region containing

the point $(0,0)$.

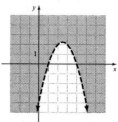

7. $9x^2 + y^2 \ge 36$

The boundary line is solid.

$\dfrac{9x^2}{36} + \dfrac{y^2}{36} = \dfrac{36}{36}$

$\dfrac{x^2}{4}+\dfrac{y^2}{36}=1$ $\dfrac{x^2}{2^2}+\dfrac{y^2}{6^2}=1$ $a=2$ $b=6$

An ellispe

x-intercepts: $(\pm2,0)$ or $(2,0)$ and $(-2,0)$

y-intercepts: $(0,\pm6)$ or $(0,6)$ and $(0,-6)$

Test point is $(0,0)$.

$9(0)^2+(0)^2\overset{?}{\geq}36$

$0+0\overset{?}{\geq}36$

$0\geq36$ False, shade the region not

containing the point $(0,0)$.

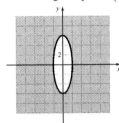

9. $16x^2+36y^2<144$

The boundary line is dashed.

$\dfrac{16x^2}{144}+\dfrac{36y^2}{144}=\dfrac{144}{144}$

$\dfrac{x^2}{9}+\dfrac{y^2}{4}=1$ $\dfrac{x^2}{3^2}+\dfrac{y^2}{2^2}=1$ $a=3$ $b=2$

Ellipse

x-intercepts: $(\pm3,0)$ or $(3,0)$ and $(-3,0)$

y-intercepts: $(0,\pm2)$ or $(0,2)$ and $(0,-2)$

Test point is $(0,0)$.

$16(0)^2+36(0)^2\overset{?}{<}144$

$0+0\overset{?}{<}144$

$0<144$ True, shade the region containing

the point $(0,0)$.

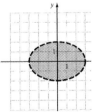

11. $4x^2-y^2>100$

The boundary line is dashed.

$4x^2-y^2=100$

$\dfrac{4x^2}{100}-\dfrac{y^2}{100}=\dfrac{100}{100}$ $\dfrac{x^2}{25}-\dfrac{y^2}{100}=1$

$\dfrac{x^2}{5^2}-\dfrac{y^2}{10^2}=1$ $a=5$ $b=10$

Hyperbola

x-intercepts: $(\pm5,0)$ or $(5,0)$ and $(-5,0)$

Equation of asymptotes are

$y=\dfrac{10}{5}x=2x$ and $y=-2x$

Test point is $(0,0)$.

$4(0)^2-(0)^2\overset{?}{>}100$

$0-0\overset{?}{>}100$

$0>100$ False, shade the region not

containing the point $(0,0)$.

13. $y>x^2-3$ $y\leq-x+1$

$y>x^2-3$

The boundary line is dashed.

$y=x^2-3$

$y=(x-0)^2-3$

Parabola opening up with vertex: $(0,-3)$.

x	$y=x^2-3$	(x,y)
-3	$(-3)^2-3=6$	$(-3,6)$
-1	$(-1)^2-3=-2$	$(-1,-2)$
0	$(0)^2-3=-3$	$(0,-3)$
1	$(1)^2-3=-2$	$(1,-2)$
3	$(3)^2-3=6$	$(3,6)$

Test point is $(0,0)$.

$0\overset{?}{>}0^2-3$

$0>-3$ True, shade the region

containing the point $(0,0)$.

$y\leq-x+1$

The boundary line is solid.

$y=-x+1$

x	$y=-x+1$	(x,y)
0	$-0+1=1$	$(0,1)$
2	$-2+1=-1$	$(2,-1)$

Test point is $(0,0)$.

$0\overset{?}{\leq}-(0)+1$.

$0\leq1$ True, shade the region

containing the point $(0,0)$.

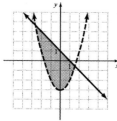

15. $x^2 + y^2 \geq 9$ $x^2 + y^2 < 25$

$x^2 + y^2 \geq 9$

The boundary line is solid.

$x^2 + y^2 = 9$

$(x-0)^2 + (y-0)^2 = 3^2$

Circle: center: $(0,0)$ Radius $r = 3$

Test point is (0,0); $0^2 + 0^2 \overset{?}{\geq} 9$

$0 \geq 9$ False, shade the region not containing the point (0,0)

$x^2 + y^2 = 25$

The boundary line is dashed.

$(x-0)^2 + (y-0)^2 = 5^2$

Circle: center: $(0,0)$ radius $r = 5$

Test point is $(0,0)$; $0^2 + 0^2 \overset{?}{<} 25$

$0 < 25$, shade the region containing the point $(0,0)$.

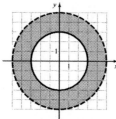

17. $y < x^2 + 2x + 1$ $y < -x^2 - 2x - 4$

$y < x^2 + 2x + 1$

The boundary line is dashed.

$y = x^2 + 2x + 1$

$y = (x+1)^2 = (x-(-1))^2$

Parabola opening up, vertex: $(-1, 0)$

x	$y = x^2 + 2x + 1$	(x, y)
-3	$(-3)^2 - 2(-3) + 1 = 4$	$(-3, 4)$
-2	$(-2)^2 - 2(-2) + 1 = 1$	$(-2, 1)$
-1	$(-1)^2 - 2(-1) + 1 = 0$	$(-1, 0)$
0	$(0)^2 - 2(0) + 1 = 1$	$(0, 1)$
1	$(1)^2 - 2(1) + 1 = 4$	$(1, 4)$

Test point is $(0,0)$

$0 \overset{?}{<} (0)^2 + 2(0) + 1$

$0 \overset{?}{<} 0 + 0 + 1$

$0 < 1$ True, shade the area containing the point $(0,0)$.

$y < -x^2 - 2x - 4$

The boundary line is dashed.

$y = -x^2 - 2x - 4$

$y = -(x^2 + 2x) - 4$

$y = -\left(x^2 + 2x + \left(\dfrac{2}{2} \right)^2 \right) - 4 + \left(\dfrac{2}{2} \right)^2$

$y = -(x^2 + 2x + 1) - 4 + 1$

$y = -(x^2 + 2x + 1) - 3$

$y = -(x+1)^2 - 3$

$y = -(x-(-1))^2 - 3$

Parabola opening down, vertex: $(-1, -3)$

x	$y = -x^2 - 2x - 4$	(x, y)
-3	$-(-3)^2 - 2(-3) - 4 = -7$	$(-3, -7)$
-2	$-(-2)^2 - 2(-2) - 4 = -4$	$(-2, -4)$
-1	$-(-1)^2 - 2(-1) - 4 = -3$	$(-1, -3)$
0	$-(0)^2 - 2(0) - 4 = -4$	$(0, -4)$
1	$-(1)^2 - 2(1) - 4 = -7$	$(1, -7)$

Test point is $(0,0)$.

$0 \overset{?}{<} -(0)^2 - 2(0) - 4$

$0 \overset{?}{<} 0 - 0 - 4$

$0 < -4$ False, shade the region not containing the point $(0,0)$.

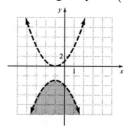

19. $8x^2 + 2y^2 \leq 72$ $x^2 + 4y^2 \leq 36$

$8x^2 + 2y^2 \leq 72$

The boundary line is solid.

$8x^2 + 2y^2 = 72$

$\dfrac{8x^2}{72} + \dfrac{2y^2}{72} = \dfrac{72}{72}$

$\dfrac{x^2}{9} + \dfrac{y^2}{36} = 1 \quad \dfrac{x^2}{3^2} + \dfrac{y^2}{6^2} = 1 \quad a = 3 \quad b = 6$

Ellipse

x-intercepts are $(\pm 3, 0)$ or $(3, 0)$ and $(-3, 0)$

y-intercepts are $(0, \pm 6)$ or $(0, 6)$ and $(0, -6)$

Test point is $(0, 0)$.

$8(0)^2 + 2(0)^2 \overset{?}{\le} 72$

$0 + 0 \le 72$ True, shade the region

containing the point $(0, 0.)$

$x^2 + 4y^2 \le 36$

The boundary line is solid.

$x^2 + 4y^2 = 36$

$\dfrac{x^2}{36} + \dfrac{4y^2}{36} = \dfrac{36}{36}$

$\dfrac{x^2}{36} + \dfrac{y^2}{9} = 1 \quad \dfrac{x^2}{6^2} + \dfrac{y^2}{3^2} = 1 \quad a = 6 \quad b = 3$

Ellipse

x-intercepts are $(\pm 6, 0)$ or $(6, 0)$ and $(-6, 0)$

y-intercepts are $(0, \pm 3)$ or $(0, 3)$ and $(0, -3)$

Test point is $(0, 0)$.

$(0)^2 + 4(0)^2 \overset{?}{\le} 36$

$0 + 0 \le 36$ True, shade the region

containing the point $(0, 0.)$

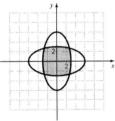

21. $x^2 - 4y^2 < 16 \quad x^2 + y^2 \ge 1$

$x^2 - 4y^2 < 16$

The boundary line is dashed.

$x^2 - 4y^2 = 16$

$\dfrac{x^2}{16} - \dfrac{4y^2}{16} = \dfrac{16}{16}$

$\dfrac{x^2}{16} - \dfrac{y^2}{4} = 1 \quad \dfrac{x^2}{4^2} - \dfrac{y^2}{2^2} = 1 \quad a = 4 \quad b = 2$

Hyperbola

x-intercepts are $(\pm 4, 0)$ or $(4, 0)$ and $(-4, 0)$

Equation of asymptotes are

$y = \dfrac{2}{4}x = \dfrac{1}{2}x$ and $y = -\dfrac{1}{2}x$

Test point is $(0, 0)$.

$(0)^2 - 4(0)^2 \overset{?}{<} 16$

$0 + 0 < 16$, Shade the region

containing the point $(0, 0)$.

$x^2 + y^2 \ge 1$

The boundary line is solid.

$x^2 + y^2 = 1$

$(x - 0)^2 + (y - 0)^2 = 1^2$

Circle, center: $(0, 0)$, radius $= 1$

Test point is $(0, 0)$.

$0^2 + 0^2 \overset{?}{\ge} 1$

$0 \ge 1$ False, shade the region not

containing the point $(0, 0)$.

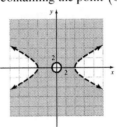

23. $4x^2 + 9y^2 \le 144$

The boundary line is solid.

$4x^2 + 9y^2 = 144$

$\dfrac{4x^2}{144} + \dfrac{9y^2}{144} = \dfrac{144}{144}$

$\dfrac{x^2}{36} + \dfrac{y^2}{16} = 1 \quad \dfrac{x^2}{6^2} + \dfrac{y^2}{4^2} = 1 \quad a = 6 \quad b = 4$

Ellipse.

x-intercepts are $(\pm 6, 0)$ or $(6, 0)$ and $(-6, 0)$

y-intercepts are $(0, \pm 4)$ or $(0, 4)$ and $(0, -4)$

Test point is $(0, 0)$.

$4(0)^2 + 9(0)^2 \overset{?}{\le} 144$

$0 + 0 \le 144$ True, shade the region

containing the point $(0, 0)$.

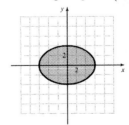

25.   a. $x^2 + y^2 \le 2500 \quad y \ge x + 2$

      b. $x^2 + y^2 \le 2500$

The boundary line is solid.

$x^2 + y^2 = 2500$

$(x-0)^2 + (y-0)^2 = 50^2$

Circle. Center: $(0,0)$, radius $= 50$

Test point is $(0,0)$.

$0^2 + 0^2 \overset{?}{\le} 2500$

$0 \le 2500$ True, shade the region

containing the point $(0,0)$.

$y \ge x + 2$

The boundary line is solid.

$y = x + 2$

x	$y = x+2$	(x, y)
0	$0+2=2$	$(0,2)$
20	$20+2=22$	$(20,22)$

Test point is $(0,0)$.

$0 \overset{?}{\ge} 0 + 2$

$0 \ge 2$ False, shade the region not

containing the point $(0,0)$.

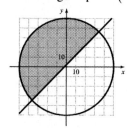

c. No, only points in Quadrant I are possible solutions since the lengths of the gardens cannot be negative.

27.   a. $x^2 + y^2 \le 900$ $(x-50)^2 + y^2 \le 1600$

b. $x^2 + y^2 \le 900$

The boundary line is solid

$x^2 + y^2 = 900$

$(x-0)^2 + (y-0)^2 = 30^2$

Circle, center: $(0,0)$ radius $= 30$

Test point is $(0,0)$.

$0^2 + 0^2 \overset{?}{\le} 900$

$0 \le 900$ True, shade the region

containing the point $(0,0)$.

$(x-50)^2 + y^2 \le 1600$

The boundary line is solid.

$(x-50)^2 + y^2 = 1600$

$(x-50)^2 + (y-0)^2 = 40^2$

Circle, center: $(50,0)$ radius $= 40$

Test point is $(0,0)$

$(0-50)^2 + 0^2 \overset{?}{\le} 1600$

$2500 + 0 \le 1600$ False. Shade the region

not containing the point $(0,0)$.

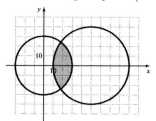

Chapter 10 Review Exercises

1. $y = -2(x+3)^2 + 5$

$y = -2(x-(-3))^2 + 5$

$h = -3, \ k = 5$

Vertex: $(-3,5)$

Axis of symmetry: $x = -3$

x	$y = -2(x+3)^2 + 5$	(x, y)
-5	$-2(-5+3)^2 + 5 = -3$	$(-5,-3)$
-4	$-2(-4+3)^2 + 5 = 3$	$(-4,3)$
-3	$-2(-3+3)^2 + 5 = 5$	$(-3,5)$
-2	$-2(-2+3)^2 + 5 = 3$	$(-2,3)$
-1	$-2(-1+3)^2 + 5 = -3$	$(-1,-3)$
0	$-2(0+3)^2 + 5 = -13$	$(0,-13)$

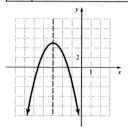

2. $x = 3(y-2)^2 - 10$

$h = -10 \ \ k = 2$

Vertex: $(-10,2)$

Axis of symmetry: $y = 2$

y	$x = 3(y-2)^2 - 10$	(x, y)
5	$3(5-2)^2 - 10 = 17$	$(17, 5)$
4	$3(4-2)^2 - 10 = 2$	$(2, 4)$
3	$3(3-2)^2 - 10 = -7$	$(-7, 3)$
2	$3(2-2)^2 - 10 = -10$	$(-10, 2)$
1	$3(1-2)^2 - 10 = -7$	$(-7, 1)$
0	$3(0-2)^2 - 10 = 2$	$(2, 0)$

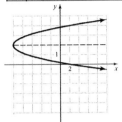

3. $x = 4y^2 + 32y + 64$

$x = 4(y^2 + 8y + 16)$

$x = 4(y + 4)^2$

$x = 4(y - (-4))^2$

$h = 0, \ k = -4$

Vertex: $(0, -4)$

Axis of symmetry: $y = -4$

y	$x = 4y^2 + 32y + 64$	(x, y)
-2	$4(-2)^2 + 32(-2) + 64 = 16$	$(16, -2)$
-3	$4(-3)^2 + 32(-3) + 64 = 4$	$(4, -3)$
-4	$4(-4)^2 + 32(-4) + 64 = 0$	$(0, -4)$
-5	$4(-5)^2 + 32(-5) + 64 = 4$	$(4, -5)$
-6	$4(-6)^2 + 32(-6) + 64 = 16$	$(16, -6)$

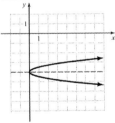

4. $y = -x^2 - 6x - 7$

$y = -(x^2 + 6x) - 7$

$y = -\left(x^2 + 6x + \left(\dfrac{6}{2}\right)^2\right) - 7 + \left(\dfrac{6}{2}\right)^2$

$y = -(x^2 + 6x + 9) - 7 + 9$

$y = -(x + 3)^2 + 2$

$y = -(x - (-3))^2 + 2$

$h = -3, \ k = 2$

Vertex: $(-3, 2)$

Axis of symmetry: $x = -3$

x	$y = -x^2 - 6x - 7$	(x, y)
-6	$-(-6)^2 - 6(-6) - 7 = -7$	$(-6, -7)$
-5	$-(-5)^2 - 6(-5) - 7 = -2$	$(-5, -2)$
-4	$-(-4)^2 - 6(-4) - 7 = 1$	$(-4, 1)$
-3	$-(-3)^2 - 6(-3) - 7 = 2$	$(-3, 2)$
-2	$-(-2)^2 - 6(-2) - 7 = 1$	$(-2, 1)$
-1	$-(-1)^2 - 6(-1) - 7 = -2$	$(-1, -2)$
0	$-(0)^2 - 6(0) - 7 = -7$	$(0, -7)$

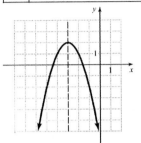

5. $y = 8x^2 - 56x + 74$

$y = 8(x^2 - 7x) + 74$

$y = 8\left(x^2 - 7x + \left(\dfrac{-7}{2}\right)^2\right) + 74 - 8\left(\dfrac{-7}{2}\right)^2$

$y = 8\left(x^2 - 7x + \dfrac{49}{4}\right) + 74 - 8\left(\dfrac{49}{4}\right)$

$y = 8\left(x - \dfrac{7}{2}\right)^2 + 74 - 98$

$y = 8\left(x - \dfrac{7}{2}\right)^2 - 24 \quad h = \dfrac{7}{2}, \ k = -24$

Vertex: $\left(\dfrac{7}{2}, -24\right)$

6. $x = 5y^2 + 15y + 7$

$x = 5(y^2 + 3y) + 7$

$x = 5\left(y^2 + 3y + \left(\dfrac{3}{2}\right)^2\right) + 7 - 5\left(\dfrac{3}{2}\right)^2$

$x = 5\left(y^2 + 3y + \dfrac{9}{4}\right) + 7 - 5\left(\dfrac{9}{4}\right)$

$x = 5\left(y + \dfrac{3}{2}\right)^2 + \dfrac{28}{4} - \dfrac{45}{4}$

$x = 5\left(y - \left(-\dfrac{3}{2}\right)\right)^2 - \dfrac{17}{4} \quad h = -\dfrac{17}{4} \quad k = -\dfrac{3}{2}$

Vertex: $\left(-\dfrac{17}{4},-\dfrac{3}{2}\right)$

7. $d = \sqrt{\left(x_2 - x_1\right)^2 + \left(y_2 - y_1\right)^2}$

$d = \sqrt{\left(6-9\right)^2 + \left(1-(-5)\right)^2} = \sqrt{\left(-3\right)^2 + \left(6\right)^2}$

$d = \sqrt{9+36} = \sqrt{45}$

$d = 3\sqrt{5} = 6.7082... \approx 6.7$ units

8. $d = \sqrt{\left(x_2 - x_1\right)^2 + \left(y_2 - y_1\right)^2}$

$d = \sqrt{\left(-2-(-8)\right)^2 + \left(11-10\right)^2}$

$d = \sqrt{\left(6\right)^2 + \left(1\right)^2} = \sqrt{36+1}$

$d = \sqrt{37} = 6.0827... \approx 6.1$ units

9. $d = \sqrt{\left(x_2 - x_1\right)^2 + \left(y_2 - y_1\right)^2}$

$d = \sqrt{\left(-1.8-(-1.3)\right)^2 + \left(0.5-(-0.7)\right)^2}$

$d = \sqrt{\left(-0.5\right)^2 + \left(1.2\right)^2} = \sqrt{0.25+1.44}$

$d = \sqrt{1.69} = 1.3$ units

10. $d = \sqrt{\left(x_2 - x_1\right)^2 + \left(y_2 - y_1\right)^2}$

$d = \sqrt{\left(-2\sqrt{7}-\sqrt{7}\right)^2 + \left(-5\sqrt{2}-(-\sqrt{2})\right)^2}$

$d = \sqrt{\left(-3\sqrt{7}\right)^2 + \left(-4\sqrt{2}\right)^2} = \sqrt{9\bullet 7 + 16 \bullet 2}$

$d = \sqrt{63+32} = \sqrt{95} = 9.7467... \approx 9.7$ units

11. $\left(\dfrac{-16+24}{2},\dfrac{9+17}{2}\right) = \left(\dfrac{8}{2},\dfrac{26}{2}\right) = (4,13)$

12. $\left(\dfrac{-7+10}{2},\dfrac{-13+(-5)}{2}\right) = \left(\dfrac{3}{2},\dfrac{-18}{2}\right) = \left(\dfrac{3}{2},-9\right)$

13. $\left(\dfrac{\dfrac{5}{2}+\left(-\dfrac{3}{4}\right)}{2},\dfrac{\dfrac{1}{5}+\dfrac{3}{10}}{2}\right) = \left(\dfrac{\dfrac{10}{4}-\dfrac{3}{4}}{2},\dfrac{\dfrac{2}{10}+\dfrac{3}{10}}{2}\right) =$

$\left(\dfrac{\dfrac{7}{4}}{\dfrac{2}{1}},\dfrac{\dfrac{5}{10}}{\dfrac{2}{1}}\right) = \left(\dfrac{7}{4}\bullet\dfrac{1}{2},\dfrac{5}{10}\bullet\dfrac{1}{2}\right) = \left(\dfrac{7}{8},\dfrac{1}{4}\right)$

14. $\left(\dfrac{-0.35+(-1.05)}{2},\dfrac{-2.8+(-4.5)}{2}\right) =$

$\left(\dfrac{-1.40}{2},\dfrac{-7.3}{2}\right) = (-0.7,-3.65)$

15. $x^2 + y^2 = 64$

$\left(x-0\right)^2 + \left(y-0\right)^2 = 8^2$

$h = 0, \ k = 0$

Center: $(0,0)$, radius $= 8$

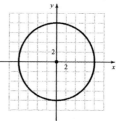

16. $\left(x+2\right)^2 + \left(y-4\right)^2 = 4$

$\left(x-(-2)\right)^2 + \left(y-4\right)^2 = 2^2$

$h = -2, \ k = 4$

Center: $(-2,4)$ radius $= 2$

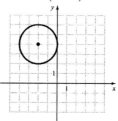

17. $x^2 + y^2 - 4x + 6y - 12 = 0$

$x^2 - 4x + y^2 + 6y = 12$

$x^2 - 4x + \left(\dfrac{-4}{2}\right)^2 + y^2 + 6y + \left(\dfrac{6}{2}\right)^2 =$

$\hspace{3cm} 12 + \left(\dfrac{-4}{2}\right)^2 + \left(\dfrac{6}{2}\right)^2$

$x^2 - 4x + 4 + y^2 + 6y + 9 = 12 + 4 + 9$

$\left(x-2\right)^2 + \left(y+3\right)^2 = 25$

$\left(x-2\right)^2 + \left(y-(-3)\right)^2 = 5^2$

$h = 2, \ k = -3$

Center: $(2,-3)$ radius $= 5$

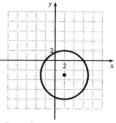

18. $x^2 + y^2 + 8x - 2y + 8 = 0$

$x^2 + 8x + y^2 - 2y = -8$

$x^2 + 8x + \left(\dfrac{8}{2}\right)^2 + y^2 - 2y + \left(\dfrac{-2}{2}\right)^2 =$

$\hspace{3cm} -8 + \left(\dfrac{8}{2}\right)^2 + \left(\dfrac{-2}{2}\right)^2$

$x^2 + 8x + 16 + y^2 - 2y + 1 = -8 + 16 + 1$

$\left(x+4\right)^2 + \left(y-1\right)^2 = 9$

$\left(x-(-4)\right)^2+\left(y-1\right)^2=3^2$

$h=-4,\ k=1$

Center: $(-4,1)$ radius $=3$

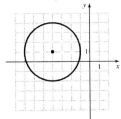

19. $h=9,\ k=0$

$(x-9)^2+(y-0)^2=13^2$

$(x-9)^2+y^2=169$

20. $h=-6,\ k=10$

$\left(x-(-6)\right)^2+(y-10)^2=\left(2\sqrt{5}\right)^2$

$(x+6)^2+(y-10)^2=4\bullet5$

$(x+6)^2+(y-10)^2=20$

21. $x^2+y^2-12x-14y-35=0$

$x^2-12x+y^2-14y=35$

$x^2-12x+\left(\dfrac{-12}{2}\right)^2+y^2-14y+\left(\dfrac{-14}{2}\right)^2=$

$\qquad\qquad 35+\left(\dfrac{-12}{2}\right)^2+\left(\dfrac{-14}{2}\right)^2$

$x^2-12x+36+y^2-14y+49=35+36+49$

$(x-6)^2+(y-7)^2=120\ \ h=6,\ k=7$

Center: $(6,7)$ radius $=\sqrt{120}=2\sqrt{30}$

22. $x^2+y^2+16x+10y+9=0$

$x^2+16x+y^2+10y=-9$

$x^2+16x+\left(\dfrac{16}{2}\right)^2+y^2+10y+\left(\dfrac{10}{2}\right)^2=$

$\qquad\qquad -9+\left(\dfrac{16}{2}\right)^2+\left(\dfrac{10}{2}\right)^2$

$x^2+16x+64+y^2+10y+25=-9+64+25$

$(x+8)^2+(y+5)^2=80$

$\left(x-(-8)\right)^2+\left(y-(-5)\right)^2=80$

$h=-8,\ k=-5$

Center: $(-8,-5)$ radius $=\sqrt{80}=4\sqrt{5}$

23. $\dfrac{x^2}{64}+\dfrac{y^2}{9}=1\ \ \dfrac{x^2}{8^2}+\dfrac{y^2}{3^2}=1\ \ a=8\ \ b=3$

x-intercepts: $(\pm8,0)$ or $(8,0)$ and $(-8,0)$

y-intercepts: $(0,\pm3)$ or $(0,3)$ and $(0,-3)$

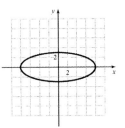

24. $\dfrac{x^2}{16}-\dfrac{y^2}{36}=1\ \ \dfrac{x^2}{4^2}-\dfrac{y^2}{6^2}=1\ \ a=4\ \ b=6$

x-intercepts are $(\pm4,0)$ or $(4,0)$ and $(-4,0)$

Equation of asymptotes are

$y=\dfrac{6}{4}x=\dfrac{3}{2}x$ and $y=-\dfrac{3}{2}x$

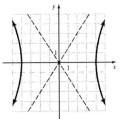

25. $y^2-4x^2=4$

$\dfrac{y^2}{4}-\dfrac{4x^2}{4}=\dfrac{4}{4}$

$\dfrac{y^2}{4}-\dfrac{x^2}{1}=1\ \ \dfrac{y^2}{2^2}-\dfrac{x^2}{1^2}=1\ \ a=2\ \ b=1$

y-intercepts: $(0,\pm2)$ or $(0,2)$ and $(0,-2)$

Equation of asymptotes are

$y=\dfrac{2}{1}x=2x$ and $y=-2x$

26. $4x^2+y^2=64$

$\dfrac{4x^2}{64}+\dfrac{y^2}{64}=\dfrac{64}{64}$

$\dfrac{x^2}{16}+\dfrac{y^2}{64}=1\ \ \dfrac{x^2}{4^2}+\dfrac{y^2}{8^2}=1\ \ a=4\ \ b=8$

x-intercepts: $(\pm4,0)$ or $(4,0)$ and $(-4,0)$

y-intercepts: $(0,\pm8)$ or $(0,8)$ and $(0,-8)$

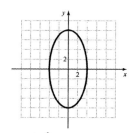

27. $y = 2x^2 + 1 \quad y = 2x + 5$

$2x^2 + 1 = 2x + 5$

$2x^2 - 2x - 4 = 0$

$2(x^2 - x - 2) = 0$

$2(x - 2)(x + 1) = 0$

$x - 2 = 0 \qquad$ or $\quad x + 1 = 0$

$x = 2 \qquad\qquad\qquad x = -1$

$y = 2(2) + 5 = 9 \qquad y = 2(-1) + 5 = 3$

$(2, 9) \qquad\qquad\qquad (1, 3)$

28. $x^2 + y^2 = 10 \quad y = 3x$

$x^2 + (3x)^2 = 10$

$x^2 + 9x^2 = 10$

$10x^2 = 10$

$x^2 = 1$

$x = \pm\sqrt{1} = \pm 1$

$y = 3x \quad y = 3(1) = 3; \quad y = 3(-1) = -3$

$(1, 3), (-1, -3)$

29. $x^2 + 4y^2 = 16 \quad x = y^2 - 4$

$y^2 = x + 4$

$x^2 + 4(x + 4) = 16$

$x^2 + 4x + 16 = 16$

$x^2 + 4x = 0$

$x(x + 4) = 0$

$x = 0 \qquad$ or $\quad x + 4 = 0$

$y^2 = 0 + 4 \qquad\qquad x = -4$

$y = \pm\sqrt{4} = \pm 2 \qquad y^2 = -4 + 4$

$(0, 2), (0, -2) \qquad\quad y^2 = 0$

$\qquad\qquad\qquad\qquad y = 0$

$\qquad\qquad\qquad\qquad (-4, 0)$

30. $x^2 + y^2 = 8 \xrightarrow{\times(-1)} -x^2 - y^2 = -8$

$3x^2 + y^2 = 12 \xrightarrow{} \underline{3x^2 + y^2 = 12}$

$\qquad\qquad\qquad\qquad 2x^2 \qquad\;\; = 4$

$x^2 = 2$

$x = \pm\sqrt{2}$

$2 + y^2 = 8$

$y^2 = 6$

$y = \pm\sqrt{6}$

$\left(\sqrt{2}, \sqrt{6}\right), \left(-\sqrt{2}, \sqrt{6}\right)$

$\left(\sqrt{2}, -\sqrt{6}\right), \left(-\sqrt{2}, -\sqrt{6}\right)$

31. $6x^2 + 2y^2 = 16 \xrightarrow{\times\left(\frac{1}{2}\right)} 3x^2 + y^2 = 8$

$2x^2 - y^2 = 17 \xrightarrow{} \underline{2x^2 - y^2 = 17}$

$\qquad\qquad\qquad\qquad 5x^2 \qquad\;\; = 25$

$x^2 = 5$

$x = \pm\sqrt{5}$

$2(5) - y^2 = 17$

$-y^2 = 17 - 10$

$y^2 = -7$

$y = \pm\sqrt{-7} = \pm i\sqrt{7}$

$\left(\sqrt{5}, i\sqrt{7}\right), \left(-\sqrt{5}, i\sqrt{7}\right)$

$\left(\sqrt{5}, -i\sqrt{7}\right), \left(-\sqrt{5}, -i\sqrt{7}\right)$

32. $4x^2 - 9y^2 = 36 \xrightarrow{} 4x^2 - 9y^2 = 36$

$6x^2 + 6y^2 = 54 \xrightarrow{\times\left(\frac{3}{2}\right)} \underline{9x^2 + 9y^2 = 81}$

$\qquad\qquad\qquad\qquad 13x^2 \qquad\;\; = 117$

$x^2 = 9$

$x = \pm\sqrt{9} = \pm 3$

$4(9) - 9y^2 = 36$

$-9y^2 = 36 - 36$

$-9y^2 = 0$

$y^2 = 0$

$y = 0$

$(-3, 0), (3, 0)$

33. $y < -x^2 + 1$

The boundary line is dashed.

$y = -x^2 + 1$

$y = -(x - 0)^2 + 1 \quad h = 0, \;\; k = 1$

Vertex: $(0, 1)$, axis of symmetry: $x = 0$

x	$y = x^2 + 1$	(x, y)
-3	$-(-3)^2 + 1 = -8$	$(-3, -8)$
-2	$-(-2)^2 + 1 = -3$	$(-2, -3)$
-1	$-(-1)^2 + 1 = 0$	$(-1, 0)$
0	$-(0)^2 + 1 = 1$	$(0, 1)$
2	$-(2)^2 + 1 = -3$	$(2, -3)$
3	$-(3)^2 + 1 = -8$	$(3, -8)$

Test point is $(0, 0)$

$0 \overset{?}{<} -(0)^2 + 1$

$0 < 1$ True, shade the region

containing the point $(0, 0)$.

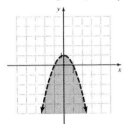

34. $(x + 3)^2 + y^2 \geq 4$

The boundary line is solid

$(x + 3)^2 + y^2 = 4$

$(x - (-3))^2 + (y - 0)^2 = 2^2$

$h = -3 \quad k = 0$

Center: $(-3, 0)$ radius $= 2$

Testpoint is $(0, 0)$

$(0 + 3)^2 + 0^2 \overset{?}{\geq} 4$

$9 + 0 \geq 4$ True, shade the region

containing the point $(0, 0)$.

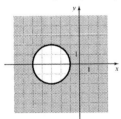

35. $8x^2 + 2y^2 \leq 32$

The boundary line is solid.

$8x^2 + 2y^2 = 32$

$\dfrac{8x^2}{32} + \dfrac{2y^2}{32} = \dfrac{32}{32}$

$\dfrac{x^2}{4} + \dfrac{y^2}{16} = 1 \quad \dfrac{x^2}{2^2} + \dfrac{y^2}{4^2} = 1 \quad a = 2 \quad b = 4$

x-intercepts: $(\pm 2, 0)$ or $(2, 0)$ and $(-2, 0)$

y-intercepts: $(0, \pm 4)$ or $(0, 4)$ and $(0, -4)$

Testpoint is $(0, 0)$.

$8(0)^2 + 2(0)^2 \overset{?}{\leq} 32$

$0 + 0 \leq 32$ True, shade the region

containing the point $(0, 0)$.

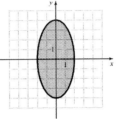

36. $9y^2 - 36x^2 > 144$

The boundary line is solid.

$9y^2 - 36x^2 = 144$

$\dfrac{9y^2}{144} - \dfrac{36x^2}{144} = \dfrac{144}{144}$

$\dfrac{y^2}{16} - \dfrac{x^2}{4} = 1 \quad \dfrac{y^2}{4^2} - \dfrac{x^2}{2^2} = 1 \quad a = 2 \quad b = 4$

y-intercepts: $(0, \pm 4)$ or $(0, 4)$ and $(0, -4)$

Equation of asymptotes are

$y = \dfrac{4}{2}x = 2x$ and $y = -2x$

Test point is $(0, 0)$.

$9(0)^2 - 36(0)^2 \overset{?}{>} 144$

$0 + 0 > 144$ False, shade the region not

containing the point $(0, 0)$.

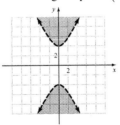

37. $x^2 + y^2 \leq 64 \quad y \geq \dfrac{1}{2}x + 3$

$x^2 + y^2 \leq 64$

The boundary line is solid.

$x^2 + y^2 = 64 \quad (x - 0)^2 + (y - 0)^2 = 8^2$

Circle. Center: $(0, 0)$, radius $= 8$

Test point is $(0,0)$.

$$0^2 + 0^2 \overset{?}{<} 64$$

$0 < 64$ True, shade the region

containing the point $(0,0)$.

$$y \geq \frac{1}{2}x + 3$$

The boundary line is solid.

$$y = \frac{1}{2}x + 3$$

x	$y = \frac{1}{2}x + 3$	(x, y)
0	$\frac{1}{2}(0) + 3 = 3$	$(0,3)$
4	$\frac{1}{2}(4) + 3 = 5$	$(4,5)$

Test point is $(0,0)$.

$$0 \overset{?}{\geq} \frac{1}{2}(0) + 3$$

$0 \geq 3$ False, shade the region not

containing the point $(0,0)$.

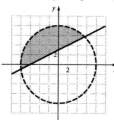

38. $x \geq y^2 - 4$ $x \leq -y^2 + 4$

$x \geq y^2 - 4$

The boundary line is solid. $h = -4,\ k = 0$

Vertex: $(-4,0)$ Axis of symmetry: $y = 0$

y	$x = y^2 - 4$	(x, y)
-3	$(-3)^2 - 4 = 5$	$(5,-3)$
-2	$(-2)^2 - 4 = 0$	$(0,-2)$
-1	$(-1)^2 - 4 = -3$	$(-3,-1)$
0	$(0)^2 - 4 = -4$	$(-4,0)$
1	$(1)^2 - 4 = -3$	$(-3,1)$
2	$(2)^2 - 4 = 0$	$(0,2)$
3	$(3)^2 - 4 = 5$	$(5,3)$

Test point is $(0,0)$

$$0 \overset{?}{\geq} (0)^2 - 4; \quad 0 \geq -4 \text{ True,}$$

shade the region containing the point $(0,0)$.

$x \leq y^2 + 4$

The boundary line is solid. $h = 4,\ k = 0$

Vertex: $(4,0)$ Axis of symmetry: $y = 0$

y	$x = -y^2 + 4$	(x, y)
-3	$-(-3)^2 + 4 = -5$	$(-5,-3)$
-2	$-(-2)^2 + 4 = 0$	$(0,-2)$
-1	$-(-1)^2 + 4 = 3$	$(3,-1)$
0	$-(0)^2 + 4 = 4$	$(4,0)$
1	$-(1)^2 + 4 = 3$	$(3,1)$
2	$-(2)^2 + 4 = 0$	$(0,2)$
3	$-(3)^2 + 4 = -5$	$(-5,3)$

Test point is $(0,0)$

$$0 \overset{?}{\leq} -(0)^2 + 4$$

$0 \leq 4$ True, shade the region

containing the point $(0,0)$.

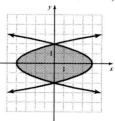

39. $x^2 + y^2 < 16$ $x^2 + y^2 > 49$

$x^2 + y^2 < 16$

The boundary line is solid.

$x^2 + y^2 = 16$

$(x-0)^2 + (y-0)^2 = 4^2$ $h = 0$ $k = 0$

Center: $(0,0)$ radius $= 4$

Test point is $(0,0)$.

$$0^2 + 0^2 \overset{?}{<} 16$$

$0 < 16$, shade the region

containing the point $(0,0)$.

$x^2 + y^2 > 49$

The boundary line is solid.

$x^2 + y^2 = 49$

$(x-0)^2 + (y-0)^2 = 7^2$ $h = 0$ $k = 0$

Center: $(0,0)$ radius $= 7$

Test point is $(0,0)$.

$$0^2 + 0^2 \overset{?}{>} 49$$

$0 > 49$ False, shade the region not

containing the point $(0,0)$.

No points satisfy both conditions (inside the smaller circle and outside the larger circle).

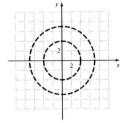

40. $4x^2 + 25y^2 \le 100 \quad 9x^2 - y^2 \ge 9$

$4x^2 + 25y^2 \le 100$

The boundary line is solid.

$4x^2 + 25y^2 = 100$

$\dfrac{4x^2}{100} + \dfrac{25y^2}{100} = \dfrac{100}{100}$

$\dfrac{x^2}{25} + \dfrac{y^2}{4} = 1 \quad \dfrac{x^2}{5^2} + \dfrac{y^2}{2^2} = 1 \quad a = 5 \quad b = 2$

x-intercepts: $(\pm 5, 0)$ or $(5, 0)$ and $(-5, 0)$

y-intercepts: $(0, \pm 2)$ or $(0, 2)$ and $(0, -2)$

Test point is $(0, 0)$.

$4(0)^2 + 25(0)^2 \overset{?}{\le} 100$

$0 + 0 \le 100$ True, shade the region containing the point $(0, 0)$.

$9x^2 - y^2 \ge 9$

The boundary line is solid.

$9x^2 - y^2 = 9$

$\dfrac{9x^2}{9} - \dfrac{y^2}{9} = \dfrac{9}{9}$

$\dfrac{x^2}{1} - \dfrac{y^2}{9} = 1 \quad \dfrac{x^2}{1^2} - \dfrac{y^2}{3^2} = 1 \quad a = 1 \quad b = 3$

x-intercepts: $(\pm 1, 0)$ or $(1, 0)$ and $(-1, 0)$

Equation of asymptotes are

$y = \dfrac{3}{1}x = -3x$ and $y = -3x$

Test point is $(0, 0)$.

$9(0)^2 - (0)^2 \overset{?}{\ge} 9$

$0 - 0 \ge 9$ False, shade the region not containing the point $(0, 0)$.

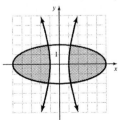

41.   a. $R = 20x - 0.5x^2$

$R = -0.5x^2 + 20x$

$R = -0.5(x^2 - 40x)$

$R = -0.5\left(x^2 - 40x + \left(\dfrac{-40}{2}\right)^2\right) + 0.5\left(\dfrac{-40}{2}\right)^2$

$R = -0.5(x^2 - 40x + 400) + 0.5(400)$

$R = -0.5(x - 20)^2 + 200$

$h = 20, \ k = 200$

Vertex: $(20, 200)$ This shows that the manufacturing plant will make a maximum revenue of \$200 when it sells 20 units.

42.   a.   The parabola has a vertex at $(0, 50)$ and passes through the point $(40, 0)$.

$h = 0 \quad k = 50$

$y = a(x - 0)^2 + 50$

$y = ax^2 + 50$

$0 = a(40)^2 + 50$

$1600a = -50$

$a = -\dfrac{50}{1600} = -\dfrac{1}{32}$

$y = -\dfrac{1}{32}x^2 + 50$

b.   Find y when $x = 24$

$y = -\dfrac{1}{32}(24)^2 + 50$

$y = -\dfrac{576}{32} + 50 = -18 + 50 = 32$

The height of the arch 24 ft from the center is 32 ft.

43.   The student ends up at

$((8 - 4), (-15 + 7)) = (4, -8)$

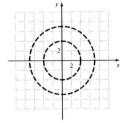

The distance from $(0, 0)$ to $(4, -8)$ is:

$d = \sqrt{(x_2 - x_1)^2 + (y_2 - y_1)^2}$

$d = \sqrt{(4 - 0)^2 + (-8 - 0)^2} = \sqrt{(4)^2 + (-8)^2}$

$d = \sqrt{16+64} = \sqrt{80} = 4\sqrt{5} = 8.9442...$

The distance between the student's apartment and work is $4\sqrt{5}$ or approximately 8.9 mi.

44. $h = 0, \ k = 0, \ \text{radius} = 60$

$(x-0)^2 + (y-0)^2 = 60^2$

$x^2 + y^2 = 3600$

45. $h = 0, \ k = 0, \ \text{radius} = 4000 + 500 = 4500$

$(x-0)^2 + (y-0)^2 = 4500^2$

$x^2 + y^2 = 20{,}250{,}000$

46. $\dfrac{x^2}{16} + \dfrac{y^2}{15} = 1 \quad \dfrac{x^2}{4^2} + \dfrac{y^2}{(\sqrt{15})^2} = 1$

$a = 4 \quad b = \sqrt{15}$

x-intercepts: $(\pm 4, 0)$ or $(4, 0)$ and $(-4, 0)$

The distance between x-intercepts is $4 + 4 = 8$ billion km. The distance from the sun to one vertex is 3 billion km making the distance from the sun to the other vertex $8 - 3 = 5$ billion km.

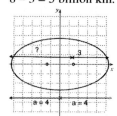

47.   The length is $8 = 2a$. $a = 4$.

The width is $4 = 2b$. $b = 2$.

$\dfrac{x^2}{4^2} + \dfrac{y^2}{2^2} = 1 \quad \dfrac{x^2}{16} + \dfrac{y^2}{4} = 1$

48. $-16t^2 - 32t + 120 = -16t^2 + 80$

$-32t = -40$

$t = \dfrac{40}{32} = \dfrac{5}{4} = 1.25$

They will be at the same height $\dfrac{5}{4}$ sec, or 1.25 sec. after they are released.

49.   a.   Center: $(0,0)$, $h = 0, \ k = 0$

Radius > 1

$(x-0)^2 + (y-0)^2 > 1$

$x^2 + y^2 > 1$

b.   The boundary is dashed.

Test point is $(0,0)$.

$0^2 + 0^2 \overset{?}{>} 1$

$0 > 1$ False, shade the region not containing the point $(0,0)$.

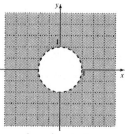

50.   a. $x^2 + y^2 \le 225$ and $x < y$

$x^2 + y^2 \le 225$

The boundary line is solid.

$x^2 + y^2 = 225$ Circle, center $(0,0)$, radius $= 15$.

Test point is $(0,0)$.

$0^2 + 0^2 \overset{?}{\le} 225$

$0 \le 225$ True, shade the region containing the point $(0,0)$.

$x < y$

The boundary line is dashed.

$x = y$

x	$y = x$	(x, y)
0	$0 = 0$	$(0,0)$
2	$2 = 2$	$(2,2)$

Test point is $(0,2)$

$0 < 2$ True, shade the region containing the point $(0,2)$.

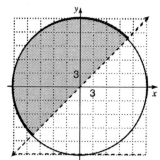

b.   No, only the points in Quadrant I are possible solutions since the lengths of the sandboxes must be non-negative quantities.

Chapter 10 Posttest

1. $x = -2y^2 + 16y - 91$

$x = -2(y^2 - 8y) - 91$

$x = -2\left(y^2 - 8y + \left(\dfrac{-8}{2}\right)^2\right) - 91 + 2\left(\dfrac{-8}{2}\right)^2$

$x = -2(y^2 - 8y + 16) - 91 + 32$

$x = -2(y-4)^2 - 59$ $h = -59,\ k = 4$

Vertex: $(-59, 4)$

2. a. $d = \sqrt{(x_2 - x_1)^2 + (y_2 - y_1)^2}$

$d = \sqrt{(-4 - (-2))^2 + (1 - (-1))^2}$

$d = \sqrt{(-2)^2 + (2)^2} = \sqrt{4 + 4} = \sqrt{8}$

$d = 2\sqrt{2}$ units

b. $d = \sqrt{(x_2 - x_1)^2 + (y_2 - y_1)^2}$

$d = \sqrt{(-4.1 - 7.9)^2 + (2.6 - (-2.4))^2}$

$d = \sqrt{(-12)^2 + (5)^2} = \sqrt{144 + 25} = \sqrt{169}$

$d = 13$ units

3. a. $\left(\dfrac{-8 + (-4)}{2}, \dfrac{-15 + 9}{2}\right) = \left(\dfrac{-12}{2}, \dfrac{-6}{2}\right) =$

$(-6, -3)$.

b. $\left(\dfrac{-3 + (-6)}{2}, \dfrac{7 + 3}{2}\right) = \left(\dfrac{-9}{2}, \dfrac{10}{2}\right) =$

$\left(-\dfrac{9}{2}, 5\right)$

4. $h = -2,\ k = 8,\ \text{radius} = 3\sqrt{2}$

$\left(x - (-2)\right)^2 + (y - 8)^2 = \left(3\sqrt{2}\right)^2$

$(x + 2)^2 + (y - 8)^2 = 9 \bullet 2$

$(x + 2)^2 + (y - 8)^2 = 18$

5. $x^2 + y^2 + 10x - 2y + 14 = 0$

$x^2 + 10x + y^2 - 2y = -14$

$x^2 + 10x + \left(\dfrac{10}{2}\right)^2 + y^2 - 2y + \left(\dfrac{-2}{2}\right)^2 =$

$\qquad\qquad -14 + \left(\dfrac{10}{2}\right)^2 + \left(\dfrac{-2}{2}\right)^2$

$x^2 + 10x + 25 + y^2 - 2y + 1 = -14 + 25 + 1$

$(x + 5)^2 + (y - 1)^2 = 12$

$\left(x - (-5)\right)^2 + (y - 1)^2 = 12$ $h = -5,\ k = 1$

Center: $(-5, 1)$, radius $= \sqrt{12} = 2\sqrt{3}$

6. $x = 3(y - 1)^2 - 5$ $h = -5,\ k = 1$

Vertex: $(-5, 1)$ axis of symmetry: $y = 1$

y	$x = 3(y-1)^2 - 5$	(x, y)
3	$3(3-1)^2 - 5 = 7$	$(7, 3)$
2	$3(2-1)^2 - 5 = -2$	$(-2, 2)$
1	$3(1-1)^2 - 5 = -5$	$(-5, 1)$
0	$3(0-1)^2 - 5 = -2$	$(-2, 0)$
-1	$3(-1-1)^2 - 5 = 7$	$(7, -1)$

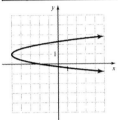

7. $x^2 + y^2 = 144$

$(x - 0)^2 + (y - 0)^2 = 12^2$ $h = 0,\ k = 0$

Center: $(0, 0)$, radius $= 12$

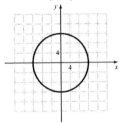

8. $(x - 4)^2 + (y + 5)^2 = 1$

$(x - 4)^2 + \left(y - (-5)\right)^2 = 1^2$ $h = 4,\ k = -5$

Center: $(4, -5)$ radius $= 1$

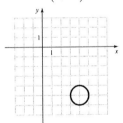

9. $\dfrac{x^2}{100} + \dfrac{y^2}{64} = 1$ $\dfrac{x^2}{10^2} + \dfrac{y^2}{8^2} = 1$ $a = 10\quad b = 8$

x-intercepts: $(\pm10, 0)$ or $(10, 0)$ and $(-10, 0)$

y-intercepts: $(0, \pm8)$ or $(0, 8)$ and $(0, -8)$

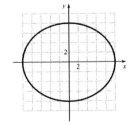

10. $64x^2 + 4y^2 = 256$

$$\frac{64x^2}{256} + \frac{4y^2}{256} = \frac{256}{256}$$

$$\frac{x^2}{4} + \frac{y^2}{64} = 1 \quad \frac{x^2}{2^2} + \frac{y^2}{8^2} = 1 \quad a = 2 \quad b = 8$$

x-intercepts: $(\pm 2, 0)$ or $(2, 0)$ and $(-2, 0)$

y-intercepts: $(0, \pm 8)$ or $(0, 8)$ and $(0, -8)$

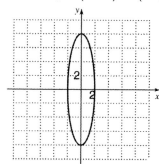

11. $\dfrac{y^2}{49} - \dfrac{x^2}{25} = 1 \quad \dfrac{y^2}{7^2} - \dfrac{x^2}{5^2} = 1 \quad a = 5 \quad b = 7$

y-intercepts are $(0, \pm 7)$ or $(0, 7)$ and $(0, -7)$

Equation of asymptotes are

$$y = \frac{7}{5}x \text{ and } y = -\frac{7}{5}x$$

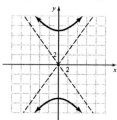

12. $6x^2 - 54y^2 = 216$

$$\frac{6x^2}{216} - \frac{54y^2}{216} = \frac{216}{216}$$

$$\frac{x^2}{36} - \frac{y^2}{4} = 1 \quad \frac{x^2}{6^2} - \frac{y^2}{2^2} = 1 \quad a = 6 \quad b = 2$$

x-intercepts: $(\pm 6, 0)$ or $(6, 0)$ and $(-6, 0)$

Equation of asymptotes are

$$y = \frac{2}{6}x = \frac{1}{3}x \text{ and } y = -\frac{1}{3}x$$

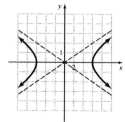

13. $x^2 + y^2 = 25 \quad y = x + 5$

$x^2 + (x+5)^2 = 25$

$x^2 + x^2 + 10x + 25 = 25$

$2x^2 + 10x = 0$

$2x(x+5) = 0$

$2x = 0 \qquad\qquad x + 5 = 0$

$x = 0 \qquad\qquad x = -5$

$y = x + 5 \quad$ or $\quad y = x + 5$

$y = 0 + 5 = 5 \qquad y = -5 + 5 = 0$

$(0, 5) \qquad\qquad (-5, 0)$

14. $y = x^2 + 4 \quad y = 2x^2 - 6$

$x^2 + 4 = 2x^2 - 6$

$x^2 = 10 \quad x = \pm\sqrt{10}$

$y = x^2 + 4 = 10 + 4 = 14$

$(\sqrt{10}, 14), (-\sqrt{10}, 14)$

15. $3x^2 + y^2 = 9 \xrightarrow{\times 3} 9x^2 + 3y^2 = 27$

$9x^2 + 2y^2 = 15 \xrightarrow{\times(-1)} \dfrac{-9x^2 - 2y^2 = -15}{y^2 = 12}$

$y = \pm\sqrt{12} = \pm 2\sqrt{3}$

$3x^2 + y^2 = 9$

$3x^2 + 12 = 9$

$3x^2 = -3$

$x^2 = -1$

$x = \pm\sqrt{-1} = \pm i$

$(i, 2\sqrt{3}), (-i, 2\sqrt{3}), (i, -2\sqrt{3}), (-i, -2\sqrt{3})$

16. $x^2 + 9y^2 > 36$

The boundary line is dashed.

$x^2 + 9y^2 = 36$

$$\frac{x^2}{36} + \frac{9y^2}{36} = \frac{36}{36}$$

$$\frac{x^2}{36} + \frac{y^2}{4} = 1 \quad \frac{x^2}{6^2} + \frac{y^2}{2^2} = 1 \quad a = 6 \quad b = 2$$

x-intercepts: $(\pm 6, 0)$ or $(6, 0)$ and $(-6, 0)$

y-intercepts: $(0, \pm 2)$ or $(0, 2)$ and $(0, -2)$

Test point is $(0, 0)$.

$(0)^2 + 9(0)^2 \overset{?}{>} 36$

$0 > 36$ False, shade the region not containing the point $(0,0)$.

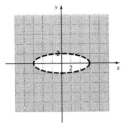

7. $4x^2 + 16y^2 \le 64$

The boundary line is solid.

$4x^2 + 16y^2 = 64$

$\dfrac{4x^2}{64} + \dfrac{16y^2}{64} = \dfrac{64}{64}$

$\dfrac{x^2}{16} + \dfrac{y^2}{4} = 1 \quad \dfrac{x^2}{4^2} + \dfrac{y^2}{2^2} = 1 \quad a=4 \quad b=2$

x-intercepts: $(\pm 4, 0)$ or $(4, 0)$ and $(-4, 0)$

y-intercepts: $(0, \pm 2)$ or $(0, 2)$ and $(0, -2)$.

Test point is $(0,0)$. $4(0)^2 + 16(0)^2 \overset{?}{\le} 64$

$0 + 0 \le 64$ True, shade the region

containing the point $(0,0)$.

$4x^2 - y^2 \le 100$

The boundary line is solid.

$4x^2 - y^2 = 100$

$\dfrac{4x^2}{100} - \dfrac{y^2}{100} = \dfrac{100}{100}$

$\dfrac{x^2}{25} - \dfrac{y^2}{100} = 1 \quad \dfrac{x^2}{5^2} - \dfrac{y^2}{10^2} = 1 \quad a=5 \quad b=10$

x-intercepts: $(\pm 5, 0)$ or $(5, 0)$ and $(-5, 0)$

Equation of asymptotes are

$y = \dfrac{10}{5}x = 2x$ and $y = -2x$

Test point is $(0,0)$.

$4(0)^2 + (0)^2 \overset{?}{\le} 100$

$0 + 0 \le 100$ True, shade the region

containing the point $(0,0)$.

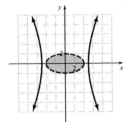

18.   The vertex is at $(0, 2)$

$y = a(x - 0)^2 + 2 = ax^2 + 2$

It passes through $(450, 110)$

$110 = a(450)^2 + 2$

$108 = a(202500)$

$a = \dfrac{108}{202500} = \dfrac{1}{1875}$

$y = \dfrac{1}{1875}x^2 + 2$

19. $2a = 130, \quad a = 65$

$2b = 120, \quad b = 60$

$\dfrac{x^2}{65^2} + \dfrac{y^2}{60^2} = 1 \quad$ or $\quad \dfrac{x^2}{4225} + \dfrac{y^2}{3600} = 1$

20.   **a.** $C \ge -0.5x^2 + 500$

$R \le 50x$

b. $C \ge -0.5x^2 + 500$

The boundary line is solid.

$C = -0.5x^2 + 500$

x	$C = 0.5x^2 + 500$	(x, C)
0	$0.5(0)^2 + 500 = 500$	$(0, 500)$
10	$0.5(10)^2 + 500 = 550$	$(10, 550)$
30	$0.5(30)^2 + 500 = 950$	$(30, 950)$
50	$0.5(50)^2 + 500 = 1750$	$(50, 1750)$
90	$0.5(90)^2 + 500 = 4550$	$(90, 4550)$

Test point is $(0,0)$.

$0 \overset{?}{\ge} 0.5(0)^2 + 500$

$0 \ge 0 + 500$ False, shade the region not

containing the point $(0,0)$.

$R \le 50x$

The boundary line is solid.

$R = 50x$

x	$R = 50x$	(x, R)
0	$50(0) = 0$	$(0, 0)$
50	$50(50) = 2500$	$(50, 2500)$

Test point is $(0, 500)$.

$500 \overset{?}{\le} 50(0)$

$500 \le 0$ False, shade the region not

containing the point $(0, 500)$.

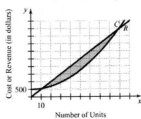

Cumulative Review Exercises

1. $y = \dfrac{3}{4}x - 1, \quad m = \dfrac{3}{4}$

Perpendicular line has slope $m = -\dfrac{4}{3}$

$y - 4 = -\dfrac{4}{3}(x - 9)$

$y - 4 = -\dfrac{4}{3}x + 12$

$y = -\dfrac{4}{3}x + 16$

2. $(2x + y)(x - 3y)^2 =$

$(2x + y)(x^2 - 6xy + 9y^2)$

$\begin{array}{r} x^2 - 6xy + 9y^2 \\ 2x + y \\ \hline x^2y - 6xy^2 + 9y^3 \\ 2x^3 - 12x^2y + 18xy^2 \\ \hline 2x^3 - 11x^2y + 12xy^2 + 9y^3 \end{array}$

3. $\sqrt{2n+5} - 2 = \sqrt{4n - 7}$

$\left(\sqrt{2n+5} - 2\right)^2 = \left(\sqrt{4n-7}\right)^2$

$(2n+5) - 4\sqrt{2n+5} + 4 = (4n - 7)$

$-2n + 16 = 4\sqrt{2n+5}$

$2(-n + 8) = 2\left(2\sqrt{2n+5}\right)$

$-n + 8 = 2\sqrt{2n+5}$

$(-n + 8)^2 = \left(2\sqrt{2n+5}\right)^2$

$n^2 - 16n + 64 = 4(2n + 5)$

$n^2 - 16n + 64 = 8n + 20$

$n^2 - 24n + 44 = 0$

$(n - 22)(n - 2) = 0$

$n - 22 = 0 \quad n - 2 = 0$

$n = 22 \qquad n = 2$

Check $n = 22$

$\sqrt{2(22)+5} - 2 \overset{?}{=} \sqrt{4(22)-7}$

$\sqrt{49} - 2 \overset{?}{=} \sqrt{81}$

$7 - 2 \overset{?}{=} 9$

$5 = 9$ False, $x = 22$ is not a solution.

Check $n = 2$

$\sqrt{2(2)+5} - 2 \overset{?}{=} \sqrt{4(2)-7}$

$\sqrt{9} - 2 \overset{?}{=} \sqrt{1}$

$3 - 2 \overset{?}{=} 1$

$1 = 1$ True

4. $(f \circ g)(x) = f(g(x)) = 2\left(\dfrac{x+3}{2}\right) - 3 =$

$(x + 3) - 3 = x$

$(g \circ f)(x) = g(f(x)) = \dfrac{(2x - 3) + 3}{2} =$

$\dfrac{2x}{2} = x$

$(f \circ g)(x) = x = (g \circ f)(x)$, The functions are inverses of each other.

5. $32^{x-4} = 16^{2x}$

$\left(2^5\right)^{x-4} = \left(2^4\right)^{2x}$

$2^{5(x-4)} = 2^{8x}$

$5(x - 4) = 8x$

$5x - 20 = 8x$

$-3x = 20$

$x = -\dfrac{20}{3}$

6. $x^2 + y^2 - 10x - 4y + 25 = 0$

$x^2 - 10x + y^2 - 4y = -25$

$x^2 - 10x + \left(\dfrac{-10}{2}\right)^2 + y^2 - 4y + \left(\dfrac{-4}{2}\right)^2 =$

$\qquad\qquad -25 + \left(\dfrac{-10}{2}\right)^2 + \left(\dfrac{-4}{2}\right)^2$

$x - 10x + 25 + y^2 - 4y + 4 = -25 + 25 + 4$

$(x - 5)^2 + (y - 2)^2 = 2^2 \qquad h = 5, \quad k = 2$

Center: $(5, 2)$, radius $= 2$

7.   Let $h =$ the amount of money invested in the high risk fund and $l =$ the amount of money invested at 4%.

$h = 2l$

$0.055h + 0.04l \geq 1500$

$0.055(2l) + 0.04l \geq 1500$

$0.11l + 0.04l \geq 1500$

$0.15l \geq 1500$

$l \geq \dfrac{1500}{0.15}$

$l \geq 10,000$

$h = 2l \geq 20,000$

She must invest at least \$10,000 in the fund with a guaranteed return of 4% and \$20,000 in the fund that has a guaranteed rate of return of $5\dfrac{1}{2}\%$.

8. $\text{time} = \dfrac{\text{distance}}{\text{rate}}$

$\dfrac{192}{r} + \dfrac{224}{r-8} = 7$

$\dfrac{192}{r}r(r-8) + \dfrac{224}{r-8}r(r-8) = 7r(r-8)$

$192(r-8) + 224r = 7r(r-8)$

$192r - 1536 + 224r = 7r^2 - 56r$

$7r^2 - 472r + 1536 = 0$

$a = 7 \qquad b = -472 \qquad c = 1536$

$x = \dfrac{-(-472) \pm \sqrt{(-472)^2 - 4(7)(1536)}}{2(7)}$

$r = \dfrac{472 \pm \sqrt{222784 - 43008}}{14}$

$r = \dfrac{472 \pm \sqrt{179776}}{14} = \dfrac{472 \pm 424}{14}$

$r = \dfrac{896}{14} = 64, \quad r - 8 = 56$

$r = \dfrac{48}{14} = \dfrac{24}{7}, \quad r - 8 = -\dfrac{32}{7}$

A negative answer makes no sense in this problem. The average speed during the first part of the trip was 64 mph, and the average speed during the second part of the trip was 56 mph.

9.   a. $h(t) = -16t^2 + 24t + 144$

$h(2) = -16(2)^2 + 24(2) + 144$

$h(2) = -16(4) + 48 + 144 = -64 + 192$

$h(2) = 128 \text{ ft.}$

b. $h(t) = -16t^2 + 24t + 144$

$h(t) = -16\left(t^2 - \dfrac{24}{16}t\right) + 144$

$h(t) = -16\left(t^2 - \dfrac{3}{2}t + \left(\dfrac{1}{2} \bullet \dfrac{3}{2}\right)^2\right) + 144$

$\qquad\qquad\qquad + 16\left(\dfrac{1}{2} \bullet \dfrac{3}{2}\right)^2$

$h(t) = -16\left(t^2 - \dfrac{3}{2}t + \dfrac{9}{16}\right) + 144 + 9$

$h(t) = -16\left(t - \dfrac{3}{4}\right)^2 + 153$

Vertex: $\left(\dfrac{3}{4}, 153\right)$

The object reaches its maximum height of 153 ft $\dfrac{3}{4}$ sec, or 0.75 sec, after it is thrown.

c. $104 = -16t^2 + 24t + 144$

$-16t^2 + 24t + 40 = 0$

$-8(2t^2 - 3t - 5) = 0$

$-8(2t - 5)(t + 1) = 0$

$2t - 5 = 0 \quad t + 1 = 0$

$2t = 5 \qquad t = -1$

$t = \dfrac{5}{2} \qquad t = -1$

A negative answer makes no sense in this problem.

The object is 104 ft above ground $\dfrac{5}{2}$ sec, or 2.5 sec, after it is thrown upward.

10. $A = Pe^{rt}$

$10000 = 6800e^{0.0385t}$

$e^{0.0385t} = \dfrac{10000}{6800} = \dfrac{100}{68} = \dfrac{25}{17}$

$0.0385t = \ln\left(\dfrac{25}{17}\right)$

$t = \dfrac{\ln\left(\dfrac{25}{17}\right)}{0.0385} = \dfrac{0.385662...}{0.0385} = 10.017...$

It would take approximately 10 yr for the amount in the account to grow to 10,000.